# Ezekiel's Hope

# Ezekiel's Hope

## *A Commentary on Ezekiel 38–48*

Jacob Milgrom *and* Daniel I. Block
IN CONVERSATION

CASCADE *Books* · Eugene, Oregon

EZEKIEL'S HOPE
A Commentary on Ezekiel 38–48

Copyright © 2012 Jacob Milgrom and Daniel I. Block. All rights reserved. Except for brief quotations in critical publications or reviews, no part of this book may be reproduced in any manner without prior written permission from the publisher. Write: Permissions, Wipf and Stock Publishers, 199 W. 8th Ave., Suite 3, Eugene, OR 97401.

Cascade Books
An Imprint of Wipf and Stock Publishers
199 W. 8th Ave., Suite 3
Eugene, OR 97401

www.wipfandstock.com

ISBN 13: 978-1-61097-650-3

*Cataloging-in-Publication data:*

Milgrom, Jacob, 1923–2010.

    Ezekiel's hope : a commentary on Ezekiel 38–48 / Jacob Milgrom and Daniel I. Block in conversation.

    xxiv + 314 p. ; 23 cm. Includes bibliographical references and index.

    ISBN 13: 978-1-61097-650-3

    1. Bible, O.T. Ezekiel—Commentaries. 2. Bible. O.T. Ezekiel—Criticism, interpretation, etc. I. Block, Daniel Isaac, 1943– . II. Title.

BS1545.53 M55 2012

Manufactured in the U.S.A.

*For Moshe Greenberg*

— *ărî šebbaḥăbûrâ (Sanhedrin 8b)*

*A lion among his peers*

# Contents

*Lists of Figures and Tables / x*

*List of Excurses / xii*

*List of Abbreviations / xiii*

*Preface and Acknowledgments by Jacob Milgrom / xv*

*Preface by Joel Duman / xvii*

*Preface and Acknowledgments by Daniel Block / xix*

*Preface by Shira, Etan, Asher, and Jeremy Milgrom / xxiii*

## PART ONE: Ezekiel 38–39: The Gog Pericope

Introduction: Structure and Message / 3

Unit 1: YHWH's Program for Gog's Attack against Israel in the Distant Future (38:1–13) / 7

    Preface (38:1–2b) / 7
    Frame 1: YHWH's Conscription of Gog (38:2c–9) / 7
    Frame 2: The Motives of Gog (38:10–13) / 12

Unit 2: YHWH's Anger in View of Gog's Advance against Israel (38:14–23) / 15

    Frame 3: YHWH's Counterplan: His Goal (38:14–16) / 15
    Frame 4: YHWH's Counterplan: His Strategy (38:17–23) / 17

Unit 3: The Annihilation of Gog's Army and Its Armaments (39:1–16) / 20

    Frame 5: The Slaughter of Gog (39:1–8) / 20
    Frame 6: The Spoiling of Gog (39:9–10) / 22
    Frame 7: The Burial of Gog in Hamonah (39:11–16) / 23

Unit 4: The Corpses of Gog's Army Devoured by Birds and Beasts (39:17–29) / 27

    Frame 8: The Victory Banquet (39:17–20) / 27
    Frame 9: The Final Word (39:21–29) / 29

## Contents

### PART TWO: Ezekiel 40–48: The Visionary Sanctuary and Land

1. The Visionary Sanctuary (40–43) / 41

    Introduction: The Sanctuary / 41
    - a. Ezekiel's Temple: Its Dimensions / 41
    - b. The Delphi Temple / 44
    - c. Separation / 53
    - d. The Laws of Ezekiel's Sanctuary / 55

    The New Temple and Its Precincts: Measurement of Boundaries and Spaces (40–43) / 60

    Preamble: A Visionary Flight to a High Mountain in Israel—The Celestial Guide (40:1–4) / 60

    The Perimeter Wall, Gatehouses, and Court (40:5–27) / 66

    The Outer Gatehouses and Court (40:28–37) / 74

    The Slaughtering Tables and the Priestly Chambers (38–47) / 76

    The Temple and its Auxiliary Structures (40:48—41:26) / 82

    The Priestly Sacristies for Dressing and Dining (42:1–14) / 97

    The Measurement of the Perimeter Wall (42:15–20) / 101

    YHWH Returns to the New Temple (43:1–12) / 103

    The Altar Measurements (43:13–17) / 118

    The Purgation of the Altar (43:18–27) / 122

2. The Sanctuary Personnel and the *Nāśî'* (44–46) / 132

    Foreigners Forbidden (44:1–8) / 132

    Protecting the Sacred Space (44:9–14) / 153

    Ezekiel's Zadokite Priests (44:15–31) / 163

    The Priestly and Princely Lands Foreshadowed (45:1–8) / 187

    The Regulations of the *Nāśî'* (45:9–17) / 193

    The *Pesaḥ* and Its Prelude (45:18–25) / 198

    Other Fixed Festivals (46:1–15) / 209

    The Prince's Land (46:16–18) / 220

    The Temple Kitchens (19–24) / 223

3. The Land (47–48) / 227

    Healing Waters from the Temple (47:1–12) / 227

    The New Boundaries of the Land (47:13–20) / 234

    The Resident Aliens (47:21–23) / 243

The New Tribal Allocations (48:1–7, 23–29) / 246
The *Tĕrûmâ* "District" (48:8–22) / 250
The New City (48:30–35) / 257

*Bibliography* / 267

*Biblical Reference Index* / 279

*Ancient and Jewish Sources Index* / 305

*Author Index* / 307

*Subject Index* / 311

# Figures and Tables

## FIGURES

1. The Plan of the Holy Precinct / 42
2. Cross Section of the Temple of Delphi / 45
3. The Supporting Wall of the Temple of Delphi / 45
4. Ground Plan of the Temple of Delphi / 46
5. Aerial View of the Temple of Apollo, Podium and Supporting Wall / 47
6. Reconstruction of the *Temenos* at Delphi / 47
7. Ground Plan of the Tabernacle / 48
8. Ezekiel's Temple Tour / 67
9. The Outer Gatehouse of Ezekiel's Temple / 70
10. Plans of Two Solomonic Gates / 70
11. The Ground Plan of the Temple / 84
12. The Ground Plan of the Ain Dara Sanctuary / 88
13. The Auxiliary Structures of the Temple Building / 89
14. The Holy Spine of the Temple / 92
15. The Doors of the Great Hall / 96
16. Ezekiel's Altar of Sacrifice / 119
17. The Horned Altars from Meggido and Beer Sheba / 121
18. The Dimensions of the Priestly Area / 190
19. The Tribal Territories, Ezekiel 47–48 / 238
20. The Sacred District (Reserve) / 252
21. The Gates of "The City" / 260

## TABLES

1. The Links between Ezekiel and Moses / 215
2. Sabbath and New Moon Sacrifices / 219
3. Accompaniment / 219
4. Sabbath Sacrifices and Accompaniment / 219
5. New Moon Sacrifices and Accompaniment / 219
6. Tamid Sacrifices / 220
7. A Comparison of Three Accounts of Israel's Northern Border / 240
8. A Synopsis of Ezekiel 45:3–4 and 48:10b–12 / 253
9. The Tribal Encampment and Gates / 261

# Excurses

1. Ezekiel and the Levites / 141
2. Terminology (44:9–14) / 148
3. The Leadership Groupings / 167
4. The Sins of the High Priest and Other Leaders / 174
5. The Purification Offering (*ḥaṭṭā'ṭ*) / 201
6. The *ḤAG* / 207
7. Daily Public Sacrifices During Pesaḥ / 208
8. Ezekiel, the New Moses? / 214
9. The Mosaic Torah and Ezekiel Compared / 219
10. The *GĒR* / 244

# Abbreviations

| | |
|---|---|
| *AB* | Anchor Bible |
| *AfO* | *Archiv für Orientforschung* |
| *AHw* | W. von Soden, *Akkadisches Handworterbuch*, 3 vols. Wiesbaden: Harrassowitz, 1965–81 |
| *ANEP²* | *The Ancient Near East in Pictures*. 2nd ed. by J. B. Pritchard. Princeton: Princeton University Press, 1969 |
| *ANET* | *Ancient Near Eastern Texts Related to the Old Testament*. 3rd ed. by J. B. Pritchard. Princeton: Princeton University Press, 1969 |
| *ARAB* | Daniel David Luckenbill, *Ancient Records of Assyria and Babylonia*. 2 vols. Chicago: University of Chicago Press, 1926–1927. |
| *ASTI* | *Annual of the Swedish Theological Institute* |
| *BASOR* | *Bulletin of the American Schools of Oriental Research* |
| *BDB* | F. Brown, S. R. Driver, and C. Briggs, *A Hebrew and English Lexicon of the Old Testament*. Oxford: Clarendon, 1907 (corrected impression, 1952) |
| *BHS* | *Biblia Hebraica Stuttgartensia*. Edited by K. Elliger and W. Rudolph. Stuttgart: Deutsche Bibelstiftung, 1977. See also MT. |
| *BT* | Babylonian Talmud |
| *B-Y* | E. Ben Yehuda, *A Complete Dictionary of Ancient and Modern Hebrew*, 17 vols. Jerusalem, 1910–59 [rpt. in 8 vols., New York: Yoseloff, 1960] |
| BZAW | Beihefte zur *Zeitschrift für die alttestamentliche Wissenschaft* |
| *CAD* | *The Assyrian Dictionary*. The Oriental Institute, the University of Chicago, 1956– |
| DJD | Qumran Cave I, Discoveries in the Judaean Desert-I Edited by D. Barthelemy et al. Oxford: Clarendon, 1955 |
| *EJ* | *Encyclopaedia Judaica*. Jerusalem: Keter, 1971 |
| *EM* | *Encyqlopedia miqrait* [Encyclopedia Biblica]. Jerusalem: Bialik Institute, 1950– |
| *GB* | W. Gesenius, *Hebräisches und aramäisches Handwörterbuch über das alte Testament*. Edited by F. Buhl. 17th ed. Neudruck, Berlin: Springer, 1949 |
| *GKC* | *Gesenius' Hebrew Grammar,* as edited and enlarged by the late E. Kautzsch, revised by A. E. Cowley. Oxford: Clarendon, 1910. Cited by section |
| *GL* | The Lucianic revision of the Greek text (fourth century C.E.), as presented in G (Ziegler's edition of the Septuagint) |
| HAT | Handbuch zum Alten Testament |

## Abbreviations

| | |
|---|---|
| *IB* | *The Interpreter's Bible* |
| ICC | International Critical Commentary |
| *IDB* | *The Interpreter's Dictionary of the Bible.* 4 vols. Nashville: Abingdon Press, 1962. Cited by entry (s.v.) and author |
| *IDB Suppl.* | *The Interpreter's Dictionary of the Bible.* Supplementary Volume (1976) |
| *K* | *Kethib,* "[what is ] written"; form of a word in MT (indicated by the consonants in the main text); contrast Q |
| *KAI* | *Kanaanäische und aramäische Inschriften,* von H. Donner und W. Röllig. 3 vols. Wiesbaden: Harrassowitz, 1964 |
| KAT | Kommentar zum Alten Testament |
| *K.T.U.* | *Die keilalphabetischen Texte aus Ugarit* |
| *LXX* | Greek (Septuagint), according to J. Ziegler, ed., *Ezechiel, Septuaginta . . . auctoritate Societatis Litterarum Gottingensis editum,* XVIII. Gottingen: Vandenhoeck und Ruprecht, 1952 |
| NRSV | The New Revised Standard Version, 1989 |
| MT | Masoretic Text, according to *Biblia Hebraica Stuttgartensia,* [fasc.] 9, Liber Ezechiel. K. Elliger praep. Stuttgart: Württembergische Bibelanstalt, 1971 |
| NAB | The New American Bible, New York: Kennedy, 1970 |
| NEB | The New English Bible. Oxford and Cambridge, 1970 |
| NJPS | The New Jewish Publication Society of America translations of the Holy Scriptures: *The Torah.* 2d ed. Philadelphia, 1967; *The Prophets: Nevi'im.* Philadelphia, 1978; *The Writings: Kethubim.* Philadelphia, 1982 |
| *OtSt* | *Oudtestamentische Studiën* |
| *PEQ* | *Palestine Exploration Quarterly* |
| Q | *Qere,* "[what is] read"; form of a word in MT (indicated by the vowel signs and the consonants in the margin); contrast K |
| REB | Revised English Bible, 1989 |
| RSV | The Holy Bible, Revised Standard Version. New York: Nelson, 1952 |
| SBLDS | Society of Biblical Literature Dissertation Series |
| *VTSup* | Supplements, *Vetus Testamentum* |
| TDOT | G. J. Botterweck and H. Ringgren, eds. *Theological Dictionary of the Old Testament* |
| Vulg | Vulgate, as in *Biblia sacra vulgatae editionis.* Monachorum Abbatiae Pontificiae Sancti Hieronymi in Urbe, Ordinis Sancti Benedicti. Roma: 1959 |
| WCJS | World Congress of Jewish Studies |

# Preface and Acknowledgments
# by Jacob Milgrom

During one of my frequent visits with Moshe Greenberg, friend and colleague for over half a century, I talked about my readiness for a new project, now that my one volume Leviticus was done. Moshe suggested that I complete his Ezekiel. He had already published the Anchor Bible *Ezekiel* 1-20 (1987) and *Ezekiel* 21-37 (1997). But he felt that his health would not enable him to complete the final chapters. Since these chapters dealt with the structure and rules of Ezekiel's visionary sanctuary, a topic whose antecedents were my expertise (Leviticus and Numbers), I was an ideal candidate to succeed him.

The offer was frighteningly irresistible. My interest in Ezekiel 38-48 had been piqued as early as 1970 (*Studies in Levitical Terminology*), and since then the plethora of its enigmas and contradictions had not been satisfactorily resolved. But the challenge was overwhelming. Greenberg's two volumes were acknowledged classics. They were immediately translated into German, the European center of biblical scholarship. Could I measure up to the Greenberg standard?

Merely to scan my commentaries on *Numbers* (1990) and *Leviticus* (1991, 2000, 2001) is sufficient to indicate that, like Greenberg (1983, 11-27), I too have adopted a holistic exegetical approach. This holds even more so for Ezekiel, which I aver was written by him (and/or his tradents). Even where his theology totally shifts, such as the surprising absence of repentance in 38-48, the cause is not due to the insertion of a later redactor but to the circumstances that impel Ezekiel to change his mind.

The research on Ezekiel 38-48 is enormous and I acknowledge my indebtedness especially to Daniel I. Block, the Ezekiel scholar from whom I have learned the most. His comprehensive coverage of the versions has eased my path, as demonstrated in the textual notes below. Critical encounter with Block's *Ezekiel* has quickened the writing of this book. Where my conversation partner and I disagree is indicated in the commentary and the notes.

A gift of magnitude has been the sustained presence of Joel Duman, my colleague, research assistant, and dedicated study partner who coaxed my no. 3 pencil micrography into electronic luster. Then there is Richard Tupper ("Tup"), careful reader of my writings who carries my offprints in his briefcase for distribution. Tova

*Preface and Acknowledgments by Jacob Milgrom*

Ganzel, co-researcher on the thought of Ezekiel, full time lecturer, and young mother of five, found time to read my manuscript and comment meaningfully. What would I have done without Batya Kaplan, chief librarian of Hebrew Union College, and her able and willing staff who helped me find what I needed and allowed me long-term lease on everything pertaining to my research?

I am humbly thankful to our Creator who provided me with a body strong enough to cope with incessant insults threatening completion of the work. Second only to the Creator is my life partner of sixty-two years, Jo, who propels me daily to my "holy of holies," past all the domestic trivia. When she reads my work she rigorously questions my thinking, and brightens and lightens my language.

> "As water mirrors one face to another face, so her heart speaks to mine"
> (Proverbs 27:19).

Jacob Milgrom

# Preface by Joel Duman

Having become a frequent visitor to the home and the study of Professor Jacob Milgrom, and through my ongoing work with his wife, Dr. Jo Milgrom, in 2004 I noticed that Professor Milgrom was collecting materials on the book of Ezekiel. Knowing of his long-term concentration on Leviticus and the Holiness Code, I asked him what brought him to Ezekiel and he told me of his plan to complete Professor Moshe Greenberg's commentary on Ezekiel. I volunteered to assist Professor Milgrom in his work; thus began my involvement in the present volume. Over the course of the following years, I served as Milgrom's study partner, reader, transcriber, typist, and research assistant, as he worked through Ezekiel 38–48, overcoming the challenges of this most perplexing text and his own declining health.

Jacob Milgrom brought to this monumental project his world-renowned erudition regarding the Priestly and Holiness Codes, as well as a number of studies he had already published on Ezekiel. As a long-time colleague and friend, he also brought Greenberg's approach and methodology, as well as the influences of Mary Douglas and other scholars. A particularly important contribution that Milgrom wanted to make regarding Ezekiel was to reference and build on medieval Jewish scholarship that is often neglected by critical scholars, especially the Aramaic Targums and the commentaries of R. Eliezer of Beaugency and R. Joseph Kara.

From the first day of my work with Professor Milgrom, I was introduced to Professor Daniel Block's commentary on Ezekiel. I quickly perceived that Milgrom considered Block's book to be the authoritative work currently available on the subject. I was frequently given the assignment of combing Block's commentary for references and additional insights, in preparation for Milgrom's own analysis. Eventually I realized that in essence a conversation was being created between these two scholars. While Milgrom sought out every piece of research on these final chapters of Ezekiel, Block's work was consistently Milgrom's point of departure. Our discussions of each section of Ezekiel would often center on Milgrom's judgments regarding Block's conclusions: frequently, Milgrom adopted Block's suggestions—regarding textual difficulties, Ezekielian concepts and English translations of Ezekiel's idiosyncratic Hebrew; at other times, Milgrom was delighted to do battle with Block, especially regarding Ezekiel's grounding in his Pentateuchal sources.

*Preface by Joel Duman*

It is, therefore, particularly fitting that this final form of Professor Milgrom's work has become a conversation between Milgrom and Block, echoing in a deep and moving sense the inter-personal and inter-generational conversations of much of traditional Jewish scholarship. The interfaith character of the dialogue between Milgrom and Block is a truly significant innovation to such collaborative scholarship.

Joel Duman<br>
January 2012, Jerusalem

# Preface and Acknowledgments by Daniel Block

EARLY IN 1983 I received a telephone call from R. K. Harrison, inviting me to write a commentary on Ezekiel for the New International Commentary on the Old Testament series. At the time I could not have known how critical that call would be for setting the course of my life as a teacher and scholar. Nor did I anticipate that this would be the beginning of a fifteen-year conversation with Ezekiel, by common consent the most enigmatic of the Hebrew prophets. In my work on this prophet I was deeply indebted to Moshe Greenberg, the foremost Jewish authority on the book, both for his holistic approach to biblical interpretation and for his understanding of particular texts. We were all saddened when we learned that Moshe would be unable to finish his commentary on Ezekiel. It is right that Professor Milgrom took it upon himself to complete the project by writing a commentary on Ezekiel 38–48. With his background in the study of the books of Leviticus and Numbers and his profound understanding of all things cultic in ancient Israel, this was a perfect assignment. Earlier, in my own work, the close links between Ezekiel and Leviticus inevitably drew me to the work of Jacob Milgrom, the fruits of which are represented in his magisterial three-volume commentary on Leviticus in the Anchor Bible Commentary series. Unfortunately Professor Milgrom's labors on Ezekiel would not appear in published form during his lifetime.

While I was on sabbatical leave in Cambridge in the winter of 2010, Jacob Milgrom called to inquire if I would consider working together with him in preparing his manuscript for publication. Sadly, his untimely death brought the conversation to a halt. This was a deep personal loss for his wife Jo and his family, but it was also a loss for the whole world of biblical scholarship, causing me to wonder if the world would ever gain access to his work on Ezekiel. In the fall of that year, at the annual convention of the Society of Biblical Literature in Atlanta, I was delighted to meet Dr. Jo Milgrom and their sons Jeremy and Etan. Jo and Jeremy had come from Israel, and Etan from California to explore whether or not we could find a way to publish Professor Milgrom's work. This volume represents the product of that conversation. When I first saw his manuscript I was both surprised and humbled that a scholar of his stature should have found my work helpful. At Professor Milgrom's request, his commentary on Ezekiel 38–48 is presented as a conversation between the two of us.

*Preface and Acknowledgments by Daniel Block*

In preparing this document for publication our greatest challenge has been to polish the manuscript without losing Dr. Milgrom's voice in the process. We have generally left his discussion exactly as we found it. It has not been our role to check for accuracy every primary and secondary reference that the author cites. On the one hand this was precluded by the pressures of my life and my other projects. On the other hand, out of respect for Dr. Milgrom, it seemed imperative to make this work available as quickly as possible. We hope readers will be forgiving of the author and the editor when they encounter mistakes. The changes we have introduced involved primarily the following: (1) bringing the manuscript into conformity with Wipf & Stock's house style; (2) reformatting the translation and textual notes on each literary unit; (3) smoothing out readings where the composition was awkward or sentences were incomplete; (4) filling in lacunae, especially by identifying secondary sources to which Milgrom refers. Since we did not have access to Milgrom's originals, in some instances [especially figures and tables] the images are imperfect; some we have reproduced as we found them in his manuscript. Given his ubiquitous references to my commentary, we have generally signaled his use of or response to my earlier work by placing a number in square brackets at the end of a sentence or paragraph: e.g., [596]. Unless otherwise indicated, this means page 596 of the second volume of my NICOT commentary, *The Book of Ezekiel Chapters 25–48*.

I wish Jacob Milgrom's work on Ezekiel would have been available to me twenty years ago when I was wrestling with this prophetic book. Although we obviously do not agree on all matters, I gladly accept his correction in many instances, and have grown greatly from his contribution to the conversation, including his incorporation of insights from the long history of Jewish scholarship. I am encouraged by those moments when my approach to the text as a Christian interpreter have matched not only the impulse of this giant in modern biblical scholarship, but also the perspectives of R. Eliezer of Beaugency and R. Joseph Kara, to which I did not have access. It is a great honor to engage in this inter-faith conversation, and a privilege to have a small hand in making Jacob Milgrom's significant work on Ezekiel available to the broader community of biblical scholars.

The Milgrom family and I owe special thanks to Robin Parry and Christian Amondson at Wipf & Stock for their enthusiasm for this project and the efficiency with which they have handled all the business and editorial matters. From the first conversation after the annual meeting of the Society of Biblical Literature in Atlanta, they have encouraged us and offered the help we needed to produce it to their specifications. I am also grateful to Alan Myers, editor of the NICOT series and Tom deVries at Eerdmans Publishing Company for granting permission freely to reproduce images that had been used in my own commentary. The original location of these and all other images used have been duly acknowledged. Closer to home, I am thankful to Bud and Betty Knoedler, who have given so generously to underwrite my professorial chair, which allows me time and resources to work on stimulating projects like this. My assistants, Jason Gile, Matt Newkirk, Austin Surls, and Carmen Imes, have provided excellent aid in proofreading and indexing this volume and in offering suggestions for its improvement. I also eagerly acknowledge the support of Ellen, the delight of my life, who has spent many hours on the indexes to this volume. She has patiently stood by me as a gracious friend and counselor for more than four decades.

Most of all, I am humbled and grateful to the Milgrom family for their invitation to enter into a conversation that had engaged their family for the past eight or nine years. No one is more familiar with the conversation that was going on between her husband and me than Jo Milgrom, who has supported this project with enthusiasm and wise counsel all along the way. I must extend a particular word of thanks to Jeremy Milgrom, who worked through the manuscript scrupulously to ensure that all the links between his father's comments and my work were duly noted. I am also grateful for the assistance Dr. Joel Duman graciously provided in the end as we were trying to solve a series of issues involving credits, images, and bibliographic riddles in the footnotes. This has been a team effort, and I am privileged to have been a part of this team. Our common prayer is that through our scholarship and the tone of our conversation, readers of the book of Ezekiel will see the benefits that arise from conversations involving people from different faith commitments in wrestling with this enigmatic book, and that they will be enlightened and blessed by its message.

Daniel I. Block<br>
Wheaton College, Illinois<br>
July, 2012

# Preface by Shira, Etan, Asher, and Jeremy Milgrom

> *. . . Rather, his delight is in God's Torah,*
> *in which he is steeped night and day*
> *Like a tree planted on streams of water*
> *bearing fruit regularly, his leaves not wilting*
> *he succeeds in everything that he does.*
> (Psalm 1:2–3)

Throughout his life, *Yaacov Avinu* = Jacob Milgrom demonstrated his devotion to Torah; living in his household provided an ongoing lesson in *talmud torah k'neged kulam*—the priority of learning Torah over all other commandments. Over a span of fifty years, from our early childhood to the birth of our grandchildren/grand nieces and nephews, we can vividly recall his constant retreat/pilgrimage/exile into his study in Richmond, Berkeley and Jerusalem where he engaged and created holiness. As we all know, from each of these oases of Torah emerged first articles, then monographs and finally commentaries that have enriched the world of biblical scholarship.

For his very last commentary he seamlessly wove two important conversations into his work. One included the ongoing conversation that he had through the conventional assistance that Joel Duman, his faithful study companion and scribe provided, for which we owe endless gratitude. The second embodied an ongoing conversation with Block's NICOT commentary on Ezekiel which bore an amazing resemblance to the one-sided conversations between earlier and later medieval scholars (think: Rashi and Ramban) in which one work is grafted onto the other. While distinct and innovative, they are actually inseparable from each other! Daniel Block recognized the value of this conversation, and with an open heart and generous spirit, joined in publishing the manuscript as the conversation the two of them could have shared, in the spirit of the following teaching:

אמר רב אחא בר אדא אמר רב
ואמרי לה אמר רב אחא בר אבא אמר רב המנונא אמר רב
שאפילו שיחת חולין של תלמידי חכמים צריכה תלמוד
שנאמר ועלהו לא יבול וכל אשר יעשה יצליח

*Preface by Shira, Etan, Asher, and Jeremy Milgrom*

R. Aha bar Ada quoted Rav (perhaps it was R. Aha bar Aba who quoted R. Hamnuna quoting Rav) who said that even informal conversations between scholars are worth studying, as it is written, "his leaves not wilting, he succeeds in everything he does." (*Abodah Zara* 19b)

מה אהבתי תורתך כל היום היא שיחתי
*ma ahavti toratecha, kol hayom hi siḥati*
How I love your Torah, it is my conversation all day long (Ps 119:97)

In the end, it pretty much comes down to this: the conversations you have, the ones you should have, and the ones you wish you had . . .

Shira, Etan, Asher, and Jeremy Milgrom
White Plains, Los Angeles, Irvine and Re'ut
(half way between Tel Aviv and Jerusalem)
February, 2012

Part One

# Ezekiel 38–39
*The Gog Pericope*

Introduction

# Structure and Message

Ezekiel 38–39 deals with the demolition of hostile peoples surrounding Israel who invade the land of Israel and are buried there. These chapters have been inserted between the miraculous return of exiled Israel to their homeland (36–37) and the description of Ezekiel's visionary sanctuary (40–46). A chronological, if ahistorical, picture emerges: the resurrection, restoration, and resettlement of all twelve tribes of Israel (47–48).

In the Jewish tradition, these chapters provide the earliest treatment and sources upon which all subsequent projections are based. Magog is mentioned in Gen 10:2 as a descendant of Japheth, together with Meshech and Tubal who are mentioned in verse 3. The Targumic source (*Tg. Ps.-J*) on Exod 40:11 refers to the final struggle of Gog against Israel, and to the Messiah, son of Ephraim, who will vanquish him and his rabble.

*Fg. Tg* on Num 11:26 reads, "two men remained in the camp, the name of one Eldad and the name of the other Medad, and the Holy Spirit rested upon them ... and the two of them prophesied together saying, 'At the end, the very end of days, Gog and Magog and their armies shall go up against Jerusalem, but they shall fall by the hand of the King Messiah. For seven full years, the children of Israel shall use their weapons for kindling, without having to go in the forest to cut down trees.'" This prophecy is also referred to in *b. Sanh.* 17a and *Num. R.* 15:19.[1]

Ezekiel 38–39 comprises a single extract, opening with a divine revelation (38:1) and closing with final recognition and signatory formulae,[2] henceforth naming and signing patterns, 39:28–29. The naming pattern appears seven times (38:16, 23; 39:6, 7, 22, 23, 28). The extract consists of two panels (A and B), each containing two units which address the prophet as *ben 'ādām*, "human":

Unit 1   YHWH's program for Gog's attack against Israel in the future (38:2–13)

Unit 2   YHWH's anger in view of Gog's advance against Israel (38:14–23)

Unit 3   The annihilation of Gog's army and its armaments (39:1–16)

Unit 4   The corpses of Gog's army devoured by birds and beasts (39:17–29)

---

1. Details in Levey, *Targum of Ezekiel*, 105–7, n. 1.
2. On *nĕ'um ădōnāy YHWH*, as a signatory formula, see Block, *Ezekiel 1–24*, 33–34.

## EZEKIEL'S HOPE

The first and third units are alike (38:2-3; 39:1-2). Certain words occur in all four units: *lābeṭaḥ*, *'im*, and the roots *'lh* and *bw'*. Others occur in three units: *yarkĕtê ṣāpôn*, *ăgāpîm*, *yāda' baggôyîm*, *qdš*. A number of idioms from other biblical passages have found their way into the Gog extract: e.g., *ḥereb'îš bĕāḥîw*, "self destruction," (38:21) in Gideon's war against Midian (Judg 7:22); *yôm 'ădōnāy YHWH*, "the day of Lord YHWH," indicated by a collapsing (perimeter) wall at Jericho (38:18; Josh 6:20) and Aphek (1 Kgs 20:30); *haggôy miṣṣāpôn*, "the foe from the north," (38:9, 16; Jer 1-6; 10:22-25; 13:20-27; 25:46-51); Gog is destroyed on the mountains of Israel (39:4; Isa 14:25). The destruction of Gog and his allies takes place by realistic and mythical forces, e.g., fire, brimstone, and earthquake, due to the appearance of YHWH, and the feasting of birds and wild life on the unburied carcasses.[3]

As demonstrated by Moshe Greenberg,[4] Ezekiel's style is dominated by the literary device "halving," according to which the first (usually longer) part expounds an oracular theme, and the second follows with another theme but ends with a coda that links elements from both parts. Symmetrical patterns are achieved occasionally by composing halves virtually identical in length. Thus, in the Gog oracle, panel A (38:2-23) consists of 365 words, and panel B (39:1-29), 359 words (below). Their parallel opening is represented diagrammatically as follows [adapted from Block, 424-25]:

### "HALVING" in Ezekiel 38:1-4aα and 39:1-2aα

| 38:1-4aα | 39:1-2aα |
|---|---|
| *wayĕhî dĕbar YHWH ēlay lē'mōr* | |
| *wĕattâ* | |
| *ben 'ādām* | *ben 'ādām* |
| *śîm pānêkā 'el gôg 'ereṣ hammāgôg* | |
| *nĕśî' rōš mešek wĕtubāl* | |
| *wĕhinnābē' 'ālāyw wĕāmartā* | *hinnābē' al gôg wĕāmartā* |
| *koh 'āmar 'ădōnāy YHWH* | *koh 'āmar 'ădōnay YHWH* |
| *hinĕnî ēlêkā gôg* | *hinĕnî ēlekā gôg* |
| *nĕśî'* | *nĕśî'* |
| *rōš mešek ûtubāl* | *rōš mešek ûtubāl* |
| *wĕšôbabtîkā* | *wĕšôbabtîkā* |

---

3. Aharoni, *Structure of the Prophecy*, 52-53, would rather divide chapters 38-39 into the six portions beginning with *kōh 'āmar 'ădōnāy YHWH*, "Thus declared Lord YHWH" (38:3-9, 10-13, 14-16, 17-23; 39:1-16, 17-24).

4. Greenberg, *Ezekiel 1-20*, 25-27, 137-38.

## Introduction: Structure and Message

| 38:1–4aα | 39:1–2aα |
|---|---|
| The word of YHWH came to me saying, | |
| "As for you, | |
| "Human, | "Human, |
| set your face toward Gog, | |
| of the land of the Magog, | |
| the prince, | |
| chief of Meshech and Tubal. | |
| Prophesy against him and say: | prophesy against Gog and say: |
| 'Thus has the Lord YHWH declared: | 'Thus has the Lord YHWH declared, |
| Lo, I am against you, O Gog, | Lo, I am against you, O Gog, |
| prince, | prince, |
| chief of Meshech and Tubal, | chief of Meshech and Tubal, |
| I will turn you around . . .'" | I will turn you around . . .'" |

As pointed out by Daniel Block, "The opening word-event formula (henceforth word-action pattern) serves as a general heading for both chapters, but the echo strategy thereafter suggests that chs. 38 and 39 function as a diptych, two leaves of a single document."[5] More precisely, 38:1–4 and 39:1–2 are "halving" equivalents.

The integral unity of Ezekiel 38–39 and its tie to chapters 40–45 are demonstrated by emphasis on the number seven, the integer of fullness and completion. For examples consider (1) the recorded dates: the seventh month (45:25), the seventh day (45:20), seven days (43:25, 26; 44:26; 45:23, 25), seven months (39:12, 14), seven years (39:25); (2) specified objects: seven kinds of weapons (39:9–10), seven steps (40:22, 26); seven bulls (45:23), seven rams (45:23); (3) seven references to knowing God (38:16, 23; 39:6, 7, 22, 23, 28); (4) measures: seven cubits (41:3). Especially significant is 45:23. Instead of the graded series of whole burnt sacrifices that mark P's Tabernacle (*Sukkot*, Num 29:12–34), Ezekiel ordains that all prescribed burnt offerings are seven in number: seven bulls and seven rams on the seven days of the seventh month (beginning on the fifteenth day, 45:23). Finally, the seven attacking nations—again the number symbolizing totality and completion—form a merism: Meshech, Tubal, Gomer, and Beth-Togarmah, which represent the northern extreme of the world known to Israel; Persia, Cush, and Put, the southern (and eastern) extreme, suggesting that the *whole world* is involved in this invasion.

A major question remains concerning Ezekiel's theology. As a priest he is the scion of the Holiness School, which projects the following blessing for Israel: "I will grant peace in the land, so that you shall lie down, and no one shall make you afraid; I will eliminate vicious beasts from the land, and *no sword shall traverse your land*" (Lev 26:6).[6] This means that the enemy will be stopped at the border; God will not

---

5. Block, *Ezekiel 25–48*, 424–25.
6. See Milgrom, *Leviticus 23–27*, 2295–99.

permit a hostile force to penetrate his land. Why then were Gog and his fully armed cohorts permitted to enter? The question is especially acute because subsequent to their annihilation on the mountains of Israel (38:8; 39:4) the Israelites would have to expend much energy and time (at least seven months, 39:12) burying the strewn enemy corpses and purifying the land (39:16). In keeping with Lev 26:6,[7] why would the enemy not be held at bay at the land's borders? As soon as Israel is resettled (miraculously) in its land (chs. 36–37), it can engage in learning the architecture and laws of the visionary sanctuary that YHWH has revealed to Ezekiel (chs. 40–46). Thereafter it can fertilize the barren parts of the land and reallot it equally among the twelve tribes (chs. 47–48). In other words, according to the view of the redactor(s) of Leviticus ($H_R$), the Gog chapters would be entirely superfluous!

The answer lies in the explicit objective of the divine intervention in 38–39. Not only does it propose to rescue Israel from its avowed enemies, but also to enlarge and sanctify the name of YHWH among the nations (38:23). These nations have witnessed YHWH inviting the Babylonians (or lacking the ability to prevent the Babylonians) to enter the land, raze its temple, and exile its inhabitants (chs. 1–11). Now YHWH will again enter the land and destroy the very nations that have entered the land to plunder it (38:12). The divine principle of "measure for measure" is in operation. The nation(s) that entered the land to devastate it will now be devastated on Israel's mountains. Indeed, Ezekiel 38–39 is a quintessential element in the structure and plot of the story.

Alternatively, as suggested by Kaufmann, the plot of the Gog pericope is based on the tradition of Israel's crossing of the Red Sea (Exod 14:2–4, 8, 17–18).[8] Israel lies helpless on unprotected banks/country, but when Egypt/Gog enters the sea/land, God intervenes and the enemy is annihilated.

There is yet another message devolving from the placement of chapters 38–39. Ezekiel is telling his progeny that Israel's settlement on its land cannot be secure unless the inimical nations that surround it are neutralized or destroyed, a lesson that informs international history to this very day.

---

7. Ibid., 2295–96.
8. Kaufmann, *Religion of Israel*, 446.

UNIT 1

# YHWH's Program for Gog's Attack against Israel in the Distant Future (38:1–13)

*Preface and Frame 1: YHWH's Conscription of Gog (38:1–9)*

TRANSLATION

*Preface (38:1–2b)*

1 The word of YHWH came to me: 2 Human, set your face against Gog of the land of Magog,¹ prince, chief of Meshech and Tubal.²

FRAME 1: YHWH's Conscription of Gog (38:2c–9)

2c Prophesy against him, 3 saying: Thus the Lord YHWH has said: Look, I am coming at you, O Gog, prince, chief of Meshech and Tubal. 4 I will turn you around³ and put hooks into your jaws; I will bring you forth, you and all your army, horsemen and charioteers,⁴ all handsomely outfitted,⁵ a vast assembly,⁶ armed with bucklers and shields, all of them wielding swords.⁷ 5 Persia, Cush,

---

1. Tg. and Vulg. follow MT, but LXX and Pesh. add the copula (as above), suggesting that Magog was treated as the name of a people; cf. Rashi. Magog occurs with an article only here (cf. 39:6; Gen 10:2; 1 Chr 1:5); [432, n. 29]; cf. Radak.

2. The Versions are inconsistent in their renderings of *nāśî' rōš mešek wĕtubāl*. LXX ρως treats *rōš* as a proper name. Tg. apparently follows MT's pointing as an extended construct chain with two genitives. Pesh. understands the first two terms as a coordinate pair. Vulg. *principem capitis* sees in *rōš* an intensification of the title *nāśî'*. Many delete *nāśî'* as a secondary interpretation of *rōš*, though the present construction recurs in verse 3 and 39:2 [432, n. 28]. For further discussion see the COMMENT.

3. The Polel of *šûb* recurs in 39:2 and 29:27 [436, n. 50]; "induce" (magically) cf. Hos 8:6; Menahem ben Simeon; Eliezer of Beaugency.

4. On the word pair, *sûsîm* and *pārāšîm*, see above on 26:7. Cf. also 23:6, 12, where *pārāšîm* is followed by *rōkĕbê sûsîm* "riders of horses" [437, n. 52].

5. LXX ενδεδυμενους θωρακας παντας, "dressed in breastplates," and Pesh. *zyn'*, "weapon," for *miklôl* render the military imagery more explicit [437, n. 53].

6. Cf. *qāhāl gādôl wĕḥayil rāb* in verse 15. *qāhāl rāb* also occurs in 17:17; 26:7; 32:3, 38 [437, n. 54].

7. Without a connective particle, *ṣinnâ ûmāgēn tōpĕśê ḥărābôt kullām* is cryptic and intrusive. Pesh. smooths the text, reading *bnzk' wbskn*, "with lances and shields," and linking the following *klhwn* (MT

# EZEKIEL'S HOPE

and Put joining them, all armed with shields and helmets. **6** Gomer and all its hordes,[8] Beth-Togarmah[9] from the distant[10] north, and all its cohorts—many peoples with you.

**7** Get ready, prepare yourselves![11]—you and the whole mob that has crowded[12] about you. You will become their[13] guard.[14] **8** Much later you will be summoned;[15] in the distant future[16] you will invade a land that has survived[17] the sword, and [whose population] has been assembled[18] from many peoples on the mountains of Israel, which had long been devastated. Now they [its inhabitants] have been freed from the peoples;[19] they are all living in safety. **9** You will rise up[20] like a tempest advancing like the storm cloud that blankets the land—you and all your troops, and many peoples with you.[21]

## COMMENT

**1-2.** The word-action pattern is followed by the direct address to the prophet as *ben-ʾādām*, "Human," and an order to the prophet to orient himself toward Gog. This is

---

*kullām*) to verse 5. Tg. clarifies by inserting the particle *dmzyynyn*, "who are armed," to go with the added preposition b. LXX appears to read *māgēn wěqôbāʿ*, "hand shield and helmet," while dropping *tōpěśê* [437, n. 56]. Following Tg., read *běṣinnâ*. Add *b* to *ṣinnâ* by haplography. Most commentators delete the whole line as a gloss.

8. *ʾaggāpîm* is a genuinely Ezekelian word, occurring outside this context (cf. vv. 9, 22; 39:4) only in 12:14 and 17:21 [437, n. 58].

9. Beth-Togarmah. A city-state in NE Anatolia, Akkadian *Tîl-Garimmu*.

10. *yarkětê ṣāpôn*, "distant north." Read with LXX and Pesh. *miyyarkětê*.

11. Note the assonance of *hikkōn wěhākēn lěkā*, a combination of Niphal and Hiphil imperatives of the same root [437, n. 60]; see Rashi.

12. *hanniqhālîm*, defines the collective *qāhāl*. Cf. GKC §145c. Num 10:7 and 20:10 contain similar constructions. The coordination of nominal and verbal forms of *qāhāl* recurs in verse 13 [437, n. 61].

13. MT *lāhem*, "for them," (also Tg. and Pesh.) is difficult, but is preferable to "for me," reflected in LXX (cf. REB), on the principle of *lectio difficilior* [437, n.62].

14. *mišmār*, "guard." "You will guard them" (Rashi), though Radak renders "they will guard you," i.e., they will guide you on the right path. LXX renders "agent" (*měšārēt*) of YHWH.

15. In military contexts, *pāqad* means "to summon, muster"; see 23:22; Isa 10:28 [437, n. 63].

16. Yet, judging from 39:8, the comeuppance to Gog is about to occur.

17. *měšûbebet*, "survived," is a Polel fem. participle of *šûb*. Cf. Holladay, *The Root šûb*, 106-7 [438, n. 64]. Alternatively, "spared by the sword," Menahem ben Simeon.

18. Following Pesh. and Vulg., which smooth out MT by adding the copula before *měqubbeṣet* (see Menahem). Elsewhere in Ezekiel the verb *qibbēṣ*, "gather," is associated only with living objects: the house of Israel, 22:19-20; the entire people of Israel or portions thereof, 11:17; 20:34, 41; 28:25; 34:13; 36:24; 37:21; 39:27; Jerusalem lovers, 16:37; Egyptians, 29:13; animals, 29:5; 39:17 [438, n. 65]. The reader might note in verse 8b the sequence of *segolim* creating the rhymed verse of a song.

19. The fem. form, *wěhî*... *hûṣāʾâ* assumes the land as the subject, but the following *kullām*, "all of them," has the people in mind [438, n. 67].

20. Arise, *wěʿalîtâ*, lit., "go up"; so too in verses 11 and 16. The literal meaning "ascend, go up" may be the best, since Gog and his hordes are located in the lowlands, and they are headed for the mountains of Israel (v. 8).

21. On MT *ʾōtāk* as a stylistic variant of *ʾittāk*, see Block, *Ezekiel 1-24*, 114, n. 7.

## Unit 1: YHWH's Program for Gog's Attack against Israel (38:1–13)

the last of the six occurrences of the (hostile) orientation formula (cf. 6:2; 13:17; 21:7; 25:2; 28:21) [432].

**Gog.** Gyges, king of Lydia, is probably the historical person linked to the name Gog. Ashurbanipal (668–631 BCE) authorized the inclusion of his name in six inscriptions. Gyges' name also appears in a sixth-century ashlar inscription discovered at Bin Tepe (Akkadian, *gugu*) thought to be located in the heart of Lydia. Sometime between 668–665, Gyges of Lydia sought Assyrian military support against Cimmerian pressure. Other Anatolian states, including Tabal, joined the Assyrian camp. Ashurbanipal signed a nonaggression pact with the Cimmerians and in ca. 650 Gyges met a violent death at the hands of the Cimmerians.[22] In the time of Gyges' great-grandson, Alyattes, a contemporary of Ezekiel, Lydia once again became the dominant power in western Anatolia. As pointed out by Zimmerli,[23] "Gog is introduced not as a ruler of a great empire but as a leader of a number of national groups," a political-historical situation corresponding to the relation of Alyattes/Gyges. Possibly Gyges/Gugu may actually have been the throne name of the dynasty; Ezekiel may have known it not only as the name of a legendary ruler but also as the name of a living rule—Alyattes/Gyges of his time. Hence, the latter is called *nāśî'*, "chief" (below).

**of the land of Magog (*'ereṣ hammāgôg*).** This name, which recurs in 39:6, as the name of a people (Rashi), appears the Hebrew Bible only in Gen 10:2 and 1 Chr 1:5, where Magog is named as the second of Japeth's seven sons. Magog as a personal name in LXX anticipates later writings in which he and Gog, are caught up in the final "end of days" battle (Rev 20:8; *Sib. Or.* 3:319–20, 512).[24] Some see *māt gūgi* "land of Gog" shortened to Gog as associated with the land of Lydia in western Anatolia.[25]

**chief of Meshech and Tubal (*rō'š mešek wětubāl*).** MT *něśî' rō'š* (followed by LXX) reads as a broken construct, "prince of Rosh, Meshech, and Tubal," whereby *něśî'* is vocalized as the construct of *nāśî'*, and is so translated.[26] Alternatively, the construct can be retained: Gog's title is *gôg něśî' hārō'š*, "Gog the chief prince," modeled after *śěrāyâ kōhēn hārō'š* (Jer 52:24). Once a second construct is added *hārō'š* becomes *rō'š*. Odell relates the expression to *nōśē' 'et-rō'š*, lit., "head-counter" (Num 1:2, 44; 4:34, 46).[27] Even if one would change the verb *nōśē'* into the noun *nāśî'*, it is unlikely that an of-

---

22. For details, see "Gyges and Ashurbanipal," M. Cogan and H. Tadmor, 65–85, and Block, *Ezekiel 25–48*, 731, n. 32.

23. Zimmerli, *Ezekiel 2*, 305.

24. Cf. Block, *Ezekiel 25–48*, 434, n. 35.

25. Josephus (*Ant.* 1.6.1§123) identified Magog with the Scythians: "Magog founded the Magogians, thus named after him, but who by the Greeks are called Scythians." The name has no geographic or ethnographic analogies in ancient Near Eastern literature, though Albright, "Contributions to Biblical Archaeology," 383, proposed a blend with Manda, an abbreviation of Umman Manda, the common Mesopotamian designation for "barbarian."

26. The attempt of politicians and religionists to equate *rō'š* with Russia is briefly described and debunked by Block, *Ezekiel 25–48*, 434–35.

27. Odell, "Defeat of Gog," 168.

ficial who on rare occasions merely conducts a census might be delegated to command an international military coalition. Although Gog is less than a king, at least he is not a census taker. Gog's title remains a puzzle. Was he not a king? *Rōš*, "chief," is best perceived as a lower case noun, defining the preceding *nāsî*', "prince." The names Meshech and Tubal have turned up earlier in the commercial inventory of Tyre (27:13) and among the casualties in Sheol (32:26). Neo-Assyrian sources mention both Meshech (Musku/Mušku) and Tubal (Tabal). Meshech (Muski) was subject to King Mitas (the legendary Midas) during the reign of Sargon II. Tubal/Tabal, bounded on the west by Meshech, had no access to the sea. Gog (Lydia), further west, headed an alliance with Meshech on her east, and Tubal still further east of Meshech. Block [436] conjectures that these distant nations were mentioned because the fame of Gyges and Midas had spread as far as Babylon and the report of its mysterious people spoke of its wildness and brutality. My conjecture, on the other hand, proposes that these far off nations in all directions—north, south, and east—create a literary merism, indicating that Israel was invaded by all its surrounding nations.

**2c-3.** In previous oracles, YHWH had challenged Judah/Israel (5:8; 21:8 [Eng 3]), the false prophets (13:8), Pharaoh (29:3; 30:22), and Edom (35:3); this time the duel will be between YHWH himself and Gog and his confederates. The initial phrase, a call to battle, orders Gog into the fray (vv. 4–6), and details his required military strategy [438].

**3b–6.** *So I am coming at you* (*hinĕnî 'ēlêkā* = *'alêkā*; cf. 8:5). According to verse 4b Gog's forces are well-equipped, clothed and armed defensively (buckler and shield, either carried or worn on the arm) and offensively (swords), with cavalry and horse-driven chariots. Gog is not alone. The forces that join Meshech and Tubal include the African nations Cush (Ethiopia) and Put (Libya) and Paras (Persia) to the east. But it is unlikely that African nations would join an Anatolian coalition. Additionally, the mention of Persia—a people hardly known in Ezekiel's time—suggests deleting this trio in verse 5 as a late gloss[28] [439]. However, as suggested earlier, these nations form an imaginary merism, and Persia, though not yet a kingdom, was a well known conglomerate of tribes.[29] Also, these nations may comprise a mercenary force, cf. 27:10; Jer 46:9.

Other allies, *Gomer* and *Beth-Togarmah* are identified in verse 6. Gomer is a brother of Meshech, Tubal, and Magog and father of Togarmah (Gen 10:2–3). Gomer, rendered Gimmeraia in Akkadian and Cimmerian in Greek, is known as a savage tribe occupying foggy territory north of the Black Sea [440]. According to Strabo (*Geography*, 1.61), King Midas took his life in despair over the loss of the Phrygian capital Gordion to the Cimmerians. The latter were finally defeated by the Assyrians,

---

28. E.g., Zimmerli, *Ezekiel 2*, 306.

29. See also the pointed arguments of Odell, "Are you of whom I spoke," 103–6, but her arguments for an unknown Paras are unacceptable.

## Unit 1: YHWH's Program for Gog's Attack against Israel (38:1–13)

their people assimilating into the native Anatolian population. An earlier list of Tyrian trading partners provides reference to Beth-Togarmah (27:14).

The expression, *yarkĕtê sāpôn* (v. 6 and 39:2), indicates that the Gog oracle reflected prophecies of Jeremiah and Isaiah, unrealized, concerning "the enemy from the north."[30] The texts most often cited are Jer 1:13–14; 4:6–17; 6:1–30. However, see below.

Seven is the number of allies, the same symbolic number as in the oracles against the nations (chs. 25–32). The term *'aggāpîm*, "rabble," occurs seven times, only in Ezekiel. Note also the enemy's seven weapons (39:9), the seven years worth of fuel these provided (39:9), and the seven months needed to bury the enemy corpses (39:12). The artificiality of this list offers further evidence that these nations are a merism forming a universal conspiracy against Israel. Gog's every move is controlled by YHWH (vv. 4–6). He is pictured with hooks in his jaws being dragged to the mountains of Israel [441]. The image is taken from real life. See, for example, the Zincirli Stele.[31] Esarhaddon, a towering figure, holds two miniscule kings (Egypt and probably Tyre) by hooks inserted into their mouths. Esarhaddon describes himself as one "who holds the reigns of princes." The fitting biblical analog is: "They took Manasseh captive in hooks (*ḥôḥîm*), bound him with fetters, and brought him to Babylon" (2 Chr 33:11).

**7–8.** Verse 7 is YHWH's formal call to Gog, emphatically expressed as a double command (*hikkōn wĕhākēn lĕkā*) plus a purpose clause constructed of lamed plus noun/infinitive construct, cf. *hikkōn liqra't 'ĕlōhêkā*, "Prepare to meet your God" (Amos 4:12; cf. Jer 46:14; for the same construction, cf. 14:6; 18:30). Although the singular of the imperative shows the oracle's main concern with Gog, the following phrase amplifies the call to his allies: "Your assembly that has been mustered about you" [442]. YHWH charges Gog to assume leadership by serving as the *mišmār*, "guard," of the allied forces. Gog's initial commission omits any reference to Israel. The divine summons to Gog is not to be expected in the near future, but *miyyāmîm rabbîm*, "after a long time,"[32] and *bĕ'aḥărît haššānîm*, lit., "in later years." This is a stylistic variant of *bĕ'aḥărît hayyāmîm*, "in later days," in verse 16, a frequently occurring expression (Gen 49:1; Num 24:14; Deut 4:30; 31:29; Isa 2:2=Mic 4:1; Jer 23:20=30:24; 48:47; 49:30; Dan 2:28; 10:14). An exact counterpart is found in Akk *ina/ana aḫ-ri-a-at ūmī*; see *AHw* 21; *CAD* 1/1:194 [443].

According to verse 8, two conditions will precede Gog's invasion. First, the land itself will have recovered from the slaughter of its people. Second, the population will have been ingathered from the many peoples of the diaspora (*'ammîm rabbîm*) and planted securely within the land. The condition of the population at the time of the invasion is reflected in *yāšab lĕbeṭaḥ*, "living securely," derived from Lev 25:18, 19;

---

30. Aharoni, "The Gog Prophecy," 14–15; Zimmerli, *Ezekiel 2*, 299–300.
31. See Pritchard, *ANEP*[2], 154 and 300.
32. This expression is found only once elsewhere, in Josh 23:1, where it defines the period between Israel's entrance into the land and Joshua's farewell address.

26:5 (H), a key term in this oracle (vv. 11, 14; 39:26). As pointed out by von Rad,[33] the premise of Israel's covenant with its God is that Israel need but stand firm and YHWH will fight its battles, as Moses counsels his people: "Do not be afraid, stand firm and see the deliverance that YHWH will do for you today . . . YHWH will fight for you, and you have only to keep still" (Exod 14:13–14). This advice was followed by subsequent prophets, e.g., Isa 30:15; Mic 4:11–13; Ezek 38–39; Hag 2:21–22. The restoration of the population is highlighted in 36:24, 33–36 and in 34:25–29. Gog's invasion underlies the realization of the salvation oracles in chapters 34–37.

**9.** Ezekiel's use of *šō'â*, "storm," may be derived from Isa 10:3: "what will you do on the day of punishment (*pĕquddâ*) in the storm (*šō'â*) that will cover the land?" cf. Prov 1:27. *šō'â*, literally "devastation"—used today to identify the Holocaust—when paired with *'ānān*, a destructive "storm cloud" (30:3),[34] becomes a metaphor for the storming attack of many soldiers (cf. Jer 4:13).

### *Frame 2: The Motives of Gog (38:10–13)*

TRANSLATION

> 10 Thus said the Lord YHWH: On that day, thoughts will occur to you[35] and you will plot an evil scheme.[36] 11 You will say to yourself: I will rise up against a land of open towns; I will strike[37] the complacent people, all living safely[38] in unwalled towns without bolted double doors[39] 12 to seize booty and to cart off the spoils[40]—to turn your hand[41] against the resettled[42] ruins and against

---

33. Von Rad, *Holy War in Ancient Israel*.

34. For a discussion of the metaphor in Ugaritic and Hebrew (including this text), see de Moor and de Vries, "Hebrew *hādād* 'Thunder-Storm,'" 176–77.

35. On the idiom *'ālâ 'al-lēb*, see Block, *Ezekiel 1–24*, 425, n. 35 [445, n. 100].

36. *ḥāšab maḥšebet*, "to scheme schemes," is a standard Hebrew idiom (2 Sam 14:14; Jer 11:19; 18:11, 18; 29:11; 49:20, 30; Dan 11:24; Esth 8:3; 9:25. In Exod 31:4; 35:32, 33, 35; 2 Chr 2:13; 26:16 the idiom has the positive meaning "to be skilled in a craft" [445, n. 101]. Hence, an "evil scheme" requires the addition of *rā'â*.

37. The anticipated cohortative after *'e'ĕleh* requires redividing *'bw hšqtwm* as *'bwh šqtym* (Zimmerli, *Ezekiel 2*, 287), but *bô'* in the sense of "attack," may tolerate a direct object, see 32:11. The pairing of *'ālâ*, "to go up against," and *bô'*, "to enter," provides an intentional link with verse 9 [445, n.103].

38. The construct state (*yōšĕbê*) followed by a prepositional phrase (*lābeṭaḥ*) occurs also in the next verse (*yōšĕbê 'al ṭabbûr*). For the syntactic structure, see Isa 5:11.

39. *dĕlātayîm*, "gates." The dual construction is a reminder that the gate constituted two doors and that a bar (*bārîaḥ*) was inserted between the doors to bolt them.

40. Gog's quest is not conquest and rule, but plunder.

41. LXX "my hand" continues the internal monologue [445, n.106]. *lĕhāšib yādĕkā 'al*, "To turn your hand," "to strike" (cf. Amos 1:8; Zech 13:7; Ps 81:15).

42. Menahem ben Simeon refers us to *wĕnôšăbû hē'ārîm wĕhehărābôt tibbānênā*, "the cities will be repopulated and the ruins will be rebuilt" (36:10b). Here the "ruins will be repopulated."

## Unit 1: YHWH's Program for Gog's Attack against Israel (38:1-13)

the people ingathered from the nations, who have gotten[43] cattle and goods, and live at the navel[44] of the earth. **13** Sheba and Dedan and the merchants of Tarshish, and all its leaders,[45] will ask you, "Is it to despoil that you have come?—Is it to plunder that you have mustered your allies? To rip off silver and gold? To confiscate cattle and goods? To loot everything?"

### COMMENT

**10-11.** A new formula marks the beginning of the second frame. Gog's schemes shift the focus away from YHWH's plan. He aims to attack an innocent country, a land of *pĕrāzôt*, found only in Zech 2:8 (Eng 4) and Esth 9:12, rural settlements unwalled and ungated.[46] The aggressor's plot and the target's illusion of safety recall Jer 49:30-31:

> Nebuchadrezzar king of Babylon has devised a plan against you—
> he has conceived a scheme against you (*ḥāšab ʿălêkem maḥăšābôt*)
> Arise, attack a nation at ease (*gôy šĕlēyw yôšeb lābeṭaḥ*)—
> the declaration of YHWH—
> That has no gates or bars (*lōʾ-dĕlātayim wĕlōʾ-bĕrîaḥ lô*)
> That dwell alone [446].

**12.** Gog admits his lust for booty. The oracle addresses Gog in the second person. The target land has been resettled in fulfillment of 36:10: the people have been ingathered from their diaspora, are rich with abundant cattle and goods, fulfilling 34:26-27, and are living at the navel of the land of Israel. The common rendering, "navel of the earth," based on LXX ομφαλος, is questioned [447].[47]

**13.** Merchants trading via overland routes across the Arabian Desert (e.g., Sheba and Dedan) and sailing the Mediterranean to the west (Tarshish) trail Gog's armies to plunder. These three extreme east and west names probably compose a merism, i.e., all the surrounding nations either join Gog's armies or follow in their wake, for com-

---

43. The sg. form *ʿōśeh* is influenced by the preceding collective *ʿam*. The following *yôšĕbê* calls for a pl. form. So too Pesh. and Tg. [445, n.107].

44. *ṭabbûr*, "center," or "navel," or "highest point"; cf. *BDB*, 375. Tg. renders the term *tuqba*, "stronghold," which Radak [448, n. 120] explains geographically as a reference to the land of Israel being located higher than any surrounding country. For further discussion, see Levey, *Targum of Ezekiel*, 107, n. 8 [447-48].

45. LXX, Pesh., and Vulg. mistranslate *kĕpirêhā*, "young lions," as from *kĕpārêhā*, "her villages," so Eliezer of Beaugency. So also RSV (but not NRSV), NASB, NIV. Cf. Josh 18:24; 1 Sam 6:18; 1 Chr 17:25; Cant 7:25. But MT's vocalization and Tg. *wkl mlkh*', "and all her kings," point in a different direction. BHS, Zimmerli, *Ezekiel 2*, 2, 287, and others (e.g., NJPS) see here a corruption for *rklyh*, "its traders." Cf. *sḥr* parallel to *rkl* in 27:12-13, 15-16, 17-18, 20-21a, 21b-22 [445, n. 109]. Rashi renders "outstanding merchants" and Radak leans to "powerful officials" on the basis of 32:2; cf. also Menahem Ben Simeon.

46. A standard triad; cf. Deut 3:5; 2 Chr 8:5; 14:6. Strangely, the future city will have gates (48:30-35), though their function will not be military. Cf. gentilic *pĕrîzî* for the residents of unwalled villages (Deut 3:5; 1 Sam 6:28; cf. Naʾaman (1991), 72-75 [446, n. 111].

47. Cf. B. W. Anderson, "The Place of Shechem," 10-11. Note also that Greek oracle sanctuaries, such as in Dydima, Miletus, and Delphi, were viewed as the navel or the center of the earth. However, the etymology and, hence, the meaning of *ṭabbûr* is uncertain [447]. Cf. *EM* 3:362.

mercial gain. *Sōḥărîm*, "traders," recalls the Tyre trade list in chapter 27, and *kĕpirîm*, (lit., "lions") leading traders, also have their eyes on the spoil (*šālāl*), booty (*baz*), silver (*kesep*), gold (*zāhāb*), cattle (*miqneh*), and movable goods (*qinyān*) [449]. These two frames (38:2–9, 10–13) dealing with Gog's armies and their merchant vultures are now followed by YHWH's counterplans (38:14–16) and strategy (38:17–23).

# UNIT 2

# YHWH's Anger in View of Gog's Advance against Israel (38:14–23)

*Frame 3: YHWH'S Counterplan: His Goal (38:14–16)*

### TRANSLATION

**14** So, prophesy, human, speaking to Gog: Thus the Lord YHWH has said: Surely,[1] you know the day, when my people, Israel, dwell in safety![2] **15** You will come from your home in the distant north—you and many peoples with you, all of them on horseback; a vast mob, a huge army. **16** You will storm against my people, Israel, like a thick cloud blanketing the earth. It is in the distant future, that I will set you against my land so that the nations may know me,[3] when I reveal my holiness through you before their very eyes, O Gog.[4]

### COMMENT

**14a.** Therefore, *lākēn* connects this frame with the preceding: YHWH's anger is provoked by Gog's self-importance [450]. The association of the two frames is further supported structurally, by the inverse chiasm of verses 8–9 and 15–16:

---

1. *hălō'* here is an emphatic particle; see Brown, "Is It Not?" 201–19, esp. 216 [449, n. 124].

2. MT *tēdaʿ* is supported by Pesh., Vulg, and Tg. Many emend it *tēʿōr*, "you will be roused," with LXX, on the assumption that MT misread *r* for *d* and transposed the last two letters; cf. NRSV, REB, NJPS (Allen, *Ezekiel 20–48*, 200) [449, n. 125]. However, MT is plausible: "you will know (the punishment of my might)"; Tg., Rashi: "you will know (who is protecting them when you are overcome by their God)"; Kara: "you will know (who indeed I am)," Menahem ben Simeon.

3. Tg.'s paraphrase, "they will know the punishment of my might," may have recognized the anomalous form of the naming pattern, *lĕmaʿan daʿat haggôyim ʾōtî* [449, n. 126]. God cannot be seen directly by the nations but they can observe his intervention in history by observing his acts within Israel.

4. The vocative heightens the speaker's emotion. Pesh.'s omission of the vocative and LXX's attachment of it to verse 17 are insufficient grounds for its deletion [449, n. 127].

# Ezekiel's Hope

## Frames 2 and 3

| vv. 8–9 | vv. 15–16 |
|---|---|
| a. *miyyāmîm rabbîm tippāqēd<br>bĕ'aḥărît haššānîm<br>tābô' 'el-'ereṣ<br>mĕšôbebet mēḥereb* | c.' *ûbā'tā mimmĕqômĕkā<br>miyyarkĕtê 'āreṣ<br>'attâ wĕ'ammîm rabbîm 'ittāk* |
| b. *wĕ'ālîtā kaššô'â<br>lābô' kĕ'ānân<br>lĕkassôt hā'āreṣ* | b.' *wĕ'ālîta 'al-'ammî yiśrā'ēl<br>ke'ānān<br>lĕkassôt hā'āreṣ* |
| c. *'attâ wĕkol-'ăgappêkā<br>wĕ'ammîm rabbîm 'ōtĕkā* | a.' *bĕ'aḥărît hayyāmîm tihyeh<br>wahăbi'ōtîkā 'al-'arṣî* |
| a. After a long time you will be summoned, in the distant future you will march against a land that has been reclaimed from the sword. | c.' You will come from your homeland in the remotest parts of the earth— you and many people's with you. |
| b. You will advance like a thunderstorm; you will come like the storm cloud covering the land. | b.' You will advance upon my people Israel, like a storm cloud covering the land. |
| c. You and all your allies, and many people with you. | a.' In the distant future, when it happens, I will bring you against my land. |

Seidel is credited with the discovery of this inverse chiasm found variously in the Ezekiel text,[5] confirming that YHWH, not Gog and his rabble, designed the attack against the unsuspecting people of Israel, whereby Israel's erstwhile enemies would be destroyed and YHWH's reputation among the nations restored.

**14b–16a.** YHWH's intervention is motivated by Gog's attack against "my people Israel" (vv. 14, 16) and against "my land" (v. 16). For Gog to assault YHWH's people and to invade YHWH's land equals declaring war against YHWH. Moreover, Gog will ambush Israel while it is enjoying its safety. The real adversaries in this oracle are not YHWH and Israel but YHWH and Gog, who is YHWH's puppet. YHWH is again carrying out his contractual threats against his people. However, the puppet will feel divine retribution [451]. Joyce suggests that it is reminiscent of Isa 10, when the "puppet" Assyria (YHWH's rod, v. 5) is punished for arrogantly overstepping its mission. Gog too "has no commission to devastate YHWH's people."[6] The analogy is incorrect; Gog does what he is told.

**16b.** Gog's invasion is planned according to YHWH's timetable; it is pushed off into the distant future, *bĕ'aḥărît hayyāmîm*, "at the end of days," once Israel is established and flourishing. However, YHWH is dissatisfied that only Israel would learn the lesson from its full restoration. The nations that ridiculed YHWH for his impotence in protecting his people and his land motivate his intervention. Israel's ingathering on its own land will be a sign of YHWH's omnipotence and his holy name (36:22–23). There

---

5. Seidel, "Parallels Between Isaiah and Psalms," 1–97.
6. Joyce, *Ezekiel*, 214, and 215, on 38:18.

Unit 2: YHWH's Anger in View of Gog's Advance against Israel (38:14–23)

is indeed an operative agent in this scenario, but it is not Gog, who is solely manipulated by YHWH. In saving his people and his land YHWH convinces the world of his incomparable power and holiness [450].

## Frame 4: YHWH's Counterplan: His Strategy (38:17–23)

### TRANSLATION

17 Thus announced the Lord YHWH: Aren't you the one[7] of whom I spoke in the early days[8] through my servants, the prophets of Israel, who prophesied for many years[9] that I would set you against them?

18 Now on that day, when Gog sets foot on the land of Israel—announced the Lord YHWH—I will fume with rage.[10] 19 In my zeal and burning passion I have said: For sure, on that day, a terrible earthquake will strike the land of Israel. 20 The fish of the sea, the birds of the sky, the animals of the field, every creature that crawls on the ground, and every human being on earth will tremble before me. The mountains will come crashing down, the terraced cliffs[11] will break apart, and every wall will crumble to the ground. 21 Then I will call upon the sword to terrorize him, everywhere,[12]—declared the Lord YHWH—one man's sword will be turned against his fellow. 22 I will punish him with plague and blood, with torrential rain, hailstones, fire, and brimstone upon him and the masses with him.

23 Thus will I flaunt my grandeur and my holiness[13] making myself known in the sight of many nations. Then they will know that I am YHWH.

### COMMENT

**17.** At the command of YHWH, Gog and his allies are marching on the land of Israel with the intent to sack and pillage every corner of this unsuspecting country. YHWH now sets before Gog a leading question: Are you the one handed down by the prophets

---

7. Many follow LXX, Pesh., and Vulg in reading an affirmative statement, assuming the *hē* on *hă'attâ* is a dittography (*BHS*, followed by NJPS, NAB, NIV, REB, most recently Kasher, *Ezekiel* 2:147). But haplography in the Versions is more likely; see COMMENT [452, n. 132].

8. *bĕyāmîm qadmônîm* answers to *bĕ'aḥărît hayyāmîm* (v. 16) [452, n. 133].

9. Radak, Mitrani, LXX, and Pesh. smooth out MT's awkward asyndetic construction of *bayyāmîm hāhēm šānîm* by adding the copula to *šānîm*. Talmon ("Double Readings in the Massoretic Text," 171) plausibly proposes a conflation of two synonymous readings: *bymym hhm* and *[b]šnym* [452, n. 134].

10. MT *ta'ăleh ḥămātî bĕqirbî*, lit., "my wrath shall go up in my nostrils." *bĕ'appî* is best taken with verse 19 [452, n. 135]. However, *bĕ'appî* is found frequently with *ḥămātî* (e.g., Jer 7:20; 32:31; 33:5; 42:18; Ezek 22:20; 25:14).

11. *BHS* suggests emending *hammadrēgôt* to *hammigdālôt*, "towers" with Pesh. and Tg. Note the pairing of *ḥômâ* and *migdāl* (Isa 2:15) [452, n. 137].

12. MT *wĕqārā'tî 'ālāyw lĕkol-hāray ḥereb*, lit., "I will summon against him to all my mountains a sword," is difficult. LXX φοβον, "fear," presupposes *ḥărādâ* [452, n. 138].

13. LXX intensifies the reading by adding ενδοξασθησομαι, "and my glory," viz. "I will magnify myself, sanctify myself, and glorify myself" [452, n. 139].

to be the divine agent to devastate the land and people of Israel? That is, not only is Gog the present choice of the divinity to destroy Israel, but also the destroyer designated throughout history. The question is rhetorical: its purpose to further aggrandize Gog's inflated ego, that his invasion of Israel is the fulfillment of an age-old universal prophecy expressed by the words *hāāreṣ/haggôy miṣṣāpôn*, "the land/foe from the north," prophesied at-large throughout Jeremiah's career (e.g., Jer 4–6, esp. 6:22). Thus, apart from being motivated by personal greed, Gog's ego would have been bolstered by the conviction that he was the one *historically designated* as the destroyer of Israel. Moreover, as Nebuchadrezzar was identified by Jeremiah as "the foe from the north" for his own generation (Jer 25:9), so Gog was now divinely chosen as the "foe from the north" to wreak even further devastation on Israel at some future time.

If Gog had overlooked that he was dragged by his jaws to be Israel's conqueror (38:4) and, instead had persuaded himself that his military campaign was an act of his free will and desire (38:10–13), he would have answered the prophet's question unhesitatingly in the affirmative. Of course, had he realized from the start that he was only a pawn in the divine scheme, that his real purpose was to aggrandize YHWH's holiness before the very nations that had spurned it (38:23; 39:7, 27), that he was not YHWH's "foe from the north" sent to punish Israel for its national and moral sins, but chosen to be punished for all his sins against Israel, then Gog's answer would have been unambiguously negative.[14] Yet, the true answer was neither positive nor negative. The question was only rhetorical, requiring no response. It was tinged with mockery and colored with sarcasm. Its goal was to sharpen the contrast between the prophet—authentic divine agent, commissioned to bring YHWH's word to Israel—and Gog, who was about to be lashed for his iniquities.[15]

**18–19a.** Divine fury at first spent against Israel now moves against Gog.[16] "I have spoken in my zeal" expresses YHWH's implacable resolve.[17]

**19b–20.** Divine wrath first affects the invaded territory then echoes throughout the universe. YHWH warns in advance: a fearful earthquake will rock the land that Gog plans to conquer.[18] All living things will quake with the quaking of the earth.[19] The

---

14. See Block, "Gog in Prophetic Tradition," 154–72.

15. Kasher, *Ezekiel*, 741, renders *ha'attâ*, "behold you." That is, Gog, indeed, is the person predicted by the ancient prophets. However, the ten occurrences of *ha'attâ* (Gen 27:21; Judg 13:11; 2 Sam 2:20; 7:5; 9:2; 20:17; 1 Kgs 13:14; 18:7, 17; Ezek 38:17) are all interrogative.

16. All these expressions of divine anger have appeared earlier in the book: *ḥēmâ*, "fiery anger" (thirty-three times in Ezekiel, esp. 24:8 with the verb, *'ālâ*, to rise'); *'ap*, "anger" (Ps 18:9 [Eng 8]), which speaks of smoke rising from YHWH's nostrils, *ēš 'ebrātî*, "the fire of my overflow" (cf., 21:36; 22:21, 31) [457, n. 159].

17. On *dibbartî bĕqin'ātî*, see 5:11; 36:6; cf. *bĕēš qin'ātî dibbartî*, "in the fire of my passion I have spoken" [457, n. 160].

18. This is the first time Ezekiel has used *ra'aš* for an earthquake: cf. 31:12–13 (rumbling noise); 12:18 (trembling body); 37:7 (rattling of dry bones); 26:10, 15 (the din of the armies attacking Tyre); 27:28 (the sound of her fall); 31:16 (the collapse of the great tree) [457, n. 161].

19. The catalogue of creatures resembles Gen 1:26, 28; though by virtue of their special status humans are excluded. Similar catalogues of animals occur in Gen 7:14, 21, 23; 8:17; 1 Kgs 5:10 [457, n. 163].

## Unit 2: YHWH's Anger in View of Gog's Advance against Israel (38:14–23)

quake will shatter mountains (symbolic of divine power against nature's stability, albeit of divine origin) and terraced cliffs and crumbling walls (symbols of human creativity) *wĕnehĕrsû*, "they will be hurled down" [457–58]. Ezekiel expands Isaiah's prophecy (Isa 2:12), *kî yôm laYHWH ṣĕbā'ôt 'al kol-gē'eh wārām wĕ'al kōl niśśā' wĕšāpāl*, "for YHWH of Hosts has ready a day against all that is proud and arrogant, against all that is lofty," to include the impact of the divine quake that embraces every living creature, in addition to every man-made and divinely created height.

**21–22.** The Lord YHWH proclaims the sword against Gog.[20] "My mountain" as the target occurs in Isa 14:35 and Zech 14:5 but is unprecedented in Ezekiel. Like our text, Isaiah imagines YHWH destroying a foreign presence in his land whereas Zechariah links earthquake with foreigners fighting in the land of Israel [458], disguising God's participation.

The armies of Gog and his allies turn their weapons against each other, a scene recurring in Zech 14:13. But YHWH punishes Gog beyond the sword: verse 22 lists three disastrous pairs. Fire (*'ēš*) and burning sulfur (brimstone [hell-fire], *goprît*) are known to us from Gen 19:24, but new to Ezekiel. *Goprît* is a yellow crystalline non-metallic substance that burns readily in air, giving off pungent suffocating fumes. Why these calamities? One word summarizes their purpose: *wenišpaṭtî*. The Niphal denotes "to enter into judgments" or "to commit to trial" (cf. 17:20; 24:35–36), but since the guilt has already been established it must mean the carrying out of the sentence [459].

**23.** The purpose of YHWH's revelation is proudly proclaimed in triplicate: to demonstrate his greatness (*hitgaddiltî*), his holiness (*hitqaddištî*), and his *presence* (*nôda'tî*). This verse summarizes YHWH's program for all the events of "that day" (v. 18), opening with YHWH's enlisting of Gog and closing with his termination [459].

---

20. According to Block [458, n. 168], "Even if *ḥăraddû* occurs in 26:16, . . . it is difficult to imagine how scribes could have mistakenly reproduced it as *hāray ḥereb*."

# Unit 3

# The Annihilation of Gog's Army and Its Armaments (39:1–16)

## Frame 5: The Slaughter of Gog (39:1–8)

### Translation

**1** And you, human, prophesy against Gog, and say: Thus has the Lord YHWH proclaimed: See, I am coming at you, O Gog, prince, chief of Meshech and Tubal! **2** I will turn you around,[1] drive you forward,[2] raise you up from the far distant north, and bring you to the mountains of Israel, **3** I will knock your bow from your left hand, and scatter your arrows from your right hand. **4** You will plunge down the mountains of Israel—you and all your masses with you. I will hand you over as carrion to every scavenger bird[3] and wild animal. **5** You will topple over in the open field, for I have spoken—announced the Lord YHWH. **6** And I will set fire against Magog, and on those who live complacently[4] on the coast and islands. Then they will know that I am YHWH. **7** And I will proclaim my holy name among my people Israel. Never again will I allow my holy name to be violated. And the nations will know that I am YHWH, the Holy One of Israel. **8** See! It is here—it has come to pass! The declaration of the Lord YHWH—this is the day of my edict.

---

1. On *wěšōbabtîkā* see 38:4 [460, n. 1].

2. *wěšiššē'tîkā*, "is an inexplicable hapax form." *BDB* (1058) and GKC §55o explain the form as an abbreviated Pilpel from the root *š'*. A similar sense is achieved by emending *wšštyk* to *whš'tyk* on the basis of Tg. *w't'ynk*, "and I will lead you astray" (*BHS*, *HALAT*, 153) [460, n. 2]. Others derive the word from *nś'*, "to lift." AV "to leave the sixth part" follows the medieval derivation of the word from *šiššâ* (Radak, Menahem ben Simeon) or "to deceive, deflect," as in Gen 3:12 (Kara, Eliezer of Beaugency). Block favors "to lead," or "to drive," LXX "to lead" [460, n. 2].

3. *ṣippôr kol-kānāp* is appositional to *lě'ēṭ*, cf. GKC §130e [460, n. 4].

4. LXX transforms the declaration of judgment into a promise of salvation for the coastal lands by reading *wbyšby* as *wyšbw*, "and they will return" [460, n. 6]. Why single out coastal lands for punishment (MT)? LXX reading is preferable.

## Unit 3: The Annihilation of Gog's Army and Its Armaments (39:1–16)

COMMENT

The introduction to the second half of the oracle against Gog echoes 38:2 and applies to the entire chapter 39 [461]. Indeed, the repetition of 38:2 in 39:1, and especially the repetition of *wĕsōbabtîkâ*, "I shall turn you around" (38:4 in 39:2), would give the impression that chapter 39 is an independent variant of chapter 38, were it not for Greenberg's discovery of Ezekiel's halving pattern that proliferates in his book.[5]

Although there is no reference to YHWH's action against Gog—as is the case in 38:1–9—YHWH is the subject of nearly every verse in this frame. The emphasis on YHWH's presence is punctuated by the repeated use of two patterns: naming, "I am YHWH" (vv. 6, 7, 22, 28), and signing, "the declaration of the Lord YHWH" (vv. 5, 8, 10, 13, 20, 29). The repeated chorus of his involvement is a vociferous forecast of his strategy to demolish Gog: He will turn him around, drive him, lead him, knock out his weapons, make his corpses carrion and finally burn up the coastal lands (vv. 2–6).

4–5. Because eating birds of prey was forbidden among the Israelites,[6] the phrase *'ēṭ ṣippôr kol-kānāp* seems perverse. Ezekiel's plan to include vultures, ravens, and crows from his wide experience of carrion-eating birds probably suggests the extent of the losses; there will be enough corpses to feed them all [462].

6a–b. YHWH will send fire against the lands from which Gog and his allies have come: Gog is represented by Magog, his place of origin (38:2), and *yōšĕbê hā'iyyîm*, "the inhabitants of the coastal lands and islands," refers to those who inhabit the Mediterranean coastal regions (cf. *'iyyîm* in Ezek 26:15, 18; 27:3, 6–7, 15, 35), represented by Tarshish (38:13). The coastlands refer to land and sea forces directed by the Anatolian powers. In 38:13 the prophet suggests sarcastically that these merchant nations were jealous observers of Gog's enterprises against the (ironically) "secure" (*lābeṭaḥ*) residents, whereas in fact they have actually taken their stand with Gog against YHWH [463].

6c–8. Verses 7–8 contain a threefold occurrence of the root *qdš*, referring to the divine holy name (*šēm qodšî*), which disallows the frame to end with 6c. The second occurrence recalls 20:39 and 36:20–23; the third reference to YHWH's holiness occurs in verse 7c, *qādōš bĕyiśrā'ēl*, "the Holy One in Israel," the divine title [464], which recalls many texts in Isaiah.[7] Kasher aptly points to the parallel language in Lev 22:31–32, *ûšĕmartem miṣwōtay . . . wĕlō' tĕḥallĕlû 'et-šēm qodšî wĕniqdaštî bĕtôk bĕnê yiśrā'ēl 'ānî YHWH mĕqaddiškem*, "You shall heed my commandments . . . You shall not desecrate my holy name that I may be sanctified in the midst of the Israelites. I am YHWH who sanctifies you."[8] However, he errs in claiming that YHWH's promise is dependent on Israel's obedience to the divine commandments in Leviticus, since Ezekiel opts for holiness, stemming from YHWH, *independent of Israel obedience*. When Israel is

---

5. Cf. n. 3 above.
6. Cansdale, *Animals*, 140–41.
7. Isa 1:4; 5:19, 24; 10:20; 12:6; 17:7; 29:19; 30:11, 12, 15; 31:1; 37:23; 41:14, 16, 20; 43:3, 14; 45:10; 47:4; 48:17; 54:5; 55:5; 60:9, 14.
8. Kasher, *Ezekiel*, 2:753.

more scrupulous in preventing the desecration of God's commandments it appears as if Israel has supplemented YHWH's holiness.[9]

***Never again will I let my holy name be desecrated (wĕlō' 'aḥēl 'et-šēm-qodšî 'ôd).*** This promise renders a recurrence of the exile impossible.

Like "the day of Midian" in Isa 9:3 [Eng 4], "the day [of Gog]" represents the moment of YHWH's decisive intervention on his people's behalf against this enemy. Contrary to a common opinion,[10] according to Block, "the day of which I have spoken," does not pick up on 38:17, which has referred to an earlier prophecy by Ezekiel's precursors. The antecedent pronouncements are Ezekiel's own declarations of the coming of Gog and his demise at the hands of YHWH [464].

***See! It is here—it has come to pass! (hinnēh bā'â wĕnihyātâ).*** Ezekiel's language of surprise (e.g., 21:12), verifies that the Gog oracle was not intended for the distant future but for imminent fulfillment—even in Ezekiel's time.

## Frame 6: The Spoiling of Gog (39:9–10)

### Translation

9 Then the residents of Israel's cities will go out and set fire to the weapons:[11] hand and body shields,[12] bows and arrows, clubs and spears, which will burn for seven years.[13] 10 They will neither carry in wood from the field nor cut from the forests, because the weapons will fuel the fire. They will plunder those who plundered them and ravage those who ravaged them. The declaration of the Lord YHWH.

### Comment

For the first time Israelites enter the picture, emerging (yāṣĕ'û) from their homes to dispose of the weapons of the annihilated foe. But where were the people during the conflict? If they "were holed up behind the walls of their towns, this would contradict the picture of a nation without any defensive structures (38:10–13)" [465]. However, Block mistakenly defines the term "city" as "a settlement surrounded by defensive walls" [465, n. 27]. In the legal corpus of H, upon which Ezekiel continuously depends, the term 'îr ḥômâ occurs (Lev 25:29), implying that towns ('îr) without walls do exist. Thus the Israelite settlements ('ārîm) were unwalled, and there is no contradiction between the settlements ('ārîm) described in 38:10–19 and in 39:9.

---

9. Cf. Milgrom, *Leviticus 23–27*, 488–89.

10. Cf. Zimmerli, *Ezekiel 2*, 312; Odell, "Are you of whom I spoke?" 135.

11. *ûbi'ărû wĕhiśśîqû*, lit., "they will ignite and burn" (see *m. Shab.* 3:2). LXX telescopes the pair into a single term [464, n. 24] *or* hendiadys (Radak); see the Comment.

12. The preposition *bĕ* should be prefixed to *māgēn* and *ṣinnâ* (cf. the preceding *bĕnešeq* and the following *bĕqešet*) [464, n. 25].

13. Lit., "they will fuel the fire for seven years" [464, n. 26].

## Unit 3: The Annihilation of Gog's Army and Its Armaments (39:1–16)

Ezekiel uses four stylistic devices to highlight the fervor of the post-war clean up. First, he speaks of igniting as well as burning the weapons. The two verbs in succession (*ûbi'ărû wĕhiśśiqû*, "they will burn and set on fire") do not function as a hendiadys, where two elements work as a single unit, as claimed by Block [465], but reflect the intense process of building a fire by increments.[14] Similar descriptions of burning the equipment of enemy soldiers may be found in Isa 9:4 (Eng 5) and Ps 46:10 (Eng 9), perhaps known to Ezekiel. Second, Ezekiel records seven different weapons, seven being a number of completion and suggesting that Ezekiel inventoried the quartermaster to show how well equipped and how great the defeat of the enemy. The generic term for armor, *nešeq*, is followed by three appropriate pairs: small shields (*māgēn*) and body shields (*ṣinnâ*); bows (*qešet*) and arrows (*ḥiṣṣîm*); clubs (*maqqēl yād*) and spears (*rōmaḥ*). Third, to show how huge was the number of enemy armaments, Ezekiel observes that the burning will last for seven years, rather than being a single massive conflagration. In effect he has devised a double sabbatical; the people will rest from the labor of cutting and carrying wood, and the land will rest and recover its vitality. Fourth, he invokes the biblical principle of measure for measure: literally, the plunderers have become the plundered, and the ravagers have become the ravaged.[15] YHWH ends the frame with his reverberating oral signature, *nĕ'um 'ădōnāy YHWH*, "the declaration of the Lord YHWH."

### Frame 7: The Burial of Gog in Hamonah (39:11–16)

TRANSLATION

**11** On that day I will appoint a grave site[16] for Gog there in Israel—the Valley[17] of the Travelers, east of the Sea.[18] It will block the path of the travelers,[19] for there Gog and his rabble will be buried. It will be called the Valley of Gog's Rabble. **12** Seven months the house of Israel will set aside to bury them, in order to cleanse the land. **13** All the people of the land will take part in burying them; and I will bring them honor[20] on the day I will manifest my Glory, de-

---

14. G. R. Driver, "Linguistic and Textual Problems," 60–69, 175–87, recognizes that fuel must be kindled *before* it is burned; for details, see Block, *Ezekiel 25–48*, 465, n. 28.

15. One cannot help comparing Ezek 39:9–10 with Isa 2:4 and Mic 4:3. The use of weapons as fuel is a lot more possible and practical than eschatological fantasies.

16. LXX and Vulg misread *mĕqôm šām* as *mĕqôm šēm*, "a famous place"; cf. Tg. *'tr kšr*, "a proper place." On MT's asyndetical clause in place of the expected *māqôm 'ăšer šām*, "a place where there is…" (e.g., 21:35), cf. GKC §130 c, d [466, n. 33].

17. *gê* is defectively written for *gê'* [466, n. 34].

18. For its geographical location, see the COMMENT.

19. MT *wĕḥōsemet hî' 'et-hā'ōbĕrîm* is rendered freely by Tg., "and it is near the two mountain cliffs," etc. [467, n. 36].

20. *wĕhāyâ lĕhem lĕšēm*, lit., "and it will become a name for them" [467, n. 39].

clares the Lord YHWH. **14** And they[21] will select men for long-term service,[22] to traverse the land and bury any corpses (invaders[23]) still remaining[24] above ground, in order to cleanse it. The search will continue for seven months. **15** As the searchers pass through the land, anyone who sees a human bone will set up a marker beside it, until the gravediggers[25] have interred it[26] in the Valley of Gog's Rabble. **16** There will also be a city named Rabble (Hamonah).[27] Thus, they will cleanse the land.

## Comment

The Israelites now face a series of problems regarding the many enemy corpses scattered about "the mountains of Israel." (1) Shall they respect the bodies of the enemy with a proper burial or leave them to the elements and to scavenger animals as 37:1–10 had portrayed the bones of Israel? Certainly, early Israelite law required that all the dead, even criminals, be buried promptly (Deut 21:22–23). (2) What gravesite was large enough to contain the myriad slain? (3) Shall foreigners (the victims) be buried within the borders of Israel, or be placed outside its boundaries so as to maintain the sanctity of the land?

Verses 11–13 respond to these questions [468]. Verse 11 tackles the second question with devious clues: (a) YHWH chooses the site. (b) The burial place is "in Israel," answering the third question. (c) The site is identified as $gê\ hā'ōbĕrîm$, "Valley of the Travelers."[28] Block prefers to render $hā'ōbĕrîm$, "those who have passed on"; that is, the deceased heroes, referred to as Rephaim in Ugaritic literature [469].[29] However, this solution is unlikely. First, Ugaritic netherworld imagery is not characteristic of Ezekiel. Second, above all one would expect to encounter some reference to the inhabitants of

21. I.e., the people of the land.

22. The form of MT $'anšê\ tāmîd$ ("men to serve permanently," idiomatically, for "long-term service") resembles $'ōlām\ tāmîd$, "regular, on-going burnt offering," in 46:15 [467, n. 40], and it is the object of the sentence.

23. Alternatively, (a) $'et$, "with," so rendered by Tg. $'im\ dĕ'ādēn$, "with a mobile group" [467, n. 42] (Rashi; cf. Kara, Eliezer of Beaugency, Radak); (b) Men for long-term service ($'anšê\ tāmîd$) is the subject, but it leaves the clause $'et$-$hā'ōbĕrîm$, superfluous (Isaiah of Trani, Menahem ben Simeon); c) this clause is omitted in LXX and Pesh.

24. $hannôtārîm$, "those who remain," which in context refers to the unburied corpses [467, n. 43].

25. $mĕqabbĕrîm$, "the buriers" (grave diggers), are a different group than the $'ōbĕrîm$, "searchers."

26. $'el$-$gê'$, in the Valley" ($bĕgê'$). The discovered body parts are brought to the mass grave site $gê'\ hămôn\ gôg$, "Valley of Gog's Rabble," where they are buried, contra Kara, who holds they are buried where they are found.

27. See Odell, "The City of Hamonah," 479–89.

28. NRSV, NJPS. For possible locations, see Zimmerli, *Ezekiel 2*, 317. On the suggestion that $'ōbĕrîm$ is a variant spelling of Abarim, which identifies a site east of Galilee (Jer 22:20) as well as one in the Moabite highlands (Num 27:12), both identifications are ruled out by the present emphasis on burial "in Israel" (vv. 11, 15, 17).

29. K.T.U. 1.22.1. 12–17 associates $'brm$ with $mlkm$, departed kings, on which see Levine and de Tarragon, "Dead Kings," 649–59. Pope ("Review of K. Spronk," 462) describes the $'ōbĕrîm$ as "those who cross over the boundary separating them from the living, so that, from the viewpoint of the living, they "go over," rather than "come over." For further evidence, see Block 469, n. 47.

## Unit 3: The Annihilation of Gog's Army and Its Armaments (39:1–16)

the netherworld, the Rephaim (as in Prov 2:18; 9:18; Job 26:5), but the Rephaim appear not even once. Finally, the same term *ʿōbĕrîm* occurs further down this verse and in verses 14–15, where it can only mean "travelers."[30] (d) The burial place is "east of the sea," most likely the Mediterranean.[31] (e) It is the site of a common grave, which "shall block the path of the travelers," that is, be filled to capacity.[32] (f) The site will be renamed "the Valley of Hamon-Gog [Gog's Rabble]," associated phonetically with *gêʾ hinnōm*, "the valley of Hinnom," where children were sacrificed to Molek (e.g., Jer 2:23).[33] Thus, just to sound the name that commemorates the destruction of Israel's enemies is to remember the crime and the idol worship.[34] But where is this place? Each of the above clues is vague, yet, in agreement with Block, "their cumulative weight places the burial site within the vicinity of Jerusalem" [470], on which see below.

12–13. The effect of Gog's burial is described in these verses. First, the land undergoes cultic purification based on Num 19:11–22. According to Ezekiel, the land already had been polluted by *moral* impurity, namely, prostitution (23:17), promiscuity, bloodshed, and idolatry (36:17–18),[35] which YHWH had healed by exiling the people and allowing the land to rest and recuperate[36] for a sabbath of years (2 Chr 36:21). The people have now been permitted to return from exile, cleared by YHWH of moral impurity. But the land and especially the mountains, littered with the bodies of Gog and his rabble, are polluted once again, this time not by moral impurity but by *cultic* impurity. Purification is required by the steps outlined above in Num 19:11–22 (cf. also Ps 79), starting with the burial of all the scattered remains and lasting for a week of months rather than a week of days. Ezekiel has previously shown great interest in the "name" (i.e., the reputation) of YHWH. Now for the first time he shows interest in *Israel's* name. Whereas YHWH's action is intended to bring honor (*kābôd*) to him, the people of Israel's total dedication to the gruesome task of burying the enemy corpses will provide honor for Israel itself [470]. Indeed, as noted by Odell (1994, 488), "the diligence of the people of the land implies a contrast between the failure of the former [people of the land, 7:27; 12:19] and the obedience of the latter. Whereas the historic people of the land have defiled the land, the eschatological people will cleanse it (39:12, 13, 16)."[37]

---

30. The same strictures apply to Odell, "The City of Hamonah," 485; Odell, "Defeat of Gog," 475.

31. As pointed out by Block [469, n. 48], "east of 'the (Dead) sea' contradicts 'in Israel.'" Furthermore, in the oracles against "the nations," "the sea" designates the Mediterranean (25:16; 26:5, 16, 17, 18; 27:3, 4, *et passim* in the chapter; cf. 47:8); see Eliezer of Beaugency.

32. The word *ḥāsam* occurs elsewhere in the Hebrew Bible only in Deut 25:4, which describes the muzzling of an ox. Also cf. Sir 48:17, which refers to Hezekiah creating a reservoir by damming up a stream.

33. Cf. Milgrom, *Leviticus 17–22*, 1551–65, on Lev 18:21.

34. For greater detail, cf. Block, "Gog in Prophetic Tradition," 113–41, esp. 127–29.

35. Cf. Frymer-Kensky, "Pollution, Purification, and Pugation," 406–9.

36. Details in Milgrom, *Leviticus 23–27*, 2322–25 on Lev 26:33–36; cf. also Ackroyd, *Exile and Restoration*, 242.

37. For the meaning of *ʿam hāʾāreṣ*, "people of the land," cf. Lev 20:2, 4.

**14–16.** These verses expand the theme raised in verse 12, that is, the cleansing of the land by its people, a process that will require four steps: (1) Long-term service men shall be appointed to oversee the burial of Gog's remains. (2) These men shall move up and down the length of the land, to find remains of the defeated foe. A second group of gravediggers (*mĕqabbĕrîm*), accompanying the "inspectors," is charged with the responsibility of disposing of the discovered remains. The search team will work for seven months, presumably the same seven months mentioned in verse 12. (3) Wherever the inspectors find so much as a single unburied bone, that spot will be marked conspicuously (see 2 Kgs 23:17 for *ṣîyûn* as a grave marker) to be transported for burial to the Valley of Hamon-Gog [471].[38] Note that the language and ideas follow those of Num 19:16.

The assertion that the slain armies are to be buried in a city called Hamonah leads to the identification of this city with Jerusalem. As shown by Odell,[39] and followed by Block [472], *hāmôn*, the symbolic name of Jerusalem (5:7; 7:12–14; 23:40–42) also alludes to the Valley of Hinnom outside of Jerusalem, where child sacrifice was practiced,[40] further intimating that the common grave of Gog's masses is located in the Jerusalem area. Once the land is purified ritually by Israel's energetic efforts (accomplished in seven months), preceded by the moral purification of the land (and people) effected by the deity, the stage is set for YHWH's permanent return (43:1–7). Hamonah is gone; "the name of the city from that day is 'YHWH is there'" (48:35).

---

38. That Ezekiel is speaking in realistic terms is strikingly confirmed by ZAKA, a volunteer organization founded in the 1990s and approved by the Israeli government to identify victims of acts of terrorism, road accidents and other disasters, and where necessary to gather body parts and spilled blood for proper burial. ZAKA is now called upon for assistance in international disasters, such as helping forensic teams in Thailand, Sri Lanka, India, and Indonesia in the aftermath of the 2004 Indian Ocean earthquake.

39. Odell, "The City of Hamonah in Ezekiel 39:11–16," 479–89.

40. Cf. Milgrom, *Leviticus 17–22*, 1552–65, 1729–38.

UNIT 4

# The Corpses of Gog's Army Devoured by Birds and Beasts (39:17–29)

*Frame 8: The Victory Banquet (39:17–20)*

TRANSLATION

17 As for you, Human, thus has the Lord YHWH said: Proclaim to every winged scavenger bird and every animal in the field:

Gather yourselves, come and convene from all over for my banquet, which I am preparing for you—a huge banquet—on the mountains of Israel. You shall eat meat and you shall drink blood. 18 The flesh of brave men you shall consume, and drink the blood of the earth's princes: rams, fattened lambs, and male goats, bulls and fatlings of Bashan—all of them. 19 You will stuff yourselves with fat and get drunk on blood from the banquet I have set before you. 20 And you will be sated at my table with horses and charioteers,[1] warriors and all men of war—proclaims the Lord YHWH.

COMMENT

17. All commentators have noted the incongruity of feasting on human cadavers (v. 17–20) after they are presumably buried (vv. 12–13). The obscene barbarism of verses 17–20 defies logical sequence. Dining on buried cadavers befits a surreal nightmare and steels the reader against anything that might follow. Taking objective distance from the horror, Odell surmises that the expansions of the three subunits (above) "contribute toward the definition of relationships among Yahweh, Israel, and Gog."[2] Stavrakopoulou proposes that the buried bodies of Gog and his cohorts were disinterred and then offered to the wild beasts and birds to prevent them from joining their family sepulchers, in effect denying them afterlife.[3] Her solution resembles *mutatis mutandis* the priestly punishment *kārēt*.[4] Such, indeed, is the punishment imposed

---

1. *rekeb*, lit., "chariot"; LXX, Vulg, and Pesh. read *rôkēb*, "riders" [473, n. 67]. Zimmerli (*Ezekiel 2*, 294) prefers "chariot horses." *sûs wārekeb* are frequently paired, e.g., Deut 20:1; Josh 11:4; 1 Kgs 20:1.
2. Odell, *Ezekiel*, 474.
3. Stavrakopoulou, "*Gog's Grave* and the Use and Abuse of Corpses in Ezekiel 39:11–20," 67–84.
4. Literally "cut off" from the afterworld; cf. Milgrom, *Leviticus 1–16*, 457–60.

on captured enemy kings: their corpses are disinterred and exposed.[5] However, there is no indication in the text that the corpses of Gog and his masses were disinterred. Block, Odell, and others may have overlooked a logical answer. As seen by Eliezer of Beaugency, the bones were picked clean by the scavenger animals, *ṭerem qĕbûrātām*, "before they were buried." That is, first, burial plans are set forth for the future, "on that day" (vv. 11–16), but the actual burial (of their remains, the bones) takes place *after* the victory banquet (vv. 17–20).

YHWH invites the animal scavengers of the world to a giant banquet (*zebaḥ*) on the mountains of Israel. This is not a "sacrificial banquet" (the customary translation of *zebaḥ*). YHWH has nothing to do with the meal offered to his scavenger guests. True, the imagery resembles the sacrifice: Gog and his rabble are spread on *šulḥānî*, "my table," a term that is poetically used on occasion for the altar (44:16), but this does *not* imply that YHWH partakes of the offering. Moreover, the *zebaḥ* sacrifice is eaten "before YHWH" (e.g., Deut 27:7), not "with YHWH."[6] All the more so, since sacrificial imagery and vocabulary are nonexistent in this pericope. YHWH does not partake of the sacrifice when it is offered to him on the altar, and he certainly takes no share in a (secular) banquet of human (Israel's) enemies (Isa 34:6; Jer 46:10; Ezek 39:17–19; Zeph 1:7). Note especially the similar bestial imagery in Isa 34:6: *ḥēleb, dam, kārîm, ʿattûdîm, ʾêlîm, zebaḥ*. It is not unreasonable to maintain that Ezekiel 39 was influenced by Isaiah 34.

**18. rams, fattened lambs, and male goats, bulls, and fatlings of Bashan** (*ʾêlîm, kārîm, wĕʿattûdîm, pārîm, mĕrîʾê bāšān*). These animals are not found on Israel's mountains nor are they mentioned anywhere as victims for YHWH's banquet. In chapter 32, denizens of the underworld also include *gibbôrîm*, "valiant men," (vv. 12, 21, 27) and *nĕśîʾîm*, "princes," (v. 29), who contrast the same category of men in Gog's army, who never taste "the joy of burial."[7] Tg. should be credited with its metaphoric rendering: "kings, rulers, and governors, all of them mighty men, rich in possession" (echoed in Rashi, Kara, Eliezer of Beaugency).[8]

**19. the banquet I have prepared for you.** This statement's irony should not be missed: suet and blood belong to the deity in normal sacrifices. Here they are given by God to scavenger animals. To mock the tradition: Instead of human worshipers slaughtering animals in YHWH's presence, YHWH slaughters humans for the sake of animals.

---

5. Cf. most recently Olyan, "Some Thoughts," 424–25.

6. Perhaps the most vivid description of a divine *zebaḥ* is Exodus 24, where the invitees "see God and eat and drink," verse 11b; cf. verses 9–11; cf. Milgrom, *Leviticus 1–16*, 22. Block: Note, however, that nowhere in the Hebrew Bible does anyone eat "with YHWH"; eating always occurs "before him" (*lipnê YHWH*), the divine host: Deut 12:7, 18; 14:23, 26; 15:20; 27:7; Ezek 44:3; 1 Chr 29:22.

7. Kasher, *Ezekiel*, 2:758.

8. Another apt example is Isa 34:6–7, where "lambs, he-goats and rams" probably represent the common people, while "wild oxen . . . young bulls with mighty steers" represent the leaders; Kissane, *Book of Isaiah*, 370.

## Unit 4: The Corpses of Gog's Army Devoured by Birds and Beasts (39:17–29)

### Frame 9: The Final Word (39:21–29)

TRANSLATION

21 Thus I will sustain my glory among the nations, and all the nations will perceive the judgments that I have executed, and my power[9] that I have laid on them. 22 From that day forward the house of Israel will know that I am YHWH their God. 23 And the nations will recognize that the house of Israel went into exile because of their own evil. Because they committed sacrilege against me, I hid my face[10] from them. I handed them over to their enemies to fall to the sword—all of them.[11] 24 I treated them as befitting their defilement and sacrilege. Therefore, I hid my face from them.

25 Therefore, the Lord YHWH has announced: Now I will reclaim the fortunes[12] of Jacob; I will show tenderness to the whole house of Israel and still be zealous for my holy name. 26 They will forget/bear[13] their shame[14] and all the sacrilege they committed against me when they lived safely on their own land fearing nothing.[15] 27 When I rescue them from the peoples and gather them in from the countries of their enemies, I will be sanctified through them, in the sight of many nations.[16] 28 And they will know that I am YHWH their God who, having sent them into exile[17] to the nations, will return them to their own land. I will never again abandon any of them out there.[18] 29 Nor will I ever again hide my face from them, for[19] I will have poured out my Spirit[20] on the house of Israel. The declaration of the Lord YHWH.

---

9. *yādî*, lit., "my hand"; cf. Tg. *gbwrty*, "my strength" [477, n. 80].
10. Tg. interprets the hiding of YHWH's face as removing his shekinah [477, n. 81].
11. "All" means "most," a literary exaggeration; cf. Gen 41:57 (Radak).
12. Kethib, *šbyt*; Qere *šbwt*. On the variations, see Block, *Ezekiel 1–24*, 512–14 [477, n. 83].
13. Block notes that MT *wĕnāśû* is pointed as if from *nāśā'* "to bear." Most translations, however, read *wĕnāšû*, as if from *nāšâ*, "to forget," by changing the diacritical point (NJPS, BHS, NRSV, REB, NASB). For the staunch defense of MT, see Zimmerli, *Ezekiel 2*, 295. Note especially 16:53–54 where *šûb šĕbût* is followed by *nasa' kĕlimmâ*, "bear shame" [478, n. 84].
14. Fulfilled in Ezek 44:13.
15. Promised in Lev 26:6 and Ezek 34:28.
16. Block notes that *haggôyîm rabbîm* is odd, not only because these two words are rarely conjoined but also for the article on *goyîm*. For its defense, see Davidson, *Syntax*, §32, Rem 2 [478, n. 85].
17. MT *bĕhaglôtî ōtām*. Tg. justifies each of YHWH's actions: He exiled them "because they sinned against me"; he restored them "because they repented" [478, n. 86].
18. These last two clauses are missing in LXX [478, n. 87]. The allusion here is to the historic fact that most Jews did not return, palpable evidence of a later insertion (Eliezer of Beaugency).
19. Treating *ăšer* causally, in the sense of *ya'an ăšer* (for, because), with LXX and Vulg, contra Zimmerli (*Ezekiel 2*, 295), who interprets the particle temporally. Alternatively the rendering "(in) that" is also possible [478, n. 88].
20. Block observes that LXX reads τον θυμον μου "my wrath," a harmonization with Ezekiel's stereotypical phrase *šāpak ḥēmâ*, "pour out wrath" [478, n. 89]. Tg. *rwḥ qdšy*, "my holy Spirit," is more specific than MT.

# EZEKIEL'S HOPE

## Comment

One can see verses 21–24 and verses 25–29 as two panels of a balanced and symmetrical whole, as demonstrated below [adapted from Block, 479]:

|    | TOPIC | 39: 21–24 | 39: 25–29 |
|----|-------|-----------|-----------|
| A  | The actions of YHWH | 21a | 25 |
| B  | The response of the object | 21b | 26–27 |
| B' | The recognition formula | 22–23a | 28 |
| A' | The hiding of YHWH's face | 23b–24 | 29 |

| Ezekiel 39:21–24 | | Ezekiel 39:25–29 | |
|---|---|---|---|
| A | wĕnātattî 'et-kĕbôdî baggôyîm (21a) | A | 'attâ 'āšîb 'et-šĕbut ya'ăqōb (25) |
| B | wĕrā'û kol-haggôyîm 'et-mišpāṭî | B | wĕnāśû 'et-kĕlimmātām (26) |
| B' | wĕyādĕ'û bēt yiśrā'ēl . . . wĕyādĕ'û haggôyîm | B' | weyādĕ'û kî 'ănî YHWH 'ĕlōhêhem (28) |
| A' | wā'astîr pānay mēhem . . . wā'astîr pānay mēhem | A' | wĕlō'-'astîr 'ôd pānay mēhem (29) |
| A | I will establish my glory among the nations (21a) | A | Now I will restore the fortunes of Jacob (25) |
| B | and all the nations will see my justice (21b). | B | They will bear their shame (26) |
| B' | The house of Israel will know . . . the nations will acknowledge (22a, 23a) | B' | And they will know that I am YHWH their God (28) |
| A' | I hid my face from them . . . I hid my face from them (23a, 24b) | A' | I will never again hide my face from them (29) |

Chiasm characterizes the internal organization of each panel. Divine action marks both the start and the conclusion; between them lies the human response, evidence for intention in the composition. These two parts form another example of Ezekielian "halving."[21] The first panel addresses YHWH's judgment of Israel's rebellion; the second, his saving action on her behalf. One might conclude that verses 20–29 are to chapter 39 as 38:23 is to chapter 38; each summarizes YHWH's management of his people.

**21–22.** These verses are in flux, modulating between the past—YHWH's victory over Gog (e.g., "the judgments that I have executed," "my power that I have laid on them" [that is, Gog and his rabble])—and the future—"from that day [YHWH's victory] forward" (e.g., "I will sustain my glory among the nations," "all the house of Israel will know that I am Lord YHWH"). Gog's oracle is mainly about revelation: to expose the person and character of YHWH [480].

As Block has observed, "The use of *nātan be* (lit., "to put in place") with the substantive *kābôd*, "glory," treats the latter as a concrete reality (cf. Exod 40:34–38; 1 Kgs

---

21. Cf. Greenberg, *Ezekiel 1–20*, 25–27, 137–38, 150–51.

## Unit 4: The Corpses of Gog's Army Devoured by Birds and Beasts (39:17-29)

8:10-12). Ezekiel had witnessed the departure of this glory (in a vision, Ezek 8-11), so will he announce its return to the rebuilt temple (43:1-5)" [480]. The translation of *mišpāṭî* as "my justice," rather than the usual, "my judgment," is justified because (1) *'āśâ mišpāṭ*, "to execute justice" (18:8); (2) the execution of judgment requires the plural in Ezekiel: against Israel (5:10, 15; 11:9; 14:2; 16:4); against the nations (25:11; 28:22, 24; 30:14, 19); (3) In the Gog oracle "to execute judgment" is rendered with the verb *šāpaṭ* (niphal; cf. *nišpāṭĕtî*, 38:22); (4) the present context requires that Gog's greed be met with justice (cf. 38:10-13); (5) *'āśâ šĕpāṭîm* has to do with punitive execution of divine judgment (Exod 12:1; Num 22:4; 2 Chr 24:24). In 23:24 YHWH commits justice (*mišpāṭ*) into the hands of Oholibah's lovers, who are then authorized to judge (*šāpaṭ*) her according to their *mišpāṭîm*, that is, the stipulations of sovereignty treaties [481]. "Even though the Gog debacle is considered an eschatological event (38:8, 16), it does not occur at the end of time. Rather, it marks the beginning of a new era" [482].

**23-24.** The events described here happened long ago. The cause for Israel's exile is broken down into four sins. These are: (1) *'āwôn*, "iniquity, perversion," the privileges of the covenant relationship were perverted into a just claim; (2) *ma'al*, "sacrilege," unfaithfulness to the covenant. The verb *mā'al* reappears with its cognate accusative in verse 26;[22] (3) *ṭum'à*, "uncleanness, defilement." Their idol worship and spilling of blood had polluted the land (36: 17-18) [482]; (4) *peša'*, "transgression, offensive trespass," intentionally violating the covenant. The nations had concluded that YHWH was either impotent or fickle regarding his covenant commitments. However, neither explanation was correct. Rather, Israel had brought this fate upon herself, provoking the exile by brazenly betraying the covenant relationship [482-83].

The people's behavior brought on YHWH's direct action against them. First, YHWH hid his face (*wā'astîr pānāy*) from them, echoed three times (vv. 23 and 24, and again in v. 29).[23] The human notion of YHWH hiding his face has a positive counterpoint, "to cause the face to shine towards someone" (*hē'îr pānîm*) and "to lift up the face toward someone" (*nāśā' pānîm 'el*), both of which occur in the Aaronic blessing (Num 6:25-26) [483].[24]

When royalty turns their face away, the subject faces calamity, "I shall turn (and) die if the crown prince, my lord, turns away his face from me."[25] The hidden face usually reflects the attitude of the deity as does the fallen face, that of the supplicant, as in this excerpt from A Prayer of Lamentation to Ishtar [483]:

---

22. Cf. *mā'al ma'al* in 14:13; 15:8; 17:20; 18:24; 20:27 [482 n. 103].

23. Cf. Block, "Divine Abandonment," 15-42.

24. The expression *histîr pānîm*, "hid the face," occurs thirty times in the Hebrew Bible. Cf. the related Akkadian idioms *pāna šākānu* and *pāna nadānu*, "to give the face" as well as *pāna nabâlu*, "to bring the face (near)"; cf. Oppenheim, "Idiomatic Akkadian," 256-57 [483, n. 104].

25. Waterman, *Royal Correspondence*, 114-15.

> Accept the abasement of my countenance . . .
> Look upon me and accept my supplication . . .
> How long will you be angered so that your face is turned away?
> Turn your neck which you have set against me
> Set your face [toward] good favor"[26]

The people conveniently excuse their own infidelity with the lament, "YHWH does not see us; YHWH has abandoned his land" (Ezek 8:12; 9:9). Now the nation will understand that the hidden face of YHWH was the anticipated response to their betrayal of the covenant [484].

In verse 24 Israel is charged with the severest crime in the priestly inventory: *kĕṭumātām ûkĕpîš'âhem*, "according to their defilement and their transgression." *Ṭum'à* refers to the worst ritual offense. Their commission causes contagious impurity, and those leaders of the first temple days charged with *ṭum'à* "impurity" (e.g., the king, the false prophet) are barred from holding office in Ezekiel's proposed (second) temple. The term *peša'* means "rebellion" and refers to a vassal's break with his sworn loyalty to his suzerain and is reflected in Israel's breach of its covenantal oath. Thus Ezekiel accuses his previous generation of the worst possible sins, which justify the hiding of YHWH's face. When the nation is ready to recognize the justice of the way YHWH has handled his people's acts in the past, a new fate awaits them (vv. 25–29).

**25. Therefore,** alternatively, "assuredly" (*lākēn*). God's mercy (vv. 25–29) is not the consequence of his punishment (vv. 21–24). Rather, just as the covenant warned of dire punishment for betrayal, so it stipulated that YHWH would never violate his covenant, and that he would be ready to reaccept his people once they regretted their past and turned to YHWH in fidelity—as stated explicitly in the covenant:

> But if they confess their iniquity . . . then I will remember
> my covenant . . . I will remember the land. (Lev 26:40–42)

> for YHWH your God is a compassionate (*raḥûm*) God . . .
> He will not forget the covenant which he made on oath. (Deut 4:31)

**Now** (*'attâ*). The focus is no longer "on that day" (38:10, 14, 18, 19; 39:8, 11), or "from that day forward" (39:22), but *now*. "These are the people who are asking, 'In the light of YHWH's abandonment of us in 586 [BCE] and our present hopeless condition, what basis for hope is there?'" [485]. The prophet responds: Though the destruction of Israel's enemies is a matter for the future, Israel's return to its land, its material benefit from the land, and YHWH's twice-expressed promise never to hide his face from them, and that not a single person will be left behind in the diaspora (vv. 25–29) is a matter of the immediate present; it will be fulfilled *now*.[27]

---

26. ANET, 385; cf. the complaint of the afflicted in *Ludul bêl nêmeqi* ("The Babylonian Job"): "I cried to my god (Marduk) but he did not look to me," Lambert, *Babylonian Wisdom*, 38, line 4, which resembles the reaction of Job to God in the face of a similar plight in Job 13:14: "Why do you hide your face and count me as your enemy?" Cf. Deut 31:17–18; see Friedman, "Biblical Expression," 139–47; Friedman, *The Hidden Face*, 1–140; Balentine, *Hidden God*; [484, nn. 106–7].

27. On the use of *lākēn* in previous oracles, see 5:7–8; 11:7; 13:13, 20, etc.

## Unit 4: The Corpses of Gog's Army Devoured by Birds and Beasts (39:17–29)

"The idiom *hēšîb šĕbût/šĕbît* encountered earlier in 16:53–58 (with reference to Israel) and 29:14 (with reference to Egypt) functions as a technical reference 'to a model of restoration most frequently characterized by YHWH's reversal of his judgment—*restitution integrum*'" [485].[28] The unanticipated appearance of the verb *rḥm* comes as a great surprise. Nowhere else in the entire book does *rḥm* and its synonymous *ḥml* and *ḥûs* appear in a positive sense (cf. 5:1; 7:4, 9; 8:11; 9:5; 16:5) [486]. YHWH is *ʾēl raḥûm wĕḥannûn* (Exod 34:6). As Ezekiel's Babylonian contemporary prophesies, "For YHWH has comforted his people, and has taken back his afflicted people in love (*yĕraḥēm*)" (Isa 59:13), "But with kindness everlasting I will take you back in love (*riḥamtîk*)" (Isa 54:8).[29] The association of zeal and compassion with the holy name is found in Joel 2:18: *wayyĕqannēʾ YHWH lĕʾarṣô wayyaḥmōl ʿal-ʿammô*, "YHWH was roused on behalf of his land and had compassion upon his people."

**26–27.** "*They will bear/forget their shame and all their perfidy* (*wĕnāśĕʾû ʾet-kĕlimmātām wĕʾet-kol-māʿălām ʾăšer māʿălû-bî*). The antonym of *maʿal*, "perfidy," is *qōdeš*, "sanctity, holiness,"[30] representing the totality of the violations against the covenant between Israel and its God. Thus Israel will bear/forget the shame of breaking the covenant.[31] If "bear," this polemical phrase is repeated in accounting for the failing of the Levites and their restoration, *wĕnāśĕʾû kĕlimmātām wĕtôʿăbôtām ʾăšer ʿāśû*, "and they will bear their shame for all the abominations they committed" (44:13). There is a nuance of difference, whereas the plural *tôʿăbôt* refers to the sum of individual violations of the covenant, *maʿal* is perpetually in the singular, a common noun for the totality of covenantal violations. Thus, Israel persistently violated the covenant while it enjoyed God-given prosperity on its land. The theme of verse 27 is the restoration of Israel, a theme reiterated in many passages (cf. 22:28; 34:13; 36:24; 37:21). The restoration from exile involves the return to security and knowledge of God.

**28.** The nations will now know that Israel is YHWH's covenanted people. It was he who scattered them among the nations, and it is he who will restore them to their land. Ezekiel's customary word for "gather," *qibbēṣ*, is replaced by the rare *kinnēs*.[32] The promise that not a single individual will be left behind is without parallel in the Hebrew Bible. The Hiphil of *ytr* was used of survivors of YHWH's judgment (6:8; 12:16). YHWH's restoration is perfect and everlasting [487].[33]

---

28. Bracke, "'*šûb sebût*': A Reappraisal," 244.

29. Sperling claims the homonym *rḥm* I, "to be compassionate," and *rḥm* II, "to take back, love." "Biblical '*rḥm*' I and '*rḥm*' II," 156.

30. See Milgrom, *Leviticus 1–16*, 345–56.

31. And all their sacrilege = for all their sacrilege, GKC §104.

32. Ezekiel used this root earlier in 22:21. Elsewhere both Qal and Piel forms of this verb are restricted to late writings (Neh 12:14; Esth 4:16; 1 Chr 22:2) or texts that are difficult to date (Pss 33:7; 147:23; Sir 2:8; 3:5). The Hithpael (Isa 28:20), like the noun *miknās* (Exod 28:42; 39:28; Lev 6:13; 16:4; Ezek 44:18), derives from a different root, Hurvitz, *Linguistic Study*, 124, n. 201 [487, n. 116].

33. Cf. Zech 10:10, LXX, "none of them will be left behind," in place of MT, "Till there is no room for them."

**29.** *for I will have poured out my Spirit on the house of Israel* (*'ăšer šāpaktî 'et-rûḥî 'al-bēt yiśrā'el*). The *rûaḥ YHWH*, "Spirit of YHWH," represents the divine power, which is metaphorically an independent force. In creation, the Spirit takes the form of the wind, *'ōśeh mal'ākāyw rûḥôt*, "he made the *winds* his agents," to blow the waters to their assigned place (Ps 104:4, 8). The *rûaḥ* can also be a lying spirit (*šeqer*) and deceive all the king's prophets (1 Kgs 22:22). This Spirit, moreover, has the power to effect the nature of man; as an artist, Bezalel is endowed with *rûaḥ 'ĕlōhîm bĕḥokmâ ûbitĕbûnâ ûbĕda'at ûbĕkol-mĕlā'kâ*, "divine Spirit or skill, ability and knowledge in every craft" (Exod 31:3); as a warrior, *wattiṣlaḥ rûaḥ-'ĕlōhîm 'al-šā'ûl*, "the Spirit of God gripped Saul" (1 Sam 11:6); as a ruler, *wĕnāḥâ 'ālāyw rûaḥ YHWH rûaḥ ḥokmâ ûbînâ rûaḥ gĕbûrâ rûaḥ 'ēṣâ ûda'at wĕyir'at YHWH*, "the Spirit of YHWH shall alight upon him: a Spirit of wisdom and insight, a Spirit of counsel and valor, a Spirit of devotion and reverence for YHWH" (Isa 11:2); in prophecy, *wayyā'ṣel min-hārûaḥ 'ăšer 'ālyāw wayyittēn 'al šibĕ'îm hazzĕqēnîm*, "he [God] drew upon the Spirit that was in him and put it upon the seventy elders . . . and they spoke in ecstasy" (Num 11:25). A survey of the verb *hitnabbē'* shows that it sometimes designates ecstatic or trance behavior. The precise nature of the behavior is not clear, although it is recognized by the people as prophetic. In any event, the divine Spirit is unstinting in its endowment, *kî 'eṣṣāq-mayim 'al ṣāmē' wĕnôzĕlîm 'al-yabbāšâ 'eṣṣōq rûḥî 'al zar'ekā*, "Even as I pour water on thirsty soil, and rain upon dry ground, so I will pour my Spirit on your offspring" (Isa 44:3).

The expression *šāpak ḥēmâ/za'am*, "pour wrath," with YHWH as its subject, recurs frequently (nine times) throughout Ezekiel (7:8, 9, 28; 14:19; 21:13, 21, 33; 22:22, 31; 36:18). Only once does it occur as a blessing, *šāpak rûaḥ*, "pour [divine] Spirit" (39:29). It appears twenty-four more times outside of Ezekiel, all in a negative sense except for twice in a positive sense: *wĕšāpaktî 'al-bêt dāwîd . . . rûaḥ ḥēn wĕtaḥănûnîm*, "and I shall pour on the house of David . . . a Spirit of pity and compassion" (Zech 12:10), and, notably, *'ašpōk 'et-rûḥî 'al-kol-bāśār wĕnîbbĕ'û bĕnêkem . . .*, "I shall pour my spirit on all flesh and your sons . . ." (Joel 3:1 [Eng 2:28]), both, I believe, under the influence of Ezek 39:24.

The editor(s) of chapters 38 and 39 graded the Gog invasion and annihilation so that in chapter 38 it was predicted for the far off future *miyyāmîm rabbîm*, "after a long time" (38:8); *bĕ'aḥărît haššānîm*, "in the distant future" (38:8); and *bĕ'aḥărît hayyāmîm*, "in the distant future" (38:16). But in halving chapter 39, the advent of Gog narrows in time. At first, Gog and his masses are turned and brought to the mountains of Israel, *wĕšōbabtîkā . . . wahăbi'ôtîkā 'al-hārê yiśrā'ēl*, "I have turned you around . . . and brought you to the mountains of Israel" (39:2). Then the day of the annihilation of Gog and his masses has come: *hinnē bā'â wĕnihyātâ*, "it has come" (39:8). Finally, the victory banquet follows: *'ĕmōr lĕṣippôr kol-kānāp*, "announce to every winged scavenger bird" (39:17). The immediate consequence is the restoration of Israel's fortunes: *'attâ 'āšîb 'et-šĕbî[û]t ya'ăqōb*, "now[34] I will return the fortunes of Jacob" (39:25); the

---

34. Ezekiel frequently updates his prophecies by use of *'attâ*, "now": 7:3, 8; 19:13; 23:43; 26:18; 43:9.

## Unit 4: The Corpses of Gog's Army Devoured by Birds and Beasts (39:17–29)

restored people of Israel was showered with YHWH's Spirit—*wěšāpaktî ʾet-rûḥî ʿal-bêt yiśrāēl*, "for I will have poured[35] out my Spirit on the house of Israel" (39:29).[36] Note the use of *bêt yiśrāēl*, "the house of Israel," that is, "women as well as men," a point that is picked up by the prophet Joel. By including the entire *bayit*, "household,"—including the slaves—as recipients of the gift of the divine Spirit, i.e., of prophecy (Joel 3:1–2; see below), Joel clearly has Ezek 39:29 in mind.[37]

Ezekiel avers that the divine Spirit has already been poured out over the house of Israel. He is not referring to the gift of life, which was endowed upon Israel by YHWH's *rûaḥ* (37:14, employing a different verb, *nātan*). Here I agree with Duguid[38] that YHWH's Spirit (*rûaḥ*) in 37:10 provides life (*wiḥĕyîtem*), not prophecy, but I differ with his claim that Ezekiel remains as the prophet. Ezekiel indeed remains a prophet, but on the same level as the rest of Israel—he is no longer YHWH's intermediary with Israel. It seems clear that in 39:29, Ezekiel alludes to the Spirit of prophecy in answer to the challenge enunciated by Moses, *ûmî-yittēn kol-ʿam YHWH nĕbîʾîm kî-yittēn YHWH ʾet-ruḥô ʿălêhem*, "Would that all YHWH's people were prophets, that YHWH put his Spirit upon them" (Num 11:29). The prophet Joel prophesies that Moses' fervent hope will be fulfilled in the future: "I will pour out (*ʾešpōk*) my Spirit on all (Israelite) flesh; your sons and daughters shall prophesy; your men shall dream dreams, and your young men shall see visions. I will even pour out my Spirit upon male and female slaves in those days" (Joel 3:1–2 [Eng 2:28–29]). Joel's vision is a distant eschatological vision, but Ezekiel is bestowing the gift of prophecy on his own generation. By what measure do they merit it?

Ezekiel has good reason to presume that his (exiled) generation is worthy of responding to the Mosaic challenge. First, like the Mosaic generation, it experienced exile and redemption and is poised to enter, possess, and allocate the Promised Land (Ezek 48). Second, unlike the Mosaic and every other generation, his generation is incapable of sinning. It has been purified and given a new heart and a new Spirit: *ăšer bĕḥuqqay tēlēkû ûmišpāṭay tišmĕrû waʿăśîtem*, "I will cause you to follow my laws and faithfully to observe my rules" (Ezek 36:25–27; cf. 11:17–21). Ezekiel had already inherited Jeremiah's prophecy that exiled Israel will be restored to its land and will be given "a single heart and a single nature to revere me [YHWH] for all time . . . and I will put into their hearts reverence for me so that they do not turn away from me" (Jer 32:39–40); "I will make a new covenant with the house of Israel and the house of Judah. Not like the covenant that I made with their fathers . . . which covenant of mine they violated . . . But this is the covenant that I will make with the house of Israel . . .

---

35. The distinction must be carefully made between *nātan rûaḥ* and *šāpak rûaḥ* in Ezekiel. The former is used when the divine Spirit placed (*nātan*) in the heart provides life to the carcass (37:14) or prevents the human being from sinning (36:27). As indicated above, when the divine Spirit is poured (*šāpak*) on a person, he is elevated to prophetic status.

36. Cf. Block, "Gog and the Pouring Out of the Spirit," 257–68.

37. Following Cogan, *Joel*, 1–66 (Hebrew); Crenshaw, *Joel*, and most recent commentators.

38. Duguid, *Ezekiel and the Leaders of Israel*, 105.

I will put my teaching inside of them and write it on their hearts" (Jer 31:31–34 [Eng 30–33]).[39]

Ezekiel both incorporates and expands Jeremiah's prophecy. "I will sprinkle pure water upon you and you shall be clean . . . and I will give you a new heart and I will put a new spirit into you . . . Then I will cause you to follow my laws and faithfully to observe my rules" (Ezek 36:25–27). What Jeremiah and Ezekiel prophesied, Ezekiel himself realizes. The exiles will have been restored to their land (Ezek 38:8, 11, 14) and its enemies will have been destroyed (39:1–21). YHWH then promises: "Never again will I hide my face from them, for I will have poured out my Spirit[40] upon the house of Israel" (39:29). Just as *miyyāmîm rabbîm*, "after a long time," and *bĕaḥărît haššānîm*, "in the distant future" (38:8), turn out to be an imminent now (39:8), so the final chorus of the Gog oracle moves the action forward. Possessing a new heart (36:25)—meaning that Israel is unable to sin—renders it capable of being endowed with *rûaḥ YHWH*, the ability to prophesy.

Ezekiel also maintains that the redeemed Israel will be governed by a non-hierarchical (lit., "ranking of holiness") principle. All superior offices and office holders will be abolished. Thus, there is no king—his duties will be reduced to that of the civil leader called *naśîʾ*, "prince" (Ezek 44:15–31). There will be no high priest—his duties and prohibitions will be shared among all the priests (45:15–27). The Promised Land will be allocated in equal measure among all the tribes. Every resident, including the alien, will receive inheritable landed property, (47:22–23; chapter 48, *et passim*). The national city will be accessible to *all* Israel; its maintenance the equal responsibility of *all* the tribes (48:30–35). Except for Ezekiel, all of his contemporary prophets are false prophets (13:1–23); they will be redeemed from exile with the rest of Israel, but they will not be admitted into the land (13:9).

This non-hierarchical doctrine also holds for the prophetic office—Ezekiel is slated to be the last messenger prophet. Henceforth, *every* Israelite—women as well as men (note *bêt yiśrāʾēl*, "the house of Israel," 39:29)—will be a "prophet" (cf. Joel 3:1–2 above) eligible to receive the divine word directly, because all intermediaries between Israel and God will disappear. In the post-Gog world, every Israelite, suffused by YHWH's *rûaḥ*, "Spirit," will be directed by the will of YHWH.[41]

In Ezekiel the list of nations slated for punishment (chs. 25–32) is comprehensive. But the name of Babylon, the arch-destroyer of the country of Judah, is missing! However, one should recall that Ezekiel lives in exile, in Babylon, and precisely because he is a community leader (the elders consult him regularly [8:1]), his words are carefully monitored, if not censored, by the authorities. Moreover, as noted by Greenberg,[42] Babylon is adumbrated in Ezekiel's prophecy against the Ammonites (21:33–36). His words could only have been spoken at the heyday (Nebuchadrezzar) of the neo-Babylonian Empire, that is, during the lifetime of the prophet Ezekiel.

39. For further details, see Greenberg, "Design and Themes," 735–40.
40. *ʾăšer šāpaktî ʾet-rûḥî* is so rendered by NAB; cf. REB, taking account of the perfect.
41. Cf. Tg.; cf. the COMMENT on 39:29.
42. Greenberg, *Ezekiel 1–20*, 435–38.

## Unit 4: The Corpses of Gog's Army Devoured by Birds and Beasts (39:17–29)

Another puzzling omission is that in contrast to Ezekiel's ample attention to Israel's role in the future (ʾaḥărît), Ezekiel ostensibly lacks a worldview of Israel's neighbors. There is one notable exception: matching Judah's forty-year exile (Ezek 4:6), Egypt will also suffer a forty-year exile (Ezek 29:13). However, in contrast to Israel's glorious future as a nation of prophets, wěšāpaktî rûḥî ʿal-bêt yiśrāʾēl (39:29), Egypt's future will be humble, lowly—incapable of aiding Israel as it did in the past (29:16). As for the other nations, no future is predicted, but their inconspicuous position is also presumed (29:15).

The Gog chapters (38–39) provide an answer to this dilemma. In chapter 38, the ʾaḥărît is far-off, remote; in chapter 39, with Gog's invasion of Israel, the ʾaḥărît turns imminent. God and his allies initiate a cosmic war, ushering in the eschaton. The annihilation of Israel's neighbors (prophesied in Ezek 25–32) also constitutes their ʾaḥărît. As noted above, Israel has been transformed into a nation of prophets as its role in the ʾaḥărît (39:29). The yearning of Moses to found a nation of prophets (Num 11:29) is realized in the generation of Ezekiel.

PART TWO

# Ezekiel 40–48

*The Visionary Sanctuary and the Land*

# 1

# The Visionary Sanctuary

## Ezekiel 40–46

### INTRODUCTION: THE SANCTUARY

#### A. Ezekiel's Temple: Its Dimensions

It is well accepted that Ezekiel's visionary sanctuary (Ezek 40–48) is a riddle in spatial design. Spaces measure divisions in Ezekiel's sanctuary to separate the holy from the common (42:20). This is effectively accomplished by a massive circumferential wall (43:12). The *temenos* on the inside of the wall contains three spatial divisions, effected vertically by graded platforms. One arrives at the first platform by climbing seven steps (40:22) and passing through three gatehouses in the outer wall, facing respectively east, north, and south. The gatehouses lead into an outer court accessible only to Israelites. The second platform is the inner court of the priests, who climb eight steps from the outer court (40:37), passing through three gatehouses, which also face east, north, and south (see Fig. 1). The highest platform, reserved for the sanctuary building, is reached by climbing ten steps (40:49) from the inner court. Not even the priests entered the sanctuary, except possibly on the Sabbath to exchange the stale loaves for fresh ones (Lev 24:8) on *haššulḥān 'ăšer-lipnê YHWH*, "the table before the presence of YHWH" (41:22b). The table—not gold plated (cf. Exod 25:23–29) and differing in size from *šulḥan (leḥem) happānîm*, "the table of (the bread of) presence," in the tabernacle (Exod 25:30)—, called *hammizbeaḥ*, "the altar" (Ezek 41: 22a), is most likely identified with its nearest tabernacle counterpart. The bread was always present on this tabernacle

# PART TWO: EZEKIEL 40-48—THE VISIONARY SANCTUARY AND THE LAND

FIGURE 1: The Plan of the Holy Precinct[1]

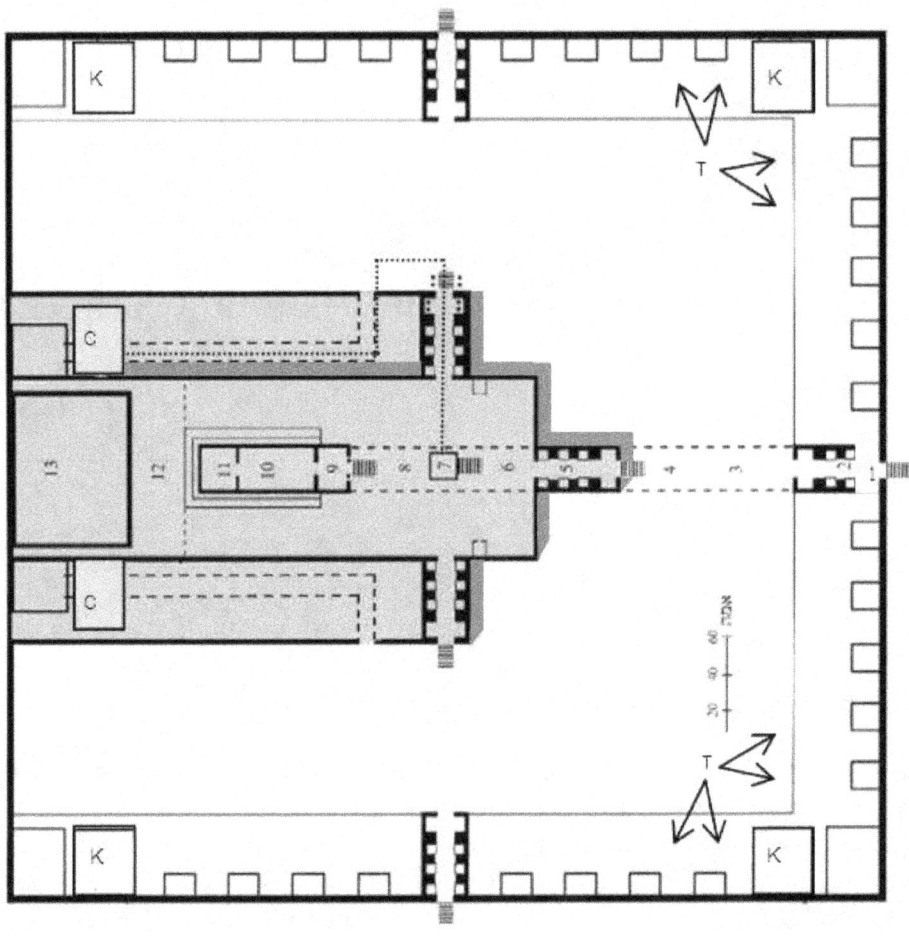

1. Eastern Steps
2. Outer court gate
3. Outer court
4. Inner court steps
5. Inner court gate
6. Inner court
7. Altar
8. Vestibule steps
9. Vestibule
10. Temple hall
11. YHWH's throne room
12. "Restricted space"
13. "The building"
C. Priestly chambers
K. Priestly kitchens
T. Tables

table, even when the table was in transit (Num 4:7b), which is why it was the most important sanctum except for the ark. It follows the ark in all accounts (prescription, Exod 25:29–30; construction, Exod 37:10–16; installation, Exod 40:4, 22; and transport, Num 4:7–8). It joins the ark in meriting three coverings, whereas the other sancta—the menorah and the two altars—rate only two coverings (cf. Num 4:5–8 with vv. 9–14). The absence of a candelabrum and incense altar from Ezekiel's sanctuary may imply that no daily ritual took place inside the sanctuary building, but only on the sacrificial altar in the inner court (Ezek 46:14–15). How can Ezekiel's sanctuary

1. Adapted from Block, *Ezekiel 25–48*, 508.

differ from its tabernacle predecessor? First, it should be noted that Ezekiel's sanctuary has no inner (barrier) wall, but only a sustaining wall. Yet, I will show that an inner wall is not only pointless but, if postulated, then the major objective of the *temenos* design—the separation of the sacred from the common, specifically the priests from the people—is irrevocably undone.

I begin with this latter point. Assuming the existence of an inner wall, the priest who officiates at the most sacred (*ḥaṭṭā't*, "purification," or *'āšām*, "reparation") offering will employ the following route (see dotted line, Fig. 1): From the altar, where he has offered the blood and suet (Lev 4:25–26), he proceeds to the inner north gatehouse where he picks up his sacrificial perquisites (Lev 6:19 [Eng 26]; 7:7) from the vestibule table on which the animal had been slaughtered (Ezek 40:39), descends eight steps into the outer court, and turns left into a passageway that leads to the *liškat haqqōdeš*, "sacristies or sacred rooms," at the western end of the *temenos* where the priests cook and eat their sacred perquisites (42:13; 46:19). This is the precise route of the divine "man" who twice conducted the prophet (42:1; 46:19).

As a consequence, the priest—blocked by the alleged inner wall—has been forced to trespass on the forbidden outer court while wearing his sacred vestments. Not only is he in imminent danger of contact with the laity (44:1–6; 46:20), but he is also liable to desecrate the most sacred perquisite he is carrying (Lev 5:14–16). In sum, Ezekiel's major purpose in redesigning the sanctuary—to distance the holy from the nonholy—will be irreparably vitiated because of this putative inner wall.

However, once the inner wall is erased from the design, the officiating priest makes a beeline to the sacristies without leaving the inner court. He descends the staircase located inside the three-tiered structure of the sacristies to the lower room (located on the platform of the outer court), where he cooks and eats his perquisite (46:19–20). This route would explain the otherwise unexplained purpose of having three tiers of sacristies—to provide access to and from the sacristies without trespassing on the outer court.

The question nonetheless remains: Does not the open space between the inner three gatehouses invite incursions by the laity, who might attempt to scale the priestly platform and thereby precipitate major desecration?

Ezekiel's sanctuary is not a chance appendix to his book; it is a logical and fitting climax to all that has preceded it. First comes the reunification, restoration, and purification of Israel, ending with a promise of a Davidic ruler and a new sanctuary (chaps. 36–37). Then follows the purification of the land after the slaughter and burial of Israel's enemies (chaps. 38–39, esp. 39:12–16). Once the peoples and the land have been purged, the new, divinely built sanctuary can be dedicated and operational (chaps. 40–46). Moreover, Israel will be elevated to the level of prophecy, thereby obviating the need for intermediaries. All Israel will have direct access to God (see the COMMENT on 39:29 and 48:35).

Thus, the Israelites who worship in the sanctuary are no longer prone to sin. Their inner nature will have changed. Filled with a new heart and spirit (36:26–27), they will be stricken with remorse for their cultic and moral failings (43:10-11; cf. 16:52-54, 61-63; 36:32). "They shall never again (intentionally) defile themselves with their idols and detestable things or with any of their transgressions" (37:23a).

The only specified exclusion from the sanctuary *temenos* concerns the non-Israelite: "no foreigner, uncircumcised in heart and uncircumcised in flesh, may enter my sanctuary" (44:9a). Hence, a prodigious perimeter wall encloses the *temenos*. The *temenos* itself, however, is filled solely with penitent Israelites. Their remorse and shame for their sinful past qualify them for worshiping YHWH in his sacred precinct. They are of no mind or heart to penetrate into the forbidden inner court. Besides, the eight-step high platform suffices to prevent even accidental access into the inner court.

In that case, why the need for guarded inner gatehouses? The thought immediately comes to mind that forbidden incursions might occur not by rebels against YHWH but by zealots of YHWH. One need only think of the example of Nadab and Abihu who, in their zeal to worship YHWH, penetrated into the shrine itself burning incense on profane coals (Lev 10:1-3). Thus, guarded gatehouses are barriers against the impetuous passion of the unqualified to get *qārôb*, "near," to YHWH.

It would be helpful to compare the status of Ezekiel's redeemed Israel with the status of worshipers, according to P, who have offered expiatory sacrifices (either the *ḥaṭṭāʾt*, "purification," or *ʾāšām*, "reparation"). The worshipers are also contrite (*weʾāšēm*, Lev 4:12, 22, 27; 5:2-5, 17, 23, 24); their remorse and confession transform their advertent sins into inadvertent ones (*bišĕgāgâ*, 4:2, 13, 22, 27; 5:15, 18), rendering them eligible for sacrificial expiation (e.g., 5:20-26). So too, exilic Israel's shame and contrition render them eligible to worship YHWH in his new sanctuary. Thus, Ezekiel is informed: "When they [the people] are ashamed of all they have done, make known to them the plan of the sanctuary" (Ezek 43:11a).

Consider the religious and spiritual upgrade of a sanctuary without an inner wall. As noted by Kalinda Stevenson,[2] the worshipers are able to witness the priestly rituals on the altar (see Fig. 1). Envisage the following scenario: The *naśîʾ*/king ascends the inner east gatehouse on sabbaths and new moons to offer the prescribed sacrifices (46:1-8). When the smoke of the sacrifices begins to rise, he prostrates himself in unison with the masses in the outer court below (46:9-10). This joint participatory and visual experience would concretize for the people the promise vouchsafed to the prophet: "I will set my sanctuary among them forever. My presence shall rest over them. I shall be their God, and they shall be my people" (37:36b-37).

## B. The Delphi Temple

Finally, one must ask: Is it possible that Ezekiel's sanctuary, constructed on graded platforms minus an inner wall, was simply the product of the prophet's fertile, visionary mind independent of external influence? Below are a floor plan and a reconstruction of the *temenos* of the Apollo temple at Delphi (Figs. 4 and 2, respectively).[3]

---

2. Stevenson, *Vision of Transformation*, 44.
3. Maaß, "Delphi," *New Pauly* 4.216-23; Hale et al., "Questioning the Delphic Oracle," 67-73.

FIGURE 2: Cross Section of the Temple of Delphi[4]

FIGURE 3: The Supporting Wall of the Temple of Delphi

Founded in the eight century, overlapping the time of Ezekiel, it also has a raised platform for its temple and *no inner wall!* There are other even more striking parallels.

(1) The Delphi *temenos*, enclosed atop a massive wall (Fig. 3), is located on the southern slope of Mount Parnassus. Ezekiel's *temenos*, enclosed within a more massive wall ("a structure like a city," Ezek 40:2), was also built on the southern slope (*minnegeb*) of a "high mountain." The reading of the LXX *minnegdî*, "opposite me," must now be rejected.

---

4. David Fierstein, illustrating the article by Hale, et al., "Questioning the Delphic Oracle," 71. Used with permission.

## PART TWO: EZEKIEL 40–48—THE VISIONARY SANCTUARY AND THE LAND

FIGURE 4: Ground Plan of the Temple of Delphi[5]

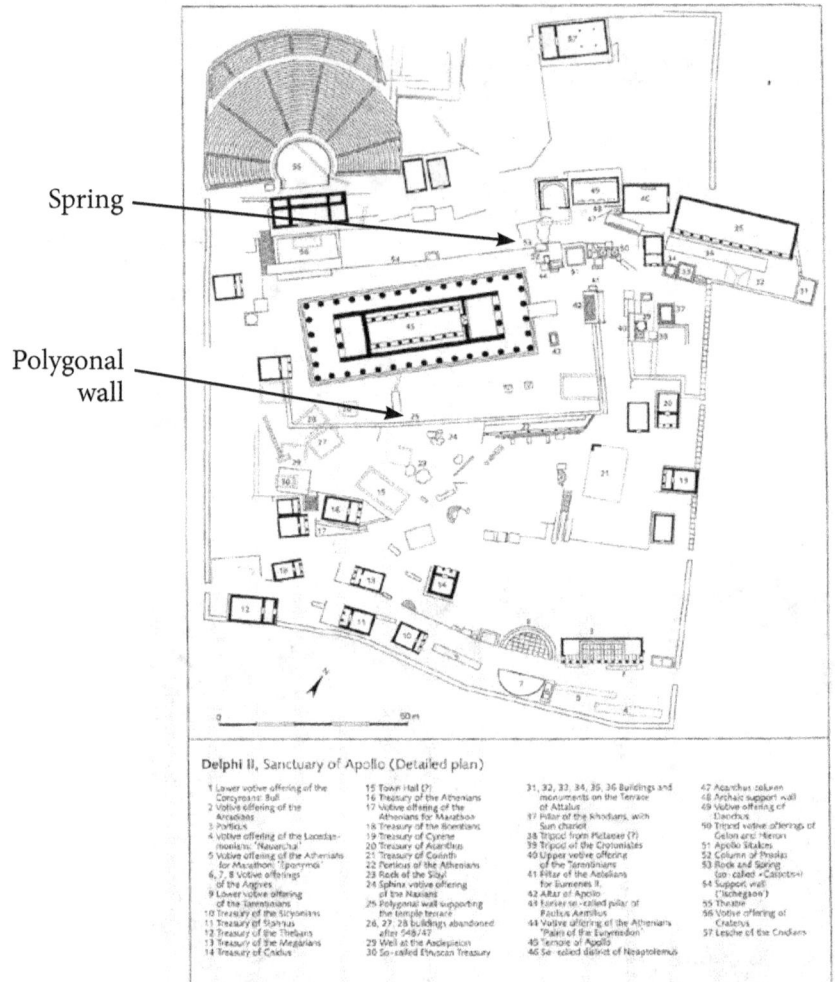

(2) The polygonal wall surrounding Delphi's temple platform (Fig. 3; Fig. 4, #25) is a supporting wall, not a barrier wall. Thus, as mentioned above, the most sacred areas of both temples are situated on unwalled raised platforms.

(3) A spring ran under the Delphi temple surfacing outside the *temenos* (Fig. 4, #53). So too, Ezekiel saw in his vision a spring emanating from within the sanctuary, running underground on the side of the altar and surfacing outside the *temenos* (Ezek 47: 1–2).

(4) The absence of the bronze laver alongside the altar (Exod 30:17), called "sea" (1 Kgs 7:23–26), or ten basins (1 Kgs 7:38–39) in Ezekiel's sanctuary is startling. Where did the priests wash their hands and feet—the neglect of which was a capital crime (Exod 30:20–21)? Delphi provides a satisfying answer. Near the altar—which

---

5. Maaß, "Delphi," New Pauly 4.219–20.

stood at the entrance (i.e., outside) of the temple—there was a spring (Fig. 3) called "Cassotis" (Fig. 4, #53), which served as the priestly laver. Thus, it may be surmised that in Ezekiel's sanctuary an equivalent facility was located in the *temenos*, possibly in the northern sacristies (50 x 100 cubits, 42:7–8), where the priests would wash and dress before ascending to the altar.

FIGURE 5: Aerial view of the Temple of Apollo Podium and Supporting Wall[6]

FIGURE 6: Reconstruction of the Temenos at Delphi

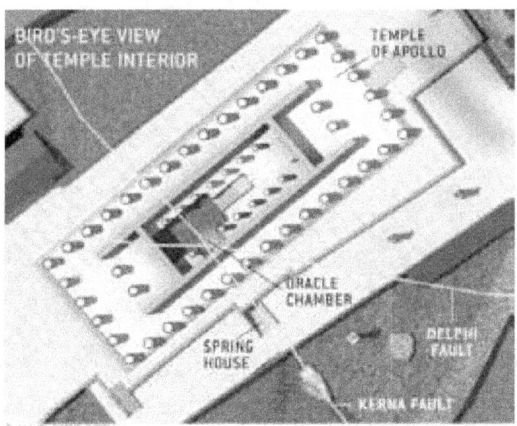

(5) Vapors from the subterranean stream emerged in the adytum of the Delphi temple where the Pythia sat inhaling ethylene—a trance-inducing gas that could have risen, according to the investigating scientists, from the fissures created by the two faults that intersected underneath the adytum. Ezekiel's sanctuary, to be sure, had no Pythia, but Israel's God also spoke from the adytum (Exod 25:22; cf. Num 7:89), and

---

6. David Fierstein, illustrating the article by Hale, et al., "Questioning the Delphic Oracle," 71. Used with permission.

## PART TWO: EZEKIEL 40-48—THE VISIONARY SANCTUARY AND THE LAND

Ezekiel received a direct divine revelation in his sanctuary vision only after YHWH entered the sanctuary and took his place in the adytum between the cherubim (Ezek 43:2-3; cf. chaps. 1, 10, and 11).

(6) As far as we know, there were no images in the Delphi temple, neither of Apollo nor of any other god. There were two places for communication with the deity: at the great altar atop the raised platform at the entrance to the sacred court (Fig. 3, #42), and in the oracular room (the adytum, Fig. 6). Is it a coincidence that Ezekiel's sanctuary was devoid of sacred objects (namely the menorah, the incense altar, and the ark), except for a wooden table, probably the table of the bread of presence (cf. Exod 25:23-30)? This would have left only the great altar in the inner court and the oracular presence of the deity in the adytum.

FIGURE 7: Ground Plan of Tabernacle[7]

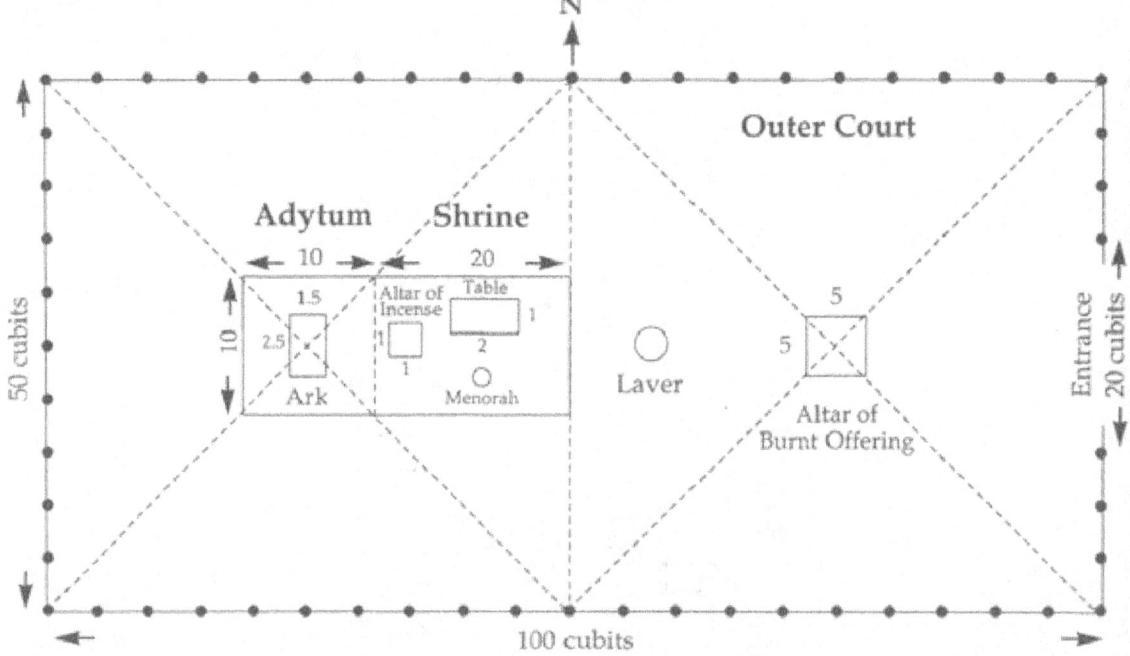

(7) Nothing could be more illustrative of the change of worship patterns in Ezekiel's sanctuary than the shift that occurs in the architectural center of the sacred compound or *temenos*. In the Mosaic tabernacle, the center is the entrance into the shrine; its *temenos* can also be construed as comprising two squares whose concentric centers are respectively, the Ark and the altar (Fig. 7). The impact of this tabernacle design was so powerful on later generations that the *temenos* of the Temple Scroll document, a millennium later, also puts it center at the entrance to the great hall.[8] By contrast, in Ezekiel's sanctuary the altar becomes the architectural center of the

---

7. Adapted from Milgrom, *Leviticus 1-16*, 135.
8. Maier, "Die Hofanlagen im Tempel-Entwurf des Ezechiel," 55-67.

compound. This shift tells a powerful historical and theological story: The liturgy has abandoned the great hall for exclusive worship at the altar. In this respect it is entirely like—and perhaps influenced by—the Delphi temple, whose worship was also confined to the sacrificial altar. Inscriptional and archaeological evidence amply testify to the probable early contact of the Greek world with the ancient Near East. During the final century of the Neo-Assyrian Empire (720–620 BCE), the names of Greek craftsmen, seafarers, robbers, plunderers, mercenaries, and merchants appear in these documents. In addition, "distinguished positions in the local societies . . . involved in land transmissions . . . selling and buying . . . acting as witnesses"[9] certify that Greeks were not only engaged in transient economic pursuits but were also permanently settled as productive "citizens" within the Assyrian empire. If this is the case in the eight–seventh century, it must be even more so a century later at the height of the Neo–Babylonian empire, the time of Ezekiel. Unfortunately, there is little documentation of Greek contacts during the Neo–Babylonian period.[10]

Had Ezekiel been able to observe a Greek sacrifice, he would have registered his familiarity with most of the proceedings. As detailed by Burkert[11] and summarized by Brown, the particulars include:

> Washing and putting on clean clothes and wreaths; a procession with song "departing from the everyday world" to the place of sacrifice; a girl with a basket (containing barley and a hidden knife) leading the way; the sacrificial animal accompanying as if willingly, decorated, with gilt horns. At the place of sacrifice is the altar which is bloodied, with a fire on top, a censer, a water jug. The sacrifice is begun by washing the participants and the animal with water; eliciting its apparent agreement; throwing the barley on the altar and on the animal, a gesture of dismissal; cutting hairs from the animal and throwing them in the fire. Then the animal is killed; the women scream; the blood is caught and poured on the altar. The animal is carved up: the heart is placed on the altar; a diviner interprets the form of the liver; the organs are quickly roasted and eaten. The bones with the tail and fat, along with token pieces of meat, are burned; the skull is preserved; the skin is sold to benefit the sanctuary; the fire blazes up as cakes and wine are put on it. The participants have a feast on the roasted meat of the animal.[12]

As pointed out by West,[13] these procedures are precisely matched by their Semitic counterparts as follows: bloodless food offerings, hair, burning of incense, killing without eating, killing and eating, oxen and sheep as the preferred victims (provided they never bore a yoke); sacrificers being bathed and wearing clean clothes; the ceremony beginning by leading the animal to the altar in a musical procession into a

---

9. Rollinger, "Ancient Greeks and the Impact of the Ancient Near East," 233–64; Helms, *Greeks in the Neo-Assyrian Levant*. I am indebted to my colleague Israel Eph'al for this reference.
10. Weidner, "Hof-und Harems-Erlasse assyrischer Könige," 257–93.
11. Burkert, "*Lescha-Liškah*," 19–38.
12. Brown, *Israel and Hellas*, 183.
13. West, *The East Face of Helicon*, 39–42.

## PART TWO: EZEKIEL 40-48—THE VISIONARY SANCTUARY AND THE LAND

sacred circle; and the victim being slaughtered over the altar.[14] In the Greek ritual, the victims' thighbones were burned for the gods, and libations were poured over them; in Babylonian ritual, "you will slaughter a sheep (or bull), you will offer the shoulder, the fat round the intestines, and some roast meat; you will make a libation of best beer, wine, and milk."[15] The god was supposed to delight in the smell of the barbecue.[16] The meat had to be eaten at the feast, or else destroyed; the victim's hide went to the priest. Moreover, Ezekiel would have understood much of the technical vocabulary in Greek sacrifice. According to West, there are over one-hundred common words in Greek and Semitic languages, including "the names of animals, insects and fishes, plants and plant products, minerals, vessels and containers, fabrics and garments, various other manufactured articles, prepared foods, terms used in commerce and religious cult, and the names of the letters of the alphabet."[17] For example, the Greek word for wine, *woinos*, corresponds to Semitic **wainu* as well as Hittite *wiyana*.[18] Akkadian *tem(m)en(n)u* (from Sumerian *temen*) is the source of Greek *temenos*, "sacred precinct." The *leskhai* at Delphi were social centers in the sanctuary,[19] corresponding with Heb. *liškâ*, "rooms." The terms *mōmos/mōmar/mūmar* are equivalent to Hebrew *mûm*,[20] "flaw, blemish"; *plinthos*, "clay brick," derives from **libintu, libittu*;[21] so too *burmos = bāmâ*, "sacral platform"; *maza = maṣṣâ*, "bread." The same Greek equivalences hold especially in Babylonian hepatoscopy: *mazzazu*, "place"; *dananu*, "strength"; *murtu*, "gall"; *padānu*, "path"; *padan šumal martí*, "the left path of the gall"; *bab ekalli*, "gate of the palace"; *ubanu*, "finger"; *ṣibtu*, "appendix"; *reš amutim*, "head of the liver"; *nar amutim*, "river of the liver." Greek and Semitic sacrifices agree on certain features: oxen and sheep as preferred victims; sacrificing first born (humans, too); musical procession; victims slaughtered on altar; victims' thighbones with some meat for the gods and libations over them; similarly in Babylon, "offer the shoulder, the suet round the intestines, and the roast meat; you will make a libation of best beer, wine, and milk";[22] the skins are for the priest; the sacrifice must be totally consumed at the feast.[23] Indeed the best parallels come from the Hittite and Mesopotamian worlds.[24]

It is important to keep in mind the totally unambiguous westward direction in which the above-mentioned sacrificial terms and procedures moved. In a word, the

---

14. In P, however, the slaughtering took place in the court (Lev 1:5, 11; 3:2, 8).
15. *ANET*, 335.
16. Ibid., 334–38; Lev 3:5, 16; Gen 8:21; Exod 29:18; 25:41.
17. West, *The East Face of Helicon*, 14.
18. In north-west Semitic initial *w-* turned into *y-*, hence Ugaritic *yēnu*, Hebrew *yayin*.
19. Cf. Burkert "*Lescha-Liškah*," 19–38.
20. Burkert, *Ancient Mystery Cults*, 3–7; Burkert, *Greek Religion*, 63–64.
21. *CAD* 9.176–79.
22. *ANET* 335.
23. Cf. details in West, *The East Face of Helicon*, 41–42.
24. Ellis, *Foundation Deposits*, 147–50; Ellis, "Gründungsbeigabe," 655–61; Burkert, *Orientalizing Revolution*, 53–55.

## The Visionary Sanctuary

Semitic world permeated Hellas. Perhaps the most influential borrowing, which impacted all the others, is the adoption of the Phoenician scripts by the Greeks.[25]

To be sure, this sizeable onomastic evidence may only attest to Greeks from the Ionic (Anatolian) and Philistine coasts and not from the Greek mainland. But contact with Greek civilization and not just with Greek individuals was inevitable. It is highly probable that both Greek travelers and merchants, and Babylonian travelers and merchants, brought information about the reputed oracular wonders of the Delphi temple. Thus, Ezekiel could have known about Delphi. By Ezekiel's time the fame of the Delphic oracle had spread beyond the borders of Greece.

Why would Ezekiel have been infatuated and influenced by the architectural details of the Delphi temple? The Delphi temple would have offered no opposition to Ezekiel's monotheistic and aniconic convictions. Instead of a statue of Apollo, the adytum of the Delphi temple contained a natural spring. The Pythia who transmitted the oracle is reminiscent of Israel's high priest, who interpreted the Urim and Thummim in the sanctuary (Num 27:21; Exod 28:30), indeed, of Moses (Num 7:89), of his successors the prophets (Deut 18:18), and of Ezekiel himself, who was commissioned to relay YHWH's message to the people (e.g., Ezek 43:10–11).

Furthermore, the Delphi characteristics would have fit Ezekiel's major architectural aim: a sanctuary design that would permanently separate the sacred from the common. It would indeed be ironic if Israel's priests, whose basic pedagogic responsibility was to teach the distinction between the sacred and the common (and between the impure and pure (Lev 11:10; Ezek 44:23), would (and did) violate this distinction while serving in the Jerusalem temple (Ezek 22:26). Hence, Ezekiel envisioned a temple with a mighty perimeter wall (which from afar looked like a fortified city, 40:2) to keep out non-Israelites (especially of hostile military strength). Three gatehouse towers built into the walls, ascended by seven steps, led into the first elevated platform, the area reserved for the Israelite laity and forbidden to foreigners. A second elevated but unwalled platform, also entered through three gatehouses and ascended by eight steps, was the domain of the priests and excluded all lay Israelites (including the *nāśîʾ*/king). A third unwalled and untowered platform, ascended by ten steps, contained the sanctuary building and was the exclusive reserve of the deity. It separated YHWH from the priests. Since the sanctuary contained no cultic objects served by a high priest, there was no need for a high priest; nor does Ezekiel ever mention one.[26] Whether the wooden table (mentioned above) represents an actual or symbolic bread offering, it would have been served not by the high priest but by ordinary priests—and only once weekly on each Sabbath (cf. Lev 24:8–9). In disagreement with Kasher,[27] who claims that the sanctuary was always void of humans, the presence of the bread table implies that it was served by the priestly cadre every Sabbath by exchanging the bread. Moreover, ten steps led up to the sanctuary from the priestly platform. Surely the steps

---

25. Burkert, *Orientalizing Revolution*, 169, n. 1.
26. For a similar deduction, see Kasher, "Anthropomorphism, Holiness and Cult," 192–208.
27. Ibid.

were used at some point by the priests. The space within the sanctuary compound is also based on the principle of separation (see below).

Thus, the Delphi temple was tailor-made for Ezekiel's theology. Israel would worship its God only at the altar. The Levites would assist by slaughtering the offering and in other preliminary ways. The *nāśî'*/king, seated on the priests' platform—though confined to the gatehouse—could observe the people's sacrifices and his own ascending in flames from the altar, thereby assuring that the worshipers' praise of and requests to their resident God in "the house of YHWH" were being received with favor.

Are these parallels between the Delphi and the Ezekielian sanctuary mere coincidences? There are too many parallels to be coincidental. After all, the features of Ezekiel's sanctuary mentioned above are unique. There is nothing known thus far among the sanctuaries of Israel and the ancient Near East that duplicates or even resembles the following features: a sanctuary complex on the southern slope of a high mountain, a sanctuary building raised on an elevated platform uncircumscribed by a wall, a sanctuary building containing no sacred object, worship limited to a sacrificial altar in the inner priestly court, a subterranean spring surfacing outside the *temenos*, and a human intermediary who hears a message for the people from the voice of the deity emanating from the adytum.

Thus, there is no point in seeking the origins of Ezekiel's sanctuary in the myths of Mount Sinai, the Garden of Eden, and Mount Zion.[28] There is nothing miraculous about the structure. Even the prodigious dimensions of the perimeter wall (ca. 10 ft. high by 10 ft. thick) are feasible (note the size of parts of the "Wall" separating present day Israeli and Arab populations). Indeed, the height of 10 feet is hardly a deterrent to a determined enemy. However, the area outside the temple is replete with miraculous data, e.g., the fertilization of all the land east of the central range (Ezek 47), and the equivalent distribution of the land to all the tribes (Ezek 48).

Therefore one must treat the possibility that news and details of the Delphi temple, transmitted by the oral reports of travelers or merchants, influenced the design of Ezekiel's visionary temple. The mental images of the Delphi temple percolated inside his creative, imaginative mind and became transmuted *mutatis mutandis* into the basis of the divinely-ordained sanctuary for a redeemed Israel on its redeemed land.

The seventh-century sanctuary of Apollo at Delphi was totally destroyed by fire during the first half of the sixth century (during the time of Ezekiel), but was rebuilt and expanded in 548/47 BCE. The data presented here is from the second Delphi temple (Figs. 2–6), which was *rebuilt on the ruins* of the first temple. Thus the influence of the first temple conjectured about may be considered probable.

Nor was it necessary to cross the Dardanelles and climb Mount Parnassus to witness first hand the wonders of Delphi. Another famous oracular site was more handily available at Didyma, the most important sanctuary in Asia Minor. Located on the Aegean coast of Turkey, only 10 km south of the city of Miletus, pilgrims would disem-

---

28. Levenson, *Theology of the Program of Restoration of Ezekiel 40–48*, 1–53.

bark at the nearby port of Panomas and walk the short distance along the Sacred Way, lined with sculptures and statues, to the oracle of Apollo.

Didyma sat astride a sacred hot spring that emitted sulfurous fumes; a smaller, older temple *naiskos* was actually constructed over the sacred spring. It was enclosed by a wall approximately 24 x 10 meters, containing an open–air sanctuary, a portico 16 meters in length, a sacred well, and a votive altar. Unfortunately, there is much less literary information on Didyma than on Delphi, but the standard structure of Apollonian oracular sanctuaries makes it feasible for the easily accessible Didyma, even more than the remote Delphi, to have influenced the visionary sanctuary of Ezekiel.

## C. Separation

It was demonstrated above that the fundamental doctrine of separation in Ezekiel's sanctuary resides in the vertical dimension, namely in its three concentric platforms, each smaller than the one below, with the sacrificial altar as its center. The lowest platform, surrounded by the perimeter wall, is entered through three gatehouses (though the eastern gate will be shut once YHWH enters it, cf. Ezek 44:1–3). This level is accessible only to Israelites; non-Israelites (*běnê nēkār*) are prohibited. The middle platform is open only to priests; not even Levites or the *nāśî'*/king, may enter. The third and highest platform is reserved for the temple building, *bêt YHWH*, "the house of YHWH" (Ezek 43:6), which is off-limits to all humans, even priests (except possibly for the weekly bread offering). Thus, the three ascending platforms create different levels of holiness in the sanctuary. Sectioning the sanctuary perpendicularly produces the following categories (from bottom to top): non-Israelite wall, Israelite platform, priestly platform, YHWH's platform (sanctuary). These constitute the vertical separations of Ezekiel's sanctuary. They are matched by horizontal separations, namely, by spaces, the exposition of which now follows.

Ezekiel's sanctuary design is not a ready-to-build blueprint. It lacks many structural details. It avoids mention of all vertical dimensions, except for the height of the perimeter wall (Ezek 40:5). The measurements in Ezekiel's skeletal design only describe spaces. Spaces indicate separation. The shape of the spaces in Ezekiel's sanctuary expresses the basic principle of separation between the holy and the common. As discerned by Stevenson,[29] a square shape signifies that its area is holy in contrast to its surroundings. Thus, the entire sanctuary complex (*temenos*) is 500 x 500 cubits, "to separate between the holy *temenos* and the common exterior" (Ezek 42:20; cf. 43:12; 45:2). The sanctuary *temenos* is subdivided into smaller squares: the laity's outer court (400 x 400 cubits) congruent with the first elevated platform (Ezek 40:19, 23; cf. 47); the priestly inner court (100 x 100 cubits) atop the second elevated platform (Ezek 40:47); the uppermost platform comprising two squares: the sanctuary building (100 x 100 cubits),[30] *bêt YHWH*, "the House of YHWH" (44:4), and the mysterious, unex-

---

29. Stevenson, *Vision of Transformation*, 26–30.

30. The actual breadth of the Building is 50 cubits, but a 25 cubit margin on each side up to the edge of the platform brings the total to 100 cubits. The protean term, *bêt YHWH*, refers either minimally to

plained *binyān* (41:12–15), with its frontal open space called *gizrâ*, forming a square (100 x 100). The double square is hardly an accident, for it duplicates the double square construction of the tabernacle (Fig. 7).

The great altar situated at the center point of the entire *temenos* is constructed of five concentric squares (12, 14, 16, 18, 20 x 12, 14, 16, 18, 20 cubits).[31] The apex of holiness, the sanctuary adytum, is also a square (20 x 20 cubits)—"and he [the guide] said to me, 'this is the holy of holies'" (Ezek 41:4). The three-tiered sacristies of the priests flanking the sanctuary building platform on both sides are each 50 x 100 cubits (Ezek 42:2, 8). Together they form a square (100 x 100 cubits; see Fig. 1). Thus there is no need to postulate, with Jonathan Smith, that these rooms maintain an intermediate status of "priestly domestic activities."[32] Rather, their (combined) square is attached to the square of the inner priestly court and possesses the same degree of holiness (cf. Fig. 1).[33]

As correctly noted by Stevenson,[34] the square areas are completely defined. In contrast, the structures in the outer people's court are rectangular and less defined—for example, the cooking areas for the people in the four corners of the outer court (40 x 30 cubits; Ezek 46:22–24) and the horizontal dimensions of all six gates (50 x 25 cubits). True, the perimeter wall (and the outer court) is "most holy" (Ezek 43:12), but only in contrast with the area immediately outside. It should not be overlooked that the symbolism of the square continues to dominate the landscape outside the sanctuary. The *těrûmâ*, "contribution," the portion of the land donated to the deity, measures a square (25,000 x 25,000 cubits), comprising living space for the priests and Levites, and a city of YHWH: "YHWH is There" (Ezek 48:35). This area also forms a square (4500 x 4500 cubits)—an obvious polemic against "The City of David," i.e., Jerusalem, that it seeks to replace.

One should not overlook the remaining application of Ezekiel's separation principle. Religiously the *nāśî*/king is only a layman with a very limited privilege. He is granted access to the outer east gatehouse (44:1–3) and the inner east gatehouse (46:2, 12), but like every layman he is barred from the inner court. Furthermore, his landed property, while extensive (Ezek 48:21–22), is distant from the sanctuary, thereby obviating the abuses of the Solomonic temple caused by its juxtaposition with the king's palace (43:7–9). Moreover, in contrast to the king's cultic rights in the Solomonic temple (e.g., 1 Kgs 8:63; 2 Kgs 16:12–14), Ezekiel's *nāśî*/king has no access to the inner court and its altar. From a position in the inner east gateway he may only witness his sacrifice being immolated by the priests (Ezek 46:1–2). The *binyān*, "building," annexed to the sanctuary, is not the royal palace, as was its erstwhile Solomonic prede-

---

the sanctuary building (Ezek 44:4), or maximally to the *temenos*, the entire sanctuary complex (Ezek 44:5, the contiguous verse; cf. v. 7; 23:39).

31. Block, *Ezekiel 25–48*, 598.

32. Smith, *To Take Place*, 59.

33. Bennett Simon's, "Ezekiel's Geometric Vision of the Restored Temple," 11–38, arrived too late to incorporate its contributions to the discussion.

34. Stevenson, *Vision of Transformation*, 30.

cessor (see the discussion in Ezek 43:6–9), but an extension of the sanctuary building, "the House of YHWH." The City is no longer the royal *'îr dāwîd*, "the city of David," but YHWH's city called, "YHWH is There" (Ezek 48:35). It is freely accessible to all the tribes of Israel (vv. 30–34). Above all, "until Ezekiel, every Near Eastern text that described the building or restoration of a temple attributed the project to the glorification or shame of the reigning king."[35] Ezekiel's sanctuary is *built by YHWH, not by a king*. As summarized by Stevenson, "there is no human king responsible for building the house of YHWH in Ezekiel's vision. This House is already built. The point cannot be overstressed. YHWH builds this house as a claim to kingship."[36]

## D. The Laws of Ezekiel's Sanctuary

With the exception of the bread of presence (*lehem happānîm*, see below), all rituals ordained by P in the shrine are eliminated in Ezekiel's sanctuary. Hence, Ezekiel has no need for a high priest. But how could he have dispensed with the high priest, the sole day-long officiant in the temple on Yom Kippur? To be sure, Yom Kippur—the tenth of Tishri (Num 29:7)—is absent from Ezekiel's calendar. But surely an annual day of purgation for the temple was essential. Such a day was associated with among other ancient Near Eastern sanctuaries; it could hardly be missing in Israel's yearly cycle, as well. Indeed, an equivalent day did exist in Ezekiel's calendar—the first of Nisan, and its repetition seven days later (Ezek 45:18–20). This ritual prescribes that the blood of an unblemished *ḥaṭṭā't* bull will be smeared on *mĕzuzat habbayit*, "the doorpost of the temple building," on the four corners of *hā'ăzārâ*, "the [altar] ledge," and on the doorpost of the (eastern) gatehouse of the inner court (Ezek 45:19). Thus *wĕkippartem 'et habbayit*, "you (pl.) will purge the temple *temenos*" (v. 20b).

Three features need to be mentioned here. First, the purgation takes place on the second and third elevated platforms, specifically at the entrance to *bêt YHWH*, "the House of YHWH," at the altar, and at the eastern, inner gatehouse. It should be borne in mind that the officiating priest may never enter the outer court. Nonetheless, the latter is purged (Ezek 45:18b, 20b), even though it receives no purgation blood. It can hardly be overlooked that the path taken by the *ḥaṭṭā't* blood—temple doorpost, altar ledge, eastern gatehouse doorpost—corresponds to the path taken by YHWH when he enters the sanctuary (Ezek 43:1, 4). Another point is that the officiating priest purges the sanctuary building at its entrance. He does not enter it. This demonstrates once again that the entire sanctuary building was "the House of YHWH," into which no human, not even a priest, had access, thus precluding the need for the office of the high priest. Also to be noted is that the altar is purged on its *'ăzārâ*, "ledge," not on its horns, as prescribed by P (Lev 4:25; 16:18). The altar, comprising five platforms, resembles a miniature Ziggurat, like the sanctuary compound, and the *'ăzārâ*, "ledge," which receives the purgation blood, corresponds to the altar located on the second level.

---

35. Patton, *Ezekiel's Blueprint*, 180.
36. Stevenson, *Vision of Transformation*, 116.

Ezekiel's *tāmîd*, "regular (daily) offering," differs from the Torah's prescription. The latter *tāmîd* is one whole burnt-offering lamb, and as a *minḥâ*, requires a tenth of an *ēpâ* of semolina, mixed with a quarter of a *hîn* of olive oil and accompanied by a quarter of a *hîn* of wine as a libation (Num 28:3–8). Ezekiel's *tāmîd* also comprises one whole burnt offering lamb but requires an adjusted *minḥâ*, consisting of a sixth of *ēpâ* semolina mixed with a third of a *hîn* of olive oil (Ezek 46:13–15). The major difference is that P's *tāmîd* is repeated in the evening, whereas Ezekiel's *tāmîd* is only offered in the morning. There seem to have been variant traditions of the *tāmîd* during pre-exilic times. The *tāmîd* was indeed offered twice daily, but the whole burnt offering was only sacrificed in the morning, and the *minḥâ*, "the meal offering," in the evening (2 Kgs 16:15; cf. 1 Kgs 18:29, 36). This evidence renders it feasible that Ezekiel may have adopted his prescription for the *tāmîd* from one of the extant traditions of the First Temple period. The elimination of the evening *tāmîd* would allow the priests to offer up all the required public sacrifices in the morning hours and free the rest of the day for the individual sacrifices of the *nāśî'* and the people.

In the main, the people's sacrifice refers to the *šĕlāmîm*, "well-being offering," which, in accordance with Lev 17:3–5 [H], is required for eating meat. The dining area in the sanctuary for the *nāśî'* was inside the eastern outer gate (Ezek 44:3) and presumably for the people in the surrounding thirty rooms spaced along the outer wall (Ezek 40:17). It must also be presumed that the *šĕlāmîm* meats were eaten only *within* the sanctuary. This seems to have been the case in the Shilo sanctuary and in others,[37] in distinction to P, which allowed the *šĕlāmîm* portions to be eaten outside the *temenos* as long as its consumers were not in an impure state (Lev 7:15–21).

The sacrifices for *New Moon* day provide another standard of comparison: an unblemished bull, an unblemished ram, and six lambs as whole burnt offerings; an *ēpâ* (of semolina) for the bull, the same for the ram, and a voluntary amount of semolina for each lamb, mixed with one *hîn* of olive oil per *ēpâ* (of semolina) as meal offerings (Ezek 46:6–7). This compares with two bulls, one ram, and seven lambs as whole burnt offerings and three tenths of an *ēpâ* of semolina for each bull, two tenths for the ram, and one tenth for each lamb, together with one half a *hîn* (of wine) for each bull, a third of a *hîn* for the ram, and a fourth of a *hîn* for each lamb as a libation, as well as a he-goat as a *ḥaṭṭā't*, "purification," offering in addition to the daily *tāmîd* (Num 28:11–15). Since the new moon sacrifices are provided by the *nāśî'*/king rather than the sanctuary, it is understandable that a different standard is employed.

The same holds for the Sabbath. Ezekiel requires the *nāśî'* to offer six unblemished lambs and one ram as whole burnt offerings and an *ēpâ* (of semolina) as a *minḥâ*, "meal offering," for the ram, a voluntary amount for each lamb, all mixed with a *hîn* of oil per *ēpâ* (Ezek 26:4–5). This compares with P's prescription of two unblemished lambs as a whole burnt offering, accompanied by two tenths of an *ēpâ* of semolina mixed with oil as meal offerings, together with its wine libation (Num 28:9; cf. 15:4–5). It is no accident that Ezekiel imposes a heavier, more expensive burden upon the *nāśî'*.

---

37. Milgrom, *Leviticus 1-16*, 227.

## The Visionary Sanctuary

Considering the vast lands under the latter's control (see Ezek 45:7–8; 48:21–22), he is in an affordable financial position to supply the increased quota of Sabbath offerings. Besides, this law reflects the paramount importance of the Sabbath in the Babylonian diaspora, as demonstrated in the book of Ezekiel.[38] It should also be noted that the *nāśî'* is responsible for the sacrifices mandated on all the festivals in addition to the sabbaths and the new moons.

The pilgrimage festivals are represented by the Festival of Unleavened Bread (Nisan 15–21) and the Festival of Booths (Tishri 15–21). Both require the same fixed sacrifices: seven bulls and seven rams as whole burnt offerings and one purification he-goat each day, accompanied by an *'ēpâ* (of semolina) mixed with a *hîn* of oil for each bull and ram as a meal offering (Ezek 45:23–25). P, however, prescribes for the Feast of Unleavened Bread two bulls, one ram and seven lambs per day as whole burnt offerings and one purification he-goat per day, accompanied with three tenths (of semolina) for each bull and two tenths for the ram, one tenth for each lamb (Num 28:19–24). For the Festival of Booths, P requires an entirely different regimen: a total of seventy whole burnt bulls and for each day two whole burnt rams and fourteen whole burnt lambs (Num 29:13–34) and a meal offering in accordance with Num 15:2–12. The *nāśî'* is also responsible for a purification bull on Nisan 14, the day each Israelite family head offers up the *pesaḥ* lamb or goat (Ezek 45:2), whereas no purification bull is required by P. Again, the far larger number of (and more expensive) animals and larger semolina quantity (an *'ēpâ* is approximately 20 liters) reflect the fiscal responsibility for the upkeep of the sanctuary imposed on the *nāśî'*.

The reason for similar treatment of the Festival of Unleavened Bread and the Festival of Booths can only be conjectured. Perhaps it is the realization that Israel observes two calendars—the older autumnal agricultural calendar, beginning on 7/1, and the more recent Babylonian spring calendar beginning on 1/1. The adoption of the latter may have been accelerated in the Babylonian diaspora where a number of city-states observed both the spring and autumn calendars simultaneously.[39] Nonetheless, since Ezekiel does not observe P's Alarm Blast festival on 7/1 (Lev 23:23–25; Num 29:1), it is likely that he would have observed only one New Year's day on 1/1. As for the unprecedented purification bull required during the *pesaḥ* offerings of the people on 1/14 (Ezek 45:22), it can only be surmised that the altar had to be purged by a purification bull for fear that illicit flock animals (blemished, stolen?, cf. Hag 1:13) offered for the *pesaḥ* may have contaminated the altar.

It is no accident that the Festival of Weeks/Harvest (cf. Exod 23:16; 34:22; Num 28:26; Deut 16:10) is omitted. This already had been done by H (Lev 23:21).[40] Thus, it is understandable that Ezekiel followed his own priestly (H) tradition—which on pragmatic grounds realized that the Festival of Weeks was being ignored by Israel-at-

---

38. Ezek 20:12, 13, 16, 20, 21, 24; 22:8, 26; 23:38; 44:24. See the discussion in Milgrom, *Leviticus 17-22*, 1954-64 on Ezek 44: 24; Greenberg, *Ezekiel 1-20*, 366-67.
39. Milgrom, *Leviticus 17-22*, 1966.
40. Ibid., 2009.

large. They were reluctant to leave their homes during the wheat harvest season, for fear of damage wrought by the unpredictable, deadly sirocco winds.[41]

The obligation of the *nāśî'* for maintaining the sacrificial cult of Ezekiel's visionary temple is stated explicitly: "The *nāśî'* is responsible for the whole burnt offerings, the meal offerings, and the libations on the festivals, the new moons and the sabbaths—indeed all of Israel's fixed occasions. He will provide the purification offering, the meal offering, the whole burnt offering, and the well-being offering (the *šĕlāmîm*, "well-being," offering is not an expiatory sacrifice, since it is brought only for joyous reasons).[42] Block[43] suggests that the reparation offering (*'āšām*) was either omitted by mistake, or that this list was not intended to be inclusive. However, the *'āšām* is an exclusively private offering. It is never included in any of the fixed public offerings. Indeed, the *'āšām* mentioned in Ezek 40:39; 42:13; 44:29; and 46:20 all refer to the priestly prebends from *private* offerings of the *'āšām*.

The *nāśî'* is granted two honorific privileges: He is privileged to eat his *šĕlāmîm* offering while seated in the vestibule of the eastern gatehouse of the outer court (Ezek 44:1–3), and he offers the public sacrifices on the Sabbath and new moon as well as his own sacrifices while stationed in the eastern gatehouse of the inner court (Ezek 46:2, 12). These privileges are exclusive. Otherwise, these two eastern gates are closed; they mark the path taken by YHWH when he returns to his people and reenters his sanctuary (Ezek 43:4–6).

The laws concerning the behavior and perquisites of the priests (Ezek 44:17–31) show once again that Ezekiel did not envision the office of a high priest. Not only is there no role for the high priest in Ezekiel's empty shrine, but the stricter rules imposed on individual priests compared with those imposed by H demonstrate that H's regulations concerning the high priest have been partially absorbed by those of Ezekiel's ordinary priest. For example, H allows a priest to marry a widow, but Ezekiel allows the marriage only if she is the widow of a priest (Ezek 44:22). H, however, mandates that the high priest may marry a priestly virgin (Lev 21:14). Thus, Ezekiel adopts an intermediate position between H's priest and high priest.[44]

H ordains no distinction between the purificatory rites for corpse-contaminated priests and Israelites. That is, the sprinkling with ashes of a red cow on the third and seventh day, followed by ablutions (Num 19:19) are the same for both priest and Israelite in H. Ezekiel, however, ordains that the priest shall wait an additional seven days following his seven-day purification (presumably until his impurity is completely removed) and then purify the altar with a purification offering (being a priest he had

---

41. Ibid., 1999–2001.

42. But see my discussion of Lev 17:11 to effect expiation for the house of Israel (Ezek 45:17). Ibid., 1472–78.

43. Block, *Ezekiel 25–48*, 659.

44. For other solutions, cf. Zimmerli, *Ezekiel 2*, 457; Greenberg, "Design and Themes," 208; Zeitlin, "Titles High Priest and the Nasi," 1–5; Lang, *Kein Aufstand in Jerusalem*, 139; Mackay, "Why Study Ezekiel 40–48?" 155–67; Douglas, "Ezekiel's Temple," 365–67, 420–22, 468–70, 515–18; Lane, *The Cloud and the Silver Lining*, 143.

contaminated the altar with more severe impurity) before he is allowed to resume his priestly functions.

The wide ranging discrepancies between the priestly laws of H and Ezekiel have led scholars to assume that Ezekiel (or his tradents) had no knowledge of H.[45] This position, however, must be contested. First, it can be shown that Ezekiel had the text (probably a form that underlies the MT) of H before him.[46] Then, on logical grounds, one may ask: What were the rules governing the priestly cadre of the Jerusalem temple? Unfortunately, textual evidence is nonexistent. However, it can be shown that during the last century of the first temple there was a continuous Zadokite high priest (2 Kgs 12:11; 22:4, 8, 10; 23: 4, 24). Thus, Ezekiel, who eliminates the high priestly office from his temple, could not be citing some independent position. Rather, he is *opposing* the prevailing practice of the Jerusalem temple of which he, a Zadokite, is fully aware.

H (or P) declares twice, firmly and unambiguously, that the Levites *lo' yinḥălû naḥălâ*, "may not possess any inheritable land" (Num 18:23b–24b), in place of which *tĕrûmâ nātatî lalĕwiyyîm lĕnaḥălâ*, "an inheritable land gift have I given to the Levites," which amounts to *ma'ăśēr*, "a tenth," of the people's major crops (Num 18:24; cf. Deut 14:22–23). However, H also allocates to the Levites forty-eight cities and their surrounding *migraš*, "livestock enclosures,"[47] thus allowing Ezekiel to fuse theoretically all these properties into a single *'ăḥuzzâ*, "possession," for their *'ārîm lāšebet*, "city dwellings" (Ezek 45:5, LXX; cf. 48:13–14). Ezekiel says nothing about the tithe, but it must be assumed. Otherwise, how would the Levites survive? Alternatively, and preferably, they were granted ample pasturage for full-time animal husbandry, which would obviate the need for the tithe.

The priests would exhibit the same economic development. Originally (H) they too were denied possession of landed inheritance (Num 18:20; Deut 18:1–2). But they were assigned dwellings in nine settlements located in the tribes of Judah and Simeon (Josh 21:13–16), which are also collapsed into a single block of land (Ezek 45:3–4; 48:10–12). Their income continues to derive from the sacrifices, the first fruits, first-processed foods, proscriptions, and the first dough (Ezek 44:29–30).

The separation between the priests and Levites (and the laity), which prevails as a key element in the structure of Ezekiel's sanctuary, continues in the allocation of the tribal lands. First, the priests and Levites are awarded sacred property, "YHWH's contribution" (*tĕrûmâ laYHWH*). Then the priests and Levites are assigned separate lands (Ezek 45:1–5; 48:8–14).

The revelation to Ezekiel of unique sanctuary dimensions (Ezek 40–43) and unique laws concerning the sanctuary personnel (Ezek 44–46) has led a number of critics to regard Ezekiel as a second Moses.[48] Indeed, it cannot be overlooked that, like Moses, Ezekiel receives a revelation containing the construction of a sanctuary (cf.

---

45. Haran, "Law-Code of Ezekiel 40–48," 66–67.
46. See Milgrom, *Leviticus 23–27*, 2348–57.
47. Milgrom, *Leviticus 23–27*, 2204; Num 35:1–8.
48. Levenson, *Theology of the Program of Restoration*, 638–39; Duguid, *Ezekiel and the Leaders*, 105–7; Block, *Ezekiel 25–48*, 498–500.

Exod 25–40) and a law code (e.g., Leviticus). He is vouchsafed a vision of the reapportioned land from a high mountain, but does not enter this land (cf. Deut 34). However, that Ezekiel is a second Moses is a blatant exaggeration. Where is Ezekiel's equivalent to the Decalogue and the Covenant Code (Exod 19–24)? Ezekiel's laws are restricted to Israel's leaders: the priests, Levites, and *nāśî'*. The latter, however, is mainly limited to his relationship with the sanctuary. Aside from his prohibition to annex land (Ezek 47:18) and his responsibility to control honest weights and measures (45:10–15), the *nāśî'* plays no role in serving his people. Moreover, the people, it seems, are a blank in Ezekiel's law code. Where are the laws of slavery (Exod 21:1–11), homicide (Exod 21:12–15), and injury (Exod 21: 18–27)—to cite the initial examples from the oldest Mosaic law corpus? At best, Ezekiel is a *partial Moses*, who is mostly interested in the sanctuary structure, priestly laws, and sacred land (*tĕrûmâ*, Ezek 45:1–5; 48:9–14). Ezekiel's utopia of the equal subdivision of the land is pure fantasy, but it is the required conclusion to the book because it represents the fulfillment of YHWH's oath that he will resettle his people in their land (Ezek 20:41–44; 36:24–36; 48). But the laws concerning the sanctuary, its personnel, and the *nāśî'* are viable and enforceable. For the people, however, the Mosaic laws necessarily remain in force (mainly P and H; secondarily D) until a new Moses ("one like me," Deut 18:15) makes his convincing appearance. For further discussion, see Excursus 8.

## THE NEW TEMPLE AND ITS PRECINCTS: MEASUREMENT OF BOUNDARIES AND SPACES (40–43)

### *Preamble: A Visionary Flight to a High Mountain in Israel. The Celestial Guide (40:1–4)*

TRANSLATION

**1** At the beginning of the twenty-fifth year[49] of our exile, on the tenth[50] [day] of the month, fourteen years after[51] the city had been subjugated, on that very day, YHWH's hand lay upon me, and brought me there. **2** In a heavenly vision[52] he brought me to the land of Israel and set me down on a very high mountain, on which there was a structure[53] like a city, to the south.[54] **3** When

---

49. LXX adds "in the first month" [511, n. 49], presumably Nisan. The rabbis see it as Tishri (*b. 'Arak.* 12a), the tenth of which is Yom Kippur and the beginning of the jubilee year (Lev 25:8).

50. The rare cardinal form *'āśôr*, instead of *'ăśîrî*, e.g., 29:1; 33:21, occurs in 20:1 and 24:1 [511, n. 50].

51. *'aḥar 'ăšer*, instead of conventional *'aḥărê 'ăšer*, occurs in Ruth 2:2 [511, n. 51].

52. *bĕmar'ōt* is not a true plural; see the discussion on 1:1 in Greenberg, *Ezekiel 1–20*, 41.

53. *mivneh* from *bānâ*, "build," is a biblical hapax, but its meaning is found in a late Phoenician inscription (*KAI*, 60.2; *TSSI*, 3:148–50), which contains the phrase *mbnt ḥṣr bt 'lm*, "the building of the court of the temple" [511, n. 57].

54. *minnegeb*, "to the south," is rendered *minnegdî*, "opposite me" (LXX). Elsewhere in chapters 40–45 [512, n. 58], "south" is always represented by *dārōm*. For the further justification of MT, see above, p. 45.

he brought me over to it, there[55] was a man standing at the gate who looked like burnished copper. He held a linen cord[56] in his hand, and a measuring rod. 4 The man spoke to me: "Human, see with your eyes, hear with your ears, and pay attention with your heart to everything I am going to show you—for in order to be shown have you been brought[57] here, and tell everything you see to the House of Israel.

## Comment

Three major literary units comprise chapters 40–48: In the first, 40:1—43:27, following the order of the priestly chapters of the Pentateuch YHWH sets up his home in the temple; in the second, 44:1—46:24, Israel is delegated responsibility for the temple; in the third, 47:1—48:35, the fertile land is divided among the twelve tribes [498]. The priestly chapters of the Pentateuch determine the order of this sequence: YHWH's sanctuary is centrally located in Israel's midst (Exod 25:1—40:38), and Moses delivers YHWH's cultic requirements (Lev 1:1—Num 10:28), ending with the division of the land (Num 34:1—35:34). Parallel details follow: (1) In both cases an intermediary receives the Torah, and conveys it to the people (Exod 19:3; 24:12; Ezek 40:4; 43:7; etc.). (2) A high mountain is the location of the revelation (Exod 24:12-18; Ezek 40:2; 48:35). (3) The plans for the sanctuary are revealed only after a covenant is established between YHWH and Israel (Exod 24:1-11; 25:1-40; Ezek 37:26; 40:3—43:12) [499]. (4) The people visually experience the entrance of YHWH's *kābôd* into the temple. (Exod 40:34-38; Ezek 43:1-9). (5) Both prophets are privileged to view the land from atop a mountain (Ezekiel in a vision) but neither is permitted to enter it: Moses dies there (Deut 32:48-52) and Ezekiel "returns" to Babylon [500].

**40:1 twenty-fifth year.** Multiples of twenty-five occur frequently in Ezekiel. The number fifty refers to the jubilee (*b. 'Arak. 12a*; Rashi), which Ezekiel recognizes as *šěnat haddĕrôr*, "the year of liberation" (46:17). Thus, symbolically, Israel has reached the turning point in its exile in Babylonia; henceforth they can expect to receive good news of their impending return to their land. Since Ezekiel dates the exilic period beginning with his personal deportation (597), Ezekiel's vision of the temple must therefore be dated in 573 [Block, 513, calculates the exact date to be April 28, 573 BC]. This verse constitutes a further example of the dating pattern found throughout Ezekiel (cf. 1:1; 8:1; 20:1; 24:1; 26:1; 29:1; 31:1; 32:1) [512].

*At the beginning of the year* (*běrôš haššānâ*). All other dates (listed above) indicate the month by number; here the month is specified by the time of the year, a designation also found in Akkadian *re-eš šatti* (*CAD 18*). The probable reference of the "twenty-

---

55. *hinnēh*, lit., "behold" [512, n. 59]; see Block, *Ezekiel 1–25*, 381, 506.

56. *pětîl* from *pātal*, "twist," a rope of various sizes and shapes comprising of twisted cords, e.g., decorative cord of the ephod (Exod 28:28, 37) or of the *ṣiṣṣyôt*, "fringes," at the hems of the outer garment (Num 15:38). It also denotes the rope to bind Samson (Judg 16:22) [512, n. 60].

57. The only attested occurrence of the *hophal* form of *bô'* (GKC, §74d). The Tg. renders impersonally *ětyûkā*, "they have brought you," i.e., the divine powers; LXX reads "you have come" [512, n. 64].

## PART TWO: EZEKIEL 40–48—THE VISIONARY SANCTUARY AND THE LAND

fifth year" to the jubilee year (above), which begins in the fall (Lev 25:9), may imply that the intended year here also occurs in a fall calendar.[58] However, Ezekiel bases all his date notices on the spring calendar (beginning in Nisan, not in Tishri). Moreover, Ezekiel's New Year is expressly designated in the 1st of Nisan when the sanctuary is purged; when, on the fourteenth of the month, the *pesaḥ* is offered; and when, during the following week, the Festival of Unleavened Bread is celebrated (Ezek 45:18–27) [513].

A numbered-month calendar is employed throughout the priestly calendars (Lev 23:5, 24, 27, 39, 41; Num 28:16; 29:1, 7, 12) as well as elsewhere in the priestly texts (Gen 7:11; 8:4, 5, 13, 14; Exod 12:2; 16:1; 19:1; 40:2, 17; Num 1:1, 18; 9:1, 11; 10:11; 20:1; 33:3, 38). Levine[59] argues that its use in Jeremiah, in 2 Kgs 25:1, 25, and in contemporary epigraphy shows that it came into existence close to the exilic period. De Vaux[60] contends that since the numbered-month calendar system assumes a spring New Year, its adoption is due to the influence of the Babylonian calendar, which also begins in the spring. According to de Vaux, this must have occurred after the death of Josiah when Judah became a vassal state of Babylonia. Elliger[61] holds that the calendar with a spring New Year first arrived under Assyrian influence in the seventh century BCE. Nonetheless, he argues that the numbered-month system was taken over from the Babylonians, but only in the exile. Ginsberg[62] suggests the earlier date of the reign of Manasseh, who, as a submissive vassal of Assyria, also may have used the Babylonian calendar.

It is possible the changeover could have occurred as early as the eighth century, under Ahaz, to curry favor with his Assyrian overlord (2 Kgs 16:7, 10). This would account for the few P references to the numbered-month system in the story of the Flood (Gen 7:11; 8:4, 5, 13, 14) and in P's cultic calendar (Num 28:16; 29:1, 7, 12), both of which may stem from the pre-centralized (pre-Hezekian) Jerusalem temple. All the other numbered months in the Torah derive from H, and we must consider the possibility that the citations attributed to P may actually be the product of H's editing. In any event, it is clear that the spring calendar using a numbered-month system was in place by the seventh century and, possibly, as early as the eighth century.

Tadmor[63] maintains that the northern and southern kingdoms differed in their respective calendars in regard to the beginning of the year: the north in the fall and the south in the spring. Especially telling is his demonstration that a number of synchronizations between the two—beginning in the eighth century, particularly between the reigns of Zechariah, the son of Jeroboam II, and Uzziah—can be reconciled only by positing a difference of six months in their calendrical reckoning.[64] Indeed, with

---

58. So Zimmerli, *Ezekiel 2*, 346–47; Gese, *Verfassungsentwurf des Ezechiel*, 9–10.
59. Levine, *Leviticus*, 267.
60. De Vaux, *Ancient Israel*, 191–92.
61. Elliger, *Leviticus*, 312.
62. Ginsberg, *Israelian Heritage of Judaism*, 67, 122–27.
63. Tadmor, "Chronology," 264–67.
64. Ibid., 267.

Tadmor, it seems likely that this difference between the two calendrical systems was in place from the beginning of the history of the divided kingdom. In any case, it can be stated affirmatively that with the loss of the northern kingdom at the end of the eighth century, the spring calendar of Judah prevailed, and that is what is reflected in our priestly texts.

***On the tenth [day] of the month*** (*běʿāśôr laḥodeš*). On the tenth day of the first month, Israel is commanded to take an unblemished lamb or a kid for each family or household (Exod 12:3–5) and keep it under guard until the fourteenth day when it is slaughtered as a *pesaḥ* sacrifice (v. 6). The purpose of the tenth day is not clear. Philo speculates that allowing the victim to be selected closer to the fourteenth may result in a hurried and blemished choice.[65] Philo may be on the right track. Ordinarily, an individual's sacrifices can be exchanged with ease up to the moment it is brought to the altar, but the *pesaḥ* must be brought by every Israelite family. All available unblemished sheep and goats would no longer be available on the market. Therefore, it must be set aside in advance.

The tenth day seems to have special significance. The tenth of the seventh month is *yôm hakkippurîm*, "the Day of Purgation" (Lev 16; 23:26–32). The Israelites entered Canaan on the tenth of the first month (Josh 4:19), and may have been circumcised on that day.[66] As noted by S. R. Driver,[67] the tenth of the twelfth month in the Muslim calendar is the great sacrifice of the Mecca pilgrimage, thought it may have been inspired by Yom Kippur.[68] Astronomical data may also have played a dominant role in designating this date.[69]

A more plausible reason for Ezekiel is that on the tenth day of the first month the Babylonian New Year's festival reached its climax when Marduk, the god of Babylon, took up residence in the *Akitu* temple, the day that YHWH, God of Israel, took up residence in his new temple [496].

The MT on Exod 12:3 actually lends itself to a different interpretation. The major pausal sign, the *ʾathnak*, falls under the word *hazzeh*, thus creating the reading, "Speak unto the entire congregation of Israel saying on the tenth of this month: 'each of them shall take . . .'" (Exod 12:3). This means that the command will be ushered on the tenth, but the Israelites will have until the fourteenth to secure the sacrificial victim. The MT was adopted by the Karaite Japhet[70] and by Saadiah Gaon (agreeing with a Karaite!), though it is not followed by the Tannaites (*m. Pes.* 9:5). However, this reading is palpably wrong: *lēʾmōr*, "saying," is always followed by direct quotation, and it should be the bearer of the *ʾathnak*. Thus, there remains no doubt that the victim should be chosen on the tenth and kept under guard until the fourteenth.

65. Philo, *Quaest. in Exod* 1.2.
66. Jacob, *Second Book of the Bible*, 300–302.
67. S. R. Driver, *Book of Exodus*, 88.
68. Dalman, *Arbeit und Sitte in Palästina*, 1–27.
69. Cf. Propp, *Exodus 1–18*, 388.
70. Recorded in Ibn Ezra [long].

PART TWO: EZEKIEL 40–48—THE VISIONARY SANCTUARY AND THE LAND

*the fourteenth year after the city had been conquered.* This happened eleven years after Ezekiel's deportation together with the leading economic, cultural, and religious classes of Israel, adding up to the twenty-five years after Ezekiel's deportation [597].

*the city,* i.e., Jerusalem, which in chapters 40–48 is never mentioned by name.

*on that very day* (*bĕʿeṣem hayyôm hazzeh*). A common priestly expression, also favored by Ezekiel 2:3; 24:2; 40:1;[71] probably, April 28, 573.

*the hand of YHWH lay upon me* (*hāyĕtâ ʿālay yad YHWH*). This sentence opens each of Ezekiel's three visions: "And the hand of YHWH lay upon him there (1:3; 3:22); "the hand of YHWH lay upon me" (40:1). "Susceptibility to seizure is characteristic of Ezekiel, distinguishing him from other literary prophets who never employ this expression in describing the onset of their prophecy."[72] The hand falling upon him, seizing him by the hair, and carrying him off in 8:1 is less forceful than its resonance in 1:3 [514]. The verb indicates the immediate reaction of Ezekiel to the revelation.

*And he brought me there* (*wayyābēʾ ʾōtî šāmmâ*). This wording is deliberately phrased to create an inclusio with the last sentence of chapters 40–48, *wĕšēm-hāʿîr miyyôm YHWH šāmmâ*, "and the name of the city from that day on shall be 'YHWH IS THERE.'" Thus, from the start Ezekiel was brought there, i.e., to a temple complex that looked like a city (v. 2).

**40:2** *In a heavenly vision* (*bĕmarʾôt ʾĕlōhîm*). *marʾôt* is not a true plural but a "plural of generalization,"[73] frequently rendered as a singular (Ezek 1:1; 8:3; Gen 46:2). In Ezekiel *ʾĕlōhîm* is usually an appellative, a common noun, "divinity," not a proper noun "god."[74] Thus the sense of this expression is "a glorious or divine vision."[75] This is not a day vision but a night dream (Menahem ben Simeon).

*he brought me to the land of Israel* (*hĕbîʾanî ʾel-ʾereṣ yiśrāʾēl*). The destination, "the land of Israel," determines the verb, *hĕbîʾanî*, "brought me," in contrast with *wayyôṣiʾanî*, "he carried me away," to the valley of bones (Ezek 37:1). The "land of Israel" here includes Jerusalem; in Ezek 27:17 the land includes the (former) kingdom of Northern Israel (e.g., 2 Kgs 5:2, 4), and in Ezek 47:18, the land includes all of Cisjordan (approximately the boundaries of Num 34).

*very high mountain . . . like a city.* Both toponymous sites are unnamed, so that they should *not* be identified with Jerusalem and its temple mount. The temple, uniquely, is surrounded by a fortified wall; hence, it resembles a fortified city.

---

71. See Greenberg, *Ezekiel 1–20*, 496–97.
72. Ibid., 42.
73. Joüon and Muraoka, *Grammar of Biblical Hebrew* §136.
74. GKC §124e.
75. Greenberg, *Ezekiel 1–20*, 41; Block, *Ezekiel 25–48*, 85; Kasher, *Ezekiel*, 149.

*The Visionary Sanctuary*

*to the south, minnegeb.* The temple of Apollo at Delphi, the projected model for Ezekiel's temple, is also located on the southern slope (of Mount Parnassus); see the discussion above in the introduction.

**40:3** *When he brought me there, wayyābē' 'ōtî šāmmâ.* A repetition of v. 1bγ, which would be entirely redundant were it not for the possibility that it was a relative clause, as rendered above. This repetition is not for the sake of redundancy, but for the opportunity to stress the word *šāmmâ*, the name of the divine city (Ezek 48:35b).

*Who looked like burnished copper (mar'ēhû kĕmar'ēh nĕḥōšet).* The figures supporting the throne of YHWH were also of copper (Ezek 1:7), adding to the impression that the copper-coated man is a *supernatural* figure. Judging by Ezekiel's past experience, the divine figure would serve two functions: Like the guide who showed Ezekiel around the old temple (Ezek 8) he would escort the prophet around the new temple, and like the man with the writing case (Ezek 9:2), he would be a *surveyor* [515]. It is striking that both Gudea and Ezekiel see in their visions a man who is in charge of the plans of their respective temples. Gudea's divine assistant is named Ninurta, literally, "Lord of Copper," while Ezekiel's guide is described as bearing the appearance of copper.[76]

*A linen cord and a measuring rod, ûpĕtîl-pîštîm . . . ûqĕnēh hammiddâ.* To perform this latter (surveying) task, he held two measuring instruments in his hand: a linen cord, the equivalent of the modern carpenter's tape, to measure long distances, and a measuring rod (*qĕnēh hammiddâ*; see *ḥebel middâ,* Zech 2:5), the equivalent of the carpenter's yardstick, for short distances.[77]

**40:4** *I am going to show you . . . in order to be shown you have been brought here ('ănî mar'eh 'ōtĕkā . . . kî lĕma'an har'ōtĕkāh hūbā'tāh hēnnâ).* The comparison with the wording of God's command to Moses is striking: *kĕkōl 'ăšer 'ănî mar'eh 'ōtĕkā,* "all I am going to show you" (Exod 25:9), except that Moses is commanded, *wĕkēn ta'ăśeh,* "so shall you do," whereas Ezekiel is commanded, *haggēd 'et-kol-'ăšer-'attāh rō'eh lĕbêt yiśrā'ēl,* "tell everything you see to the House of Israel." Ezekiel is not a second Moses in this instance; nor, indeed, a second Solomon, who also erected a temple (1 Kgs 6–8). However, Ezekiel is instructed to pass on the vital (but incomplete) statistics of the temple that Israel—the people!—will heed once they have been restored to their land and feel remorse for their past sins (see Ezek 43:11).

*Human, see with your eyes, hear with your ears, . . . tell everything you see to the House of Israel (ben-'ādām rĕ'ēh bĕ'ênêka ûbĕ'oznêkā šema' . . . haggēd 'et-kol-'ăšer-'attāh rō'eh lĕbêt yiśrā'ēl).* Note the similar language and thought to *'attâ ben-'ādām haggēd 'et-bêt-yiśrā'ēl 'et-habbayit . . . hôda' 'ōtām ûkĕtōb lĕ'ênêhem,* "You, human, report to the House of Israel concerning the temple . . . inform them and write (it) before

---

76. Sharon, "A Biblical Parallel?" 106.
77. Radak; Block, *Ezekiel 24–48*, 515.

## PART TWO: EZEKIEL 40-48—THE VISIONARY SANCTUARY AND THE LAND

them" (43:11). This inclusion is one of the literary marks that indicate the larger unit of the temple construction (40:1—43:12).[78]

### *The Perimeter Wall, Gatehouses, and Court (40:5-27)*

### The Outer (Perimeter) Wall (40:5)

#### TRANSLATION

5 Along the outside ran a wall all around[79] the temple area.[80] The rod that the man held was six cubits long, plus one hand span for each cubit (a long cubit).[81] When he measured the structure,[82] it measured one rod deep[83] and one rod high.

#### COMMENT

The outer wall is measured again in 42:15-20, but there the measurement focuses on the perimeter; here the focus is on depth and height. The two measurements are separated in order to create an inclusion for the tour conducted by the divine guide, which begins and ends at the eastern gate of the outer wall (Fig. 8). Another indication of the possible editorial authorship of this inclusion is that its term *bayit* refers to the temple *compound*, whereas all the other references to *bayit* in chapters 40-42 (twenty times) refer to the temple *building*.[84]

---

78. See Talmon and Fishbane, "Structuring of Biblical Books," 129-53.

79. The duplication of *sābîb sābîb*, found frequently in chapters 40-41 [516, n. 2], is found elsewhere only in 2 Chr 4:3. The duplication is stylistic and not emphatic, as confirmed by Targumic Aramaic, which renders the sg. *sābîb* (Lev 8:15) as *sĕḥôr sĕḥôr* (Onqelos) and *ḥăzôr ḥăzôr* (Pseudo-Jonathan). For details see Hurvitz, *Linguistic Study*, 84-87.

80. In contrast to the term *bayit*, "house," which throughout chapters 40-42 consistently means "the temple building," i.e., the house of YHWH, here it refers to the *temenos*, the temple compound [516, n. 3]. See the COMMENT.

81. *'ammâ* refers to the normal cubit. Adding to it, a *ṭepaḥ*, "a span," produces the long, royal cubit, see Tg. Ps.-J.

82. *binyān*, an Ezekielian neologism under Aramaic influence [516, n. 5]; cf. Hurvitz, *Linguistic Study*, 132-35. Haran's rendering "wall" ("Ezekiel," 213) must be rejected.

83. *puṭya'*, "deep." Tg. Aramaic term meaning "broad," but also "deep, thick."

84. Ezek 40:8, 9, 43, 45, 46, 48; 41:5, 6, 7, 8, 9, 10, 13, 14, 17, 19, 26; 42:15.

*The Visionary Sanctuary*

FIGURE 8: Ezekiel's Temple Tour (a-m)[85]

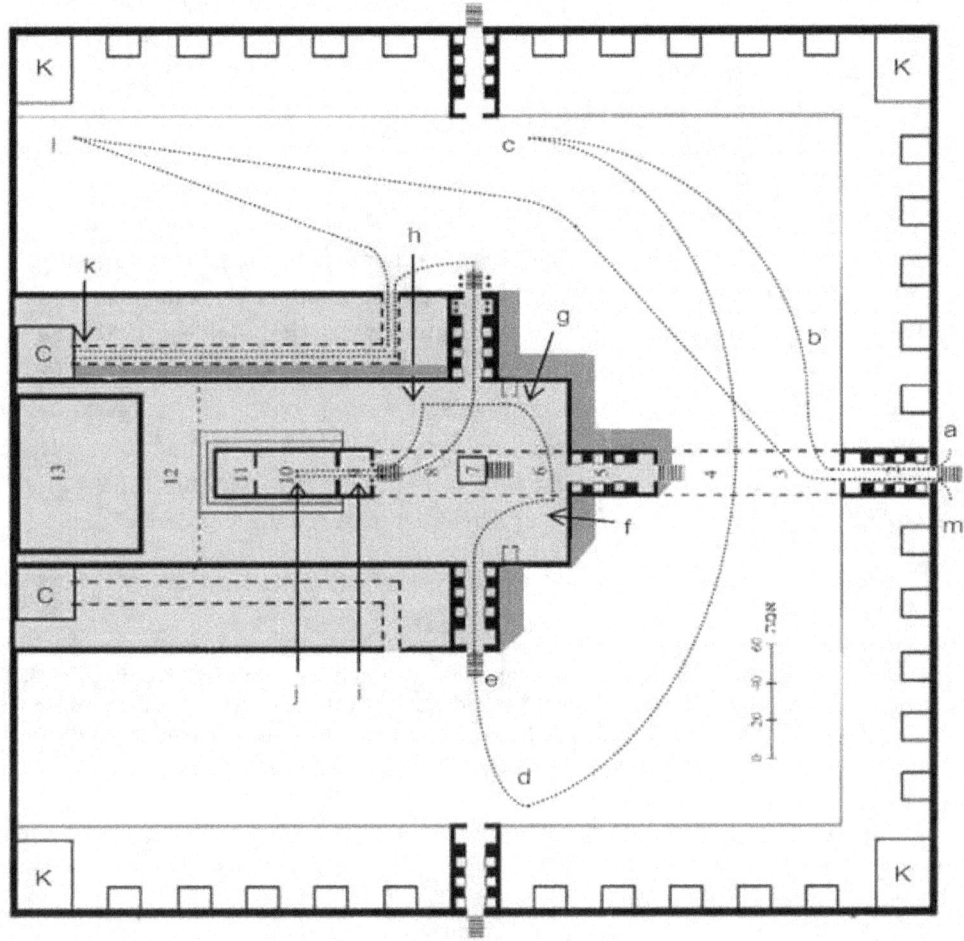

K = Kitchen
C = Sacred Chambers
: = Slaughtering Tables
7 = Altar

85. Adapted from Block, Ezekiel 25–48, 509.

## PART TWO: EZEKIEL 40-48—THE VISIONARY SANCTUARY AND THE LAND

### The Outer East Gatehouse (40:6-16)

TRANSLATION

6 Then he came to the gatehouse[86] that faced east and mounted its steps.[87] He measured the threshold[88] of the gateway; it was one rod deep.[89] 7 Each alcove was one rod wide and one rod deep, with a [partition][90] of five cubits between the alcoves. The threshold of the gateway, next to the vestibule of the inside gate, was one rod. 8 Then he measured the vestibule of the [inside] gate, which was one rod. 9 Then he measured the vestibule of the gate;[91] which was eight cubits, and its jambs were two cubits. The vestibule of the gatehouse was on the inside. 10 There were three alcoves on either side of the gatehouse facing east.[92] The jambs on either side also measured the same. 11 Then he measured the opening of the gate, which was ten cubits wide. The total length[93] of the gateway was thirteen cubits. 12 In front of the alcoves on either side was a barrier one cubit wide. The alcoves on either side were six cubits deep. 13 Next he measured the gateway from the ceiling of one alcove to the ceiling [opposite it];[94] which measured a total of twenty-five[95] cubits. The openings [of the alcoves] were opposite each other. 14 Then he measured the vestibule,[96] which

---

86. Anarthrous *ša'ar* is rendered as definite by the Versions (as in 43:4) and appears in a definite form elsewhere (see 40:20, 22; 42:15; 43:1) [517, n. 11].

87. Qere correctly reads Kethib's *bm'lwtw* as pl. According to Andersen and Forbes, *Spelling in the Hebrew Bible*, 323-28, the defective spelling *w* for *yw* which occurs frequently in this chapter (40:6, 26, 31, 37, 47) represents an archaic convention. LXX reads, "and he entered by seven steps," corresponding to verses 22 and 26 [517, n. 13]. According to Rashi, there were twelve steps, citing *m. Midot* 2:3.

88. LXX renders *sap* as αιλαμ, confusing this structural feature with *ĕlim*, "vestibule," in verses 9-10 [517, n. 14].

89. NJPS notes correctly that *rōḥab*, usually rendered "width," may represent the measurement from an outer surface inward, hence "depth" here. *wĕ'et-sap haššaʻar qāneh 'eḥād rōḥab* MT (also Tg.) is incomprehensible and looks like a dittography [517, n. 15].

90. Tg. logically inserts *kūtlā'*, "wall."

91. The repetitious bracketed material is missing in numerous Hebrew mss., LXX, Syr, and Vulg, and should probably be deleted as a dittography [518, n.18].

92. The idiom *mippōh . . . mippōh*, "from here . . . from here," is unique to chapters 40-41 (e.g., 40:12, 21, 16, 41, 48) [518, n. 19].

93. The term *ōrek* usually denotes length, but it is used here to indicate the full width of the gate inclusive of the jambs and the sockets [518, n. 20].

94. *miggag hattā' lĕgaggô*, lit., "from the roof of the alcove to its roof." NRSV and REB follow the common emendation of *miggag* as *miggaw*, "from the back wall," based on LXX τοῖχος, which frequently translates *qîr*, "wall." But the major versions follow the MT. Since each alcove is 6 cubits and the gateway is 13 cubits wide, yielding a total of 25 cubits, the measurement was taken from the points at which the roof and the walls met [518, n. 21].

95. The Tg. renders MT's *wayyaʻaś 'et-ĕlîm*, as *waʻăbad yāt ēlēyā'*, "he made the jambs," but it is incomprehensible. Rather, *wayyaʻaś* should be taken as a synonym of *wayyāmod*; an abbreviation of *wayyaʻaś 'et-[middat hā]'ĕlîm*, "and he performed the measurement of the vestibule" (reading *'ulām* for *ĕlîm*) [518, n. 23].

96. Zimmerli (*Ezekiel 2*, 335) follows Gese (*Der Verfassungsentwurf*, 140-48) in deleting the entire verse as a corruption containing elements of verses 15-16; see Allen's reconstruction of verse 14 (*Ezekiel*

was sixty[97] cubits. [The gate went around facing the jambs of the court.][98] **15** The distance from the front of the outer gate,[99] to the front of the interior vestibule was fifty cubits.[100] **16** The alcoves and the jambs[101] had sealed niches[102] on all sides of the interior gateway. The vestibules also had niches[103] all around, and each jamb[104] was decorated with palm trees.

## Comment

The structure of the outer east gatehouse (Fig. 9) reflects familiarity with architectural conventions of Ezekiel's time, as shown by the archaeological remains of the city gatehouses of Gezer, Hazor, Ashdod, Lachish, and Timnah (cf. Fig. 10).[105] The tour of the

---

20–48, 220) [518, n. 24]. The simple orthographic emendation *ēlîm* > *'ulām*, "vestibule," offers a satisfactory solution.

97. *šiššîm*, "60," is an impossible measurement [518, n. 25] (about 30 meters!). Besides, it refers to the height of the *ēlîm*, "jamb," a part of a floor plan that contains no vertical measurements. The LXX reading *wayyāmod 'et-hā'ulām 'eśrîm 'ammâ*, "he measured the vestibule, 20 cubits," is preferable not only because all the difficulties are removed, but because it adds a measurement not found elsewhere—the inner width of the vestibule.

98. *wĕ'el-'ēl heḥāṣēr haššaʻar sābîb sābîb*. The literal bracketed translation is gibberish [518, n. 26]. The LXX renders it *wĕ'el-'ulām haššaʻar heḥāṣēr sābîb sābîb*, lit., "and close to the vestibule of the gate the court ran round about." That is, after exiting from the vestibule one was exposed to the entire platform that comprised the court of the Israelites.

99. *wĕ'al pĕnê haššaʻar hāy'îtôn*, lit., "and against the face of the gate" is senseless. The measurement is from a beginning to an end. Hence, the reading *millipnê* is required (Zimmerli, *Ezekiel*). *yi'tôn* [Qere *'îtôn*] is a hapax, probably an architectural term [519, nn. 27–28)], meaning "opening, entrance," (see below) i.e., "The distance from the opening (façade) of the gatehouse" (Radak). The hapax *'îtôn* (perhaps an Aramaic term from the root *'t'*, "enter," and *'al pĕnê* should be rendered *'ad pĕnê*, "until." However, the frequent occurrence of *'al* meaning *'el*, "to," obviates the need for an emendation. Rashi maintains that the height of this gate was 50 cubits. Radak takes vigorous exception to Rashi on this score. According to Levey (*Targum of Ezekiel*, 111, n. 13), Rashi's error may be based on his misreading of the Tg. *gaboah* for *gawaʻah* "inner."

100. This is the length of the gateway, calculated as follows: outer threshold, 6 cubits; three recesses, 18 cubits; two spaces between the recesses, 10 cubits; inner threshold, 6 cubits; vestibule, 8 cubits; jamb, 2 cubits. Total 50 cubits (see Fig. 8; adapted from Block, [530]).

101. *Their supports*, *ĕlêhēmâ*, equivalent to *ĕlēhēmâ*. A spelling frequent in Qumran writing (note *gĕwiyōtêhenâ*, 1:11); see Burrows. "Orthography, Morphology, and Syntax," 209; Gese, *Der Verfassungsentwurf*, 148). On the form, see GKC §91l; Joüon and Muraoka §94l. See the discussion on *gĕwiyōtêhenâ*, (1:11) [519, n. 30].

102. *wĕhallōnôt 'ăṭumôt*, "closed niches" (Radak). The LXX renders the phrase, "secret windows," which has no philological basis, since the meaning of the root *'ṭm* is clear: Isa 33:15; Ps 58:5; Prov 21:13 the closing of the ears; Prov 17:28 the closing of the lips [522, nn. 40–41]. *Num. R.* 15:7 cites this verse to prove that the windows were narrow within and widened outward, so that the sacred light, which issued from the temple, could spread out to the world. However, Levey points out (*Targum of Ezekiel*, 111, n. 14) that Tg. 1 Kgs 6:4 read the comparable sentence: "And he made for the temple windows, which were wide on the inside and narrower on the outside."

103. Since *wĕkēn* introduces the second half of the verse, the *'athnak* on *lāēlāmmôt* should be transferred to *lipnîmâ* (not to *sābîb*, as Block argues [519, n. 31]). Also *wĕhallōnôt* should read *ḥallōnôt*.

104. *wĕ'el-'ayil* should read *wĕ'al-'ayil*, lit., "and on each jamb." The palm tree decorations are a direct imitation of the Solomonic temple (1 Kgs 6:29) [523, n. 45].

105. Mazar, *Archaeology of the Land of the Bible*, 384–87, 465–70.

PART TWO: EZEKIEL 40–48—THE VISIONARY SANCTUARY AND THE LAND

FIGURE 9: The Outer Gatehouse of Ezekiel's Temple (Ezekiel 40:5–16)[106]

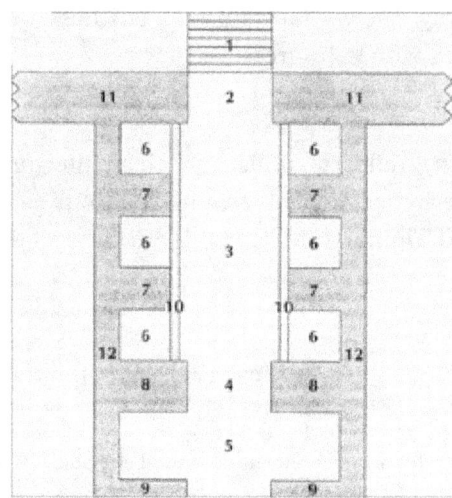

1. Steps
2. Threshold (outer)
3. Gateway
4. Threshold (inner)
5. Vestibule
6. Recesses
7. Walls (between recesses)
8. Wall (between vestibule and recess)
9. Jambs
10. Boundary
11. Outer Wall
12. Back Walls

FIGURE 10: Five Six-Chamber Gates

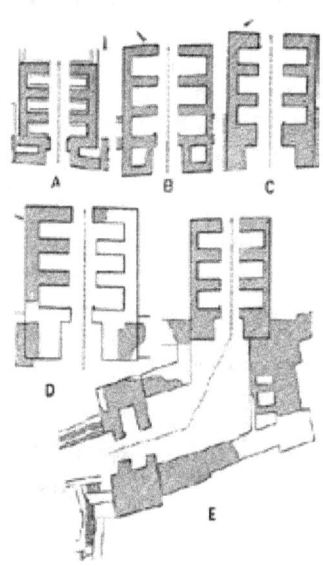

A. Gezer
B. Hazor
C. Ashdod
D. Lachish
E. Megiddo (with the outer gate an offsets-insets city wall)

temple grounds at this gate (Fig. 9). The prophet follows the man as he measures the objects and spaces before him. The gatehouse is measured, mostly in sharp detail, as indicated by numbers 1–12 in Fig. 9, as follows [519–23].

**40:6–7.** They ascend the steps (*ma'ălôt*, #1), seven in number (vv. 22, 26). The guide measures the outer threshold (*sap*, #2) one rod deep (6 long cubits, about 10 foot), the same width as the wall itself (*ḥômâ*, #11). Attention is drawn to the square alcoves (*tā'*,

---

106. Adapted from Block, *Ezekiel 25–48*, 520.

#6), one rod wide and one rod deep, on each side. There are six such alcoves, three on each side, a pattern well attested in Iron Age II city walls (Fig. 10).[107] The alcoves are separated by walls (*bên hattā'îm*, #7), 5 cubits thick. The alcoves most likely serve as guardrooms. As told in verse 16, the alcove walls contain niches to hold the special weapons and clothing of the guards [519, 521].

**40:8–10.** Traversing the gateway, the guide reaches the inner threshold (*sap*, #4) separating the guardroom from the vestibule (*'ûlām/'ulām*), a large room just inside the gate (#5). The wall between the vestibule and the alcoves area (#8) is thicker than those between the alcoves. The vestibule is rectangular in shape, 8 cubits deep. It is supported by two jambs (*'êlîm*, #9).

**40:11–15.** The guide returns to the gate opening (#2) and measures it, 10 cubits (17 ft.) wide and the gateway (#3), 13 cubits (about 22 ft.) wide. He also measures the roof, 25 cubits (about 43 ft.) wide. The height of the ceiling is not given. The term *gag* (v. 13) is better rendered here as "ceiling" than "roof." The width of the back walls (#12) is undetermined. The guide measures the length of the gateway (v. 15); the total 50 cubits (about 86 ft.) coincides with the cross-section measurements, as follows:[108]

#11 + #6 + #7 + #6 + #7 + #6 + #8 + #5 + #9
6 + 6 + 5 + 6 + 5 + 6 + 6 + 8 + 2 = 50

**40:16.** The meaning of *ḥallōn* here is problematic. On *ḥallōnê šĕqāpîm 'ăṭumîm* (1 Kgs 6:4) Rashi and other medieval exegetes (based on *Num. R.* 15:7) claim that these words describe windows that are wide from without and narrow from within. The Tg. and Radak claim the reverse: the windows were narrow from without (*sĕtîmân milibārâ*) and broad from within (*pĕtîḥān milqāw*). Radak argues that *'ăṭumôt* cannot mean "completely closed/shut," since it modifies the noun "windows." These medieval exegetes are preceded by Peshitta's expansion, "windows open on the inside, narrow on the outside," and Vulgate's, "slanted windows." Yadin proposes that engraved ivories of building in Israel and Syria show windows having interlocking, stacked frames, one deeper than the next.[109] Another suggestion is that these words (in 1 Kgs 6:4) do not represent windows but the *bît ḥilāni*, an Assyrian broad room structure with two chambers, but as attractive as this is in 1 Kings, it has no meaning in Ezekiel.[110]

Finally, keeping the rabbinic interpretation *'ăṭumîm*, "LORD YHWH's exalted house," *ḥallōnôt* are found inside the alcoves, inside the vestibules, and on the jambs and this implies that the *ḥallōnôt* are not windows but niches;[111] that is, niches in the shape of windows or frames, carved into the walls of the alcoves. This, indeed, is the meaning

---

107. Adapted from Mazar, *Archaeology of the Land of the Bible*, 384.
108. Correcting Block, *Ezekiel 25–48*, 522.
109. Yadin, "The First Temple," 181; cf. also Karageorghis, "Chronique de fouilles et decouvertes archeologiques a Chypre en 1969," fig. 80.
110. See the discussion by Hurowitz, "LORD YHWH's Exalted House," 70.
111. Eliezer of Beaugency; Block, *Ezekiel Chapters 25–48*, 522–23.

of *ḥallōnôt* in tannaitic literature (e.g., *m. Tam.* 5:3; *m. Toh.* 7:7; *t. Suk.* 4:27). The most striking verification of this interpretation is in Qumran's Temple Scroll, 11QT 33:11, "All the wall of this House (of Utensils) have ḤLWNYM PNYMH ʾṬWMYM, "inner blocked niches in their inner faces." These three Hebrew terms are clearly borrowed from Ezek 40:16. Moreover 11QT 33 states that the niches are two cubits deep. This depth must be based on Ezek 40:7, namely that the walls between the recesses were five cubits. This allowed for a one-cubit separation between the niches. (Block, 523, assumes that the walls were three cubits thick. The niches would collide!). The enormous size of the Qumran *ḥallōnôt* (2 x 4 x 2 cubits) may be utopian, but it lends credence to viewing the alcoves as large, the size of windows. And the description of these niches in Qumran's House of the Laver and House of (altar) Utensils[112] makes it certain that we are dealing not with artistic design but with practical structural elements, probably, with compartments for the clothing and weapons of the Levitic guards.

### The Outer Court (40:17–19)

TRANSLATION

> **17** Then he took me to the outer court where there were rooms,[113] as well as a pavement,[114] all[115] around the entire court.[116] There were thirty rooms on the pavement. **18** The pavement flanked the gatehouses,[117] the lower pavement corresponding to the length of the gatehouse. **19** Then he measured the width of the court from in front of the inner gate[118] to in front of the outer court;[119] it measured 100 cubits. So much for the eastern [gatehouse]; now to the northern [gatehouse].[120]

112. See Yadin, *The Temple Scroll*, 227, Fig. 11.

113. The term for the sanctuary room, *liškâ*, seems to be related to Greek λέσχη, where banquets were held (Brown, *Israel and Hellas*, 151–53). However, it is more likely related to Akkadian *aslukkatu/ašrukkatu* (Hurowitz, "Inside Solomon's Temple," 57, n. 18). *liškâ* appears first in the Bible (1 Sam 9:22; 1 Sam 1:18 LXX).

114. The spiranted *p* is regular in *riṣepâ*, "pavement" (cf. vv. 18; 42:3; 2 Chr 7:3; Est 1:6), distinguishing this feature from *rișpâ*, "glowing coal" [524, n. 48]; classic Hebrew *qarqaʿ* (Num 5:17).

115. *ʿāśûy* recurs again in disagreement with its subject (41:18, 20, 25). Zimmerli (*Ezekiel 2*, 337) suggests it is a technical term used as a noun (like *mĕḥuqqeh*, 8:10; 23:14) [524, n. 49].

116. *hattaḥtônâ* (fem) clashes with its antecedent *haššaʿar* (msc). Based on the LXX, many emend *hattaḥtônâ lipnê* to *hattaḥtôn ʾel pĕnê* [524, n. 52].

117. *ketep haššĕʿārîm*, lit., "the flank of the gatehouses," as defined by Haak ("The 'shoulder' of the Temple," 271–78. "*ketep* refers to the façade of the gate, which is perpendicular to the passageway of the gate" (cf. 40:40, 41, 44; 46:19).

118. See Fig. 1.

119. *lipnê* > *ʿal pĕnê*.

120. To resolve the awkward phrase, *haqqādîm wehaṣṣāpôn* (lit., "the east; the north"), the LXX inserts the guidance formula: "and he brought me to the gate" (cf. v. 24) [524, n. 54]. Note the stylistic equivalence *wĕhaššaʿar ʾăšer pānāw derek haṣṣāpôn lĕḥāṣēr haḥîṣônâ* (20a) // *wĕhabbinyān ʾăšer ʿal-pĕnê haggizrâ*, "As for the Building that was in front of the sacred space" (41:12aβ). Thus, beginning the verse with the guidance formula (LXX) is unnecessary.

## Comment

While moving from the east gate to the north gate (Fig. 8), the prophet receives a glimpse of the outer court. He is enabled to count thirty rooms attached to the outer wall (North, East, and South), ten rooms per wall. There are columned porticos (42:6) used by worshipers as dining and meeting places during religious events [524]. These are important rooms in the sanctuary (Jer 35:4; 36:10; 1 Chr 28:12; 2 Chr 36:11; Neh 10:38–40). Block suggests [525] that the thirty rooms were divided 8, 8, 8, 6 (North, East, South, West). However, the westerly view may have been blocked by the inner platform (Fig. 1).[121]

## The Outer North and South Gatehouses (40:20–27)

### Translation

20 Next he measured the length and breadth of the outer court gatehouse facing north. 21 It had three alcoves on either side, as well as its own jambs and vestibule.[122] It measured the same as the first gate: 50 cubits long and 25 cubits wide. 22 The niches of its vestibule[123] and its palm decorations were the same size as those of the gatehouse facing east. People would climb seven steps to reach it,[124] its vestibules being in front of them.[125] 23 Like the east gate, the north gate faced a gateway leading to an inner court. The distance from one gateway to the other measured 100 cubits.

24 The he led me[126] to the south side to the gate, which measured the same as before for its jambs and vestibule. 25 It [the gatehouse] and its vestibule had niches all around just like the previous niches. Its length was 50 cubits and its width 25 cubits. 26 Seven steps[127] led up to it, its vestibule being before them.[128] On either side of its jambs were palm ornaments. 27 The inner court

---

121. Block's recommendation that the term *riṣĕpâ*, "pavement," implies that there were "at least two levels to this (outer) court" (525) should be rejected. To be sure, the two other instances of this spiranted term refer to the richly appointed temple (2 Chr 7:3) and Persian palace (Esth 1:6), but there is no analogy here. As will be argued, Ezekiel's sanctuary has neither silver nor gold and is void of luxuries. The *riṣĕpâ* is a stone pavement, not a platform. Moreover, measurements are never taken from the pavement. As exemplified here, the space (100 cubits) of the inner court includes the pavement.

122. The defective *'lm* for *'ylm* recurs in verse 24 (cf. vv. 29, 31, 33, 36) [526, n. 59].

123. Since *ḥallôn/ḥallônîm(ôt)* is never construed with a pronominal suffix and a copula, the emendation *wĕḥallônôt(îm) 'ēlammô* is recommended [526, n. 61].

124. The plural verb is interpreted impersonally [526, n. 63].

125. The antecedent of *lipnêhem* is not *ma'ălôt* but the "people" [526, n. 64].

126. *wayyôlikēnî*. As in 23:1; 47:6; 20:26, LXX.

127. *'ōlōtāw*, is a unique form, equivalent to *ma'ălōtāw*. Eliezer of Beaugency (on v. 24) points out that the verb *wayyĕsibbēnî*, lit., "and he took me around" (see 47:2), defines their route precisely because the root *sbb* is used for turning outside (e.g., Josh 6:3), but the root *hlk*, hip'il, is used for moving on the inside.

128. Instead of *lipnêhem*, "before them," follow the LXX *lipnîmâ*, "its interior (corridor)." Otherwise, as in verse 22, the masculine suffix on *lipnêhem* refers to the people climbing the stairs [526, n. 70].

also had a gatehouse facing the south. The distance from one gateway to the other on the south side was 100 cubits.

**COMMENT**

Despite the absolute symmetry of the three outer gates, their descriptions exhibit a wide variety of terms, as shown by the following synopsis:

| Eastern Gatehouse | Northern Gatehouse | Southern Gatehouse |
|---|---|---|
| 40: 6–18 | 40: 20–23 | 40: 24–27 |
| m'lwt |  | t'y |
| sp | 'ylym, 'wlm | 'ylym, 'wlm |
| t' |  | 'wrk wrwḥb ḥṣr |
| 'wlm |  | ḥlwnwt lš'r wl'wlm |
| 'ylym |  | ḥlwnwt l'wlm |
| gbwl |  | tymwrym |
| rwḥb ḥṣr |  | 'wrk wrwḥb ḥṣr |
| 'ylym |  | šb' m'lwt |
| 'wrk ḥṣr | šb' m'lwt | tmwrym |
| ḥlwnwt | hmrḥq lš'r šbḥṣr | hmrḥq lš'r šbḥṣr |
| tymwrym | hpnymyt | hpnymyt |

40:19  wymd rḥb m/pny ḥš'r htḥtwnh lpby hḥṣr hpbyny mḥws m'h 'mh

40:23  wš'r lḥṣr hpnymy ngd ḥš'r lṣpwn wlqdym wymd mš'r 'l š'r m'h 'mh

40:27  wš'r lḥṣr hpnymy drk hdrwm wymd mš'r 'l ḥš'r drk hdrwm m'h 'mwt

40:19  *Then he measured the width of the court from in front of the inner gate to in front of the outer court; it measured 100 cubits.*

40:23  *Like the east gate, the north gate faced a gateway leading to an inner court. The distance from one gateway to the other measured 100 cubits.*

40:27  *The inner court also had a gatehouse facing the south. The distance from one gateway to the other on the south side was 100 cubits.*

## The Inner Gatehouses and Court (40:28–37)

**TRANSLATION**

**28** Then he took me into the inner court through the south gateway,[129] which measured the same as the previous gateway. **29** Its alcoves, jambs, and vestibule[130] measured the same as the others. Both it [the gateway] and its vestibule had niches all around. It was 50 cubits long and 25 cubits wide. **30** There were

---

129. ḥāṣēr is treated as definite by the versions and numerous Hebrew mss (GKC 126w) [527 n. 71].

130. w'lmw is found in the Genizah ms. G-B Eb 22. Cf. Goshen-Gottstein and Talmon, *Book of Ezekiel*, 186, and is preferred over w'lmyw (Q, pl).

vestibules on all sides, 25 cubits long¹³¹ and 5 cubits wide.¹³² **31** Its vestibule, however, faced the outer court,¹³³ and palms decorated its jambs on either side. Its staircase had eight steps.

**32** Then he took me into the inner court on the east side.¹³⁴ He measured the gatehouse there whose dimensions were the same as the previous [gatehouses]. **33** Its alcoves, jambs, and vestibule also measured the same as the previous one. It [the gateway] and its vestibule had niches all around. It was 50 cubits long and 25 cubits wide. **34** Its vestibule faced the outer court¹³⁵ and palms decorated its jambs on either side. Its staircase had eight steps.

**35** Then he brought me to the north gatehouse whose measurements were the same, **36** with the same alcoves, jambs, and vestibule. It also had niches¹³⁶ all around. It was 50 cubits long and 25 cubits wide. **37** Its vestibule¹³⁷ faced the outer court, and palms decorated its jambs on either side. Its staircase had eight steps.

## Comment

The tour takes Ezekiel up to the second platform, which, as will be shown (40:38–46), belongs exclusively to the priests. Its greater holiness is also marked by its elevation, eight steps—one step higher than the seven-step lower platform (v. 22). Figure 1 illustrates the relative symmetry of the three inner gatehouses, which are either traversed (South and North) or only measured (East; cf. Fig. 8). The entrance to the third and highest platform is reached by ten steps (40:49, LXX). The number of steps is not arbitrary. Not only do they indicate the increased holiness of the platforms but their sum, 7 + 8 + 10 = 25, is the base number of Ezekiel's architectural system (see the Comment on verse 1).

The reluctance to enter the eastern gatehouse anticipates its special sanctity associated with the forthcoming arrival of (and possession by) YHWH (43:4–5), or perhaps in memory of the departure of YHWH from the Solomonic temple, which also took place via the eastern gate (an indication that the vertical path between the temple and the outer eastern gate is *a priori* divine property and off limits to humans). The northern gatehouse is entered subsequently (Fig. 8). Or the prophet anticipates the sacrificial route permitted to laity, south to north (46:9).¹³⁸ Nearly all critics explain the

---

131. *wĕrōḥab ḥāmēš 'ammôt*. Again, the LBH order; details in 40:5.

132. Block writes as follows [528, n. 73]: "V. 30 is suspect for several reasons: (1) It is missing in LXX; (2) a counterpart is lacking in the descriptions of the other two gates; (3) the pl. "vestibules" is inappropriate for the context; (4) the dimensions of the vestibule(s) are inconsistent with the previous statements. I suspect dittography."

133. A true vestibule since it is the entrance to the gatehouse, as opposed to the inner vestibule of the outer court cf. NJPS.

134. I.e., in order to measure the inner eastern gatehouse.

135. *leḥāṣēr* is equivalent to *'el-ḥāṣēr* in verse 31 [528, n. 76].

136. LXX harmonizes the wording with verses 29 and 33 by adding "and its vestibule" [528, n. 77].

137. MT *wĕēlāw* should be emended to *wĕēlammô* with LXX; cf. verses 31 and 34 [528, n. 78].

138. Thus Kasher, s.v.

PART TWO: EZEKIEL 40–48—THE VISIONARY SANCTUARY AND THE LAND

absence of any mention of an inner barrier wall connecting the three gatehouses by assuming that it exists and must be presumed. As argued in the Introduction (section A), there is no inner wall.

## *The Slaughtering Tables and the Priestly Chambers (40:38–46)*

### The Slaughtering Tables (40:38–43)

TRANSLATION

> **38** There was a room which opened into the vestibule[139] of the gatehouse where the whole burnt offering was to be washed.[140] **39** Two tables were placed on either side of the vestibule [of the gateway] on which to slaughter the whole burnt offering, the purification offering, and the reparation offering. **40** Off to the side[141] were two more tables, outside as one climbs[142] to the entrance of the gateway facing north. Off to the other side of the vestibule of the gatehouse were two (more) tables. **41** (Thus) four tables fronted the gateway on either side—eight tables in all—on which the slaughter would take place. **42** The four tables[143] for whole burnt offerings were [made of] hewn stone. They were 1½ cubits long, one and a 1½ cubits wide, and 1 cubit high. On them were arranged[144] the tools with which to slaughter both whole burnt offerings and (well-being) offerings.[145] **43** Shelves,[146] one hand-span wide, were fixed in place all around on the inside. The flesh of the offering was to be laid out on the tables.[147]

139. Both the context (v. 39) and the sg. *liškâ* demand that MT *bĕʾēlîm haššĕʾārîm*, "into the jambs, the gatehouses," be emended to *bĕʾulām haššaʿar*, "into the vestibule of the (northern) gateway" [530, n. 82].

140. See the COMMENT.

141. *kātēp*, "side." The façade of the tables is perpendicular to the staircase. The outside tables were probably against the outside wall; Haak, "The 'Shoulder' of the Temple," 274–75.

142. Emend *lĕʿōleh*, "as one goes up," to *lĕʾulām*, rendering verse 40a parallel with verse 40b, and reading: "Off the side, on the outside of the vestibule at the entrance of the gateway facing north." Cf. Block, 530, n. 85. Fig. 8 will quickly clarify the instruction. See COMMENT for details.

143. The definite article *h* was accidentally dropped from *šulḥānôt* by haplography from preceding *wĕʾarbāʾâ* [531, n. 87].

144. *ʿălêhem wĕyannîḥû*. There is no need to omit the conjunction (with the major Versions and Block). Like *bōqer wĕyōdaʿ* (Num 16:5), the emphasis is on *ʿălêhem* (= *ʿălêhem*).

145. It would make better sense if verse 42b were transposed after verse 43a (see NJPS, note t–t) [531, n. 89].

146. LXX γεόσπς, "projection," Vulg. *labia* and Pesh. *spwthwn* assume a derivation of *haššĕpātayim* from *śāpâ*, "lip." Most translations follow Tg. *ʿwnqlyn*, "hooks," envisioning a series of hooks attached to the jambs on which the carcasses were hung while being skinned; see Levey, *Tg. Of Ezekiel*, 113, n. 19. This interpretation, however, requires altering *haššĕpātayim* from a dual to a plural [531, n. 91]. Therefore Radak's derivation of the word from *špt* (Ezek 24:3; cf. 2 Kgs 4:38) is more attractive: "an object on which pots are arranged." Thus, in keeping with MT, two long boards for containing the sacrificial tools are attached to the walls on either side of the tables.

147. LXX rewrites this sentence, "above the tables were roofs to give protection from the rain and the heat" [531, n. 93].

## COMMENT

**40:38.** The proximity of the slaughtering to the washing rooms indicates that the Levites who were assigned to slaughter the sacrificial animals (44:1) were also in charge of washing them. To be sure, P assigns the task of washing the whole burnt offering to the lay offerer (Lev 1:9, 16), but in Ezekiel's system all the gateways are under the exclusive control of the Levites and, hence, the washing room is inaccessible to lay offerers. Presumably, the sacrificer of a whole burnt offering would bring the sacrificial animals to the steps of the northern inner gate, and the Levite guards would take over and drag the animal up the eight-step staircase into the vestibule, where it would be washed and slaughtered.

I have presumed that the sacrificial animal is an ovid (sheep or goat), which, according to Lev 1:12, must be slaughtered on the northern side of the altar—which explains the designated north gatehouse as the slaughtering site. Bovids, however, which are not required to be slaughtered north of the altar (only *lipnê YHWH*, "before the LORD"; Lev 1:5, i.e., anywhere within the sacred compound) would not only have to be hauled up the fifteen stairs of two flights, but would have to be stretched atop one of the slaughtering tables in the vestibule. For bovids we must presume another slaughtering procedure on which the text is silent.

What sacrificial animals or animal parts require washing? The rule, I submit, is that whatever is laid out upon the altar requires prior washing. According to P, only the shins and entrails of a whole burnt offering need to be washed. This rule is based on hygiene, not on ritual. But, as perceived by Kasher, according to Ezekiel, the *entire* burnt animal has to be washed. Indeed, I presume, for Ezekiel whatever ascends the altar must initially be washed.[148]

**40:39.** The sacrifices eligible for slaughtering, according to the above procedure, are the three most holy sacrifices, listed according to their order in P: whole burnt offering, purification offering, and reparation offering (Lev 1, 4, 5). The only omitted blood offering—that of well-being (cf. Lev 3), which has the lower status of *qodeš*, "holy" (not *qodeš qodāšîm*, "most holy")—is discussed below. Since I have discussed all these sacrifices at length elsewhere,[149] here a précis should suffice.

### THE WHOLE BURNT OFFERING

The ritual procedure with the whole burnt offering can be reconstructed as follows: After the offerer has performed the hand-leaning rite, the Levite slaughters his/her animal and the officiating priest dashes the animal's blood—collected by his fellow priest(s)—upon all the sides of the altar, while the offerer skins and quarters the animal and washes it. Once the priests have stoked the altar fire, laid new wood upon it, and then laid the animal parts on the altar, the officiating priest supervises the incineration of the sacrifice (cf. Lev 1:1–13). If the offering is unblemished it will be acceptable on the offerer's behalf, but "if you present a lame or sick one—it does not matter! Just

---

148. Kasher, *Ezekiel*, 795.
149. Milgrom, *Leviticus 1–16*, 172–345.

offer it to your governor: will he accept you?" (Mal 1:13). From this citation we can derive two things. First, to be acceptable to God (or the governor), the sacrifice must be *unblemished*. Just as a king expects perfection in his gifts, so does the divine King of Kings. Second, the function of the whole burnt offering here is to *elicit the favor of the Deity*.

### THE PURIFICATION OFFERING

Biblical rituals are symbolic acts that, in the main, contain within them ethical values. This axiom is nowhere better illustrated than in the purification offering (often wrongly translated as "sin offering"). According to Leviticus, the purification offering is prescribed as a response to moral impurity—defined as an unintended breach of prohibitions (Lev 4:2)—and to severe cases of physical impurity. Physical impurity in this context applies to either gender and has to do only with *ritual*, not with one's character or morality. Two examples of such physical impurity are the genital flow from a parturient mother and from a gonnorhean (Lev 12 and 15).

The first question to ask is naturally: *Who* or *what* is purified? Surprisingly, it is not the person with the moral or physical impurity. According to Leviticus, if his or her impurity is physical, only bathing is required to purify the body; if the impurity is moral (the unintended breach of a prohibition), a remorseful conscience clears the wrongdoing. In neither case does the offering purify the person bringing the offering.

### THE REPARATION OFFERING

The reparation offering seems at first glance to be restricted to offenses against the property of God, either God's sancta or God's name. It reflects, however, wider theological implications, revealed by looking at the linguistic roots of the word *ʾāšām*, "reparation offering." The noun *ʾāšām*, "reparation/reparation offering," is related to the verb *ʾāšam*, "feel guilt." Feeling guilt dominates the description of the reparation offering (Lev 5:17, 23 [Eng 6:4], 26 [Eng 6:7]) and the purification offering (Lev 4:13, 22, 27; 5:4, 5). The compilers of Leviticus use the reparation offering to help develop a moral conscience in the young Israelite nation by allowing intentional sins, usually irremediable, to be expiated through sacrifice so long as the sinner is unapprehended and feels guilt for his or her actions.

As a general matter, expiation by sacrifice depends on three factors: (a) the unintentionality of the sin, (b) the remorse of the worshiper, and (c) the reparation the worshiper brings to rectify the wrong. Intentional crimes cannot be remedied by sacrifice. This sacrifice, however, breaks the mold. If someone falsely denies under oath having defrauded his/her fellow—an intentional crime—and subsequently feels guilt (although not apprehended), restores the embezzled property, and pays a 20 percent fine, he/she may then bring a reparation offering to expiate his/her false oath (Lev 5:20–26 [Eng 6:1–7]). Here we see the priestly legists in action, bending the sacrificial rules in order to foster the growth of individual conscience. They permit sacrificial expiation for a deliberate crime against God (in this case, knowingly taking a false oath), provided the person repents (without being apprehended). Thus they ordain that repentance converts an intentional sin into an unintentional one, thereby making it eligible for sacrificial expiation.

Both the purification and reparation offerings are exclusive expiatory sacrifices, but they differ totally in their effect. The former expiates the pollution of sancta, the latter the desecration of the transgressor. What is the difference between pollution and desecration? The difference may seem semantic, but its roots are deep. Desecration is noncontagious, affecting only the transgressor, and is expiated by a reparation offering; pollution, on the other hand, is contagious and can drive Israel out of its land and even God out of his sanctuary unless it is expiated by a purification offering.

**40:40–41.** By reading *lĕʿulām* instead of *lĕʿōleh* in verse 40a, the entire verse is balanced and the scene becomes clarified. The prophet and his guide are standing at the edge of the vestibule at the northern inner gateway, from which they see two tables on either side of the staircase as they look down. These tables may be flat against the outside wall as well as perpendicular to it.[150] Thus MT of verse 40a is acceptable as, "And on the outside, as one goes up to the entrance of the north gate" (Tg.). In sum, there is a total of eight slaughtering tables: four on one side and four on the other or, to enumerate more specifically, four in the vestibule (of the inner court) and four below in the outer court.[151] As will be demonstrated below, the tables in the outer court are for the *zebaḥ*, the well-being offering.[152]

**40:42–43.** Though the four tables located in the vestibule are assigned to the whole burnt offerings, they are also for the purification and reparation offerings. I suggest that these tables were called "whole burnt offering tables," because these sacrifices were preponderant. According to Lev 1:4, people would bring whole burnt offerings for purposes of expiation as well as joy. Thus, just as the altar was called *mizbaḥ haʿōlâ* because the *ʿōlâ* was the predominant immolated sacrifice, so these tables were called the *ʿōlâ* tables because of the preponderant number of *ʿōlâ* sacrifices that were washed and slaughtered on them prior to their immolation.

The height of only three sacred objects is given: the slaughtering tables (1 cubit, 40:42), the table of the bread (3 cubits, 41:22) and the altar's hearth (4 cubits, 43:15). The heights are cited because their surfaces must be used in the worship service. One cubit height is ideal for slaughtering; three cubits are also the ideal height for removing and replacing loaves of bread; and four cubits, to be sure, are out of reach of human hands. However, this height—the altar hearth—is accessible by a staircase. The four tables used for slaughtering the most sacred animals (whole burnt, purification, and reparation offerings) were constructed as a perfect square (1½ x 1½). It is no accident that the table of the bread (2 x 2) and the altar (12 x 12) are also perfect squares. All these—and only these three—are employed in the worship of Ezekiel's sanctuary. It was mentioned above (n. 297) that verse 42b should be transferred after

---

150. See Haak, "The 'Shoulder' of the Temple," 271–78.
151. Haran, "Ezekiel," 210.
152. Contra Block, *Ezekiel 25–48*, 533.

verse 43a (so NJPS), so that the tools could be laid out on the shelves, rather then taking up space on the tables. These instruments would also be used for sacrificing the *zebaḥ*, "the well-being offering,"[153] on the four tables on the lower outside court. In sum, the slaughtering tools for all the sacrifices (from all eight tables) were laid out on the ledges (43a–42b), whereas the animal's flesh would be laid out on the tables; the carcasses of the purification and reparation offerings would not be on these tables because they were priestly prebends; the carcass of the *zebaḥ* would revert to its owner, and their blood and suet would be presented to God on the altar. However, the entire burnt offering animal—all but its skin (Lev 7:8)—is given to God on the altar. It must be quartered—on the table upon which it was slaughtered with the proper instruments located on the shelves above—before being incinerated.

### The Priestly Chambers (40:44–46)

TRANSLATION

> 44 Outside[154] the inner gateway in the inner court were two rooms;[155] one[156] beside the north gateway, facing[157] south, and the other[158] beside the south[159] gateway, facing north. 45 He said to me, "The room[160] facing south is for the priests who guard the temple. 46 And the room facing north is for the priests who guard the altar—they are the descendants of Zadok, who alone of the descendants of Levi may approach YHWH to serve him.

COMMENT

In the inner court the prophet sees two rooms, one on the north side facing south and the other on the south side facing north (Fig. 1). The guide tells him that both rooms are assigned to Zadokite priests.[161] As shown by Duke,[162] there is no need to posit two kinds of priests—non-Zadokites in the north and Zadokites in the south (as it appears superficially). The designation, "the descendants of Zadok" (v. 46b), applies to both priestly groups, those assigned to the northern as well as the southern rooms.

---

153. See Milgrom, *Leviticus 1–16*, 172–76.

154. LXX begins this paragraph with the guidance formula, followed by REB, NAB, NEB and others [535, n. 110].

155. Reading *liškôt šĕtayim*, "two rooms," with LXX in place of MT, "rooms for singers" [535, n. 112].

156. Reading MT *ăšer* as *'aḥat* with LXX and Vulg. [535, n. 112].

157. Emend MT *ûpĕnêhem*, "and their face," to *ûpānêhā*, "and its face" [535, n. 114].

158. The subject *liškôt* (fem.) requires *'aḥat* in place of MT *'eḥād* [535, n. 115].

159. Reading *haddārôm*, "south," with LXX in place of MT *haqqādîm*, "east" [535, n. 116].

160. *zōh halliškâ*, lit., "this the room," is awkward. *zōh* is a later variation of *zō't*. See Cooke, *Ezekiel*, 445 [535, n. 118].

161. Independently suggested by Berry, "Priests and Levites," 237; cf. Duguid, *Ezekiel and the Leaders*, 89, n. 677.

162. Duke, "Punishment or Restoration?" 61–81.

## The Visionary Sanctuary

An alternative exegesis is propounded by Eliezer of Beaugency. Reserving the Zadokite identification for the priests charged to guard the altar—the customary reading of 40:46—he assigns *lakkōhănîm šōměrê mišmeret habbāyit*, "to the priests the guard duty of the temple grounds," to the non-Zadokite priests. These are the priests who, in Eliezer of Beaugency's interpretation of Ezek 22:26, "violated my torah, desecrated my sanctuaries . . . and caused me to be desecrated in their [the people's] midst." Their punishment was that they no longer qualify to officiate at the altar (44:13). Instead they joined the Levites in guarding the temple grounds (44:14). Thus, these non-Zadokites retained their priestly status and were eligible to occupy a room on the priestly platform, but were banned from officiating at the altar and partaking of the sacrifices. (Presumably they were also banned from occupying their own sacristy, since they were ineligible to partake of the sacrifices or wear the sacred priestly clothing). They were theoretically priests but functionally they were Levites.

The problem with this interpretation is that we never hear of the alleged non-Zadokite priests again. Indeed, there is no place for them in Ezekiel's sanctuary. Moreover, the priestly land is allocated to the Zadokites (48:11); nothing is left over for the non-Zadokites. Furthermore, the second sacristy is left without an occupant. Because of these unassailable objections, I side with Duke's reading of Ezek 40:45–46 and its implications.[163]

As shown above (COMMENT on 40:5), in chapters 40–42 the term *bayit* refers to the temple house. The same phrase, *šōměrê mišmeret habbāyit*, "who guard the temple," occurs in 44:14, where the service is also attributed to the Levites (44:14). Many critics have claimed that the Levitic text is original and this priestly text (40:45) is erroneous. However, these two expressions are not in conflict. The term *bayit* is subject to two different meanings. Whereas in 40:45, it is restricted to "the temple building," in 44:14 it signifies "the temple grounds, the *temenos*." These terms all derive from Num 18:5a, *ûšěmartem 'ēt mišmeret haqqōdeš wě'ēt mišmeret hammizbeah*, "You (the priests) will guard the sanctuary and the altar." Ezekiel thus follows a hallowed priestly tradition that the priests are divided into two groups, one guarding the "holy place" (*qōdeš*)/"house" (*bayit*), i.e., the temple, the other guarding the altar. Since only priests have access to the inner court why is there such stringent need for guard duty? One can only conjecture that the altar was carefully guarded to prevent deviations from the prescribed ritual. And the other priestly group stands in and around the ten-step staircase to prevent entry into the temple building (Ezekiel's innovation), except on the Sabbath, when priests were allowed to enter the temple to exchange the bread on the wooden table (see at 41:22).[164]

---

163. For greater detail, see Excursus 1: Ezekiel and the Levites.
164. For greater detail, see Excursus 1: Ezekiel and the Levites.

PART TWO: EZEKIEL 40–48—THE VISIONARY SANCTUARY AND THE LAND

*The Temple and Its Auxiliary Structures (40:47—41:26)*

## The Measurements of the Second (Priestly) and Third (Divine) Platforms (40:47—41:4)

### Translation

**47** Then he measured the court, which was 100 cubits long by 100 cubits wide, a square,[165] with the altar in front of the temple.[166] **48** He then took me to the vestibule of the temple where he measured the jambs, 5 cubits on either side. The gateway was 14 cubits wide,[167] and the sidewalls were 3 cubits wide on every side. **49** The vestibule measured 20 cubits wide[168] and 20[169] cubits long, accessed by ten[170] steps. There were columns on either side of the jambs.

**41:1** He then led me into the great hall. The jambs he measured were 6 cubits wide on either side. This was the width of each jamb.[171] **2** The entrance was 10 cubits wide, and the walls that flanked the entrance were each 5 cubits wide. Its [i.e., the great hall's] depth, he measured at 40 cubits, and its width, 20 cubits. **3** He then entered the inner room and measured the jamb of the (next) entrance, which was 2 cubits. The entrance was 6 cubits wide and the walls[172] flanking on either side[173] of it were each 7 cubits deep. **4** Its depth measured 20 cubits, and its breadth 20 cubits. He said to me, "This is the Holy of Holies."

### Comment

**40:47.** Block and others continue to assume the existence of an inner barrier wall and a pavement surrounding the inner wall—analogous to the pavement surrounding the outer wall. However, as demonstrated in the Introduction (section A), the supposition of the inner wall would have undermined Ezekiel's basic principle of separation. As for

---

165. *mĕrubbāʿat* is late Biblical Hebrew that displaces *rĕbûaʿ* in Mishnaic Hebrew. Cf. Hurvitz, *Linguistic Study*, 27–31 [539, n. 1].

166. The only way to see the entrance to the temple while standing at the altar is if the latter is located in the center of the inner court, thus confirming that the altar is set at the very center of the entire sanctuary complex.

167. Following LXX, MT seems to have dropped *ʾarbaʿ ʿeśrê ʾammâ wĕkitĕpôt haššaʿar* by homoioteleuton [539, n. 3].

168. The terms *ʾōrek* and *rōḥab* are again being used loosely. The former refers to the width from the standpoint of the observer (the longer side); the latter to the distance to the wall in front of him [539, n. 4].

169. In light of 41:13, MT *ʿaštê ʿeśrēh*, "eleven," is impossible. LXX reads correctly, *šĕtēm ʿeśrēh*, "twelve" [539, n. 5].

170. Reading *ʿeśer* with LXX instead of MT's meaningless *ʾăšer* [539, n. 7].

171. Read *hāʾayilāyim* with LXX instead of MT *hāʾohel*, though Tg., Syr, Vulg. attest to the latter, apparently linking it with the *ʾohel môʿēd*, "tent of meeting," though meaningless in this context [539, n. 8].

172. Reading *wĕkitĕpôt* with LXX and the analogue in verse 2 [540, n. 10].

173. Reading *mippōh wĕšebaʿ ʾammôt mippōh* with LXX [540, n. 11].

a pavement around the inner wall, it would have no purpose. The pavement around the lower wall was bounded by thirty rooms. Presumably lay worshipers would use these rooms for eating their well-being sacrifices and for social purposes such as meeting and strolling with associates and friends. Thus this lower pavement was indispensable. But the upper, priestly court was intended strictly for worship at the altar. It was meant exclusively for "priestly business," which requires silence. A surrounding pavement would be irrelevant and disturbing.

The guide also notices an altar "in front of the temple," which places the altar in the very middle of the inner court, and indeed, in the very center of the sacred grounds, the *temenos*. However, the guide does not stop to measure the altar's dimensions. That text is reserved for chapter 43—after the deity has passed over it on the way to his permanent resting place in the sanctuary. Here it seems the guide is in a rush to take the prophet into the highest platform to enter the temple. There is another possible reason for his haste. The measurement of the altar (43:13–17) is followed by its purification rite (43:18–27). Instead of first measuring and returning later to perform its rite of purification, the author/redactor decided to combine both altar pericopes into one (43:13–27). The inner court is a perfect square, and the altar is a series of perfect squares, see the COMMENT on chapter 43 and the discussion in the Introduction (section C).

**40:48–49.** The details of the temple are best understood by viewing the design in Figure 11. First, as one penetrates deeper into the temple, the entrances become correspondingly narrower: The entrance to the vestibule is 14 cubits, to the great hall, 10 cubits, and to the adytum (Holy of Holies), 6 cubits [544]. Second, the adytum is a square, indicating by its shape its greater holiness. Third, the temple structure is located on the third, highest platform, up ten steps, giving a total of twenty-five steps in height, from outside the *temenos* [542].

**41:1–4.** From the vestibule, Ezekiel and his guide enter the *hêkāl*. This word derives ultimately from its source in Sumerian É. GAL, "big house," having evolved through Ugaritic and Canaanite, and finding its cognate in Akkadian *êkallū*. This is a nonsacral term, used to describe a large luxurious house such as a palace. When applied to Israel's sanctuary, it designates YHWH's palace [543].[174]

According to the guide's measurements, the jambs of the entry were 6 cubits wide, even larger than the 5 cubit jambs of the vestibule (Fig. 11). The doorways are beginning to narrow: vestibule 14 cubits, *hêkāl* 10 cubits, and *děbîr* 6 cubits. The *hêkāl*, indeed, is a "big room," 40 cubits by 20 cubits, a correctly proportioned rectangle.

Having measured the *hêkāl*, the guide now measures the *děbîr*. Ezekiel does not follow; he observes from the outside. Even though the temple has not been dedicated (i.e., YHWH has yet to enter the *děbîr*), the ancient tradition holds: No man may enter the *děbîr* (Lev 16:14–16). The adytum is a perfect square of 20 cubits—quintessential holiness (see Introduction, section C. Separation).

---

174. Cf. Ezek 8:16; also 2 Kgs 6:5, 17; 7:21; Isa 6:1.

Solomon's temple (1 Kgs 6–7) and Ezekiel's are alike in many ways. Each is fronted by two freestanding columns with three interior rooms. The *hêkāl* and *qōdeš haqqŏdāšîm*, "holy of holies," measure alike. The difference between the two buildings is mainly in the way Ezekiel guards his temple: (1) the temple building is ten steps higher than the inner, priestly court; (2) the entryways shrink as one moves toward the adytum; and (3) the prophet is accompanied through the first two rooms but may not enter the third, the holiest room [544].

FIGURE 11: The Ground Plan of the Temple[174]

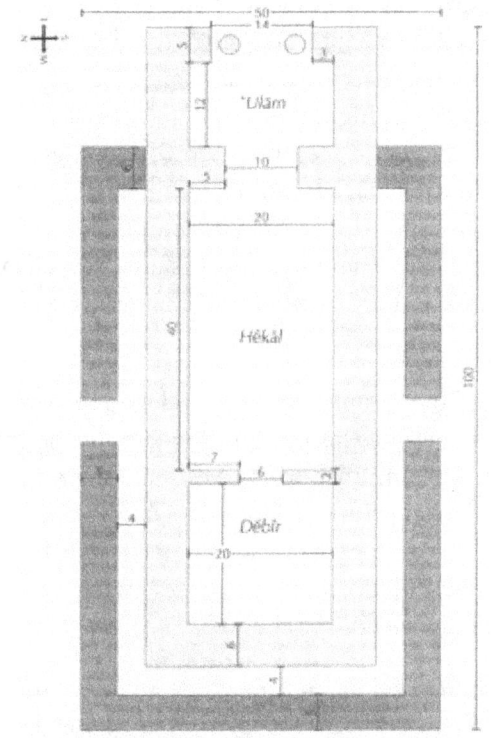

**40:4.** The superlative expression, *qōdeš haqqodāšîm*, "the holy of holies,"[176] refers to the inner room of the house of YHWH (41:4) in relation to the outer room (*qōdeš*, 41:21). Ezekiel employs related expressions to identify other sacred objects and places as well:

1. In 42:13 *qōdšê haqqodāšîm* occurs twice, referring to the offering that the priests eat and deposit in relation to the room (*haqqōdeš*).

2. In 43:12 *qōdeš qodāšîm* relates to the area (*temenos*) inside the perimeter wall in relation to the (*ḥōl*) outside the *temenos*.

---

175. Adapted from Block, Ezekiel 25–48, 541.

176. *haqqodāšîm/qodāšîm* is a relative term in comparison with the juxtaposed *qōdeš*. The expressioin occurs six times, but may appear with or without the definite article, and with or without the possessive suffix.

*The Visionary Sanctuary*

3. In 45:3 *qōdeš qodāšîm* refers to a strip of land reserved for the sanctuary (*miqdāš*) and the Levites (48:12).

4. In 45:3 *qōdeš qodāšîm* refers to YHWH's portion (the temple, *hammiqdāš*) in relation to the priests' portion (45:4).

5. In 44:13a *qōdeš qodāšîm* is used in relation to *qodāšay*, "'my holy things/areas" (44:13a).

6. In 48:12 *qōdeš qodāšîm* refers to the priests' sacred land in relation to the Levites' contiguous sacred land (cf. 45:3).

## The Auxiliary Structures of the Temple (41:5–12)

TRANSLATION

> 5 Then he measured the wall of the temple, which was 6 cubits [thick] on each side,[177] with side-rooms that measured 4 cubits [across]. 6 The side rooms, 30 units, were built one above the other on three stories.[178] Ledges on the wall of the temple served as supports for the side rooms all around, the supports not being part of the temple wall itself. 7 The circular ramp[179] at the side rooms widened[180] with each story; and since the structure had circular ramps throughout,[181] each story was wider than the one below. In this manner one ascended from the bottom story to the top story by way of the middle one.[182] 8 Then I saw a raised platform[183] all around the temple—the base of the side rooms. Its height[184] measured a full[185] rod, 6 cubits.[186] 9 The outer wall of the

---

177. Tg. *shur shur mqp lbyt' shur shur* is even more cumbersome than MT *sābîb sābîb labbayit sābîb* [544 n. 23].

178. MT *ṣēlā' 'el- ṣēlā' šālōš ûšělōšîm pě'āmîm*, lit., "side room over side room, thirty-three times," is difficult. Reversing the numbers and omitting the copula yield the most likely sense: "thirty (side rooms), three times." Cf. LXX, "room over room, thirty and three times," which suggests two stories, each with thirty-three diminutive cells (cf. Vulg. *bis triaginta*). Tg. *tltyn wtlt ḥd' 'sry bsydr'* reflects a three-story construction with eleven per story. Many (e.g., Zimmerli, *Ezekiel 2*, 370; Gese, *Verfassungsentwurf*, 165) delete *ûšělōšîm* as a gloss [544 n. 24]. *šālōš*, "three"; Radak suggests that the side chambers are located on three sides (N, S, W).

179. MT vocalizes *wěrāḥăbâ* as a verb, "to be/become wide," but a subject is lacking. Many follow Tg. and read a noun *rōḥab*, "width, widening." [544 n. 25].

180. The absence of the *dagesh* in *wěnāsěbû* (from *sbb*, "surround, turn") reflects Aramaic influence. Cf. GKC §67dd. Whereas LXX drops the word, Tg. reads a noun *msybt'*, "winding staircase" [544 n. 26].

181. Repointing *mûsab* as a Hophal participle, *mûsāb*. [544 n. 27].

182. On the basis of Tg. *b'wrḥ* and Vulg *in mediam*, Gese (*Verfassungsentwurf*, 168) proposes *btykwnh* instead of *ltykwnh* [544 n. 30].

183. Elsewhere *gōbah* denotes "height" (40:42; 43:13). BHS and many commentators repoint it as *gabbâ*, "back elevation" (cf. 10:12; 16:24, 31, 39) [544 n. 32].

184. *'aṣṣîlâ* is apparently another technical building term of unknown meaning [544 n. 34].

185. On *mlw'*, defectively spelled from *mlw'*, "full," see GKC §23f. Cf. the measurement espressions, *ml' qwmtw* in 2 Sam 28:20, and *ml'-rḥb* in Isa 8:8 [545 n. 35].

186. *mûsdôt* (Q. *mîsdôt ḥaṣṣěla'ôt mělô haqqaneh šēš 'ammôt 'aṣṣîlâ*); "from the base [reading

side rooms was 5 cubits thick. The open walkway[187] between[188] the side rooms of the temple 10 and the other rooms around the entire temple complex was 20 cubits wide. **11** The side rooms opened onto the open walkway,[189] which was 5 cubits wide all around with one entrance to the north and another to the south. **12** And the structure that was in front of the open space[190] on the west side [of the temple] was 70 cubits wide. Its wall was 5 cubits thick all the way around and 90 cubits long.

## Comment

Despite their abstruseness, the architectural terms in 41:5–12 clarify the auxiliary structures of the temple. The following terms will be deciphered: *bā'ôt*, "ledges"; *ăḥûzîm*, "supports"; *měsibbâ*, "stairwell"; *munnaḥ*, "open space"; *gōbah*, "raised platform"; *ṣēlāʿ*, "side chambers"; *môsĕdôt*, "foundations"; *aṣṣîlâ*, "elevation"; *qîr*, "wall"; *lěšākôt*, "rooms"; *petaḥ*, "entrance"; *binyān*, "building"; *gizrâ*, "open space."

**41:5. wall of the temple (*qîr-habbayit*).** The term *qîr* refers to the "inner wall," in contrast to *ḥômâ*, "outer (city) wall."

**side room (*haṣṣēlaʿ*)** has been variously interpreted.

> **Rashi:** *rōḥāb haṣṣēlaʿ*: "appendage" in Old French; the cell beside it was 4 cubits in depth, while in the second temple it was 6 cubits deep.

> **R. Eliezer of Beaugency:** *rōḥāb haṣṣēlaʿ*: its meaning: the width of the wall of a flank—the compartments that were along the northern, southern, and western flanks of the temple. **4 cubits**—all **around the temple**, i.e., surrounding **the temple** in its three directions. And one should not explain *rōḥāb haṣṣēlaʿ* to mean the interior of a compartment of the **flank**. If this were the case, the length of the *gizrâ* and the *binyān* on the west side would not add up to 100, as reported below (vv. 9–13).

> **M. Midot 4:3:** There were thirty-eight cells there: fifteen on the north, fifteen on the south and eight on the west. On the north and the south there were three tiers of five cells, while on the west there were two tiers of three cells, and above them a tier of two cells. Each cell had three openings: one to the cell on the right, one to the cell on the left, and one to the cell above. At the northeast corner there were five openings: one to the cell on the right, one to the cell above, one to the *měsibbâ* (staircase), one to the *pišpeš* and one to the *hêkāl*.

---

*miyyĕsôdôt*, as suggested by Duman] of the side rooms [using] a full rod [*qāneh*] of 6 cubits, to its top." Read *'aṣṣîlāh*, perhaps "its height." Cf. *wĕ'el-'aṣṣîlê bĕnê yiśrāēl*, "and to the Israelite heads" (Exod 24:11). *'aṣṣîl* is a synonym of *rōš*, "head, leader."

187. *waăšer munnaḥ*, lit., "that which is left to rest," in the sense of "free space" [545 n. 36].

188. *bet ṣĕlāʿôt* is suspicious. On the analogy of verse 10 and LXX, "in the middle of the sides," *byt* is probably a corruption of *byn* [545 n. 37].

189. In place of *mĕqôm hammunnāḥ*, lit., "place of the open space," LXX reads τοῦ φωτόν, "window," which in 42:7, 10, 12, translates *gādêr*, "wall" [545 n. 39].

190. *gizrâ* is a synonym for *munnāḥ* [545 n. 40].

## The Visionary Sanctuary

> **B.B. 61a**: What does *yeṣî'â* mean? Here it was explained as αετο—gable. R. Joseph taught: We find two additional names to *yeṣî'â*, mentioned in 1 Kgs 6: 5: "And he built on the wall of the house a gallery (*yeṣî'â*) round about." It is also named *ṣēlā'* [Ezek 41:6]: "And the side rooms—*ṣēlā'*," etc. And also *ta'* [ibid. 40:7]: "And every cell (*ta'*)," etc.

All the sources cited above refer, at the earliest, to the second temple. There is no evidence that in the first temple there was a surrounding second wall, as proposed by most commentators. Furthermore, Haran writes as follows:

> Most commentators and scholars tend to imagine the temples of Solomon and Ezekiel as if surrounded by two walls—the main wall of 6 cubits, enclosing the *hêkāl* and the *dĕbîr*, and after this supposedly another wall of 5 cubits, parallel to the first wall and enclosing it in three directions. Between these two walls were supposedly erected three stories of cells—which, according to this assumption, are called the *ṣĕlā'ôt* and *yeṣî'â*. Actually, such cells are mentioned in the Second Temple (*m. Midot* 4.3–4) . . . but not in any of the texts connected with the First Temple, and it is highly questionable if we may make an analogy from the later sources to the earlier ones. Nor is there any evidence in the First Temple of an outer wall . . . and the simple meaning of *ṣēlā'* and *ṣĕlā'ôt* cannot accord with *ta'îm*. It is much more likely that the said *ṣĕlā'ôt* in Solomon's temple were *panels made of wooden planks* (emphasis mine) that were attached to one another . . . [S]uch panels could serve as the sides of the Ark, the Golden altar or for the siding of the Tabernacle. In Solomon's Temple they served as covering of the floors and the interior walls, as they did for the *bêt ya'ar halĕbānôn* . . . Thus is appears that *the ṣĕlā'ôt that were put on the outer walls of the Temple were no more than a covering* (emphasis mine). This covering was *intended to provide an aesthetic look* (emphasis mine) . . .[191]

Despite its attractiveness, the problem with this solution is that *haṣṣēla'* (four cubits) describes the width of the wall, not the width of its cover. Moreover, the decorative paneling from floor to ceiling refers only to *inner* walls of the temple (41:15b–26), but not to the outer walls, which are assumed to be bare. Indeed, the picture of a barestone structure is accentuated by the bare-wooden table in the middle of the *hêkāl*. A paneled outer wall would be totally at variance with the deliberate austerity—without precious metals or tapestry—of its interior. Thus the traditional interpretation, "side room," must be given full accord. Furthermore, the structures of the Ain Dara (ninth–eighth century BCE) and Deir Alla (1300–740 BCE) sanctuaries indicate that a second wall enclosed three sides of the sanctuary (Fig. 12). Thus, the theoretical reconstruction of Ezekiel's auxiliary temple structure is stunningly corroborated by the remains of the Deir Alla and Ain Dara sanctuaries. Additional support for *ṣēlā'* as "side room"

---

191. Haran, "Ezekiel," 212.

is provided by the frequently attested architectural structure of the casemate wall (cf. also Isa 22:11) located all around the temple.[192]

FIGURE 12: The Ground Plan of the Ain Dara Sanctuary[193]

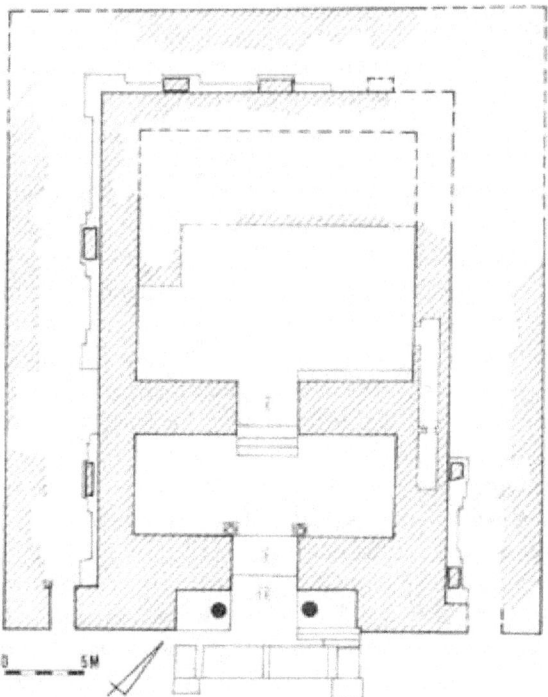

**41:6. on the wall of the temple for the side rooms** (*baqqîr ʾăšer-labbayit laṣṣĕlāʿôt*). Rashi, followed by Eliezer of Beaugency, proposes that this phrase *bayit* does not mean "temple," but "inside," and the phrase would be rendered, "on the inside wall of the side rooms," an improved rendering. However, as *bayit* consistently (twenty times) means "temple" in chapters 40–42, this interpretation here must stand.

The parallel in 1 Kgs 6:6 (below) suggests that three stories are envisaged; that there were three *ṣĕlāʿôt*, *šĕlōšîm pĕʿāmîm*, "thirty times," yielding a total of ninety rooms [547]. The meaning of *baʿot*, a technological architectural term, is unknown. It may be analogous to *migrāʿôt* (1 Kgs 6:6). Since the outer wall was uniformly five cubits thick, from bottom to top, the size of the cells must have increased from the bottom to the top floors. The joists that held up the respective stories rested on the ledges (*bāʿôt*) in the temple wall that served as *ʾăḥûzîm*, "supports" (v. 6) [549].

192. Cf. MT, *sābîb sābîb labbayit sābîb*, lit., "encircling, encircling, encircling the house." Tg. *sĕḥôr sĕḥôr maqap lĕbêtāʾ sĕḥôr sĕḥôr,* lit., "encircling, encircling round about the temple, encircling, encircling." LXX κύκλοθεν, "round about."

193. Reprinted with permission of John M. Monson, from "Solomon's Temple and the Temple at 'Ain Dara," 35. For an illustrated discussion of this temple, see Monson, "The New 'Ain Dara Temple: Closest Solomonic Parallel."

## The Visionary Sanctuary

| Ezekiel 41:6 | 1 Kings 6:6 |
|---|---|
| wĕhaṣṣĕlāʿôt ṣēlāʿ ʾel-ṣēlāʿ šālôš ûšĕlōšîm pĕʿāmîm ûbāʾôt baqqîr ʾăšer-labbayit laṣṣĕlāʿôt sābîb sābîb lihyôt ʾăḥûzîm wĕlō-yihyû ʾăḥûzîm bĕqîr habbayit | hayyāṣiwa hattaḥtōnâ ḥāmēš baʾammâ roḥbāh wehattîkōnâ šēš baʾammâ roḥbāh kî migrāʿôt nātan labbāyit sābîb ḥûṣâ lĕbiltî ʾăḥōz bĕqîrôt habbāyit |
| The side chambers were constructed one above the other, three units in three stories. There were ledges on the wall of the temple for the side chambers all around, to serve as supports, without the supports being integral to the temple wall itself. | The bottom story was 5 cubits wide; the middle story was 6 cubits wide; the third story was 7 cubits wide, for he allowed offsets for the temple all around the outside to prevent them from being attached to the walls of the temple. |

FIGURE 13: The Auxiliary Structures of the Temple Building[194]

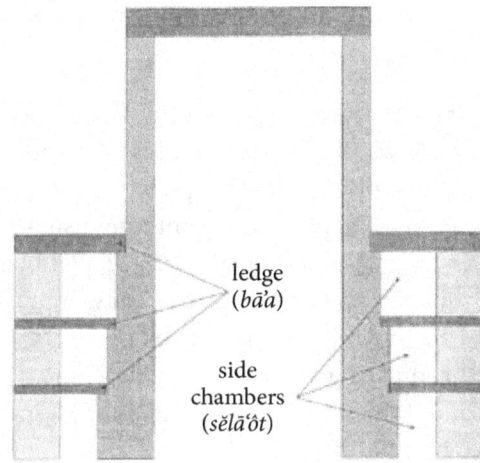

"Drawing support from the rabbinic use of *msbh* for 'gallery,' some recognize a single, large exterior ramp or stairway running around the north, west, and south sides of the Building... Rather than using an exterior ramp, 1 Kgs 6:8 states specifically that access to the upper stories was gained through *lûllîm*, probably to be understood as interior spiral staircases (i.e., progressing upward with 90 degree turns)" [549, 551]. One need not search for evidence in non-Israelite neighboring civilizations to make sense of this. The Temple Scroll (11QT 30:3—31:9) prescribes a special stairwell, apart from the temple but connected to it through a viaduct from above. What is relevant here is that the staircase is interior.[195]

**41:7A.** 1 Kgs 6:6 provides the model for this verse: "the lowest story was 5 cubits wide, the middle one 6 cubits wide, and the third 7 cubits wide; for he had provided recesses (*migrāʿôt*) around the outside of the temple so as not to penetrate the walls of the temple (*lĕbiltî ʾăḥōz bĕqîrôt-habbayit*)."

194. Adapted from Block, *Ezekiel 25–48*, 550.
195. For details, see Yadin, *The Temple Scroll* 1.211–17, esp. Fig. 6.

PART TWO: EZEKIEL 40-48—THE VISIONARY SANCTUARY AND THE LAND

**41:7B.** *Therefore* (*'al-kēn*); i.e., in order to construct such a staircase, the side rooms (*ṣĕlaʿôt*) must widen as one ascends (see Fig. 13). So one ascends from the bottom story to the upper one (only) through the middle one.[196]

Why is Ezekiel so obsessed with these minutiae about the staircase, especially the fact that in climbing the staircase from the bottom to the top level one must pass through the middle story (NJPS, NRSV)? Isn't that obvious? My colleague, Joel Duman, suggests an attractive answer. What Ezekiel is saying is: Don't think that you can ascend to the top via an outside ramp, even though it would allow for a rapid ascent to the top by bypassing the middle level. No, the ascent must be through an inner staircase, and the middle level cannot be avoided. What difference does it make if one uses a ramp or a staircase? The key difference is that the staircase is *inside* the Building and the ramp is on the *outside*; or to put it functionally, the staircase is inside the Building, therefore *part of its sanctity* (*qodeš*), whereas the ramp is outside the sacred area, and is therefore *ḥōl*, "common." As noted earlier, Ezekiel is concerned that all the property and activity assigned to the priests should occur within the central, sacred spine of the *temenos*.

**41:8-9A.** The width of the structure is exactly 50 cubits. By supplementing the inside measurements of the temple, another 85 cubits, plus the width of the real cells including the measurements of the walls, the total length is 100 cubits. This creates a correctly proportioned rectangle (100 x 50 cubits) and continues using multiples of 25 [551].

The temple stands on a *gōbah*, "height, raised platform," which is the base (*môsĕdôt*) for the side rooms, and increases the already impressive height a full 6 cubits. Verse 9a adds that the outer walls are 5 cubits wide [551]. The number of one story and many storied rooms is greater than the number of rooms in the Egyptian temples of Merneptah and Rameses,[197] or the temples of Mesopotomia.[198]

Sacks of grain, amphorae of oil and kegs of wine required enormous space, because revenue was in kind, not in money [552]. Storage space, peripheral but not connected to sancta was required for the booty of war, such as weapons and valuable textiles.

**41:10.** These rooms are in the outer court surrounding and contiguous with the outer wall (see Rashi).

**41:12. *the Building* (*habbinyān*).** This is a large structure located west of the temple. The *open space* (*gizrâ*) totals 100 by 80 cubits, an area larger than the temple itself. Since the Building was located in the "sacred space,"[199] it was divine property. Originally, it was the kings' palace connected to the royal burial site, but in the new visionary

---

196. Many commentators and translators, old and new, claim that this passage asserts that the structure is at the middle story, which makes no sense.
197. Kitchen, "Two Notes on the Subsidiary Rooms," 108*-109*.
198. Stevenson, *Vision of Transformation*, 30-33.
199. Cf. J. Z. Smith, *To Take Place*, 59.

## The Visionary Sanctuary

temple, the erstwhile palace of the king is henceforth the *divine* palace. No longer will the kings' palace be attached to or be larger than the property of God (cf. 43:6–9).[200]

### The Total Dimensions of the Temple Compound (41:13–15a)

#### Translation

13 Then he measured the temple, which was 100 cubits long. The open walkway and the Building[201] including its wall were also 100 cubits long. 14 The width of the front of the temple, including the open walkway on the east side, was also 100 cubits. 15A He also measured the length of the Building facing the open walkway at the back,[202] which together with its balconies[203] on either side was 100 cubits long.

#### Comment

The calculations that follow (vv. 13–15a) demonstrate that the temple plus its side rooms yield a square, 100 x 100 cubits. This proves that the side rooms are of equivalent holiness to the temple and are off limits to non-priests. Diagrammatically, (Fig. 14), the side rooms join the temple in forming the central spine.[204]

### The Temple Dimensions

| 41:13 Length | |
|---|---|
| The jamb of the vestibule | 5 cubits |
| The vestibule | 12 |
| The jamb of the great hall | 6 |
| The length of the great hall | 40 |
| The joist of the adytum | 2 |
| The length/width of the adytum | 20 |
| The temple's western wall | 6 |
| The side chamber | 4 |
| The open space | 5 |
| Total: | 100 cubits |

---

200. There is no basis or need for Zimmerli's surmise (*Ezekiel 2*, 121) that "its [the Building's] only task is apparently to protect the rear of the temple in which Yahweh is present."

201. *binyâ* is a feminine variation of *binyān*, recurring in verse 15 [553, n. 62].

202. MT *'aḥărêhā* should be repointed *ăḥôrêhā*; see Tg. on 8:16 [553, n. 63]. *'aḥărêhā*, "back," that is the west side (Isa 9:11; cf. Deut 34:27).

203. Tg. renders the word *zewi*, which Jastrow describes as "a projection of a wall formed by abruptly reducing its thickness so as to give space for a balcony." The Masoretes recognized the irregularity of the Kethib *w'twgyh'* pointing the *taw* with a *ḥiriq* (cf. Qere *'tygyh'*). On the Aramaic influence reflected in the final aleph see Hurvitz, *Linguistic Study*, 88, n. 105 [553, n. 64]. *'attîqêhā* is an unknown architectural term. Block surmised "ledges" or "walkways" [554]; cf. Akkadian *etēqu*.

204. J. Z. Smith, *To Take Place*, 59.

### 41:13 Length

| | |
|---|---|
| The restricted area | 30 cubits |
| The walls | 10 (2 x 5) |
| The building | 60 |
| Total: | 100 cubits |

### 41:14 Width (north to south)

| | |
|---|---|
| The temple | 20 cubits |
| The temple walls | 12 (2 X 6) |
| The side chambers | 8 (2 X 4) |
| The open space | 10 (2 X 5) |
| The restricted area | 50 |
| Total: | 100 cubits |

41:15a. The exterior measurements of the temple confirm the length of the Building to be 100 cubits. The open walkway at the rear of the temple is the same on the north and south sides (v. 10). The north-south direction is 100 cubits (v. 12).

FIGURE 14: The Holy Spine of the Temple[204]

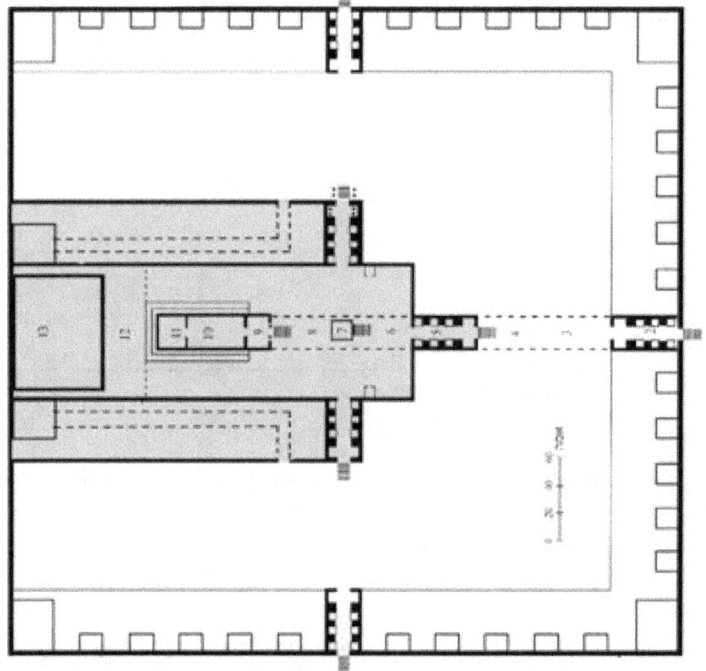

1. Eastern Steps
2. Outer court gate
3. Outer court
4. Inner court steps
5. Inner court gate
6. Inner court
7. Altar
8. Vestibule steps
9. Vestibule
10. Temple hall
11. YHWH's throne room
12. "Restricted space"
13. "The Building"

205. Adapted from Block, *Ezekiel 25–48*, 573.

## The Interior Decorations and Furnishings (41:15b–26)

TRANSLATION

**15B** Both the inside[206] of the great hall and the vestibules of the court,[207] **16** as well as the thresholds, the framed windows, and balconies on all three sides[208] of the closed niches,[209] were paneled[210] with wood all around from the ground,[211] including the covered niches, **17** and continuing to[212] the top[213] of the entrance. Both the interior and exterior of the temple, including all the surrounding walls, were carefully crafted[214] **18** with carved[215] cherubim and palm fronds, each pair of cherubim flanking a palm between them. The cherubim had two faces.[216] **19** The human face turned toward the side of one palm while the leonine face turned to the palm on the other side. Cherubim and palms covered the entire temple, **20** carved from the ground to the tops of the doorways in the great hall as well.[217]

**21** Regarding the great hall, it had squared[218] doorposts.[219] In front of the holy place[220] was something resembling[221] **22** a wooden altar,[222] which was 3

---

206. LXX wrongly reads *hpnymy* as *hpnwt*, "the corners" [554, n. 70].

207. Although Tg. and Vulg. follow MT's pl. *w'lmy hḥṣr*, LXX correctly reads sg., suggesting that we read *w'lmw hḥṣr*. However, this form is found in poetry (e.g., *hayĕto-*: Gen 1:24; Isa 56:9; Zeph 2:14). LXX assumes *wh'lm hḥyṣwn*, "and the outer vestibule" [554, n. 71].

208. The antecedent of *lišloštām* is unclear. The most likely guess is that the *ăṭumîm* had either three parts or three sides [554, n. 74].

209. On *haḥallônîm hāăṭumôt*, see n. 2 on 40:16. LXX translates, "closed off with netting" [554, n. 73].

210. The hapax, *šĕḥîp*, is cognate to Akkadian *siḫpu*, "overlay," and describes a veneering technique using wood [554, n. 76]. Tg. renders, "overlaid with boards of cedar."

211. Reading *'wmh'rs'* with LXX, instead of MT *wh'rs'* [554, n. 77]; see Radak.

212. Reading *'ad* instead of *'al* with Tg. and on the analogy of verse 20 [555, n. 79].

213. *'al-mē'al happetaḥ*. Though missing in LXX, this is a sensible conclusion to verse 16. The area between the ground and the tops of the entrances is referred to again in verse 20 [555, n. 80].

214. *middot* probably refers to a measured off area on the walls where the reliefs occur (Rashi, Zimmerli, *Ezekiel 2*, 384) or the reliefs themselves [555, n. 82]; cf. Tg. "sketched patterns."

215. Both here and in verse 19 MT *wĕ'ăśûy* is awkward (cf. 40:17). Tg. reads *glyp krwbyn*, "engraving of cherubs" [555, n. 83].

216. According to Eliezer of Beaugency the palm fronds extend outwards so they touch each other and hide the faces of the cherubim, i.e., the face of the man and the lion on each cherub. The cherubs in Isaiah's vision (Isa 6:2) cover their bodies by spreading their own wings. The tabernacle cherubs touch each other with their outspread wings. In Ezekiel's temple, the wings of the cherubs are folded and they take their place by the spread palm fronds.

217. The *puncta extraordinaria* over *hahêkal*, repeated in verse 21, recognizes the textual difficulty. If this word were a dittograph, then *wĕqîr* should have been written *baqqîr*, "on the wall" [555, n. 86].

218. On the form *rĕbu'â*, see Hurvitz, *Linguistic Study*, 27–30 [555, n. 89].

219. Repointing *mĕzûzat* as a pl. *mĕzûzôt* [555, n. 88].

220. Tg. interprets *haqqôdeš* correctly as *byt kpwry*, "place of atonement"; i.e., the *adytum*, which is synonymous with *qōdeš haqqodāšîm*, "holy of holies" (v. 4) [556, n. 90].

221. *hammareh kammareh*, lit., "something that looked like."

222. Joüon-Muraoka, *Grammar* §131a treats *hammizbēaḥ 'eṣ* as appositional, but the article appears suspect due to dittography [556, n. 91].

## PART TWO: EZEKIEL 40–48—THE VISIONARY SANCTUARY AND THE LAND

cubits high,[223] 2 cubits[224] deep, and 2 cubits wide.[225] Its corners, base,[226] and sides were made of wood. Then he said to me, "This is the table that stands before YHWH." **23** The great hall and the holy place (adytum) each had double doors, **24** each designed with two swinging panels. **25** Similarly cherubim and palm fronds were also carved[227] on these walls of the great hall. And there was a wooden lintel[228] facing the vestibule. **26** There were sealed niches[229] and palms on the sidewalls of the vestibule, the side rooms, and the lintels.

### Comment

**41:15b–20.** Beginning with a survey of the interior walls of the great hall, this part of the description focuses on the temple's interior design. The room's "threshold" (*hassipîm*), "closed niches" (*haḥallônîm ha̓ăṭumôt*), and "balconies" (*hā̓attîqîm*) constitute the triad of features running all around the room. Block cites Busink,[230] who argues that the threshold is a wooden beam that jutted out underneath the niches. The expression for *closed niches* was encountered first in 40:16, and the term for *balconies* was an educated guess for some exterior feature of the *binyān*. The modifier, *lišloštām*, suggests a three-tiered sill around the room. Thus, every inch of wall space was paneled with wood, from the thresholds below at the entrances to the closed niches above. The outside vestibule (*laḥûṣ*) was paneled similarly. Carvings of cherubim and palm trees (vv. 17b–20), motifs borrowed from Solomon's temple (1 Kgs 6:20–36), covered the walls of the temple, from floor to ceiling. Unlike the tetramorphed creatures of the prophet's earlier visions (Ezek 1 and 10), these cherubim are not three-dimensional freestanding sculptures, and they are reduced to only two faces: one human and the other leonine. Furthermore, they are carved bas-reliefs, incorporated into the walls. Pairs of rampant animals facing each other and centered on a palm tree are seen not only on ancient ivories but in other art forms as well.[231] An aesthetic principle belittles their meaning. The palm tree is a Near Eastern tree of life and the cherubim symbolize divine oversight. In Israelite thought the God who resided in this house controlled both [558].

223. Reading *gbwh* with LXX, Tg. and Pesh. [556, n. 92].

224. Whereas Early Biblical Hebrew expressed "two cubits" as the dual *'ammātayim*, Ezekiel prefers *šĕtayim 'ammôt*; see Hurvitz, *Linguistic Study*, 30–32 [556, n. 93].

225. Reading *wĕrāḥĕbô šĕtayim 'ammôt* with LXX. The phrase may have dropped out of MT by homoioteleuton [556, n. 94].

226. Reading *waădānāyw* with LXX καὶ ἡ βάσις αὐτοῦ, in place of MT *wĕ'orkô*, "and its length" [556, n. 96].

227. *wa'ăśûyâ*, "carved," sg. instead of pl. [556, n. 98]; see the Notes on 40:17; 41:18, 19; 46:23.

228. An architectural term of unknown meaning; see the Comment.

229. See 40:16, n. 18

230. Block, *Ezekiel Chapters 25–48*, 558, n. 103; cf. Busink, *Tempel* 2.755.

231. Cf. the ivory carving from Arslan Tash showing a tree between two ram sphinxes facing each other (Barnett, *Ancient Ivories*, plate 47b; and Busink, *Tempel*, 267–86). From within Israel, see the scene painted on one of the large Ajrud storage jars in Beck, "Drawings from Ḥorvat Teiman," 13–16, and Fig. 4.

**41:21–22.** *Square (rĕbu'â, a variant form of rābûa', the common word for "square")*.[232]

*Table (šulḥān)*. The guide's explanation for the table resembles his explanation of the adytum: *zeh qōdeš haqqŏdāšîm*, "This is the holy of holies" (v. 4). *zeh haššulḥān 'ăšer lipnê YHWH*, "This is the table before YHWH" (v. 22). The prophet's puzzlement evokes the guide's explanation. True, the table is different from any of the tabernacle sancta, even from its closest sanctum, the table of presence (Exod 25:23–30); the latter's dimensions are 2 cubits long, 1 cubit wide, and 1½ cubits high, whereas Ezekiel's table is 2 cubits long, 2 cubits wide, and 3 cubits high. Moreover, the tabernacle table is overlaid completely with gold whereas Ezekiel's table is made of exposed wood [559], and Ezekiel's table is twice the height of the tabernacle table (3 cubits versus 1½ cubits).

Nonetheless, one should keep in mind that the tabernacle table was the second most important sanctum in the shrine, superseded only by the ark (see Exod 25:25–30; 35:12–13; 37:10–16; Num 4:7). The tabernacle's rectangular table has been redesigned as a square (2 x 2 cubits), in keeping with Ezekiel's architectonic principle that all holy objects should occupy square spaces. The height of the table is given, as is that of the altar, the only sancta with this stated dimension of height. Furthermore, they are the only sancta in service: their surfaces (3 x 10 cubits; cf. 43:14–15a) are in use—bread is on the table and sacrifices are on the altar. Thus the two times that the guide offers an explanation of the sancta—the holy place (adytum) and the table—he is not trying to resolve the prophet's "puzzlement" [Block, 559] (surely, the prophet was fully knowledgeable about the location of the holy place). Rather, the guide's pronouncement was a statement of the *importance* of these two sancta; after all they are the most important in the temple.

---

232. Cf. the five-sided doorposts at the entrance to the adytum of Solomon's temple (1 Kgs 6:31).

PART TWO: EZEKIEL 40-48—THE VISIONARY SANCTUARY AND THE LAND

FIGURE 15

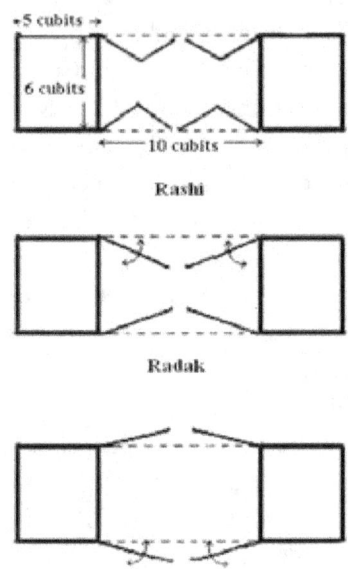

Doors of the Great Hall

Ezekiel 41: 23 - 24

Rashi

Radak

Asher Milgrom

**41:22.** *a wooden altar* (*hammizbēaḥ ʿēṣ*). The article may be a dittograph. Clearly, the table is not an incense altar, as claimed by Kasher and others; a wooden altar would go up in flames during its first day of service. Possibly Ezekiel's alleged puzzlement is the table's resemblance to an altar, due to its *miqṣōʿôt*, "corners," which Kasher claims are "horns," i.e., horns of an altar (see 43:15).[233] But it is clear that Ezekiel has "corners" in mind, as demonstrated by 46:21-22. Nonetheless, its meaning here is obscure. NJPS suggests that this word apparently means "that it had a rim around the top, like the table of Exod 25:25" (41:22, n. 5). Unfortunately, there is no evidence that *miqṣōʿôt* means anything but "*corners.*"

**41:23-25A.** The temple doors. One entered both the great hall and the adytum through swinging double doors, as in Solomon's temple (*šětayim mûsabbôt dělātôt*; 1 Kgs 6:34), each of which was fixed in its own hinge hole next to the jamb (see Fig. 15). These two rooms were decorated with palm and cherub reliefs, similar to the rest of the interior [560]. [typesetter: Fig 15 needs to be somewhere near here]

**41:25B-26.** *a thick supporting beam* (*ʿāb*). This is another architectural term whose meaning is unknown [560]. The most attractive suggestion is the rendering of Tg.

---

233. Kasher, *Ezekiel*, 810.

## The Visionary Sanctuary

*sqwpt'*, "lintel," i.e., a thick beam that is the lintel, or is above it, intended to support the structure. Thus, Radak states, "*'āb* is a large beam called *mārîš* by the sages (*m. Git.* 5:5; *b. B.K.* 67a), a 'thick beam' set into the building in the wall [or above the lintel, Milgrom] of the vestibule, visible from the outside and facing the altar." Rashi (on 1 Kgs 7:6) cites the Mishna for explanation, "Cedar beams were set into the wall of the great hall and the wall of the vestibule, lest the walls collapse" (*m. Mid.* 3:8).

**closed niches and palms** (*wĕḥallônîm 'ăṭumôt*). But no cherubs are mentioned [560]. This proves that the vestibule, side rooms, and the supporting lintel beams were of lower sanctity than the walls of the great hall, which were also decorated with cherubs.

**41:26. Lintels** (*hā'ubbîm*). The plural would refer to the two entrances, one to the great hall and the other to the adytum (v. 21a), both of which require fortifying beams above or part of the lintels to support the structure.

### The Priestly Sacristies for Dressing and Dining (42:1–14)

TRANSLATION

1 Then he took me to the north[234] into the outer[235] court, to the room [area][236] facing both the vacant space and the Building. 2 The side of the façade[237] of the northern entrance[238] measured 100 cubits[239] in length and 50 cubits in width. 3 A three-tiered terrace[240] area[241] lay facing the 20 [cubits][242] of the inner court as well as the pavement of the outer court.[243] 4 Facing the room

---

234. *hadderek* before *derek haṣṣāpôn* is a dittograph and should be deleted [560, n. 112]. Both LXX and Tg. refer explicitly to the northern gate, perhaps reading *derek šă'ar haṣṣāpôn*, "by way of the northern gate."

235. Tg. retains the dittograph interpreting harmonistically "by way of the gate that faces northward" while LXX deletes *hadderek* and adds κατὰ ἀνατολὰς κατέναντι, "to the east, opposite," before the phrase, "the northern gate . . ." Several LXX mss. read "inner" [560, n. 113]; the sense of the verse, according to these readings, may be that the observation of the chamber area is from the inner court looking north, rather than from the outer court looking south.

236. MT should be read as a collective sg. [cf. 560, n. 114].

237. So NJPS. MT *'el-pĕnê* at the beginning of verse 2 cannot support an independent sentence [cf. 560, n. 115]. Perhaps it should be read as a continuation of the preceding verse; see LXX. Alternatively, drop the first word *'el* and read *pĕnê 'ōrek pĕ'at*, "the length of its northern face."

238. *petaḥ haṣṣāpôn*, lit., "the entrance of the north" is often deleted as a gloss. Others emend *petaḥ* to *pĕ'at*, following LXX, πρὸς βορρᾶν, and the analogy of 41:12 [560, n. 116], to produce "the northern flank"

239. Block reconstructs the reading *'orkâ mē'â 'ammôt*, "its length 100 cubits," corrupted by incorrect word division and transposition [561, n. 117].

240. *'attîq* must be read as a collective sg. in this context [561, n. 119].

241. MT *baššĕlišîm*, "tripart," is a variant form of *mĕšullāšîm* in v. 6 [561, n. 120].

242. "Cubits" is understood in MT, as in Tg. [561, n. 118].

243. Cf. 40:17.

## PART TWO: EZEKIEL 40–48—THE VISIONARY SANCTUARY AND THE LAND

whose entrances[244] were on the north side was a walkway[245] 1 cubit wide[246] and 10 cubits long on the inner side. **5** The upper rooms were narrower[247] than the middle and lower levels because the terraces took away [more space] from them.[248] **6** Because they were built as three stories, they had no pillars like the pillars of the courts.[249] Thus, it [the third story] was set back[250] from the ground more than the lower and middle ones. **7** There was a wall 50 cubits long outside, parallel and in front of the rooms, facing the outer rooms, **8** since the rooms of the outer court were 50 cubits long, whereas [the wall] in front of the great hall[251] was 100 cubits long. **9** At the base of these rooms was an entryway, from which one could enter (the rooms) from the outer court, **10** where the wall of the court began.[252] On the south[253] side facing opposite[254] the vacant space and opposite the Building were more rooms, **11** with a walkway in front of them as well. They looked exactly like the rooms on the north side; their length, width,[255] exits;[256] their layout and entrances were identical.

---

244. In LBH there is a tendency to use the masculine plural suffix for the feminine. In Ezekiel the masculine plural suffix is used for the feminine in eighty cases, whereas the feminine plural suffix (where the antecedent is feminine) occurs sixty-four times. The irregularity is a sign that Ezekiel marks the transition period between EBH and LBH; cf. Rooker, *Biblical Hebrew in Transition*, 78–81.

245. *riṣĕpâ* (with a spiranted *peh*), "pavement" (Ezek 22:4)—which replaces EBH *qarqaʿ*—should not be confused with *rispâ* (with a labial stopped *peh*), "coal"; cf. Rooker, *Biblical Hebrew in Transition*, 162–63.

246. *derek 'ammâ 'eḥāt* is obscure, since a path or opening of 1 cubit in width is highly unlikely. LXX and Pesh. point to an original *wĕ'ōrek mē'â 'ammâ*, "and its length was 100 cubits," envisioning a walkway running the entire length of the Building [561, n. 122].

247. MT *qĕṣurôt*, lit., "cut short"; Tg. renders *dhyqn*, "pressed, narrowed"; Pesh. *zʿwryn*, "diminished" [561, n. 123]. Note that the temple's side rooms (*ṣĕlāʿôt*) also had three stories which, in contrast, widened on the top (41:7).

248. The sense of MT's obscure *kî-yôkĕlû 'attîqîm* is rendered by Tg., "The balconies took space away from them." Several Hebrew mss. have a Qere reading *y'klw*, "they ate up," a more vivid picture [561, n. 124].

249. NRSV follows LXX in reading *haḥăṣērôt haḥîṣônôt*, "the outer courts" [561, n. 127]. The ceilings were supported by the walls.

250. *neʾĕṣal*, a Niphal participle of *āṣal*, "to be topped," is probably a technical building term [561, n. 128]. Cf. above on 41:8.

251. LXX καὶ αὐταί suggests a repointed original *wĕhēnnâ*. *'al-pĕnê hahêkāl* is generally emended on the basis of LXX to *'al-pĕnêhâ hakkōl*, and together with *wĕhēnnâ* read something like, "and they were facing it, the whole [measured] 100 cubits" [562, n. 130].

252. Reading *bĕrōš* with verse 12 and LXX ἐν ἀρχῇ, in place of MT's meaningless *bĕrōḥab* [562, n. 134].

253. The context demands reading *derek haddārôm*, with LXX in place of MT *haqqādîm*, "east" [562, n. 135].

254. Here *'el-pĕnê* is equivalent to *neged* in verse 1 [562, n. 136].

255. MT reads *kĕ'orkān kēn roḥbān*, lit., "like their length so their width," but LXX probably reflects the original *ûkĕroḥbān* [562, n. 137].

256. Most scholars emend MT *wĕkol môṣāʾêhen* to *ûkĕmôṣāʾêhen*, "and like their exits" [562, n. 138].

12 Accordingly, one entered the rooms on the south side corresponding to the passage, from the east, along the matching[257] wall.

13 Then he said to me, "The northern and southern rooms that face the vacant area are the sacred rooms where the priests qualified to come before YHWH will eat the most sacred offerings. There they will place their most sacred offerings—the meal offering, purification offering, and reparation offering—for the place is holy. 14 Having once entered,[258] the priests must lay aside the vestments in which[259] they officiate before leaving this sacred area to the outer court, because they are holy; they shall put on other clothes before entering the area assigned to the people.[260]

## Comment

There are two sets of sacristies on either side of the Building (*binyān*), of symmetrical shape, each being of graded heights, the highest being three stories tall and covering an area of 100 x 50 cubits. Together they would form a square, 100 x 100 cubits—a guarantee of holiness. Indeed, these are priestly quarters and are off limits to non-priests.

Haran presumes that any priest who wanted to enter these rooms from the inner court had to first exit by way of an inner wall.[261] However, as was demonstrated earlier (Introduction, section A), if the gateway leads into the outer court this could mean contact with the laity while wearing sacred vestments and bearing most sacred sacrificial portions. This forms a major reason for denying the existence of an inner wall, outside the fact that this alleged wall is absent from the text all along. Thus far, it has only been a conjecture. As shown (see Fig. 1), the priest merely has to proceed to the west where he finds an entrance into the upper level of the sacristies and descends on the inner staircase to the ground floor room (north or south) where he consumes his sacrificial prebends or deposits his priestly clothing. Thus the whole time he has remained within priestly bounds and has preserved the basic floor plan of Ezekiel's temple—keeping apart the holy from the common (v. 20).

The actual design of these sacristies is subject to controversy: there are as many interpretations as interpreters. This stems from too many corrupted phrases and unknown architectural terms in the text. The position I have adopted is, I believe, the simplest, though it is just as conjectural as all the others.

257. The variations in rendering of *hăgînâ* in the versions indicates that the meaning of this technical term was lost early [563, n. 141]. The translation of *haggĕderet hăgînâ* follows NJPS and NRSV [563, n. 142] and refers to verses 7–8.

258. *bĕbōʾām hakkōhănîm*, lit., "when they enter, the priests." On the infinitive construct with proleptic pronominal suffix, see Joüon-Muraoka, *Grammar*, §146e; GKC §131n; Rooker, *Biblical Hebrew in Transition*, 92–93 [563, n. 146].

259. Zimmerli (*Ezekiel 2*, 397) considers the feminine suffix on *bāhen* and the independent pronoun *hĕnnâ* corruptions, but inconsistencies of gender (and number) are common in these chapters [563, n. 148].

260. LXX reads "before touching the people"; Tg., "and then mingle with the people" [563, n. 149].

261. Haran, "Ezekiel," 215.

**42:1-6.** The tour of the inner court and its structures (Fig. 8) having been completed, the celestial guide leads the prophet through the inner north gateway, down its eight steps into the outer court. Turning sharply to the west, they take a position to view the sacristies. It is a three-tiered structure at the western wall of the temple compound. Being 100 cubits long (deep) it is parallel to the length of the Building (80 cubits) plus the *gizrâ*, "the vacant space" (20 cubits). The sacristies building is terraced, each story indented, smaller, than the one below [564]; they are connected by an inner staircase.[262] Entrance to the sacristies was gained by doorways located on the north side, facing the outer court [566] and also from the inner court into the third tier of the sacristies.

**42:7-12.** A path (*mahălak*) separated the outer court from the sacristies. This term is Late Biblical Hebrew, a synonym of *derek* and found only in Jon 3:3, 4; Zech 3:3; and Neh 2:6. The path was separated from the outer court by a wall (*gādēr*) running parallel (*le'ummat hallěšākôt*) to the sacristies [566]. Block[263] surmises that since the sacristies were 100 cubits long and the wall was only 50 cubits long, "its western end apparently abutted the corner of the other structures along the perimeter of the complex" [566]. However, there is no evidence for the existence of such structures; there is only Block's hypothesis that six of the laity's thirty rooms that hugged the perimeter wall were located at the west (three on each side of the Building, *binyān*). However, if my construction of the sacred compound (Fig. 1) is correct, there is no place for lay rooms at the western perimeter (see at 40:17). The entrance to the sacristies would be located at the far end (at the perimeter) and a wall of 50 cubits length would be more than enough to protect it.

The southern sacristies (vv. 10b-12) are described without indicating their measurement. None, however, is needed. They are mirror images of their northern counterpart. The text only lists the symmetrical features: the rooms, their entrances, the passageway, the protective wall, and the doorway [566].

**42:13-14.** Once again the celestial guide stops to comment on the special features of the sacred compound (cf. 40:45-46; 41:4, 22), emphasizing the sanctity of the objects [566]: They are located opposite the open space (*haggizrâ*) behind the temple; "They [i.e., the chambers] are holy" (*hēnnâ liškôt haqqōdeš*); "they are reserved for the priests who have access to YHWH" (*'ăšer qěrôbîm laYHWH*), elsewhere identified as descendants of Zadok (40:46; 44:15; 48:11); they constitute the only place where the priests eat their prebends from the most holy sacrifices; they serve as storage rooms for the meal (*minhâ*), purification (*hattā't*), and reparation (*'āšām*) offerings. The *minhâ* replaces the whole burnt offering (*'ōlâ*) in the earlier sacrificial list (40:39) [567]. The *'ōlâ* is not mentioned here because it was entirely consumed on the altar; the *minhâ* is absent in 40:39 where only the blood offerings on the altar are listed. These rooms

---

262. For a different view of the sacristies structure, see Block, *Ezekiel 25-48*, 566, and Maier, "Die Hofanlagen im Tempel-Entwurf," 60.

263. Block, *Ezekiel 25-48*, 565, Fig. 6.

*The Visionary Sanctuary*

also serve as storage rooms for the sacred priestly vestments when they are not in use [567]. Stevenson rightfully stresses that the threefold mention of *šām*, "there," in verses 13–14[264]—the priests will eat *there*, the most holy offerings will be brought *there*, the priestly vestments will be deposited *there*. The priests and no one else will enter these rooms and these actions *will transpire nowhere else*. Also it should not be overlooked that the two sets of rooms are each perfect rectangles (100 x 50) [568], and together they form a perfect square (100 x 100), a key indicator that we are dealing with a sacred area which, though grounded in the outer court, belongs in the domain of the priests.

## The Measurement of the Perimeter Wall (42:15–20)

TRANSLATION

15 When he had completed measuring the inside of the temple,[265] he brought me out through the east[266] gate. Then he measured all around [the temple compound]. 16 Using the measuring rod, he measured the east side, which was 500 [cubits[267]] rods.[268] Then he turned around[269] 17 and measured[270] the north side, which was 500 [cubits] rods. Then he turned around 18 and measured the[271] south side, which was 500 [cubits] rods. 19 He turned and measured the west side, which was 500 [cubits] rods. 20 Thus he measured it [i.e., the temple compound] on four sides. It was surrounded by a wall 500 [cubits] long and 500 [cubits] wide to separate the holy [area] from the common.[272]

---

264. Stevenson, *Vision of Transformation*, 61.

265. This includes the inner (priestly) court and the temple platform.

266. Exiting through the same gate by which he entered; see the COMMENT.

267. Reading *ḥmš m'wt* with Qere and the versions instead of Kethib's *ḥmš 'mwt*, "five cubits," an error of metathesis; cf. verses 17–19 [568, n. 160]. On the other hand, the Qere's *ḥmš m' wt* may be followed by Kethib's *'mwt*, the latter replacing the inscrutable *qānîm*, "rods" (also in vv. 17–19), yielding *ḥmš m'wt 'mwt*, "500 cubits." Note that the word *qānîm* is absent in LXX (see below).

268. As pointed out by Block [568, n. 162], there are mathematical inconsistencies with MT. Since 1 rod equals 6 cubits (40:5), each side of the temple compound would be 3000 (500 x 6) cubits, which would be incompatible with the 500 x 500 cubits perimeter specified in 40:15—41:13. Either *qānîm* is to be deleted here and throughout verses 16–19 (with LXX) as an erroneous gloss on *biqnēh hammiddâ* (so Allen, *Ezekiel 20–48*, 227), or MT may be defended first, as the *lectio difficilior*, and second, as being unlikely that this error would have been made four times [568, n. 161]. Block's suggestion, however, that *qānîm* identifies "an instrument rather than a unit of measurement" lacks support. Perhaps, as I surmise above, replacing *qānîm* with Qere's *'ammôt* in verse 16 yields the essential *ḥāmēš mē'ôt 'ammôt*, "500 cubits."

269. Following Tg., LXX, and Vulg, read *sābab* in place of MT *sābîb* (cf. v. 19) [568, n. 162].

270. Add the copula with LXX and Pesh. to smooth the reading [568, n. 163].

271. Block defends MT *'et* over LXX *'el*, favored by many critics, but which may reflect a secondary harmonization with verse 19 [569, n. 164].

272. On Late Biblical *bên . . . lĕ* replacing *bên . . . bên*, see Hurvitz, *Linguistic Studies*, 113; Rooker, *Biblical Hebrew in Transition*, 117–19. Cf. 22:26; 43:23 [569, n. 165].

PART TWO: EZEKIEL 40-48—THE VISIONARY SANCTUARY AND THE LAND

COMMENT

This unit comprises three parts: opening statement (v. 15), detailed description (vv. 16–19), and conclusion (v. 20). The latter "performs double duty, as an inclusio with 40:5 (note the reference to the wall), and as a conclusion with 43:12 to the tour narrative, with which it may have been linked prior to the editorial insertion of the *kābôd* pericope (43:1–9)" [569].[273]

**42:15–20.** The celestial guide leads the prophet out the very gateway (east) through which they entered. The tour of the temple compound is over, except for the report on the priestly and lay kitchens (46:19–24). The perimeter is measured in the following sequence: east, north, south, and west.[274] The measurement confirms that the temple compound is one large square (500 x 500 cubits). Note the computation of the east-west direction:

The East-West Dimensions of Yhwh's Temple[275]

| | |
|---|---|
| depth of the exterior eastern gate | 50 cubits |
| distance between exterior and interior gatehouses | 100 cubits |
| depth of the inner eastern gateway | 50 cubits |
| depth of the inner (priestly) court | 100 cubits |
| length of the temple and its auxiliary structures | 100 cubits |
| depth of the vacant area at the rear of the temple | 20 cubits |
| depth of the Building (*binyān*) and its walls | 80 cubits |
| total distance east to west | 500 cubits |

Verse 20 provides the rationale for the perimeter wall: "to separate the holy from the common," i.e., to protect the sanctity of the sacred temple compound [570]. In 43:12 the distinction between the temple compound and the outside is called *qōdeš qādāšîm*, "most holy." The contrast expresses the supreme holiness of YHWH's sacred grounds. This does not conflict with our verse 42:20, which cites the older formula (Lev 10:10; cf. Ezek 22:22). See the details in the COMMENT on 43:12. It had been noticed that the height of this wall, 1 rod or 6 cubits (40:25), would suffice to keep out an inquisitive pilgrim but by no means would it block an invading army. The wall, then, was not built for defense. Its function, as stated expressly by this verse, is to repel the common—not to speak of the impure (*ṭāmē'*)—from desecrating the sacred compound. Verse 20 forms an inclusion with 20:5, and, as observed by Joyce,[276] it signals the end of the initial tour of the temple and the first section of chapters 40–48.[277]

273. See Talmon and Fishbane, "Structuring of Biblical Books," 142–46.
274. LXX measures counterclockwise by reversing verses 18 and 19.
275. Adapted from Block, *Ezekiel 25–48*, 570.
276. Joyce, *Ezekiel*, 22b.
277. Block, *Ezekiel 25–48*, 571–73, following J. Z. Smith, *To Take Place*, 56–58, subdivides the temple compound into rings of holiness. His two maps are erroneous and misleading. In the first (his Fig. 7),

## The Visionary Sanctuary

## YHWH Returns to the New Temple (43:1–12)

### YHWH Returns Home (43:1–5)

TRANSLATION

1 Then he brought me to the gatehouse[278] that faces[279] east. 2 And then the Presence of Israel's[280] God, coming from the east, thundering like the roar of mighty waters,[281] lit up the earth with his Presence. 3 It was the same as the vision[282] I had seen when he[283] came to destroy the city, and the same vision I saw[284] by the Chebar canal, and I fell upon my face. 4 YHWH's Presence entered the temple[285] by the east gateway. 5 Then a spirit wind picked me up and brought me inside,[286] and behold, YHWH's Presence filled the temple.

---

the altar is declared a sphere of the Levites. But the altar is found in the middle of the inner, priestly court, into which Levites have no access. Furthermore, the entire temple building is YHWH's home; it is off limits even to Zadokites (except each Sabbath when they exchange the bread offering). Turning to the second map (his Fig. 8), the outside court cannot be set apart for "sacred activities." The laity cross through it as they enter and exit (46:9). Furthermore, the *gizrâ* and *binyān* (his nos. 10 and 11) are surely not holier than the temple itself (nos. 7–10). As suggested, they belong to YHWH and at the outmost they bear the same holiness as the temple building. Smith's spine image is helpful (cf. Fig. 14), but it must be re-designated: 1–3, Israel; 4, Levites; 5–6, priest; 7–11, YHWH.

278. The absence of the article increases the suspicion of dittography. LXX, Vulg, and Pesh. drop the second *ša'ar* [574, n. 1].

279. *'ăšer pōneh* occurs only here in the book. Ezekiel's style varies, cf. *'ăšer pānāyw* (40:6, 20), *'ăšer mopneh* (9:2), and the participle *happōneh* alone (8:3; 11:1; 44:1; 46:1, 12) [574, n. 2].

280. The full name of the deity who is approaching occurs at the beginning of an important event. The divine title, *kĕbôd 'ĕlōhê yiśrā'ēl* (v. 2) alternates with Lord YHWH, *'ĕlōhê yiśrā'ēl* (4:2), indicating that *kābôd* is an equivalent name of Lord YHWH.

281. In chapter 1 the same sounds emanate from the wings of the cherubim (1:24). There too the prophet identifies these sounds with the divine presence [579]. Here, however, the sight of the cherubim precedes their sound (43:2). The close-up of the cherubim in chapter 1 allows the prophet to describe their appearance in detail. Here the total appearance of the cherubim is all that he can make out, but it suffices to identify it with the cherubim in Chebar and Jerusalem's destruction (v. 3).

282. The root *r'h* is found eight times in this verse.

283. MT *bĕbō'î*, "when I came," is difficult: Ezekiel had no part in the destruction of Jerusalem; he was in Babylon together with many of the exiles of 597. Nonetheless, MT is supported by LXX and Pesh. Most scholars prefer the slight emendation *bĕbō'ô*, "when he came." This reading is supported by several Hebrew MSS, Theodotion, and Vulg. It also has been suggested that MT may preserve a miswritten abbreviation *bb' y[hwh]*, "when YHWH came" (Galling in Fohrer-Galling, *Ezechiel*, 241). However, YHWH was present in Jerusalem/the temple for many years before he decided to destroy it. This reading, then, is no better than MT. The meaning may be in keeping with Tg. *b'tnb'wty*, "when I prophesied [concerning]" [574, n. 5].

284. Ezekiel is vouchsafed a vision of the deity like the one he witnessed at the Chebar canal (1:1) and within the city (10:1). According to the Tg., the double mention of *rā'îtî*, "I saw," should be rendered, "in my prophecy."

285. Since Ezekiel, the priest/prophet, is now in the priestly court, the term *bayit* in verses 4–6 refers to the temple building. See the discussion, Excursus 2.

286. Ezekiel, an ordinary mortal, was not allowed entrance into the inner court through the inner east gateway, which had just been traversed and, thereby, possessed by YHWH. However, Ezekiel was entitled to have access to the inner, priestly court since he was a priest. It was important for him to be

PART TWO: EZEKIEL 40-48—THE VISIONARY SANCTUARY AND THE LAND

Comment

**43:1-2.** The climax of the construction project of the new sanctuary is the return of the divine presence. Thus, the *kābôd*-Presence enters the tabernacle (Exod 40:34-38) only after it is completely built (Exod 35-40). Similarly, the divine Presence enters Solomon's temple (1 Kgs 6:10-11; 1 Chr 7:1) when it is ready for occupancy. The kings of the ancient Near East took great pains to rebuild destroyed temples, not only of their own gods but also of their enemies. However, as noted by Block, "the present placement of this segment creates some tensions within the broader context. After the statistical description of the perimeter wall of the temple in 42:15-20, the present narration of an event is unexpected. Furthermore, the sketch of the temple provided in 40:2—42:20 appears incomplete. Several items undoubtedly observed during the visit to the inner court, specifically the altar (43:13-17) and the priestly kitchens (46:19-24) are yet to be described" [577].

The climactic moment of the twelve-day Babylonian New Year's festival involved the re-entry of Marduk into his *akītu* temple.[287] Herein lies a significant distinction between Babylon and Israel. Israel's tabernacle was thoroughly purified once a year (on Yom Kippur), but YHWH did not leave its premises. His residence in the adytum was only symbolically cleansed with 7 + 1 drops of *ḥaṭṭāʾt* blood, but his Presence did not budge from his cherubic throne. So too, Ezekiel's sanctuary was cleansed once yearly (Ezek 45:18-20), but no ritual detergent touched the interior of the sanctuary structure (contrary to Lev 16:12-20). Not just the adytum, but all of Ezekiel's sanctuary building was the symbolic residence of YHWH. No human ever entered to contaminate it even accidentally.

The entry (return) of the deity into his sanctuary was marked both by rejoicing and apprehension. Would the deity be happy in his terrestrial dwelling? Would he accept the offerings of his worshipers? Note that earlier Moses alone had witnessed the entry of the *kābôd*/Presence into the tabernacle (Exod 40:34). But for the people the celebratory day was not the day the deity entered the tabernacle, but when he consumed their offerings. Thus, the people at large witnessed the *kābôd*/Presence emerge from the adytum to incinerate the offerings of the priests and the people on the altar (Lev 9:2-7), *wayyarʾ kol-hāʿām wayyārōnnû wayyippĕlû ʿal-pĕnêhem*, "the entire people saw, rejoiced, and fell on their faces" (Lev 9:24b). According to the Chronicler's version of the initiation of Solomon's temple, the divine fire, which consumed the altar's sacrifices, emanated not from the adytum (P)[288] but from heaven (1 Kgs 8:54 [D]; 2 Chr 7:1).

Besides Moses, Ezekiel is the only mortal who witnesses the entrance (or return) of YHWH into his sanctuary (Exod 40:34-35; Ezek 43:1-6). But whereas the community is gathered around the tabernacle altar awaiting the appearance of the *kābôd*

---

there in sight of the Presence inside the temple. Ironically, but deliberately, Ezekiel occupied the same position when, in an earlier vision, he witnessed YHWH's departure and abandonment of the temple (chap. 10). In both visions, however, Ezekiel is not permitted to enter the temple itself, since it is occupied by God.

287. See Stevenson, *Vision of Transformation*, 52-53.
288. Ibid.

(Lev 9:4, 6), in Ezekiel's visionary sanctuary, the people never appear at all. The *kābôd*/Presence enters the sanctuary (43:1–9) and consecrates the altar (43:12–27) through the medium of the Zadokite priests, but the presence of the people is neither required nor desired. The people throng about the altars of the tabernacle and the Solomonic temple hoping for a sign that the sanctuary they have erected is acceptable to their God. Thus, when the *kābôd*-fire incinerates their sacrifice, they shout for joy (*wayyārōnnû*, Lev 9:24). But Ezekiel's sanctuary is not built by the people but by God. Moreover, the people will have undergone a change of nature; they will no longer be able to sin intentionally. They will only bring private expiatory sacrifices (*ḥaṭṭā'ōt* and *'ăšāmîm*) and "whole burnt and well-being offerings" (*'ōlôt* and *šĕlāmîm*, Ezek 43:27)—that is, offerings of praise and thanks for God's beneficence. Indeed, the people learned of the temple's dimensions and sacred spaces as revealed to them by Ezekiel (43:10–12), and only then—if they expressed shame for their past sins—would their sacrifices by acceptable at God's altar. Even then, they could only bring their sacrifices into the outer court; the Levites would slaughter them within (and below) the inner north gatehouse, and the priests would incinerate them on the sacrificial altar in the inner court in the sight of the people (see the Introduction, section C).

The celestial guide could have led Ezekiel outside the *temenos* through the nearby outer north gateway; instead they both exit the sanctuary through the eastern gateway. The purpose of choosing this exit is immediately apparent. The *kābôd*/Presence left Jerusalem from the east, where "it stood on a hill" (11:23), and it was returning via the same route. It was initially recognizable by its sound—Ezekiel had the same auditory experience at the Chebar canal—"a roar like the roar of mighty waters" (1:24; 43:2). The choice of the eastern gate is clarified by the route of the *kābôd*/Presence within the sanctuary: The outer eastern gatehouse forms the beginning of the sacred spine leading to YHWH's Holy of Holies [578] and *binyān* (see Fig. 14), an area traversable by no human, not even by a priest, but only by God himself.

The Presence of the God of Israel, *kĕbôd 'ĕlōhê yiśra'el* (43:2), is also termed YHWH *'ĕlōhê-yiśra'el*, "YHWH the God of Israel" (44:2). Thus, *kābôd* is a synonym for YHWH. This identical expression for YHWH, *kĕbôd 'ĕlōhê yiśra'el*, is found in 8:4, forming a triple identification with the God of the valley (3:22–23), the God of destruction (8:4), and the God of restoration (43:2)—the same triple identification spelled out in 43:3.

Verse 4 repeats verses 1b–2a but in reverse order: *ša'ar 'ăšer pōneh derek haqqādîm . . . kĕbôd 'ĕlōhê yiśra'el bā' . . . ûkĕbôd YHWH bā' . . . ša'ar 'ăšer pānāyw derek haqqādîm*, "the gatehouse that faces towards the east (1b) . . . the Majesty of the God of Israel came (2a) . . . the Presence of YHWH entered (4a) . . . the gateway that faced eastward (4b)."

Ezekiel and the celestial guide exit the sanctuary via the outer eastern gateway. The *kābôd*/Presence enters the sanctuary via the same gate. The inversion follows Seidel's law, namely, the God who entered via the outer east gate (v. 2a) is the same God who enters the temple via the inner east gate (v. 4). The area covered by the *kābôd*/Presence—from the seven-step outer east gate through the eight-step inner east gate into the ten-step temple (total twenty-five steps)—is the permanent home of the deity.

PART TWO: EZEKIEL 40–48—THE VISIONARY SANCTUARY AND THE LAND

As noted by Eliezer of Beaugency, even before Ezekiel sees a representation of the deity, he hears the deity's familiar voice, "the roar of mighty waters," which he first had heard at the Chebar canal (1:24). Whereas the sound of waters is at first part of the apparatus of the *kābôd*, the second time it is a mark of recognition: Ezekiel knows it is the *kābôd*. That YHWH is recognizable as the sound of waters is the subject of an entire psalm (Ps 93).

Kasher argues that when the *kābôd* of YHWH filled the temple, it thereby rendered all the sacred objects, including the ark, superfluous.[289] However, when the same phenomenon is reported to occur in the tabernacle (Exod 40:35) and in the temple (1 Kgs 8:10; 2 Chr 5:14), the sacred cultic objects in the shrine remain unaffected and are not withdrawn.

Defiling the Lord YHWH's Holy Name (43:6–9)

TRANSLATION

6 I heard someone speaking[290] to me from the temple,[291] though[292] the man[293] was standing[294] beside me.[295] 7 It said to me, Human, this[296] place is for my chair and for the soles of my feet,[297] where I will live among the progeny of

289. Kasher, "Anthropomorphism, Holiness and Cult," 192–98.

290. *middabbēr*, lit., "speak to oneself," (Hithpael). According to Rashi, the Piel is used in conversation between humans, but the Hithpael occurs in describing the internal speech of the Shekinah overheard by a messenger (Gese, *Verfassungsentwurf*, 34) [574, n. 8] Thus, the speech addressed to the prophet sounded like the speech was addressed to oneself. Either God is speaking with his *kābôd* and Ezekiel overhears (Rashi) or, more likely, the voice of the *kābôd* comes out of the temple and Ezekiel, standing in the inner court, hears it (Radak). See the COMMENT on 40:1.

291. *mēhabbāyit*, "from the temple." While Ezekiel was standing before the deity in the inner court.

292. *wĕ'îš > wĕhā'îš*, "although, but the man." The *w* can introduce an antithesis (e.g., *wĕ'ānōkî*, "but I," Gen 19:19; *wĕ'el-hammizbēaḥ*, lit., "but to the altar," Lev 2:12) or when one of the two clauses is subordinated to the other. GKC §154a.

293. Reading *wĕhā'îš* with the versions instead of MT *wĕ'îš* [575 n. 10].

294. *hāyāh 'ōmēd*, "was standing," a late Hebrew form instead of *'āmad*, "stood," as in *'ăšer hāyû rō'îm 'ōtām* (34:2) [575 n. 11]. The transition may be due to Aramaic influence; cf. *wahăwāt bāṭĕlā'*, cf. Rooker, *Biblical Hebrew in Transition*, 108.

295. Up to this point the only words heard by Ezekiel have stemmed from the celestial man. This time, the speech could not have emanated from the man, since he was standing silently next to the prophet.

296. Most English translations follow Tg. in interpreting *'et* as "this" (NJPS, NRSV, NIV, NASB, NAB, IB), but Tg.'s reading may have been influenced by Isa 66:1. REB, "Do you see the place of my throne," is based on LXX, which inserts ἑώρακας (= *hărā'îtā*) before *ben-'ādām*. Some scholars treat *'et* as an emphatic particle, equivalent to a demonstrative pronoun, as in Mishnaic Hebrew. Gese, *Verfassungsentwurf*, 34; Zimmerli, *Ezekiel 2*, 409; Joüon-Muraoka §125j. But this is better recognized as an anacoluthon, whereby all the objects of the verb *lō' yĕṭammĕ'û* were brought forward to the beginning of the sentence. Muraoka, *Emphatic Particles*, 155; Barthélemy, et al., *Preliminary and Interim Report*, 170 [575 n. 12] See 17:21.

297. The anthropomorphism expressed here impels the Tg. to render "this is the place of the abode of my throne of glory, and this is the place of my abode where my *šěkînâ* dwells, for I will make my *šěkînâ* dwell there" [575 n. 13].

# The Visionary Sanctuary

Israel forever. The house of Israel including their kings[298] will no longer defile my holy name[299] with their whoring[300] and the burial gardens[301] of their dead kings.[302] 8 Whenever they set their thresholds next to mine and their doorposts next to my doorposts, with only a wall separating them[303] from me, they defiled my holy name with their abominations. So I devoured them in my rage. 9 Now,[304] they will distance[305] from me[306] their whoring and the burial gardens of their kings, and I will reside among them forever.

## Comment

**43:6.** Assuming that the man standing next to the prophet was his celestial guide, why is he there? After bringing Ezekiel into the outer eastern gateway, through the sacred spaces of the sanctuary, and out again through the same outer eastern gate, the guide clearly was no longer needed. Ezekiel's newest entry into the sanctuary is carried out by a divinely sent wind. However, the measurements of the altar (vv. 13–17) were made by the man (Eliezer of Beaugency). A further reason: Why is the guide needed at all, especially since thereafter the guide disappears mysteriously from view? Block suggests that "Ezekiel would have been reassured by the guide's presence."[307] A more "reassuring" answer emerges by rendering the word wĕ[hā]'îš as "although the man"

---

298. In chapters 40–48 the ruler is called *nāśî'*. The only exception is 43:7, 9 where the ruler is entitled *melek*, "king," but these are two past historic references. See further the Comment to verse 6.

299. Only here (and in the following verse 8) is the divine name defiled (*ṭm'*). Otherwise (in the seventeen remaining occurrences), the divine name is desecrated (*ḥll*); Lev 18:21; 19:8, 12; 20:3; 21:6; 22:24, 32; Ezek 20:9, 14, 22, 39; 36:20, 23; 39:7; Isa 48:9, 11; 52:5; Amos 2:7; Jer 34:15–16; Mal 1:11–14). The burial of kings Manasseh and Amon in the garden connecting the temple and palace (2 Kgs 21:26; cf. Rashi on Ezek 43:7; Radak), although separated by a wall, sufficed for Ezekiel to regard the temple as having been corpse-defiled—the most severe degree of defilement, called by the rabbis: *ăbî ăbôt haṭṭumʾâh*, "the father of the fathers of impurity." Cf. Milgrom, "The Desecration of YHWH's Name," 69–82. Hence, the stronger verb *ṭm'* was chosen, see the Comment.

300. *zĕnûtām*, "their harlotry," Ezekiel's general term for idolatry (6:9; 8:27; 16:16, 17, 26, 282, 34; 20:30; 23:32, 5, 19, 30, 43), a term that stems from the Torah literature (e.g., Exod 34:15–16 [JE]; Lev 17:7; 19:29; 20:5, 6; Num 15:39 [H]). A synonymous metaphor is *tôʿăbôtām*, "their abominations" (v. 8).

301. *pigrê*, "corpses of." See the discussion in the Comment to verse 7b.

302. Vulg, Pesh., and Tg. (Sperber) interpret MT *bāmôtām*, "on their high places." LXX reads *bĕtôkām* "in their midst." Some medieval exegetes (e.g., Ibn Janah; Menahem ben Simeon) and most modern translations repoint *bĕmōtām*, "in their deaths," with numerous Hebrew mss, Theodotian, and several rabbinic editions of Tg. See Gese, *Verfassungsentwurf*, 34 [575 n. 15].

303. A wall would normally suffice to separate the burial grounds from the living quarters, but for Ezekiel it was not enough. The corpses and stelae of the royal dead were visible through the wall in his imagination, i.e., in his vision, and deep defilement would have ensued.

304. This new temple, as YHWH's permanent residence, is separated at a great distance from the royal palace (cf. 45:4, 7; 48:11–12, 21); see the next Note and n. 16.

305. *yĕraḥăqû*, "put far, remove, banish." The meaning of the Piel, *riḥēq*, is best illuminated by its semantic opposite *qērēb*, "bring near, give access, admit." Thus, the implication of physical distancing is social banishment. Cf. Milgrom, *Studies in Levitical Terminology*, 16–22, 33–43; Rattray and Milgrom, "*qarab*," 135–52.

306. *mimmennî*, "from me." Now that YHWH has entered the sanctuary, he is located there (Radak).

307. Block, *Ezekiel 25–48*, 580.

(see n. 433). Ezekiel is addressed directly *by God* for the first time. Heretofore he had been addressed *by the man*. Lest one think that the divine message, which confronts him from the sanctuary (vv. 7–9), continues to emanate from the guide, the text states explicitly that the guide stood silently alongside him, so the voice could only emanate from the *kābôd*/YHWH inside the temple.

**43:7. The place of my throne and place of my feet** (*'et-mĕqôm kis'î wĕ'et-mĕqôm kappôt raglay*). The language is royal (e.g., Isa 6:1; Jer 3:17; Isa 1:26; 10:1; Ps 47:9; 2 Chr 7:19) [580]. One would have expected a reference to the ark as *hădôm raglāyw*, "his footstool" (e.g., Isa 66:1; Pss 99:5; 132:7; Lam 2:1; 1 Chr 28:2). However, the ark's absence in Ezekiel's temple may reflect the fulfillment of Jeremiah's prediction: "in those days . . . they shall no longer say, 'The ark of the covenant of YHWH.' It shall not come to mind or be remembered, or missed; nor shall another one be made. At that time Jerusalem shall be called the throne (*kissē'*) of YHWH" (Jer 3:16–17) [581]. Indeed, as suggested in the Introduction, Ezekiel's visionary sanctuary will be void of all sacred objects (except for a wooden table).

Moreover, as Ezekiel's temple will have no high priest, so the people of Israel will have no human king. Only YHWH will be king. As assertively stated: "As I live—the declaration of the Lord YHWH—surely with a strong hand and with an outstretched arm, and with outpoured fury, I will reign over you" (Ezek 20:33). Israel, to be sure, will be led by a human king, a Davidide (37:24). In the main, however, he will be called *nāśî'*, "chief," a reflex of an ancient tribal leader (e.g., Lev 4:22–26; Num 2:3, etc.). The *nāśî'* will be given ample land on either side of the sacred land afforded the priests and Levites (45:7–9; 48:21–22) and capital city (45:6). The land of the *nāśî'* will be withdrawn from the sacred land (*tĕrûmâ*)—containing the sanctuary, priests and Levites, and the capital city—belonging to all the people (45:6) under the sovereignty of YHWH (48:30–35).

**43:7.** In Ezek 1–39, foreign kings are called *melek*, as is the future Davidide (37:22, 24); the present and immediate past kings of Judah are called *nāśî'*, "chief, prince."[308] In Ezek 40–48, the future rulers of Israel are called *nāśî'*.[309] The only exception is the occurrence of *melek* in this pericope, 43:7–9 [584, n. 54].

In Ezek 1–39, *melek* is found thirty-one times, two of which refer to the future Davidide king (37:22, 24). Oddly enough both passages are rendered *archon* in LXX. Similarly, two additional verses in the same pericope (34:24; 37:25) also render *nāśî'* as *archon* for the future Davidic ruler. Possibly, the term *melek* refers back historically to the early rulers who merited the title *melek*.[310] The seventeen times the term *nāśî'* is found in chapters 40–45 are rendered quite uniformly. The future Davidide ruler is not only called *nāśî'*, "chief, prince," but also YHWH's *'ebed*, "servant" (Ezek 34:23–24; 37:24–25). YHWH's kingship over Israel is stated unambiguously: *ḥay-ānî nĕ'um*

---

308. Duguid, *Ezekiel and the Leaders*, 18–20.
309. Ibid., 26–27.
310. Ibid., 26.

*ădōnāy* YHWH *'im-lō' bĕyād ḥăzāqâ ûbizĕrōaʻ neṭûyâ ûbĕḥēmâ šĕpûkâ 'emlōk 'ălēkem*, "By my life, declares the Lord YHWH, surely with a strong hand, with an outstretched arm, and with outpoured fury, I will be king (*'emlôk*) over you" (20:33).

The Davidide ruler will be entitled *naśi'*, a title drawn from the premonarchic, tribal rulers (Lev 4:22; Num 7:2, 3, 10, 11, 18). However, the king will be YHWH himself. There will be no human king, only a human *naśi'*. The disparity between God/king and human/prince is further attested in verse 7. God is pictured on a throne (*kissē'*) and a footstool (*mĕqôm kappôt raglay* = *hădôm raglāyw*, Ps 99:5; 132:7; Lam 2:1). Especially noteworthy are Isa 60:13, which pairs *mĕqôm miqdāšî*, "the place of my sanctuary" with *mĕqôm raglay*, "the place of my feet," and 1 Chr 28:2, where the footstool (*hădôm*) is associated with the ark of the covenant [581].

In Ezek 43:7-9, three demands are made on Israel so that the sanctuary (or the divine holy name) will remain holy. The first is that the *zĕnût* of the former kings will cease. *Zĕnût* frequently functions as a metaphor for idolatry (Exod 34:15-16) and for any defection from God's commandments (Num 14:33; 15:39). The egregious idolatry of King Manasseh must surely be a reference point, but the opposition of King Jehoiakim to the prophet Jeremiah (Jer 36:9-26) may also be kept in mind.

As noted by Kasher, the first person possessives—*kis'î*, "my throne"; *raglay*, "my feet"; *sippî*, "my threshold"; *mĕzûzātî*, "my doorpost" (43:7-8)—indicate that YHWH resides in his terrestrial home *lĕʻôlām*, "forever" (vv. 7-9), a concept borrowed from H (cf. Lev 15:31; 26:12).[311]

**Where I will dwell in the midst of the descendants of Israel forever, never again will the house of Israel defile my holy name** (*'ăšer 'ĕškān-šām bĕtôk bĕnê-yiśrā'ēl lĕʻôlām welō' yĕṭammĕ'û 'ôd bêt-yiśrā'ēl šēm qodšî*). As noted by Kasher, these two sentences may be structured on Num 35:34, *wĕlō' yĕṭammĕ'û 'et-hā'āreṣ . . . 'ăšer 'ănî šōkēn bĕtôkāh kî 'ănî YHWH šōkēn bĕtôk bĕnê yiśrā'ēl*, "you shall not defile the land . . . in which I myself abide. For I, YHWH, abide among the Israelite people."[312] However, whereas the defilement (*ṭm'*) of the land is an idiom of H (e.g., Lev 18:25, 27), the defilement (*ṭm'*) of YHWH's *name* is unique to Ezek 43:7-8. Ezekiel may have deliberately chosen the stronger verb (*ṭm'*) over the standard verb (*ḥll*, "desecrate") because of the intensity of defilement within the sanctuary; namely, the penetration of (royal) corpse contamination into the sanctuary building, indeed, into the adytum itself. The standard verb (*ḥll*) occurs seven times in H (Lev 19:8, 12, 18, 21; 20:3; 21:5; 22:2, 32) and is borrowed seven times in Ezek 20:9, (14, 22), 39; 36:20, 23; 39:7. The exceptional defilement of God's name in 43:7-9 is figurative, not ritual.[313]

As noted by Zimmerli,[314] the blame is placed on "the house of Israel," and not only on the errant kings. That these kings set their burial tombs adjacent to the sanctuary and worshiped idols (43:7b, 9) is laid at the feet of the people. As a result, they defiled

---

311. Kasher, "Anthropomorphism, Holiness and Cult," 204; cf. Knohl, *Sanctuary of Silence*, 124-64.
312. Kasher, *Ezekiel*, 827.
313. See Milgrom, "Desecration of YHWH's Name."
314. Zimmerli, *Ezekiel 2*, 415.

(*ṭm'*) YHWH's name (v. 7b) and will be far distant from the new sanctuary[315] where their cultic damage will be eliminated (36:31).

YHWH's resolve to reside in his sanctuary *lĕʻôlām*, "forever," is repeated in *wĕšākantî bĕtôkām lĕʻôlām*, "and I will dwell amidst them forever" (v. 9), and confirmed by YHWH's command to close the eastern outer gate permanently (44:1–2), signifying that he has no intention ever to leave. As pointed out by Kasher,[316] here Ezekiel is inverting the meaning of the verb *šākan*: whereas it refers to YHWH's *temporary* residence (in the temple), Ezekiel adds the adverb "forever," thereby reversing its meaning.

*and the mortuary gardens of the kings at their deaths* (*ûbĕpigĕrê malkēhem bāmôtām*). The second demand made on Israel is that no longer will kings be allowed to be buried adjacent to the sanctuary. Maiberger[317] cites Obermann[318] that Hebrew *peger* is a denominative from Semitic *pgr*, "lifeless mass," which evolved into "corpse" (Hebrew, Aramaic, and Akkadian), and "a stone, heap of stones, altar" (Ugaritic). Akkadian *pagru* means "body"—both living and dead, human and animal. Hebrew *peger* only designates a human corpse, chiefly in the context of war, but it also denotes memorial stele or stone heaps.[319] This double entendre was developed by Neiman,[320] who rendered it "your funerary steles," which was accepted by Albright[321] and de Vaux.[322] Alternatively, *peger* has been rendered as "funerary offerings."[323] However, this view is contradicted by Ezekiel, the first interpreter of Lev 26.[324]

It is commendable of Radak (eleventh–twelfth centuries) to have stated the entire exegetical problem in a few words. He gives two derivations for the *bāmôtām*: 1. *Bāmâ*, "high place"; 2. *Māwet*, "death." The first accords with MT and the second seems more suitable to the context of burial in the King's Garden (2 Kgs 21:18, 26). The Garden of Uzza (2 Kgs 21:18, 26) is commonly regarded as a pleasure garden in or near Jerusalem, which came to be used as a royal burial ground once the tombs in the City of David had become full. Alternatively, royal graves adjacent to the temple offended the temple priests.[325] However, on the basis of comparative evidence from the ancient Near East, Stavrakopoulou has recently demonstrated that mortuary gardens

---

315. Duguid, *Ezekiel and the Leaders*, 41.

316. Kasher, "Anthropomorphism, Holiness and Cult," 195.

317. Maiberger, "*pāgar, paegaer*," 477–82.

318. Obermann, *Votive Inscriptions*.

319. Ibid., 3a.

320. Neiman, "*PGR*: A Canaanite Cult-Object," 55–60.

321. Albright, *From the Stone Age to Christianity*.

322. De Vaux, *Ancient Israel*, 287; see also Noth, *Leviticus*.

323. Malamat, "Prophecy in the Mari Documents," 77–78; Malamat, *Mari and the Early Israelite Experience*, 97, n. 91; cf. Moran, "New Evidence from Mari," 43, n. 1.

324. Cf. Milgrom, *Leviticus 17–22*, 2318–19.

325. Naʾaman, "Amarna *ālāni pu-ru-zi* (EA 137) and biblical ʻ*ry hprzy-hprzwt*' ('rural settlements')," 245–54.

played an ideological role within perceptions of Judahite kingship.[326] Thus, Manasseh and Amon are expressly buried in the Garden of Uzza (2 Kgs 21:18, 26). The negative connotation of this Garden may have played a part in a tradition assigning Jehoiakim's grave to the κήπῳ Οζα, "garden of Oza" (4 Kgdms Lucianic 24:6), or Γανοζα, "Ganoza" (2 Par 36:8). Biblical texts such as Isa 65:3-4; 66:17; and perhaps 1:29-30 refer not to goddess worship but to practices and sacred sites devoted to the royal dead. Thus, the possibility exists that the Garden of Uzza was located adjacent to the temple (Ezek 43:7-9), where the royal ancestors were buried and worshiped.

**43:8. when they placed their threshold next to my threshold and their doorposts next to my doorposts, with only a wall between me and them** (*bĕtittām sippām 'et-sippî ûmĕzûzātām 'eṣel mĕzûzātî wĕhaqqîr bênî ûbênêhem*). Threshold and doorpost are repeated, "threshold to threshold," and "doorpost to doorpost," a stylistic device, a kind of crescendo, emphasizing his encroachment. The image provides easy access between the palace and the sanctuary via the mortuary gardens (the Garden of Uzza, above). Thus, the impurity of the palace is perpetually carried on foot into the sanctuary, intervening wall notwithstanding. The relationship between palace and sanctuary would have been familiar to denizens of biblical Jerusalem.[327]

In the ancient Near East it was customary for kings to be buried in tombs dug under the floor of their palace, referred in Assyrian texts as "the baked-brick rooms beneath."[328] The tombs of four kings from the eleventh to the ninth centuries have been excavated beneath the palace.[329] Similarly at Kalhu, Assurbanipal built four well-preserved royal tombs, probably for the queens of Assyria, below the floor of the domestic quarter of the palace.[330] A probable reference to this practice is echoed in Isa 14:18, *kol-malkê gôyim kullām šākĕbû bĕkābôd 'îš bĕbêtô*, "all the kings of the nations are all reposing each one in his house."

Two tombs were recently discovered under the royal palace of Samaria, one for Omri and the other probably for his son Ahab or his wife.[331] This phenomenon was less likely to be found in the country of Judah. There, where the priestly source had a greater impact on the cultic mores of the palace, the Omride palace would have been regarded as perpetually impure. The royal cemetery would have adjoined the palace, but alongside it not below it. A millennium later, workers had to be amply bribed to build the city of *tbry* (Tiberias) because they had to build it on a graveyard.[332] Thus, it was no offense to the deity that the king might be buried under his own palace, even if it meant that, in the priestly view, he would continually be impure. But if he was buried next to the sanctuary or came into contact with its sancta (i.e., its sacrifices),

---

326. Stavrakopoulou, "Exploring the Garden of Uzza," 1–21.
327. Cf. Beitzel, *Moody Atlas of Bible Lands*, 159; and Pritchard, *ANEP²*, 86–87.
328. Ellis, *Foundation Deposits in Ancient Mesopotamia*.
329. Andrae, *Das Widerstandene Assur*.
330. J. Oates and D. Oates, *Nimrud: An Assyrian Imperial City Revealed*.
331. Franklin, "Lost Tombs of the Israelite Kings," 26–35.
332. Josephus *Ant.* 18.2.3. §36; *b. Shabbat* 33b.

that was a different matter. For Ezekiel, this violation was the supreme reason why the temple had become polluted, YHWH was forced to leave, and the people were exiled. In Ezekiel's visionary sanctuary, for sure, the position of the king was abolished, and his replacement, the *nāśî'*, "chief," was removed far from the sacred area.

***their abominable practices*** (*bĕtô'ăbôtām*). The third demand made on Israel concerns the elimination of their "abominations." This word, *tô'ăbôt*, appears more than thirty-six times, referring to a wide range of idolatrous crimes or to major offenses that terminate in idolatry, including sexual crimes that ultimately are associated with idolatrous practices (cf. Ezek 16). Israel will not be expected to seek repentance, but "Then you shall remember your evil ways and your doings that were not good, and you shall loathe yourselves on account of your iniquities and your abominations (*tô'ăbôtêkem*)" (Ezek 36:31; cf. 20:43). If Israel only keeps in mind that the net effect of its abominations and evil deeds has been the desecration/defilement of God's name, and consequently will remove itself (physically and spiritually) from such shameful acts, YHWH will assuredly abide in Israel's midst forever.

**43:9. they will put far from me** (*yĕraḥăqû . . . mimmennî*). This verb, *rḥq* (Piel), has both a physical and spiritual connotation, both of which are present in this verse. Israel will place itself widely between the holy and the common. Thus, its future rulers (*nĕśî'îm*) will reside far (48:21–22) from the *tĕrûmâ*, "the sacred contribution" (i.e., land-gift), embracing the sanctuary, the priestly land, the Levitic land, and the capital city (48:9–20, 30–35). Specifically, Israel's rulers will no longer be buried adjacent to the sanctuary. Since the priestly land, as well as the temple mount, is declared holy (45:1–5), their burial places and other impurities will be far removed (Eliezer of Beaugency). But *riḥēq* most frequently also carries the figurative meaning, "banish, remove, eliminate" (e.g., Ps 88:19). Since verse 9 is addressed to all Israel (note "the mortuary gardens of their kings"), it is urging all Israel to remove its cultic and moral abominations, which kindled the divine wrath and led to its exilic punishment [586]. Whereas the priests were authorized to "come near" (*qāreb*, the antonym of *riḥēq*) to YHWH (40:2, 6; 42:13; 43:19), and offerings were to "be brought near" (*hiqrîb*) to him (see 43:24), the evils cited here were to be banished [586].

Epilogue to the Temple Vision (43:10–12)

TRANSLATION

> 10 As for you, human, describe the sacred compound to the house of Israel so they may be ashamed of their crimes. Let them assess its proportion.[333]

---

333. *tāknît*, "proportion," stems from the root *tkn*, related to measure. For example, *mî-mādad bĕšā'ălô mayim wĕšāmayim bazzeret tikkēn*, "Who has measured the waters in the hollow of his hand and marked off the heavens with a span" (Isa 4:12). Zimmerli (*Ezekiel 2*, 410) emends MT *tknyt* (elsewhere only in 28:12) to *tkntw*, "its layout" [586, n. 66]. Even though the temple is already built, Israel measures its spaces so that it makes no mistakes over its separations. Greenberg (*Ezekiel 21–37*, 580; on 28:12) suggests that *toknî* is related to token, "measure," i.e., perfectly proportioned. Cf. *BDB*.

## The Visionary Sanctuary

11 And if[334] they will indeed become ashamed of everything they have done, make known to them[335] the design of the temple compound and its layout, exits[336] and entrances (and its entire[337] design), and its laws and its instructions. And write [them] down in their sight so they may observe all my rulings and all my ordinances and perform them. 12 This is the Torah of the temple compound on top of the mountain: The entire area of its enclosure shall be distinctively holy. This is the Torah of the sanctuary compound.

## Comment

That 43:10–12 forms an inclusion to 40:1–5 is demonstrated by their parallels:

*haggēd 'et-bêt-yiśrā'ēl 'et-habbayit* (43:10)
*haggēd 'et-kol-'ăšer-'attâ rō'eh lĕbêt-yiśrā'ēl* (40:4b)
Describe the sacred compound to the house of Israel.
Report everything you see to the House of Israel.

*habbayit 'al-rōš hāhār kol-gĕbulô sābîb sābîb* (43:12)
*wĕhinnēh ḥômāh miḥûṣ labbayit sābîb sābîb* (40:5a)
the temple compound on top of the mountain—the entire area of its enclosure.
I noticed a wall running all around the temple compound.

As pointed out by Kasher,[338] the instruction to describe the dimensions (and spaces) of the *temenos* in the conclusion (43:10–11) is purposeful—to generate shame. Moreover, whereas the sanctuary is located atop a high mountain (40:2; 43:12), the conclusion highlights its distinctive holiness: *qōdeš qodāšîm* (43:12).

A major change in this inclusion refers to the active role of the people: They not only hear the sanctuary's dimensions from the prophet (40:4–6), but they have to repeat them (43:10). The purpose of this double lesson is also stated: Hearing and vocalizing the measurements allows for the feeling of shame to sink deeper into the people's consciousness (43:10, 11), fortifying earlier prophetic calls for shame (16:54, 61; 36:31–32). Lapsley suggests cogently that the people's sense of shame splits the directions to the prophet.[339] Shame is motivated by beholding the perfect *overall* pro-

---

334. Most scholars read *wĕhēm yikkālĕmû*, "and they will be ashamed," with LXX and Vulg., instead of *wĕ'im-niklĕmû*, "and if they will be ashamed" (v. 11a) with MT. According to Block, "the unconditionality of the foregoing renders a conditional clause at this point improbable" [586, n. 67]. But the MT is perfectly sensible—indeed essential—and no emendation of MT is required. See the Comment on verse 11.

335. *'ōtām* can refer to all the preceding objects, but the context more plausibly indicates that the reference is to the Israelites.

336. *ûmôṣā'āyw ûmôbā'āyw*, "exits and entrances." The latter should be vocalized *ûmĕbô'āyw* (see 44:5; 46:19), but its juxtaposition with *ûmôṣā'āyw* influenced its change to *ûmôbā'āyw* [587, n. 70].

337. *wĕkol-ṣûrōtayw*, "and its entire design." The repetition of this phrase for a second and third time is entirely superfluous. Note their absence in LXX. Besides, this word *ṣûrâ* is a hapax in this verse.

338. Kasher, *Ezekiel*, 829.

339. Lapsley, *Can These Bones Live?* 178.

portions of the temple, and this shame generates a readiness to receive the *details* of the temple structure. Also, the measuring of the holy spaces will accentuate the separation between the holy and the common (Eliezer of Beaugency). However, since the measurements must be written down, memory plays no role. Kasher[340] is correct in suggesting that the people have been elevated as the prophet's partners: His instructions must be coupled with the people's action—fulfilling commands (43:11b). Here again, Ezekiel is a second Moses: He carries with him a written record of the laws and measurements of the divinely revealed sanctuary. Israel is not only to learn them (*hôdaʿ ʾōtām*) but to perform them (*wěʿāśû ʾōtām*, 43:11b; see Excursus 8)

**43:10.** As shown above, "all that you see" (1:4b) is replaced with *habbayit*, "the temple precincts, *temenos*." The enthusiastic detailing of the sanctuary's specifications recognizes the people's hope that indeed YHWH's sanctuary will be realized.

The prophet's vision in 40:1—43:11 is similar in structure and details to his inaugural vision and call in 1:4—3:11. These are the parallels as noted by Block [587, n. 72]:

1. YHWH encounters Ezekiel in a theophanic vision, followed by a direct charge to communicate with his compatriots.
2. The vision climaxes in the appearance of the *kābôd* of YHWH.
3. The vision is accompanied by a sound like the rumbling of waters.
4. The vision is connected with the Chebar River.
5. The prophet responds to the *kābôd* by falling on his face.
6. The divine Spirit picks him up and prepares him for future interaction.
7. Special reference is made to the throne.
8. YHWH speaks to Ezekiel directly, addressing him in both instances as *ben-ʾādām*, "Human."
9. The spiritual condition of the Israelites is described, albeit in different terms.
10. The prophet is commanded to pass on to his compatriots a divine message.
11. The commissioning involves a written document: In the first instance, it is a scroll with the message already transcribed; in the present, the prophet is instructed to record the message himself.

If the people are ashamed of their prior deeds (that led to their exile), they will be eligible to measure the details of the sanctuary design. The people's remorse will qualify them to follow the path of the man (and the prophet) and measure the sacred spaces of the sanctuary grounds themselves. In other words, the shame that will be generated among the people when Ezekiel relates to them the details of the sanctuary grounds will increase manifold, when the people themselves perform these measurements.

---

340. Kasher, *Ezekiel*, 830.

**43:11.** MT *wĕ'îm*, "and if, indeed," makes it evident that the principle of free choice will be embodied in the lives of redeemed Israel. That is, even though Israel will no longer be capable of sinning (36:26–27) and, ostensibly, will lose its freedom of choice, the prerequisite of shame will not be imposed by YHWH but will be a matter of individual choice. That is, Israel will no longer sin *intentionally*. However, comprised of humans and their failings, they will continue to sin *inadvertently*. When discovered, they will invoke shame. The altar and its expiatory sacrifices (*ḥaṭṭā't* and *'āšām*), which specify a prerequisite of *bišĕgāgâ*, "inadvertence" (Lev 4:2, 12, 22, 27; 5:15), will be just as busy as before.[341]

The divine charge to the prophet consists of three elements: The first, *ṣûrat habbayit*, "the design of the sanctuary compound," pays exclusive attention to the boundaries and sacred spaces [588]. The term *ṣûrâ* is a hapax in this verse; it is assumed to be closely synonymous to the neighboring terms *tāknît* and *tĕkûnâ*, but its precise meaning is uncertain. The second element concerns access to platforms of sacred space and to spaces occupied by authorized personnel [589]. The two terms, *tāknît* and *tĕkûnâ*, have some connection with the term *mîdâ*, "measurement" (cf. v. 10), though according to Neh 2:10, *tĕkûnâ* refers to a "treasure, precious trove." The third element is embodied in the *ḥuqqôt*, "laws" and *tôrôt*, "instructions." Thus far little has been said in this regard [589]. It is anticipatory of chapters 44–46, which provide the cultic duties within the sanctuary compound. Here we are informed that these requirements are yet to be commanded.

*and write [them] down in their sight* (*ûkĕtōb lĕ'ênêhem*). By the end of the First Temple period, writing was fairly widespread (cf. Isa 29:11–1).[342] The exiles of 597 BCE, which included Ezekiel and his compatriots, surely constituted the educated and literate classes.[343] It is possible that "in their sight" implies that Ezekiel will only draw a sketch of the sanctuary compound (see 4:1–3). However, an outline will not do. As explicitly stated in verses 10–11, the man's purpose in drawing the exact measurements of the sacred space was to relate these figures to the people (40:4); they needed exact numbers, not an approximate design or delineation.

*so they may observe . . . and do them* (*wĕšāmĕrû . . . wĕ'āśû 'ōtām*). The combination of verbs, *šāmar* and *'āśâ*, yields the idiom "observe carefully" (e.g., Deut 4:6).

God returns to his earthly domicile before his people are informed of its basic laws. This follows an ancient pattern: Israel learns how to worship God in the tabernacle (Exod 25—Lev 7), even before the latter is consecrated (Lev 8:10–11)—although not before God enters it (Exod 40) and from there decrees its laws.

**43:12.** Is this verse a closure for 40:1—43:11 or an opening for 43:13—46:24? Structurally, it resembles other closures:

---

341. Cf. Milgrom, *Numbers*, 373–78.
342. Cf. Lachish Ostraca 3, *ANET*, 322b.
343. Cf. 24:2; A. Lemaire, "Writing and Writing Materials," 999–1008, esp. 1005; Tigay, *Deuteronomy*, 359, n. 39.

1. Lev 14:54-57

*zō't hattôrâ lĕkol-negaʿ haṣṣāraʿat wĕlannāteq*
*ûlĕṣāraʿat habbeged wĕlabbāyit*
*wĕlaśĕʾēt wĕlassappaḥat wĕlabbehāret*
*lĕhôrōt bĕyôm haṭṭāmēʾ ûbĕyôm haṭṭāhōr*
*zōʾt tôrat haṣṣāraʿat*

This is the procedure for all [fleshy] scale diseases, for scales,
for mold in fabrics and houses
for discolorations, for scabs, or for shiny marks
to determine when they are impure and when they are pure.
This is the procedure for scale disease.

It can be shown that these concluding verses of Lev 13–14 subdivide into two groupings:

A. Summation

54a   *zō't hattôrâ*
54b   *lĕkol-negaʿ haṣṣāraʿat wĕlannāteq*
55    *ûlĕṣāraʿat habbeged wĕlabbāyit*

B. Inclusions

56    *wĕlaśĕʾēt wĕlassappaḥat wĕlabbehāret*
57a   *lĕhôrōt bĕyôm haṭṭāmēʾ ûbĕyôm haṭṭāhōr*
57a   *zōʾt tôrat haṣṣāraʿat*

Thus the first two of the final four verses of this chapter sum up all varieties of scale disease discussed in chapters 13–14. The last two verses comprise inclusions—with the beginning of chapter 13, with the beginning of chapter 14, and with the summation (vv. 54–55). Thereby, the subscript has skillfully and effectively locked in and enveloped chapters 13–14, the entire unit on scale disease.

2. Num 7:84-88

Another priestly example of this concluding structure is Num 7:84-88

84a   *zō't ḥănukkat hammizbēaḥ bĕyôm himmāšaḥ 'ōtô*

(A summary of tribal chieftains' gifts to the altar)

88b   *zō't ḥănukkat hammizbēaḥ 'aḥărê himmāšaḥ 'ōtô*

The obvious function of this structure is to enclose a large listing. However, this criterion would not apply to Ezek 43:12. Why, then, was it employed? It can be surmised that the first *tôrat habbāyit* has in mind the prior list of instructions that have been imparted to the prophet by the guide, concerning the dimensions of sacred space in the sanctuary compound (Ezek 40–42). The second *tôrat habbāyit*, however, may be anticipatory of the cultic instructions for the priests, *nāśîʾ*, and people (Ezek 44–46).

*The temple* (*habbāyit*). The key term that unlocks the meaning of this structure is the subtle change that takes place in the meaning of *bayit*. Whereas in 40:1—42:12 it referred to the temple of stone—a secular building that had no sanctified import—from 43:10, the meaning of *bayit* may change to "the sanctuary compound," namely, the *temenos*, the entire enclosed area, the sanctuary.[344] Alternatively, the synonym *miqdāš*, "sanctuary, sanctified place," is frequently used.[345] Note that 21:12, 23; 23:38–39; 24:21 refer to the first temple before it was abandoned by God, and 37:26, 28 look forward to the future temple. Haran[346] argues that these terms are symbolic and not literal, but Hurowitz counters: The sanctuary was YHWH's residence, and "symbols" were physical aspects of the divine presence. The sanctuary was filled with dangers: contagious holiness. *kābôd* is not an abstract concept but visual and anthropomorphic.[347] Although Haran is right in protesting that the *bayit* is not a warehouse of divine needs, nonetheless God himself is present within.[348] Thus, the entrance of the deity suffices to change the temple from a building of stone to a building of sanctity.

**the entire area of the enclosure** (*kol-gĕbullô sābîb sābîb*). The term *gĕbûl* generally means boundary, but it also denotes the area within the boundary (cf. Ezek 11:10–11; Num 21:13, 23). Hence, *gĕbûl* refers here to the area encompassed by the prominent, perimeter wall [591–92].

**shall be distinctively holy** (*qōdeš qodāšîm*). This phrase should not be confused with *qōdeš haqqŏdāšîm*, "the holy of holies" (41:4), the adytum [592]. Thus, the adytum is most holy in comparison with the lower degree of holiness enjoyed by the rest of the sanctuary. And the entire sanctuary compound is declared as distinctively holy in comparison with the common, non-holy area of its surroundings. As noted by Kasher, "nowhere else in biblical literature do we find the term 'holy of holies' as a designation for an area outside the temple proper."[349] Moreover, Kasher proposes that Ezekiel's spatial notion of holiness is fluid: strong holiness will spill over its bound and effect the contiguous area.[350] The diffusion of holiness is also attested in 45:3; 48:12. However, it should not be overlooked that in all these verses *qodāšîm* is written without the definite article. Hence, this nuance implies a *comparative* sense; that is, in comparison with its surroundings it is most holy.[351]

---

344. E.g., 3:12; 4:11, 14; 5:5; 6:24; but see my strictures, Excursus 1.
345. Cf. 44:1, 5, 7, 8, 9, 11, 15, 16; 45:3, 4, 18; 47:12; 48:10, 18.
346. Haran, "Biblical Topics: Yahweh's Presence in Israel's Cult and the Cultic Institutions," 109.
347. Hurowitz, "Temple of Solomon," 136–38.
348. Cf. Ganzel, *Concept of Holiness*, 87, n. 6; Kasher, "Anthropomorphism, Holiness and Cult," 192–203.
349. Kasher, "Anthropomorphism, Holiness and Cult," 201–7.
350. Ibid.
351. Cf. also Joyce, "Temple and Worship in Ezekiel 40–48," 156–57.

PART TWO: EZEKIEL 40–48—THE VISIONARY SANCTUARY AND THE LAND

## The Altar Measurements (43:13–17)

### Translation

**13** The altar is measured in cubits (a cubit being one normal cubit[352] plus a handbreadth). Its trench was 1 cubit [deep[353]] and 1 cubit wide, with a rim of 1 span around its edge.[354] This is the base[355] of the altar. **14** From the bottom on the ground to the smaller ledge was 2 cubits, and its width was 1 cubit. From the smaller ledge to the greater ledge was 4 cubits, and its width was 1 cubit.[356] **15** The altar hearth[357] was 4 cubits [high],[358] and from the hearth four horns pointed upwards. **16** The hearth was 12 cubits long by[359] 12 cubits wide, a four-sided square.[360] **17** The [greater] wall[361] was 14 cubits long and 14 cubits wide, with four equal sides. The rim around it was 1/2 cubit [high],[362] and together with its trench[363] 1 cubit wide all around, its steps facing[364] east.

### Comment

**43:13.** *a cubit . . . handbreadth* (*'ammâ . . . wāṭōpaḥ*). The size of the (royal) cubit is given again (40:5) because the intervening passage (43:1–9) might lead to the conclu-

---

352. Several Kennicott mss., LXX, and Pesh. drop one member of MT *'ammâ 'ammâ*, but Tg. and Vulg retain the redundancy [592, n. 10].

353. Qere *wĕḥēqāh 'ammâ*. MT *whyq h'mh* arose from incorrect word division. Vulg and Pesh. read a smooth *whyqh 'mh*. Bracketed words fill in ellipses [592, n. 11]. Cf. *wĕrōḥab 'ammâ* > *wĕroḥbāh 'ammâ*, verse 14.

354. *śĕpātāh*, lit., "its lip," but *śāpâ* is used here in the derived sense of "rim, edge." Zimmerli (*Ezekiel 2*, 423) correctly observes that the feminine suffixes on *ûgĕbûlāh* and *śĕpātāh* refer not to the altar but to the trench (*ḥêq*) [592, n. 13], which according to Albrecht ("Das Geschlecht der hebräischen Hauptwörter," 80) is construed as a feminine.

355. *wĕzeh gab*, "This is the base." This is the only place in Scripture where a summary is mentioned this way. Many read *gōbah* "height" with LXX τo ὕψος (NJPS, NRSV, REB, NAB, NIV, JB), but the final *hē* reflects a dittography from the previous *hammizbēaḥ* [592, n. 14].

356. Read *wrḥbh 'mh* for MT *wrḥb h'mh* [593, n. 18].

357. Qere reads *h'ry'l*, "the lion of God" (cf. Isa 29:1–2), for Kethib *hhr'l*, "the mountain of God." The *plene* spelling *h'ry'l* also occurs in verse 16. Tg. reads *mdbḥ*, "altar," throughout [593, n. 19]. On the etymology see the Comment.

358. M. Dijkstra ("The Altar of Ezekiel," 24–36) argues strongly that *wĕhahar'ēl 'arbaʿ 'ammôt* (15a) is a gloss, that the altar has no third platform, that the hearth is situated on the same level as the substructure, and that the height of the altar is 6 cubits.

359. On the preposition *beth* in the sense of "by," see verse 17; 45:2; 48:20 [593, n. 21].

360. Cf. *rābûʿa* "square" with the form *mĕrubbāʿ* (40:47; 45:12). On the forms, see Hurvitz, *Linguistic Study*, 27–30 [593, n. 22].

361. The unsure etymology of *'ăzārâ* is discussed in the Comment. *haggĕdôlâ*, "greater," may have dropped out by homoioteleuton, cf. verse 14, but Block suggests that the description is cryptic throughout [593, n. 23]. The context leaves no doubt that the upper part of the altar is being described.

362. "Wide" is also possible, but this interpretation of *gĕbûlâ* is consistent with verse 13 [593, n. 26].

363. On *wĕhaḥēq lāh* as an abbreviation for *wĕhaḥēq 'ăšer lāh* (cf. 41:9; 42:3), see Cooke, *Ezekiel*, 476 [593, n. 27].

364. MT infinitive construct (*pĕnôt*) should be repointed as a participle (*pōnôt*) [593, n. 29].

sion that another cubit size is intended. According to Eliezer of Beaugency, a cubit trench was dug surrounding the altar.

FIGURE 16: Ezekiel's Altar above the figure

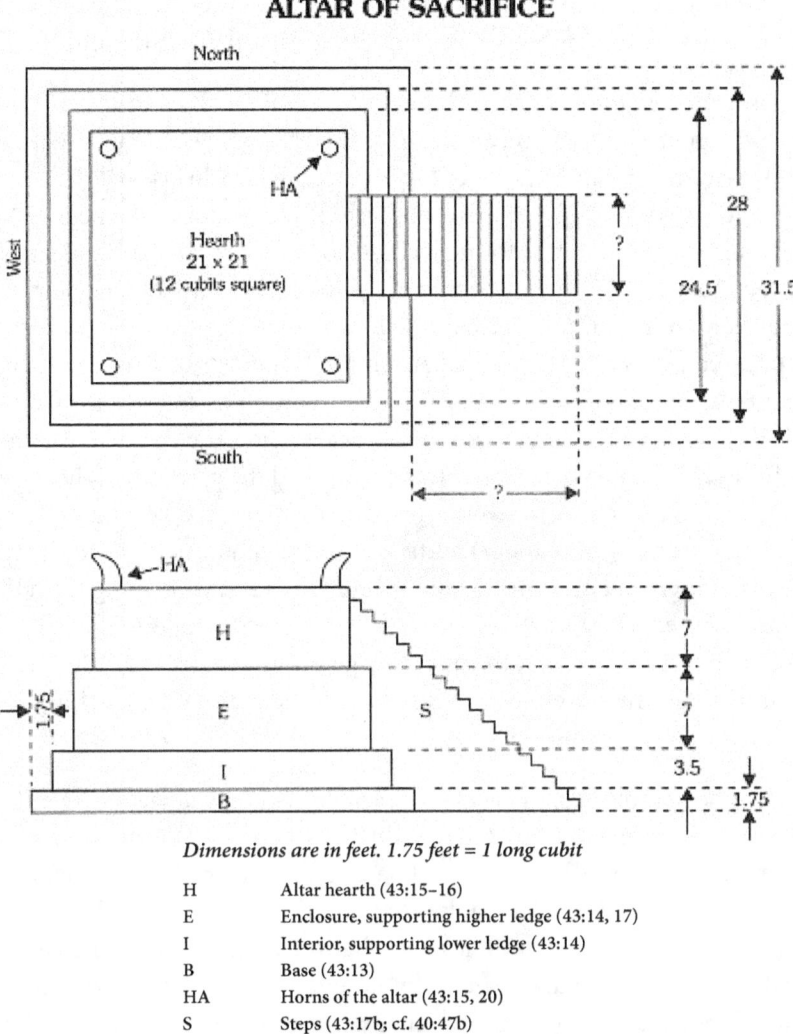

Dimensions are in feet. 1.75 feet = 1 long cubit

| | |
|---|---|
| H | Altar hearth (43:15–16) |
| E | Enclosure, supporting higher ledge (43:14, 17) |
| I | Interior, supporting lower ledge (43:14) |
| B | Base (43:13) |
| HA | Horns of the altar (43:15, 20) |
| S | Steps (43:17b; cf. 40:47b) |

The altar was bypassed while measuring the temple (40:47). The reason is not completely clear. First, it should be recalled that the pentateuchal priests were divided into two groups: *mišmeret haqqōdeš*, "the sancta/temple guards," and *mišmeret hammizbēaḥ*, "the altar guards" (Num 18:5a). This division is honored by Ezekiel, *mišmeret habbayit*, "house [i.e., temple] guards," and *mišmeret hammizbēaḥ*, "altar guards" (40:45–46). These two groups of priestly guards are completely separated in regard to the location where they dress, eat, and sleep (cf. 40:44–46). It is thus only natural that the guide would first measure all the items of the *bayit* before turning to the altar. Secondly, measuring the altar separately and in such extravagant detail adds to the altar's importance, demonstrating that the altar is indeed equivalent to the total of the rest of the sancta.

**43:14.** *ḥēq hāʾāreṣ* is best understood as a trench sunk into the ground; *hāʾāreṣ*, "of the ground," distinguishes this trench from another one at the top of the altar (v. 17; cf. Fig. 16). This trench functioned as a receptacle for the blood and gore of incinerating, sacrificial animals, preventing the defilement of the sacred ground [599].

*from the bosom of the land (ûmiḥēq hāʾāreṣ).* A possible allusion to the altar being located at the center of the earth.[365] *ḥēq hāʾāreṣ* is the precise Hebrew equivalent of Akkadian *irat erṣitti/ kigalle*, "bosom of the earth/underworld" [597].[366]

The etymology of the term *ʿăzārâ* is obscure. The best clue to its meaning is found in 2 Chr 4:9; 6:13 where it refers to the wall-enclosed court, and so in Sir 50:2 and in later rabbinic literature. Here, however, it refers to two "walls" of the altar. Since the sides of the altar, built on top of the base (*gab*), were shorter than the base, to the observer it appeared as a ledge running all around the altar [599]. Thus the term, *ʿăzārâ*, can refer to the altar ledges (smaller and greater) as well as to their respective walls. Nothing is said about the composition of the walls. Block suggests that large stones were "carefully set to support the upper framework and the earth fill of the altar." Block further suggests that "a real altar would presumably have had one or more conduits draining the liquids from the (upper) gutter to the bottom trench." Indeed, one would expect the two gutters to be connected and to contain a funnel leading from the lower "earth-bound" gutter away from the altar.[367] The "lower" ledge is *haqqěṭannâ*, "the smaller," i.e., two cubits high, and the upper ledge is the "greater," i.e., four cubits high. As shown in Fig. 16, there were two ledges with sunken areas for catching the blood drained from the altar [599–600].

**43:15–16.** The hearth of the altar is called *harʾēl* (v. 15), or *hāʾărîʾēl* (v. 16). Elsewhere Ariel appears as a personal name of two individuals (2 Sam 23:20 = 1 Chr 11:22; Ezra 8:16), and as a cryptic name for Jerusalem (Isa 29:1–2, 7b). The folk translation of Ariel as "lion of God" is difficult to relate to the altar hearth. The name *harʾēl* (lit., "mountain of God") may refer to a common folk belief that the altar stands at the center of the earth.[368] It derives from Akkadian *Arallu*, "mountain of the gods/underworld" [600].[369]

The altar's horns are right-angle tetrahedrals projecting upward from the four corners. They are not added to the altar but are of one piece with it (Exod 27:2; 30:2), as illustrated by the incense altar from Megiddo and the sacrificial altar from Beer Sheba (see Fig. 17).

---

365. Cf. Levenson, *Sinai and Zion*, 139; Levenson, "The Temple and the World," 275–98.

366. Cf. Langdon, *Die Neubabylonische Kǫnigsinschriften*, i.1.36 (Nabopolassar) and i.2.31; v.2.1–2, xii.2.23 (Nebuchadrezzar).

367. For an example, see the altar at Dan and its drainage system.

368. Levenson, "The Temple and the World," 275–98.

369. Albright, *The Archaeology of Palestine*, 146–47; cf. consonantal *ʾryʾl* in Isa 29:11 and Ezek 43:15–16.

FIGURE 17: The Horned Altars from Megiddo and Beer Sheba[370]

Horned altar
from Megiddo

Horned altar
from Beer Sheba

The daubing of the horns of the sacrificial altar with the blood of the purification offering implies that the entire altar is being purged, on the principle of *pars pro toto*. The choice of the horns to represent the altar is not arbitrary. The significance of this choice can be deduced through a series of analogies with other uses of sacrificial blood, such as the purification rite of a healed *mĕṣōrāʿ* (Lev 14:14–17, 25–28), the consecration rite of the new priests (Lev 8:23–24; Exod 29:20) and of the new altar (Lev 8:11; Exod 29:21), and the smearing of the lintel and doorposts with the blood of the paschal sacrifice (Exod 12:7, 22). The things that receive the blood are extremities, the very points of an object, which a hostile force would strike first in attacking it.

In the ancient Near East, temples were periodically smeared with magical substances at precisely the same vulnerable points, such as entrances and corners, in order to expel the malefic force from those points and to protect them against future demonic incursion. In Israel, the monotheistic revolution had banished the world of demons, but the sancta were still vulnerable to the malefic power of humans.[371] The physical and spiritual impurity of human beings is capable of polluting the sanctuary altar by attacking its extremities, namely its horns. Support for this thesis stems from the purgation rite prescribed for the sacrificial altar in Ezekiel's visionary temple. It calls for daubing the purification blood not only on the altar's horns but also on the corners and rim of the ledge that circumscribed it in the middle (Ezek 43:20; cf. vv. 13–17). Like the horns, it was an extremity and, hence, vulnerable to pollution. The

---

370. Photographs by J. Marr Miller. Used with permission.
371. Cf. Milgrom, *Leviticus 1–16*, 226–61.

indispensability of the altar horns is confirmed by the rabbinic rule that if even one of the altar's horns is missing, the sacrificial service is invalidated.[372]

There is abundant attestation of ritual daubing in the ancient Near East. The incantations recited during the ritual smearing of persons, statues of gods, and buildings testify that their purpose is purifying and apotropaic, namely to wipe off and ward off the incursions of menacing demonic forces. Always it is the vulnerable parts of bodies (extremities) and structures (corners, entrances) that are smeared with magical substances.[373] Thus it can be seen that the blood-daubing of the altar's extremities—its horns—closely resembles the blood-daubing of the extremities of priests being consecrated (Lev 8:23). But it is the dedicatory rite of Ezekiel's altar that most closely corresponds to the daubing of the priests, for the purifying blood is daubed not only on the altar's horns but also on the corners of its two gutters, located at its middle and bottom (Ezek 43:20). These points correspond to a person's earlobe, hand thumb, and big toe. It is safe then to conclude that these two congruent rites share the same purpose, which in the case of Ezekiel's altar is made explicit: *wĕḥiṭṭē'tā 'ōtô wĕkippartāhû*, "and you shall decontaminate it and thus purge (*kpr*) it" (Ezek 43:20). Note the same phraseology in Exod 29:36: *yĕkappĕrû 'et-hammizbēaḥ wĕṭihărû 'ōtô*, "they shall purge (*kpr*) the altar and thus purify it" (Ezek 43:26). Therefore, the daubing of the priest at points of his body and the daubing of the comparable points on the altar must possess a similar goal: *kippûr*, "purgation."

**43:17.** The hearth was reached by steps on the east side. This feature flies in the face of the Mosaic proscription on steps for an altar (Exod 20:26). This is another indication in favor of seeing Ezekiel as a new Moses (see Excursus 8). The altar proper was as wide as the entrance to the temple, and the overall width was the same as the vestibule. From the bottom of the gutter to the top of the altar the structure measured 6 cubits (about 10 ft.). In height, it was equivalent to Solomon's altar (2 Chr 4:1). A staircase was required. In accordance with Exod 20:24–25, the altar frame was probably from uncut stone, and then filled with soil. The horizontal surfaces (hearth and "ledges") would have been paved with flat stones or plastered with lime. Josephus' reference to a ramp (*kbš*) reflects respect for the Mosaic taboo on steps and a repudiation of Ezekiel's design (*J.W.* 5.5.6 §§222–26) [601–2].

*The Purgation of the Altar (43: 18–27)*

TRANSLATION

18 Then he said to me, "Human, this is what the Lord YHWH has declared: These are the ordinances of the altar on the day it is constructed for offering up whole burnt offerings on it[374] and for dashing blood upon it. 19 You shall

---

372. *Sipra*, Ḥobah, par. 4:12.
373. E.g., *ANET*, 338; Wright, *The Disposal of Impurity*, 34–36.
374. Note the assonance of *lĕha'ălôt 'ālāyw 'ōlâ* [593, n. 31].

deliver a young bull from the herd as a purification offering to the Levitical priests who are from the line of Zadok, and thus have access to me[375]—the declaration of the Lord YHWH—to serve me. 20 You shall take some of its blood and daub it on its four horns, the four corners of the [greater] wall, and the surrounding curb [on the base]. Thus you shall decontaminate it and purge it. 21 Then you shall take the (carcass of the) purification bull and have it burnt[376] at the guardpost[377] [located] outside the sanctuary. 22 On the following day you shall sacrifice an unblemished male goat as a purification offering. They shall decontaminate the altar as they had decontaminated [it] with the bull. 23 When you have completed the decontamination ritual, you shall sacrifice an unblemished bull from the herd and an unblemished ram from the flock. 24 When you sacrifice them before YHWH, the priests shall sprinkle salt on them and incinerate them as a whole burnt offering to YHWH. 25 For each of seven days you shall sacrifice an unblemished male goat as a purification offering and an unblemished bull of the herd and a ram of the flock shall be sacrificed. 26 For seven days they shall purge the altar by purifying it and ordaining it.[378] 27 When these days are over from the eighth day onward, the priests may sacrifice on the altar your whole burnt offerings and your well-being offerings, and I will accept[379] you—the declaration of the Lord YHWH.

## Comment

Ezekiel's altar consists of four different sized square blocks piled on top of each other and located in the exact center of the 500 cubits x 500 cubits sanctuary compound. Thus the square, Ezekiel's symbol of holiness, is quadruple cubits (or quintuple cubits) the holiness of the temple hall, and double the holiness of the most holy (holy of holies) adytum. This constitutes the major shift from the Mosaic altar.[380] The elliptic tabernacle contains two equivalent centers: the adytum and the altar.[381] Ezekiel's temple omits the adytum's centrality and concentrates the central holiness on the *altar*. The symbolism is clear: Israel worships her God exclusively at the altar, and the erstwhile service inside the temple (tent) has been eliminated, as demonstrated by the absence of sacred objects inside the temple and the abolition of cultic service by the high priest (see Introduction, section C). The isolation of this pericope from the guided tour

---

375. With *haqqĕrōbîm ʾēlay*, cf. *haqqĕrēbîm . . . ʾel-YHWH* (40:46) [593, n. 32].

376. Allen, *Ezekiel 20–48*, 238, proposes an indefinite subject for *śĕrāpô*. Cf. Zimmerli's (*Ezekiel 2*, 434) comparison with Lev 16:27–28 [594, n. 37]. Cf. also Milgrom, *Leviticus 1–16*, 239–40.

377. The meaning of *mipqād* is unclear. Most translations follow the versions in treating it as a place. Cf. LXX and Vulg *in separato loco*, "in the separate place." Cf. Tg. *bʾtr dḥzy*, "in its proper place" (so Levey, *Tg. Of Ezekiel*, 118) [594, n. 38]. See the Comment.

378. Lit., "they shall fill its hand." See further the Comment. Qere reads pl. *ydyw*, "his hands," as if the priests are being dedicated. Cf. LXX, "their hands" [594, n. 41].

379. On *rāṣāʾ*, an Aramized variant of *rāṣâ*, see GKC, §75rr. Cf 20:40–41 [594, n. 43].

380. Cf. Milgrom, *Leviticus 1–16*, 135, Fig. 7.

381. See Fig. 3.

(40–42) and its details is an indication of its importance. Also the altar differs from the other sacred objects in that its height, though not stated, can be calculated: From the top of the horns to the bottom of the gutter it is 10 cubits. The text contains no orders to build; it assumes an existing, divinely constructed structure in the middle of sacred space [597].

As pointed out by Paul,[382] placing the altar at the beginning of a law corpus follows the pattern found in each of the major law codes of the Torah: (1) Exod 20:22–23 at the head of the Book of the Covenant (Exod 20:22—23:33), (2) Lev 17:1–9 at the head of the Holiness Code (Lev 17–26/27), (3) Deut 12: 1–27 at the head of the Deuteronomic Code (Deut 12:1—26:15). However, Ezekiel's altar differs from its predecessors in that it contains no instructions to build and reveals no interest in its composition (stone or earth). All that matters is its size and shape [597].

**43:18–27.** For the first time in 40–48, YHWH speaks. The ritual is outwardly structured as a prophetic oracle, beginning with *kōh ʾāmar YHWH* and concluding with *nĕʾum ʾădōnay YHWH*. These formulae have not appeared in 40–48 prior to this point but occur frequently thereafter (44:6, 9, 12, 15, 27; 45:9, 15, 18; 46:1, 16; 47:13, 23; 48:29). According to Block, the absence of a named subject to *wayyōʾmer* may indicate that God's message was relayed to Ezekiel via the celestial man [604]. But this can hardly be the case; YHWH has already spoken directly to the prophet in 43:7–9, 10–12. God's speech does not comprise remonstration—the usual content of prophetic messages—but a new law. The formulaic parallel is clear: *ʾēlleh ḥuqqôt hammizbēaḥ*, "these are the altar ordinances" (43:18)//*zōʾt ḥuqqat happāsaḥ*, "this is the pesaḥ ordinance" (Exod 12:43). The construction of the altar follows the lines of Exod 29:36–37; 40:10; Lev 16:18–19 [605].

> *Purgation vs. Consecration of the Altar*
>
> There is one puzzling distinction between the treatment of Ezekiel's altar and the treatment of the Mosaic altar. The latter is sanctified; the term *qādōš* predominates. This word (and its root *qdš*) is totally absent in Ezek 43:18–27. (Hence this pericope is entitled "The *Purgation* of the Altar," not "The *Consecration* of the Altar"; cf. Lev 8.) Nothing could be more surprising: the priestly quarters are *qōdeš* (42:13–14; 44:1, 27), and the temple adytum is expressly *qōdeš haqqŏdāšîm*, "holy of holies" (41:4). As noted, Ezekiel's altar is the center of the *temenos*, which, in turn, is the center of a series of concentric squares. This theoretically would make the altar the holiest object within the temple compound, and yet there is no indication that the altar is a sacred object! The answer is that the texts of the pentateuchal and Ezekielian altars are not alike. The former is a consecration rite; hence, the root *qdš*. The latter is not a consecration; the repeated usage of *ḥiṭṭēʾ*, "decontaminate" (4x); *ṭihēr*, "purify" (1x); *kipper*, "purge" (2x), indicates that the

---

382. Paul, *Studies in the Book of the Covenant*, 34.

altar is not being consecrated, but purified (i.e., being readied for use). There can be no doubt that the altar is holy, indeed most holy (cf. Exod 30:28–29), but this fact is irrelevant to the fundamental task of the altar—to receive the sacrifices of the people of Israel and find acceptance for them by God (43:27).

The question still remains: Why was the tabernacle altar sanctified, but Ezekiel's altar was not? Indeed, the very centricity and squareness of Ezekiel's altar—quintessential hallmarks of structural holiness—would lead one to assume that the altar should expressly be *qādōš* (indeed, *qōdeš qŏdāšîm*!). The likely answer is provided by the nature of the consecration ritual. Consecration is performed with *šemen hammišḥâ*, "the anointment oil" (Exod 30:22–33). But in the inauguration ritual of Ezekiel's altar there is no anointment ceremonial. This accords with the rabbinic tradition that at the end of the First Temple period the anointment oil disappeared and was never again reconstituted (*b. Yoma* 2:15; *t. Soṭa* 13:1; *ʾAbot R. Nat.* A 40). Thus, Ezekiel had no choice: he decontaminated (and purged) the altar so that it could be put to cultic use, but he had to abstain from consecrating it as a sacred object. Was the power of the altar in any way diminished because of this deficiency? According to P, *kol-hannōgēaʿ yiqdaš*, "whatever touches (it) is sanctified."[383] That is, the sanctified altar could transfer its holiness to whatever contacted it—*what*ever, but not *who*ever.[384] It must be assumed that this unanointed altar possessed effective sacral force. After all, the priestly clothing (Ezek 46:20) possessed contagious holiness even though it was not anointed. Possibly, the very placement of the altar in the "sacred spine," indeed in dead center of the temple compound, may have provided it with sacral power.

If Ezekiel's altar was not consecrated because there was no longer any sacred anointment oil, how can we account for the existence of the "holy" (*qādōš*) temple hall (41:2), the "holy" (*qōdeš*) sacred spine (42:13), the "most holy" (*qōdeš qŏdāšîm*) adytum (41:4), and even the "most holy" (*qōdeš qŏdāšîm*) mountain (43:2)? A possible answer is that Ezekiel used the term *qōdeš* figuratively. A concrete example of such usage is his declaration that the entire mountain, on top of which is the sanctuary, is most holy (43:12).[385] To be sure the mountain does not bear "most holy" properties. This is only a *figure of comparison*. In relation to the surrounding geography, this mountain is most holy. Similarly, the sanctuary hall is "holy" in relation to its outside environment, and the sacred spine is holy in comparison with the other areas of the sanctuary. It must be admitted that the adytum does possess "most holy" qualities. Otherwise, one could not explain Ezekiel's reluctance to enter the adytum while it was being measured by his angelic guide, even though it had not yet been occupied by the divine *kābôd*. Thus, one must assume that the sanctuary sancta (in particular, the table of the bread's presence) were (most) holy without being anointed with the sacred oil, and that this constitutes one of Ezekiel's ritual innovations as the "second Moses" (see below, Excursus 8).

---

383. Milgrom, *Leviticus 1–16*, 553–55.
384. See the details in ibid, 446.
385. See Levenson, *Sinai and Zion*, particularly part 2, "Zion, The Mountain of the Temple," 111–45.

### Comparing Ezekiel, Leviticus, and Numbers

Kasher astutely notes that in P, YHWH enters the tabernacle only *after* it is built by his specification (Lev 8–9), whereas in Ezekiel, YHWH *first* enters the sanctuary (43:1–12) and *then* the cleansing and purging ceremonies follow (43:18–27). Indeed, since the latter is built by God—and not like P's tabernacle, by man—"the prophet can guarantee that God will reside in the sanctuary forever."[386] But this is more than an indication that "God's presence is quite independent of Israel's actions,"[387] it is evidence that YHWH has despaired of Israel's ability (not will) to build a sin-free sanctuary, so he does the job himself.

Ezekiel's rite prescribes a purification bull on the first day and a whole burnt offering bull and ram on each of the following seven days. The tabernacle altar, in contrast, is initiated with a purification bull and a whole burnt offering ram on each of the seven days (Exod 29:15–18, 36; Lev 8:11, 13–17). At stake here are two different traditions concerning the purification of the altar on behalf of the community: Ezekiel follows Num 15:22–26, and the tabernacle account is based on Lev 4:13–21.[388] Also, the length of the initiation differs: the tabernacle altar for seven days (Exod 29:35, 37; Lev 8:33) and the Ezekielian for eight.[389]

The formation of the Num 15:22–26 passage must have occurred early, for not only has its procedure become the rule for all public purification offerings (e.g., Num 28–29), but it is also incorporated into Ezekiel's rite for the initiation of the altar (Ezek 43:18–27). The latter passage is significant because it adopts both procedures: that of Lev 4 for the first day (Ezek 43:19–21) and that of Num 15 for the following seven days (Ezek 43:22–27). By contrast, the consecration of the tabernacle altar calls for the Lev 4 procedure only—during all seven days (Exod 29:36–37)! Thus the Num 15 rite must have crystallized into its present form after Lev 4—a deduction that concurs with the literary analysis presented above—and before Ezek 43. If it turns out that Num 15:22–31 is the product of H, as Knohl (1995:53) has strongly argued,[390] then it provides further evidence of the preexilic provenance of all priestly material.

### The Redaction of Ezekiel 43

Another oddity is even more disturbing. As shown by Block, in Ezek 43 the subject regularly changes in number and person [605]:

| | |
|---|---|
| vv. 19–21a | second person singular |
| v. 21b | third person singular |
| v. 22a | second person singular |

---

386. Kasher, "Anthropomorphism, Holiness and Cult," 205.

387. Ibid.

388. Milgrom, *Leviticus 1–16*, 264–69. That the altar was "initiated" or "inaugurated," in other words, put into use, and not "dedicated," is discussed in ibid., 535–38.

389. Ibid., 281–84.

390. Knohl, *Sanctuary of Silence*, 53.

| v. 22b | third person plural |
| vv. 23–24a | second person singular |
| v. 24b | third person plural |
| v. 25a | second person singular |
| vv. 25b–27b | third person plural |
| v. 27c | first person singular |

The differences in person are hardly random; five times second and third person are climaxed by the first person YHWH. It would seem that a single redactor rearranged these verses this way even if necessarily changing the person or number to fit the system. However, such a theory would fail by comparing *wĕḥiṭṭē'tā 'ōtô*, "and you (sg.) shall decontaminate it" (v. 20b; cf. v. 23a), with *ka'ăšer ḥiṭṭĕ'û bappār*, "as they have decontaminated [it] with a bull" (v. 22b). Thus the singular subject, (i.e., Ezekiel) changes abruptly to a third person plural (probably the priests), though referring to the same act (the same verb). No single redactor would have used the same verb bearing two different and contradictory persons and numbers in the same pericope. Kasher suggests that verses 19–27 combine two sources, one singular, the other plural.[391] The singular subject's position is described by Radak (on v. 19) as follows: "he is the priest . . . who will splash the blood and purge the altar in the future, since he will be the high priest even though Aaron may be present." As noted, Radak's problem is nonexistent, since Ezekiel's temple dispenses with the high priest. The other tradition (pl.) attributes the cleansing and purgation to the priestly cadre. LXX reads all the second person verbs as third person plural, demonstrating that the first tradition (sg.) is the older one. In any event, the redactor took whatever traditions were at hand and found that they could not be set in a logical order: 2, 3-2, 3-2, 3-2, 3-2, 1.

As the officiant of the altar decontamination Ezekiel would be part of the literary tradition holding that Ezekiel is a second Moses. Like Moses he decontaminates the altar with a *ḥaṭṭā't* bull (Lev 8:14–17) for seven days (Exod 29:36); cf. Ezek 43:19–27. The following are Ezekiel's other officiating acts:

1. Ezekiel delivers the sacrificial bull to the Zadokite priests (19).

2. He performs the blood-daubing ceremony (20; but not blood-sprinkling, Block, 606).

3. He has the *ḥaṭṭā't* carcass burned outside the *temenos* (21; Ezekiel is the only officiant, *contra* Block, 607–8).

4. He decontaminates the altar with a male goat (22)

5. He sacrifices a bull and a ram (22).

6. He decontaminates the altar (or has the altar decontaminated) for seven days with a bull and a ram (25)

---

391. Kasher, *Ezekiel*, 834.

As a recipient of direct speech from YHWH, Ezekiel is the founder of a new cult, i.e., as a second Moses. Side by side with Ezekiel's activity are the following acts of the priests:

1. They receive the *ḥaṭṭā't* bull whose blood will be used in the decontamination rite. (v. 10).
2. They have the bull burned (*contra* Block, 607, v. 21).
3. They decontaminate the altar with a male goat (correcting Block, "bull," 607, v. 22).
4. They sacrifice a bull and ram as whole burnt offerings (v. 24).
5. For seven days, purge the altar by purifying it and ordaining it (v. 26).
6. From the eighth day onward, sacrifice the people's whole burnt and well-being offerings (v. 27).

## *The Seven-Day Ritual in Ezekiel and Elsewhere*

I have discussed briefly the ritual significance of the number seven in Israel and the ancient Near East elsewhere.[392] Of special interest is the dedication of Eninnu, the temple of Ningirsu, which also lasted seven days (Gudea II, 16–18).[393] But it is the initiation of Ezekiel's altar that affords the nearest parallel. The text reads, "Every day, for seven days, you shall present a goat of purification offering, as well as a bull of the herd and a ram of the flock; they shall present unblemished ones. Seven days they shall purge the altar and purify it; thus they shall ordain it" (Ezek 43:25–26). There can be no question that Ezekiel's demand that the new altar be purged with a purification offering each day for seven days is based on a passage contained in the account of the consecration of the tabernacle and its priesthood: "You shall ordain them [i.e., Aaron and his sons] through seven days, and each day you shall sacrifice a bull of purification offering for purgation; you shall decontaminate the altar by performing purgation upon it, and you shall anoint it to consecrate it. Seven days you shall purge the altar and consecrate it" (Exod 29:35b–37a).

Both rites are in accord in stating that the altar's initiation lasts for seven days. They differ, however, in three significant details. First, Ezekiel's altar is not consecrated, because it is not anointed. But this is not surprising because after the destruction of the first temple, the anointment oil was not reconstituted. Then, the sacrificial animals differ. It can be shown, however, that this difference rests on two variant traditions concerning the purging of the altar on behalf of the community: Ezekiel relies on Num 15:22–26 and the tabernacle account relies on Lev 4:13–21. More precisely, Ezekiel has fused two traditions: He calls for a purification bull (Lev 4:14) for the first day (Ezek 43:21) and a purification goat (Num 15:24) for the following seven days. Finally, the length of the

---

392. Milgrom, *Leviticus 1–16*, 234.
393. See Falkenstein and von Soden, *Sumerische und akkadische Hymnen und Gebete*, 137–82.

## The Visionary Sanctuary

initiation, in fact, also differs: Ezekiel's actually runs for eight days. Yet this deviation is not traceable to a variant tradition concerning the number of days but is due to Ezekiel's attempt both to conflate the two purification offering traditions (cited above) and to equate the altar initiation to his eight-day spring festival (Ezek 45:21-23).[394] The initiation of Solomon's altar (*ḥănukkat hammizbēaḥ*) also lasted seven days (2 Chr 7:9; cf. 1 Kgs 8:65 LXX, 66), a clear attempt by the Chronicler to equate the Solomonic temple with the tabernacle[395]—as demonstrated by his attribution of a theophany on the Solomonic altar (2 Chr 7:1a) similar to that on the tabernacle altar.

**43:18. He said to me ... "These are the ordinances of the altar"** (*wayyōʾmer ʾēlay ... ʾēlleh ḥuqqôt hammizbēaḥ*). Who is speaking? It must be the celestial guide who is standing next to him (Eliezer of Beaugency).

**This is what the Lord YHWH has declared** (*kōh ʾāmar Lord YHWH ʾĕlōhîm*). As pointed out by Stevenson,[396] this formula does not necessarily introduce punishment judgment; it is used in 43:18; 44:6, 9; 46:1, 16; 47:13 to introduce a command or regulation.

**and for dashing blood upon it** (*wĕlizrōq ʿālāyw dām*). The reference is mainly to the *šĕlāmîm*, "the well-being offering," sacrificed by the layperson whenever he wanted meat (Lev 17:3-5), and rarely the *ʾāšām*, "the reparation offering" (Lev 7:2), the two sacrifices whose blood offering is specified (Tg., Radak).

**43:19-21.** The first day is characterized by three activities. Ezekiel is to initiate the week-long activities by procuring a bull and presenting it as a purification offering to the Zadokite priests, who slaughter it [608] on the designated table (40:39) in the priestly court (*contra* Block, not on the altar). The blood is collected and Ezekiel daubs it on the four horns, on the four corners of the larger wall, and on the surrounding base curb. Block (608) renders *pinôt hāʿăzārâ*, "the four sides of the altar" [608]. However, the priestly consecration (Lev 8) to which the altar's decontamination is most closely compared, indicates that *pinôt* must be rendered "corners" (v. 20). Block also claims that the *mipqād* is located "within the temple grounds." However, the *ḥaṭṭāʾt* carcass, bearing in full the absorbed impurity, is expressly burned outside the camp (Lev 4:12, 21).

There are three sources of pollution: contact with a corpse (Num 19:13, 20); affliction with a chronic genital discharge (Lev 15) or certain skin diseases (Lev 13); and inadvertently violating any prohibitive commandment (Lev 4) [610]. Block avers that the contamination may have been conveyed to the sacrificial animal and then to the altar. However, the altar would then have been defiled *ab initio* and it would have been ruled out of use. Why then was the altar considered contaminated even before the

---

394. Details in Milgrom, *Leviticus 1-16*, 264-69.
395. Japhet, *Ideology of the Book of Chronicles*, 69.
396. Stevenson, *Vision of Transformation*, 69.

PART TWO: EZEKIEL 40-48—THE VISIONARY SANCTUARY AND THE LAND

blood of the sacrificial animal contacted it? No reason is given. Perhaps the altar was inadvertently defiled by its builders. The altar, therefore, had to be decontaminated from all human contact.

**43:19.** *And you shall deliver* (*wĕnātattâ*). Ezekiel, who functions as high priest (Radak), or "you," as the people's representative (Eliezer of Beaugency).

**43:20.** *you shall decontaminate it and purge it* (*wĕḥiṭṭētā ʾōtô wĕkippartāhû*). Its meaning is clarified explicitly by *wayĕḥaṭṭēʾ . . . lĕkappēr ʿālāyw*, "he decontaminated it . . . [in order] to purge it" (Lev 8:15). That is, the altar was prepared for its expiating role: First it must be cleansed (*wayyĕqaddĕšēhû*, "and he sanctified it"), and then it can provide expiation for Israel's (future) sins. In Ezek 43:26, the order of the verbs is reversed, *yĕkappĕrû . . . wĕṭihărû*, "they shall purge . . . and you shall purify" (*ṭiher = ḥiṭṭēʾ*); perhaps an example of Seidel's law, that the reversal of the normal order is a reference to an earlier quotation where the correct order occurs.

**43:21.** *the guardpost of the sanctuary outside the sanctuary grounds* (*mipqad habbayit miḥûṣ lammiqdāš*). According to Garfinkel[397] the *mipqad* is synonymous with *mišmār*, "guardpost," which in turn is related to *pĕquddôt*, "guard duty" (44:11); *mipqad* rather implies a specific guardpost, namely, the one outside the sanctuary next to the dumping ground for impure sacrifices. Possibly, this was the first guardpost before the ones at the entrances to the guardways of the sanctuary wall.

*Sanctuary* (*miqdāš*). This is the first occasion when the entire area within the perimeter wall is called *miqdāš*. As will be noted (44:1), once the divine presence has entered, then the *bayit*, "the house," is transformed into a *miqdāš*, i.e., it has become sanctified.

**43:22-24.** On the second day the altar is once again cleansed, this time with the blood of a *ḥaṭṭāʾt* male goat. This is followed by the *ʿōlâ* sacrifice of a second bull and a ram (23). The sprinkling of the sacrifices with salt is not limited to this ritual since all sacrifices must be sprinkled with salt while on the altar (cf. Lev 2:13). That is, the *melaḥ bĕrît ʾĕlōhêkā*, "the salt of the covenant of your God" (Lev 2:13) implies longevity: Just as the salted covenant between Israel and YHWH is imagined to be eternal, so is the person of the deity in his sanctuary and his reception of Israel's offerings [610–11].

**43:25-27.** During days three to seven, the purgation rituals are prescribed for the entire week (v. 25). To the expiatory verbs *kipper* and *ḥiṭṭēʾ*, a third verb is added, *millēʾ yādāw*, lit., "fill the hand" (v. 26). This metaphoric expression stands for "to ordain." While Exod 29:22, 26, 27, 31; Lev 8:22, 29 speak of an *ʾēl hammilluʾîm*, "an ordination ram," the present ordination speaks uniquely of an inanimate ordination, that of the altar. With the eighth day and onwards the priests sacrifice the whole burnt offering and the well-being offering on the altar. It must be assumed that the expiatory sacrifice, *ḥaṭṭāʾt*, is omitted because Israel is incapable any longer of committing sin, since, as demonstrated, this sacrifice applies only to deliberate sin. But the possibility

---

397. Garfinkel, *Studies in Akkadian Influences*, 19–27.

of inadvertent, accidental sin (e.g., both moral, Lev 4, and physical, Lev 12–15) always recurs [611].

***and I will accept you*** (*wĕrāṣi'tî 'etkem*) is a most satisfying climax to preparing the altar for future outreach to God. The summit of the consecration ritual of the tabernacle altar was the incineration of the sacrifices by a fiery ray from the adytum (Lev 9:24). Here, however, no miracle is given or requested, only the assurance that the bond between Israel and YHWH, via the altar, will never be broken.

# 2

# The Sanctuary Personnel and the Nāśî' (Ezekiel 44–46)

## THE TEMPLE PERSONNEL AND THE *NĀŚÎ'* (44–46)

### *Foreigners Forbidden (44:1–9)*

#### The Closed Outer East Gate (44:1–3)

TRANSLATION

1 Then he[1] led me back by way of [2] the outer gate of the sanctuary that faces east; but it was closed. 2 Then YHWH[3] said to me, "This gate[4] will remain closed;[5] it must not be opened! And no one may go through it because YHWH, Israel's God, has gone through it. Therefore, it must remain closed. 3 But the

---

1. Who is leading Ezekiel in verse 1? In verse 2, God is the subject. Does this mean that God is also the subject of verse 1, or that Ezekiel is stressing that God, not the guide, is speaking to him? Since all the leading within the sanctuary is done by the celestial guide, this is no exception (see n. 540). The term *ša'ar hammiqdāš*, "gate of the sanctuary," only appears here.

2. The *derek* can hardly take its ordinary adverbial meaning "through," since, as the text states explicitly, the eastern gate was shut. However, *derek* also denotes "destination of, the road to, by way of, towards" (cf. 40:5, 6, 10, 24). The altar faces due east of the east gatehouse. But Ezekiel finds that the east outer gate is closed, and he must seek another exit from the sanctuary.

3. The MT is not ungrammatical, as claimed by Gese (*Verfassungsentwurf*, 50–51), Zimmerli (*Ezekiel 2*, 437), Allen (*Ezekiel 20–48*, 244) and others. This reading is attested in virtually all Hebrew mss, and the versions (except LXX[239]). On the principle of *lectio difficilior* the MT should be retained [613, n. 1]. Moreover, this reading is essential since up to this point the speaker was the celestial guide (Eliezer of Beaugency).

4. This gate is located at the top of the seven-step staircase.

5. *sāgûr yihyeh*. LBH usage [613, n. 2] replacing EBH *yissāgēr*. Cf. also 3:6; 46:1.

*nāśîʾ*,[6] and only the *nāśîʾ*,[7] may be seated there to dine[8] before YHWH. He will enter by way of the vestibule to the gate and exit the same way.

## Comment

The use of *hēšîb*, "he brought back, led back," links Ezekiel's present experience with a previous visit to the same gate (40:6–23; cf. Fig. 8), as well as the spectacular initial departure (11:23) with the return of the *kābôd* through the same gate [613]. This fact is mentioned here to let us know that Ezekiel's original intention was to ascend to the priestly platform to hear the word of YHWH emanating from the temple building (v. 4). Since he was at the outside eastern gatehouse to witness the entry of the *kābôd* (43:1) he might have been expected to ascend the two eastern gates (the seven-step outside Israelite platform and the eight-step inner priestly platform). However, he finds that atop the first stairwell, the gateway is shut, which prompts YHWH to speak to the prophet directly (v. 2).

It seems that Ezekiel took the initiative to stand on the priestly platform before YHWH. Nowhere do we read that YHWH asked Ezekiel to stand before him. However, Ezekiel has already been told—and in almost identical language—that YHWH has a message for his people (40:4). Besides, the heavenly guide led him there [613].

We meet the term *miqdāš* "sanctuary," (40:1, as in 23:21) at a strategic point. Its occurrence here is no accident. YHWH has just entered his terrestrial home and transformed it from a house (*bayit*) of stone to a house of holiness, i.e., sanctuary (*miqdāš*). Block has suggested this transition may be responsible for the deity's full title, "YHWH the God of Israel" (v. 2) [614]. His suggestion may be debated, but explicit statements in this pericope are beyond question. Twice it is emphasized that the entrance to the eastern gate is henceforth permanently closed, and though the *nāśîʾ* has the right to eat the specified portion from his sacrifices in the corridor of the gatehouse, his entrance to and exit from it must always be through the outer court. This means that his access to the eastern inner gatehouse can only take place by first ascending either the northern or southern outer gateway and then traversing the outer court to the vestibule entrance of the outer eastern gatehouse. And this is precisely what happens here: Ezekiel is brought through the northern outer gate (v. 4) in view of the priestly platform. The closed eastern gate indicates that the area beyond it constitutes the "sacred spine," the area belonging exclusively to YHWH, stretching from the closed inner gate at the base of the priestly platform up to the temple building situated atop the sanctuary (see Fig. 14). To be sure, the priests occupy the middle platform of the sacred spine, but only by divine permission; their area still belongs to YHWH.

6. The particle *ʾet* plus nominative occurs twelve times in Ezekiel, and with increasing frequency in Mishnaic Hebrew [613, n. 3].

7. Most commentators follow LXX and Pesh., deleting the second occurrence of *nāśîʾ* as a dittograph. Cf. BHS; Zimmerli (*Ezekiel* 2, 438). However, on *ʾet* with the emphatically repeated subject used in a limited sense, see G. R. Driver, "Ezekiel: Linguistic and Textual Problems," 308–9; L. Boadt, *Ezekiel's Oracles Against Egypt*, 10 [613, n. 4].

8. The *leḥem*, "meal," eaten by the *nāśîʾ* most likely consists of his *šĕlāmîm*, "well-being offering," which he would have brought to the sanctuary as his sacrifice (Eliezer of Beaugency).

Another purpose of the closed gate is to indicate that YHWH will reside within forever, as promised explicitly (43:7, 9). Block [615], following many scholars,[9] holds that 44:3 is repeated in 46:8, but he is hard pressed to justify the MT here. However, since these two verses speak of two different gates, the outer east gate (44:3) and the inner east gate (46:8), it is not surprising, indeed, it is to be expected, that the same rule—to enter and exit by the same gate—holds for both gates.

The introduction of the *nāśî'* (v. 3) is sudden, but necessary: the *nāśî'* is the only exception to the rule that no human enters the closed outer east gate—however, the entrance is not via the stairs and the (closed) gate, but through the other side of the gate—from the outer court (see the fuller treatment of the *nāśî'*, 45:7—46:12). Here, in his first appearance in the Ezekielian Torah, the *nāśî'* is a non-cultic figure, radically different from his appearance in chapters 1–39, where he poses as a Davidic figure (cf. 34:24; 37:25). Here he holds several subservient ranks: YHWH occupies the uppermost (third) platform; the priests, the middle platform; the Levites in all the gateways and in the outer court (see below); but the *nāśî'* has no role in the cultic service. His only privilege is to eat his meals while seated in the vestibule of the outer eastern gatehouse. That is, he is enabled to observe the immolation of the very sacrificial animals that he has presented [615–16].

### The Violation of Sacred Space (44:4–8)

TRANSLATION

4 Then he led me through the north gateway to the front of the temple. I looked and lo! The Presence of YHWH filled the temple of YHWH, and I fell upon my face. 5 YHWH said to me: "Human, mark well.[10] Look closely[11] and listen carefully[12] to everything I have to say to you about[13] all the laws of the temple of YHWH and about all its teachings.[14] Mark well those who may enter[15] the temple and all[16] those excluded[17] from the sanctuary. 6

---

9. E.g., Gese, *Verfassungstenwurf,* 86; Zimmerli, *Ezekiel 2,* 439.

10. *śîm libběkā*, lit., "set your heart" [618, n. 22].

11. *ûrĕēh bĕ'ênêkā*, lit., "and see with your eyes."

12. *ûbĕ'āznêkā šěmā',* lit., "and hear with your ears."

13. On the *lamed* used to identify the topic of a verb of saying, see Waltke-O'Connor, *Syntax* §11.2.10g [618, n. 24].

14. Reading the pl. *twrtyw* with Qere in place of sg. *twrtw*, Kethib [618, n. 22].

15. Since this verse clearly distinguished between *habbayit* and *hammiqdāš*, the former refers to the temple building, which has only one entrance; hence the MT is preferable. However, since Tg., Pesh., and Vulg. read pl. *lmbw'y*, MT may be in error, either as a metathetical corruption with *yod* miswritten as *waw* or the final vowel letter has been mistakenly omitted [618, n. 22].

16. One would expect *ûbĕkol* or *ûlĕkol* [618, n. 22].

17. The pl. *môṣā'ê,* "exits," is necessary since the exit had to be other than the entrance (46:9; Eliezer of Beaugency).

## The Sanctuary Personnel and the Nāśî' (Ezekiel 44–46)

You will say to the rebellious [House],[18] the House of Israel: 'Thus has my Lord YHWH proclaimed: Enough of your abominations, O House of Israel: 7 When you invited aliens of uncircumcised spirit and uncircumcised flesh to my sanctuary, to desecrate my temple;[19] when you sacrificed my food[20]—suet and blood—to me, you[21] broke my covenant with all[22] your abominations. 8 You did not guard my sancta, and appointed them[23] to guard my sanctuary in your stead.'"[24]

### Comment

#### Entrances and Exits of the Sanctuary in Chapter 44

The entrances and exits of the sanctuary form the common denominator of the units that comprise chapter 44, demonstrated by the root *bw'*, which occurs twelve times, as follows:

1. The entrance to the outer eastern gate should be closed permanently. No person may enter (*yābô'î*) it since YHWH entered (*bā'*) it (v. 2). Hence, the *nāśî'* enters (*yābô'*) and exits it on its other side (v. 3). For the laity, access to the outer eastern gatehouse is totally forbidden (vv. 4–5). Ezekiel is brought (*wayyĕbî'nî*) thought the northern gateway and told to pay attention to the entrance (*limĕbô'*) of the temple.

2. It is forbidden to bring (*bahăbî'ăkem, yābô'*) a non-Israelite into the *temenos* where they have served as sanctuary guards. Their place will be taken by the Levites who assisted the Israelites in their idol worship (vv. 7, 9, 10).

3. Only Zadokite priests are permitted to enter (*yābô'û*) and officiate in the temple (v. 16).

4. When they enter (*bĕbô'ām*) the sanctuary, the priests must wear linen vest-

---

18. Read *'el bêt hammerî* with LXX and BHS; the duplicated *'el* and added *yiśrā'ēl* are a homoioteleuton error [618, n. 28]. Cf. Duguid, *Ezekiel and the Leaders*, 122, n. 105, for evidence that *bêt/bĕnê yiśrā'ēl* usually means "the laity," exclusive of the priests and Levites (but is inclusive in 44:22).

19. Tg., Vulg, and Pesh. smooth out the reading by dropping the suffix on the object *'et-bêtî*. This object renders the suffix on *lĕhallĕlô* superfluous. LXX drops it and also begins the verse with the conjunction rather than the preposition [621, n. 37].

20. Tg. *qwrbn*, "sacrifice," grasps the significance of *leḥem*. LXX and Vulg read more literally "bread" [621, n. 38].

21. Reading second person pl. *wattāpērû*, "you have violated," with LXX, Vulg, and Pesh., in place of MT third person pl. *wayyāpērû* [621, n. 40].

22. On *'el* in the sense of *'al*, see Block, *Ezekiel 1–24*, 99, n. 67 [621, n. 41]; also Rooker, *Biblical Hebrew in Transition*, 127–31.

23. The feminine suffix on MT *wattĕśîmun* probably confused a final *mem* for *nun* prior to the shift from the old Hebrew script, when the *mem* and *nun* resembled each other, to the square script when *mem* and *nun* were sharply distinguished [621, n. 43]. Also, in order to avoid two consecutive labial consonants (*mm*) one was changed to *mn*.

24. Many read *lākēn*, "therefore," with LXX (διά τουτο) in place of MT *lākem*, and connect it with the beginning of verse 9, but this is probably a harmonious alteration [621, n. 44].

## PART TWO: EZEKIEL 40–48—THE VISIONARY SANCTUARY AND THE LAND

ments. They don and divest them in assigned sacristies (v. 17)—followed by rules about outer appearances and mourning (vv. 21, 25, 27).

5. It is forbidden to priests to enter (*bĕbô'ām*) the priestly platforms with liquor breath (v. 21)—followed by marital restrictions (v. 22) and their pedagogic and legal obligations (vv. 23–24).

6. Corpse-contaminated priests are forbidden to enter (*yābô'*) the *temenos*, and for their purification they must enter (*bō'ô*) and sacrifice a purification offering (vv. 25, 27).

### Ezekiel 44 and Numbers 18

Ezekiel 44 consists of a series of independent units that are founded linguistically and ideologically on Numbers, chapter 18, as follows:

| Ezekiel 44 | Numbers 18 |
|---|---|
| *wĕāmartā 'el-[bêt ham]merî* | |
| *'el-bêt yiśrāēl* | *lĕōt libĕnê merî* (17:25) |
| *rab-lākem* | *rab-lākem* (16:3, 7) |
| *mikkol tô'ăbôtêkem bêt yiśrāēl* | *wĕlō'-yiqrĕbû 'ôd bĕnê yiśrāēl '* |
| *bĕhăbî'ăkem bĕnê-nēkār...* | *el 'ōhel mô'ēd* |
| *kol-ben-nēkār... lō' yābô' 'el-miqdāšî...* | *lāśē't ḥēṭ'lāmût* |
| *kî 'im-hallĕwiyim...* | *wĕ'ābad hallēwî hû' 'et 'ăbōdat 'ōhel mô'ēd* |
| *wĕnāśĕ'û 'ăwōnām* (vv. 6–10) | *wĕhēm yiśĕ'û 'ăwōnām*, etc. (18:22–23) |
| *bĕhaqrîbĕkem 'et-laḥmî* (v. 7) | |
| *kol-ben nēkār... lō' yābô' 'el-miqdāšî* | *lō'-yiqrab 'îš zār* (17:5) |
| | *wĕzār lō'-yiqrab 'ălēkem* (18:4) |
| *kî 'im-hallĕwiyim...* | *wĕhazzār haqqārēb yāmût* (18:7) |
| *wĕnāśĕ'û 'ăwōnām* (vv. 9–10) | *tiśĕ'û 'et-'ăwōn hammiqdāš...* |
| *...wĕnāśĕ'û 'ăwōnām* (v. 12) | *tiśĕ'û 'et 'ăwōn kĕhunnatĕkem* (18:1) |
| *wĕhēmmā ya'ămĕdû lipnêhem lĕšārĕtām* (v. 11) | *wĕla'ămōd lipnê hā'ēdâ lĕšārĕtām* (16:9) |
| *'et-habbayit... wĕhēmmā ya'ămĕdû lipnêhem* | *wĕgam 'et 'aḥêkā maṭṭēh lēwî...* |
| *lĕšārĕtām* (v. 11) | *wĕyillāwû 'ālêkā wîšārĕtûkā* (18:2) |
| *wĕlāgešet 'al-kōl qādāšay* (v. 13) | *wa'ănî hinnēh nātattî lĕkā e't-mišmeret* |
| *'el qodšê haqqŏdāšîm* (v. 13) | *tĕrûmōtay lĕkol-qōdšê bĕnê yiśrāēl* (18:8) |
| *wĕnātattî 'ōtām šōmĕrê mišmeret habbayit* (v. 14) | *zeh yihyeh lĕkā miqqōdeš haqqodāšîm* (18:9) |
| *wĕhāyĕtā lāhem lĕnaḥălâ* | *wĕšāmĕrû mišmartĕkā ûmišmeret kol-hā'ōhel* (18:3) |
| *'ănî naḥălātām* | *bĕ'arṣām lō' tinḥāl* |
| *wa'ăḥuzzâ lō' titnû lāhem bĕyiśrāēl* | *'ănî ḥelqĕkā* |
| *'ănî 'ăḥuzzātām* (v. 28) | *wĕnaḥălātĕkā bĕtōk bĕnê yiśrāēl* (18:20) |
| *hamminḥâ wĕhaḥaṭṭā't wĕha'āšām* | *lĕkol-minḥātām ûlĕkol-ḥaṭṭā'tām ûlĕkol-'ăšāmām* (18:9) |
| *hēmmâ yo'kĕlûm* | *kol-ḥērem bĕyiśrāēl' lĕkā yihyû* (18:14) |
| *wĕkol-ḥērem bĕyiśrāēl lāhem yihyû* (v. 29) | *wĕzeh-lĕkā tĕrûmat mattānām...* |
| *wĕrē'šît kol-bikkûrê kol wĕkol tĕrûmat* | *rē'šîtām 'ăšer yitĕnû laYHWH lĕkā nĕtattîm...* |
| *kol mikkōl tĕrûmōtēkem* | *bikkûrê kol-'ăšer' bĕ'arṣām...* |
| *lakkōhănîm yihyû* (v. 30) | *lĕkā yihye* (18:11–13) |

| | |
|---|---|
| you shall say to the rebellious [House], the House of Israel | a lesson to rebels (17:25) |
| Enough | Enough (16:3, 7) |
| of your abominations, when you admitted aliens . . . to be in my sanctuary the Levites and will bear their punishment (vv. 6–10) | Henceforth, Israelites shall not trespass on the Tent of Meeting, and thus incur guilt and die Only Levites shall do the work of the temple and they shall bear their punishment, etc. (18:22–23) |
| when you sacrificed my food (v. 7) | An unauthorized person may not serve (17:5) an unauthorized person may not be associated with you (18:4) |
| no foreigner . . . may enter my sanctuary | an unauthorized person who encroaches shall be put to death (18:7) |
| Rather the Levites . . . will bear their punishment (vv. 9–10) . . . will bear their punishment (v. 12) | they will bear the punishment (for encroaching) against the sancta/against your priesthood (18:1) |
| and they shall be the ones to stand before to serve them (v. 11) | to stand before the congregation to serve them (16:9) and also your brother Levites . . . shall be attached to you (18:2) |
| have access to any of my sancta (v. 13) and I will appoint them as guards of the temple compound (v. 14) | I hereby appoint you to guard my gifts, Including all the sancta of the Israelites (18:8) This shall be yours from the most holy sacrifices (18:9) |
| And it shall be their inheritance; I shall be their inheritance And you shall not give them a possession in Israel. I am their possession (v. 28) | Perform your guard duty and the guard duty of the entire congregation (18:3) You shall have not territorial share in their land . . . I am your portion and your share among the Israelites (18:20) |
| the cereal, the purification, the reparation offerings (v. 29) they are the one who will eat | including all your cereal, purification and your reparation offerings (18:9) |
| And they will possess all proscriptions in Israel (v. 29) | Everything proscribed shall be yours (18:14) |
| The first of all produce, the first of all the fruit, and the first gift of all the gifts shall be for the priests (v. 30) | This shall be yours: the gift offerings of their contributions . . . the first processed they bring to YHWH shall be yours (18:11–13) |

As indicated by the parallel wording in Ezek 44 and Num 16–18, the former is based on the latter.[25] Ezekiel may have been attracted to Num 16–18 at this juncture because both the unauthorized (*zār*) Israelite (Num 18:22) and the foreigner (*ben-nēkār*, Ezek 44:9) are banished from the sanctuary. Even more so, it should be noted that these two pericopes are parallel because in both the Levites are "rewarded" as sanctuary guards (Num 18:3–4; Ezek 44:10–11) even though they have assisted the Israelites in defying YHWH (Num 16, Korah; Ezek 44:12; see Excursus 1). Ezekiel follows his priestly predecessors: Korah and his Levite allies, who were assigned the life-

---

25. Kasher, *Ezekiel*, 844–45.

## PART TWO: EZEKIEL 40–48—THE VISIONARY SANCTUARY AND THE LAND

endangering roles as sanctuary guards; so too, the Levites who assisted the Israelites in their idolatrous worship are assigned similar perilous guarding roles in Ezekiel's visionary temple.[26]

**44:4. then he brought me** (*wayĕbîʾēnî*). The subject is YHWH. It cannot be the guide, since Ezekiel is taken from the Israelite to the priestly platform, over the inner gate. The purpose of stating the subject is to let us know that at this point Ezekiel is separated from the celestial guide and he stands alone before YHWH. Ezekiel could reenter the temple grounds either through the north or south outer gateway; the choice is irrelevant. In "front of the temple" means in front of the eastern inner gatehouse from which he would have a clear view of the temple building on the divine platform and the altar on the priestly platform below it. Recall that the sanctuary has no inner wall, allowing for an unobstructed view of the priestly and divine platforms from the Israelite (outer) court below. Alternatively, the celestial guide took the prophet through the northern inner gateway—past the slaughtering tables in the vestibule—and they took their stand between the altar and the ten-step staircase (see Fig. 8) where Ezekiel fell on his face.

***in front of the temple*** (*ʾel-pĕnê habbayit*). This would have to be between the altar and the staircase to the divine platform. Being a priest himself, Ezekiel would have had the right to be anywhere on the priestly platform. For the priestly idiom *ʾel-pĕnê*, see Lev 9:5.

**44:5. YHWH said to me** (*wayyōʾmer ʾēlay YHWH*). Ezekiel stresses that it is YHWH (and not the celestial guide) who addresses him.

***Look closely and listen carefully*** (*śîm libĕbkā ûrĕʾēh bĕʿênêkā ûbĕʾoznĕkā šĕmaʿ*), i.e., "Pay attention." This same wording is written chiastically (*bʿaʾ*) in 40:4. There the reference is to "what I will show you." Here, the reference is the laws that follow immediately.

***temple . . . sanctuary*** (*habbayit . . . hammiqdāš*). Kasher claims that these two words are synonymous in the context, both referring to the entire temple grounds. The result is confusing.[27] Rather, *bayit* refers to the temple into which there is only one entrance (*mābôʾ*), and *miqdāš* takes its usual meaning, "*temenos*, sanctuary, temple grounds" (see n. 551). The use of foreign temple guards as "a breach of the covenant may imply the existence of legislation for a class of lawful keepers of the sanctuary, such as found in Numbers 18:3f."[28]

---

26. For details see Milgrom, *Studies in Levitical Terminology*, 8–36. Fishbane (*Biblical Interpretation in Ancient Israel*, 139) sets up parallels of some of these verses, namely Num 18:1–4, 22–23, and Ezek 44:9–16, but some of the basic terms are, in my opinion, erroneously rendered, specifically (1) *nāśaʾ*, "bear the guilt," rather: "punishment" (Num 18:1); (2) *haqrēb*, "draw near," rather: "associate" (Num 18:2); (3) *lōʾ yiqrab*, "shall not draw near," rather: "encroach" (Num 18:4, 22). Cf. Ezek 44:10–12, 15.

27. Kasher, *Ezekiel*, 856.

28. Duguid, *Ezekiel and the Leaders*, 77; Abba, "Priests and Levites in Ezekiel," 6.

**44:6.** Kasher makes the attractive suggestion that the following prophecy was uttered before the destruction of the first temple; note Israel's description as *merî*, "rebellious," in 2:7; 12:9; 17:12.[29] Also, *rab-lākem*, "enough [of your abominations]," is a phrase borrowed from the Korah pericope (Num 16:3, 7). As suggested by Kasher,[30] just as this phrase is central in the debate about the legitimacy of those who seek the right to officiate in the temple, so here the same struggle ensues—the right of aliens to serve in the sanctuary.

As shown by Block [619], the two times that Ezekiel confronts the *kābôd* at and in the sanctuary terminate with awed prostration, as follows:

| Ezekiel 44:4 | | Ezekiel 43:3, 5 |
|---|---|---|
| | 5 | *wattiśśāēnî rûaḥ* |
| *wayĕbîēnî* | | *wattĕbîēnî* |
| *derek ša'ar haṣṣāpôn* | | |
| *'el-pĕnê habbayit* | | *'el-haḥāṣēr happĕnîmî* |
| *wāēre'* | | |
| *wĕhinnēh* | | *wĕhinnēh* |
| *mālē' kĕbôd-YHWH 'et-bêt YHWH* | | *mālē' kĕbôd-YHWH habbayit* |
| *wāeppōl 'el-pānāy* | 3 | *wāeppōl 'el-pānāy* |
| | 5 | Then the Spirit picked me up |
| Then he brought me | | and brought me |
| through the north gate | | |
| to the front of the temple. | | into the inner court, |
| I looked | | |
| and look, | | and look, |
| the glory of YHWH | | the glory of YHWH |
| filled the temple of YHWH | | filled the temple! |
| Then I fell down on my face. | 3 | and I fell down on my face. |

Almost the same language and order are used when YHWH and the celestial man commission Ezekiel:

---

29. Kasher, *Ezekiel*, 856.
30. Ibid.

PART TWO: EZEKIEL 40-48—THE VISIONARY SANCTUARY AND THE LAND

| Ezekiel 44:5 | Ezekiel 40:4 |
|---|---|
| wayyōʾmer ēlay YHWH | wayĕdabbēr ēlay hāʾîš |
| ben-ʾādām | ben-ʾādām |
| śîm libbĕkā | |
| ûrĕʾēh bĕʿênêkā | rĕʾēh bĕʿênêkā |
| ûbĕʾoznêkā šĕmaʿ | ûbĕʾoznêkā šĕmaʿ |
| | wĕśîm libbĕkā |
| ʾēt kol-ʾăšer ʾănî mĕdabbēr ʾōtāk | lĕkol ʾăšer ʾănî marʾeh ʾōtāk |
| YHWH said to me, "Human, set your heart, and look with your eyes and with your ears hear | And the man said to me, "Human, look with your eyes and with your ears hear and set your heart |
| everything that I tell you." | to all that I show you."[31] |

**44:7. When you admitted aliens** (*bĕhăbîʾăkem bĕnê-nēkār*). There is ample evidence that aliens were employed to perform labor within the first temple (e.g., Josh 9:27; Zech 14:21; cf. Ezra 2:47–58; Neh 7:46–60). Instead of employing *bĕnê yiśrāʾēl*, "Israelites," they employed *bĕnê-nēkār*, "foreigners." The terminological balance may account for the choice of *bĕnê-nēkār*, "foreigners," the only attestation of this term in Ezekiel. However, Duguid suggests that this term betrays its association with Gen 17 and its emphasis on circumcision and the breach of covenant.[32] The clearest example of foreigners serving in the temple is that of the Carians, members of the royal guard in Jerusalem, whose duties included guarding the temple—the royal chapel attached to the palace (2 Kgs 11:4–8). That these foreigners served as "armed guards" in the temple compound is demonstrated by verse 11, which states that they were replaced by Levitic *pĕquddôt*, "armed guards," in place of the banished foreigners. The chief offenders in this crime, however, are not the Levites, but the *people*. Indeed, according to H, the priests are under the control of the laity (Lev 21:24). Thus, it is of no surprise that the people are of primary blame for the sanctuary's sins.

But what is the specific sin of hiring foreign temple guards? It is the violation of the express command of YHWH: *wĕšāmĕrû ʾet-mišmeret ʾōhel môʿēd lĕkōl ʿăbōdat hāʾōhel wĕzār lōʾ-yiqrab ʾălêkem*, "They (the Levites) shall guard the Tent of Meeting including all the work of the tent but the unauthorized should not encroach upon you" (Num 18:4). Thus the responsibility rests with the people to appoint only Levites as sanctuary guards (and handle any work regarding the temple compound) and see to it that no foreigner or any other unauthorized person encroaches upon the sanctuary.

---

31. Adapted from Block, *Ezekiel 25–48*, 619, n. 30.
32. Duguid, *Ezekiel and the Leaders*, 76, n. 103.

## The Sanctuary Personnel and the Nāśî' (Ezekiel 44–46)

***uncircumcised of spirit*** (*'arlê-lēb*), lit., "thickened of heart" (cf. Lev 19:23–25; 26:4), a metaphor denoting a dull, insensitive heart, which can be opened by metaphoric circumcision (Deut 10:16; 30:6).

***uncircumcised of body*** (*'arlê-bāśār*), i.e., a foreigner. May a foreigner offer sacrifices at the sanctuary? If he were a resident alien (*gēr*), the answer would be positive (Lev 17:8–9; Num 15:14, 30–31). Because the alien is obliged to observe all the prohibitive commandments, he is trusted as much as the Israelite to enter the sacred compound in a pure state with an unblemished sacrifice. Not so the foreigner. He, therefore, can only send his sacrifices which would be carefully inspected, as implied by Lev 22:25; cf. Rashi on this verse: an unblemished animal you should accept from them (*b. Hulin.* 13b), to which the verse above alludes: *'ish' 'ish* (Lev 22:18)—to include foreigners who make (sacrificial) vows and donations like Israelites.

**44:8.** ***You have failed to guard my sancta*** (*wĕlō' šĕmartem mišmeret qădāšāy*). The charge is directed at the people who are responsible for guarding the sanctuary and its sancta. The latter refers to the sacred objects in the sanctuary. However, since there are no sacred objects inside Ezekiel's sanctuary, the sancta refer solely to the altar, its utensils, and its sacrifices.

***in your stead*** (*lākem*). Once again, but even more firmly, stressing that the guarding of the sanctuary is the responsibility of the laity.

### EXCURSUS 1: EZEKIEL AND THE LEVITES

Ezekiel 44:9–14 is the only pericope on the Levites' duties in the book.[33] As will be shown, this text contains several key terminological cruces, which have never failed to give engaged scholars a collective exegetical headache and whose questionable resolutions have stood in the way of understanding this pericope. This was my experience too in my first book, when I analyzed the role of the Levites in the wake of the Korahite rebellions (Num 16–18) and referred to Ezekiel's Levites in several footnotes.[34] Except on one point I have not changed my mind on their resolution. My perspective, however, has altered. Instead of Ezekiel supporting Numbers, now it will be Numbers supporting Ezekiel.

As will be shown, the function and placement of the priests and Levites in Ezekiel's temple are based on Num 18:3a and 5a, with one distinction: Whereas in Num 3:7 and 18:3a the Levites and priests share the guarding duties at the entrance to the court, in Ezekiel's temple the Levites and priests are strictly separated: the Levites are in charge of the outer court and all the gatehouses, and the priests are in control of the inner court.

---

33. The Levites' land allotment is mentioned in 45:5 and 48:11–13, which, however, says nothing about their responsibility.

34. Milgrom, *Studies in Levitical Terminology*, nn. 41, 43, 226, 310, 316.

That is why the priests are assigned both rooms of the inner court (40:45–46), as will be demonstrated immediately below, as stations for their armed guards.

First, I must discuss Ezek 40:45–46 because many commentators have assumed that this text actually deals with the Levites:

*zōh halliškâ 'ăšer pānêhā derek haddārôm lakkōhănîm šōmĕrê mišmeret habbāyit*

*wĕhalliškâ 'ăšer pānêhā derek haṣṣāpôn lakkōhănîm šōmĕrê mišmeret hammizbēaḥ*

*hēmmâ bĕnê-ṣādôk haqqĕrēbîm mibĕnê-lēwî 'el YHWH lĕšārĕtô*

This is the room that faces south for the priests who perform guard duty[35] for the temple,

and the room that faces north for the priests who perform guard duty for the altar—

they are the descendants of Zadok, who alone of the descendants of Levi have access to YHWH to serve him.

The assignment of the northern room to the priests, *šōmĕrê mišmeret habbāyit,* "who perform guard duty for the temple," seems erroneous. These allegedly non-Zadokite priests occur nowhere else. Furthermore, their described function is the *ipsissima verba* for the function of the Levites: *šōmĕrê mišmeret habbāyit* (44:14a). Hence, these scholars reason, the term *lakkōhănîm* may be an error for *lallĕwiyyim*.[36] One of these scholars, Menahem Haran, retains the MT, claiming that *lakkōhănîm* betrays a slip of the writer's pen. These priests originally sided with King Manasseh and his idolatrous program.[37] The exile of Jehoiachin (597 BCE) left a shortage of Levites in the Jerusalem temple, which Ezekiel tried to fill by demoting the idolatrous priests to Levites.[38]

These Levite solutions must be rejected out of hand. The two rooms are situated in the inner court to which only priests have access. To ascribe one of them to Levites would undermine the basic premise undergirding the architectural structure of Ezekiel's temple: Priest and non-priests invariably occupy discrete spheres.[39] The MT must be correct.

Another solution is proposed by Eliezer of Beaugency: The priests *šōmĕrê mišmeret habbāyit,* "who perform guard duty in the sanctuary," are the non-Zadokites who *ḥāmĕsû*

---

35. That *šāmar mišmeret* denotes "perform guard duty" was demonstrated in Milgrom, *Studies Levitical Terminology,* 8–16.

36. Even most recently Kasher, *Ezekiel, 25–48,* 797 (Hebrew); ibid., 201.

37. Haran, *Temples and Temple Service,* 104–5. Haran's theory must also be questioned on historical grounds: Why didn't Josiah remove these idolatrous priests—the more so since they allegedly served in the Jerusalem temple? Moreover, Josiah slaughtered priests of YHWH elsewhere (1 Kgs 13:2; 2 Kgs 23:20)—and they are not even accused of being idolatrous! Would he have not done the same to idolatrous Jerusalem priests?

38. Ibid., 224–25.

39. Milgrom, *Studies in Levitical Terminology,* nn. 14, 47.

*tôrātî . . . bēn-qōděš lěḥōl lo' hibdîlû,* "violated my teaching . . . [and] did not distinguish between the sacred and the common" (22:26). They were punished by being denied the priestly right to officiate on the altar (44:13), but were associated with the Levites who also *šōměrê mišmeret habbāyit,* "perform guard duty in the sanctuary" (44:14). That is, the non-Zadokites, being priests, had the right to be quartered on the priestly platform but they were barred from performing sacrifices.

One can hardly overlook the remarkable resemblance between Eliezer of Beaugency's solution and that of Julius Wellhausen. Both postulate that Levites were erstwhile priests who were punished for their idolatrous worship by being demoted to the status of Levites. But here is where the resemblance ends. According to Wellhausen, the demoted priests form a new lower clergy, called "Levites." On the other hand, Eliezer of Beaugency proposes that the "demoted" priests are non-Zadokites who retain their priestly status, but whose workload consists of Levitic guard duty (perhaps on the priestly platform).

There are several problems with Eliezer of Beaugency's solution. The first is that the sinning priests of 22:26 are not called *non-Zadokites*; the *entire priestly cordon* is excoriated. The same objection applies to the alleged identification of the priests of 40:45 as non-Zadokites. In fact, the non-Zadokites appear nowhere in Ezekiel; they are the invention of the commentators. Is there a solution that does not do violence to the text?

The way to unravel the exegetical knot of Ezek 40:45–46 is, first, to tackle the problem of the unattested "non-Zadokite" priests who occupy the northern, south-facing rooms. That problem was, in my opinion, definitively laid to rest by Rodney Duke, who posited that the pronoun *hēmmâ* (v. 46b) refers back to *both* sets of priests, implying that both priestly groups are Zadokites.[40] I would add three items for support: First, note that only the Zadokite priests are granted a land allotment (Ezek 48:11; cf. 45:4), *without mention of any other priestly group*. Thus, all the priests granted a place in the temple personnel are Zadokites. Second, two sacred rooms for eating the most sacred sacrifices are assigned to the priests, *'ăšer-qěrôbîm la YHWH,* "who have access to YHWH" (Ezek 42:13), an expression that denotes the Zadokites (40:46; 44:15, 16; 45:4). These two chambers are reminiscent of the two rooms in the inner court for the priestly guards (40:45–46). Finally, 40:45–46 is modeled on Num 18:5a: *ûšěmartem 'ēt mišmeret haqqōdeš wě'ēt mišmeret hammizbēaḥ,* "You [i.e., the priests] shall do guard duty over the sanctuary and guard duty over the altar."[41] There is no hierarchical distinction between these two classes of priests. Similarly, there is no distinction between the two classes of priests in 40:45–46. Both must be Zadokites. The conclusion is unavoidable: *All* priests granted a place among the sanctuary personnel in the inner court are Zadokites.[42]

---

40. Duke, "Punishment or Restoration?" 75.

41. The foundation of the two classes of priestly guards in Num 18:5 undermines the two source theory of Tuell, *Law of the Temple in Ezekiel 40–48*, 121–46, 175.

42. For Zimmerli it appears unthinkable (*undenkbar*) "that a whole class, united in one family, should be designated as having held true in a time of error and be adjudged worthy of subsequent reward." Zimmerli, *Ezekiel* 2, 456. Which raises doubts whether the priests who were participants in the state of affairs in chapter 8 (cf. 22:26) should be exonerated in 44:15. But the answer is clear: In chapter 8 (and 22:36) the priests are non-Zadokites while in 44:15 the priests are Zadokites.

## PART TWO: EZEKIEL 40–48—THE VISIONARY SANCTUARY AND THE LAND

Ezekiel specifies or alludes to these priests as Zadokites (he himself probably was one), because in his view the Zadokites were, in the main, loyal to the priestly tradition (despite Ezek 22:26). However, the non-Zadokite priests in the countryside allowed idolatrous elements to penetrate into their services, and hence, would have been excluded from Ezekiel's sanctuary.

A word on the alleged power of the Zadokites is in order. It is true that in addition to their demonstrably total control of all ritual connected with the sacrificial altar they also were teachers and judges (44:23–24). As Deut 17:8–11 implies, the priestly role of judging takes place in the Jerusalem supreme court, composed of joint lay and priestly judges, where the former is in charge of *mišpāṭ*, "secular law," and the priests are in charge of *tôrāh*, "religious law." According to Ezekiel, these priests are exclusively Zadokites. However, their power is limited to the sanctuary. They do not form a hierocracy. They are dependent on the good will and trust of the people (44:28–31). Moreover, their land (45:4; 48:11–12) is neither *naḥălâ*, "inheritance," nor *ʾăḥuzzâ*, "possession." Thus they must abide by the unambiguous priestly prohibition against ownership of inheritable land: *běʾarṣām lōʾ tinḥāl*, "you shall not own any inheritable land."

**neither shall you possess any (land) portion in their midst** (*wěḥēleq lōʾ-yihyeh bětôkām*; Num 18:20; cf. Deut 18:1). The same restrictions hold for the Levites except for their cities, which are called *ʾăḥuzzâ*, "possession" (45:5 LXX). This allowance is also in keeping with priestly tradition, which assigned forty-eight fixed cities to the Levites (Num 35:6; Josh 21). Thus, the cities, now centripetally condensed inside the Levitical land track *are* the Levites' *ʾăḥuzzâ*, "possession," but the rest of the Levites' land and all of the priestly lands are inalienable, neither salable nor transferable (i.e., as gifts, Eliezer of Beaugency on 48:14). In any event, in this instance, Ezekiel is obeying the law!

Who are the Zadokites?[43] My own reading begins with 2 Sam 8:17;[44] 15:35, 39; and 20:25, where Zadok and Abiathar are joint high priests during the reign of David. Solomon, son of David, banishes Abiathar from his office, as told in 1 Kgs 2:26–27 (see 1 Sam 2:27–36) leaving the high priesthood exclusively to the line of Zadok. The conflict is strictly political: Abiathar had sided with his rival (older) brother Adonijah (1 Kgs 1:7). The subsequent history of the Zadokites is murky. The only assured development is that the Zadokites seize control of the Jerusalem temple. They were invariably loyal to the Davidic line (2 Sam 15:16; 19:22; 20:25; 1 Kgs 1:8; 4:2; 1 Chr 15:11; 16:39; 18:16; 29:22). Thus, the progeny of Zadok the high priest become the sole priests of the temple, whereas the line of Abiathar settled in Anathot (1 Kgs 2:26–27) and probably in the countryside. The latter clergy were suddenly thrown out of work as a consequence of the deuteronomic reform (621 BCE). Despite the outspoken demand of the deuteronomist school that the status of the entire Levitical house be of equal validity (Deut 18:1–6), the

---

43. There are as many answers as answerers. A brief survey can be found in Milgrom, *Numbers*, 476–82.

44. See McCarter, *II Samuel*, 253, n. 17.

Zadokites of Jerusalem, in defiance of their own torah, Deuteronomy, would not allow non-Zadokite (i.e., non-Jerusalem) priests to officiate in the temple (2 Kgs 23:9).

It is, therefore, no accident that Ezekiel (most likely a Zadokite) continues the policy of his Zadokite predecessors in his visionary temple: only Zadokites may officiate as priests. Ezekiel, however, adds an explicit *religious* rationale: "because they [the Levites] used to serve them [the people] before their idols" (44:12). The "Levites" here maybe an oblique, indirect reference to the erstwhile non-Zadokite priests outside of Jerusalem. Indeed, the fact that the officiating priests in Ezekiel's temple are exclusively Zadokites implies that the non-Zadokites are banished from the altar of the new temple as they were banished from the (Josianic) altar of old. It is not too difficult to presuppose that the people, deprived of their local sanctuaries, continued to turn to their former spiritual leaders for religious counsel. The latter continued to serve them, not as priests (which was disallowed) but as Levites. They may have been defrocked as priests, but their status as Levites (lit., Levitical priests, Deut 18:1; cf. Ezek 13:19; 44:15) could not be withdrawn. These Levites (erstwhile non-Zadokite priests), however, are excoriated by Ezekiel for assisting their lay charges in their worship of idolatry. How was this possible after the deuteronomic reform?

A distinction must be made between the official, state-endorsed religion and the private, clandestine practices of the people (*bassēter*; Deut 7:13; 27:15). Thus, Deuteronomy also anticipates (or reflects) a situation that even after the obliteration of the state-sponsored cults (in the Josianic reform), private ones continued furtively, as evidenced by the worship of the queen of heaven (Jer 7:18; 44:17–18, 25),[45] the astral gods on rooftops (Jer 19:13; 32:39), the "image rooms" (Ezek 8:12) and child sacrifice in the open country (Isa 57:5; cf. Ezek 20:31). That these cults were private and unofficial is substantiated by the absence of a clergy, the quintessential component of an officially sponsored cult.[46] Is it not likely that the erstwhile non-Zadokite priests, now reduced to the status of Levites, would offer their expertise in worshiping Israel's national deity, YHWH; would—for the sake of needed income—allow their heretofore religious practices to be infiltrated by the people's idolatrous rituals while worshiping with them in their own localities.

The recent archaeological discovery of figurine hordes in the very shadow of the Jerusalem temple corroborates the few textual references on the people's idolatry. The distribution of nearly 2,000 figurines over the eighth to the sixth centuries is homogeneous.[47] This means that after the Josianic reform, profusion and practice of figurine worship continued unabated. Thus Ezekiel fires his verbal missiles at the idolatry of his own time in Jerusalem and Judah, an idolatry (*gillûlêkem*, 44:10, 12) practiced by the people and supported by their Levite advisors.

---

45. M. Smith's objections notwithstanding, "A Note on Burning Babies," 477–79.
46. Cf. Kaufmann, *The Religion of Israel*, 3:274–75; Greenberg, *Ezekiel 1-20*, xxiii, n. 47.
47. Kletter, *Judean Pillar-Figurines*, 384–85, Fig. 3; D. M. Sharon, "A Biblical Parallel?" 100–108, esp. 105.

Because of their defection, the Levites will be punished: *wĕnāśĕ'û 'ăwōnām*, lit., "they will bear their (own) punishment" (44:10, 12; cf. 14:10), namely, they will be barred from officiating at the altar or handling the sancta (44:13). Also, the absence of the Levitic prebend, the tithe (cf. Num 18:21–24), may imply that it was an additional penalty imposed on the Levites.[48] This is the rendering of all commentators and translators. But there is another rendering, which I find preferable: "they [the Levites] will bear their punishment," i.e., they will bear the responsibility if they fail to prevent encroachment. The nature of their punishment is not specified. However, the standard penalty is *napeš taḥat nepeš*, lit., "life for life" (cf. 2 Kgs 10:24), except that in the case of sanctuary encroachment, that is, encroaching on the property of YHWH, the penalty would be death by divine agency.

A third rendering is possible: "they [the Levites] bore their punishment."[49] The Levites have *already* paid for their sin; namely, they have been exiled alongside their fellow Israelites and, together with them, they will be redeemed without requiring their repentance but only their shame (v. 13b). They may no longer serve as priests (v. 13a). Instead, they will be assigned their ancient, venerable role as sanctuary guards at every gateway (Num 18:3) and as assistants to lay worshipers and their sacrifices (Num 16:6).[50] However, the problem alluded to above continues to persist: The Levites are assigned the same function as the priests *šōmĕrê mišmeret habbāyit*, "who perform guard duty for the temple" (40:45; 44:14a; cf. 45:5).

The resolution of this problem, perhaps, lies in realizing that the term *bayit* (lit., "house") means two different things in 40:45 and 44:14. In the architectural chapters 40–42, *habbāyit* refers only to the temple building (twenty-one times). The meaning, "temple compound/sacred precinct/*temenos*," appears beginning with chapter 43. When YHWH enters the temple, the *bayit*, "house," is transformed into the *bayit*, "the sanctuary" (see 43:12). Thus, 40:45 refers to the *priestly* cordon responsible for guarding the temple building (including the altar, the inner court, and its gatehouses, see below) whereas 44:14 refers to the Levitic cordon responsible for guarding the outer court (and its gatehouses).[51] As theoretically satisfying as this solution appears, it does not satisfy textually. The term *bayit* possibly refers to the sanctuary enclosure only in *ša'ărê habbayit*, "the gate of the sanctuary" (44:11), namely, all the gates and *mĕšārĕtê habbayit*,

---

48. Kaufmann, *Religion of Israel*, nn. 190, 434.

49. Treating *wĕnāśĕ'û* as a perfect. So also Fishbane, "Sin and Judgment," 140, but without corroboration or discussion of its implications.

50. For fuller detail, see below.

51. Duguid, *Ezekiel and the Leaders*, 88–90 argues that just as the priests are overseers (more precisely, "guards") of the *qdš*, "sancta" (Num 18:3), and the same term *qdš* is used for the guardianship of the Levites (Num 3:32), the same fluidity is evidenced with the term *bayit* in Ezek 40:45 and 44:14, the former verse referring to the responsibility of the priests and the latter of the Levites. His conclusion is correct but for the wrong reasons. In Num 3:32 Kohathite Levites carry the *qdš*, "sancta" (v. 3), on the wilderness march. But once the camp rests, the sancta revert to the charge of the priests. Thus, the term *qdš* does not change in meaning. The Kohathite Levites are given a higher, holier status than the rest of the Levites (cf. Num 18:1) only during the movement of the camp. Besides, one cannot reason from Numbers (P) to Ezekiel: P does not indulge in protean terminology.

"servitors of the sanctuary" (45:5; 46:24). However, in the remaining twelve attestations of *bayit* in chapters 43–48, it can only mean "house," i.e., YHWH's residence, the temple. Outside of the book of Ezekiel, *bayit* never appears as a synonym of the entire enclosed sanctuary. This solution, at best, is an attractive conjecture.

But why is there a need for two priestly cordons, one for the temple building and one for the altar (40:45–46), and correspondingly for two priestly rooms for eating their meals and changing their clothing (42:13–14)? The answer comes to light upon examining two priestly pentateuchal verses:

*'ak-'el-kĕlê haqqōdeš wĕ'el-hammizbēaḥ*, "to the *sanctuary* vessels and to the *altar*" (Num 18:3b)

*mišmeret haqqōdeš weēt mišmeret hammizbēaḥ*, "guarding the *sanctuary* and guarding the *altar*" (Num 18:5a)

As I noted back in 1970,[52] P postulates two areas for priestly guard duty, hence the necessity for two cordons—the (entrance to) the sanctuary (and its sancta) and the altar (and the inner court). Thus, Ezekiel, who bases the reconstruction of his temple on the priestly pentateuchal prototype (Num 18:1–7), also prescribes two priestly cordons of guards for precisely the same areas—the sanctuary building and the altar.

Is it possible to settle on a single solution for the crux of 40:45–46? The proposal that *šōměrê mišmeret habbāyit*, "performers of guard duty of the temple" (40:46), refers to the Levites—that is, *lakkōhănîm* is an error for *lallĕwiyyim*—must be rejected out of hand; there is no basis for it in the versions. We need not give it further thought, since we have two other solutions that do not do violence to the text. The first, as demonstrated, is the proposal of Eliezer of Beaugency, that the "priests" of 40:45 are the non-Zadokite priests who are contrasted with the Zadokite priests of verse 46. It is assumed that the priestly group condemned for flirting with idolatry, i.e., *ḥāmĕsû tôrātî*, "doing violence to my Torah" (22:26), are the non-Zadokites, who are being punished by being barred from the altar, (i.e., the priestly platform) and assigned Levitic duties, such as doing guard duty (perhaps limited to the inner altar). Otherwise they retain their priestly privileges. In this respect, the sinning non-Zadokite priests would resemble H's physically blemished priests, who were barred from officiating at the altar but *leḥemĕlōhāyw miqqodšê haqqŏdāšîm ûmin-haqqŏdāšîm yō'kal*, "He may eat the food of his God, of the most holy and of the holy" (Lev 21:22). Therefore, Ezekiel's non-Zadokite priests, though ineligible to offer sacrifices, were granted separate kitchens (46:10–20) and separate dining rooms (42:13).

The other (preferable) solution (as alluded to above) distinguishes not between "priests" but between the two *bayit* terms: In 40:45 *bayit* stands for the temple, and in 44:14 it stands for the temple grounds, i.e., the *temenos*. Thus some priests perform guard duty at the temple (40:45)—just as they were commanded in P, *ûšĕmartem ʾēt mišmeret haqqōdeš*, "to perform guard duty at the shrine" (Num 18:5aα)—whereas the others, *mišmeret hammizbēaḥ*, guarded the altar area (40:46), again following the

---

52. Milgrom, *Studies in Levitical Terminology*, 14, n. 47.

priestly (pentateuchal) prototype, *mišmeret hammizbēaḥ* in Num 18:5aβ. Following Duke's insight, the advantage of this interpretation is that *hēmmâh bĕnê ṣādôq*, "they are the descendants of Zadok," (40:46) refers back to both sets of priests. Thus, the non-Zadokite priests are eliminated from this pericope. All priests are Zadokites, some guarding the altar area, others guarding the sacred compound. Both groups divide into separate rooms for donning their sacred (contagious) clothing, for preparing their food (separate kitchens), and for eating their most sacred prebends (42:8; 46:20). However, they unite into one Zadokite entity when assigned a land allotment (48:11). Indeed, there is no place for non-Zadokites in Ezekiel's sanctuary. They probably must be identified with the egregiously sinning priests (22:26). Note the difference between the sinning priests and the sinning Levites. The sinning priests were idolaters; *hāmĕsû tôrātî*, "they violated my torah," *wayĕhallĕlû qŏdāšay*, "and desecrated my sancta." The sinning Levites, on the other hand, were only assistants to the priests and the people; *yĕšārĕtû 'ōtām lipnê gillûlêhem*, "they served them before their gods" (44:12), Hence, the non-Zadokite priests are banished from Ezekiel's sanctuary, but the Levites are retained.

Thus, there is no conflict between 40:45–46 and 44:14. The latter—which speaks of the Levites as *šōmĕrê mišmeret habbāyit* (or *mĕšārtîm 'et habbayit*, "who serve the sacred precinct/*temenos*," 44:11; 45:5; 46:24)—refers only to the Levites' guard duty in the sanctuary gatehouses and Levitic assistance with the laity's animal sacrifices (slaughtering them) in the outer court. In sum, the Levites are not mentioned either by error or design in 40:45–46. This passage deals only with the Zadokite priestly guards in the inner court. We can now turn to the only pericope dealing with the Levitic custodial responsibility in the sacred precinct—44:9–14.

## EXCURSUS 2: TERMINOLOGY (44:9–14)

As was the case with 40:45–46, the precise understanding of 44:9–14 will depend upon the deciphering of its terminology. The key terms are *ben-nēkār*, *bayit*, *miqdāšî*, and *wĕnāśā' 'āwōn*.

1. *ben-nēkār*, "foreigner." This term has been identified with Gibeonites (Josh 9:27); Solomon's Canaanite slaves (1 Kgs 9:20), referred to as Solomon's slaves among the returnees to Zion (Ezra 2:55; Neh 7:57); the *nĕtinîm* (Ezra 2:43–54; Neh 7:47–56), and others.[53] I prefer to identify them with the Carites[54] (2 Kgs 11:4), who served as mercenary guards of the palace, and since the temple served as a royal chapel, it was a simple matter for the Carites to take up position there. It is only natural that the illegitimate guards of Solomon's temple/palace, the Carites, should be replaced by legitimate, Torah-ordained guards, the Levites.[55] See further on verse 7.

2. *habbayit*, "the temple compound, *temenos*" (44:11, 14). It was shown (in v. 12) above that *bayit* in this pericope refers not to the temple building—its exclusive meaning

---

53. See Milgrom, *Studies in Levitical Terminology*, 9.
54. Ibid., 149, n. 78.
55. Ibid., 9.

in chapters 40–42—but to the temple compound, the *temenos*—though not in its entirety. The Levites, like the laity, have no access to the inner court, the exclusive domain of the priests. There may be a hairline difference between the Levites and the laity; the Levites have access to the northern inner gatehouse, where they slaughter the laity's most holy sacrifices. But this locus (rather than its function) is no innovation. As temple guards, they are stationed in all the gatehouses. Indeed, their function is defined with precision: *měšārtîm pěquddôt 'el ša'ărê habbayit ûměšārtîm 'et habbāyit*, "performing guard duty at the gatehouses of the sacred precincts and serving the sacred precinct" (44:11a). The latter duty refers to slaughtering the sacrificial animals (44:11b), cooking the meat of the well-being offering (46:24), and probably to other minor ways the Levites could be of assistance to the worshiping laity (44:11b). All this is subsumed under the locus *bayit*, the temple compound.[56]

3. *miqdāšî*, "my sanctuary, sacred compound." This word occurs seventeen times in the book of Ezekiel.[57] Contrariwise, the word *bētî* occurs only once, in 44:7—*lihyôt běmiqdāšî lěhallělô 'et-bêtî*, "to be in my sanctuary, to desecrate my house" (44:7), where *bētî* was necessitated as a synonym of *běmiqdāšî*, and *bētî* more precisely means "my temple precincts." The synonymity of these two words leads to the question: Why the exclusivity of *běmiqdāšî*, or rather, why the avoidance of *bētî*? The answer already has been given (44:12). Once YHWH enters the temple it is transformed from a house of stone to a structure of holiness, or a sanctuary. But when the sanctuary is referred to as *miqdāšî*, "my sanctuary," i.e., it is as if God is in *his house*; it is his "sanctuary," even if he does not occupy it.

The near equivalence of these two terms is exhibited in 45:18, 20: *wěḥiṭṭē'tā 'et-hammiqdāš* is balanced by *wekippartem 'et-habbayit*, "you shall decontaminate the sanctuary . . . you shall purge the house," that is, "the sanctuary," where the equivalence of *miqdāš* and *bayit* is enhanced by the (close) equivalence of *ḥiṭṭē'*, "de-sin," and *kipper*, "purge," and in *yěkappěrû 'et-hammizbēaḥ wěṭihărû 'ōtô*, "they shall purge the altar and you shall cleanse it" (43:26), where *ṭihēr*, "cleanse," is the precise equivalent of *ḥiṭṭē'*.

There is one case where *miqdāš* denotes, not the "sacred compound" of YHWH, but "the (reduced) sacred compound" of the priests (45:18), i.e., their middle platform and sacristies (Ezek 42), where *wěḥiṭṭētā 'et-hammiqdāš*, "you shall decontaminate the sacred precincts," is executed by smearing the decontaminating blood on the entrance to the temple building, the corners of the altar and the entrance to the priestly platform (45:19), which corresponds precisely to the vulnerable extremity points of the priestly consecrands (Exod 29:20; Lev 8:23). If this is correct, then *miqdāš* would be an attempt to separate the priestly area as a "sanctuary" in relation to the lower Israelite level, which would be a nonsanctuary. However, this verse can be interpreted unexceptionally; see the COMMENT on 45:18–20.

---

56. For this meaning of *bayit*, see 43:11, 12 (2), 21; 44:5, 11, 14; 45:5, 20; 46:24; 48:21; see further Milgrom, *Studies in Levitical Terminology*, 14, n. 47.

57. Ezek 5:11; 8:6; 9:6, 11; 21:2; 23:38, 39; 24:21; 25:3; 28:18; 37:26, 28; 44:7, 8, 9, 15, 16.

4. *wĕnāśĕ'û 'ăwōnām* (44:10b, 12b).[58] In Ezekiel there are two justifiable renderings of this clause. First, "*they [the Levites] will bear their [own] punishment.*" The idiom *nāśā' 'āwōn*, where *'āwōn* means punishment, occurs twenty-seven times in the Hebrew Bible.[59] The "punishment" here (vv. 10b, 12b) is explained twice by the idiom *wĕnāśĕ'û 'ăwōnām*. The Levites are assigned the perilous task of guarding the sanctuary (vv. 11, 14) against all unauthorized incursions, advertent and inadvertent alike. If they fail the penalty is death by divine agency.[60] Moreover, the penalty falls on the entire Levitic cordon. As for the intrusive prohibition not to serve as priests (v. 13), it is not a punishment, as claimed by the school of Wellhausen, but a statement of the responsibility of the Levites, as based on Num 18:3aβ (see no. 2, below). Indeed, it must be acknowledged that Ezekiel grounds his provisions for the Levites on Num 18:1–7, 23, as follows:

1. The division of the priests into two groupings (40:45–46) is based on *ûšĕmartem 'et mišmeret haqqōdeš wĕ'et mišmeret hammizbēaḥ*, "you (the priests) shall perform guard duty of the sanctuary and guard duty of the altar" (Num 18:5a), as shown above.

2. The prohibition against Levitic access to the sacred and most sacred objects and to officiate on the altar (44:13a) is based on *'ak 'el-kĕlê haqqōdeš wĕ'el-hammizbēaḥ lō' yiqrābû*, "but to the sanctuary vessels and to the altar they (the Levites) shall have no access" (Num 18:3aβ).

3. Levitic guard duty (44:14) is founded on *wĕšāmĕrû 'et mišmartĕkā ûmišmeret kol-hā'ōhel*, "And they shall perform your guard duty and the guard duty of the entire Tent" (Num 18:3aα, cf. 4aβ).

4. The banning of foreigners (*bĕnê-nēkār*) from the sanctuary (44:9) is grounded on *wĕzār lō' yiqrab 'ălêkem*, "the unauthorized should not encroach on you" (Num 18:4b).

5. The priestly guard duty of the inner court (44:15a, 16b) is based on *tišmĕrû 'et-kĕhunnatkem lĕkol-dĕbar hammizbēaḥ*, "you shall guard your priestly obligation in everything regarding the altar" (Num 18:7a).

6. The Levitic responsibility for encroachment upon the *temenos* by the unauthorized (foreigners on the outer court and Israelite laity—including Levites—on the inner court) is founded on *wĕhēm yiśĕ'û 'ăwōnām*, "and they (the Levites) will bear their (own) punishment" (Num 18:23aβ).

---

58. For a comprehensive discussion of this term, cf. B. Schwartz, "Term or Metaphor: Biblical *nasa' 'awon*," 149–71; B. Schwartz, "Bearing of Sin in Priestly Literature," 3–21.

59. Exod 28:38, 43; Lev 5:1, 6, 17; 7:18; 10:17; 17:16; 19:8, 17; 20:17, 19; Num 5:31; 14:34; 18:1, 23; 30:15; Isa 33:24; Ezek 4:4, 5, 6; 14:10; 24:23; 44:10, 12; Hos 4:8.

60. See Milgrom, *Leviticus 17–22*, 1488–90. Whereas the encroacher is put to death by the armed Levitic guards, the failed Levitic guards obviously cannot be killed by human agency, but only by God; see Milgrom, *Studies in Levitical Terminology*, 21; Milgrom, *Numbers*, 342–43, 423–24.

As pointed out by Duke,[61] the responsibility of the Levites to guard the sanctuary is commensurate with the role of the watchman/prophet in Ezek 3:16–21. Both bear the penalty of death if they fail as guards. Thus, guard duty (vv. 11, 14) indeed bears a punishment. The perilous lot of the cordon of guards is exemplified by "Now Jehu had stationed eighty men outside, saying, "Whoever allows any of those to escape whom I deliver into your hands shall forfeit his life" (2 Kgs 10:24b). The Levites need be eternally vigilant—their *lives* are at stake.

Moreover, Ezekiel is basing his notion of Levitic responsibility squarely on precedent. The Korahite Levites have sinned by demanding the status of priests (Num 16:10). Nonetheless, they are appointed sanctuary guards! Is this a case of appointing the fox to guard the chicken coop? This conundrum is resolved by Num 18:3–5, 23. The Levite guards will pay with their lives whenever encroachment occurs. So too Ezekiel's Levites are appointed sanctuary guards, *šōměrê mišmeret habbāyit* (Ezek 44:14), for their sin in abetting the people's worship of idolatry (44:12). Presumably, they face death when they fail to prevent encroachment. Thus, guard duty in the sanctuary is far from being an award; rather, it is a punishment.

However, Ezekiel does not slavishly imitate his priestly (P) precedent. In two matters he flatly reverses the explicit laws of P. First, P ordains that priests and Levites share the guarding duty—*wěšāměrû mišmartām*, "they (the Levites) will perform your (the priestly) guard duty" (Num 18:3aα). The custody of the Tabernacle was neatly divided between the two sacred orders: priests on the inside, Levites on the outside, and *both at the entrance*. Ezekiel rejected the latter; priests and laity were sharply separated, and contact between them strictly forbidden. Priests controlled the inner court, an eight-stepped platform above the outer court where the Levites held sway, as well as in all the gatehouses.[62]

A more radical change in the status of the Levites is contained in Ezekiel's prescription that the Levites (and the priests) are to be allocated territory (48:13–14) when the holy land is re-divided among all the twelve tribes. This constitutes an unqualified contradiction of the express prohibition against the Levites (and the priests) possessing any inheritable land (Num 18:20, 24b).

This reading of *wěnāśěʾû ʿăwōnām*, namely, that the Levite guards are responsible for their mistakes, resolves a number of difficulties: (1) It is no longer necessary to follow the interpretation of Ezek 44:13a, namely, that the prohibition against the Levites officiating (on the altar) implies that hitherto they were priests;[63] Ezekiel is merely applying the Levitic prohibition of Num 18:3bα (no. 2, above). (2) As demonstrated above, there

---

61. See Duke, "Punishment or Restoration?" 66, n. 8.

62. However, the priests themselves obviously use the Levite-controlled gates. Therefore, it must be assumed that the prohibition against contact between the two applies when the priests are officiating; namely, when they are wearing their sacred and *contagious* vestments. The gate entrances would only be used on entering and exiting; namely, when they are not officiating.

63. Either of countrywide small sanctuaries (high places; see Wellhausen, *Prolegomena to the History of Ancient Israel*, 124–26, n. 24), or in the Jerusalem temple (see Haran, *Temples and Temple Service*, 104–7. For this possible interpretation, see verse 13.

is no need to posit a missing Levitic group in 40:45; Num 18:5a shows that there was a priestly tradition of two groupings of priests in the Tabernacle. (3) The exclusive right and responsibility of the priests to guard the inner court (44:15a, 16b) is not Ezekiel's innovation; it is grounded in Num 18:7a. (4) The presence of (probably God-fearing) foreign guards (*běnê-nēkār*) in the sanctuary (cf. 2 Kgs 11:6) may not be a sin in itself but an exegetical extension of the *zar*, "unauthorized" (Num 18:4b) (no. 4, above). (5) The Levites' punishment for their failure to guard the sanctuary (*wěnāśě'û 'ăwōnām*, 44:10bβ, 12bβ) is not for their complicity in Israel's idol worship, but the theoretic application of their responsibility in guarding the tabernacle, as explicitly stated in P; namely, they will take responsibility for their errors, *wěhēm yiśě'û 'ăwōnām*, "and they [the Levites] will bear their [own] punishment" (Num 18:23aβ).[64]

A second justifiable rendering of the clause renders *wěnāśě'û 'ăwōnām* as "they [the Levites] bore their own punishment."[65] The verb *nś'* occurs either as imperfects or as perfects attached to a *waw*. The context invariably bears a future sense; hence, the *waw* is sequential. There is one exception: The context of Ezek 44:10 and 12 is in the perfect. It speaks of Israel's past sins, before they were exiled, when they engaged in idol worship. Hence, the initial *waw* is not consecutive but copulative, meaning when the Levites bore their punishment, namely, when they were exiled together with their people. Thus, both Israel and the Levites were punished and restored—Israel to its land and the Levites to their former assigned position (according to P) as temple guards. Moreover, just as Israel is redeemed without further punishment or the need to repent (but only to express shame, e.g., 16:52, 54, 62, 63) so too the Levites will neither be punished nor required to repent (but only to be ashamed, 44:13).

Therefore, the idiom, *wěnāśě'û 'ăwōnām*, in Ezekiel is not a statement about the future, declaring that the Levites will be punished for aiding their fellow countrymen to worship idols. The Levites have paid for their idolatrous collusion. And as God will restore Israel to its land where they will allocate the land among the twelve tribes more equitably (45:1–8; 48:1–29) than in the past (Josh 15–21), so God will fulfill for the Levites the role that he set out for them in the priestly tradition—to be the temple guards (Num 18:3a, 4a) and assistants to the lay worshipers (Num 16:9). Moreover, Ezekiel is basing himself on a priestly, pentateuchal precedent: The Levite rebel chieftains led by Korah were slain by God (Num 16:35), and the Levites themselves were assigned perilous guard duties in the sanctuary (Num18:3a, 4a).[66] The Levites' workload, however,

---

64. These strictures also strike at the rendering I offered in 1970, "They [the Levites] will bear their [the Israelites'] punishment" (*Studies in Levitical Terminology*, 22–32 n. 2). Besides, I was subsequently convinced by Duguid's argument (*Ezekiel and the Leaders*, 77, n. 114), who follows Whybray (*Thanksgiving for a Liberated Prophet*, 31–57), that the prevention of encroachment is the sin of the Levite guards, and, by the rule of Occam's razor, this is the simplest and, hence, the most accurate reading. Indeed, I admitted as much when I wrote that the principle "was not vicariousness" (*Studies in Levitical Terminology*, 32, n. 2).

65. To the best of my knowledge, only Fishbane (*Biblical Interpretation in Ancient Israel*, 134) adopts this rendering, but without annotation or discussion.

66. Cf. also Cook, "Innerbiblical Interpretation in Ezekiel 44," 199.

undergoes a slight change. They will supplant the lay worshipers as slaughterers of every sacrificial animal, and, in stark contradiction to Num 18:24, they will be granted a block of contiguous inheritable property for themselves and their descendants.

Thus, there are two viable interpretations of the idiom, *wĕnāśĕ'û 'ăwōnām* (Ezek 44:10b, 12b). Each may be subject to challenge. Both, however, share a common basis, which, I aver, is beyond question: Ezekiel construed the function of the Levites and their distinction from the priests largely on the basis of the priestly tradition embodied in Num 18. Thus, the Levites were not former priests who were demoted because they colluded with the people in their idol worship. The Levites are merely assuming the tasks assigned to them by the priestly tradition (P)—as guards in the sanctuary (Num 18:3a, 4a).

Since Ezekiel posits absolute separation between priests and non-priests, he takes pains to confine the Levites within the outer, lower court and in the gatehouses. The laity is also restricted even further, to the outer court; it has no access to the gatehouses of the inner court; its erstwhile right of slaughtering its sacrificial animals is transferred to the Levites, and the slaughtering takes place either inside or below the (northern) inner gate. This cultic change, though slight, shows that Ezekiel was not slavishly chained to his priestly tradition. His relative independence of imagination and thought can be demonstrated further by his divergence from the tradition, such as in the allotment of land to the Levitic tribe (48:13–14) and in the right granted to resident aliens (*gērîm*) to own and bequeath landed property (47:22–23). Thus, Ezekiel was not engaged in abstract hermeneutics when he based the function of the Levites (and the priests) on the theoretical prescriptions of Num 18. Rather, he applied himself creatively and innovatively to these priestly precedents as the basis of his vision of the Levitic (and priestly) functions in the sanctuary.[67]

## Protecting the Sacred Space (44:9–14)

TRANSLATION

9 This has Lord YHWH proclaimed: No alien, uncircumcised of spirit[68] and flesh found among the descendants of Israel[69] may come into my sanctuary.
10 But[70] the Levites, who deserted[71] me when Israel strayed from me,[72] stray-

---

67. See Milgrom, *Studies in Levitical Terminology*, nn. 40–41, 47.

68. Foreigners are categorically outside of the covenant community. Hence they are not spiritually ("uncircumcised of heart") and physically ("uncircumcised of flesh") identified as Israelites.

69. Even the children of *gērîm*, "foreign residents," whom you have brought, retain the status of permanent slaves (Lev 25:25–26). So too even the descendants of resident foreigners retain their foreign status and are banned from entering the sanctuary.

70. The verbal idea of *kî 'im hallĕwiyyîm* is picked up from *yābô'* in the previous verse (cf. 33:11; 36:22; 44:22). See Duke, "Punishment or Restoration?" 65 [624, n. 60].

71. *rāḥăq*, "defected." A metaphoric rather than a literal meaning (e.g., "so far from," Ezek 8:6; 11:15); antonym of *qārab*, "come spiritually closer" (to God; e.g., Num 27:1–3; 36:1).

72. LXX's omission of *'ăšer tā'û* may be homoioteleuton, the scribe's eye having skipped from one

ing from me after their fetishes, they will bear their punishment.[73] **11** They will serve inside my sanctuary doing guard duty at the gatehouses of the sanctuary and doing the sanctuary chores. They will do the slaughtering[74] of the whole burnt offerings and the well-being offerings for the people;[75] standing before them[76] and serving them.[77] **12** Because they served them in the presence of their idols, who caused the house of Israel[78] to stumble into sin, I raised my hand in oath against them[79]—the proclamation of my Lord YHWH—that they will bear their punishment.[80] **13** They will not have access[81] to me to perform priestly duties for me, or come near to any of my sancta or to the most holy offerings.[82] They will endure the disgrace of their loathsome acts. **14** And I will appoint them as guards of the temple compound, janitors for its maintenance and all the work that is done there.[83]

---

*ăšer* to the other, though most scholars delete the phrase in MT as a gloss [624, n. 61]. Alternatively, MT can plausibly be rendered "who strayed from me after . . ."

73. Lit., "bear their guilt"; cf. Milgrom, *Studies in Levitical Terminology*, 22–28; Schwartz, "Bearing of Sin in Priestly Literature," 3–21. Most translations read, lit., "they will bear their guilt."

74. Slaughtering the sacrificial animal is the duty of the offerer (Lev 1:5; 3:2). So is flaying, quartering, and washing the carcass (Lev 1:6, 9). Since the slaughtering of the *ʿōlâ*, "whole burnt offering," was performed inside the inner (northern) gate, it seems probable that the other acts performed on the carcass—flaying, quartering, and washing—were also done by the Levites. Since the slaughtering of the well-being offering occurred in the outer court, there was no difficulty for all the other preliminary sacrificial acts to be carried out by the offerer.

75. *ʿōlâ wāzebaḥ*, lit., "the whole burnt and well-being offerings," is the common expression for all the blood sacrifices, including the *ḥaṭṭāʾt*, "purification offering," and the *ʾāšām*, "reparation offering." Originally, I presume, the *ʿōlâ*, "whole burnt offering," was the sole expiatory sacrifice, hence the origin of the term, *ʿōlâ wāzebaḥ* (Lev 7:8; Josh 22:26, 28, 29; 2 Kgs 5:17; Jer 7:22; 17:28; Ezek 40:42). This last citation (Ezek 40:42) proves that this idiom is an abbreviation of all the blood sacrifices, because three verses earlier, in Ezek 40:39, the same list includes the *ʿōlâ*, the *ḥaṭṭāʾt*, and the *ʾāšām*. This idiom is also found in Num 15:3, 5, but the subject there is the votive and freewill sacrifices, which preclude expiatory sacrifices (i.e., the *ḥaṭṭāʾt* or the *ʾāšām*).

76. It is fitting to compare *wĕhēmâ yaʿămōdû lipnêhem lĕšārĕtām* (44:11) and its pentateuchal model, *wĕlaʿămōd lipnê hāʿēdâ lĕšārĕtām* (Num 16:9), to realize that the term *ʿēdâ*, which proliferates in LBH passages (except in 2 Chr 5:6, where it copies its *Vorlage*, 1 Kgs 8:5) is substituted by *qāhāl* or, as here, by it. For its socio-political significance. Cf. Milgrom, "Priestly Terminology," 66–76. Note also that *hāʿēdâ* (Lev 24:10) is replaced by *qāhāl* (Ezek 23:47); cf. Rooker, *Biblical Hebrew in Transition*, 143–46.

77. There is no need to regard *yĕšārĕtû* as a scribal error for the perfect *šērĕtu*, Radak; *BHS*; Zimmerli, *Ezekiel 2*, 449. The imperfect also has a customary case, cf. Cooke, *Ezekiel*, 481 [625, n. 64].

78. On MT *wĕhāyû*, see Rubenstein, "The Anomalous Perfect," 62–69 [625, n. 65].

79. *nāśaʾtî yādî ʿălêhem*, lit., "I raised my hand against them" [625, n. 66].

80. Cf. n. 610.

81. As a possible rendering of *qārēb*, see Milgrom, *Studies in Levitical Terminology*, 31–34.

82. Cf. ibid., 83–86.

83. For this verse signifying the transition of the meaning of *ʿăbōdâ* from "work" to "(cultic) sevice," see ibid., 83–86, on Ezekiel's midrash on *ʿăbōdâ*.

## Comment

**44:10.** The foreign guards and persons were henceforth barred from entering the sanctuary, but the Levites who served alongside them became temple guards and assistants to lay worshipers (cf. Num 16:9). F. M. Cross[84] claims that Ezek 44:10 is one of three passages in the book of Ezekiel (in addition to 8:6 and 11:15–17) where the idiom *rāḥaq mēʿalay* has the legal meaning "forfeited the right." A. F. Botta,[85] however, has shown convincingly that in all three Ezekielian passages *rāḥaq* carries the plain meaning "abandon" (my sanctuary, 8:6; YHWH, 11:5; 44:10).

*They will bear their punishment* (*wĕnāśĕʾû ʿăwōnām*). See Excurses 1 and 2.

*their idols* (*gillûlêhem*). This word derives from *gālâ*, "dung, dung balls,"[86] and the denominative *gālal*, "be dirty" (2 Sam 10:12; Isa 9:4). The vocalization has been assimilated to *šiqqûṣîm*, "detested objects." That this is Ezekiel's favorite term for idols is shown, in contrast, by his use of *ĕlîlîm* only once (30:13) and the other derisive synonym *šiqqûṣîm*, seven times (5:11; 7:20; 11:18; 20:7, 8, 30; 37:23).[87]

**44:11.** *They shall be inside my sanctuary performing guard duty at the gatehouses of the sanctuary and serving the sanctuary* (*wĕhāyû bĕmiqdāšî mĕšārĕtîm pĕquddōt ʾel-šaʿărê habbayit ûmĕšārĕtîm ʾet-habbāyit*). The double occurrence of the participle *mĕšārĕtîm* emphasizes that the Levites will resume their previous position, in contrast to the imperfect verbs of verse 11b (*yišḥăṭû; yaʿamĕdû*), which imply that this is a new Levitic task.

Numbers 18:1–7, and especially verses 22–23, provide the basis for verse 11a. Henceforth, priests and Levites alone will bear responsibility for lay encroachment. This responsibility is divided into three groupings: (1) priests and Kohathites are liable for Israelites (Num 18:1a); (2) priests and Levites for Levites (18:3); and (3) priests for priests (18:6). A fourth grouping, Levites for Israelites, is postponed to 18:22–23.[88] Originally, I thought that Levites bore responsibility for Israelite encroachment (18:22b). This may still be true. But the emphasis of this passage is *wĕʿābad hallēwî . . . wĕhēm yiśĕʾû ʿăwōnām*, "The Levite will perform [guard duty] . . . and they [the Levites] will be punished for their own sins" (18:23a). The Levites are henceforth responsible for their own mistakes, and for the mistakes of laypersons. Therefore, laypersons will

---

84. Cross, "A Papyrus Recording a Divine Legal Decision," 311–20.
85. Botta, "*rḥq* in the Bible, a Re-evaluation," 418–20.
86. *ʾAbot R. Nat.*2 38; Ibn Janaḥ, Radak; cf. 1 Kgs 14:10; Ezek 4:12, 15; Zeph 1:17.
87. See the discussion in Haran, *Temples and Temple Service*, 104–6. Greenberg (*Ezekiel 1–20*, 132, on Ezek 6:4) attributes to Baudissin (cited in *BDB*, 1122a) the suggestion, on the basis of a Palmyrene bilingual inscription, in which *gĕlālāʾ* is rendered as "stela" in Greek, that originally *gillûlîm* referred to pillars (*maṣṣēbôt*), explicitly forbidden in H (Lev 26:1). Tigay (*Deuteronomy*, 398, n. 32) adds that in Akkadian, *galālu* refers to a large type of stone (cf. Babylonian Aramaic *gĕlal*, "stone") on which inscriptions and pictures were carved (cf. *CAD* 5.11).
88. Cf. Milgrom, *Studies in Levitical Terminology*, 22–27.

no longer fear approaching (*qrb*) the tabernacle, because the Levite guards will take full responsibility for layperson encroachment[89] and for their own errors (Num 18:22–33).

Hence, being a sanctuary guard means holding a perilous job; it can easily result in *lāśē't ḥē't lāmût*, "suffering a deadly punishment" (18:22b). When the Levites are appointed sanctuary guards they are not "rewarded" for assisting the Israelites in their idolatrous practices, but given a chance to redeem themselves by keeping apart holy and common. *pĕquddot*, "performing guard duty," is a synonym of *šāmar mišmeret*; cf. verse 8.

Eliezer of Beaugency interprets these verses as dealing with erstwhile priests who were turned into Levites because they aided Israelites in their idolatrous service. Astoundingly, the Wellhausenian hypothesis posits the same thing, namely, that non-Zadokite (countryside) priests were turned into the Levites, but only Zadokite (Jerusalem) priests retained their loyal worship of YHWH.

Both interpretations presume that the Levites are demoted priests, yet one (Wellhausen) forms the basis of the radical reconstruction of Israel's religious history most current today, while the other (Eliezer of Beaugency) remains in perfect consonance with the orthodox Masoretic text. How is that possible? Both versions exhibit a similar exegesis of verse 11. The Wellhausenian presumes, through many steps, that the demotion of the non-Zadokite priests led to the creation of the Levites (for details see the COMMENT on verse 13), whereas the exegesis of Eliezer of Beaugency needs but one assumption: the priests (or part of them) were turned into the Levite guards of Ezekiel's sanctuary. There is no evidence that Wellhausen ever heard of Eliezer of Beaugency or his exegesis. But the history of exegesis ought to state that the Wellhausenian thesis—that the Levites were the demoted idolatrous priest (2 Kgs 23:6–16)—was a premise set forth over 500 years earlier by Eliezer of Beaugency.

Israelite worshipers enter the outer court with an animal. They are accompanied by Levites (Num 16:9; cf. Ezek 44:1), who assist the sacrificer in slaughtering, preparing, and cooking the sacrificial animal. The slaughter takes place on tables set inside the northern inner gatehouse (for the *'ōlâ*, "whole burnt," *ḥaṭṭā't*, "purification," and *'āšām*, "reparation" offerings) and below them (for the *šĕlāmîm*, "well being," offerings), in the outer court. The priests must take precautions lest their sacred vestments or sacrifices come into contact with a lay worshiper and sanctify him.

Even when the object of *mišmeret* is YHWH, the context is always "guarding" against violations. Citing examples only from P and H: Lev 8:35 (the priestly consecration); Lev 18:30 (sexual violation); Lev 22:9 (defiled priest and his food); Num 9:19, 23 (God directs the March); Num 18:7a (priestly taboos concerning the altar and the shrine; Num 18:8 (the priestly gifts). In Ezekiel, guard duty also holds both in similar and different ways.

1. The priest wears linen while officiating (44:17–19).

2. His hair shall always be trimmed (44:20).

---

89. Ibid.

3. No wine shall be imbibed before entry into the inner court (44:21).

4. He may not marry a widow or a divorcee, but may marry only a virgin of true Israelite descent or the widow of a priest (44:22).

5. His lifetime responsibility is to instruct between the sacred and the common, the clean and the unclean, and competently guide the fulfillment of God's laws, especially the Sabbath (44:23–24).

6. He must purify himself from contact with the dead (44:25–27).

7. He may not possess landed inheritance, but may benefit from all sacrificial offerings and proscriptions (44:28–29).

8. The first vegetable offerings are for the priest (44:30).

9. He may not eat of a naturally dead or predatorally torn animal (44:31).

The Levite guards of the tabernacle were mainly stationed outside the only entrance into tabernacle.[90] The Levite guards of Ezekiel's temple were stationed inside the three gatehouses of the outer court, located on the lower, seven-step Israelite platform. The function of the Levites in the tabernacle and the Ezekielian sanctuary was nearly identical: to exclude the impure (*ṭāmēʾ*) Israelite and the non-Israelite (*zār, ben-nēkār*). The key term is *qrb*, "encroach." The Levites must guard against encroachment of the tabernacle altar. Since the Israelite had access into the tabernacle court and could bring his sacrifice up to the altar, he slaughtered and cleansed his sacrifice and transferred it to the officiating priest. During this process, the sacrificer was under the watchful eye of the Levitic guard lest he commit encroachment (e.g., officiate on the altar). This fear has been virtually eliminated in the Ezekielian temple. The Levite guards stationed in the seven-step lower gatehouses have complete control of the access of both humans and their animals. This, indeed, is the purpose of the three-platform temple: the Levites (and Israelites) are separated from the priests and the altar, located above on the eight-step middle platform. The Levites (and Israelites) are barred from the priests' platform: A Levite slaughters the animal, and after it is sacrificed as a well-being offering by a priest, it is cooked by the Levite on the lower, Israelite platform. This change between the tabernacle and Ezekiel's sanctuary is explored below.

Both the Pentateuch and Ezekiel's sanctuary require or imply that the sacrificial animal must, or may be slaughtered by a Levite (see Num 16:9; Ezek 44:11). The lay worshiper must pass through a Levitical cordon at the entrance of the tabernacle or sanctuary. It then becomes the responsibility of the Levite to keep him under guard lest he encroach upon the sancta (Num 3:7; 16:9; Ezek 44:11). It is only natural that this Levitic guard also assists him with the preliminary noncultic acts of preparing the sacrifice: slaughtering, flaying, and washing the animal, tasks that normally are performed by the offerer him- or herself (cf. Lev 1:5, 6, 9). Thus, there is a nuance of difference between the responsibilities of the pentateuchal and Ezekielian Levite: The

---

90. Cf. Milgrom, *Numbers*, 9–11.

latter is *required* to slaughter the animal; the former slaughters the animal *whenever requested*.

But of all the preliminary sacrificial tasks, why does Ezekiel specify slaughtering as a required Levitic task? It has been shown that the sacrificial animal becomes sacred (*qādôš*) whenever it is so designated, usually before the hand-leaning ritual is performed.[91] Thus, the animal is sacred even before it is slaughtered, and it is of prime importance, especially under Ezekielian criteria, that the animal be separated from the nonsacred and safeguarded in the sacred realm—a task that is assigned to the Levite guards.

The assignment of the cooking of the *šĕlāmîm*, "the well-being" sacrifice, to the Levites (46:24) has a more pragmatic basis. Whereas the pentateuchal *šĕlāmîm* is removed from the tabernacle and is distributed to whomever is pure, the Ezekielian *šĕlāmîm* is cooked in one of the four corner kitchens on the lower platform and is eaten within the sanctuary premises at one of the thirty tables at the perimeter wall on the lower platform. It should be recalled that the Levites are in charge of the complete lower platform, including the corner kitchens. It is within their responsibility to keep these kitchens immaculate, so that their sacrifices retain their sacred status, and that they remain under the ultimate control of the Levite guards.

In summary, Ezekiel's sanctuary must be conceived visually and three-dimensionally. The animals chosen for the *šĕlāmîm*, "well-being" offering, are slaughtered by the Levites on the tables on the lower seven-step platform. The Levites raise the blood and suet to the priestly (middle) platform, where the priests bring these portions to the altar. The officiating priest receives the chest and the right thigh as his prebend. Since these prebends fall into the category of *qodšê qallîm*, "lesser holiness," they are brought by the Levites directly to the priestly rooms on the lower platform where they are cooked and eaten by the priest. The remainder (and main portion) of the meat is brought to a corner kitchen (Fig. 1) by the Levites, where it is cooked by the Levites and brought to one of the thirty perimeter wall rooms, where it is eaten by the offerer and his guests provided they are in a pure state.

Thus, the priests and Israelites are totally separated even during the sacrifice of the well-being offering. The connection between them is conveyed by a Levite. The animal is slaughtered on a table located at the base of the eight steps to the inner northern platform (below the tables located in the vestibule of the inner northern gatehouse), where the most holy offerings are slaughtered. The blood and suet are brought up the stairs to the altar (Fig. 1) and the chest and right thigh (the priestly prebend) are probably dispatched to a priestly chamber (42:1–13) via a Levitic emissary into the sacred spine (Fig. 14) on the same platform where it is cooked and eaten. The rest of the sacrificial meat is cut up and distributed among the four corner kitchens on the lower platform by the Levite guards, where it is cooked by the Levitic guards and turned over to the sacrificial owner and his guests, who eat the meat in one of the thirty rooms located along the perimeter wall.

91. Milgrom, *Leviticus 1–16*, 150–53, 320–22; Wright and Jones, "Gesture of Hand Placement," 433–46.

**44:11b.** *They shall be the ones to slaughter the whole burnt offering and the well-being offering for the people and it is they who shall attend to them by serving them* (hēmmâ yišḥăṭû ʾet-hāʿōlâ wěʾet-hazzebaḥ lāʿām wěhēmmâ yaʿămědû lipnêhem lěšārětām). These itemized duties of the Levites stem from an earlier pentateuchal verse: *laʿăbōd ʾet-ʿăbōdat miškan YHWH wělaʿămōd lipnê hāʿēdâ lěšārětām*, "to perform the guard duty of the tabernacle of YHWH and to stand before the congregation to serve them" (Num 16:9b). Thus, the guard duty of the tabernacle/Ezekiel's sanctuary and the service advanced to the people have been increased to the people by the addition of the sacrificial slaughter. That is, both the most holy animal (*ʿōlâ, ḥaṭṭāʾt, ʾāšām*, "whole burnt," "purification," "reparation") and the holy animal (*zebaḥ šělāmîm*, "well-being") offerings are henceforth to be slaughtered exclusively by the Levites. The change is phenomenal. Hitherto, slaughter had been performed by the animal's owner (e.g., Lev 1:5, 11). This new arrangement means that the Levites will control the slaughter tables in and below the north gateways, thereby *separating permanently the priests and Israelites*. Once the sacrificial animal is approved for slaughter it is transferred to the hands of the Levites, who slaughter it on the tables within or below the inner northern gateway, thereby creating a barrier between the priests on the altar platform and the Israelites on the lower platform.

The mention of the *ʿōlâ*, "whole burnt offering" (v. 11b) presumes the existence of the much rarer purification and reparation offerings. This is explicitly shown in "And in the vestibule of the gatehouse were two tables on either side [of the gateway] to slaughter the whole burnt offering, the purification offering, and the reparation offering" (40:39). Thus it is clear that the mention of the slaughtering table of the whole burnt offering automatically presumes the purification and reparation offerings. This confirms my theory regarding the history of the whole burnt offering: that originally the whole burnt offering was the exclusive expiatory offering,[92] and only subsequently were the *ḥaṭṭāʾt*, "purification," and *ʾāšām*, "reparation," offerings introduced to supplement it. But it sufficed to say *ʿōlâ*, "whole burnt offering," to imply that the purification and/or reparation offering were included.

*The well-being offering for the people* (*hazzebaḥ lāʿām*). The addition of the word *lāʿām*, "for the people," implies that this sacrifice is intended for public service; that is, other than the priestly prebends, the chest and right thigh, the meat of the animal belonged to the owner, his family, and his guests for a two-day (and two nights)[93] banquet. The animal was slaughtered on the tables located aside the eight-step staircase (Fig. 1).

In Ezekiel's sanctuary design, the laity is confined to the lower (Israelite) platform. If the animal is "most holy" (whole burnt, purification, or reparation offering) it is brought up the eight-step staircase and is slaughtered on one of the tables in the vestibule of the inner north gatehouse. If the animal is designated as "holy," its meat is intended for the offerer, his family, and guests, and the sacrificial meat must be eaten (or burnt) within two days (and two nights, Lev 7:16–18). If, however, the animal is a

---

92. See Milgrom, *Leviticus 1–16*, 172–77.
93. Lev 19:5–8.

## PART TWO: EZEKIEL 40–48—THE VISIONARY SANCTUARY AND THE LAND

thanksgiving offering, its meat must be eaten (or burnt) within that day (and night, Lev 7:11–15). The chest and right thigh are priestly prebends (Lev 7:30–36). Presumably, they are brought directly to the priestly chambers on the lower platform where they are eaten by the priests. Thus, the Levites in the inner gatehouses separate the priests (and the "most holy" animals), located on the middle platform, from the Israelites (and their "holy" well-being offering), located on the lower platform.

*and they shall be the ones who shall attend to them by serving them* (*wěhēmmâ ya'ămōdû lipnêhem lěšārětām*, v. 11bα). The concluding Levite wording is a copy of the older wording, *wěla'ămōd lipnê hā'ēdâ lěšā'ērtām*, "and to attend before the congregation by serving them" (Num 16:9b). Both formulae indicate that the Levites stand at the service of the Israelites who come there with their sacrifices and need subsequent advice and aid from the attending Levites.

However, this Levite assistance, whereby he slaughters holy and most holy sacrifices before they are brought to the priests at the altar, is a task fraught with danger. The priestly text warns the people explicitly: *wělō'-yiqrěbû 'ōd běnê yiśrā'ēl 'el 'ōhel mô'ēd lāśē't ḥēṭ' lāmût*, "henceforth, Israelites shall not encroach upon the Tent of Meeting, and thus incur sin and die" (Num 18:22). Thus, when the Levites are appointed as temple guards (in place of the *běnê-nēkār*, "foreigner," Ezek 44:7), this position is fraught with mortal danger, as the text explicitly states, *wě'ābad hallēwî hû' 'et-'ăbōdat 'ōhel mô'ēd wěhēm yiśě'û 'ăwōnām*, "and he the Levite will perform the work of the tabernacle and they [the Levites] will pay [with death] for their own sin" (Num 18:23a).

It is of interest to note the historical development between the preparation of the well-being offering in Ezekiel's sanctuary and in Jerusalem's second temple and Dead Sea Temple Scroll. In Ezekiel's sanctuary, the slaughter of the well-being offering takes place on tables located on the lower platform at the base of the eight-step staircase. In the second temple, the slaughter may take place anywhere in the temple court (cf. *m. Zebaḥ*. 5:7). In Ezekiel's sanctuary, the well-being offering is eaten on one of the thirty tables within the sacred perimeter (Fig. 1). In the Second Temple period the well-being offering was eaten anywhere within the perimeter of Jerusalem's walls (*m. Zebaḥ*. 5:7). In Ezekiel's sanctuary the well-being offering was cooked in one of the four corner kitchens (*hammĕbašĕlôt*) on the lower platform (Fig. 1). In the Temple Scroll,[94] *mĕbašĕlôt*, "the cooking places" (39:9), were located at the sides of the staircases of the inner court.[95]

The rules Ezekiel prescribes for the well-being offering in his sanctuary (44:10) are eased in the authentic rules of the Second Temple period: Slaughter can take place anywhere in the temple court, and the sacrifice may be eaten anywhere within the walled city. Thus, the wall of the inner platform theoretically spreads out to encompass the inner city. There is no such evidence of wall expansion, but it makes sense: the sanctuary *temenos* has theoretically expanded to embrace the entire walled city.

---

94. 11 QT 20:6–8; 206, map.
95. Cf. *bêt hammĕbašĕlôt*, 46:24.

**44:12. used to serve them in front of their idols** (*yĕšārĕtû 'ōtām lipnê gillûlêhem*). The Levites are the servants of the people, assisting them in all their sacrificial preparations, in contrast to the priests, who, for the sake of protecting their sacred status, must keep apart from the people. Indeed, the priests are enjoined to teach the people (44:23), but from a distance.

**which were iniquitous stumbling blocks for the house of Israel** (*wĕhāyû lĕbêt-yiśrā'ēl lĕmikšôl 'āwōn*). The subject is the idols, not the Levites. The phrase *mikšôl 'āwōn* occurs six times in Ezekiel and each time in reference to idols (7:19; 14:3, 4, 7; 18:30; 44:12).

**I raised my hand against them** (*nāśā'tî yādî 'ălēhem*). Two images of oath taking come to light: either the destruction is about to take place or the destruction has already occurred (cf. the discussion on *wĕnāśĕ'û 'āwōnām*, verse 10).

**44:13. They shall have no access to me to perform priestly duties for me** (*wĕlō' yigšû 'ēlay lĕkahēn lî*). Dead center in Ezekiel's sanctuary is the altar (see Fig. 14). As already noted, Israel is not required to repent in order to earn divine salvation, but it must express remorse and shame for its earlier sins.

**nor to have access to any of my holy offerings or to the most holy offerings** (*wĕlāgešet 'al-kol-qŏdāšay 'el-qodšê haqqŏdāšîm*). This constitutes a blanket prohibition denying the Levites any access to the altar (above) or to any of the sacrifices either brought to or taken from the altar. In other words, the Levites are henceforth barred from the priestly platform, no differently than the Israelites. Implied is that prior to their demotion, the Levites had a priestly status, that is, they could offer both holy and most holy sacrifices at the altar. When did they have this right, and why did they lose it?

Such an event could not have been recorded in the priestly corpus, which limits the priesthood to the descendants of Aaron. However, a possible answer may be reflected within in the idiom *wĕhakkōhănîm wĕhallĕwiyyim*, "the Levitical priests" (v. 15; cf. 43:19). This is an unmistakable and exclusive term for the priests in Deuteronomy (Deut 17:9, 18; 18:1; 24:8; 27:9) and in the Deuteronomic history (e.g., Josh 3:3; 8:33; Jer 33:18). D does not restrict priestly service to one Levitic family, the Aaronides. All descendants of the tribe of Levi have an equal right to enjoy sacrificial prebends as priests. There is only one restriction placed upon Levites: only in the central, divinely chosen sanctuary may sacrifices be offered.

There are some indications that D's Levites could exercise some priestly duties, even outside Jerusalem. Thus we read that the Levite priest assists in atoning for a community adjacent to an unidentified corpse: *wĕniggĕšû hakkōhănîm bĕnê lēwî kî bām bāḥar YHWH 'ĕlōhêkā lĕšārĕtô ûlĕbārēk bĕšēm YHWH we'al-pîhem yihyeh kol-rîb wĕkol-nāga'*, "Then the priests, the descendants of Levi, shall come forward, for YHWH your God has chosen them to serve him and pronounce blessing in the name of YHWH, and by their decision all cases of dispute and assault shall be settled" (Deut 21:5; cf. 10:8; 17:9; 18:5). Thus, we see the Levites had a national, judicial responsibility, which they exercised outside of the sanctuary. They also were held in high spiritual regard by the people to pronounce the priestly benediction (Num 6:22–27), presumably outside as well as within the temple.[96] Similarly, Deut 24:8 gives the responsibility for diagnosing and treating skin disease to the Levitical priest. Surely, this action was not performed inside the temple!

Ezekiel was influenced not only (though mainly) by his priestly source but also by the idioms and language of Deuteronomy. This expression, the Levitical priest, declares unequivocally that the priest must be a descendant of Levi (not of Aaron), and one verse in particular stresses further, "the Levitic priests, the entire tribe of Levi" (Deut 18:1a) . . . 'iššēy YHWH wěnaḥălātô yōʾkělûn, "they will eat the food-gifts of YHWH [from the altar]." In other words, they are priests.

The centralization of the sanctuary effected by the Josianic reform disenfranchised all the Levitical priests that served in the invalidated, countryside sanctuaries and transformed them into wards of society. The common expression for the indigent was expanded to lallēwî laggēr layyātôm wěla'almānâ, "to the Levite, alien, orphan, and widow" (Deut 26:12, 13). Deuteronomy ordains that the Levites have the right to officiate at the central sanctuary and benefit from its priestly prebends (Deut 18:6–9). However, the entrenched clergy at the central sanctuary refused to allow the displaced country priests to officiate or to share the altar's gifts, but only to eat the donated unleavened bread that required no altar sacrifice.

Ezekiel provides a religious as well as economic reason for disqualifying D's Levitical priests from a priestly status. Perhaps, as a young Zadokite priest in Jerusalem, he was witness to the idolatrous rites that had penetrated into the cultic practices of the Levitical (non-Zadokite) priests, and they even assisted the people in their idolatrous ways (44:10). Henceforth, they are barred from the priesthood. In effect, they are barred from access to the priestly platform. They are returned to their traditional status as guardians of the sanctuary by their control over all the gateways (see the discussion on verses 7–10).

On the other hand, in addition to this historical explanation of verse 13a, there is an intertextual explanation, universally overlooked by the critics, which may be preferable.[97] **They shall bear their disgrace for the loathsome acts which they performed, wěnāśě'û kělimmātām wětô'ăbôtām 'ăšer 'āśû.** Shame occurs in the context not of judgment but of salvation (44:14b; cf. Num 18:4aα; Ezek 44:13; Num 18:3bα). As explicated by Lapsley,[98] shame is a gift from God. "It strips the people of their delusions about themselves . . . paving the way for the people's identity to be shaped in a new way." Shame is evoked by a loss of status, rather than guilt. Levites will bear these "abominations." The meaning is not clear, but cf. 20:30ff; 23:36. That Israel will experience shame for its sinful ways is reiterated by Ezekiel: gam-'at śě'î kělimmātēk, "bear your shame you also" (16:52), lěma'an tiśě'î kělimmātēk wěniklamt, "in order that you

---

96. Thus two silver amulets from the biblical period on which copies of the priestly blessing were inscribed were found in Jerusalem outside the city walls; cf. Barkay, *Ketef Hinnom*, 29–31.

97. See Excurses 1 and 3.

98. Lapsley, "Shame and Self-Knowledge," 145.

### The Sanctuary Personnel and the Nāśî' (Ezekiel 44–46)

may bear your disgrace and be ashamed of all that you have done" (16:54). But here resides a burning question: Israel's (i.e., Judah's) shame will be coupled with her restoration. That is, the restoration of Israel's fortune will generate her shame (16:53–54), a process reiterated in 44:13.

Why does the prophet stop at sorrow, remorse, shame? With his prophetic predecessors' (Isaiah and Jeremiah) sharply crafted doctrine of *těšûbâ*, "repentance," available to him, why was it ignored here (though included elsewhere, e.g., Ezek 18; 33)? Here, I submit, is one of the cardinal incidents where Ezekiel resorts to the theology of his priestly ancestors, particularly H. In Lev 26:40–41 we read that all that YHWH demands of exiled Israel is *wěhitwaddû*, "confession," and *yikkānāʿ lěbābām*, "a submissive heart"—a step that precedes prophetic *těšûbâ*.[99] To be sure, Ezekiel resorts to the prophetic term, *kělimmâ*, "shame," and its denominative *hikkālēm*, "be ashamed," rather than H's, *hikkānaʿ*, "be humbled," but their sense is the same.

**44:14.** The summation of the new Levite responsibilities in the sanctuary: guard duty and maintenance in every part of the lower (Israelite) platform. Presumably, all the gatehouses are also under the supervision of the Levites. Stevenson[100] and Duguid[101] argue that the Levites were not degraded but even promoted. Nonetheless, if they were erstwhile priests, their transposition into Levites—regardless of the meaning of the term—is nothing but a demotion. However, it was suggested (on v. 13) that, as shown by the phrase, *hakkōhănîm hallěwiyyîm*, "the Levitic priests" (v. 15), according to the book of Deuteronomy (D), all Levites had the genetic right to officiate as priests, and that is what is reflected here—not a punishment or demotion of the Levites, but a statement of Levitic history: Levites were disqualified as priests, except for "Aaronide Levites" and in Ezekiel's sanctuary, only the Zadokites.

### Ezekiel's Zadokite Priests (44:15–31)

Introduction (44:15–16)

TRANSLATION

> 15 But the Levitical priests,[102] of the family of Zadok, who did guard duty for my sanctuary while the people of Israel were deserting me, they[103] are the ones who have access to me and serve me. They will be in my presence and offer me suet and blood—the proclamation of my Lord YHWH. 16 They alone will

---

99. Milgrom, *Leviticus 1–16*, 373–78.

100. Stevenson, *Vision of Transformation*, 66–78.

101. Duguid, *Ezekiel and the Leaders*, 83–87.

102. CD 3:21—4:2 omits the conjunction on *whkhnym*, but attaches it to *halwym*; see Rabin, *Zadokite Documents*, 30–33; Davies, *Damascus Covenant*, 240–41b [625, n. 70].

103. *hēmmâ*, "they," is a distinctive Ezekielian expression found repeatedly in this section (44:11 [2x], 15, 16 [2x], 19, 24, 29).

PART TWO: EZEKIEL 40–48—THE VISIONARY SANCTUARY AND THE LAND

enter my sanctuary, have access to my table[104] to serve me, and do guard duty for me.

COMMENT

**44:15–16.** The phrase *šāmĕrû mišmeret* forms an inclusion for these two verses, which stresses that the priest must be a sanctuary guard, most likely on the middle, priestly platform or in the sacristies on the lower platform. As temple (i.e., priestly) platform guards, the Zadokite priests, in contrast to the Levites, must have been successful in upholding the major function of the priesthood—one that Ezekiel stubbornly held at the heart of his visionary sanctuary—to separate the holy from the profane and to impart this difference to the people-at-large (44:23; cf. 22:26). Their virtue, therefore, was negative, i.e., they prevented the desecration of the sanctuary. Nothing is mentioned about their personal piety and behavior, namely, that they were saintly, i.e., sinless. Duguid is correct in concluding that "the faithfulness of the Zadokites was a relative characteristic and not absolute perfection."[105]

The replacement of the foreigners with the Levites employs the following language:

| Foreigners (*ben-nēkār*; 44:7–9) | Zadokites (*bĕnê ṣādôq*; 44:15–16) |
|---|---|
| *bĕhaqrîbĕkem ʾel-lāḥmî ḥēleb wādām* (v. 7) | *wĕʿāmĕdû lĕpānay lĕhaqrîb lî ḥēleb wādām* (v. 15) |
| *wattĕśîmûn lĕšōmĕrê mišmartî bĕmiqdāšî* (v. 8) | *wĕšāmĕrû ʾet-mišmartî* (v. 16) |
| *kol-ben-nēkār . . . lōʾ yābôʾ ʾel miqdāšî* (v. 9) | *hēmmâ yābōʾû ʾel-miqdāšî* (v. 16) |

The priestly and Levitic language is also comparable:

| The Levites (*hallĕwiyyim*; 44:10–14) | Zadokites (*bĕnê ṣādôq*; 44:15) |
|---|---|
| *ʾăšer rāḥăqû mēʿālay* | *ʾăšer šāmĕrû ʾet-mišmeret miqdāšî* |
| *bitĕʿôt bĕnê-yiśrāʾēl* (v. 10) | *bitĕʿôt bĕnê-yiśrāʾēl mēʿālay* |
| *wĕhēmmâ yaʿamdû lipnêhem lĕšārĕtam* (v. 11) | *hēmmâ yiqrĕbû ʾēlay lĕšārĕtēnî wĕʿāmĕdû lĕpānay* |
| *wĕlōʾ yigšû ʾēlay* (v. 13) | *hēmmâ yiqrĕbû ʾēlay* |

The priests have two main functions: they serve (*šērēt*) God in the inner court (on the priestly platform), and they teach the cultic laws to the people when they assemble on the outer court (on the lower platform). The following pericope, however, focuses on the cultic responsibilities of the priests.[106]

The expression *hakkōhănîm hallĕwiyyîm* (also in 43:19) is of exclusive deuteronomic vintage (Deut 17:9, 18; 18:1; 24:8; 27:9; cf. 21:5; 31:9) [633]. It is the only deuteronomic expression in chapters 40–48. Lest one think that this is an editorial addition, it should be kept in mind that the book of Ezekiel, in its entirety, reflects a fusion of all the edited pentateuchal sources. This is particularly evident in chapter 20,

---

104. *šulḥānî*, "my table." A euphemism for the altar. The Tg., however, renders it *lptwr lḥym ʾpi*, "table of the display bread."

105. Duguid, *Ezekiel and the Leaders*, 83.

106. Noted by Ganzel, *Concept of Holiness*, 89–90.

### The Sanctuary Personnel and the Nāśî' (Ezekiel 44–46)

which is an amalgam of the priestly (P) and deuteronomic (D)/deuteronomistic traditions in their edited (MT) form.[107] These are some of their respective words, idioms, and expressions:

*P/H and D in Ezekiel Chapter 20*

P/H

1. *wāʾeśāʾ yādî,* "raised my arm" (vv. 5, 6, 15, 23, 28, 42)
2. *wāʾiwwādaʿ lākem,* "I made myself known to them" (v. 5)[108]
3. *ănî YHWH ĕlōhêkem,* "I am YHWH your God" (vv. 5, 6, 7, 19)
4. *lĕhôṣîʾām mēʾereṣ miṣrāyim,* "to remove them from the land of Egypt" (v. 6)
5. *lĕʿênê haggôyim,* "in the eyes of the nations" (vv. 9, 14, 41)
6. *nôdaʿtî ălêhem,* "I had revealed myself to them" (v. 9)
7. *šabbĕtôtay,* "my Sabbath" (vv. 12, 13, 16, 20, 24)[109]
8. *lihyôt lĕʾôt bênî ûbênêhem,* "to be a sign between me and them" (v. 12)
9. *ănî YHWH mĕqaddĕšām,* "I, YHWH, sanctify them" (v. 12)
10. *lĕbiltî hābîʾ ōtām ʾel hāʾāreṣ ʾăšer nātattî,* "I would not bring them to the land I had given" (vv. 15, 26, 28)
11. *bĕḥuqqôtay lōʾ hālākû,* "to follow my statutes" (vv. 15, 16, 21)
12. *peṭer reḥem,* "firstborn" (v. 26)
13. *bĕmaʿălēm bî māʿal,* "by dealing treacherously with me" (v. 27)
14. *rēaḥ nîḥōḥêtām,* "their pleasing odors" (vv. 28, 41)
15. *lākēn ʾĕmōr,* "Therefore say" (v. 30)
16. *wĕhaʿăbartî ʾetkem,* "and I will make you pass" (v. 37)
17. *mēʾereṣ mĕgûrêhem,* "from the land of their sojourn" (v. 38)
18. *wîdaʿtem kî-ănî YHWH,* "you will know that I am YHWH" (vv. 38, 42, 44)
19. *wĕʾet-šēm qodšî lōʾ tĕḥallēlû,* "you shall not desecrate my holy name" (v. 39)

---

107. The dissection, translation and selected notes are by Kohn, "'With a Mighty Hand and an Outstretched Arm,'" 161–65; cf. Tuell, "Contemporary Studies of Ezekiel," 251–52.

108. The theme of YHWH making himself known either by reputation or by name is found exclusively in P (Exod 2:25) [LXX = MT Vorlage]; 6:3. For discussion of this expression in P and Ezek 20, see Propp, "Priestly Source Recovered Intact," 473, who suggests that the similarities between Ezek 20:5 and the two passages in P may indicate that the prophet knew P as an independent narrative source.

109. See Exod 31:13; Lev 19:3, 30; 26:2; and Ezek 22:8, 26; 23:38; 44:24. P requires that YHWH's Sabbaths be observed and sanctified, whereas Ezekiel repeatedly accuses Israel of profaning them. Deuteronomy never uses the plural in reference to the Sabbath.

PART TWO: EZEKIEL 40–48—THE VISIONARY SANCTUARY AND THE LAND

D

1. *lidrōš ʾet-YHWH*, "to consult YHWH" (vv. 1, 32)
2. *wayĕhî dĕbar YHWH ēlay*, "and the word of YHWH came to me" (v. 2)
3. *bĕyôm bāḥărî bĕyiśrāʾēl*, "on the day I chose Israel" (v. 5)
4. *lĕzerʿâ bêt yaʿăqōb*, "to the seed of Jacob's house" (v. 5)
5. *ʾel-ʾereṣ ʾăšer-tartî lākem*, "to a land I scouted for them" (v. 6)
6. *zābat ḥālāb ûdĕbaš*, "flowing with milk and honey" (vv. 6, 15)
7. *šiqquṣê*, "destestable things of" (v. 8)[110]
8. *lišpōk ḥămātî ʿălêhem*, "to pour out my wrath upon them" (vv. 8, 13, 15, 33)
9. *lĕkallôt ʾappî*, "to spend my anger" (v. 8)
10. *ḥuqqôtay*, "my statutes" (vv. 11, 13, 19, 25)
11. *wĕʾet mišpāṭay hôdaʿtî ʾōtām*, "I informed them of my ordinances" (vv. 13, 16, 19, 25)[111]
12. *ʾăšer-yaʿăśeh ʾōtām hāʾādām wāḥay bāhem*, "which everyone who observes them lives by them" (vv. 11, 13, 21)
13. *lišpōk ḥămātî*, "to pour out my wrath" (vv. 13, 21)
14. *ʾaḥărê . . . libbām hōlēk*, "their heart follow" (v. 16)
15. *wattāḥās ʿênî ʿălêkem*, "my eye spared them" (v. 17)
16. *ûlĕzārôt ʾōtām bāʾărāṣôt*, "and scatter them among the nations" (v. 41)
17. *gibʿâ rāmâ*, "high hill"; *wĕkol ʿēṣ ʿābôt*, "or any leafy tree" (v. 28)
18. *ʿad hayyôm hazzeh*, "to this day" (v. 29)
19. *bĕhaʿăbîr bĕnêkem bāʾēš*, "when you pass your children through fire" (v. 31)[112]
20. *nihyeh kaggôyim*, "Let us be like the nations" (v. 32)
21. *ʿēṣ wāʾeben*, "wood and stone" (v. 32)
22. *bĕyād ḥăzāqâ ûbizĕrôaʿ nĕṭûyâ*, "with a mighty hand and outstretched arm" (v. 33)
23. *pānîm ʾel-pānîm*, "face to face" (v. 35)

110. See Deut 29:16; 1 Kgs 11:5, 7; 2 Kgs 23:13, 24; Jer 4:1; 7:30; 13:27; 16:18; 32:34. In Deuteronomy and the Deuteronomistic History, this term always refers, as it does here, to idolatry. In P, the term describes various creatures unfit for consumption, but is never used in connection with idolatry.

111. The expression *ḥuqqîm umišpaṭîm* is found exclusively in D (Deut 4:1, 5, 8, 14; 5:1; 11:32; 12:1), whereas P prefers the expression *ḥuqqōt umišpaṭîm* (Lev 18:4, 5, 26; 19:37; 20:22; 25:18; 26:15, 43), contra Weinfeld, *Deuteronomy and the Deuteronomistic School*, 337.

112. Deuteronomy 18:10 prohibits passing one's child through fire, while P uses its own phraseology, "from your seed you shall not pass over to Molech" (Lev 18:21). Here Ezekiel compares Israel's current idolatrous activity to that of her ancestors following D's terminology.

## EXCURSUS 3: THE LEADERSHIP GROUPINGS

The fate of the leadership personnel was determined by a single criterion: Was the sanctuary defiled or the name of God desecrated by their sin? If the defilement/desecration did occur, then that perpetrating group was disqualified from inclusion among the sanctuary personnel (Ganzel). Thus, the king (below, 1), the high priest (2), the non-Zadokite priest (3), and the elders[113] (5) are accused of defiling/desecrating and, as a consequence, are removed. If, on the other hand, the group's sinful acts did not defile the sanctuary or desecrate God's name, although it may have suffered reduced powers, its office in the sanctuary was continued. Thus, the Levites (cf. below) and the chieftains (*něśî'îm*), with all their sins (cf. below), who did not defile the sanctuary or desecrate God's name, are given an essential function in Ezekiel's sanctuary. The Levites are guardians of the sanctuary gates and the *nāśî'*, "chieftain," replaces the king, but with lesser power (cf. below), as the following analysis will show.

Duguid has clearly demonstrated that the greater the sin of the leadership group the greater its punishment.[114] Ganzel is even more precise, having shown that those leaders who caused the pollution of the sanctuary (*ṭûmě'at hammiqdāš*) or the desecration of the divine name (*ḥillûl šēm YHWH*) are disqualified from being present in Ezekiel's visionary sanctuary and land. Their sins caused YHWH's abandonment of his sanctuary, the sanctuary's destruction, and the people's exile.[115]

The following leadership groups are totally eliminated: the king, the high priest, the non-Zadokite priests, the (false) prophets, and the lay leaders (elders and officers). Their sins are egregious, but above all they defiled the sanctuary and/or desecrated the name of God.

### (1) THE KING

"Never again will the house of Israel *defile my holy name*, neither they nor their kings with their harlotry" (*wělō' yěṭammě'û 'ôd bêt-yiśrā'ēl šēm qodšî hēmmâ ûmalkêhem biznûtām*; Ezek 43:7b). Here specifically the kings are accused of defiling the name of YHWH. Usually this sin is expressed by the verb *ḥillel*, "desecrate."[116] But here, and once again in the following verse, *wěṭimmě'û 'et šēm qodšî*, "they defiled my holy name" (v. 8), the stronger verb *ṭimmē'*, "defile," is employed to express Ezekiel's understanding of the egregiousness of the sin. The king (*melek*) is eliminated and replaced by the *nāśî'*, "chief," whose rights in the sanctuary are mainly honorary, e.g., he may observe the incineration of his sacrifices from the gateway of the eastern inner court—but he is forbidden to step into the inner court itself. That is, he must keep apart from the priestly platform and

---

113. On the *śārîm*, "officials," see below.
114. Duguid, *Ezekiel and the Leaders*, 55–56, 75–79, 98, 127–30.
115. Ganzel, *Concept of Holiness*.
116. Milgrom, "Desecration of YHWH's Name."

its priestly occupants in contrast to the Judean kings who even officiated at the temple altars (e.g., Solomon, 1 Kgs 8:64; Ahaz, 2 Kgs 16:12–15).

## (2) THE HIGH PRIEST

In Ezekiel, the high priest is a phantom figure. Not that he does not exist; Jerusalem had a high priest (called *kōhēn rōš*, "head priest") until it was destroyed (2 Kgs 25:18). But the evidence is incontrovertible that in Ezekiel's system there is *no place for a high priest*. Indeed, there is not a single mention of a high priest in the entire book of Ezekiel. Instead, many of the rules and restrictions on the high priest are now assigned to all the priests (44:17–31). Moreover, a number of oddities in the unique ritual calendar can only be explained by a concerted effort to rid the presence of the high priest from Ezekiel's sanctuary. For example, Yom Kippur on the tenth of Tishri—when the high priest is center (indeed, solo) stage—is transferred to the first of Nisan, when the ritual is conducted by an ordinary priest (25:18–19). An equally cogent example is the table of bread of presence in the shrine (*hêkāl*), the only sacred object that is retained from the Solomonic temple. It is served by the entire priestly cadre and not by the high priest;[117] the other sacred objects (the ark, incense altar, and candelabrum) are served exclusively by the high priest (see Exod 30:7, 8, 10; Lev 16:12–16; 24:3, 8; Num 8:2–3).[118] Furthermore, the high priest hired foreigners as watchmen, thereby violating the covenant (44:7–8). Though Ezekiel charges the people with this fault (v. 6), it is clear that these foreigner workers could be admitted only with the consent of the high priest.

The discovery of eighth- to sixth-century figurines in archaeological excavations in Jerusalem—in the very shadow of the temple![119]—proves that the Josianic reform may have been effective only in the state-controlled royal sanctuaries, but had little or no effect on clandestine (or even overt) idolatry practiced by the populace-at-large (cf. also Jer 7:16–19; 11:9–13). It must be conceded the high priest had no control over idolatry or any other illicitly cultic practice outside of the sanctuary. A decisive illustration is provided by Ezekiel himself: the people would sacrifice their children to Molek at the foot of the temple in the morning and *bayyôm hahû'*, "on the same day," they would ascend to the temple mount to worship (i.e., present sacrificial gifts) to YHWH (23:38).

However, Ezekiel reports that clandestine idolatry practiced by leading members of Judaean society had penetrated into the inner priestly court, which can only have occurred if tolerated by the high priest. Moreover, the *sēmel haqqin'â hammaqneh*, "the outrageous statue of jealousy" (8:3), that "stood guard" at the inner, northern gate, through

---

117. Contra Kasher, "Anthropomorphism, Holiness, and Cult."

118. Were the bread offering burned it would fall to the high priest. But it is only displayed. Hence, it may be served by any priest. Similarly, the candelabrum lamps are set up (*ya'ărōk*) by Aaron and his sons (Exod 27:21), i.e., by all the priests. However, the text relates that the twice-daily incense offering was burned by the high priest (Exod 30:7), the only one authorized to officiate in the shrine.

119. Cf. Kenyon, *Jerusalem*, 74; Shiloh, *Excavations at the City of David*; Kletter, *Judean Pillar-Figurines*.

which the sacrifices were brought to the altar, was hardly clandestine.[120] Understandably, Israel's *ʾēl qannāʾ* "impassioned God," who tolerated no other god, became furiously impassioned by the presence of another deity.[121]

In sum, the fault for the idolatry and foreigners (uncircumcised!) within the sacred precinct must be laid at the door of the high priest, who in Ezekiel's system is wholly and permanently evicted from the visionary sanctuary.

### (3) THE NON-ZADOKITE PRIESTS

The sins of the Judean priests are compressed into one verse, Ezek 22:26: *kōhănehâ ḥāmĕsû tôrātî wayyĕḥallĕlû qŏdāšay bēn-qōdeš lĕḥōl lōʾ hibdîlû ûbēn-haṭṭāmēʾ lĕṭāhôr lōʾ hôdîʿû ûmiššabtôtay heʿlîmû ʿênêhem wāʾēḥal bĕtôkām*, "Her priests did violence to my instruction and *desecrated my holy things*: They did not distinguish between the sacred and the common, or teach the difference between the impure and the pure. My sabbaths they disregarded, and *I have been desecrated* among them." The result, inevitably, was the desecration and even the defilement of the sacred, namely, the sanctuary. There is no place for them in Ezekiel's visionary sanctuary.

Due to the negligence of the priests, the sacred has been desecrated and defiled, the severity of which is elaborated in Lev 4, 5, and 16[122] This has led irreversibly to the pollution of the sanctuary, its abandonment by its God, YHWH, and the exile of Israel.[123] Since the Zadokite priests are singled out for their loyalty to YHWH (40:45-46; 43:19; 44:15; 48:11), the sinner-priests of 22:26 must refer to the non-Zadokites. And since the Zadokites are the priests of the Jerusalem temple, the non-Zadokites probably refer to the erstwhile countryside priests whose sanctuaries were abolished during the Josianic reforms (621 BCE). Because of the egregiousness of their sins (Ezek 22:26) they are not assigned any clerical functions in Ezekiel's visionary sanctuary. Neither are they allotted any land in the resettled tribes of Israel (48:11). What happens to them is not clear. Most likely they were demoted, given Levitic status (44:10-12), were forbidden thereafter to serve as priests (44:13) and turned into Levitic guards at the gatehouses (44:11), as well as sacrificial assistants to the laity (44:11).

---

120. The *sēmel* stood at the entrance of the altar (northern) gate, which menas that all sacrifice passed it by, giving the impression that the sacrifices were brought not to YHWH but to the *sēmel*.

121. Block, *Ezekiel 1-24*, 13-14, 282. There is no need to equate the *sēmel* with Manasseh's statue of Asherah (2 Kgs 21:7). The cultic chaos which prevailed in the temple during Ezekiel's time allowed for all sorts of excesses, as detailed in chapters 8-11. Besides, the Asherah was installed inside the temple building (*bayit*), whereas the *sēmel* was set up *outside* the inner gate.

122. Milgrom, *Leviticus 1-16*, 202-378.

123. The use of the verb *ḥillēl*, "desecrate," instead of the verb *ṭimmēʾ*, "defile," in relation to YHWH and his sancta, so ibid., 849.

## PART TWO: EZEKIEL 40–48—THE VISIONARY SANCTUARY AND THE LAND

### (4) THE FALSE PROPHETS

Ezekiel accuses the prophets of Israel of lies *(kzb,* 13:7, 8, 9) and the women prophets of practicing magic (vv. 17–23) and *wattĕhallelnâ 'ōtî 'el-'ammî,* "You have desecrated me among my people" (13:19).[124] Ezekiel prophesies *wĕhikratîw,* "I [YHWH] will cut them off," i.e., terminate their line (14:8) and *wĕhišmadĕtîw,* "destroy them" (14:9). And in Ezekiel's vision of the new sanctuary and settlement, the prophets are gone. Indeed, the root *nb'* in any form, e.g., the verb "to" prophesy" (Niphal or Hithpael), or the noun, "prophet" (*nābî'*), does not appear in Ezek 40–48. They will be destroyed even before Israel returns to its land, *wĕhāyĕtā yādî 'el-hannĕbî'îm haḥōzîm šāw'* ... *wĕ'el-'admat yiśrā'ēl lō' yābō'û,* "My hand will be against the prophets who see false visions ... nor shall they enter the land of Israel" (13:9). Here we see that not all the Israelites resurrected in the valley of the dry bones (37:1–15) will be restored; others in the same, sinful category as the false prophets—kings, high priest, non-Zadokite priests (above), elders and officials (below)—will also be excluded from the Promised Land. Only Ezekiel remains, but his tenure as the exclusive prophet comes to an end. As can be derived from 39:29, YHWH had poured the gift of prophecy over the household of Israel.[125] Henceforth, there is no longer a need for the mediation of Ezekiel. Each Israelite (including women? Cf. Joel 3:1–2) is a prophet, capable of communicating with or receiving instruction from the deity directly. As astutely observed by Ganzel, whereas Ezekiel is commanded to prophesy (*hinnābē' 'al*) in chapters 1–39, in chapters 40–48 he sees visions and relates them to the people.[126] Their meaning will be easily accessible by the people, who, by then, will themselves be endowed with the gift of prophecy.

### (5) THE LAITY, ELDERS, AND OFFICIALS

Ezekiel severely castigates his fellow Israelites. A typical example is 44:6–7: *wĕ'āmartā 'el-merî 'el-bêt yiśrā'ēl kōh 'āmar 'ădōnāy Lord YHWH rab-lākem mikkol-tô'ăbōtêkem bêt yiśrā'ēl bahăbî'kem bĕnê-nēkār 'arlê-lēb wĕ'arlê bāsār lihyôt bĕmiqdāšî lĕḥallĕlô 'et-bêtî,* "And you shall say to the rebellious,[127] even to the house of Israel, thus says the Lord YHWH: 'O house of Israel, let there be an end to your abominations. In admitting foreigners, uncircumcised in heart and flesh, to be in my sanctuary, desecrating my house ...'" The people (led by the high priest, see above) have desecrated YHWH's house (i.e.,

---

124. YHWH has been desecrated in the eyes of his people, not that he himself, i.e., his person, has been desecrated. So too, as a result of the priests *wayyĕḥallĕlû qodāšay,* "desecrated my sancta," *wā'ēḥal bĕtôkām,* "I was desecrated in their midst" (22:26). The added phrases, "among my people" and "in their midst," indicate that the desecration is not of God himself, but only the estimation of the people.

125. *Contra* Duguid, *Ezekiel and the Leaders,* 105, who claims that YHWH's "*rûaḥ* upon his people was to be life in the land, not prophecy." This holds true for 37:14, but not for 39:29! Also *contra* Block [488]. Block ("The View from the Top," 202–6) suggests that the liquid metaphor ("to pour out the Spirit") signifies YHWH's seal on his people as the secure covenant community.

126. Ganzel, *Concept of Holiness in the Book of Ezekiel,* 151.

127. *Bêt-merî* (44:6 LXX) is Ezekiel's frequent epithet for Israel (2:5, 6, 8; 3:9, 26, 29; 12:2, 3, 9, 25,)

the temple) by admitting foreigners into it, appointing them as watchguards, *wayyāpērû 'et bĕrîtî*, "thereby violating my covenant" (v. 8). Moreover, *'et-miqdāšî ṭimmē't bĕkol-šiqqûṣayik*, "my sanctuary you have defiled with all your detestable things" (i.e., your idols, 5:11), fallen prey to *zĕnût*, "whoring" (i.e., idolatrous worship, 43:7, 9), and thereby *yĕtammē'û . . . bēt-yiśrāēl šēm qodšî*, "they, the house of Israel, defiled my sacred name" (43:7–8; cf. 20:39; 36:20, 23).

It is generally assumed[128] that the laity is punished by the loss of the right to slaughter their sacrifices (cf. Lev 1:5, 10; 3:2, 8, 13). However, they probably would actually be thankful and relieved that the burdensome task of slaughtering was assigned to others (i.e., the Levites, 44:11). Surely, a more costly deprivation (e.g., an increase in required contributions to the public sacrifices, 45:13–16) could have been found. But in reality, the loss of slaughtering rites is no punishment at all. It represents another measure in keeping with Ezekiel's main objective, to separate the sacred from the common (22:26). Furthermore, the most sacred sacrifices are slaughtered on the vestibule tables located on the priestly platform (40:39–41), which the laity is forbidden to access. Ezekiel's innovation may refer to the *šĕlāmîm*, "the well-being offering," whose slaughter is prescribed on tables in the lower, Israelite platform, which henceforth will also be performed by Levites, in order to prevent the dedicated sacrificial animal[129] from being contaminated by the laity.

But the laity have unquestionably defiled the sanctuary and desecrated the name of YHWH. Why then are they not severely punished? The nature of the laity's "crimes" should be kept in mind. They have brought corpses into near contact with the temple (43:7–9) and they have brought foreigners into the sanctuary as watchmen (44:7–9). However, in neither case is the laity autonomous: The responsibility of burying kings up against the sanctuary wall rests with the kings (43:8), and the hiring of foreigners as guards of the sanctuary gates (as indicated above) had to occur with the concurrence of the high priest. To be sure, Jerusalem (and Judah) was saturated with idolatry, but here too the people had before them the models of their leaders, the elders and officials who worshiped idols inside the sanctuary.

In Ezekiel's visionary sanctuary, the people are distant from any contact with the sacred. They are separated from the sanctuary by the *tĕrûmâ*, "a sacred buffer zone," i.e, the tribal property of the priests. In the sanctuary, they are strictly confined to the lower, seven-step platform. Moreover, no longer may they slaughter their sacrifices (cf. Lev 1:5)—a task assigned to the Levites (44:11).[130] The people are restricted in their worship.[131] Their sacrifice is reduced to a contribution to the offering of the *nāśî'* (45:16),

---

128. E.g., Duguid, *Ezekiel and the Leaders*, 127.

129. Cf. Lev 7:19–21.

130. Thus neither a punishment nor a "downgrading" (Duguid, *Ezekiel and the Leaders*, 139). It is a most sacred offering, slaughtered on the Vestibule tables in the priestly court. The slaughter is done by the Levitic guards on the tables, which are off limits to the laity. Thus, the loss of the right to slaughter is not a punishment for their admitting foreigners into the sanctuary, but a further effort to prevent contact with the sacred.

131. Zimmerli, *Ezekiel 2*, 117 correctly points to the corridor 50 cubits long and eight steps high

a brief act of prostration in the lower court on sabbaths and new moons (46:7), and a procession through the lower court on major festivals (46:9–11).

The *zěqēnîm*, "elders," were the heads of families who assumed overall leadership in the tribe, and as the tribe became more sedentary the elders formed a village council.[132] The *śārîm*, "officials," on the other hand, were military officers who became a small council of high officials of the kings, wielding considerable power. The elders were caught red-handed: seventy of them clandestinely worship idols inside an enclosed room on the temple court (8:7–11). Nor were they afraid that their brazen pollution of the sanctuary would be punished: "For they say, 'YHWH does not see us, YHWH has forsaken the land.'" The ironic reversal is complete. The seventy elders who once "saw God" (Exod 24:9–15) and were gifted with prophecy (Num 11:24–25) are now the seventy elders who worship idols in the very house of God! The effect is explicit: "Mortal, do you see what they are doing . . . to drive me from my sanctuary" (v. 6). That idol worship is *defiling* (*ṭm'*) is the continuous refrain of the prophet (20:7, 18, 26, 31; cf. 23:7, 38).

YHWH's abandonment of his sanctuary is virtually simultaneous with Israel's entrance into exile. Surely, they will be redeemed and restored to their homeland (Ezek 36–37), excluding the egregiously sinning elders: "I will bring them out of the land where they reside as aliens, but they shall not enter the land of Israel" (20:38). Of course, not all elders are alike: "I shall judge between sheep and sheep, between rams and goats" (34:17). The result of the defection of the elders is that their place in Ezekiel's sanctuary as Israel's counselors is abolished. As suggested by Duguid,[133] their place is assumed by a single strong leader, "my servant David" (34:23).

Moreover, Duguid[134] argues that the whole bureaucracy (i.e., the *śārîm*) is swept away as well. Jaazaniah son of Azzur and Pelatiah son of Benaiah are recognized by Ezekiel among the twenty-five *śārîm*, "public officials," at the entrance to the eastern inner gate (11:1) as responsible for widespread Jerusalem murders (v. 6). Their death is prophesied (vv. 8–10), and Pelatiah falls dead during the prophecy (v. 13). "The death of Pelatiah is thus a token of the certainty awaiting all of the *śārîm* remaining in Jerusalem," just as the slaying of the twenty-five elders began the slaughter of the Jerusalemite population (9:66). Moreover, Duguid points to another reason for the decline of *śārîm*: the equitable distribution of the land (Ezek 48) and the law against the *nāśî'* dispossessing the people of their patrimony (46:16–18)—laws that militate against the class of *śārîm* from thriving. Yet is the *nāśî'* expected to govern his country on his own? The text explicitly states that the *nāśî'* will give lands to "his servants" (*'ăbādāyw*). But here too the inducement is restricted. In contrast to King Saul's practice of rewarding his loyal officers with permanent gifts of land (1 Sam 22:7), the lands that the *nāśî'* dispenses must

---

that separates the laity's worship from the priests' court as indicative of the impossibility of the laity to witness the altar service. But he overlooks the possibility of witnessing these acts by standing before the unwalled priestly platform (cf. fig 1).

132. De Vaux, *Ancient Israel*, 69; Reviv, *Elders in Ancient Israel*, 52ff.
133. Duguid, *Ezekiel and the Leaders*, 127.
134. Ibid., 125, 130.

be returned to the *nāśî'* at the jubilee (Ezek 46:17).[135] Thus, the *'ăbādîm*, "servants of the *nāśî*," are low-order officiants, and ministers of the *nāśî'*s estate (see below), a far cry from the erstwhile powerful *śārîm*.

Note, however, that the *śārîm* are not explicitly accused of causing either desecration or defilement. They are not guilty of ritual sins but of moral ones, particularly of causing bloodshed; most likely, judicial murder (e.g., 27:3, 4, 6, 9, 12, 27, 31; 23:45; 33:25; 36:18), "destroying lives to get dishonest gain" (22:27). Here Ezekiel betrays the influence of H: Murder pollutes (*ṭm'*) the land (not just the sanctuary), for which Israel is punished with exile (Num 35:34; cf. Lev 18:25, 28). Thus, for Ezekiel, both egregious sins—ritual or moral—generate Israel's destruction.

Finally, one may ask: why did Ezekiel not treat the lay leaders as he treated the high priest—with oblivion. The cultic sins of the elders and the officials in the sanctuary were surreptitious. They first had to be exposed before they were punished. Besides, though the bureaucracy as an institution was eradicated, not all of its members were guilty (see above) and that had to be singled out or implied.

## (6) THE PRINCE (HANNĀŚÎ')

The *nāśî'* is of a lower order of ruler than the king, "Nevertheless I will not take the whole kingdom away from him [Solomon] but will make him *nāśî'* all the days of his life" (1 Kgs 11:34).[136] Whereas the king rules a number of tribes, the *nāśî'* is limited in power to his own tribe (being a Davidide, probably Judah). The antiquity of the term *nāśî'* is corroborated by its occurrence only among those non-Israelite societies that are nomadic: Ishmaelites (Gen 17:20; 25:16) and Midianites (Num 25:14). The institution of the *nāśî'* persists in Israelite records only in the border tribes of Simeon (1 Chr 4:38), Reuben (1 Chr 5:6), and Asher (1 Chr 7:40), where a sedentary style of life was slow in developing. The term is artificially resurrected by Ezekiel to designate a king of lesser power. Only when YHWH restores Israel to its land will he place a *nāśî'* at its head (34:23-24). Undoubtedly, the *nāśî'* had secular authority with which to control his "chiefdom," the possessed lands and servants; yet he is not an absolute ruler: He is denied the authority to appropriate or redistribute lands. Ezekiel is mainly interested in the *nāśî'*s role in the sanctuary, where we learn that the *nāśî'*s position was strictly honorary. Mainly, he could position himself at the end of the inner eastern gateway so he could observe the incineration of his sacrifices. He was also responsible for supplying the fixed sacrifices on festivals (45:18-25), for which he was given large tracts of land and a staff (*'ăbādāyw*, 46:17), which also dampened his appetite to confiscate the land of his subjects (45:7-9). The duties of the *nāśî'* in the sanctuary are meticulously described so there is no chance for desecration (*ḥll*) to occur.

Throughout the book of Ezekiel there are references to past *něśî'îm* (erstwhile kings), a striking example of which is the following, "and my *nāśî'* shall no longer op-

---

135. Note that Saul's high officials are also called *'ăbādāyw*, "his servants" (1 Sam 22:7).
136. On the *nāśî'*, see also Block, "Transformation of Royal Ideology in Ezekiel," 234-43, esp. 241-43.

press my people . . . O *nāśî'* of Israel! Put away violence and oppression, and do what is just and right. Cease your evictions of my people" (45:8–9). Here we have a telling example of economic exploitation by the *nāśî'*, but there is no reference either to idolatry (*zĕnût*, "whoredom" = idolatry) or the desecration of YHWH's name or of the sanctuary. Ezekiel scores the past princes for their failure to prosecute transgressors (22:6–12; cf. 22–25). However, neither YHWH's name nor his residence (*miqdāš*, "sanctuary") were desecrated (*ḥll*) or defiled (*ṭm'*). In other words, even though Israel will be severely punished for its immoral acts, YHWH will not abandon his sanctuary, and the *nāśî'* will be allowed to govern, even on his limited terms.

### (7) THE LEVITES

Contrary to the Wellhausenian school, the Levites were not created by Ezekiel. They are to guard the Israelite platform of Ezekiel's sanctuary (44:14) with added responsibility to slaughter the whole burnt offerings and well-being offerings of the laity and to assist the latter in their worship preparation (44:11). To be sure, they sinned, *'ăšer rāḥăqû mē'ālay*, "distancing themselves from me," . . . *'ăšer yĕšārĕtû 'ōtām lipnê gillûlêhem*, "serving them [the laity] before their idols" (44:10, 12). In other words, the Levites continued to serve the Israelites when the latter switched from serving YHWH to serving idols. There is no accusatory word that the Levites themselves worshiped idols, but they assisted others in doing so. The sin is bad enough, but it is not so egregious to contaminate the sanctuary and drive out Israel's resident God, YHWH.

### SUMMARY

The rationale holds. The kings, non-Zadokite priests, (false) prophets, elders, and officials disappear off the screen of Ezekiel's futuristic Israel. Each in his own way has expressly desecrated the name of God or has defiled the temple, the divine residence, or has polluted God's land, and has thereby contributed to the expulsion of Israel from its land. Each is undeserving of being redeemed when YHWH restores Israel to its land. However, despite their serious shortcomings, the chieftains (*nĕśî'îm*), Zadokite priests, and Levites were never guilty of desecrating the name of God, defiling the sanctuary, or polluting the land. They are punished for their sins (except for the Zadokite priests, who in Ezekiel's account are sinless) but continue to serve in reduced capacity.

## EXCURSUS 4: THE SINS OF THE HIGH PRIEST AND OTHER LEADERS

I will share with you my line of thought. Delphi is at the end of the line, but how did I arrive at this outlandish conclusion? The beginning can be traced to my one major axiom: Nothing is taken for granted in the book of Ezekiel. If it is not explicit then it does not exist. Note that the sanctuary is empty except for the table of presence in the shrine; it is the only sacred object in the entire sanctuary. Note also that it is the only sacred object not served by the high priest. The other objects of the pre-exilic temple—the ark, menorah, incense altar—are excluded, *precisely because* they are served by the high priest, whereas the table is served by the entire priestly cadre who replace the bread of presence each Sabbath.

The difference in the service of the sacred objects should not be overlooked. The menorah is lit; the incense is burned; the ark is purged—rituals are performed by the high priest. But the bread has no ritual. In fact, nothing is done to the bread; it is simply replaced with fresh bread. Hence, it can be handled by *all* the priests. Thus, the empty shrine of Ezekiel's visionary temple is the effective ground for excluding the high priest. He is out of a job. This conclusion is verified by the laws of the sanctuary. For example, Ezekiel has no Yom Kippur. The annual purgation of the temple is transferred from the 10th of Tishri to the 1st of Nisan; from the day exclusively executed by the high priest to a day served by ordinary priests. In fact, the list of duties for the priests (44:17–31) indicates that they have usurped the austere regulations of the high priest. Again, the laws of the new sanctuary reveal a consistent and deliberate move to eliminate the high priest from the sanctuary service.

Why? What does Ezekiel have against the high priest? There is no indication that he has done wrong. In fact, there is no mention of the high priest anywhere in the entire book of Ezekiel. And that is the key. Rimon Kasher provides a simple solution. He suggests that the high priest had to be dismissed precisely because Ezekiel's anthropomorphic God had taken over the sanctuary and would not tolerate the presence of any human being. Thus the high priest has not sinned. He is simply an intruder in God's *bayit* and must vacate the premises.[137]

However attractive, this solution is ridden with problems. Why then is the priestly cadre permitted into God's *bayit*, even if only to replace the bread offering? Why indeed is the high priest not personally involved in the execution of the laws of the sanctuary, especially since most of them are performed outside the sanctuary? For example, according to 44:23 the priests constitute Israel's judiciary. Why is the high priest not the chief justice? The only answer is that Ezekiel has made a concerted attempt to rid the sanctuary of the services of the high priest. The question remains: Why?

The deuteronomic reform was effective only in the official state-controlled sanctuary, but the people at large continued to practice idolatry, even openly.[138] Thus Molekh worship thrived at the foot of the pre-exilic temple (29:38); "desecration of God's sacred name occurred by *bĕmatnôtêkem ûbĕgillûlêkem*, "with your gifts and with your idols" (20:39). Admittedly the pre-exilic high priest probably had no control over the countryside and should not be blamed for its idolatry. His bailiwick was the temple. However, Ezekiel reports that idolatry had penetrated into the temple and was practiced by Israel's leaders, the officials, and the elders. Apparently it was also tolerated (if not supported)

---

137. Kasher, "Anthropomorphism, Holiness and Cult," 192–208.
138. Milgrom, "Nature and Extent of Idolatry."

by the high priest. Therefore, the high priest is ultimately responsible for the cultic sins that defiled the sanctuary and desecrated the name of God.

Here we encounter another Ezekielian postulate. Leaders guilty of egregious sins are not heard of again. They are excluded from Ezekiel's visionary sanctuary and from the reconstructed Israel. That, I submit, is the bottom line of Ezekiel's silence on the high priest: His name and person are expunged from Ezekiel's map.

The case of the non-Zadokite priests provides a fitting analogy. First, the fact that the sanctuary is served by the Zadokite priests (44:15) implies that non-Zadokite priests are found outside the sanctuary. Where, the text does not say. Perhaps they officiated at the countryside sanctuaries that survived or were rebuilt after the Josianic reform. Perhaps they are the priests Ezekiel condemns when he charges: "Her priests did violence to my instructions and desecrated my holy things. They did not distinguished between the sacred and the common or teach the difference between the pure and the impure. My Sabbath they disregarded and I have been desecrated among them" (22:26). Surely, Ezekiel was not speaking of the faithful Zadokite priests, but of non-Zadokite priests. If so, we can understand why they are swept off Ezekiel's map. Not only are they banned from the sanctuary, but they are also excluded from the priestly territory in the future (48:11). They simply disappear. Similarly the high priest simply disappears, and so too do other leaders who are guilty of horrendous sins.

In effect, Ezekiel eliminates the entire leadership of pre-exilic Israel. This includes the king, the high priest, the prophets, the elders, and the officials—those responsible for the defilement of the sanctuary and the desecration of the divine name. As Tova Ganzel has shown, those elements allowed to remain—such as the Levites and the chieftains—have sinned but they are not accused of polluting the sanctuary.[139] In effect, Israel's hierarchy has been flattened, as Duguid has shown.[140] However, the people have not been leveled down, but leveled up. Ezekiel postulates a theocentric society in which the people were first converted into sainthood—they cannot sin ( 36:27)—and then into prophets. All persons have direct and equal access to God (39:29).

How can that be? To my knowledge, all commentators declare that the people are explicitly punished for their serious cultic and moral crimes by having their longstanding right to slaughter their sacrificial animals withdrawn from them and transferred to the Levites. A big deal! The laity's right to slaughter is not a privilege. It rests on the basic sacrificial postulate that any ritual involving the altar is the province of the priest. Any rite such as slaughter, which is independent of the altar, lies with the laity. Why then do they lose this duty to the Levites? Because, following the hand-leaning that precedes its slaughter, the sacrificial animal is quasi-sacred. Ezekiel's fundamental tenet is "to separate the common from the sacred," namely, to distance the laity from anything sacred. So the people are not punished at all. How could they be? They have been elevated to sainthood and from sainthood to prophecy.

---

139. Ganzel, *Concept of Holiness*.
140. Duguid, *Ezekiel and the Leaders*.

# The Sanctuary Personnel and the Nāśî' (Ezekiel 44–46)

> To be sure, the Levites are also laymen; however, they are under the tight control of the priests, as is written, "I have given the Levites to be under Aaron" (Num 8:9); and *wišarĕtûkâ*, "and they [the Levites] will serve you [the priests]" (18:2). In effect, they are the priests' police force, who enforce the separation postulate as part of their guarding duties; namely, the laity must be kept apart from the sacred.
>
> Thus, the overriding principle that Ezekiel meticulously follows is that *at all costs the laity must be distanced from the holy*. What Ezekiel needs is a structure that will embody this principle in which God can reside in purity forever. He seeks a model and he finds it in Delphi.

## The Priestly Duties (44:17–27)

### Translation

17 They will wear linen clothes when they go into the gates of the inner court: They must not wear wool when they serve in the gateways of the inner court. 18 They will wear linen turbans on their heads, and linen pants on their loins, loose so they do not sweat. 19 When they exit to the outer court[141] to the people, they shall take off their official garments, leaving them in the sacristies, and then put on different clothes lest they transmit holiness to people who might have touched their official garments.[142] 20 They will neither shave their heads, nor let their hair grow long but keep their hair trimmed:[143] 21 A priest[144] must not drink wine on entering the inner court. 22 They may not marry widows or divorcees, only virgins of the seed of the house of Israel[145] or widows of priests. 23 They will teach my people the difference between the sacred and the common, and the pure and impure. 24 In legal matters they will officiate as judges,[146] judging[147] according to my laws.[148] They will abide by my teachings and my decrees regarding all my fixed festivals, and maintain

---

141. MT's repetition of *'el-haḥāṣēr haḥîṣônâ* is a dittography. The second occurrence is absent from LXX, Vulg, Pesh. [637, n. 109].

142. Lit., "They shall not sanctify the people with their clothes" [637, n. 110].

143. LXX, "They shall keep their heads covered," has probably misread the root *ksh* for MT *ksm*. On the possible connection of this word with Akkadian *kasāmu*, "to cut," see Garfinkel, *Akkadian Influences*, 92–93 [637, n. 111].

144. Collective sense of *kol-kōhēn* [637, n. 112].

145. *bĕtûlôt mizzera' bêt yiśrā'ēl*, lit., "virgins from the seed of the house of Israel" [638, n. 115].

146. Kethib *y'mdw lšpṭ*, "they shall stand to judge," is supported by LXX, Pesh., and Tg., against Qere, *y'mdw lmšpṭ*, "they shall stand for judgment" [638, n. 117].

147. MT *bĕmišpāṭay*, "by my judgment." On *bet* introducing standards of measurement, see BDB, 90c [638, n. 118–19]. *yišpĕṭuhû*. LBH prefers that the suffix be attached to the verb; cf. *ya'ăbdûhû* (48:19). Note the change in parallel texts:

*wayyiś'û 'ōtô* (2 Kgs 14:20)   *wayyarkĕbû 'ōtô* (2 Kgs 25:28)   *wayyiqbĕrû 'ōtô* (2 Kgs 12:22)
*wayyiśā'uhû* (2 Chr 25:28)   *wayyilkĕduhû* (2 Chr 22:9)   *wayyiqbĕruhû* (2 Chr 24:25)

148. MT *yb'w* is a metathetical scribal error for *wyb'w*. Cf. 10:3; 36:20, etc. [638, n. 120].

the sanctity of my sabbaths. **25** They will not defile themselves by proximity to a dead person, except in the case of a father or mother, or a son or daughter, or a brother or unmarried sister. **26** Once having purified himself, he will count off[149] seven days. **27** He will bring his own purification offering on the day he returns to the inner court to serve in the sanctuary. The declaration of the Lord YHWH.

## Comment

### The Priestly Appearance (vv. 17-22)

What matters concerning the priest is his unblemished cultic appearance. For that reason, his deafness or muteness, being indiscernible, do not constitute one of the twelve blemishes which disqualify a priest from serving in the sanctuary (Lev 21:16–20).[150] So too, what designates scale disease as impure (*ṭāme'*) is its appearance.

**44:17-19.** The most obvious distinction between sacred (priestly) and common persons is seen in their clothing. It is first on the list. The priest must change into linen garments on entering the inner courtyard. Similarly, in P (see Exod 28:42–43; Lev 6:3; 16:4, 23—the term *bad* is equivalent to Ezekiel's *pištîm*). The explanation of this requirement (based on the phrase, *lō' yaḥgĕrû bayāza'*, verse 18) has been understood as deriving from the fact that wool, as opposed to linen, causes perspiration. However, it is unclear why this characteristic of wool would make it unsuitable for the priestly activities in the inner court. Is this term related to the noun *zē'â*, "sweat" (Gen 3:19; b. Yoma 5b–6a)? Eliezer of Beaugency denies it, claiming that this term refers to loosely fitting clothing.

The combination of wool and linen is found in the puzzling biblical prohibition called *ša'aṭnēz* (Lev 19:19; Deut 22:11). Paradoxically, while garments containing such combination of wool and linen are forbidden to the general population (Lev 19:19; Deut 22:11), the priests are commanded to wear such apparel, as shown by Exod 39:29 (which uses the synonym *šēš* for linen, while the reference to *'argāmān* denotes dyed wool).[151] Ezekiel's regulation states in its apodosis, *lō' yaḥgĕrû bayāza'*. Rather than viewing this as an explanation for why wool is forbidden in the inner courtyard, we should see it as another Ezekielian innovation, once again intensifying regulations on the use of the inner courtyard. Hence, Ezekiel, who is constantly concerned to protect the purity of the holy precinct, forbids the wearing of the sacral belt (Exod 39:29) because it is composed of forbidden fabric.

But the priest must avoid any possibility of coming into contact with the people with his priestly (linen) clothes, lest they (the priestly clothing) sanctify them (the people). Hence, the priest must remove his linen garments when moving from the inner to the outer courtyard. In Lev 16, these regulations refer to the high priest, but

---

149. *yispôr lô*. Sg. followed by LXX, Pesh. Kethib (followed by Vulg. and Tg.) reads pl. *yispĕrû*, either in harmony with verse 25 or as an error of metathesis for *yspwr* [638, n. 126].

150. See Milgrom, *Leviticus 17–22*, 1825–32.

151. Cf. Milgrom, *Leviticus 1–16*, 548–49.

in Ezekiel, to all priests. Thus, once again there is a spreading of the regulations for the high priest covering all of the priests. The position of the high priest has been abolished and his offices have been distributed throughout the priesthood.

In summary: Whether wool is forbidden because it causes perspiration or because it forms an integral part of prohibited *ša'aṭnēz* (Lev 19:19), all priests are forbidden to wear any substance made of wool (e.g., *ša'aṭnēz*). The priests' sacred garments must be made exclusively of linen.

**44:18.** *linen turban (pa'ărê pištîm)*, equivalent to *hammiṣnepet šeš* (Exod 29:28); Radak.

*They shall be bound loosely (lo' yaḥgĕrû bayyāz')*, lit., "They shall not gird themselves with anything that sweats" (NJPS).

**44:19.** *they will sanctify the people's clothes (yĕqaddĕšû 'et-hā'ām bĕbigdêhem)*. This requires their laundering (cf. Lev 6:20[Eng 27]; Eliezer of Beaugency). Alternatively, and preferably, "they [the priests] will sanctify the people with their [the priests'] clothes."[152]

**44:20.** Tonsorial extremes are forbidden, neither shaven nor unkempt, but trimmed and groomed (every thirty days, *b. Ned.* 51a). A shaven head would indicate pagan worship, and an unkempt appearance, a disgrace to God. According to P/H (Lev 21:10) the high priest is forbidden to shave his hair or rend his garments. According to Ezekiel here, *kāsōm yiksĕmû*, "they [the priests] must trim their hair." On the basis of Akkadian *kasāmu*, "cut," Hebrew *kāsōm* refers to a trim haircut. These two laws are equivalent but for one factor. In P it applies solely to the high priest; in Ezekiel it applies to *all* the priests. Once again the distinctiveness of the high priest is obliterated.

Leviticus 21:10 suggests the high priest donned ordinary clothes when he left the sanctuary.[153] Thus, when Mark 14:63 declares that the high priest rent his clothes because of Jesus' blasphemy, these were not his sacred vestments, since the blasphemy was uttered in the high priest's home (v. 53). Moreover, he was not in mourning, but in dismay, and these were his ordinary clothes, not priestly vestments.

**44:21.** No wine (or beer, Lev 10:9, H) is allowed the priest when ascending into the inner court. The reason for this prohibition is again because of the appearance of impropriety. The prohibition against wine applies to all priests, not just to the high priest. The effects of wine and beer are graphically depicted and condemned in Scripture (e.g., Isa 28:7; Hos 4:11; 7:5; Prov 20:1). Isa 28:7, in particular, is worth quoting in full: "But these are also muddled by wine and dazed by beer: priest and prophet are muddled by beer; they are confused by wine; they are dazed by beer; they are muddled in vision; they stumble in judgment."

---

152. Ibid., 972–85.
153. Maimonides, *Temple Service*, Temple Vessels 1:5, 7.

Therefore, the intoxication of priests (and prophets) was not a hypothetical matter; the priestly injunction recorded here can only attest to the reality that evoked it. It is also possible that cultic intoxication may have been a pagan practice,[154] and this prohibition may, in part, also be a polemic against it. It is clear from Eli's rebuke of Hannah and her defense (1 Sam 1:13–15) that it was forbidden for anyone, not just for priests, to be intoxicated inside the sacred precincts. The existence of a beer industry in Israel is attested by the prevalence of the beer jug in archaeological excavations. This vessel was equipped with a strainer spout, obviously "to strain out the beer to prevent swallowing the barley husks."[155] The fact that this vessel is Philistine in origin throws light on the story of Samson, where the Philistines engage in drinking bouts (Judg 14:10), while Samson abstains from wine and beer (Judg 13:14).

**when you enter the Tent of Meeting** (*běbōʾăkem ʾel-ʾōhel môʿēd*; cf. Lev 10:9). With the LXX add *ʾô běgištěkem ʾel-hammizbēaḥ*, "or when you make contact with the altar" (cf. Exod 28:43; 30:20).[156] The rabbis infer this addition from the analogy to Exod 30:20.[157] Indeed, it is inconceivable that inebriation would be forbidden only on entry into the tent but not while officiating at the altar. But is it true that an intoxicated priest is liable to death merely for entering the tent? The rabbis (followed by Ramban) asserted that this prohibition is strictly limited to the case of an inebriated priest who officiates in the tent.[158] Maimonides, in contrast, interprets the prohibition literally: it applies to an inebriated priest who enters the tent for any reason whatsoever,[159] but his penalty is lashes, not death.[160] Among the moderns, Haran agrees with the rabbis that this prohibition deals with officiating inside the tent, but it applies only to the high priest, for he alone may officiate there.[161]

The way out of this impasse becomes evident when this prohibition is compared with the other prohibitions falling on the priests. In Scripture there are four disqualifications of priests that forbid coming into contact with the sanctuary and outer altar on pain of death: improper washing, a physical blemish, improper dress, and drunkenness. The texts follow in order:

1. *běbōʾām ʾel-ʾōhel môʿēd yirḥăṣû-mayim wělōʾ yāmūtû ʾô běgištām ʾel-hammizbēaḥ lěšārēt lěhaqṭîr ʾiššeh laYHWH*, "When they enter the Tent of Meeting they shall wash with water, that they many not die; or when they make contact with the altar to officiate, to turn into smoke a food gift to the Lord" (Exod 30:20; cf. 40:32).

---

154. E.g., Babylonia: *ANET*, 66; *Enuma Elish* 3.134–38.
155. Albright, *Archaeology of Palestine*, 115.
156. For *nāgaš ʾel*, denoting "make contact with [for the purpose of officiating]," see below.
157. *Sipra*, Shemini, par. 1:4.
158. Ibid.
159. *Sēper Hammiṣwôt*, Prohibition 73.
160. Maimonides, "Entry to the Sanctuary" 1.15–16.
161. Haran, *Temples and Temple Service*, 206.

2. 'ak 'el-happārōket lō' yābō' wĕ'el-hammizbēaḥ lō' yiggaš kî-mûm bô, "But he shall not enter to the veil or make contact with [to officiate on] the altar, for he has a blemish" (Lev 21:23; cf. vv. 17, 18, 21).

3. wĕhāyû 'al-'ahărōn wĕ'al-bānāyw bĕbōʾām 'el-ʾōhel mô'ēd ô bĕgištām 'el-hammizbēaḥ lĕšārēt baqqōdeš, "They [the breeches] shall be worn by Aaron and his sons when they enter the Tent of Meeting or when they make contact with the altar to officiate in the sacred precinct" (Exod 28:43; cf. v 35).

4. yayin wĕšēkār 'al-tēšt 'attâ ûbānêkā 'ittāk bĕbōʾăkem 'el-ʾōhel mô'ēd, "Drink no wine or beer, you or your sons after you, when you enter the Tent of Meeting" (Lev 10:9); wĕyayin lō'-yištû kol-kōhēn bĕbōʾām 'el-heḥāṣēr happĕnîmît, "No priest shall drink wine when he enters the inner court" (Ezek 44:21).

Two preliminary observations must be made. First, the expression nāgaš 'el, "approach," (Lev 21:23; cf. 10:9) and its synonym qārab 'el (e.g., Exod 40:32) are auxiliaries to verbs denoting ministration, such as lĕšārēt, "to officiate" (Exod 28:43; 30:20), lĕhaqṭîr, "to turn into smoke" (Exod 30:20), or lĕhaqrîb, "to sacrifice" (21:17, 21 [bis]), and hence should be rendered, "make contact with [for purposes of officiating]" in positive cultic statements and "encroach" in negative, prohibitive statements.[162] Second, qōdeš (Exod 28:43) denotes the tabernacle court.

That these verses invariably and unambiguously point to the conclusion that the disqualified may not enter the tent under any circumstances is demonstrated by three pieces of evidence. First, the prohibition against serving is limited to the altar. Never do we find the verbs qārab/nāgaš or the specific ministerial acts lĕhaqṭîr, lĕšārēt, lĕhaqrîb (see above) in connection with the tent.[163] Second, Ezekiel does not mention the altar in connection with his prohibition directed against the inebriated priest, for an obvious reason. He has extended the prohibition of entering the tent (temple) to the entire sacrificial court. In Ezekiel's system, the inner court containing the altar is the private preserve of the priest. Because he prohibits "entry" to the court and not just to the altar, the conclusion is inescapable that physical entry by the drunken priest into the court is strictly forbidden. And third, despite the rabbinic statement (cited above), older, tannaitic texts unambiguously concur that "entry" must be understood literally.

Hannah represents a fitting example (1 Sam 1). Although she is not a priestess, she is suspect of being drunk within the *temenos*, which not only disqualifies her prayer, but also makes her guilty of profaning the holy. Hannah and her family have made their annual pilgrimage (1 Sam 1:3; 2:19, zebaḥ hayāmîm . . . miyāmîm yāmîmāh). Hannah's ostensible profanation would embrace her entire family. Thus, Elkanah and both his wives, Hannah and Peninnah, and the latter's children, are caught in the web of desecration. However, Hannah is making a true vow (1 Sam 1:17; Num 30:11–17), approved by the priest (1 Sam 1:17).

---

162. Details in Milgrom, *Studies in Levitical Terminology*, 33–43.
163. Provisionally, see ibid., 40 n. 154.

**44:22.** According to Ezekiel, priests may not marry widows or divorcees, but may only marry Israelite virgins and priestly widows. In comparing Ezekiel's regulations to those of H (Lev 21:13–15), note that the term *ʿam* means "nation," but the plural form, *ʿammîm*, means "clan."[164] Note also the inclusion marked by the repeated use of the word, *bĕtûlāh*, in Lev 21:13, 14b. Hence, the qualifications set in Lev 21 are slightly higher than Ezekiel's, since they limit marriage to women of the priestly clan. However, Leviticus limits this qualification to the high priest, whereas Ezekiel spreads this qualification to all priests.

In sum: Unblemished is paramount. All the rules stated above add up to *a priest without blemish*. Moreover, the high priest has been eliminated (see p. 168, above). The criteria for the high priest are nearly imposed upon all priests. The same holds true for the corpse-contaminated priests, see below.

*The Priestly Tasks (vv. 23–24)*

**44:23.** Cultic Instructions. These are similar to Lev 10:10–11, except for Ezekiel's additional verb *hôdîaʿ*. The making of distinctions (*bēn . . . ûbēn*; cf. Lev 10:10) is the essence of the priestly function. Ezekiel scores the priest of his time precisely on this point: "Her priests[165] have violated my teaching! They have desecrated what is sacred to me. They have not distinguished . . . they have not taught the difference" (22:26). The failure of the priests to distinguish between the sacred and the common has resulted in *ḥāmās*, "violence," the very sin for which God brought a flood on humankind (Gen 6:11, 13). The addition of the synonym *ydʿ* (Hiphil) to *yrh* (Hiphil) certifies that an equally primary function of the priesthood is also pedagogic: they are Israel's teachers.[166]

**44:24.** Civil Instructions. In addition to teaching differences (Ezek 22:26; 44:23), the priests are implored to teach (*ûlĕhôrōt*) all of God's laws (Lev 10:11), including his civil laws. According to Kasher, Ezekiel "also grants the priests a judicial role (44:24),"[167] but so does D (Deut 17:9, 11; 24:8), the probable precedent for Ezekiel's decree.

The new emphasis is the Sabbath, absent in verse 23. As pointed out in commenting on Lev 23:3,[168] the entire cultic calendar was crippled by the destruction of the temple. The Sabbath alone survived, and the Sabbath alone sustained Israel's ethnic identity. The failure of the priestly cordon was in, among other things, its disregard of the Sabbath, especially in the home (see Ezek 22:26). Hence, Ezekiel emphasizes that Israel's priests must sanctify the Sabbath (v. 24b).

---

164. Lipiński, "*ʿam*," 11:170–75.
165. Probably, non-Zadokite priests.
166. Cf. Lapsley, "Shame and Self-Knowledge," 109–58.
167. Kasher, "Anthropomorphism, Holiness and Cult," 207.
168. Milgrom, *Leviticus 17–22*, 1960–64.

## The Sanctuary Personnel and the Nāśî' (Ezekiel 44–46)

*Purification of Priestly Corpse Contamination (vv. 25–27)*

**44:25.** Only for his immediate family may the priest defile himself, as also ordained by Lev 21:1–3. But according to Lev 21:11–12, the high priest may neither defile himself for anyone, nor leave the sanctuary even to follow the bier. Thus Ezekiel holds the same rules as Lev 21:1–3 for corpse contamination of members of the immediate family: All close members of the immediate family are subject to the laws of purification from corpse contamination, whereas Lev 21:11–12 forbids the high priest from being contaminated by corpses of his family or exiting from the *temenos*. Ezekiel—who had eliminated the office of the high priest—places all priests on the level of the ordinary priest (Lev 21:1–3), rendering all close members of the family vulnerable to the need for corpse purification. The rabbis include the wives among the close family members (*b. Yeb* 90b on *šěʾērô haqqārôb ʾēlayw*, Lev 21:2). However, the absence of this latter phrase from the text of Ezekiel indicates that he must have excluded the wives from the vulnerable family members. Eliezer of Beaugency also rejects the rabbinic interpretation of Lev 21:2: "but he may not be defiled by [the corpse of] his wife." Were it not for this rule, which unambiguously posits the existence and force of ritual (literal) impurity, one might be led to assume that Ezekiel only accepts moral (metaphoric) impurity.

**44:26.** *he shall count off* (*yispôr lô*). Of course, the responsibility for counting lies upon the subject (cf. Lev 15:13, 28). The purpose of "counting off" is not stated. But it should be noted that it occurs where there is no other indication of the count. Thus, the *zāb* and *zābâ*, "gonorrheic" (Lev 15:13, 28) counts seven days after he/she is healed and before he/she brings a sacrifice (Lev 15:14–15, 39). It should therefore be no wonder that Ezekiel similarly demands seven days of counting between the priest's purification and sacrifice (Ezek 44:25–27).

**44:26–27.** The addition of another week for priestly purification is a special stringency in the future (Radak, Eliezer of Beaugency).

**44:27.** Afterwards, the priest contributes his personal *ḥaṭṭāʾt* before he is permitted to operate at the altar; i.e., he has contaminated the altar and needs to purify it by a personal *ḥaṭṭāʾt* on the eighth day of his counting (cf. Lev 15:14, 29)

Summary: The need for the high priest has been eliminated. Ezekiel's purification requirements for the priest make greater demands on the individual priests than in all of H (Lev 21:10–12). Ostensibly, Ezekiel's priest is in greater need of purification than H's high priest. Thus, H's statute for the high priest's marriage and purification from corpse contamination indicates, first, that Ezekiel has wiped out the cultic position of the high priest and, second, that Ezekiel's priest occupies a loftier position than the high priests in the comparable laws of H.

PART TWO: EZEKIEL 40–48—THE VISIONARY SANCTUARY AND THE LAND

The Priestly Prebends (44:28–31)

TRANSLATION

28 And this will be their patrimony; I will be their patrimony. And you will not give them an inheritance in Israel. I am their inheritance. 29 They will eat the meal offering, the purification offering, and the reparation offering. And they will possess all that has been confiscated in Israel. 30 The best of your first fruits of all kinds, and all your contributions of every kind.[169] And the first product of your dough you will give to the priest to bring a blessing upon your homes. 31 No dead animal or meat torn apart[170] by a beast will be food for the priests.

COMMENT

**44:28–30.** Only God is the priestly portion and possession (cf. Deut 18:2; Josh 13:14); *minḥâ*, *ḥaṭṭā't*, and *'āšām* are mentioned (v. 29), but not the *šĕlāmîm*—as its priestly portion is relatively miniscule; the other priestly gifts are the remaining sacrificial prebends, the produce (*rēšît*) for the priest, plus first fruits (*bikkûrîm*), plus sacral gifts (*tĕrûmâ*), plus baked goods. Unlike these others, the *ḥerem* (using a different verb phrase) cannot be gotten back by the sacrificer, but belongs to the sanctuary permanently.

**44:28.** *It shall be their inheritance* (*wĕhāyĕtâ lāhem lĕnāḥălâ*). What is the feminine antecedent of the subject? The *ḥaṭṭā't* (v. 27, Kasher)? *môtar qûrbānay*, "the remainder of my sacrifices" (Tg. cf. Eliezer of Beaugency)? "The priesthood" (Rashi and Radak)? Or should we read *wĕlō' tihyeh lāhem naḥălâ*, "and they will not have any patrimony," with Vulg, *non erit autem eis hereditas*; LXX967 καὶ οὐκ ἔσται αὐτοῖς εἰς κληρονομίαν, which strengthens the parallelism in the verse,[171] but overlooks the absence of note the deletion of *l* from *naḥălâ*/*'ăḥuzzâ*?

*you shall not give them any (land) holding in Israel; I am their holding* (*wa'ăḥuzzâ lō'-tittĕnû lāhem bĕyiśrā'ēl 'ănî 'ăḥuzzātām*). According to Radak, this verse is based on the language of Deut 18:2, *wĕnaḥălâ lō'-yihyeh-lô bĕqereb 'eḥāyw YHWH hû' naḥălātô*, "they shall not have any inherited land in the midst of Israel, YHWH, he is their inheritance."

*Holding* (*'ăḥuzzâ*). This is a priestly technical term denoting inalienable property received from a sovereign; *naḥălâ* refers to inalienable property transmitted by inheritance.[172] Leviticus (H) uses *'ăḥuzzâ* exclusively; Deuteronomy uses *naḥălâ* exclusively.

---

169. Under the influence of the key word *kōl*, *yihyeh* is masculine instead of the expected feminine after *tĕrûmâ* [639, n. 131].

170. This prohibition lies on all Israelites (Exod 22:30; Deut 14:21). Why single out the priests (cf. Lev 22:8)? For the rabbis' answer see the COMMENT.

171. Thus Block, *Ezekiel 25–48*, 639, n. 129.

172. For more on the distinction between *naḥălâ* and *'ăḥuzzâ*, see Milgrom, *Leviticus 23–27*, 2171–73.

Numbers uses both (*ăḥuzzâ* [9x];[173] *nāḥălâ* [42x][174]). The two terms are conflated (3x).[175] Ezekiel, like Numbers, uses both terms (*ăḥuzzâ* [10x][176] and *nāḥălâ* [13x][177]). These two terms embody the theology of each source. H calls YHWH's gift of land (forbidden to priests) and sacrificial prebends (granted only to priests) by the term *ăḥuzzâ*, thereby signifying that if Israel violates the covenant, the divine gifts, even inalienable inherited property (*nāḥălâ*), is subject to recall.

It is important to note that in Joshua *nāḥălâ* occurs forty-five times whereas *ăḥuzzâ* occurs six times, but four of the citations are in chapter 22, dealing with the legitimacy of the transjordanian settlement requested by two and a half tribes (vv. 4, 9, 18, 19). In contrast to the cisjordanian tribes, whose lands are called *nāḥălâ*, "inheritable land" granted by YHWH, the transjordian possessions are called *ăḥuzzâ* lit., "seized land," without divine consent, unless it is unambiguously stated as *ăḥuzzat YHWH*, "YHWH's holding" (Josh 22:19, which then refers to the divinely commanded Cisjordanian holdings).

In sum, *lĕnāḥălâ* refers to the sacrificial prebends; *ănî nāḥălātān*, "I am their inheritance," to the deity as the granter of the prebends. Priests may not receive any *ăḥuzzâ*. That is, not only is *nāḥălâ*, "inheritable land," forbidden to them but even *ăḥuzzâ*, "holding," any other land, for *ănî ăḥuzzātām*, "I am their holding." Here *ăḥuzzâ* is used synonymously with *nāḥălâ*, and, as suggested by Kasher, *ad loc.*, the purpose of the doubling is for emphasis, to strengthen the prohibition. Thus this verse is stating that sacrificial prebends are legitimate priestly inheritance (*nāḥălâ*), but landed holdings (*ăḥuzzâ*) are forbidden for God is their holding.

**44:29.** The entire *minḥâ*, "meal offering" (except its token Lev 2:1–3); the entire *ḥaṭṭā't* and *āšām*, "purification and reparation offering" (Lev 6:19 [Eng 26]); and the entire *ḥērem*, "proscription" (Lev 27:28–29), are the inheritable property—the *naḥălâ*—of the priests. The priests have no reason to *ăḥaz* ("seize, grab") property of others. God has provided them with ample land (Ezek 45:1–5; 48:11–14) and ample nutriment, i.e., these named sacrifices (cf. also Josh 13:14).

**44:30.** The ample meat from the sacrifices is matched by the ample vegetation, presumably supplied by the fertile land. The distinction between *naḥălâ*, "inherited property"; *ăḥuzzâ*, "seized property"; and *tĕrûmâ*, "gifted property," requires a redivision of the MT: *wĕrēšît kōl, bikkûrê kōl, wĕkol-tĕrûmat kōl-mikkol terumôtêkem*.

---

173. Num 27:4; 35:2, 8, 28; 32:5, 22, 28, 29.

174. Num 18:23, 24; 26:62; 27:7; 36:2, 7, 8, 9; 26:53; 34:2; 18:21, 24; 16:14; 26:7; 36:2, 3, 4(2x), 8; 35:2; 36:3, 7; 26:54 (2x), 56; 27:8, 9, 10, 11; 32:18; 33:54(2x); 35:8; 36:3, 4 (2x), 12.

175. Num 27:7; 32:32; 35:2.

176. Ezek 44:28; 45:5, 6, 7, 8; 46:16, 18; 48:20, 21, 22.

177. Ezek 45:1(2); 46:16; 47:14, 22 (2x); 46:12; 36:12; 47:28; 48:29; 35:15; 46:18.

***to the priest (lakkōhēn).*** According to Duguid,[178] Ezekiel's high priest is called, "*the priest,*" without taking into account the more obvious conclusion that Ezekiel has no high priest.

**44:31.** Ezek 4:14 demonstrates that the prophet was familiar with this proscription. It falls upon all Israel (Exod 22:30; Deut 14:21). However, according to Lev 17:15–16— the holiness source (H), which Ezekiel follows assiduously—Israelites are not forbidden to eat dead or torn animals, provided they undergo one day purification. However, the *priest* who deliberately commits this violation is punishable by death at the hands of God (Lev 22:8–9); hence, he requires this extra warning. Moreover, according to Rashi, since the required purification offering for corpse contamination (v. 27) may be in the form of birds (Lev 5:7–11), it is possible for the priest to deduce that all birds, dying naturally or torn, are permissible. Hence, this extra warning is issued against eating such birds. This warning falls regularly as the last prohibition in a list of priestly prohibitions, e.g., Lev 7:24–25; Lev 17: 15–16; see also Ezek 4:14. As observed by Fishbane, "This ruling appears disjunctive in the present collection of rules. It is contextualized by R. Eliezer of Beaugency, who regards it as dealing with prohibited priestly gifts."[179]

## Summary of Chapter 44

The division of labor in P between the priests and Levites and their location in the sanctuary are critical in understanding Ezekiel. In Num 18:1–7 there are two groups of priests (v. 5a; cf. Ezek 40:44–46; 42:13), one to guard the altar area and the other to guard the tent (sanctuary building). Also *wĕnāśĕ'û 'et-'āwōnām* (44:10, 12) "they [the Levites] will bear their punishment," i.e., they will not be permitted to enter or serve in the inner (priestly) court (cf. Num 18:3b, not based on historic reality, but on Korahite tradition [Num 16–17]). Also, the Levites are punished for aiding the Israelites in worshiping other cults/gods by having to render hard labor, e.g., the slaughtering and quartering of the sacrificial animals, as well as other labor—presumably ordered by the priests for work on the sacred grounds. Ezekiel's dependency on Num 18:1–7 is also based on:

v. 1. This is one of the two places that God speaks not to Moses but directly to Aaron. The responsibility for sins committed against the sanctuary and its sancta is vested in *bêt 'ābîkā*, "Aaronids and Kohathites" (the latter carry the sancta on the march). *'ittĕkā*, "under you, in your charge"

v. 2. *haqrēb 'ittĕkā*, "qualify in your charge" (*hā'ēdut* = *hammô'ēd*).

v. 3. *wĕšāmĕrû mišmartĕkā*, "they [the Levites] will perform your [the priestly] guard duty." That is, the Levites will replace the priest in guarding the entrance to the court. *ûmišmeret kol-hā'ōhel*, "and the guard duty of the entire courtyard." The Levites, how-

---

178. Duguid, *Ezekiel and the Leaders of Israel*, 64.
179. Fishbane, *Haftarot*, 197.

## The Sanctuary Personnel and the Nāśî' (Ezekiel 44-46)

ever, have nothing to do with the sancta, which are the exclusive responsibility of the priests.

v. 4. *lĕkōl 'ăbōdat hā'ōhel*, "including all the labor of the tent." That is, the Levites not only guard the sanctuary, but are also responsible to maintain it. *wĕzār lō'-yiqrab*, "the unqualified [i.e., the nonpriest] may not encroach."

v. 5. *ûšmartem . . . haqqodeš . . . hammizbēaḥ*, "you [the priest] shall guard . . . the shrine [and] the altar." The Levites, however, are forbidden to enter either area, namely, the tent or the altar—this is their punishment (cf. Num 16:8-9).

v. 6. *lākem mattānâ nĕtunîm laYHWH*, "That is, they [the Levites] are given to you [the priests] in dedication to YHWH."[180]

v. 7. *tišmĕrû 'et-kĕhunnatĕkem*, "you [the priests] shall guard your priestly duties," namely, the guarding of the altar and the tent (the sanctuary building), the area under the exclusive control of the priests.

### The Priestly and Princely Lands Foreshadowed (45:1-8)

TRANSLATION

1 When you apportion[181] the land as inheritable property, you will set aside a gift for YHWH. It will be a holy district through its entire extent, 25,000 cubits long[182] and 20,000[183] cubits wide. 2 The sanctuary will take up a square plot of 500 by 500 cubits with 50 cubits of this[184] area for animal corrals around it. 3 Within the measured[185] off area the sanctuary, the holy of holies, will occupy an area of 25,000 cubits in length and 10,000 in width. 4 This sacred part of the land belongs to the priests who serve in the sanctuary, and who qualify to serve YHWH. There will be place for their homes as well as the holy area for the sanctuary.[186] 5 The Levites who maintain the temple will take possession[187]

---

180. See Num 8:16, 19; Deut 28:32; Jer 26:15; Neh 12:47; 13:5; 26:11, 46.

181. *ûbĕhappîlĕkem*, lit. "when you cast [lots]" [648, n. 1].

182. According to Block, the duplication of *'ōrek* before and after the number represents a conflated reading. Either position is possible (cf. vv. 3, 5), but Ezekiel generally prefers the measurement dimension before the number, in keeping with the trend in LB Hebrew. See Rooker, *Biblical Hebrew in Transition*, 113-14 [648, n. 2]. This is probably a dittographic error, the first one being correct, cf. Eliezer of Beaugency.

183. With LXX, assuming an original *'eśrîm 'elep*, as in verses 3 and 5, contra MT and Tg., *'ăśārâ 'elep*, "ten thousand" [648, n. 3].

184. Contra Zimmerli (*Ezekiel 2*, p. 465), the antecedent of masculine *mizzeh* is *gĕbûl*, not distant feminine *tĕrûmâ* [648, n. 4].

185. Since the pl. form suits the context better, most commentators treat *tmwd* as an error of metathesis for *tmdw* [648, n. 6].

186. LXX ἀφωρισμένους τῷ ἁγιασμῷ αὐτῶν, and Tg. *wkbš lmqdš* reflect an original *wmgrš lmqdš*, suggesting that MT *wmqdš lmqdš* is dittography. But the former may just as well have been the result of careless reading of the original [648, n. 10].

187. Retaining Kethib *yhyh* rather than Qere's erroneous *whyh* (cf. vv. 4, 6) [649, n. 11].

of an additional strip 25,000 cubits long and 10,000 cubits, as their holding for urban living.[188] **6** By the side of the sacred district, you will plan a city 5,000 cubits wide and 25,000 cubits long[189] which will belong to the entire house of Israel.

**7** The prince will take possession of the land on both sides of the holy tract and the city property on the west and on the east,[190] corresponding[191] in length to a tribal portion, also extending from the western[192] to the eastern boundary **8** of the land. And it will be[193] his possession in Israel. So the princes of Israel[194] will no longer defraud my people, but will leave the land to the house of Israel according to their tribes.

## Comment

As shown by Block (650), the priestly and princely concerns are distributed as a giant chiasm, A X A¹, in chaps 44–45, as follows:

| Priestly Concerns (44:5–31) |  | Princely Concerns (45:8b—46:18) |
| --- | --- | --- |
| 44:5–8 | Description of Past Offenses | 45:9–12 |
| 44:9–27 | The New Responsibilities | 45:13—46:15 |
| 44:28–31 | Inheritance and Possession | 46:16–18 |

The text also reveals a three-stage evolution of Ezekiel's thinking on the priestly patrimony:

1. The priests have no land that they may call their own; their patrimony (*ăḥuzzâ*) is YHWH himself (44:28).

2. The priests may build their houses on the property reserved for YHWH (*tĕrûmâ laYHWH*). The area set apart as sacred (*qōdeš min-hā'āreṣ*, 45:1–5).

3. The priests' allotments shall surround the allotment on which the sanctuary is

---

188. MT *'eśrîm lĕšākōt* is attested in Tg., Vulg., and Pesh., but it makes little sense. Emendation to *'rym lšbt*, "cities to live in," following LXX πόλεις τοῦ κατοικεῖν, is preferable. Presumably, at an early date a *kaph* was mistakenly written for *beth* in the second word, and a *śin* was mistakenly inserted in the first word [649, n. 12].

189. *'ōrek*, "length," always precedes *rōḥab*, "width," except here and in 48:8 (as well as Zech 2:6 [Eng 2]) [649, n. 13].

190. *mippĕ'at yām yāmmâ ûmippĕ'at qēdmâ qādîma*, lit., "to the west westward and to the east eastward." "The *he* directive on *qēdmâ* should probably be dropped to correspond with the previous *yām*, and the word repointed as *qādîm*" [649, n. 15].

191. The pl. form *lĕ'ummôt* is unprecedented and is generally read as sg., *lĕ'ummat*. However, Rooker (*Biblical Hebrew in Transition*, 77) observes that the form agrees with the pluralization tendency found in LBH [649, n. 16]. The plural form *may have* been influenced by nearby *ḥălāqîm*.

192. LXX πρὸς θάλασσαν and the parallel *qādîmâ* support *yāmmâ* in place of MT *yām* [649, n. 17].

193. Linking *lā'āreṣ* to verse 7 with LXX, and reading *yhyh* as *wyhy* (cf. v. 5) [649, n. 18]. *lā'āreṣ* = *bā'āreṣ* (Radak). *qādîmâ lā'āreṣ*, "east of the land." Kasher, *Ezekiel*, 876.

194. Read *nĕśî'ê yiśrā'el*, with LXX in place of MT's *nĕśî'ay*, "my princes," possibly following the scribal practice of abbreviations [654, n. 31].

located, and the Levites' allotments shall adjoin these. But the ownership of all by YHWH stands (48:8–20).

This reconstruction is subject to question. There is no reason to doubt that Ezekiel was familiar with the distribution of the Levitical and priestly cities as found in Joshua 21. Of the forty-eight Levitical cities, thirteen are assigned to the Aaronide priests (vv. 4, 9–19). Of relative interest is that these thirteen priestly cities are distributed among three tribes: Judah, Simeon, and Benjamin, the closest (and most accessible) cities to the Jerusalem temple, which survived the destruction of Northern Israel (730–720 BCE).

The A X A¹ structure allows Ezekiel to drop a subject and then return to it for fuller (resumptive) exposition.[195] For example, the people's gifts for the priests occur twice in 44:30a and reappear four times in 45:1, 6–7, though with a different nuance. Indeed, the seeds of verses 1–8 were sown in 44:28–30. *'ăḥuzzâ* appears in 44:28 with YHWH's self-introduction. Thus, 45:1–8 is not "a misplaced fragment from 47:13—48:29, as many scholars maintain," but rather a summary of it.[196]

**45:1.** The use of the lot reflects the conviction that YHWH owns the land and has the authority to distribute it to whomever he pleases. The divine allotment (*tĕrûmâ*), however, is not identified by a lot. The area described here was reserved in advance by YHWH himself.

*to cast* **(lots for)** *inherited land* **(*lĕhappîl naḥălâ*).** Indeed, landed inheritance was distributed by lot (e.g., Num 33:50–56; Josh 18:6, 8, 10) [651]. However, there is nothing like this in the Bible: Instead of Israel receiving *naḥălâ* from God, God received *naḥălâ* from Israel! But actually all of Israel's offerings to God are similar, in that they are gifts that have been given to Israel by God, and are then partially returned with thanks (e.g., the *šĕlāmîm* sacrifice). What is unusual here is that it is land rather than produce that is being given to God. In a sense, the land constitutes Israel's produce of which a part (e.g., tithe) must revert to God. Compare possibly the Sabbatical Year, an admission that the land is no man's land, which therefore must be "returned" to God every seventh year.

*set aside as a gift to YHWH* **(*tārîmû tĕrûmâ laYHWH*).** Based on Num 15:19.

*when you cast* **(lots)** *for inheritable property in the land* **(*bĕhappîlĕkem 'et-hā'āreṣ bĕnaḥălâ*).** Supposedly, each Israelite tribe is not being given a predetermined piece of land, but given land according to whatever is determined by the casting of lots. However, the apportioning of inheritable land (*naḥălâ*) is entirely predetermined (Ezek 48) and the idiom here is purely metaphoric.

---

195. Block, *Ezekiel 1–24*, 24–25.
196. Tuell, *Law of the Temple in Ezekiel 40–48*, 62.

PART TWO: EZEKIEL 40-48—THE VISIONARY SANCTUARY AND THE LAND

***reserve a gift*** (*tārîmû tĕrûmâ*). The cultic use of the root *rum* Hipil means "to set aside" something (from something) for YHWH.[197] Note that the priestly land envelops the sanctuary and thereby protects it from encroachment and contamination.

The following idioms should also be noted: *naḥălâ*, land that can be bequeathed; *lĕhārîm*, "to set aside [for God]," a cultic term (e.g., Lev 2:9); *tārîmû tĕrûmâ*, "set aside a gift [to God]"; the dimensions of the *tĕrûmât YHWH*, 25,000 (length) x 10,000 (width), including both the priestly and Levitic tracts,[198] though LXX 20,000 (reflecting *'aśarîm 'ālep*) is probably preferred; *qōdeš* refers to *tĕrûmâ*, not *hāʾāreṣ*, but may also be a dittography; *gĕbûl*, not "border," but "territory."

***through its entire extent*** (*bĕkol-gĕbûlāh sābîb*). The term *gĕbûl* not only means boundary but also the area enclosed within a boundary (cf. Exod 13:7; Num 20:21; 1 Sam 11:7; 2 Kgs 18:8; Ezek 11:10–11)[591-92].

**45:2.** Précis: Out of this area, 500 x 500 (x 50 called *migrāš*) is *qōdeš*. Rashi claims that the 500 x 500 is measured in *qānîm* (*qāneh* = 6 cubits). This includes the area of the temple (100 x 50); the remainder is for the priestly dwellings. Thus Rashi explains how the *temenos* can be 500 x 500 (cubits) plus the *qōdeš* (including the area for the priestly dwellings). That is, the *qōdeš* covers the entire temple mount (500 x 500 *qānîm*), which contains the temple (500 x 500 cubits), plus the area for the priestly dwellings. It is possible that the priests live in the *migrāš*. However, as I have previously shown,[199] the *migrāš* is most likely the corral for the domestic animals (livestock pens). Radak seems to imply that all measurements are in cubits, as diagrammed:

FIGURE 18: The Dimensions of the Priestly Area

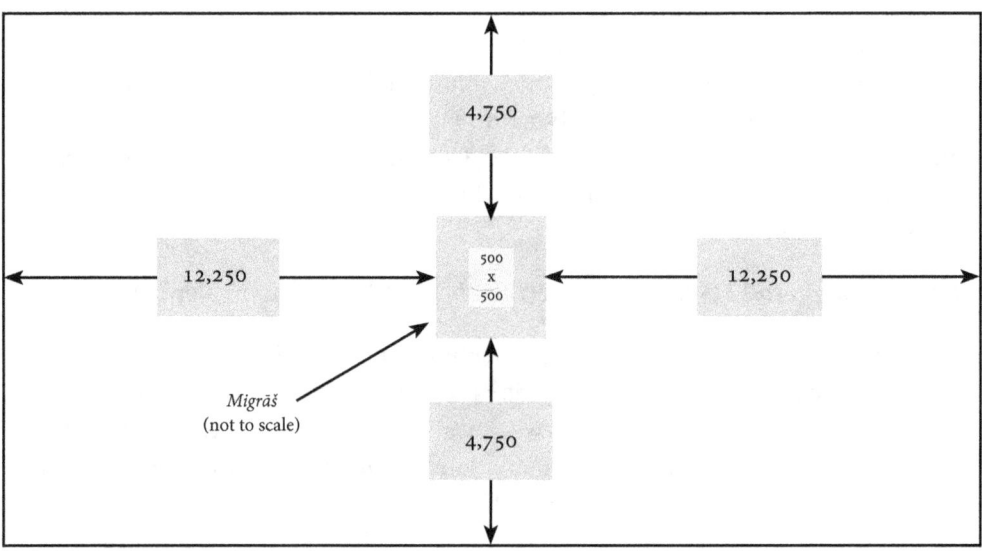

197. See Milgrom, *Leviticus 1-16*, 473–74.
198. Kasher, *Ezekiel*, 874.
199. Milgrom, *Leviticus 17-22*, 2203–7.

*Migrāš:* If this strip, which surrounded the temple, was directed for the priestly animals, this implied that the priests were cattle-breeders—and temple officiants too! The large tract for priests (25,000 x 10,000 cubits) indicates that Ezekiel had a large population of priests in mind. Surely, he could not have had all of them in the temple simultaneously. I suggest that the Chronicler's attribution of twenty-four priestly cordons, each serving two months each year (1 Chr 20) may, indeed, find its origin in pre-exilic times, so that the priests were shepherds ten months of the year. The advantage of having the Levites concentrated in one tract close to the sanctuary would, like the priests, have their numerous numbers also divided into cordons, which also enabled them to shepherd their flocks year-long and sell and redeem their *ăḥuzzâ* possessions (see the concrete law, Lev 25:33–34). Assuming that it served as a corral for the priestly cattle, according to Kasher, the purpose of the surrounding *migrāš* was to provide temporary shelter until they could be brought to the altar for sacrifice. Kasher suggests that verse 2 is out of place; it properly belongs after verse 4. But even reading 20,000 LXX for 10,000 does not solve the problem of the misplaced verse 2.[200]

The central tract—500 cubits square, protected by a 50-cubit buffer (*migrāš*)—belongs in its entirety to God. Thus, the priests possess their homes, but they do not possess the land on which the homes are built. As pointed out by Block, "the territorial scheme reflects the relative importance of the officials of state within the new constitution. The priests may not own land, but they have YHWH as their possession, and they have access to him. The relatively inferior status of the Levites is reflected in their portion being farther removed from the core . . . the location of his (the prince's) grant outside the sacred reserve reflects his relative secular nonpriestly role" [654].

**45:3.** The measurements in this verse seem redundant, but see the emendation of verse 1 based on LXX to 25,000 x 20,000. Rashi continues to claim that all measurements are in *qānîm*. Radak cites Rashi without comment. Eliezer of Beaugency also claims that this verse is in *qānîm*, thus the *qōdeš* is outside the *tĕrûmâ*. That is, he is harmonizing the 10,000 of the MT in verse 1 with verse 4.

**45:4.** Assuming the continued use of the long cubit, the length computes to slightly more than 8 miles, and the width to almost 6.5 miles, covering an area over 50 square miles [652]. These dimensions agree with the measurements of the temple compound in 42:20.

*who serve the temple (mĕšārĕtê hammiqdāš).* This refers to the total priestly corps, as in the parallel passage, 48:15. The term *miqdāš* can refer to the entire sanctuary or *temenos* (cf. 8:6; 20:3; 23:38, 39; 37:28; 44:7, 8); *haqqĕrēbîm lĕšārēt*, "those who qualify to serve" (i.e., Zadokites; cf. 44:15; 48:11); *ûmiqdāš lammiqdāš*, "the holy area for the sanctuary."

**45:5.** The Levitic tract is the same size as the priestly tract—25,000 x 10,000. The Levites are specified as *mĕšārĕtê habbayit*, "caretakers of the temple compound." Whereas the

200. Kasher, *Ezekiel*, 875.

priestly tract is called *naḥălâ*, the Levitic tract is *ăḥuzzâ*, a designation of mobility and saleable land. Whereas the priests adhere to fixed land (*naḥălâ*, "inheritable, non-saleable property") the Levites are mobile within their tract, able to sell and redeem their homes (Lev 25:33–34). Thus, the Levites' land is called *ăḥuzzâ* (cf. 48:22) and is never referred to as *naḥălâ*.[201]

**for urban living** (reading *'ārîm lāšābet*, with LXX instead of MT *'eśrîm lěšākôt*; cf. n. 722). The designation of the Levite property as cities recalls Num 35:1–8; Josh 21. Instead of being scattered throughout the land, the Levitic cites are concentrated in the Levitic sacred tract next to the priestly tract and the sanctuary itself [653]. Kasher claims that by assigning land to the Levites, Ezekiel differs with Num 35:1–8, which disperses the Levites among forty-eight cities throughout the land (cf. Josh 21 for details).[202] However, if the LXX *'ārîm lāšebet*, "cities to live in," preserves the correct text, then Ezekiel has concentrated the forty-eight Levitic cities within the assigned Levitic land, and no textual conflict need be envisaged.

**45:6.** The "city" is not Jerusalem, which is never mentioned in this part of Ezekiel. On the other hand, its location approximates Jerusalem. Was Ezekiel intimating that Jerusalem would be restored?

**it belongs to all Israel** (*lěkōl-bêt yiśrā'ēl yihyeh*). Rashi suggests that it is meant for pilgrims; so too Block [653]. We should remind ourselves of these enormous dimensions: The city tract is 5,000 x 25,000 cubits or 1.6 miles x 8 miles, but this is only miniscule compared with Jerusalem of the Dead Sea Scrolls. In contrast to the priestly tract, it is not holy.

**45:7.** The territory of the *nāśî'* is on both sides of the *těrûmâ*. *wěʼōrek lěʻumat ʼeḥad hahălākîm*, "the width is alongside one of the tribes." This must refer to Benjamin or Judah, which abut to the north and south of the *těrûmâ*, respectively. *'el pěnê*, "facing"; *litěrûmat* = *'el pěnê těrûmat*. Also Radak refers to the territory of the *nāśî'* as the thirteenth tribal area (*ḥēlek*).

The inheritable land given to the prince renders him a figure of considerable wealth (see further the COMMENT on 46:18). Out of this vast estate the prince provides the bull for the *pesaḥ* (45:22). All the required offerings for the sabbaths and new moons are also the prince's responsibility (46:4–8). See Excurses 3.6 on the *nāśî'* (46:18).

**45:8.** Haran writes:

> The '*těrûmâ*' (in other words, the offering from the land), as the prophet calls it, is a strip of land 25,000 cubits wide and the length of one of the territories from east to west (48:8); in other words: the length of the strips across the entire country, each of which is given to a different tribe. In the middle of this strip is

---

201. For a more precise distinction between these two terms, see Milgrom, *Leviticus 23–27*, 2171–73.
202. Kasher, "Anthropomorphism, Holiness and Cult," 207.

### The Sanctuary Personnel and the Nāśî' (Ezekiel 44–46)

located a square, which is also designated as "all the *terumah*" by the prophet, and whose dimensions are "25,000 by 25,000" (48:20), a square, as evidenced by the LXX to 48:9). This square is divided into three strips from north to south: the priestly lands, a rectangle of 25,000 by 10,000 (45:3–4; 48:10–12), within which is the temple; the Levitical territory, also a rectangle of the same size (45:5; 48:13); the remainder of this square, a rectangle of 25,000 by 5000, is the municipal territory, in the middle of which is found the city, common to all of the tribes. Everything on either side of this strip of territory, to the furthest extent of the territory to the west and to the east, is the *nāśî*'s territory; in other words, the royal domain (45:7–8; 48:21–22).[203]

It is worth emphasizing that the priestly territory is found at the northern side of the *tĕrûmâ*, with the Levitical territory to its south and the municipal territory on the southern side of the *tĕrûmâ*. This order is made evident by 45:1–5 and especially 48:10–13, where the priestly and Levitical strips are mentioned expressly from north to south. Many scholars assumed that the Levitical strip was north of the priestly strip, which was supposedly in the center of the square, with the Levitical portion to the left and the municipal area to the right. But this assumption has no real support, and it would appear that scholars adopted this interpretation in order to further stress the schematic character of the plan and to emphasize its symmetry.

Furthermore, the two northern strips of the *tĕrûmâ* (the priestly and Levitical strips), joined together in a rectangle of 25,000 by 20,000 (and not just the priestly strip as some assumed), are called *tĕrûmat hāqqōdeš* or *tĕrûmâ lĕYHWH*. Thus, this rectangle is differentiated from the municipal territory, called explicitly *ḥōl* (48:15), as well as from the *nāśî*'s territory, which also has no sanctity" (see Fig. 20, below).

**[He will] no longer defraud (*wĕlō' yônû*).** The custom of the *nāśî*'/king to confiscate private property is widely attested (46:18; 1 Sam 22:7).

### The Regulations of the Nāśî' (45:9–25)

#### The Prince's Obligation to the People (45:9–12)

TRANSLATION

9 Thus Lord YHWH has declared: "Enough,[204] O Princes of Israel! Stop your violence[205] and plundering.[206] Do what is just and right. End[207] your expul-

---

203. Haran, "Ezekiel," 229.

204. On *rab lākem* see 44:6 [654, n. 34].

205. On *ḥāmās* see Gen 6:11, 13. Because of *ḥāmās*, God destroyed the world.

206. A standard correlative of *ḥāmās* (Hab 1:3; in reverse order, Jer 6:7; 20:8; Amos 3:10). *ḥāmās wāšōd* may also be interpreted as a hendiadys [654, n. 36].

207. Ezekiel's uses *hērîm* for "put an end to," (lit., "lift off") which is rare (cf. Dan 8:11) [654, n. 37]. But this is Ezekiel's positive use of *hērîm* (45:1, 13; 48:8, 9, 20). Tur-Sinai emends *grštykm*, "your expulsions," to *ngystykm*, "your exactions." *Pšuto šel-Miqrā'* III, 38.

# PART TWO: EZEKIEL 40–48—THE VISIONARY SANCTUARY AND THE LAND

sions[208] of my people"—the declaration of the Lord YHWH. 10 "Keep[209] honest weights,[210] and an honest ephah [dry measure] and an honest bath [liquid measure]. 11 Keep honest balances, an honest ephah and an honest bath, with the bath holding one-tenth of a homer, and ephah a tenth of a homer. The homer will be the standard measure. 12 The shekel will weigh 20 gerahs. 20 shekels plus 25 shekels plus 15 shekels will make up the minah for you."[211]

## Comment

**45:9.** According to Radak, this verse is directed against the predestruction kings of Judah. Here it refers to political leaders' confiscation of commoners' real estate (see further 46:18). The best-known example is the seizure of Naboth's land by Ahab and Jezebel (1 Kgs 21). But Samuel's warning to the people of the "way of kings" in 1 Sam 8:14 suggests that this kind of behavior was widespread in the ancient world. To the cultic offenses of Ezek 44:6 have been added the moral sins of 45:9 [655]. In the ancient Near East, the maintenance of standard weights and measures was considered a royal responsibility. Thus, in the prologue to the ancient Sumerian law-code of Ur-Nammu we read that Ur-Nammu "fashioned the bronze *silá*-measures, he standardized the one mina weight [and] standardized the stone-weight of a shekel of silver in relation to one mina."[212] In Israel, the king was the final court of appeals (2 Sam 15:3–4; 1 Kgs 3:16–17). There is no indication that this function continued with the king's substitute, the *nāśî'*, "prince." Instead, all judicial questions are ostensibly assigned (nationally) to a system of judges and priests (Deut 17:9) that formed the judicial system in preexilic times; though it would seem that the priestly judges might have jurisdiction in religious, rather than civil cases.

Thus, it is not surprising that Ezekiel adds to the standard religious repertoire of the priesthood (44:23; cf. Lev 8:10) the following assignment: *wěʻal rîb hēmma yaʻamědû lšpṭ (K) lěmišpāṭ (Q) běmišpāṭay wšpṭh (Q) yišpṭuhû (K).* "In the context of formal disputes they shall officiate as judges" (44:24). One would presume that with the abolition of the crown, in favor of the *nāśî'*, any leadership role within the sanctuary would also involve the transfer of the judicial role from the *nāśî'* to the Zadokite priests (44:24), as mentioned above. But, as Duguid reminds us, the *nāśî'* is charged *mišpāṭ ûṣědāqâ ʻăśu*, "practice what is just and right" (45:9).[213] This is the exact at-

---

208. Tg. makes sense of the cause of the expulsions by adding "cease your taxation [of my people]." That is, confiscation of property and expulsion follow in the wake of nonpayment of taxes.

209. *yěhî lākem*, lit., "let there be for you" [656, n. 40].

210. On *mōʼznayim*, "balance, scale," see Block *Ezekiel 1–24*, 123 [656, n. 41].

211. *maneh* (Akkadian *manû*, Ugaritic *man*) totals sixty shekels, following the Babylonian sexagesimal system. But the MT is difficult: the form for fifteen, *'ăśārâ waḥămiššâ*, occurs only here (cf. GKC §97d, e) and the final *šeqel* is sg. when pl. is expected. Many commentators and translators follow LXX, "Five shekels [will be] five, and ten shekels [will be] ten, and your mina will be fifty shekels" [656, n. 42]. Cooke, *Ezekiel*, 498–99; Wevers, *Ezekiel*, 225; Eichrodt, *Ezekiel*, 567; Zimmerli, *Ezekiel 2*, 474; Hals, *Ezekiel*, 324; RSV, NEB (partially).

212. *ANET*, 523–24.

213. Duguid, *Ezekiel and the Leaders*, 54.

tribute affirmed of King Josiah by Jeremiah (22:15), who explains in the next verse as having "judged the cause of the poor and needy." Similar qualities are expected by Jeremiah of the coming "righteous Branch of David": "he shall reign as a king and deal wisely and shall execute justice and righteousness [ʾāśâ mišpāṭ ûṣĕdāqâ] in the land" (Jer 23:5). Thus, Duguid seems justified in concluding "that the nāśîʾ's responsibilities in the administration of justice have not been significantly curtailed."[214]

**45:10-12.** Similar regulations in the Holiness Code (Lev 19:36) as well as in Deut 25:15 and Prov 16:13 indicate that this was the most common way to cheat in the market place. In an economic environment lacking official norms for weights and measures, merchants were particularly tempted to cheat their customers by falsifying weights (shekels, ʾabnê ṣedeq, "just stones," Lev 19:36); the latter by false bottoms and other means of altering the size of vessels. The prophets rail against such practices (e.g., Amos 8:5-6; Hos 12:8 [Eng 7]; Mic 6:10-11; as does Deuteronomy, in 25:13-16 [Block]). The wisdom teacher advised: "A false weight [môʾznê mirmâ] is an abomination to YHWH, but a just weight [ʾeben šĕlēmâ] is his delight" (Prov 11:1; cf. 16:11; 20:10). Zech 5:5-11 envisages an ephah as a basket large enough to hold a person.

Ezekiel decrees that an ephah is one-tenth of a homer. Estimates on the size of a homer vary. ḥōmer is related to Akkadian imēr, "donkey load" (cf. Ug, ḥmr). Hebrew ḥōmer ranges from 134 liters to 230 liters.[215] The shekel is a stone arbitrarily fixed with the smallest unit of weight (20 gerahs to the shekel) and weighing about 11.4 grams. Ezekiel's minah was to be the sum of 20+25+15 = 60 shekels. Ezekiel's minah may be a metric innovation, inspired by the sexagesimal Babylonian system [657]. Eliezer of Beaugency reminds us that maʿăśēr does not refer to the tithe (i.e., to the temple) but to the king's tribute; and that three different minas are indicated here: regular (20), large (25), and small (15)

R. Hisda said (B.B. 90a-b): Samuel took as a basis for his decision the following verse [Ezek 45:12]: "And the shekel shall be twenty gerahs: [in pieces of] twenty shekels, five and twenty shekels, fifteen shekels, shall be your maneh." Was, then, a maneh sixty shekels, which makes two hundred and forty zuz? Therefore from this verse three things may be inferred: (a) That the maneh of the sanctuary was twice as much in value as the common shekel; (b) that it is allowed to increase a sixth, but not more; and (c) that the sixth may be added even from outside (e.g., to add ten to fifty, so that the sixth may be reckoned after being added, as the maneh of Ezekiel is sixty shekels, while a maneh in general contains twenty-five shekels).

---

214. Ibid.
215. Cf. Powel, "Weights and Measures," 6:897-908.

## The People's Obligation to the Prince (45:13–17)

### Translation

**13** You will levy this offering: From a homer[216] of wheat, one-sixth of an ephah; from a homer of barley, also one sixth[217] of an ephah. **14** The regular amount of oil—measured in baths[218]—will be one-tenth of a bath from each kor (because 10 baths equal 1 homer).[219] **15** [The regular quota] from the flock will be one[220] out of every 200 sheep. [These are the products] from the watered[221] areas of Israel that will be meal offerings, whole burnt offerings, and well-being offerings, to atone for you[222]—the declaration of the Lord YHWH. **16** The entire population of the land[223] is responsible to the prince in Israel to take part in this offering. **17** But the prince will be responsible for the whole burnt offerings, the meal offerings, and the libations at the pilgrimage festivals, the new moons, the sabbaths, and all the other appointed festivals of the house of Israel. He will provide the purification offerings, the meal offerings, the whole burnt offerings, and the well-being offerings, to atone on behalf of the house of Israel.

### Comment

#### *The Těrûmâ of the Nation for the Nāśî' on Behalf of the Sanctuary*

**45:13–15.** Block comments:

> The actual *těrûmâ* instructions break down into three parts, regulating the taxing of grain, olive oil, and sheep, respectively, for the regular ritual sacrifices. The difference between the present use of *těrûmâ* and verse 1, where it identified a tract of land set apart for YHWH, is obvious. But it is also distinguished from the *těrûmâ* mentioned in 44:30, where the word denoted the choice offerings of the first products of the harvest. Now *těrûmâ* is used non-technically of those gifts

---

216. Tg., Vulg, and Pesh. render *ḥōmer* as *kôr*. LXX reads γομορ here but χορου in verse 13b [657, n. 49].

217. In *wěšiššîtem* MT has created a new denominative Piel verb, "and you shall give one-sixth part," out of the ordinal *šiššît*. The versions and the parallelism of the previous phrase argue for the deletion of this final *mem*, which is probably due to wrong word division [657, n. 50].

218. Most delete the appositional phrase, *habbat haššemen*, lit., "the bath the oil," as a gloss, in spite of support from the versions. See Allen, *Ezekiel 20–48*, 247 [657, n. 51].

219. A literal reading of MT. The first occurrence of this phrase is missing in LXX and usually deleted as a dittography [658, n. 53].

220. "One [sheep]." Read *wěśeh-'eḥād* for *wěśeh-'aḥat*.

221. *mimmišqēh*, from *šāqâ*, "to drink," is used in Gen 13:10 for irrigation ditches. Tg. *mqtym*, "from the fatlings," treats the term metonymically. REB "clan" follows LXX in reading *mimmišpěḥôt*. BHS follows (Gese, *Verfassungsentwurf*, 70, n. 1) in emending to *mimmiqnēh*, "from the cattle" [658, n. 55].

222. LXX *'ălēkem*; MT *'ălêhem* [658, n. 56].

223. *hāāreṣ* is ungrammatical after *hā'ām*, and is dropped by LXX. Gese (*Verfassungsentwurf*, 72) suggests that it entered the text under the influence of *'am hāāreṣ* in verse 22 and 46:3. It is preferable, however, to read *kol-'am hāāreṣ*, dropping the article on *hā'ām* [658, n. 57].

## The Sanctuary Personnel and the Nāśî' (Ezekiel 44–46)

that are donated for the regular sacrifices. To provide for these offerings wheat and barley are to be taxed at the rate of 1/6 of an ephah for every homer of grain, which amounts to a 1/60 levy, or 1.6 percent. Since barley is cheap and wheat is expensive you give 1/6 of barley and 1/60 of wheat. The rate for olive oil is 1/10 of a bath for every homer, or 1 percent. Sheep are to be taxed at one animal per 200; that is, at the rate of 0.5 percent. The concluding statement indicates that these contributions are to be used for the grain (*minḥâ*), whole burnt (*ʿōlâ*), and well-being (*šĕlāmîm*) offerings through which expiation (*kippēr*) could be achieved for the people. The divine signatory formula brings these instructions to a close [659].

It should be noted that in verse 15 and again in verse 7 the *ʾāšām* offering is omitted. This demonstrates that the *tĕrûmâ* taxes are for the public exclusively, not for the individual.

**45:14.** 1 kur of oil equals 10 bath, which equals 1 homer—a liquid measure. Eliezer of Beaugency explains why only 1/10 is demanded for oil, as opposed to 1/6 for grain: grains are cheaper (more common); but since there is no mention of wine, apparently there was no libation of wine practiced in Ezekiel's sanctuary, except on holidays.

**45:15** *from the watered areas* (*mimmašqēh*). This word seems out of place in the context of animal offerings if its meaning is "well-watered" flocks (Eliezer of Beaugency), but see LXX, *mimmišpĕḥôt yiśrāʾēl*, "from the Israelite families." Rashi follows the rabbinic interpretation, "libation" (*Pesaḥ* 48a). Radak renders "from Israel's fatlings."

The *šĕlāmîm*, "well-being," sacrifice does not provide expiation in P. However, in H it means "ransom," i.e., the animal sacrifice ransoms its killer.[224] My study concluded: "H has initiated a new function for the *šĕlāmîm*, which differs radically from that of P. Rather than being another kind of P's *šĕlāmîm* of joy, H's *šĕlāmîm* is an expiatory sacrifice, ransoming (*kpr*) the offerer for the sin of killing (slaughtering) the sacrificial animal,"[225] thus providing a new H precedent for Ezekiel.[226]

**45:16–17.** The citizens of the land (as in 7:27, *ʿam hāʾāreṣ*, "people of the land," refers to all full citizens) are accountable to the prince for the manner in which they respond to these obligations [659 n. 42]. Ganzel observes that references to the people in the temple service are marginal; the priests and the prince are never called the people's representatives.[227]

The role of the *nāśîʾ* in these *tĕrûmâ* offerings is that he must make them available to the priests at national festivals (*ḥaggîm*), the new moon festivals (*ḥŏdāšîm*), the sabbaths (*šabbātôt*), and all other appointed celebrations (*môʿădîm*). Moreover, the *nāśîʾ* must provide the animals/produce for all the sacrifices: purification offering (*ḥaṭṭāʾt*), cereal offering (*minḥâ*), whole burnt offering (*ʿōlâ*), well-being offering (*šĕlāmîm*),

---

224. Cf. Milgrom, *Leviticus 17–22*, on Lev 17:11.
225. Ibid., 1478.
226. For another view, see Kasher, "Anthropomorphism, Holiness and Cult," 207.
227. Ganzel, *Concept of Holiness*, 131.

and libations (*nēsek*)—primarily olive oil and wine [659]. That the *nāśî'* has a major financial role in subsidizing the cult is based on a pentateuchal (priestly) source. The princes are responsible for supplying the precious stones for the ephod and the priestly breastplate (Exod 35:27); they also contributed the precious cultic offerings during the first twelve days of the initiation offerings of the tabernacle (Num 7). Conspicuous by its absence is the reparation offering (*'āšām*), which is not due to an accident (Block, 659), but due to the fact that the *nāśî'* is responsible for the public but not the private sacrifices. The *'āšām* is exclusively a private offering.

It is evident from these lists that in Ezekiel's new order, sin will continue to be a problem for the nation. Block (660) claims that the people's sin is limited by the guardianship of the patron *nāśî'*. However, in the new sanctuary there can only be accidental sin, expiated by the purification offering (*ḥaṭṭā't*). The absence of the high priest is even more conspicuous. The purification offering (*ḥaṭṭā't*) for the people is, in the Priestly Code, exclusively the responsibility of the high priest (Lev 4:13–23). Once again we have evidence that Ezekiel has eliminated the high priest from leading the cult: All priests are eligible to purify the people of their inadvertent sin.

The *nāśî'* is responsible for all the offerings on the holy days, cf. the public sacrifices in Num 28–29 where the *ḥaṭṭā't* is the final sacrifice. Here it precedes the whole burnt and well-being offerings, probably referring to its order in the service. According to MT, the *nāśî'* provides the holiday sacrifices: the whole burnt, cereal, and libation offerings, but he prepares (*ya'ăśeh*) the following sacrifices for the altar: the purification, cereal, whole burnt and well-being offerings. The active immolation is performed by the priests. According to Eliezer of Beaugency, the *nāśî'* provides the offerings from the *tĕrûmâ*, which has been donated by the people, analogous to the silver donated by the people during the days of King Joash (2 Kgs 11:5–6).

## The Pesaḥ and Its Prelude (45:18–25)

TRANSLATION

**18** Thus has Lord YHWH proclaimed: To purify the sanctuary on the first day of the first month, you will take an unblemished bull of the flock.[228] **19** The priest will take some of the blood from the purification offering[229] and smear it on the doorpost[230] of the temple and on the four corners of the altar's ledge,[231] and on the doorpost[232] of the inner court [eastern] gate.[233] **20** You will

---

228. I.e., the bull must be domesticated; cf. Milgrom, *Leviticus 1–16*, 232.
229. It is assumed that the purification offering was slaughtered.
230. LXX, Vulg, and Pesh., followed by moderns (e.g., Block, *Ezekiel 24–48*, 660, n. 4), hold that MT sg. *mĕzûzat* should be read as a pl. However, the temple contains only one door and sg. *mĕzûzat* refers to a single structure, the two posts of that one door.
231. For details, see the note on 43:20.
232. Again, the sg. MT *mĕzûzat* (n. 762) is to be preferred.
233. The sg. MT *ša'ar* is supported by the versions [660, n. 6].

do the same on the seventh day of the month[234] on behalf of the inadvertent[235] or ignorant sinner. In this way,[236] you shall purify[237] the temenos [the temple grounds].

**21** You will celebrate the *pesaḥ* when only unleavened bread may be eaten on the fourteenth day of the first month, a festival[238] of seven days.[239] **22** The prince will prepare a bull as a purification offering on that day, on his own behalf and on behalf[240] of all the people of the land. **23** He will provide a daily whole burnt offering to YHWH consisting of[241] seven unblemished bulls and seven unblemished rams and a male goat as a purification offering during the seven days of the festival **24** and a daily meal offering: an ephah for each bull, an ephah for each ram, and a hin of oil for each ephah.[242] **25** On a similar seven-day festival beginning the fifteenth day of the seventh month he will provide for the same purification, whole burnt, meal, and oil offerings.

COMMENT

**45:18–20.** There is a debate among scholars whether the present ordinance involves a one-time altar-cleansing ritual or an annual sanctuary-purgation ritual. Block, (662–64) who sides with the one-time ritual, cites these reasons, followed by my refutation:

234. LXX ἐν τῷ ἑβδόμῳ μηνὶ μιᾷ τοῦ μηνὸς (= *baššĕbî'î bĕ'eḥād laḥōdeš*), "in the seventh month on the first day of the month" [661, n. 7]. This reading assumes another purificatory ritual in the fall, matching the one in the spring. However, the following reduced qualifications render the LXX unlikely.

235. Inadvertent wrongdoing may result from two causes: negligence or ignorance. Either the offender knows the law but involuntarily violates it or he acts advertently but is unaware he did wrong. The former situation underlies the example of accidental homicide cited in Num 35:16–25 and Deut 19:5–6, and the latter is presumed in 1 Sam 14:32–34 and some nonritual texts as 1 Sam 26:21; Prov 5:23; Job 6:26; 19:4. For details, see Milgrom, *Leviticus 1–16*, 282–83 and the COMMENT here.

236. The consecutive perfect suggests a conclusion to the series begun at verse 18; cf. GKC §111k [661, n. 10].

237. *wĕkippartem*, "you shall purge," is a strange synonym for the verb *ḥiṭṭē'*, "clean," but *kipper* has the power to effect atonement, e.g., Lev 16:6, 11, 17, 24, 32; cf. Ezek 43:26.

238. Block [661, n. 12] claims that *happāsaḥ ḥag* is the inverse of *ḥag happāsaḥ* (cf. Exod 34:25), and that the missing article (*he*) may have been lost by pseudo-haplography. However, MT makes sense once it is realized that during the Babylonian exile (the time of Ezekiel) the term *ḥag* had metamorphosed from the pilgrimage festival on the seventh day of the Feast of Unleavened Bread (Exod 13:6), and to the first day of the Feast of Unleavened Bread (Exod 12:14), and finally to all seven days of the Feast of Unleavened Bread (Ezek 45:21; Ezra 6:22; 2 Chr 8:12–13; 30:13, 21; 35:17). For details, see Milgrom, *Leviticus 23–27*, 1970–76.

239. Seven, MT *šĕbu'ōt*. In several Hebrew mss. and in the versions the sg. *šib'at* appropriately appears [661, n. 13].

240. Cf. Milgrom, "*kipper 'ad/bĕ'adh*," 16–17.

241. The seven bulls and seven rams for each of the seven days are reminiscent of the same number of sacrificial animals offered up by Balaam to curse Israel, but in vain. The prevalence of the number seven in the rituals of the ancient Near East may be due to its being the first nonregular number indivisible by 2, 3, and 5. That it could not be broken down gave the number 7 the attribute of perfection, power, and permanence.

242. It is not clear why wine libations are omitted (contrary to Num 15:5, 7, 10; 28:14). Was Ezekiel afraid that his virtuous Zadokite priests might become intoxicated?

## PART TWO: EZEKIEL 40-48—THE VISIONARY SANCTUARY AND THE LAND

1. There is nothing in the Torah that resembles an annual rededication of the sanctuary on the first day of the first month (Nisan 1). However, Ezekiel was living in a Babylonian ambience where the Nisan 1 New Year festival initiates an annual renewal of the purification of the sanctuary, which may have influenced his state of mind. As he adapted the Babylonian ziggurat structure in his sanctuary, so he may have incorporated parts of the Babylonian New Year festival, especially the cleansing of the sanctuary.

2. Duguid suggests that the singular verbs are addressed to the *nāśî*', "prince,"[243] for which there is no textual evidence. The plain meaning, however, is that the singular verbs in verses 18 and 20 are directed to the prophet (*tiqqaḥ, ta'ăśeh*). If so, this pericope differs radically from the Torah's Day of Atonement (rather, Purgation), which is solely the stage for the high priest. However, Ezekiel (perhaps) sets up the *pesaḥ* celebration (vv. 18, 20), but the cleansing of the sanctuary is done exclusively by a priest (v. 19).

3. Block's main point is the parallelism that exists between this *pesaḥ* ritual and the initiation of the altar (43:18–27). His argument [663] is solid but bears criticism:

    a. The use of the Pi'el verbs *ḥiṭṭē*' and *kipper* recalls two of the key verbs in the altar initiation rite, 43:20, 22, 23, 26. But see *ḥiṭṭē*', Num 19:12, 13, 20; 31:20, 23; *kipper*, Exod 30:15, 16; Lev 1:4; 6:23; 8:34; 10:17, etc. The occurrences of these two verbs in the strict meaning of "clean" and "purge" respectively, outside of the context of the "altar" far outnumber their occurrences within.

    b. In 45:18, Ezekiel is ordered to take (*lāqaḥ*) a purification animal and cleanse the sanctuary (*miqdāš*). However, there is no proof that the subject of this action is Ezekiel rather than one of the people. Nor does it differ much from the Day of Purgation, where the requisite sacrificial animals are brought by the people (*'ădat bĕnê yiśrā'ēl*, Lev 16:5).

    c. *par-ben bāqār tāmîm* derives directly from 43:23. However, the source might as well be Lev 16:3, *bĕpar-ben bāqār*.

    d. The daubing of the *ḥaṭṭā't* blood in 45:19 resembles 43:20. However, the resemblance to Lev 16:14 is just as convincing (cf. Lev 4: 5, 18, 25, 30, 34).

    e. Here Block's suggestion is questionable. First, as mentioned above, there is only one gate with one pair of posts on the celestial platform. Secondly, the altar and the sanctuary building are an inseparable pair. Just as the priests are divided in guarding them (Num 18:5a), so here they are divided in decontaminating them. So too on Yom Kippur, the decontamination ritual is divided between the temple (Lev 16: 13–17) and the altar (Lev 16:18–19).

---

243. Duguid, *Ezekiel and the Leaders*, 64, following Biggs, "Role of *nāśî*'," 51, and H. G. May, "Ezekiel," 319.

f. Again Block is subject to question. In this respect there is no parallelism between the *pesaḥ* ritual and the initiation of the altar. The sanctuary is decontaminated on the first and seventh day of Nisan (v. 20), whereas the altar is decontaminated for seven continuous days (43:25–27).

The question still remains: What is the meaning of the seventh day of Nisan and its odd command that the sanctuary should be purged *mēʾîš šōgeh ûmippetî* (v. 20)? This question is further discussed in Excursus 4 (below) and in the COMMENT. Ezekiel then declares that this seventh day will be nationally observed on behalf of those who may have inadvertently contaminated the sanctuary during days 1–7 of Nisan.[244]

g. No comparison between cited verses 43:27 and 45:20 is given. This alleged comparison, I aver, makes it clear that 45:18–20 does not describe a one-time ritual. Indeed, the evidence shifts in the other direction once it is realized that there is no Yom Kippur in Ezekiel's calendar. It is hard to believe that he eliminated the day altogether. After all, inadvertent sins would continue to contaminate the sanctuary and the rite of 45:18–20 effectively purges it. Yet the question remains: If Nisan 1, 7, 14 is the annual replacement for Tishri 10 (*yôm hakkippûrîm*) why were three days required and not just one? It should be remembered that Ezekiel was not only changing the Day of Purgation. He was radically altering its *content*. P's Day of Purgation (Lev 16) was conducted in its entirety by the high priest. But Ezekiel had eliminated the service of the high priest in the sanctuary. The rite of purgation would now have to be carried by three purification offerings on three seven-day-apart Nisan days by the cadre of priests. In sum, on the basis of the existing evidence, one has to give the nod to the conclusion that 45:18–20 posits an annual ritual.

## EXCURSUS 5: THE PURIFICATION OFFERING (ḤAṬṬĀT) (45:18–25)

The text describing Ezekiel's visionary sanctuary refers frequently to the purification offering (Ezek 40:39; 43:19–25; 44:29; 45:17, 18–20, 23–25; 46:20). Mention has already been made of the fusion of the two kinds of *ḥaṭṭāʾt* (Lev 5; Num 15) in Ezekiel's paschal observance (45:21–24). On the fourteenth of the first month (*Pesaḥ*) a purification bull is offered up, and on each of the following seven days (of the Festival of Unleavened Bread), seven bulls and seven rams are immolated as whole burnt offerings with their cereal and oil accompaniments and one he-goat as a purification offering. The same sacrificial series is prescribed for the seven-day Feast of Tabernacles (*beḥag*, v. 25).

---

244. On days 8–14 the assumption is that all Israel is free of sin, advertently and inadvertently alike. The truth be told that during these days if a person became corpse-contaminated he could not become decontaminated in time to observe the *pesaḥ* and would of necessity have to remove him/herself from the community and await another opportunity, a month later, to observe the *pesaḥ* (Num 9:6–14).

# PART TWO: EZEKIEL 40–48—THE VISIONARY SANCTUARY AND THE LAND

The types and number of animals are at variance with P's prescriptions (Num 28:16–25). Moreover, the requirement that a purification bull be offered on the fourteenth, the same day and just before each Israelite family head offers up the paschal sacrifice (see Lev 23:5; Exod 12:1–14), is entirely novel. Still, it begins to make sense once it is realized that Ezekiel's sacrificial series for the paschal festival corresponds precisely with that prescribed for the altar initiation (43:18–27): a purification bull is offered on the first day (vv. 18–20) and a purification he-goat and a whole burnt-offering bull and ram on each of the following seven days (vv. 21–26). Yet the initiation of Ezekiel's altar is at variance with the altar initiation of the tabernacle, which prescribes a purification bull for all seven days (Exod 29:36) together with a burnt-offering ram (Lev 8:18–21; Exod 29:15–18). Also the length of the initiation service differs for Ezekiel: the tabernacle for seven days (Lev 8:33; Exod 29:35, 37) and Ezekiel's for eight.

To be sure, the text states that the ceremony for the altar initiation lasts for seven days (Ezek 43:25–26) and that the regular cult begins thereafter on the eight day (v. 27). But this seven-day period does not include the day on which the purification bull is offered; rather, it follows it. This can be deduced from the time specified for the beginning of this seven-day period, *ûbayyôm haššēnî* (v. 22), which must be rendered "on the next day" (not "on the second day"), a usage clearly attested in a number of passages (e.g., Exod 2:13; Josh 10:32; Judg 20:24–25; Neh 8:13). Thus, Ezekiel's altar initiation is prescribed for eight days precisely and with the same sacrificial ritual as his *pesaḥ* celebration. And the one illuminates the other: Just as the altar initiation unambiguously serves the purpose of purging the altar, so Ezekiel's unique requirement that a purification bull be offered by the prince (*nāśî'*) on Nisan 14 "on his behalf and on behalf of the people of the land" (45:22) can only be understood as part of a total scheme to purge the sanctuary in preparation for the following week of the Feast of Unleavened Bread (for a vivid example of the concern for the sanctuary's purity for the paschal sacrifice, see 2 Chr 30:15–20).

Undoubtedly, P is just as concerned as Ezekiel with the purity of the sanctuary, and for that reason mandates the presentation of a he-goat purification offering on every festival day (Num 28–29). The one exception is the day of the paschal sacrifice. It may be surmised that, in this matter, P reflects an earlier period—before the centralization efforts of Hezekiah and Josiah—when the paschal sacrifice was offered at local sanctuaries. Be that as it may, Ezekiel's obsession with purifying the sanctuary in preparation for the *pesaḥ* is underscored by his instructions that on the first day of the first month the blood of a purification bull is to be applied to the doorposts of the sanctuary building, the four corners of the altar's ledge (see at Lev 4:25) and the doorposts of the (eastern, Ezek 46:1) inner gateway (45:18–19).

The same purificatory ritual is enjoined "on the seventh day of the month [of the pollution caused] *mē'îš šōgeh ûmippetî*, "by an inadvertent or ignorant person" (v. 20). To be sure, LXX reads the date as "in the seventh month, on the first of the month," implying that the second purgation of the sanctuary is to fall six months later; a reading accepted by nearly every commentator since Wellhausen. Favoring the MT, however, is the added remark that the pollution has been caused by inadvertent and ignorant persons. Inadvertence[245] is familiar to us as an indispensable requirement for the purification offering (Lev 4:2). But what does ignorance (*petî*) connote? Ezekiel is drawing a finer distinction. Accidental wrong can result from two causes: negligence or ignorance. Either the offender knows the law but violates it unintentionally or he acts intentionally but does not know that he has done wrong.[246] For Ezekiel, the *šōgeh* is characterized by lack of intention, the *petî*, by lack of knowledge. The former underlies the cases of involuntary homicide (Num 35:16–18, 22–23); the latter is presupposed in non-ritual texts (e.g., 1 Sam 26:21; Prov 5:23; cf. Ps 19:15; Job 6:24; 19:4).[247]

It is assumed that after the sanctuary is purged on the first of the month, all of Israel will make a concerted effort to avoid ritual impurity during the following two weeks so that the *pesaḥ* on the fourteenth will be observed in purity. One need only recall that P requires the safeguarding of the paschal sacrifice for four days (Exod 12:3–6). Indeed, the period leading up to P's *pesaḥ* is characterized by ritual purification—the removal of leaven from the home (Exod 12:15, 19–20; 13:7). Ezekiel also demands the simultaneous purification of the temple. He therefore institutes two sanctuary purgation days, the second one on the seventh of the month for those who, despite their precautions, inadvertently or unwittingly contracted a sanctuary-polluting impurity. Thus LXX makes no sense whatever in scheduling the second sanctuary purgation six months later. If the prophet really intended a semiannual cleansing of the sanctuary, why would the second one be limited to cases of accidental pollution?

P's annual Day of Purgation (Lev 16:16, 21) is expressly devised for Israel's presumptuous sins. By the same token, it must be assumed that Ezekiel's sanctuary purgation on the first of the month effects a similar purpose: all impurity, caused by presumptuous and accidental acts, is cleansed. On the seventh, purgation is repeated lest pollution has recurred through inadvertence or ignorance. And, finally, on the fourteenth, before each Israelite family head offers up his paschal sacrifices, a third purgation takes place (45:22), but this time on the altar alone, of the lesser impurities that may have occurred during the preceding week. This would provide a final opportunity for those impurity bearers who were liable for a purification sacrifice during one of the days between Nisan 8–14 (e.g., scale diseased, Lev 14:1–32; abnormal genital discharge, Lev 15), but could not get to the sanctuary with their individual purification offering. The sanctuary's purification offering suffices to purge the sanctuary for him/her. Thus Ezekiel prescribes, in all, three purgation bulls, seven days apart, as the means of providing a ritually pure temple for the celebration of *pesaḥ*. For those whose purification is incomplete by 1/14, the *pesaḥ* sacrifice would be postponed for one month (Num 9:9–14).

The *ḥaṭṭā't* prescribed for Ezekiel's corpse-contaminated priest occurs in the following passage: *wě'aḥărê ṭohŏrātô šib'at yāmîm yispěrû-lô ûběyôm bō'ô 'el-haqqōdeš 'el-heḥāṣēr happěnîmît lěšārēt baqqōdeš yaqrîb ḥaṭṭā'tô ně'um YHWH*, "After his purification

---

245. For the verbal form *šāgâ*, see Milgrom, *Leviticus 1–16*, 242–43.
246. Milgrom, *Leviticus 17–22*, 1967.
247. Ibid.

[from corpse-contamination], seven days shall be counted off for him; and on the day he reenters the Holy Place, [namely] the inner court to officiate in the Holy Place, he shall present his purification offering—declares the Lord YHWH" (Ezek 44:26–27).

Ezekiel's variance from the Priestly text is striking. Whereas P (and H) make no distinction between priests and laity regarding purification from corpse contamination—both require the ashes of the Red Cow and ablutions (Num 19:17–19)—Ezekiel extends the purification period for corpse-contaminated priests an additional week, capped by a purification offering. Because this sacrifice is prescribed for severe cases of impurity—such as the parturient (Lev 12:6, 8), the *měṣōrāʿ* (Lev 14:19, 31), and the *zāb/zābâ* (Lev 15:15, 30)—Ezekiel obviously regards the impurity generated by the corpse to be greater for the priest than for the lay person. This is not surprising. In Ezekiel's system, the priest is subject to severer regulations: His marriage rules resemble those of H's high priest (cf. Ezek 44:22 with Lev 21:14), and his priestly clothing is contagious not only to objects but to persons (Ezek 44:19).

Moreover, his stand is logical. If a Nazirite, whose sanctity is temporary, is required to bring a purification offering for corpse contamination, all the more so a priest, whose sanctity is lifelong. In fact, the logic of Ezekiel's ruling leads one to suspect that he speaks for an older tradition, and that it was P or H that modified it. More likely, the change is the work of H, who, in opposition to P, enjoins holiness upon all Israel (Lev 19:2) and, without denying the intrinsic sanctity of the priest (Lev 21:8), does not hesitate to declare that YHWH sanctifies (*měqaddēš*) all the people (Lev 20:8; 21:8, 15, 23; 22:9, 32).

If, then, the equivalence of priests and laity was desired in this matter, why was the priest made to conform to the laity rather than the reverse: why not a purification offering for both? The answer may rest in the polemic generated by Israel's long struggle with ancestral worship:[248] the fear that sacrifices *because of* the dead might turn into sacrifices *to* the dead.

The text is silent concerning the animal required to represent the *ḥaṭṭāʾt* (44:27). On the analogy of the Nazirite (Num 6:10–11), we may assume that it was a bird.[249] The remaining references in Ezekiel to the purification offering (Ezek 40:39; 44:29; 46:20) throw no new light on the sacrifice.

Finally, as correctly noted by Patton, although he is a priest, Ezekiel never *performs* as a priest.[250] Even if he prescribes the rituals, he never officiates. Thus, he provides the *ḥaṭṭāʾt* bull for the initiation of the altar, and he hands it over to the priests (on duty). To be sure, the subject of the ritual procedure is frequently in the first person, implying that the subject is Ezekiel. However, as noted above, the subjects have been manipulated by the redactor. So too, Ezekiel provides the *ḥaṭṭāʾt* bull for the annual 1/1 purgation of the sanctuary, and again does not officiate with it but turns it over to the priests (on duty, 45:8). The conclusion cannot be avoided that the active second-person verb must be

---

248. See ibid., on Lev 19:26–28, 31; 20:1–6.
249. See further Milgrom, *Leviticus 1–16*, 986–91.
250. Patton, *Ezekiel's Blueprint*, 87–88.

understood passively, for example *wĕhiṭṭē'tā*, not "you shall purify" but "you shall have [the sanctuary] purified" (45:18).

**45:19.** It has been assumed that the *ḥaṭṭā't* has been offered up and that its blood has been daubed on the horns of the altar. Compare the smearing of blood on the altar (Ezek 43:20) with the smearing of blood on the priest during his dedication (Exod 29:21; Lev 8:30). The altar is seen as a living creature, *pars pro toto*: Blood put on the extremities stands for the entire object. Also, the extremities are the most vulnerable spots, and the blood protects them from demonic incursion. Blood is daubed on the middle section of the altar (the ledge) forming a straight line from the sanctuary entrance on the upper platform to the ledge, the middle of the altar on the priestly platform, and then to the doorposts of the eastern gateway at its entrance on the inner courtyard (the sacred spine, Fig. 14). The blood in Lev 16 also manifests an eastern movement, from greater to lesser holiness. Furthermore, on Yom Kippur the *ḥaṭṭā't* blood is sprinkled inside the adytum and the Tent of Meeting, then on the altar (Lev 16:15–19). So too the *ḥaṭṭā't* blood of Ezekiel's temple follows the same course: temple plus altar. Ezekiel adds the eastern inner gateway to cover (symbolically) all the most holy parts of the sanctuary complex.[251]

**45:20.** With Zimmerli,[252] *wĕkippartem 'et-habbāyit*, "Thus, you shall purge the temple," should be deleted as a secondary expansion because of (1) the change in number; (2) the change in terminology; *habbāyit* instead of *hammiqdaš*, and *wĕkippartem* instead of *wĕhiṭṭē'tā* (v. 18b); (3) the inner court and not the sanctuary building is decontaminated. This procedure makes sense. The entire sanctuary building on the upper platform is God's residence; no humans are allowed there, not even the high priest. I would presume that the redactor was influenced by the language of the initiation of the altar (43:20). Just as the blood daubing of the altar's horns and ledge (*'ăzārâ*) is summed up by *wĕhiṭṭē'tā 'ōtô wĕkippartāhû*, "thus you shall decontaminate it and purge it," so the decontamination of the sanctuary, *wĕhiṭṭē'tā 'et-hammiqdaš* (v. 18)—including the altar ledge (*'ăzārâ*; v. 19)—is summed up by a redactor, *wĕkippartem 'et-habbāyit*, "you shall purge the sanctuary" (v. 20). Thus *bāyit* here, as in 43:12 (twice); 44:11 (twice), 14; 45:5; 46:24 means "sanctuary."[253]

The question arises: Why does the initiation of the altar prescribe its purification for seven successive days (43:25), whereas the annual purification rite of the altar (on the cultic calendar) prescribes its purification only on the first and seventh days (45:18, 20)? The answer is that these rites are not equivalent. The altar's purgation is part of its

---

251. Kasher ("Anthropomorphism, Holiness and Cult," 206) argues that Ezekiel's purgation of the *external* sacred area (outside the building) replaces the priestly (P's) purgation of the internal sacred area, as described in Lev 16:12–16. However, inadvertent violation of prohibitive commandments inevitably continue to recur (cf. Lev 4:3–20).

252. Zimmerli, *Ezekiel 2*, 480, 483. Kasher ("Anthropomorphism, Holiness and Cult," 200) argues that *habbāyit* (25:12) implies that the entire temple is purged, including the adytum. However, Ezekiel's redeemed generation is incapable of committing intentional sins (36:26–27). Inadvertent sins, however, do not contaminate the adytum. Hence, the purgation.

253. See also n. 772 above and COMMENT.

initiation rite (43:18–26); the sanctuary's purgation (on 1/1) is in preparation for the observance of the *pesaḥ* (1/14), an event that recurs yearly.

On the seventh of Nisan, the inner court is cleansed again "on behalf of the inadvertent or ignorant sinner." According to *m. Yoma*, the high priest is carefully watched by the priestly interns for seven days. That is, for seven days the high priest is "under house arrest," lest he become defiled. So too, between days seven and fourteen, incomplete time for the seven-day purification from corpse-contamination remains. So too, one must presume, that from Nisan 1–7, some people were lax in their purity observance and the sanctuary had to be purified on their behalf. But from Nisan 8–14, the people tightened up their purity precautions. Thus, those who became corpse-contaminated did not offer up the *pesaḥ* but underwent the seven day purification ritual (Num 19:17–19) and observed the sacrificial *pesaḥ* one month later (Num 9:9–14).

**45:21.** *you shall celebrate the pesaḥ* (*yihyeh lākem happāsaḥ*). Whereas the term *ḥag* extends itself to embrace all seven days of the Feast of Unleavened Bread (see v. 23), the term *pesaḥ* remains riveted to the fourteenth of Nisan (see Excursus 6, below). The latter refers to the individual *pesaḥ* incumbent upon every family head (cf. Exod 12:3; Lev 23:5; Num 28:16). Ezekiel has no intention to change the ancient role of the *pesaḥ* required of each family whereby the family swears allegiance to the God and people of Israel. Also the *pesaḥ* no longer serves an apotropaic function. It is also hard to believe that the *ḥaṭṭā't* bull offered up by the *nāśî'* on the fourteenth of Nisan replaces the individual's *pesaḥ* sacrifice. Besides, the latter is a *zebaḥ šĕlāmîm* (Deut 16:2),[254] and not a *ḥaṭṭā't*.

As noted by Block [666], the historic changes in the *pesaḥ* sacrifice can be outlined as follows:

1. *pesaḥ* as a flock animal (lamb or goat), Exod 12:5; *ḥag* on Nisan 22 (Exod 13:6).

2. *pesaḥ* as above (Num 28:16), *ḥag* on the fifteenth of Nisan, and sacrifices of bulls and goats during the Feast of Unleavened Bread (Num 28:17–25; 2 Chr 30:15–17, 22, 24).

3. *pesaḥ* as above (2), lambs, bulls, and goats (2 Chr 35:7–17).

4. *pesaḥ* as above (1), bulls, rams, grain and goats (no mention of lambs).

The entire seven days of Feast of Unleavened Bread is called *ḥag* (Ezek 45:21–24). These are the sacrifices offered up by the *nāśî'*. The people, as individual families, offered up lambs; hence, notice of the latter is absent. Ezra 6:19–21 demonstrates that people continued to sacrifice the *pesaḥ* on the 14th of Nisan as a private familial offering.

**45:22.** Compare *ba'ădô ûbĕ'ad bêtô* (Lev 16:6, 11).[255] Whereas the high priest's Yom Kippur bull is only responsible for atoning his priestly house, the *nāśî'*'s bull is intended for the atonement of the entire Israelite nation.

---

254. Cf. Milgrom, *Leviticus 17–22*, 1965–74.
255. Cf. Milgrom, *Studies in Levitical Terminology*, 16–17.

## EXCURSUS 6: THE ḤAG

**45:23.** During the seven-day festival, *wěšibʿat yěmê-heḥag*. The verb *ḥāgag* means "turn, twist, dance out of happiness" (1 Sam 30:16; Ps 42:5), and its nominal form in Arabic (*ḥaǧǧ*) means "pilgrimage, procession, festal gathering."[256] The oldest, cultic calendar of Israel prescribed three mandatory, sanctuary appearances each year for adult males, of which the Festival of Unleavened Bread was one (Exod 23:17; 34:23; cf. Deut 16:16).

The first time *ḥag* appears in Scripture is where Moses demands of Pharaoh: "We will go, young and old. We will go with our sons and daughters, our flocks and herds, for we must observe YHWH's *ḥag*" (Exod 10:9). Thus the *ḥag* is a family affair (see Deut 16:11, 14). But Pharaoh replies: "No! You menfolk go and worship YHWH. Since that is what you want" (Exod 10:9)—keeping with the requirements of Exod 23:17; 34:23! As pointed out by Scott,[257] not all attestations of *ḥag* imply pilgrimage (e.g., Exod 32:5; Judg 21:19). The chances are that the oldest pre-centralization calendar (Exod 23:17; cf. 34:23) prescribed an appearance at a local sanctuary, which could hardly be called a pilgrimage.[258] Thus Kedar-Kopstein's rendering[259] "community festival" is more precise. Nonetheless, all other calendars mandating centralization of worship, either regionally (P and H) or nationally (D), would have pilgrimage in mind.

On what day(s) was the pilgrimage (*ḥag*)? The biblical sources provide three different answers: (1) *the first day* of the Feast of Unleavened Bread (Exod 12:14, 17; Lev 23:6 [H]; Num 23:17 [P]; Deut 16:16 [D], by inference from verses 2, and 7–8); (2) *the seventh day* (Exod 13:6 [JE]), and (3) *all seven days* (Ezek 45:21; Ezra 6:22; 2 Chr 8:12–13; 30:13, 21; 35:17). Clearly, Exod 13:6 (the Epic Source JE) is the oldest. There can be only one reason why the pilgrimage takes place on the seventh day. If the *pesaḥ* is observed at home on the fourteenth day in keeping with the regulations of Exod 12:1–13, 22–27a, 28 (all probably P, cf. Bar-On 1995), there would be no time (or energy) to make the pilgrimage the following morning. The *pesaḥ* would be offered up at local altars or, more likely, at improvised ones; in any case, near enough to bring the paschal blood back home to smear it at the entrance. The centralization of worship made a pilgrimage to the temple for the *pesaḥ* mandatory, and it necessitated the shift of the *ḥag* to the first day.

Finally, it is hardly a coincidence that the extension of the one-day *ḥag* to embrace all seven days is documented in late biblical sources beginning with Ezekiel, for it is in the Babylonian exile, when the pilgrimage to a destroyed temple could no longer be observed, that the term *ḥag* changed its meaning from "pilgrimage festival" to "festival." Henceforth, *ḥag hammaṣṣôt* refers to all seven days during which the eating of leaven is proscribed.[260]

---

256. Kedar-Kopfstein, *Biblische Semantik*, 201–3.

257. Scott, *Booths of Ancient Israel's Autumn Festival*, 29–32.

258. Contra Haran, *Temples and Temple Service*, 289–90.

259. Kedar-Kopfstein, "חַג *chagh*," 201–13.

260. The rabbis derive from the verse "You shall remove (*tašbîtû*) leaven from your houses (Exod 12:15) that the leaven must be destroyed" (*Mek. Bo'*, par 8). However, evidence that this cannot be the intent of Scripture can be adduced from a letter to the Jewish garrison of Elephantine, Egypt referring

> ### EXCURSUS 7: DAILY PUBLIC SACRIFICES DURING PESAḤ AND FEAST OF UNLEAVENED (EZEKIEL 45 AND NUMBERS 9)
>
> Ezek 45:18–20
> 1 BULL (PURIFICATION)
>
> Num 9:3
> None, only individual
>
> Ezek 45:24–25
> 7 BULLS (BURNT) + 1 EPHAH (CEREAL) + HIN (OIL)
> 7 RAMS (BURNT) + 1 EPHAH (CEREAL) + HIN (OIL)
> 1 GOAT (PURIFICATION)
>
> Num 28:17–23
> 2 BULLS (BURNT) + 3/10 (CEREAL)
> 1 RAM (BURNT) + 2/10 (CEREAL)
> 7 LAMBS (BURNT) + 1/10 (CEREAL)
>
> There is no public (i.e., sanctuary) *pesaḥ* in P's yearly calendar (Num 28:16)—only one by each family. The purpose of Ezekiel's innovation of one purification bull (45:23) is uncertain. Perhaps, its purpose, being a *ḥaṭṭā't*, is to purge the altar of its decontamination during days 7–14. This would illustrate Ezekiel's heightened sensitivity to the presence of impurity on the altar (inadvertent impurity contaminates the altar, even from afar). Thus, the presence of this *ḥaṭṭā't* provides further evidence for the Dorian Gray principle!
>
> It is assumed that after the sanctuary is purged on the first of the month (Ezek 45:18), all Israel will make a concerted effort to avoid ritual impurity during the following two weeks so that the *pesaḥ* will be observed in purity. One need only recall that P requires the safeguarding of the paschal sacrifice for four days prior to its sacrifice (Exod 12:3–6). Indeed, the period leading up to the *pesaḥ* is characterized by ritual purification—the removal of leaven from the home (Exod 12:15, 19–20; 13:7). Ezekiel also demands the simultaneous purification of the sanctuary. He therefore institutes three temple purificatory days: the 1st, the 7th, and 14th of Nisan. On the 7th, purgation is repeated lest pollution has recurred through inadvertence or ignorance (Ezek 45:20). And finally, on the 14th, before Israel offers up its paschal sacrifice, a third purgation takes place, but this time on the altar alone, because of the impurities that may have occurred during the preceding week. Thus, Ezekiel prescribes, in all, three purgation bulls seven days apart, as the means of providing a ritually pure sanctuary for the celebration of the *pesaḥ*.[261]
>
> Excursus 7 shows that Ezekiel demands more public sacrifices than P. Possibly, Ezekiel was apprehensive that the officiating priest might make a mistake and offer up an incorrect number of sacrifices. He, therefore, simplified their number as multiples of seven.

---

to a rescript of Darius II (419 BCE): [WKL ḤMYR ZY 'YLY BBTYKM H]N'LW BTWNKM WḤTMW BYN YWMY' ['LH], "And bring into your room [any leaven which you have in your houses] and seal (them) up during [these] days," Cowley, *Aramaic Papyri*, 21:8.

261. For details, see Milgrom, *Leviticus 1–16*, 281–84.

**45:25.** The identical sacrifices for each of the seven days of the Feast of Unleavened Bread balance the seven days of the Feast of Booths, which fall on days 15–21 of the seventh month, thereby dividing the calendar year into two equal halves. However, the difference between the two halves should not be overlooked: The Feast of Booths has no equivalence to *pesaḥ* (the 14th of the seventh month), and the Feast of Unleavened Bread has no *ʿăṣeret* (the 22nd of the seventh month).

## Summary of Chapter 45

There is nothing that illustrates Ezekiel's obsession with the purity of the sanctuary worship more than this chapter. Whereas the Mosaic Torah prescribes the observance of the people's *pesaḥ* on Nisan 14 without any sacrificial purification (except for P's "watchdog" guard over the *pesaḥ* during the prior four days, Exod 12:3–6), Ezekiel ordains that the temple must be purged on three occasions, seven days apart, each time with a *ḥaṭṭāʾt* bull, the most efficacious (and presumably the most expensive) purification offering.

The first time (Nisan 1) the purificatory blood is smeared on the sanctuary doorposts, then on the altar ledge, and lastly on the doorposts of the inner eastern gate—the sacred spine (Fig. 14). It cannot be overlooked that the blood is *not brought within the sanctuary*. Perhaps the reason may be that the entire sanctuary building on the upper platform is the house of YHWH, which requires no cleansing, because no human is allowed inside to decontaminate it. Also it should be noted that the purification blood avoids the lower, Israelite level, but concentrates on the middle, priestly platform. Here, Ezekiel, (who is also a priest) manifests his concern lest the altar become contaminated, especially by corpse contamination, which can only be eliminated by a seven-day purificatory ritual, which is extended to fourteen days if its bearer is a priest. Here we find Ezekiel's rule whereby the subsequent destruction of the future sanctuary can be avoided: Keep it from contamination!

The chapter begins with setting out the holy district for the sanctuary, the priests and the Levites, the people's city; the ample lands of the *nāśîʾ* will remove his temptation to add to his property by unjust eviction of its inhabitants. The chapter includes standardized weights, measures, and sacrificial offerings.

## Other Fixed Festivals (46:1–15)

TRANSLATION

1 Thus has the Lord YHWH proclaimed: The east gate of the inner court will be closed[262] during the six working days[263] but open on the Sabbath and

---

262. The expression *yihyeh sāgûr*, "it shall be closed," echoes *sāgûr yihyeh* and *wĕhāyâ sāgûr* in 44:2–3. The *hāyâ* plus participle is discussed in Rooker, *Biblical Hebrew in Transition*, 108–9 [667, n. 30].

263. The expression *yĕmê hammaʿăśeh*, "the days of work," occurs only here in the Hebrew Bible. Tg. reads *ywhy ḥwl*, "common day" [667, n. 31].

## PART TWO: EZEKIEL 40–48—THE VISIONARY SANCTUARY AND THE LAND

the new moon. **2** Having entered through the vestibule of the gatehouse[264] the prince will stand[265] by the doorpost, while the priests offer up both his whole burnt offering and his well-being offering. He will then bow low on the threshold of the gatehouse and leave; the gatehouse, however, will not be closed until evening. **3** The general population will [also] bow low before YHWH at the entrance of that gatehouse on the Sabbath and the new moons. **4** On the Sabbath day the prince will offer up to YHWH the mandatory whole burnt offering of six unblemished lambs and an unblemished ram, together with an ephah meal offering for the ram; **5** however, the meal offering for the lambs will be as much as he wishes,[266] each ephah requiring a hin of oil. **6** On the new moon, it [the sacrifice] will be an unblemished bull of the flock, six lambs, and an unblemished[267] ram **7** and an ephah meal offering with a hin of oil for each ephah for the bull and for the ram, with as much as he wishes[268] for the lambs.

**8** When the prince comes, he will enter and exit by way of the vestibule of the gatehouse. **9** However on the fixed festivals when the general population come to pray before YHWH those entering through the north gateway to bow low, will leave by way of the south[269] gateway, while those entering by way of the south gate will leave by way of the north gate. They must not exit the way they entered but must leave[270] the opposite way.[271] **10** And the prince will enter with them and leave with them when they leave.[272] **11** At the pilgrimages and the fixed festivals, the meal offering will be an ephah with a hin of oil for each ephah, for each bull and ram; But for the lambs, whatever he wishes.

**12** The east gateway will be opened for the prince whenever he offers a free-will whole burnt offering or a free-will well-being offering to YHWH, which he will offer just as he does on the Sabbath. The gate will be closed after

---

264. Block, 667, n. 32, claims that LXX "mistakenly relates *miḥûṣ* to the gate." To the contrary, the prince shall enter the gate from the outside, i.e., by way of the vestibule.

265. *weʿāmad*, "stand," should be understood literally. The prince stands at the gate, facing the altar while his sacrifices are immolated [667, n. 33].

266. "Whatever he wishes" is an idiomatic rendering of *mattat yādô*, "gift of his hand," the equivalent to *kaʾăšer taśśîg yādô*, "whatever his hand can secure" (n. 800). Ezekiel's style is influenced by the priestly text of Lev 5:11; 14:21, 31; 25:26, 49; 27:8; Num 6:27 [668, n. 36].

267. The context and versions (which read sg.) suggest that the pl. *temîmim* represents a dittographic error of the following pl. [668, n. 37].

268. See n. 801, above.

269. Here and in chapters 47–48 "south" is referred to by *negeb* instead of *dārôm*, which had been used in chapters 40–42 [668, n. 40].

270. "Whereas the previous verbs were construed as sg., the pl. occurs after the collective subject *ʿam*. Ezekiel is notoriously inconsistent in the treatment of collectives" (cf. Rooker, *Biblical Hebrew in Transition*, 94–96). *Contra* Zimmerli (*Ezekiel 2*, 488) it is preferable to view the versional sg. forms as harmonistic rather than MT as dittographic [668, n. 42].

271. *Contra* Block, *Ezekiel 25–48*, 668, n. 43, the suffix on *nikĕḥô* refers to the subject, i.e., "opposite him," rather than the gate. That is, the people will exit in the opposite direction from their entrance.

272. On the pl. *yēṣēʾû* see n. 9, above [668, n. 44].

he exits. **13** Daily, each morning you will offer²⁷³ an unblemished one-year old lamb as a whole burnt offering to YHWH. **14** And with it a meal offering of one-sixth of an ephah and one-third of a hin of oil to moisten²⁷⁴ the flour. It is a meal offering for YHWH, a perpetual edict.²⁷⁵ **15** Each morning they will offer²⁷⁶ the lamb and the meal offering and the oil a standard whole burnt offering.

## COMMENT

**46:1.** Festivals that are celebrated regularly, namely, the weekly Sabbath and monthly new moon (Ezek 46), are the days on which the eastern inner gate is open. Eliezer of Beaugency suggests that this gate is open to allow the prince to worship in the sight of the altar. It is also likely that it allows the passing crowds, below on the lower platform, a brief glimpse of the altar (see Fig. 1). The eastern outer gate by which YHWH enters the sanctuary (43:4) remains permanently closed. In the present verse, the Sabbath precedes, but there is reason to believe that originally the new moon was the more important day since it required more sacrifices and in a series was mentioned first (e.g., 2 Sam 4:23; Isa 1:13; 66:23).

*six working days* (*šēšet yĕmê hamma'ăśeh*), an expression coined by Ezekiel, but in rabbinic terminology it stands for the six days of creation.

**46:2.** *by way of the gate hall from the outside* (*derek 'ûlām haššaʿar miḥûṣ*), that is, the outside court. The prince enters the outside court through the north or south gate and then ascends the eight stairs of the eastern inner gate.

*and he will stand* (*wĕʿāmad*). While the priests immolate his sacrifices, the prince must stand at the doorpost of the eastern gateway (*ʿal-mĕzûzat haššaʿar*). This represents the deepest penetration of the prince into the sanctuary. He ascends the eight steps of the middle, priestly platform, but is forbidden to enter it since it is the exclusive domain of the priests.

*his whole burnt offering and his well-being offering.* The prince's voluntary offering (cf. v. 12). Presumably the offerer brings no expiatory sacrifice (note that P does not require public expiatory sacrifices on the Sabbath, Num 28:9–10, or, just as likely, the *ʿōlâ* and *šĕlāmîm* are the generic for all the sacrifices). The prince is responsible for all the mandatory sacrifices on the holidays (45:17).

---

273. LXX and Vulg fail to recognize the beginning of a new subsection when they harmonize the second person of MT with the preceding third person. NRSV reflects an emended text [669, n. 47].

274. *rōs* from *rāsas* is a hapax form (cf. *rāsîs*, "to moisten," parallel to *ṭal*, "dew," in Song 5:2), answering to *bālal*, "to mix," in Num 28 [669, n. 49].

275. MT *ḥuqqôt ʿôlām* should be read as sg. *ḥuqqat ʿôlām*, with many Hebrew mss. and the versions [669, n. 50].

276. Reading *w'św* with Kethib, Pesh., Tg. against Qere *y'św*. The pl. form assumes the participation of the priest [669, n. 51].

The gateway, however, should not be closed until the evening (*wĕhaššaʿar lōʾ-yissāgēr ʿad-hāʿāreb*), to allow for every one among the assembled crowds a chance to pay obeisance (by prostration) to YHWH (Rashi, Eliezer of Beaugency).

**46:3** *The general population* (*ʿam-hāʾāreṣ*), the full citizens of the nation,[277] or more limited, "the (adult) people gathered for worship."[278]

*at the entrance of that gate* (*petaḥ haššaʿar hahûʾ*). The laity crowded on the lower platform, with rare exception, are probably incapable of seeing the altar. All they can do is face the eastern gate, or wait for the signal (i.e., the prostration) of the prince that they should do likewise.

*at the new moons* (*baḥŏdāšîm*). The same would probably hold for the *môʿădîm*, "festivals," a subject that is postponed until verse 9.

**46:4.** Only the mandatory *ʿōlâ*, "whole burnt offering," is mentioned here in connection with the accompanying *minḥâ*, "meal offering." The *šĕlāmîm*, however, is always voluntary (see v. 12), with the exception of the one required on the First Wheat festival (Lev 23:19). The six lambs and one ram as the *minḥâ*, "meal offering," is a uniquely Ezekielian innovation (Radak).

**46:5.** Because of the multiple lambs (six), their accompanying *minḥâ* is left to the option of the prince.[279] The large flocks under the control of the prince encourage him to donate liberally (Eliezer of Beaugency).

**46:6.** Having begun with the Sabbath sacrifices (vv. 4–5), the text continues with the new moon sacrifices. They turn out to be the same with the addition of one whole burnt offering bull. Is this a further indication that originally the new moon was more important than the Sabbath?

**46:7.** *as much as he wishes* (*kaʾăšer tassîg yādô*; lit., "as his hand can reach") is equivalent to *mattat yādô*, with the possible nuance that the form implies something of his wealth. Note also that once again the number of sacrifices, though increased, has been simplified; compare 46:6–7 with Num 28:11–13.

**46:8.** The prince leaves the hall the way he entered. Without turning, the populace heads straight for an exit (v. 9).

**46:9.** The populace exits at the opposite gate; they go from either north to south or south to north. In other words, two lines are formed, moving in opposite directions to regulate the traffic.

---

277. See Milgrom, *Leviticus*, 251–52.
278. Cf. 45:16, 22; 46:9; Joyce, *Ezekiel*, 235.
279. Kasher, *Ezekiel*, 895–96.

**46:10.** After the prince completes his obeisance he retraces his steps in the gate, descends the eight steps, joins the throngs, and, like them, exits at the opposite gateway. Thus, in the crowd, the prince is indistinguishable. Nothing could be more illustrative of the equal cultic status of the prince and the people than this verse—the prince fuses together with the masses.

**46:11.** While this verse is related to verse 7, which describes the meal offering of the new moon festival, verse 11 deals with the pilgrimage (*ḥaggîm*) and fixed (*môʿădîm*) festivals. Thus, the new moon is turned into a *môʿēd*, a fixed festival; but cf. verse 5 on the Sabbath.

**46:12.** The prince may offer his personal sacrifice on any day (during the day time). For the free-will offering (*nĕdābâ*), cf. Num 15:3, 8; Deut 27:6b–7. The *zebaḥ šĕlāmîm* is offered for three reasons: *neder*, "vow," brought if a vow is fulfilled; *tôdâ*, "thanksgiving"; and *nĕdābâ*, "free-will."

The free-will offering of the citizens (*ʿam-hāʾāreṣ*) is omitted; they are too busy to journey to the sanctuary, except on (occasional) festivals (Rashi, Radak). Or the number of sacrifices is dependent on one's economic status.[280] The prince's free-will offering is to be accompanied by the same meal offering that he brings on the Sabbath (vv. 4–5). However, whereas the eastern inner gate is open all day on the Sabbath (v. 2), it is opened on other days just for the prince's sacrifice and closed as soon as the prince leaves.

**46:13–15.** The prescription for the daily, public offering (*tāmîd*). The first question relates to the shift from the third (v. 12) to the second person (vv. 13–14). Surely the prophet is not commanded to be responsible for *taʿăśeh*. No matter how this verb is rendered—"offer" (NJPS, NAB); "provide" (NRSV, REB)—in no way would the prophet impose such a financial burden upon himself (daily *ʿōlâ* and *minḥâ*!). The second question is why the remaining verb *wĕʿāśû* switches to the third person plural (v. 15). The answer is that Ezekiel's *tāmîd*, containing a threefold *taʿăśeh*, is based on P's *tāmîd* (Num 28:4, 8), containing a fourfold *taʿăśeh*. Just as the subject of the Numbers *tāmîd* is the people ("command the Israelites and say to them," Num 28:2), so the people are the subject of Ezekiel's *tāmîd* (shown by the third person plural in verse 15, *waʿăśû* Q; *yaʿăśû* K). Ezekiel's *tāmîd* is based on P's *tāmîd* and is not a directive to the prophet (see v. 15).

**46:13.** Ezekiel prescribes the daily *tāmîd* only for the morning. This is not surprising in view of the variable evening *tāmîd* practiced during First Temple times (cf. 1 Kgs 18:29, 36; 2 Kgs 16:15). On Sabbath and new moon the daily *ʿōla* is offered by the prince *babbōker babbōker*, "every morning" (also vv. 14–15), a different idiom than Num 28:3, which uses *layyôm* (sg. *babbōker*, "in the morning"; Num 28:4 does not convey the meaning of "daily"; cf. Ezek 12:8; 24:18; 33:22).

---

280. Ibid., 896, regarding verse 11.

**46:13–14. *you will provide (taʿăśeh)*.** Apparently the subject is still the prince, in which case the switch into the second person would be a conscious imitation of P's style, which also utilizes the second person (e.g., Exod 29; Num 28; see vv. 13–15, above).

***to moisten (lārōs)***, or "to mix" (Radak), but Eliezer of Beaugency maintains that it only means "to moisten" (cf. Num 28:5, a deliberate play on Exod 29:38, 42; Num 28:3–8, 10).

***It is a meal offering for YHWH (minḥâ laYHWH)***. As the *ʿōlâ* lamb is *laYHWH*, namely, a burnt entirely on the altar, so is the accompanying *minḥâ*.

**46:15. *they will offer (yaʿăśû,* Q; Radak).** The change from the second person singular to the third person plural implies a shift of responsibility for the *tāmîd* from Ezekiel to the priests [676]. This repetition on the *tāmîd* emphasizes its innovation. Moreover, the radical change in the *tāmîd* (from two sacrifices—morning and evening—to one sacrifice—morning only) signifies to Radak that not only on specific occasions—such as the initiation of the altar (43:25) and the altar's purification (45:18–20)—are innovations to take place, but also on all regular sacrifices such as the *tāmîd*. That is, Ezekiel's entire sacrificial system is the new revealed law—an indicator, among others, that Ezekiel is the new Moses (see below).

## EXCURSUS 8: EZEKIEL, THE NEW MOSES?

As suggested by J. D. Levenson,[281] Ezekiel's call to prophecy is validated by Deut 18:15, *yāqîm lĕkâ YHWH ʾĕlōhêkā nābîʾ miqqirbĕqâ kāmônî*, "YHWH your God will raise up for you a prophet like me from your midst." The resemblances between Moses and Ezekiel are striking. Both are preoccupied with the sanctuary and its furnishings, the cult personnel and the sacrificial system, especially the *ḥaṭṭāʾt*, "the purification offering." Levenson adds that much of the P (also H, Milgrom) material in Num 27–36 bears a striking similarity to Ezek 40–48.[282] For example, the liturgical calendar and the rules of sacrifice (Num 28:29; Ezek 45:18–29; 46:1–15), the allotment of the land (Num 32; 35:50–56; Ezek 47:13–48:29), boundaries of the land (Num 34–35; Ezek 47:13–20), land/cities for the Levites (Num 35:1–8; Ezek 45: 1–6; 48:13–14), and inheritance laws (Num 36; Ezek 46:16–18; see Table 1).

---

281. Levenson, *Theology of the Program of Restoration*, 38.
282. Ibid., 43.

TABLE 1: Links between Ezekiel and Moses

| Parallel | Detail | Source |
|---|---|---|
| 1. Preoccupation | Sanctuary, cult, and personnel | Exod 25–Num 10<br>Ezek 40–46 |
| 2. Emphasis | Purification (ḥaṭṭā't) and purgation (kippur) | Lev 4, 16<br>Ezek 43:19–26; 25:18–23 |
| 3. Levites | Guarding of the sanctuary and the sacred restricted from altar | Num 1:53<br>Ezek 44:13 |
| 4. The Torah | Law Code(s) | Exod 25—Num 10<br>Ezek 43:13—46:24 |
| 5. Revealed to . . . | The people through a human intermediary | Exod 24:3; 25:1–30<br>Ezek 43:8 |
| 6. Location | On a high mountain | Deut 32:49, 52<br>Ezek 40:2 |
| 7. Chronological context | Following the covenant ratification | Exod 24:6–11<br>Ezek 37:26 |
| 8. Goal | To separate the sacred from the common | Lev 10:10–11<br>Ezek 43:23 |
| 9. Violated | By Gog and the golden calf | Exod 32<br>Ezek 38–39 |
| 10. Priestly status | During the initiation of the altar | Exod 29:31–37<br>Ezek 45:18–27 |
| 11. Entrance of the kābōd | Visible to the prophet | Exod 40:34–38<br>Ezek 43:1–9 |
| 12. The land | Seen but not entered | Deut 34:1–4<br>Ezek 40:2–4 |
| 13. Communication with the deity | Direct | Num 7:89<br>Ezek 43:18–29 |

These precise resemblances between the Mosaic and Ezekielian law can hardly be an accident. They illustrate by themselves that Ezekiel could claim divine authority because his life-pattern duplicated his predecessor, Moses. However, Ezekiel not only resembles Moses (*nābî'* . . . *kāmôkâ*), but in most aspects, even critical ones, he differs from Moses. Although Ezekiel is Moses' successor, he is not only a clone of Moses. Ezekiel is the *new Moses*. His unique differences from his Mosaic model will now be illustrated by focusing on the new sanctuary altar.

As demonstrated in Figs. 1–2, Ezekiel has shifted the center of the sanctuary from the entrance to the Tent of Meeting in the Mosaic sanctuary to the altar hearth of his own sanctuary. And for good reason: most of the novel changes that occur in Ezekiel's sanctuary focus on the altar. The very structure of Ezekiel's altar stands in defiance of its Mosaic precedent. For example, Ezekiel's altar contains stairs (Fig. 16), in contradiction to Exod 20:26. Moreover, the altar is the *axis mundi*. It is where the prayers of Israel are directed by means of the sacrifices. Thus, during the month of Nisan, a *ḥaṭṭā't*, "purification offering," is prescribed on three occasions, seven days apart: on the 1st, 7th, and 14th. The *ḥaṭṭā't* on the first day decontaminates the *temenos* (45:18) by applying the *ḥaṭṭā't* blood to the doorposts of the sanctuary, on the uppermost divine (third) platform, to the corners of the altar's ledge, and to the inner (eastern) gate on the priestly platform (see details in the COMMENT on 45:19). This rite is repeated seven days later on behalf of the inadvertent and ignorant (see the COMMENT on 45:20). The *naśî'* is responsible for supplying the third *ḥaṭṭā't* on the 14th of Nisan, on behalf of himself and the people at large (45:22). These three *ḥaṭṭā't* sacrifices during the first half of Nisan enable nearly all Israel to be ritually pure for offering up the required lamb/goat as the family paschal sacrifice on the eve of Nisan 14. For the significance of Ezekiel's *ḥaṭṭā't* sacrifices during the month of Nisan, see Excursus 5 and the COMMENT on 45:18–25.

The sharp differences between the sacrifices offered on the altar for the Sabbath and the new moon are diagrammed below (A-E). As pointed out by Block,[283] the Mosaic Torah (P) invites the Israelite to celebrate on the first days of each month (*rāšê hŏdāšîm*), along with the appointed festivals (*môʿădîm*), with gladness and trumpet blasts and whole burnt offerings (for the former, see Num 10:10; cf. Ps 81:4; for the latter cf. 46:15, diagrams A–D). In Samuel's day everyone was expected to participate in the new moon festivals (1 Sam 20:5, 18, 24; cf. 2 Kgs 4:23), and the kings of Israel/Judah sponsored such cultic activities: David (1 Chr 23:32), Solomon (2 Chr 2:4; 8:13), and Hezekiah (2 Chr 31:3). Prophetic support is reflected in Amos' apparent prohibition against commerce on the day of the new moon (Amos 8:5). The greater sacrifice on the Sabbath (diagrams A–C) is indicative of the exclusive importance of the Sabbath with its total abstinence from work that took hold in the Babylonian diaspora. Correspondingly, the *tāmîd* offering is reduced from two lambs, morning and evening, to one lamb every morning (details in 46:13).

As pointed out only sparingly earlier,[284] one can hardly compare Ezekiel to Moses except in a limited area: the sanctuary and its laws, Ezekiel's main concern. Thus, in view of Moses' total career, Ezekiel is a *partial* Moses. Outside the sanctuary, the Mosaic Torah remains exclusively in force. Ezekiel receives a direct revelation from YHWH, which consists of a set of new laws governing the sanctuary. First and foremost, the sanctuary provides the permanent home of YHWH, the God of Israel, on its third, uppermost platform. The second, middle platform, containing the altar is the priestly platform, separate from the people (including the Levites) on the people's platform, below, and separate from YHWH's house, the sanctuary, above. In order to maintain this structure functionally, the office of the high priest is eliminated (see Introduction, section D) and among several cultic changes, the sacrificial laws for the month of Nisan are revised so that every Israelite family might bring its paschal lamb/goat to the altar in purity (above).

283. Block, *Ezekiel 25–48*, 673, n. 66.
284. See above, pp. 59–60.

## The Sanctuary Personnel and the Nāśî' (Ezekiel 44–46)

The large omissions from H's cultic calendar (Lev 23) leave room for more than one resolution. Are the details omitted taken for granted or are they deliberately deleted? For example, is *Yôm Hakkippûrîm* presumed or is it intentionally effaced? Does the triple successive *ḥaṭṭā't*, of Nisan 1, 7, and 14 suffice to cleanse the sanctuary of Israel's inadvertent sins? Since redeemed Israel no longer sins advertently (36:25–27), there is no longer any need for the traditional Day of Purgation on 10 Tishri; Nisan 1–14 suffices. Also the seven days of *ḥag* (*sukkôt*), 15–21 Tishri (45:25), is a clone of the seven days of the Feast of Unleavened Bread, 15–21 Nisan (45:23–24). Are they observances for rain as their earlier counterpart in Lev 23:33–43, or does the magical river emanating from the sanctuary (Ezek 47) suffice to fertilize the land, obviating the need for rain? For whatever reason, Ezekiel opts for two pilgrimage festivals in keeping with Lev 23. The answer to these and other festival omissions requires further investigation. But aside from the above conjectured items, Ezekiel's goal is clear: The new Israel, restored to its reassigned ancestral land according to its tribal divisions (Ezek 48) requires a revised cultic calendar, partially sketched in the laws of 45:18—46:14. These render Ezekiel the new (partial) Moses.

Ezekiel is portrayed as a true prophet, reliving the last days of Moses, standing at the brink of the Promised Land preparing for entry. Like Moses he never sets foot on the land he surveyed (in visionary form). His vision of the Promised Land is on a "high mountain" (40:2), analogous to Mount Nebo (Deut 32:49, 52). YHWH speaks directly to him from the temple (Ezek 43:6) as he spoke to Moses (Num 7:89). Ezekiel plays a central role in the initiation of the altar (43:18–27) by being involved in the sacrificial and the blood rite, just as Moses was involved in the initiation of the tabernacle altar (Exod 29:36; Lev 8). As summarized by McConville: "As in the case of Moses, God speaks directly to him. Like Moses, he has priestly status (cf. Exod 24:6ff.) Like him he is to preside over the institution of the cult, including the setting apart of the priests for their duty."[285]

J. L. Ska[286] has noted similarities between Ezekiel's call (Ezek 2:1–3; 21) and the commissioning of Moses (Exod 7:1–5). His views are summarized by Duguid: "In both God entrusts a mission to his envoy and before it begins announces the failure of that mission; the root *ḥzq* and *qšh* are found side by side, in both cases connected with *lēb*; hardening of heart is a common theme, an attitude which is catastrophic, even perhaps fatal; the recognition formula appears in both, though in very different contexts."[287]

The task assigned to Ezekiel of ordering the renewed cult is seen as a distinctly prophetic task, as shown by the repeated use of the messenger formula, *kōh 'āmar 'ădōnāy YHWH* (Ezek 43:18; 44:6, 9; 45:9, 18; 46:1, 16; 47:13). The prophetic *j'accuse* is evident in the formulas *rab lākem*, "enough" (44:6; 45:9), *lō'. . . 'ôd*, "no more" (43:7; 45:8; cf. 34:10; 37:23). However, the uniqueness of Moses the prophet is revealed in the Pentateuch

---

285. McConville, "Priests and Levites in Ezekiel," 28.
286. Ska, "La Sortie d'Egypte," 203–4.
287. Duguid, *Ezekiel and the Leaders*, 105, n. 36.

law codes attributed to his name (Exod 21–23; Lev; Num 1–10; Deut 12–26). No other prophet—or person—can make such a claim.

Ezekiel is the only one outside of Moses who authored a corpus of legislation, though Ezekiel's corpus is limited to the laws of the priests. Listed by Ezekiel (44:16–31), they give the impression that they are revealed to Moses' tradents, refining and expanding the priestly laws mainly found in Leviticus 21; for example, the priestly vestments and tonsure (44:7–19; Lev 21:10). It should be noted, however, that this priestly law (Lev 21:10, H) applies to the high priest, which Ezekiel transfers to all priests. Moreover, two laws in Ezekiel's list cannot be called the derivative work of tradents; they flatly contradict their pentateuchal counterpart, as follows.

According to H (Lev 21:7), a priest may not marry a divorcee; and in addition, a high priest may not marry a widow but must find a bride from within the priestly tribe (21:14). In contrast, Ezekiel ordains that a priest may marry an Israelite virgin or the widow of a priest (44:22). Note that the changes cannot be derived from H. They are innovations. Ezekiel imposes the starker marital prohibition of H's high priest (no widows) on all the priests, but he allows the widow of a priest and permits an Israelite virgin. These two concessions seem powered by a single motivation: to assure the continuity of the priestly stock.

For purification from the impurity incurred by contact with a corpse, there is no distinction in the procedure for a priest and high priest: both must be sprinkled with the waters containing the ashes of a red cow on the third and seventh day (Num 19:17–19) of his purification. Ezekiel adds to this law an additional seven days—followed by a purification offering—before entry into the inner (priestly) court is permitted (44:26–27). Purity is at stake here—to guarantee that the priest who works exclusively in the inner, sacred court always retains a sacred, uncontaminated status. This law jibes with the principle of separation (cf. Introduction, section C) that operates throughout Ezekiel's sanctuary. It stems from Ezekiel, not from Moses.

There is no way that these two Ezekielian laws can be derived from their pentateuchal counterparts. One has to concede that Ezekiel is more than a priestly tradent. He is an *innovator*, a lawgiver, another Moses. His purpose is to guarantee that the priestly line remains strong and pure. The priest, therefore, assumes the severer restrictions of the high priest who evanesces from the sanctuary service.

# EXCURSUS 9: THE MOSAIC TORAH AND EZEKIEL COMPARED[288]

### TABLE 2: Sabbath and New Moon Sacrifices

|  | Ezekiel 46:4–7 | Numbers 28:9–15 |
|---|---|---|
| Sabbath | 6 lambs + cereal: discretionary + oil<br>1 ram + cereal: ephah | 2 lambs + cereal: 2/10 + libation |
| New Moon | 1 bull + cereal: ephah + oil<br>1 ram + cereal: ephah + oil<br>6 lambs + cereal: voluntary | 2 bulls + cereal: 6/10 + oil<br>1 ram + cereal: 2/10 + oil<br>7 lambs + cereal: 7/10 + wine |

### TABLE 3: Accompaniment

| Ezekiel 46:11 | Numbers 28:13–14 |
|---|---|
| For the lamb voluntary + 1 hin oil per ephah | 1/10 (of ephah) + 1/4 hin oil |
| For the ram 1 ephah + 1 hin oil | 2/10 + 1/3 hin oil |
| For the bull 1 ephah + 1 hin oil | 3/10 + 1/2 hin oil |

### TABLE 4: Sabbath Sacrifices and Accompaniment

| Element | Mosaic Torah | Ezekielian Torah |
|---|---|---|
| Number of lambs | 2 | 6 |
| Number of rams | — | 1 |
| Grain per lamb | 2/10 ephah semolina | According to means |
| Grain per ram | — | 1 ephah |
| Amount of oil | Unspecified, mixed with semolina | 1 hin/ephah |

### TABLE 5: New Moon Sacrifices and Accompaniment

| Element | Mosaic Torah | Ezekielian Torah |
|---|---|---|
| Number of bulls | 2 | 1 |
| Number of rams | 1 | 1 |
| Number of lambs | 7 | 6 |
| Grain per bull | 3/10 ephah semolina | 1 ephah |
| Grain per ram | 2/10 ephah semolina | 1 ephah |
| Grain per lamb | 1/10 ephah semolina | According to means |
| Amount of oil | Unspecified<br>Mixed with the semolina |  |
| Wine per bull | 1/2 hin | 1 hin/ephah |
| Wine per ram | 1/3 hin |  |
| Wine per lamb | 1/2 hin |  |

288. Adapted from Block, *Ezekiel 25–48*, 673–77.

PART TWO: EZEKIEL 40-48—THE VISIONARY SANCTUARY AND THE LAND

TABLE 6: Tamid Sacrifices

| Element | Mosaic Torah | Ezekielian Torah |
|---|---|---|
| Time of day | Every morning and every evening | Every morning |
| Number of lambs | 2 (AM and PM) | 1 |
| Grain per lamb | 1/10 ephah semolina | 1/6 ephah semolina |
| Oil per lamb | 1/4 hin | 1/3 hin |
| Wine per lamb | 1/4 hin | — |

*The Prince's Land (46:16-18)*

TRANSLATION

**16** Thus has the Lord YHWH proclaimed: If the prince favors any[289] of his sons with a gift [from][290] his inheritance,[291] it belongs to his sons; it is their holding of family property. **17** But if he favors one of his servants with a gift from his inheritance, it belongs[292] to him [the servant] until the [Jubilee] year of liberation,[293] when it reverts[294] to the prince. However, his inheritance is the permanent property of his sons. **18** The prince may not oust[295] the people from their property in order to confiscate their inheritance. He will gift his sons from his own inheritance[296] so that none of my people will be deprived[297] of his holding.

289. *lĕʾîš*, "to any," paralleled by *lĕʾaḥad*, "to one," verse 17.

290. [*min*]*naḥălātô*, "[from] his inheritance." The *mem* is required by sense, and is paralleled by *minnaḥălātô*, verse 17. Block, 678, n. 2 justifies MT; the *mem* may be mistakenly duplicated from the beginning of the previous word.

291. For a recorded example of such a royal grant; cf. 2 Chr 21:3.

292. *wĕhāyĕtā*, "it will belong." This is the only occurrence in Ezekiel of the EBH pattern of this conditional clause: syndetic apodosis plus imperfect verb; cf. Rooker, *Biblical Hebrew in Transition*, 120–22 [678, n. 4].

293. *šĕnat haddĕrôr*, "the year of liberation," which the Tg. interprets as *št dywbyl*, "Year of the Jubilee" [678, n. 5]. This identification makes sense: 1) the reference is to a specific year, and 2) to a specific verse (Lev 25:10; cf. Jer 34:8, 15).

294. *wĕšābat*, "when it will revert," which appears to be a primitive qatalat form, replacing *wĕšābâ*. In Lev 22:13 and Isa 23:17 both forms appear together. On the form cf. GKC §72o; Joüon-Muraoka, Grammar §42f [678, n. 6].

295. *lĕhônôtām*, "oust them," (cf. 45:8–9). Alternatively, render "robbing them" (NJB), the usual meaning of this word (e.g., 18:22; 22:7).

296. *yanḥîl*, "provide an inheritance," (NAB), i.e., the prince shall provide a gift of land to his son (cf. v. 16), which will become his inheritance.

297. *yāpuṣû*, "dispossessed/deprived, lit., "scattered," i.e., without land, he will have no means of economic support.

### The Sanctuary Personnel and the Nāśî' (Ezekiel 44–46)

COMMENT

**46:16–18.** A number of details link this fragment with 45:1–8: The primary interest is the *nāśî'*, the concern is for real estate (*ăḥuzzâ*), exploitation of citizens, the shared verb *hônâ* (45:8), and Israel as "my people."[298] The message is straightforward. In order to remove temptation from the prince to rob his citizens of their holding, the prince has been given ample lands (45:7–8), and in order to preserve his own holding, transference to outsiders is only temporary; at the Jubilee (every fixed fiftieth year) they revert to the prince. Only transfers to his sons (to gift them an inheritance) are permanent, so the land remains always, within the family [678–79]. The rationale for this ordinance is clear, although naïve: By keeping the prince permanently his greed to confiscate the property of others will be lessened.[299]

Ezekiel has probably warned his people, in the words of Samuel: "He [the king/prince] will take the best of your fields and vineyards and olive orchards and give them to his courtiers" (1 Sam 8:14). His major provision is the reenactment of the Jubilee (Lev 25). Block writes: "In this 'year of the Jubilee' all enslaved Israelites were to return (*šûb*) to their patrimonial holdings (*ăḥuzzâ*)." More so, Lev 25 abolishes Israelite slavery: "do not make him [your fellow Israelite] work as a slave. He shall remain under you as a resident hireling; he shall work under you until the Jubilee year" (Lev 25:39–40) [680]. Ezekiel, however, only releases land but not persons. True, he focuses only on real estate, namely the prince's suspected avarice for lands. Yet one would expect, as in the case of Lev 25, that the prophet would declare an encompassing rule —in the name of YHWH—that the Jubilee would cancel all debts and release both indentured lands and persons.

**46:17. But if he presents a gift . . . to one of his servants** (*wĕkî-yittēn mattānâ . . . lĕaḥad mēʿăbādāyw*). This question is reminiscent of Saul's challenge to his courtiers (*ʿăbādāyw*): "Hear now, you Benjaminites, will the son of Jesse give every one of you fields and vineyards . . . ?" (1 Sam 22:7). Clearly, Saul's admission of his favoritism for his fellow Benjaminites is the realization of Samuel's warning to his people! (above).

*the year of liberation* (*šĕnat haddĕrôr*). Ezekiel is now saying: The prince is no exception to the universality of the Jubilee. All outside gifts must be returned at the Jubilee. In a document from Ḥana, analyzed by J. Lewy,[300] the partners to a deal involving royal land specify that the year of Jubilee should not apply.[301] Thus, this document demonstrates that the Jubilee was living law, and it applied—if not to the entire nation—at least to the monarch's property. In fact, that the text speaks of *šĕnat haddĕrôr*, "the year of liberation," implies that the year is fixed and the dependence of this verse on Lev

---

298. However, as argued by Block, *Ezekiel 25–48*, 678–79, any attempt at reconstruction is conjectural.

299. Tuell, *Law of the Temple*, 110.

300. Lewy, "The Biblical Institution of D'rôr," 21–32.

301. Cf. Weinfeld, *Social Justice in Ancient Israel*, 31–39, 55–56; Lipshitz, "On 'The Servant of LORD YHWH,'" 157–71.

25:10 is confirmed. Ezekiel does not use the term *yôbēl*, "Jubilee," because he wishes to focus on the main function of this institution—*děrôr*, liberation.³⁰²

**His inheritance shall [permanently] belong to his sons** (*naḥălātô bānāyw lāhem tihyeh*). Compare the phrasing in verse 16. The same word order strengthens the credibility of MT. The import of this sentence is that contrary to the prince's gifts to his servants, which return to him at the Jubilee, his gifts to his sons remain permanently theirs.

**46:18. The prince shall not confiscate any of the people's inheritance** (*welo'-yiqqaḥ hannāśi' minnaḥălat hā'ām*). A common royal practice: A king would rather expropriate the property of his citizens than part with his own.

***the people . . . my people*** (*hā'ām . . . 'ammî*). Ezekiel is not only concerned with the prince and the sanctuary. His basic concern is for all of Israel, and in this fragment for vouchsafing their landed inheritance.

Ezekiel's *nāśi'* is a far cry from the *nāśi'* of old. The latter was a tribal leader, Ezekiel's was pan-Israelite. The tribal *nāśi'* was a judge, made covenants, and apportioned land (Num 34:18–28; Josh 9:18–21; 17:4; 22:32). These are absent in Ezekiel's portfolio, with the exception of being administrator of justice. *mišpāṭ ûṣĕdāqâ*, "practice justice and righteousness" (45:3), precisely the same virtue that characterized King Josiah, according to Jer 22:15, where it is explained as *dān dîn-'ănî wĕ'ebyôn*, "he judged the cause of the poor and the needy" (Jer 15:16). Indeed, the future Davidic ruler will also be characterized by the same virtue (Jer 23:5).

Duguid correctly points to 1 Kgs 11:34, the only place outside Ezekiel where *nāśi'* denotes king, and is the probable antecedent for the *nāśi'* in Ezekiel: "I will not take the whole kingdom out of Solomon's hand. I will make him a *nāśi'* for all the days of his life."³⁰³ However, in actual fact, the Davidic dynasty was reduced to being heads of one tribe, Judah, which made them, in effect, the tribal leader, the *nāśi'*. In Ezekiel as well, the office of the king has been modified and its scope limited because of past sins, metamorphosed in *nāśi'*. Ezekiel's *nāśi'* was distanced from the sanctuary so as not to contaminate it. The precedent of the sanctuary as the royal chapel was abolished, and the *nāśi'* was provided with large tracts of land (45:7–8), which would curb his appetite for the land of his subjects. He was no longer responsible for the administration of the cult. His erstwhile power to appoint or dismiss priests, to organize or reform the worship has been abolished. In Ezekiel's vision it is *YHWH* who builds his sanctuary, organizes the priesthood, and reforms the worship; YHWH acts on his own to rescue Israel and only after that places a *nāśi'* at the head of his people (34:23–24). The land is also apportioned by divine command (Ezek 48) and not by the *nāśi'* (Num 34:18). The *nāśi'* is just warned not to undermine YHWH's plan by land-grabbing (45:8).

---

302. For a brief discussion of the Jubilee, cf. Milgrom, *Leviticus 23–27*, 3162–83.

303. Duguid, *Ezekiel and the Leaders*, 57, following Levenson, *Theology of the Program of Restoration*, 67.

## The Sanctuary Personnel and the Nāśîʾ (Ezekiel 44–46)

Nonetheless, the *nāśîʾ* is a person of privilege. The lay worshiper is limited to the lower sanctuary platform. As remarked by Duguid, even if he climbed the stairs to the priestly platform, he would face a 90 foot long access to the priestly platform, providing a dim view at the other end.[304] The *nāśîʾ*, on the other hand, was allowed to walk down this passage to the threshold at the other end, where he had a good view of everything that transpired in the inner court (46:2). Like the pre-exilic king, he is the focus for the worshiping community, but he is inseparable from it when entering and exiting the sanctuary (46:10).

### The Temple Kitchens (46:19–24)

TRANSLATION

**19** Then he took me through the entrance beside the gate to the sacristies of the priests,[305] which faced north. There I saw a space at the rear facing west.[306] **20** He said to me: This is the place where the priests will cook the reparation offering and the purification offering, and where[307] they will bake the meal offering, so as not to bring [them] out outside, thereby exposing the people to holiness. **21** Then he took me to the outer court past the four corners of the court,[308] each of which contained a small[309] enclosure **22** measuring 40 cubits long by 30 cubits wide, all the same size.[310] **23** A row [of stones][311] encircled the interior[312] of each of the four. Beneath the rows hearths were built[313] all the way

---

304. Duguid, *Ezekiel and the Leaders*, 53.

305. MT *ʾel-hakkōhănîm*, lit., "to the priests," implies that the prophet visits the priest inside their rooms, even though he never encounters anyone other than the guide in the vision. An original *lakkōhănîm* or *ʾăšer lakkōhănîm* may be proposed, *ʾel* functioning as an abbreviation for *ʾšr l*. Cf. Cooke, *Ezekiel*, 516 [681, n. 21].

306. Tg. and Pesh. support Kethib in reading—the ending of the preceding *byrktym* as a suffix, "at their far side/rear" (cf. Gen 49:13 for a similar form), but the dual absolute form represented by Qere, *yrktym*, followed by *ymh* (familiar from Exod 26:27; 36:32; cf. 26:23; 36:28) is preferable [681, n. 23].

307. *ʾăšer . . . šām* leads one to expect the adverb *šām* after the second *ʾăšer*. Cf. LXX και εκει, "and there" [681, n. 24].

308. On distributive repetition in Hebrew, see Waltke-O'Connor, *Syntax* §12:5; GKC §123d [682, n. 25].

309. Many emend MT's seemingly incomprehensible *qtrwt* to *qtnwt*, "small" (Zimmerli, *Ezekiel 2*, 499; NRSV, NAB, NEB), [685] but cf. NJPS, "unroofed" [682, n. 27]. Cf. *m. Mid* 2:5). See comments on 46:22 below for more details.

310. MT adds a denominative Hophal fem. participle *mĕhuqṣāʿôt*, "corner rooms," at the end of the verse. The absence of the word in LXX, Vulg, and Pesh. as well as the doubts of the Masoretes (the *puncta extraordinaria*; cf. GKC §5n), suggest that it may have originated as a marginal gloss on the masculine form *miqṣōʿôt* in verse 21 [682, n. 28].

311. *ṭîrâ* replaces *ṭûr* in verse 23b; see the COMMENT [682, n. 30]. Kasher, *Ezekiel*, 904, suggests reading *lĕʾarbaʿat hammiqṣāʿôt*, "the four corners."

312. MT *wĕṭûr sābîb bāhem*, lit., "around in each was a low fence." Zimmerli (*Ezekiel 2*, 499) defends MT against BHS's proposed *lāhem* [682, n. 29].

313. Uninflected *ʿăśûy* in 40:17 and 41:18 argues against BHS's emendation to *ʿăśûyôt taḥat* [682, n. 31].

around. 24 The he said to me: These are the kitchens[314] where the servants of the temple compound cook the people's well-being sacrifices.

## Comment

This pericope comprises two units, 19-20 and 21-24. It conforms to Ezekiel's "halving" style [683].[315] Moreover, there are several thematic links, which suggest that they share a common author. Thus, *mišmeret habbayit* (v. 24) is an epithet of the Levites (e.g., 44:11; 45:5) [682]. Also the list of the most holy sacrifices under priestly control: reparation (*'āšām*), purification (*ḥaṭṭā't*), and meal (*minḥâ*) in 46:20 stand in chiastic relation with the same sacrifices in 42:13, *minḥâ*, *ḥaṭṭā't*, *'āšām*. Both sites are identified as *liškôt haqqōdeš*, "the sacred rooms" (42:13; 46:19), but whereas the order of the sacrifices in 42:13 follows the list of the sacrifices in Lev 2; 4:1-5; and 5:14-26, the order of these sacrifices in 46:20 corresponds to no known system. This is no accident, but is an instance of Seidel's law;[316] namely, a chiastic repetition, which implies that the latter broken list is aware of and related to the earlier list.

The point of showing the sanctuary kitchens was not for descriptive purposes but to affirm two distinct groups: (a) the priestly kitchens in the priestly quarters[317] and (b) the people's kitchens in the outer court. Their respective functions are clear: Even in their meals, the priests and people (including the Levites) are separated. Nonetheless, the location of the kitchen pericope is at the end of the tour—it could and perhaps should have been described earlier (e.g., 42:1-14) when the kitchens were in view (Fig. 1). Greenberg is correct when he comments, "There is no evidence for dissociating arranger from author (Ezekiel), but the complex associative linkage of this division especially indicates that its composition was in stages."[318]

**46:19.** The last we heard of the prophet and his celestial guide was that they were standing on the priestly platform facing the entrance to the temple (44:4). Now they are transported back through the northern inner gate into the outer court. They turn left (west), and enter into the passageway (*mābô'*) some 20 cubits at the side (*kātēp*) of the gate, where they see the priestly chambers at the far western end of the sanctuary [684]. Since the rooms face north (*happōnôt ṣāpônâ*), it is possible that they entered the passageway to the south of the temple and beheld the southern priestly rooms, which were symmetrically equivalent to the northern rooms (42:9).[319] Their path is drawn in Fig. 1 ("wall route").

---

314. Although Tg., Pesh., and Vulg. read sg., *bêt haměbaššělîm* should be construed as pl. with LXX. For this rare construction of the pl. see GKC §124r [682, n. 32].

315. Cf. Zimmerli, *Ezekiel 2*, 500.

316. Cf. Seidel, "Parallels Between Isaiah and Psalms," 149-72, 229-40.

317. The priestly rooms *liškôt haqqōdeš* are located in the sacred spine, in the two-level structure that is attached to both the outer and inner courts.

318. Greenberg, "Design and Themes," 199.

319. Cf. Block, *Ezekiel 25-48*, 684; Kasher, *Ezekiel*, 903.

## The Sanctuary Personnel and the Nāśî' (Ezekiel 44–46)

The priests eat all their sacred (i.e., most holy) meals in their sacristies. This constitutes a severer command than the one ordained by P, which requires that the priests eat their sacred meals *bĕmāqôm qādōš*, "in a sacred place," *baḥăṣar ʾōhel môʿēd*, "in the courtyard of the Tent of Meeting" (Lev 6:19 [Eng 26]); that is, anywhere in the court (to which the laity had access!) and not in special rooms. The latter were specified by Ezekiel as a further device to separate the priests from non-priests, thereby preventing the contamination of the sacred.

**46:20.** As pointed out in the introduction to this COMMENT, above, the order of the most holy sacrifices here—reparation, purification, and meal offerings—is the inverse order of the order of sacrifices in Lev 2; 4:1—5:13; 5:14–26; and Ezek 42:13. This constitutes an editorial use of the Seidel law, whereby a chiastic revision refers the reader back to and connects with the original. Thus both this verse (46:20) and its referent (42:13) speak of the identical priestly room where the priests eat their most holy sacrificial portions—that is, their *ḥaṭṭāʾt*, *ʾāšām*, and *minḥâ* prebends—and where they deposit their priestly clothing and change to lay clothing upon entering the outer court (42:19). These precautions obviate the need to sanctify the people who may touch their most holy sacrifices (46:20) or their most holy vestments (46:20).

**46:21.** *Then he took me out* (*wayyôṣîʾēnî*). This is evidence that Ezekiel and his guide were heretofore in the inner, priestly court. Now they are in the outer, Israelite court where they survey all four lower kitchens.

*Corner* (*miqṣōʿa*). Cf. the COMMENT on 41:22.

*Court* (*ḥāṣēr*). Here this can stand for the outer court or the confined space within the outer court.

**46:22.** *fenced-in* (*qĕṭurôt*). This hapax has been variously explained: (1) from Arabic *qaṭara*, "to couple together, line up, tie" (Radak); (2) "unroofed" (*m. Mid.* 2:5; Neh 3:38 Tg.).[320] (3) Tg. *mqṭrn*, "fenced-in";[321] (4); *ḥṣrwt qṭrwt* "open courts."[322] However, courts by definition are "open."[323] The Tg. (no. 3) is most plausible [685].

**46:23.** *row* (*ṭûr*; pl. fem *ṭîrôt*), a stone wall fencing in the court. Imagine a series of ovens made of tiered stones or a stone ledge around inside the enclosure under which are fireplaces [685], though the fence/wall is higher than the cooking pots, giving the latter the appearance of being "under," *mittaḥat*.[324]

*Hearths* (*umĕbaššĕlôt*). This rare feminine plural is instanced by *mĕnaqqiyôt* (Exod 25:29); *mĕqaṭṭĕrôt* (2 Chr 30:14).

---

320. Cf. Kasher, *Ezekiel*, 904.
321. Levey, *Targum of Ezekiel*, 125; Jastrow, *Dictionary*, 135.
322. Yadin, *Temple Scroll* 2.159.
323. Busink, *Tempel* 2, 723, cited by Block [685, n. 40].
324. Kasher, *Ezekiel*, 904.

**46:24. kitchens** (*bêt hamĕbaššĕlîm*), lit., "house of the cooks," facilities for the lay worshipers to prepare their sacred meals. This rare plural is paralleled *bêt habbāmôt/bātê habbāmôt* (2 Kgs 17:29).

***those who serve the temple compound*** (*mĕšārĕtê habbayit*), namely, the Levites who are called *mĕšārĕtîm 'et-habbayit* (44:11), a further "demotion" of the laity, who no longer cook their own offerings. Analogous to the slaughtering of the sacrificial animals, which is transferred from the laity to the Levites (44:11), the cooking of the *zebaḥ hā'ām*, "the people's sacrifice" (see below), is also assigned to the Levites. The identical reason applies to both: to prevent lay contact with the sacred.

Presumably, the offerer brings his sacrifice into the Israelite platform, whence it is taken over by the Levites, who then slaughter the animal on a table beside the stairway of the northern inner gate; after the blood and suet rite on the altar, the meat is cooked by the Levites in the temple kitchen on the Israelite platform. Thus, the overall Levite profile is as the guardian of holiness, protecting against encroachment from the outside and against desecration and defilement from the inside. Controlling the slaughtering (44:11) and cooking of the sacrificial animals, one might say that, in addition to their guardianship, the Levites are the butchers and *les chefs de cuisine* of the sanctuary.

***the people's sacrifice*** (*zebaḥ hā'ām*). Originally—surely at (pre-Jerusalem temple) Shilo—the *zebaḥ* (i.e., the well-being offering) was consumed by its offerers within the temple precincts.[325] This earlier practice is now advocated by Ezekiel. Its spiritual advantage is obvious: It offers the lay worshiper the privilege to eat (rather, to share) God's meal in his courtyard. This is actually preserved by the law of the Nazirite (Num 6:18–19) and by the actual practice at the Shilo sanctuary (1 Sam 2:13–14). The detailed exposition on the sanctuary kitchens has a theological purpose: the separation between priests and non-priests even as they eat in the sanctuary.

Now that the sacrificial laws are terminated (Ezek 43–46), it is clear that only the public sacrifices are accounted for (e.g., people of the land, 46:3, 9–10; festivals, 45:18–25). But other than the *nāśî'* (e.g., 46:2, 4–15), the sacrificial needs of the individual are omitted. Galambush suggests a (partial) answer: "The metaphor of the female body must be excluded from the purified temple in chs. 40–48 because of the possibility of further defilement inherent in it."[326] Were women excluded from Ezekiel's sanctuary?

---

325. See Milgrom, *Leviticus 1–16*, 11–12, 29–34, esp. 418–20 (the note on Lev 7:15).
326. Galambush, *Jerusalem in the Book of Ezekiel*, 147–53.

# 3

# The Land (Ezekiel 47–48)

## HEALING OF THE LAND (47–48)

### Healing Waters from the Temple (47:1–12)

TRANSLATION

1 Then he brought me back to the entrance of the sanctuary. Look![1] Water was flowing out from underneath the sanctuary threshold eastward—since the sanctuary faced east; and the water flowed down below[2] the south side of the sanctuary, on the south side of the altar. 2 Then he took me out through the north gatehouse[3] and around the outside to the outer[4] gatehouse that faces east. Look,[5] water was bubbling[6] up from the right side. 3 As the [celestial] man continued eastward with a measuring line in his hand, he measured off 1,000 cubits[7] and led me through the water, which was ankle deep.[8] 4 Then he measured off another 1,000 and led me through the water, which was knee deep.[9] Then he measured off another 1,000 and led me through the water

---

1. *wĕhinnēh*, lit., "And behold" [687, n. 3].

2. *mittaḥat* is missing in LXX, Pesh., and Vulg, suggesting that it may have been copied erroneously from verse 1a (Joyce, *Ezekiel*, 201; Cooke, *Ezekiel*, 522; Fuhs, *Ezechiel 25–48*, 257). The omission may also reflect an attempt by early translators to smooth the text [687, n. 4].

3. On *derek ša'ar ṣāpônâ* without the article on the last word, see 46:9; 47:18 [687, n. 5].

4. LXX reads *heḥāṣēr* for the first *haḥûṣ*, and *haḥîṣôn* for the second (*ha*)*ḥûṣ* [687, n. 6]; cf. Eliezer of Beaugency.

5. *wĕhinnēh*, lit., "and behold" [687, n. 8].

6. On the onomatopoeic hapax *mĕpakkîm*, see the COMMENT [687, n. 10].

7. *'elep ba'ammâ*, lit., "a thousand with the cubit." On this idiom see 40:5 [687, n. 11].

8. MT *mê 'opsāyim*, "water of the ankles," involves an accusative of measure. See Joüon-Muraoka, *Grammar* §127b; GKC §128, n. 1. LXX ἀφέσεως simply transliterates *'opsāyim* [687, n. 12].

9. *mayim birkāyim*. Contextual consistency calls for *mê birkāyim*. Thus many Hebrew mss., Tg., LXX [687, n. 13].

## PART TWO: EZEKIEL 40–48—THE VISIONARY SANCTUARY AND THE LAND

waist deep. **5** Then he measured another 1,000, now it was a swollen[10] stream, which could not be crossed, which I could not cross except by swimming.[11] **6** Then he said to me, "Have you seen, O mortal?" and he brought me back[12] to the bank of the stream.

**7** As I came back, I saw a dense grove of trees[13] on both banks of the stream. **8** Then he said to me, "This water flows to the eastern region into the Arabah, and when it comes into the sea, into the sea of stagnant[14] waters, the water will be healed, **9** and every living swarming creature will thrive wherever this stream[15] flows. The fish will multiply once these waters have reached there bringing health and life where the stream flows.[16] **10** And[17] fishermen will stand[18] beside it[19] all the way from En-gedi to En-eglaim; a place for spreading nets [to dry]. The variety[20] [and] abundance of its fish[21] will equal those of the fish of the Great Sea.[22] **11** But its swamps[23] and marshes[24] shall not be healed; they will supply salt.[25] **12** All kinds of fruit trees will grow on both banks of the stream. Their leaves will not wither nor their fruit ever cease. Every month

---

10. *kî gā'û hammayim*, lit., "because the waters had risen up" [687, n. 16].

11. *śāḥû*, "swim," is a hapax form; see von Soden, "Ist im Alten Testament schon von Schwimmen die Rede?," 165–70; GKC §§24d, 93x. The verb *śāḥâ* occurs in Ps 6:7 [Eng 6:6] and possibly in Isa 25:11, 12, though von Soden doubts the latter verse [687, n. 17].

12. MT has two verbs, *wayyôlikēnî wayĕšibēnî*, lit., "he led me and took me back" [689, n. 19].

13. *'ēṣ rab mĕ'ōd* may also translate "a gigantic tree," but the collective sense is preferable, as in verse 12 [689, n. 22].

14. NJPS "foul" and REB "noxious" follow G. R. Driver's explanation ("Linguistic and Textual Problems: Ezekiel," 86–87) of *hammuṣā'îm* as a Hophal participle of "to be polluted, filthy." Similarly Pesh. reads, "stagnant" (so NRSV) [689, n. 26].

15. The versions read MT's problematic dual *naḥălayim* as sg.; Ehrlich (*Randglossen*, 158) emends it to *naḥălām* "their [viz. the waters'] stream." The dual may have influenced the two rivers of Zech 14:8. The Ugaritic texts locate the home of the god El at the source of the two rivers (*mbk nhrm*). For references see Gordon, *Ugaritic Textbook*, 42; also Clements, *God and Temple*, 107, n. 2 [689, n. 28]. The repetition of *kōl ăšer-yābō' šāmmâ hannāḥal* is not just a matter of style (so claimed by Kasher, *Ezekiel*, 910) but an emphasis on the waters, namely, they are the same waters emanating from the sanctuary.

16. While the final clause *kōl ăšer-yābō' šāmmâ hannāḥal*, "everywhere the stream flows," is commonly deleted as a dittographic variant of *kōl ăšer-yābō' šām naḥălayim* in verse 9a, it is better retained as an emphatic repetition; see the COMMENT on p. 232, below [689, n. 29].

17. LXX reads *wĕḥāyâ* as *wĕḥāyâ*, "and it will live," and places it at the end of verse 9 [689, n. 30].

18. Reading *wĕ'āmĕdû* with the versions. Cf. Kethib *y'mdw* and Qere *'mdw* [689, n. 31].

19. Block [689, n. 32] and Allen (*Ezekiel 20–48*, 274) incorrectly identify the antecedent as the stream instead of the sea.

20. MT *lĕmînā* should be read as *lĕmînāh* [689, n. 34].

21. Pl. suffix *dĕgātām* [689, n. 35].

22. *hayyām haggādôl*, lit., "the Great Sea" (cf. vv. 15, 19, 20; 48:28) [689, n. 36], i.e., the Mediterranean.

23. *biṣṣō't* (only in Job 8:11; 40:21) is related to *bōṣ*, "mud" (Jer 38:21) [689, n. 33]; cf. Radak.

24. LXX incorrectly derives *gĕbā'āyw* from *gābah* instead of *gebe'*, "cistern, pool" (only Isa 30:14) [689, n. 38].

25. Tg. expands to "salt pits" [689, n. 40].

*The Land (Ezekiel 47–48)*

they will yield fresh fruit[26] because its waters flow from the sanctuary. Their fruit will produce food and their leaves healing.[27]

COMMENT

According to Block, scholars have not taken kindly to the text of 47:1–12 because of uncharacteristic lexical forms, doublets, repetitions, grammatical anomalies, substantive inflections, and awkward interruptions. However, nothing in this subunit is unbecoming of the prophet. His excitement affected the literary quality of the report (cf. Ezek 1, 7). Ezekiel's amazement is reflected in the threefold occurrences of *wĕhinnê* (vv. 1, 2, 7) [689–90].

These are the textual difficulties encountered in 47:1–12: anomalous lexical forms: e.g., *negeb*, "south" (v. 1; cf. *dārōm* in 40:24, 27–28, 44–45; 41:21; 42:12–13, 18); *qāw*, "measuring line" (v. 3; cf. *pĕtîl pištîm* in 40:3); *miptān*, "threshold," cf. *sap* in 40:7–8; 41:16 (?); 43:9); doublets: e.g., *derek happôneh* (v. 2), both terms mean "in the direction of"; repetitions: especially *naḥal ʾăšer lōʾ-ʾûkal laʿăbōr* and *naḥal ʾăšer lōʾ-yĕʿābēr* (v. 5); *kol-ʾăšer yābōʾ šām naḥălayim* and *kol ʾăšer yābôʾ-šammâ hannaḥāl* (v. 9); *haddāgâ rabbâ mĕʾōd* (v. 9) and *dĕgātām . . . rabbâ mĕʾōd* (v. 10); *hammayim hāʾēlleh wĕyērāpĕʾû* (v. 9) and *wĕnirpĕʾû hammayim* (v. 8); grammatical anomalies: e.g., *bĕṣēʾt hāʾîš*, without a preceding *wĕhāyâ* or *wayĕhî*, in verse 3[28]; infelicities: the guidance formula in verse 1, the appearance of the celestial guide measuring the depth of the stream in verses 3–5; interruptions: the question/exclamation in verse 6a is separated from its answer in verse 8 by another guidance formula and prophetic observation in verses 6b–7 [689–90, n. 45].

As indicated by Kasher, the placement of this pericope before the subdivision of the land among the tribes (vv. 13–23) is a *sine qua non*; it is essential to make the tribal allotments equally fertile.[29] The main obstacle is the barren Judean wilderness (Fig. 18).[30] This area originally was like the Garden of Eden. Before the destruction of Sodom it was *kullāh mašqeh*, "well-watered"; *kĕgan YHWH*, "as the garden of YHWH" (Gen 13:10). That YHWH intended to restore this area to its erstwhile Edenic state is alluded in Ezek 16:53–55: *wĕšabtî ʾet-šĕbîthen ʾet-šĕbît [šĕbût, Q] sĕdōm . . . wĕăḥōtayik sĕdōm ûbĕnôtêhâ tāšōbĕnâ lĕqadmātām*, "I will restore their fortunes, the fortunes of Sodom . . . As for your sisters, Sodom and her daughters shall return to their former state." As part of creation, *wayyiṭṭaʿ YHWH ʾĕlōhîm gan-ʿēden miqqedem*, "the Lord

---

26. *yĕbakkēr* is a denominative Piel from *bĕkôr*, "firstborn," meaning "to bear early or new fruit." Cf. Milgrom "Hittite *ḫuelpi*," 575–76 [689, n. 42].

27. *tĕrûpâ* is a hapax from *rûp*, a by-form of *rāpāʾ*, "to heal" [689, n. 44]. Cf. also Sir 38:4 and Eliezer of Beaugency.

28. But on this construction see Rooker, *Biblical Hebrew in Transition*, 103–5.

29. Kasher, *Ezekiel*, 909.

30. Merely to glance at Ezekiel's map suffices to reveal its territorial inequities: The northern tribes from Dan to Ephraim are twice or thrice the size of the southern tribes. Of course, Ezekiel had no choice. The area covered forms the actual (priestly) borders of the Promised Land (Num 34:1–15). On the other hand, the Judaean desert, newly fertilized by the divine stream, may more than compensate for this small area in comparison with the size of the northern tribes.

## PART TWO: EZEKIEL 40–48—THE VISIONARY SANCTUARY AND THE LAND

YHWH planted the Garden of Eden in the east" (Gen 2:8). According to Ezekiel 28:14, 16, the Garden of Eden is located *běhar ʾĕlōhîm*, "on God's mountain," and so is Ezekiel's sanctuary (Ezek 40:2). As in the description of the Garden of Eden in Gen 2:8 and Ezek 31:7, the multiplicity and varieties of the trees are stressed, and the water that flows out of Ezekiel's sanctuary and becomes a mighty river is reminiscent of the river that flows out of the Garden of Eden (Gen 2:10).

R. Pattai[31] may have been the first to recognize the motif common to the ancient Near East that water flowing out of a temple is the source of widespread fertility. For example, on the cylinder inscription B of Gudea, after the consummation of the sacred marriage of Ningirsu and Ba'u, waters stream forth from a basin placed near the couch of the gods and bring forth waters that equal the size and fertility of the Tigris and Euphrates.[32]

**47:1.** The guide walks Ezekiel through the set-up of the sacrificial kitchens (46:21–24). Suddenly he is surprised to see a stream of water bubbling out from under the *miptān*, "threshold" [691].[33]

***From underneath*** **(*mittaḥat*).** Since this is a visionary "seeing," Ezekiel is enabled to follow the spring inside the sanctuary, presumably as it exits from the adytum and flows underground until it surfaces outside the sanctuary. The surfacing of the spring is more precisely identified, *mikketep habbayit hayĕmānît*, "from the right side of the sanctuary [façade]" *miptān* and *kātēp* are architectural terms, the latter referring to the part of the gate structure that extends horizontally from the gateway opening to the next corner. The façade of the sanctuary (like that of the tabernacle and Solomonic [first] temple) also faces east.

***From the south side of the sanctuary*** **(*mikketep habbayit hayĕmānît*).** Holding that *hayĕmānît* means "right" (rather than south), commentaries are at a loss to follow the route of the flow. How can it commence on the right (i.e., north) side of the sanctuary, and flow south of the altar? Some suggest that "right" means from the point of view of the sanctuary, in which case "right" means "south"; others retain the meaning right = north (i.e., from the perspective of the prophet-observer), but that the flow runs diagonally, right to left (e.g., Rashi, Radak). *Yāmîn* or *yĕmānî* frequently means "south," indeed in the same architectural context (1 Kgs 6:8; 7:19; 2 Kgs 11:11; 2 Chr 4:10; 23:10), and it also means "south" in Ezekiel (10:3; 16:46).

**47:2.** The guide leads Ezekiel from the sanctuary complex circuitously through the inner north gate, to the lower platform, through the outer north gate and around right outside to the outer east gate in order to observe the flow of the underground spring. This circuitous route is taken because the outer east gate is permanently closed (cf. 44:1–2; 46:1). The prophet is surprised to see that the spring has surfaced, at first in

---

31. Pattai, *Ha-Mayim [Water]*, 86–87.
32. I am thankful for this reference to D. Sharon, "Biblical Parallel?" 99–139, esp. 102.
33. A slab of stone at the base of a doorway visible to an observer, outside.

bubbles (note its onomatopoeic formation from *pak*, "bottle," *pākak* "bubble forth," conveying the sound of liquid gurgling out of a flask [691]),³⁴ and then in increased volume. The Talmud offers this imaginative description:

> R. Pinchas said in the name of R. Huna of Tzipori: The spring that issued from the Holy of Holies was at first like the antennae of a grasshopper; by the door of the sanctuary it was like a thread of the warp; at the porch it was thick as a thread of the woof; at the door of the forecourt it was as broad as the mouth of a small pitcher. [This is what we have learned in a Mishna (*m. Mid.* 2:4): "R. Eliezer b. Jacob said: Water will issue in the time to come from under the sill of the temple."] Thenceforth, it waxed in strength, and when it reached the door of David's house, it was like a streaming river, and these people bathed, as it is written [Zech 13:1]: "On that day shall there be a fountain opened to the house of David ... for cleansing from sins and for purification." (*Yoma* 77b)

**47:3–5.** The use of a new term, *qāw*, for the guide's measuring instrument "alerts the reader to a possible shift in significance." Earlier he had moved inward towards greater holiness. Now he moves outward, away from the sanctuary complex [692]. Perhaps *qāw*, in contrast to *qĕnēh hammiddâ*, "measuring reed" (40:5), or *pĕtîl pištîm*, "flax line" (40:3), is used for long distances (1,000 cubits at time, vv. 3–5).³⁵

The guide wades downstream with the prophet, pausing every 1,000 cubits to measure the depth. The repetitive style reflects the guide's methodical manner. Having begun as a bubbling spring (*mĕpakkîm*), the stream reaches his ankles at 1,000 cubits, his knees at 2,000 cubits, and his waist at 3,000 cubits. At 4,000 cubits, the waters—now a stream (*naḥal*)—is too deep for wading and deep enough for swimming (*śāḥû*). There are no further measurements. Now both prophet and reader must calculate by geometric progression the torrential rise of water every 1,000 cubits as it rushes toward the sea [692].

Reminiscent of and perhaps influenced by Ezekiel [697], Joel writes (4:18 [Eng 3:18])

> In that day,
> the mountains will drip with wine,
> and the hills will flow with milk.
> All the gullies (*ăpîqîm*) of Judah
> will flow with water;
> a spring (*'ayin*) will issue from the temple (*bayit*) of YHWH,
> and water the Wadi of the Acacias.

Also later, the prophet Zechariah predicts: "In that day living waters (*mayim ḥayyîm*) will flow from Jerusalem, one-half of them toward the Eastern [Dead] Sea, the other half to the Western [Mediterranean] Sea" (14:8). See also Isa 44:3–4; 55:1; 58:11 [698]. Few doubt that these verses, including Ezek 47:1–12, are influenced by

---

34. *Tos. Suk* 3:3, but cf. Tg. and Radak.

35. Note *qāw middâ*, "measuring line," in Jer 31:39; cf. 1 Kgs 7:21 = 2 Chr 4:2; 2 Kgs 21:13; Isa 34:11, 17; 44:13; Zech 1:16; Lam 4:8; Job 38:5 [692. n. 53].

Gen 2:10–14, which portrays paradise as a garden, rendered fruitful by a river flowing out of Eden and dividing into four branches [696].[36]

**47:6.** The verb *rāʾâ* is capable of a wide range of meanings: e.g., see, observe, gaze, discover, become aware, perceive, experience [693, n. 55].[37] Having been too busy counting off the 1,000 cubit intervals to pay attention to the prophet, the guide now turns to him and asks, "Have you seen [until now]?"

**47:7–9.** Greater sights await the prophet, signaled by the third *wĕhinnēh*. As the guide returns Ezekiel to the bank, he is astonished to see dense groves of trees on both banks of the stream. The stream flows *ʾel-haggĕlîlâ haqqadmônâ*, "to the eastern region" (cf. *gĕlîlôt happĕlištîm*, "the region of the Philistines," Josh 13:2; Joel 4:4 [Eng 3:4]; and *gĕlîlôt hayyardēn*, "the region of the Jordan," Josh 22:10–11) [693, n. 56]. The stream drops into the *Arabah*. Today, this term usually identifies the depression south of the Dead Sea that terminates in the Gulf of Aqabah, but in biblical times the name was used more generally of the rift valley that runs from the Kinneret (Lake Tiberias/Galilee) in the north to the Gulf of Aqabah in the south. The water is said to flow *hayyāmmâ*, "into the sea." [693]. Earlier, *yām* referred to the western sea, namely, the Mediterranean; here it means the Dead Sea, more precisely *hayyāmmâ hammûṣāʾîm*, "the sea of foul waters" (see n. 866) [694].[38]

The repetition of the entire clause, *kol ʾăšer-yābōʾ šām[mâ] hannahal[ayim]*, "wherever the stream flows" (v. 9), emphasizes the completeness of the "healing." In language reminiscent of Gen 1:20–21, the sea "swarms" (*šāraṣ*) with fish [694], perhaps to compensate for the absence of fish along the Mediterranean littoral.[39]

**47:10.** En-gedi is a flourishing oasis on the northwestern side of the Dead Sea, and En-eglaim, identified with Egloth-shelishiyah (Isa 15:3; Jer 48:34), is on the opposite, east side of the Dead Sea. These two points form a merism standing for the total Dead Sea coast. Thus, all around the lake, fishermen will spread their nets to catch their fish. The present expression, *mištôaḥ laḥărāmîm*, carries a different sense than *mištaḥ ḥărāmîm* in 26:5, 14. In the latter text, the image represents a warning of judgment for Tyre; the city will be reduced to a bare rock fit solely for fishermen spreading their nets. Here the image represents blessing: The fish will be famous not just for abundance but for variety (*mînâ*), comparable to all the fish of the Great Sea (*hayyām haggādôl*), the Mediterranean [695]. The economic change of this piscatorial miracle cannot be over-

---

36. Stevenson's claim (*Vision of Transformation,* 142) that the symbolism of 47:1–12 is cosmic is unwarranted. The sacrificial altar cleanses the temple of Israel's sins, and only the land of Israel is healed by its temple-originating waters.

37. See Fuhs, "*rāʾâ*," 13.208–42.

38. Rabbinic midrash parses this word as a Hophal pl. from *yāṣāʾ*, "leave, flow," connects it with Zech 14:8, and postulates that the river flowing out of Jerusalem will split into three branches: one flowing into the Sea of Tiberias (Galilee), one flowing into the Sea of Sodom (the Dead Sea), and the ultimate destination being the Great Sea (Mediterranean), encompassing the entire world; cf. Tg., Rashi, and Radak; cf. also *Exod Rab* 15:22.

39. See the account of the serendipitous discovery, Milgrom, *Leviticus 1–16,* 660–61.

## The Land (Ezekiel 47–48)

looked: Postexilic Israel will no longer be dependent on the Phoenician fleets to import fish from the distant Greek islands; henceforth, fish are a local, plentiful product.

**47:11–12.** The water in the swamps (*biṣṣō'tāw*) and marshes (*gĕbā'āyw*) will not be "healed." Apparently, the southern part of the Dead Sea—below the Lisan, a tongue shaped peninsula jutting into the sea from the eastern shore—is intended. This region, reputed to cover the destroyed cities of Sodom and Gomorrah (Gen. 19:1–24), is entirely too shallow for fish. On the other hand, it will be an even more fabulous economic resource for its salt (*melaḥ*). Corresponding to the profusion and variety of fish in the Dead Sea is the abundance and variety of fruit trees on its shores, [696] whose "leaves will never wither" (*lō'-yibbol*, cf. Ps 1:3) and whose fruit will never cease (*lō'-yittōm*; cf. Jer 17:8), more concretely "every month the trees will yield" fresh fruit (*laḥŏdāšāyw yĕbakkēr*). Even its leaves will be a vital source for human well-being: They will serve a pharmaceutical function, bring "healing" (*tĕrûpâ*) to the sickly and the wounded [696]. This entire pericope is succinctly summarized by the clause, "because its [the stream's] waters flow from the sanctuary" (*kî mêmāyw min-hammiqdāš hēmmâ yōṣĕ'îm*), emphasizing that the mighty healing stream has its origin in the trickle of water emanating from the source of the supreme-holiness, the divine residence, the sanctuary. The flow of these miraculously healing waters inspires the following rabbinic midrash:

> R. Eliezer b. Jacob says, *Through it the water comes out [on the south side]* (Ezek 47:2). This teaches that they flow outward like the water of a flask. And they are destined to flow *down from below the south end of the threshold of the temple, [south of the altar]* (Ezek 47:1). And so it says, *Going on eastward with a line in his hand, the man measured a thousand cubits, and then led me through the water, and it was ankle deep* (Ezek 47:3). This teaches that a man may go through water up to his ankles [without danger]. *Again he measured a thousand and led me through the water, and it was knee deep* (Ezek 47:4). This teaches that a man goes through the water up to his knees [without facing danger of drowning] . . . *Again he measured a thousand, and led me through the water, and it was up to the loins* (Ezek 47:4). This teaches that a man may go through water up to his loins [without danger]. *Again he measured a thousand, and it was a river that I could not pass through, [for the water had risen; it was too turbulent to swim in, a river that could not be passed through]* (Ezek 47:5). Is it possible to interpret that one might not go through by foot, but one could pass over by swimming? [No, for] Scripture say, *For the water had risen, it was deep enough to swim in*. Is it possible to interpret that one might not cross by swimming, but one might cross in a small boat? [No, for] Scripture says, *A river that could not be passed through*—even in a boat. Is it possible to interpret that one might not cross in a small boat, but one might pass over in a large boat? Scripture says, *[But there the Lord in majesty will be for us, a place of broad rivers and streams,] where no galley with oars can go, [nor stately ship can pass]* (Isa 33:21). Is it possible to interpret that one might not cross in a large boat, but one might pass in a large ship? Scripture says, *No stately ship can pass*.
> 
> And it says, *On that day water will go forth from Jerusalem* (Zech 14:8). Is it possible that they will be mixed with water from other springs? Scripture says,

## PART TWO: EZEKIEL 40-48—THE VISIONARY SANCTUARY AND THE LAND

> *On that day there shall be a fountain opened for the house of David and the inhabitants of Jerusalem to cleanse them from sin and uncleanness* (Zech 13:1). There will be a single source [of purification-water] for sin and for menstrual uncleanness. Whither do they flow? To the Great Sea, to the Sea at Tiberias, and to the sea at Sodom, so as to heal their water, as it is said, *And he said to me, This water flows toward the eastern region and goes down into the Arabah; and when it enters the stagnant waters of the sea, the water will become fresh* (Ezek 47:8). *This water flows toward the eastern region*—this refers to the sea at Sodom. *And it goes down into the Arabah*—this refers to the sea at Tiberias. *And when it enters the stagnant waters of the sea, the water will become fresh*—this is the Great Sea. And it says, *And wherever the river goes every living creature which swarms will live; and there will be very many fish; for this water goes there, that the waters of the sea may become fresh; so everything will live where the river goes* (Ezek 47:9). And it says, *fishermen will stand beside the sea; from Engedi to Ein eglaim it will be a place for the spreading of the nets; its fish will be very many kinds, like the fish of the Great Sea* (Ezek 47:10). This teaches that all the waters created at the time of Creation are destined to go forth from the mouth of this little flask. (*t. Suk* 3:3–10).[40]

### The New Boundaries of the Land (47:13–20)

TRANSLATION

**13** Thus has the Lord YHWH proclaimed: This will be the border [boundary[41]] of the land which you will divide up for the inheritance[42] among the twelve tribes of Israel, [Joseph having two portions[43]]; **14** and you will divide it equally[44] for inheritance; [it is] the land I raised my hand in oath to give to your fathers. This land will fall[45] to you as your inheritance.

**15** This will be the border of the land: As the northern border:[46] from the Great Sea[47] by way of Hethlon and Lebo-hamath to Zedad, **16** Hamath, Beratha, Sibraim[48]—which lie between the border of Damascus and Hamath—[as far

---

40. Translation by J. Neusner, *Tosefta*, 574ff.

41. *gēh gǎbûl* is an error for *zeh haggěbûl*. The first *gimel* probably was written in anticipation of the second, and the article was dropped by haplography (cf. LXX, Tg. and Vulg; see also the form of the colophon in 48:29) [705, n. 5]. Eliezer of Beaugency, however, renders "canyon" (*gēh* = *gê'*).

42. The *lamed* after *hitnaḥēl* introduces the beneficiaries of the action; cf. Lev 25:40, Num 33:54 [705, n. 7].

43. *yōsēp ḥăbālîm* is intrusive and ungrammatical, though attested in all the versions and rendered as a dual in Tg. and Vulg. If anything, read *lěyôsēp ḥăbālayim* (dual), "two portions for Joseph," i.e., for Ephraim and Manasseh [705, n. 8]; *ḥebel*, lit., "rope" is used for measuring (cf. Deut 32:9; Josh 13:5, 14; Zech 2:5).

44. *'iš kě'āḥîw*, lit., "each like his brother" (cf. Lev 7:10) [706, n. 9].

45. *wěnāpělâ*, "will fall," i.e., by lot, but since the boundaries have been fixed by God, *wěnāpělâ*, "will fall," is a metaphor for "will allot."

46. The *hē* directive on *ṣāpônâ* has lost its force after *lip'at* [706, n. 10].

47. *hayyām haggādôl*, lit., "the great sea" [706, n. 11]; i.e., "the Mediterranean."

48. MT reads simply *lěbô'*; *ṣědādâ* and *ḥāmat*, the first word in verse 16, were apparently transposed; cf. LXX and 48:1 [706, n. 13].

*The Land (Ezekiel 47–48)*

as] Hazer-hatticon,[49] which borders on Hauran. **17** So the boundary [will go] from the sea to Hazer-enon, which is the north boundary[50] of Damascus, with the region of Hamath to the north. This[51] will be the northern border.

On the east: the boundary will go from [a point][52] between Hauran and Damascus, and between Gilead and the land of Israel, with the Jordan as the border,[53] at the eastern sea as far as Tamar.[54] This will be the eastern border.

**19** On the south:[55] the boundary goes from from Tamar to the waters of Meriboth-kadesh,[56] along the Wadi[57] [of Egypt] to the Great Sea. This is the southern border.

**20** On the west: The Great Sea will be the boundary to a point opposite Lebo-hamath. This is the western border.

COMMENT

The pericope 47:13–23 comprises two sections: the boundary list of the land (vv. 15–20) and the framework (vv. 13–14, 21–23). The latter is distinguished by its key word and form. The root *nḥl* occurs six times (vv. 13, 14, 14, 22, 22, 23), four by its noun *naḥălâ* (vv. 14, 22, 22, 23). The former has *gĕbûl* as its keyword, occurring nine times (vv. 15, 16, 16, 16, 17, 17, 17, 18, 20). The opening verse of the framework also contains the term *gĕbûl*, perhaps a deliberate attempt by the redactor to tie both sections together and to raise the number of *gĕbûl* occurrences to ten, also to raise the number of occurrences of the word *naḥălâ* to seven by adding it to verse 19, where it is a proper noun. The quill of the redactor is more evident in the composition of the framework [707], as shown by the chart below:

---

49. The versions do not agree on the meaning of *ḥāṣēr hattîkôn*, "the inside court," unidentified; Tg. *brykt 'gyb'y*, "pond of Agibites," again unidentified. *BHS*' emendation to *ḥăṣērā 'ēnōn* on the basis of LXX αὐλὴ τοῦ Σαυναν, "the court of Saunon," is unlikely [706, n. 15]. See the COMMENT.

50. *gĕbûl dammeseq wĕṣāpôn, ṣāpōnâ gĕbûl ḥămat*, "the border of Damascus and north northward and the border of Hamath," is unintelligible. *Wĕṣāpon* is probably a dittography [706, n. 18].

51. *w't* is an error for *zo't* (Pesh.), repeated in verses 18 and 19; cf. v. 20 [706, n. 19].

52. This is the sense of *mibbēn*. *BHS* and RSV insert Hazer-enon; NRSV deletes it [706, n. 20].

53. *miggĕbûl* may be a scribal error for *magbîl* (Exod 19:12, 23) [706, n. 22].

54. MT *tāmôdû*, "you will measure," is out of place. Emendation to *tamrâ*, "date palm," viz., Jericho (Deut 34:3) is supported by LXX, Φοινικῶνος, and Pesh., *'l ym' mdnḥy' dtmr*; cf. v. 19 and 48:28 [706, n. 23].

55. The redundancy *negeb têmānâ* is supported by LXX and 48:28. Ezek 21:2 uses three designations for south: *negeb, dārôm*, and *têmānâ* [706, n. 24].

56. MT pl., *mĕrîbôt qādēš*, is reflected in LXX and Tg., *mṣwt rqm*. Kadesh as Reqam is found in Gen 16:14, 20. The sg. rendering is supported by 48:28 (cf. Num 27:14 and Deut 32:51) [707, n. 25].

57. Tg. *'ḥsn'* and Pesh. *ywrtn* read *nḥlh* as "inheritance" [707, n. 26]. Cf. Rashi.

PART TWO: EZEKIEL 40-48—THE VISIONARY SANCTUARY AND THE LAND

## The Framework of Ezekiel 47:13-23

| 47:13-14 | 47:21-23 |
|---|---|
| 13 kōh 'āmar 'ădōnāy YHWH<br>gēh gĕbûl<br>'ăšer titnaḥălû 'et- hā'āreṣ<br>lišnê'āśār šibṭê yiśrā'ēl<br>(yôsēp ḥăbālîm)<br>14 ûnĕḥaltem 'ōtāh 'îš kĕ'āḥîw<br>'ăšer nāśā'tî 'et-yādî lĕtittāh la'ăbōtêkem<br>wĕnāpĕlâ hā'āreṣ hazzō't lākem<br>bĕnaḥălâ | 21 wĕḥillaqtem 'et-hā'āreṣ hazzō't lākem<br>lĕšibṭê yiśrā'ēl<br>22 wĕhāyâ tappilû 'ōtāh bĕnaḥălâ lākem<br>ûlĕhaggērîm haggārîm bĕtôkĕkem<br>'ăšer-hôlidû bānîm bĕtôkĕkem<br>wĕhāyû lākem kĕ'ezrāḥ bibnê yiśrā'ēl<br>'ittĕkem yippĕlû bĕnaḥălâ bĕtôk šibṭê yiśrā'ēl<br>23 wĕhāyâ baššēbeṭ 'ăšer gār haggēr 'ittô<br>šām tittĕnû naḥălātô<br>nĕ'um 'ădōnāy YHWH |
| 13 Thus has the Lord YHWH declared<br>"This shall be the boundary of the land,<br>which you shall apportion for inheritance<br>among the twelve tribes of Israel,<br>[Joseph having two portions].<br>14 And you shall share it<br>equally for inheritance<br>(it is) the land I swore to give to your fathers<br>This land shall fall to you<br>as your inheritance. | 20 You shall divide this land<br>among yourselves<br>according to the tribes of Israel.<br>22 You shall allot it as an inheritance<br>for yourselves,<br>according to the tribes of Israel,<br>and for the aliens who reside amongst you,<br>who have fathered children among you,<br>They shall be to you as ethnic Israelites.<br>They shall share the allotment<br>[of the land] with you<br>as an inheritance<br>among the tribes of Israel.<br>23 In whatever tribes the alien may reside<br>there you shall assign him his inheritance,<br>the declaration of the Lord YHWH |

The framework makes good sense apart from the boundary list it encompasses. The supertext speaks of the past: YHWH's oath to the ancestors that this land would be their progeny's inheritance and that it would be divided equally among their twelve tribes. This does not fit the following boundary list in two ways. First, the boundaries (vv. 15-20) correspond mainly (but not exactly) to Num 34, but these boundaries were never revealed to the forefathers. Second, neither the Numbers boundaries (nor any other) were claimed to be an equal division of tribal territory. The subtext (vv. 21-23) repeats the injunction to divide the land among the tribes, but holds as its major innovation of this pericope that the resident alien should be assigned inheritable property in whatever tribe he resides. This innovation is revolutionary. According to H, no Israelite may be enslaved (Lev 25:39-42), but the alien and his offspring may be permanently enslaved (Lev 25:44-46). Not even the exilic prophet Isaiah achieved these visionary heights (on Isa 56:6-9, see below).

**47:13.** The divine injunction to divide the land among the tribes has as its initial innovation that the tribal property is inheritable. This provision is ensconced in the verb *titnaḥălû*. This means that the land may never be alienated (even by a king, cf. 1 Kgs 21), and even when economic necessity forces relinquishing of all or part of the land; in effect the usufruct has been ceded but not the land itself.[58] The law of the Jubilee is the answer provided by H to restore landed property to its original owner (Lev 25:10–13).[59] However, this contingency is not mentioned by Ezekiel. In his idealistic, utopian world will economic privation never occur? Or are H's laws concerning destitution and restitution (Jubilee) taken for granted?

Ezekiel had already prophesied that the restored tribes would be reunited (37:19). Here their number is specified—twelve [708], i.e., stemming from the twelve sons of Jacob. Does this mean that Joseph is one of the tribes? Indeed, the name Joseph is singled out in the earlier prophecy of unification (37:19). However, the tribe of Levi has been awarded its own territory within the *tĕrûmâ*, "the sacred area" (45:5), leaving their vacated spot among the twelve to be filled by the two sons of Joseph, Ephraim and Manasseh, a replacement that tradition dates back to the blessing of Jacob (Gen 48:5) [709]. Despite the patriarchal precedent, some tradent or redactor of Ezekiel found it necessary to add a reminder that the tribal territory included two portions, "double cords, for [the sons of] Joseph." The specific term is *ḥăbālim*, corrupt for *ḥăbālayim* "double cords." The term *ḥebel* "cord" refers to a surveyor's measuring rod, a metonym for the land laid out by the rod, i.e., the tribal territory.

**47:14.** The injunction to allot the land *'îš kĕ'āḥîw*, lit., "each man as his brother," implies that all Israelites should partake alike, namely, that each tribe should share the land equitably, which anticipates the tribal division of chapter 48. This expression is also found in Lev 7:10, where the Aaronide priests are informed that their sacrificial prebends should be shared by all priests equally. Here this injunction is applied to the twelve tribes. That is, each tribe should share inherited landed property alike. The boundary list follows below (vv. 15–20). This list is based on the boundary map of Num 34:15, which is what one would expect, since that map has been attributed to P; the dependency of the priest Ezekiel on the priestly source has been frequently attested. Thus the land division "indicates a significant degree of pragmatic realism."[60] This applies to the division of the tribes (Ezek 48), but not to the boundaries of the land, which are based on the detailed priestly map, Num 34.

***The land I swore to give to your fathers.*** YHWH does not contravene his oath, specifically *'el-hā'āreṣ 'ăšer nāśā'tî 'et-yādî lātēt 'ōtāh lĕ'abrāhām lĕyiṣḥāq ûlĕya'ăqōb*, "to the land I swore to give to Abraham, Isaac and Jacob" (Exod 6:8; cf. Gen 26:3; 50:24; Exod 13:5, 11; 33:1; Num 14:30; 32:11; Deut 1:8; 6:10)—even though there is no text where God's promise of land to the fathers takes the form of an oath [710]. Ezekiel refers to YHWH's earlier oath of land to Abraham (33:24), Jacob (28:25; 37:25), and to

---

58. Cf. Milgrom, *Leviticus 23–27*, 2191–212.
59. Ibid., 2241–51.
60. Joyce, *Ezekiel*, 238.

## PART TWO: EZEKIEL 40-48—THE VISIONARY SANCTUARY AND THE LAND

unidentified ancestors (*ābôt*; 20:28, 42; 36:28). Note also that "raising the hand" is still used today, particularly in the courtroom, to signify the taking of an oath. When the subject is God, the expression must be understood metaphorically.

**The land will fall** (*wĕnāpĕlâ hā'āreṣ*). This verb refers to the idiom, *lĕhappîl gôrāl*, "to cast a lot." Originally, the Canaanite territory was apportioned to the Israelite tribes by lot (Num 33:54; 34:13) [710]. The result was not equitable (see Josh 17:1–18; 18:11–28; 19:1–9).[61] Here, the boundaries of the land have already been fixed; there is no relying on the vagaries of lot-casting. The expression is purely metaphoric, namely the borders of the land assigned to you are fixed, as delineated below. To obviate complaints about inequities, the people are told that the land has been subdivided equitably.[62]

FIGURE 19: The Tribal Territories, Ezekiel 47–48. Pentateuchal (smaller font) and Ezekielian (larger font)

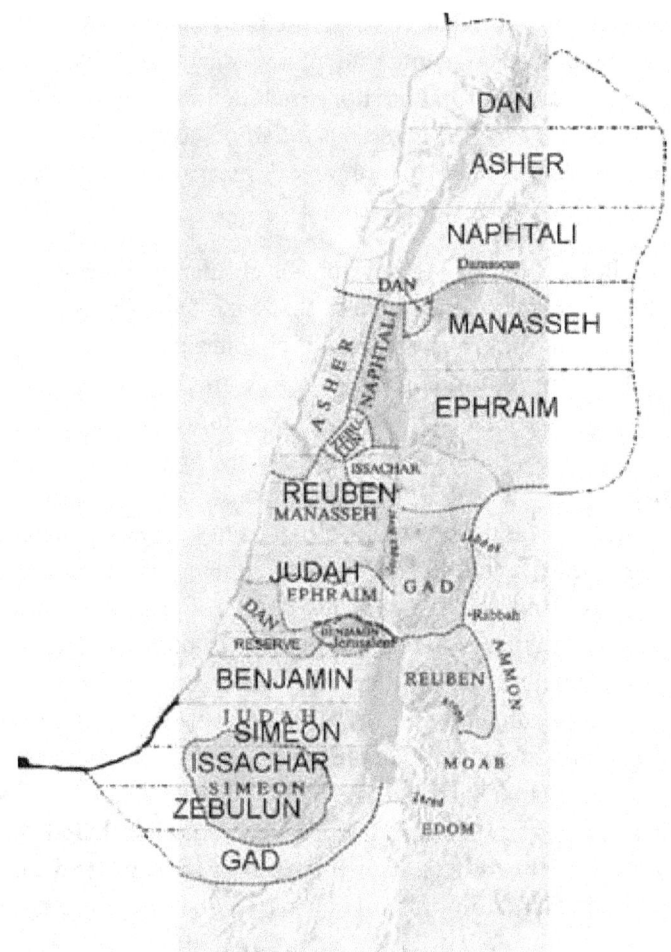

61. See Greenberg, *Ezekiel 1–20*, 500, and Block, *Ezekiel 1–24*, 778.
62. So it has been intended. The result, however, as shown above, is hardly *'îš kĕ'āḥîw*.

## The Land (Ezekiel 47–48)

**47:15–17. The northern border.** This border is replete with specific points. So is the northern border in Num 34:7–9, though less so, and even less in Ezek 48:1 (see Fig. 19). As pointed out by Galil,[63] three factors distinguish the northern borders: (1) the plethora of points, (2) phraseology, and (3) the multiple descriptions (twice in chapter 47 and once in chapter 48). Each description is composed of two stiches (each stich containing two to four border points). In most cases, the single stich does not fully describe the border, so that the additional stich bridges and completes the description, going over much of the same ground. The emphasis on the northern border—with its multiple northern points—may be due to this area being beyond the bounds of the land according to the book of Joshua and the actual borderline of the First Temple period. While Block [712] conjectures that Ezekiel perceives the land from the perspective of his own experience (he was led north into exile) and his aspirations (the exiles will return from the north),[64] the reason for this topographic excess may be that in contrast to the other borders, which were well known to the Israelites as real borders of the demographic and political states of Judah and Israel, the northern border was—except for a brief period under David (1 Kgs 8:65; 1 Chr 13:5; 2 Chr 7:8) and Jeroboam II (2 Kgs 14:25)—an unachieved utopia.

Note on the map (Fig. 19) that the territory assigned to the tribes of Dan, Asher, Naphtali, Manasseh, and Ephraim—five of the twelve tribes!—was occupied permanently, wholly or partially, by Phoenicians and Aramaeans. Of course, Ezekiel had no choice. His visionary northern border was that of the Mosaic map (Num 34). Fig. 19 shows the realistic borders of Israel superimposed on the visionary borders of the Promised Land. The latter apparently represents the northern boundary of the Egyptian province of Canaan according to the peace treaty between Ramses II and the Hittites at the beginning of the thirteenth century BCE.[65]

---

63. Galil, "Boundaries of Aram-Damascus," 242.

64. To which I respond, "Hardly. As an exile he crossed the border but was unlikely given the opportunity to survey it (the boundary was approximately 80 miles long!)." But Block's statement does not suggest he imagines Ezekiel to have had the opportunity to survey northern boundary region; only that he speaks from the perspective of having passed through this region on the way to Babylon.

65. B. Mazar, "Canaan on the Threshold," 18–32; de Vaux, "Le pays de Canaan," 23–30; Milgrom, *Numbers*, 501.

## PART TWO: EZEKIEL 40–48—THE VISIONARY SANCTUARY AND THE LAND

TABLE 7: A Comparison of Three Accounts of Israel's Northern Border

| Numbers 34:7b–9a | Ezekiel 47:15b–17 | Ezekiel 48:1 |
|---|---|---|
| tĕtā'û lākem hōr hāhār | min hayyām haggādōl | |
| mēhōr hāhār tĕtā'û | hadderek ḥetlōn | 'el-yad derek ḥetlōn |
| Lĕbō'-ḥămāt | lĕbō' | Lĕbō'-ḥămāt |
| wĕhāyû tôṣĕ'ōt haggĕbul | | |
| ṣĕdādâ | ṣĕdādâ | |
| wĕyaṣā' haggĕbul ziprōnâ | ḥămāt bērôtâ sibrayim | |
| | 'ăšer bên-gĕbûl dammeśeq | |
| | ûbên gĕbûl ḥămāt | |
| | ḥăṣēr-hattîkôn | |
| | 'ăšer 'el-gĕbûl ḥaurān | |
| wĕhāyû tôṣĕ'ōtāyw ḥăṣar 'ēnān | wĕhāyâ gĕbul min-hayyām | |
| | ḥăṣar 'ēnān | ḥăṣar 'ēnān |
| | gĕbûl dammeśeq wĕṣāpôn | gĕbûl dammeśeq |
| | ṣāpônâ ûgĕbûl ḥămāt | ṣāpônâ 'el-yad ḥămāt |
| From the Great Sea to Mount Hor you shall draw a line Lebo hamath Zedad | From the Great Sea by way of Hethlon Lebo Zedad Hamath, Beratha, Sibraim, which lies between the border of Damascus | bordering on the way of Hethlon Lebo-hamath |
| The boundary shall run to Ziphron | and the border of Hamath which is on the border of Hauran | |
| | So the boundary from the sea | |
| and terminate at Hazar-enan. | to Hazer-enon which is the northern border of Damascus. | and Hazar-enan which is the border of Damascus, with Hamath to the north. |

As shown by Kallai,[66] the term *gĕbûl* does not refer to linear boundaries, but to the territory under the jurisdiction of the specified boundary point [712]. The Mosaic map begins with the southern border (Num 34:3–15). It reflects the path of the scouts who reconnoitered the land from the south to Lebo-hamath in the north (Num 13:21). Both maps begin their northern border at the Great Sea, that is, the Mediterranean. But starting from where? The probable point lies just north of Byblos in present day Lebanon, which marked the northern boundary of the Egyptian province of Canaan. Beginning in the fifteenth century, Canaan was the official name of Egyptian holdings in Asia. Its northern boundary was fixed in the thirteenth century by the peace treaty between Ramses II of Egypt and the Hittite empire (ca. 1270), which left the city of Kadesh in Hittite hands and the Damascus region under Egyptian control [715]. These are the northern polar points:

---

66. Kallai, *Historical Geography of the Bible*, 100–101, n. 5.

*The Land (Ezekiel 47–48)*

**Hethlon**. Ezekiel gives Hethlon as a northern boundary point; it is identified with modern Heitela, northeast of Tripoli, at the foot of Jebel Akkar, and south of the Eleuthera River, which separates Syria from Lebanon.[67] The rabbis identify it with Mount Amana (Song 4:8), modern Zebedani, the source of the Amanah River (2 Kgs 5:12), modern Barada, which flows through Damascus.[68] Where Ezekiel has Hethlon Num 34:7 cites Mount Hor. It is not Mount Hor that lies near the border of Edom where Aaron died (Num 20:22–29; 33:8). It is probably one of the northwest summits of the Lebanese range north of Byblos (possibly Ras Shaqqah on Jebel Akkar) [713].

**Lebo-hamath**. Lebo, identified with Libweh, was an important point on the southern border of the kingdom of Hamath on one of the sources of the Orontes River, which flows northwest from there and turns westward to reach the Mediterranean about 45 miles north of Ugarit. Lebo coincides with the northern boundary of Israel under David and Solomon (1 Kgs 8:65) and Jeroboam II (2 Kgs 14:25; Amos 6:14) [713]. The description of the northern border in Josh 13:4 adds Aphek, modern Afqa, 15 miles east of Byblos.

**Zedad**. Present-day Sedad, east of the Sirion (Anti-Lebanese range), near the Damascus-Ohms road, 35 miles northeast of Libway (Lebo) [713].

**Berutha** is usually equated with Bereitan, situated south of Ba'albek[69] and 30 miles north-northwest of Damascus [713].

**Sibraim**. Unknown. The unfamiliarity of this place in Ezekiel's time accounts for the explanatory phrase "which is located between the territories of Damascus and Hamath" [713].

**Hazer-hatticon**. Also unknown, obscure even in Ezekiel's time. Hence the explanatory phrase "which is on the border of Hauran." A point between Hauran and Damascus, perhaps parallel with Tyre and Dan, may be proposed [714].

**Haraun**. Modern Jebel Druze, identified with the high balsamic mountains east of Galilee, which separate Bashan from the desert. The name occurs in the Bible only here and in verse 18, but it appears in Nineteenth Dynasty Egyptian texts as *Ḫu-ru-na* and in ninth-century Assyrian annals as *Ḫa-u-ra-ni* [714].[70]

**Hazer-enon** not definitely identified. Scholars tend to equate it with Qaryatein, 70 miles northeast of Damascus toward Palmyra [714].[71]

---

67. De Vaux, "Le pays de Canaan," 23–29.

68. Tg., *Midrash Songs* on 4:8; *m. Shevi'it* 6:1; *t. Ter* 2:12; cf. Albeck, *Six Orders of the Mishnah: Seeds*, 379

69. Aharoni, *Land of the Bible*, 73; Simons, *Geographical and Topographical Texts*, 333.

70. Shalmaneser III advanced as far as "the mountains of Hauran" (*šadêe mat Ḫa-u-ra-ni*) cf. *ARAB* 1:2861, §672; *ANET*, 280.

71. Aharoni, *Land of the Bible*, 37–38; Simons, *Geographical and Topographical Texts*, 102.

**Damascus.** This commercial and political center, known to the Arabs as "the pearl of the east" is located east of the Anti-Lebanon range on the Abana River. Until it fell to the Assyrians in 732, it was the base of the strongest Aramaean kingdom in Israel's north [714].[72]

**Hamath.** A major city-state on the middle Orontes River, 100 miles north of Damascus. It was successively controlled by Hittites, Aramaeans, and Assyrians. Isaiah 11:11 notes that captive Israelites were brought to Hamath by the Assyrians, and according to 2 Kgs 17:24 Esarhaddon resettled people from this place in Israel. The city fell eventually to Babylon (Jer 39:5) during the time of Ezekiel [714–15].

It should be noted that the EBH *bên . . . bên* has shifted to *bên . . . lĕ* eight times in Ezekiel (4:3; 8:3, 16; 20:12, 20; 34:20; 47:16; 48:22). Parallel texts in Leviticus and Ezekiel demonstrate this shift excellently:

| | |
|---|---|
| Lev 10:10 | Lev 10:10 |
| *lehabdîl bên haqqōdeš ûbên haḥol* | *ûbên haṭṭāmē' ûbên haṭṭāhôr* |
| Ezek 22:26 | Ezek 22:26 |
| *bên qōdeš lĕḥōl lō' hibdîlû* | *ûbên haṭṭāmē' lĕṭāhôr* |

**47:18. The eastern border.** Ezekiel describes the eastern boundary in terms of regional designation (Hauran, Damascus, Gilead). He omits any reference to Chinereth (the Sea of Galilee), and changes the name of the Dead Sea from *yām hammelaḥ*, "salt," to *hayyām haqqadmônî*, "the eastern sea." Running southward the boundary skirts the southern limits of land in Damascus' orbit (Karnaim),[74] due east of the Sea of Galilee, probably following the Yarmuk tributary to the Jordan River. From here the Jordan River serves as the border until it enters the Dead Sea. The southern limit of the eastern boundary is fixed at Tamar (Fig. 16) [716].

Ezekiel's definition of the Land of Israel, like Num 34:10–12, excludes the Transjordanian regions previously occupied by the tribes of Gad, Reuben, and one-half of Manasseh. In the priestly sources it was never recognized as integral to the Promised Land (Josh 22). For Ezekiel, as for Moses, "the holy land" stops at the Jordan River, and beyond this the land is unclean (Josh 22:19; Amos 7:17) [716]. Eliezer of Beaugency, citing Hos 6:8, suggests that the tribes of Gad, Reuben, and one-half of Manasseh were transferred to Cisjordan in Ezekiel's map so that their greater proximity to the sanctuary would deter them from sin.

**47:19. The southern border.** Tamar marks the beginning of the border, which goes to the southwest byway of the valley south of Mount Halak—the southern end of Joshua's conquest (Josh 11:17; 12:7)—to Meriboth-kadesh, another name for Kadesh-barnea (48:28; Num 27:14; Deut 32:15).

---

72. *ARAB* 1:279, §777; *ANET*, 283; Aharoni, *Land of the Bible*, 376.
73. Cf. Rooker, *Biblical Hebrew in Transition*, 117.
74. Cf. Aharoni, *Land of the Bible*, 376.

**47:20. The western border.** The Mediterranean forms the western border of the Land of Israel, as in Num 34:6. The boundary line comes full circle as it moves along the coast from the mouth of the Brook of Egypt to a point opposite Lebo-hamath [717].

## The Resident Aliens (47:21–23)

### Translation

21 You will divide up this land among yourselves, according to the tribes of Israel. 22 You will distribute[75] it as an inheritance for yourselves and for the aliens[76] who reside among you, who have fathered children among you.[77] You should treat them as native born [ethnic] Israelites. They will share[78] the division [of the land] with you as an inheritance among the tribes of Israel. 23 In whatever tribe the alien resides you must give him his portion, his inheritance. The declaration of the Lord YHWH.

### Comment

**47:21.** Does verse 21 end the pericope of the land's borders (vv. 13–20), or does it open the passage on the resident alien (vv. 22–23), as claimed by most translations and commentaries?[79] The answer, I submit, rests on structural grounds. Verse 21 forms an inclusio with verses 13–14. The subscript (v. 21) and the superscript (vv. 13–14) contain the expression *šibṭê yiśrāʾēl*, "tribes of Israel," and *hāʾāreṣ hazzōʾt*, "this land," as well as the synonyms *wĕhillaqtem*, "you shall divide" (v. 21), and *ûnĕḥaltem*, "you will share" (v. 14). Moreover, the subscript verse 21 is extended into verses 22–23 since the address continues to be directed to *šibṭê yiśrāʾēl*. Verse 21, then, forms a bridge connecting verses 13–20 and verses 22–23. Thus, the concluding verses of chapter 47 (vv. 13–23) meld into a single unit (so NJB) comprising three subunits (vv. 13–20, 21, 22–23), each focusing on *šibṭê yiśrāʾēl*, the borders of the land, the division of the land, and the alien inheritors of the land, in accordance with the preexisting tribal territories.

Since the land is subdivided according to its ancient tribal boundaries, the question remains: What of the resident aliens scattered throughout the land? Herein Ezekiel asserts his startling innovation: In contrast to his anterior priestly source (H), which avows that the resident alien and his family remain the enslaved property of

---

75. *wĕhāyâ* before *tappîlû* is dropped by LXX and Vulg. That *tappîlû* is short for *tappîlû gôrāl*, "throw a lot," is recognized by LXX βαλεῖτε αὐτὴν ἐν κλήρῳ and Vulg. *Mittetis . . . in hereditatem* [707, n. 28].

76. *haggērîm*, "the aliens." Block's rendering "proselytes" must be rejected out of hand, since there is no evidence for religious conversion in the Hebrew Bible. The *gēr*, "alien," must be sharply distinguished from *nokrî*, "foreigner." Cf. Milgrom, *Leviticus 17–22*, 1493–1501.

77. Residence is proven by the birth of a child in the land, a polemic on Lev 25:25, which declares the child of an enslaved *gēr* is also a slave.

78. MT's pointing *yippĕlû*, lit. "they will be allotted," makes little sense. With *BHS*, this word should be repointed as a Hiphil, *yappîlû* (cf. Zimmerli, *Ezekiel 2*, 521) [707, n. 29].

79. NJPS, NRSV, NEB, NAB; Block, *Ezekiel 25–48*, 717; Kasher, *Ezekiel*, 918.

his Israelite owner (Lev 25:44–46), Ezekiel avers that the resident alien shall inherit and bequeath whatever land on which he resides, provided he fathers a son on his tribe's land. That the same language and theme are invoked, namely, *hôlîdû běʾarṣěkem* (Lev 25:45). *hôlîdû . . . bětôkěkem* (Ezek 47:22) implies that a polemic is being drawn: Ezekiel is reversing the ordinance of Leviticus.

**47:22–23.** Ezekiel's non-hierarchical thrust has heretofore expressed itself in the elimination of the cultic prerogatives of the king and the high priest. An attempt will also be made to equalize the landed property of each tribe (Ezek 48). Here Ezekiel's non-hierarchical goal reaches its climax when he ordains, in the name of God, that the resident alien who fathers at least one child locally must be absorbed by the tribe in whose midst he resides and be granted inheritable land on a par with his fellow Israelite tribesman. (Coincidentally, children of foreign workers born in the US today are automatically citizens.)

## EXCURSUS 10: THE *GĒR*

Aliens could not own land and were largely day laborers and artisans (Deut 24:14–15), or were among the wards of society (Exod 23:12). Indeed, since the Levites—although Israelites—were also landless, they were also dependent on the tribes in whose midst they settled, and hence they could be termed "aliens" (e.g., Judg 17:7; 19:1; Deut 18:6). Although some aliens did manage to amass wealth (Lev 25:47), most were poor, and were bracketed with the poor as recipients of welfare (cf. Lev 19:10; 23:22; 25:6). These latter verses indicate only too clearly that the alien was landless. Thus the rabbis are at a loss as to explain Ezekiel's prophecy (47:22–23) that the alien will inherit the land on a par with the Israelite.[80]

Under biblical decree, the alien enjoyed protection with the Israelite under the law, as it is written: "there shall be one law for you and the resident alien" (Num 15:15; cf. Exod 12:48–49; Lev 24:22; Num 9:14; 15:29–30). However, granting civil equality for the resident alien should by no means be construed as a general statement of parity between Israel and the alien. Whereas civil law held the citizen and the alien to be of equal status (e.g., Lev 24:22; Num 35:15), in the religious domain the alien neither enjoyed the same privileges nor was bound by the same obligations. The religious law made distinctions according to the following underlying principle: The alien is bound by the prohibitive commandments, but not by the performative ones.[81]

---

80. *Sipre* Numbers 78, on Num 10:29.

81. For example, the alien is under no requirement to observe the festivals. The paschal sacrifice is explicitly declared a voluntary observance for the alien (Exod 12:48; Num 9:14). Whereas an Israelite abstains from the paschal sacrifice on pain of *karet*, the alien may participate in it and in the rest of the voluntary sacrificial cult if he or she follows its prescriptions (Num 15:14–16; Lev 22:17–25). Details in Milgrom, *Leviticus 17–22*, 1982.

This conclusion can be derived from the following prohibition incumbent on the alien: "Any person, whether citizen or alien, who eats what has died or has been torn by beasts shall launder his clothes, bathe in water, and remain impure until the evening; then he shall be pure. But if he does not launder [his clothes] and bathe his body, he shall bear his punishment" (Lev 17:15–16). Thus the alien and the Israelite are not forbidden to eat carrion, but are required to cleanse themselves of the impurity. Aliens living on the land must keep themselves free from impurity for the same reason that Israelites must: Failure to eliminate impurity threatens God's land and sanctuary. The welfare of all of Israel, residing in God's land and under the protection of God's sanctuary, is jeopardized by the prolongation of impurity. This principle is underscored by the requirement to bring a communal purification offering to atone for the individual wrongs not only of the Israelites but of the aliens as well (Num 15:26).

No wonder, then, that the alien and the Israelite are obligated equally to refrain from violations that produce impurity. Moreover, the requirement of a purification offering is imposed for the inadvertent violation of any prohibitive commandment (Lev 4:2, 13, 22, 27), whether the polluter is Israelite or non-Israelite. Anyone in residence on YHWH's land is capable of polluting it or the sanctuary. Since a later view is that the entire planet is YHWH's (Ps 24:1), the priestly theology would imply that physical (e.g., ecological) or moral (e.g., genocidal) crimes anywhere on earth pollute it (ultimately causing YHWH to abandon it) and render it uninhabitable (see Ezek 4).

Performative commandments, however, are violated by refraining or neglecting to do them. These violations are sins not of commission but of omission. Because these are acts of omission, of *non*observance, they generate no pollution, either to the land or to the sanctuary. Thus, while their nonobservance can lead to dire consequences, these consequences are reserved for the Israelites who are obligated by their covenant to observe them. The alien, however, is not so obligated, because the alien, the resident non-Israelite, does not jeopardize the welfare of his Israelite neighbor by not complying with the performative commandments. As a result, for example, the alien need not observe the paschal sacrifice. But if he wishes to observe it, he must be circumcised (Exod 12:48) and, presumably, must be in a state of ritual purity (Num 9:6–7, 13–14). However, under no circumstances may the alien violate the prohibition to possess leaven during the festival (Exod 12:19; 13:7).

D. L. Petersen[82] avers that the *gēr*, "resident alien," differs from the *ben-nēkār*, "foreigner," in that the former may enter the sanctuary and participate in the rituals on a par with the Israelite because he too is circumcised. Circumcision, however, is required for an alien who wishes to participate in the paschal sacrifice (Exod 12:48), but he may opt to abstain. Even if he foregoes all the Israelite rituals he still retains the status of a *gēr*, as long as he and his offspring reside in the Promised Land. It is only during the Second Temple period, when the *gēr* takes on the coloration of the convert, that circumcision becomes the *sine qua non* for conversion.

---

82. Petersen, "Creation and Hierarchy in Ezekiel," 169–78.

## PART TWO: EZEKIEL 40-48—THE VISIONARY SANCTUARY AND THE LAND

In the Hebrew Bible the alien never lost the connotation of "resident alien."[83] The first glimmer of a new status for the alien is found in the words of Second Isaiah at the end of the sixth century BCE. In the Babylonian exile, non-Jews had been attracted by the Jewish way of life, particularly by the Sabbath. Isaiah calls on these would-be proselytes to "make *aliyah*" with the Israelites. Although he cannot promise them that they will be part of the peoplehood of Israel—conversion as such was unknown—he assures them that the sanctuary service will be open to them because "My house will be called a house of prayer for all peoples" (Isa 56:7).[84] However, one postexilic passage states unequivocally that the alien will become part of the Israelite people: "and the resident aliens shall join them and attach themselves to the house of Jacob" (Isa 14:1).

The assimilation of the alien may also be intimated in Ezek 47:22-23: "You shall allot it [the land] as an inheritance for yourselves and for the aliens who are resident among you, who have fathered children among you. They shall be to you as ethnic Israelites. They shall share the allotment [of the land] with you as an inheritance among the tribes of Israel. You shall give the alien an allotment within the tribe where he resides—declares YHWH your God." With this last barrier between the social status of the Israelite and the alien removed, total assimilation is probably envisioned.

### *The New Tribal Allocations (48:1-7, 23-29)*

TRANSLATION

1 These are the names of the tribes:
First,[85] from the northern periphery, bordering[86] on the Hethlon road, Lebo-hamath and Hazar-enan (which is the border of Damascus, with Hamath to the north), going[87] from east[88] to west,[89] [the tribe of][90] Dan.
2 Second, bordering on the territory of Dan, from east to west, [the tribe of] Asher.

---

83. M. Smith, *Palestinian Parties and Politics*, 178-79.

84. See also Ezra 6:21; Neh 10:29-30 (Eng. 28-29); 2 Chr 30:25; and a discussion in Japhet, *Ideology of the Book of Chronicles*, 286-99.

85. Each of the tribal allotments ends with the number, *'eḥād*, "one," an ancient way of checking off individual items in a series (as Josh 12:9-24). English convention places the number at the beginning [719, n. 80].

86. On *'el* in the sense of *'al* and in reverse, a transitional sign from EBH to LBH, see Rooker, *Biblical Hebrew in Transition*, 127-31 [719, n. 82].

87. Reading *wĕhāyâ*, "and it will be" with LXX and Vulg. instead of MT *wĕhāyû lô*, "and they shall be for him" [719, n. 83].

88. The context and following forms support emending *pĕ'at* to *mippĕ'at* [719, n. 84].

89. *ymh* has been miswritten as *hym*; cf. LXX [719, n. 85]. The medieval exegetes Rashi, Radak, and Eliezer of Beaugency interpret MT *hym* as *'ad hayyām* "until the sea" (so, too, NJPS).

90. Here and throughout the following list "the tribe of" has been inserted for clarity [719, n. 86].

**3** Third, bordering on the territory of Asher, from east to west, [the tribe of] Naphtali.

**4** Fourth, bordering on the territory of Naphtali, from east to west, [the tribe of] Manasseh.

**5** Fifth, bordering on the territory of Manasseh, from east to west, [the tribe of] Ephraim.

**6** Sixth, bordering on the territory of Ephraim, from east to west, [the tribe of] Reuben.

**7** Seventh, bordering on the territory of Reuben, from east to west, [the tribe of] Judah.

**23** As for the remaining the tribes, eighth, from east to west, [the tribe of] Benjamin.

**24** Ninth, bordering on the territory of Benjamin, from east to west, [the tribe of] Simeon.

**25** Tenth, bordering on the territory of Simeon, from east to west, [the tribe of] Issachar.

**26** Eleventh, bordering on the territory of Issachar, from east to west, [the tribe of] Zebulun.

**27** Twelfth, bordering on the territory of Zebulun, from east to west, [the tribe of] Gad.

**28** And bordering on the territory of Gad at the south end, the boundary[91] will extend from Tamar to[92] the waters of Meribath-kadesh; [from there] to the wadi [of Egypt], and the Mediterranean Sea.

**29** This is the land that you should assign as inheritance[93] for the tribes of Israel. These are their individual allotments. The proclamation of Lord YHWH.

## Comment

Chapter 48 fulfills the expectations of 47:13–14, 21 [720]. We have an inclusion here *wĕēlleh šĕmôt haššĕbāṭîm*, "These are the names of the tribes," (v. 1), and its conclusion *zōʾt hāʾāreṣ ʾăšer-tappîlû minnaḥălâ lĕšibṭê yiśrāʾēl*, "This is the land you should assign as inheritance for the tribes of Israel" (v. 29). It is probable that the middle section dealing with the *tĕrûmâ*, the nontribal "reserve" for YHWH (vv. 8–17), is a later insertion and not part of the original tribal list, and for that reason will be dealt with separately. That this list is closed with the signatory formula *nĕʾum ʾădōnāy* LORD YHWH, "The declaration of the Lord YHWH" (v. 29), affirms that these allocations have been divinely ordained and are not subject to change (see below) [721]. Above all, the land is distributed by direct divine allocation in contrast with the land's distribution in Num 34:18 and in the days of Joshua, when it was accomplished exclusively by

---

91. LXX, Tg., and Pesh. restore the article on *gĕbûl*, which may have dropped out by haplography [719, n. 88].

92. Vulg and Pesh. assume an inserted *ʿad* (cf. 47:19) [719, n. 89].

93. Emending *minnaḥălâ* to *bĕnaḥălâ*, supported by several Hebrew mss., LXX, Tg, and Vulg. (cf. 45:1; 47:22) [719, n. 92].

the *nĕśî'îm*—another example of the departure of the *nāśî'* from a position of leadership in Israel. Ezekiel's *nāśî'* bears no similarity to the pentateuchal *nāśî'*: The former is a pan-Israelite leader and is in charge of civil, national matters. The latter is tribal, involved in judging (cf. Exod 18:13–25) and distribution of spoils (1 Sam 30:21–30), and wherever the tribal *nāśî'* (chieftain) is expressly mentioned (e.g., Num 2:3; 7:11, 24, 30; 25:14). As perceived by Duguid,[94] this new, total land division could only be envisaged in landless exile, not after the land was resettled.

Descriptive summaries of the northern and southern borders frame the list (vv. 1, 28). The northern boundary line runs along the Hethlon road through Lebo-hamath and Hazer-enan between the Damascus and Hamathite territories. The southern boundary (v. 28) runs from Tamar to Meribath-kadesh, down to the Brook of Egypt to the Mediterranean Sea. The writer of this replication of 47:19 could be the same hand (including textual corrections), as follows:

## The Southern Border

| Ezekiel 47:19 | Ezekiel 48:28 |
|---|---|
| *ûpĕ'at negeb têmānâ* | *'el-pĕ'at negeb têmānâ wĕhāyâ* |
| *mittāmār 'ad-mê mĕrîbat qādēš* | *mittāmār 'ad-mê mĕrîbat qādēš* |
| *naḥălâ 'el-hayyām haggādôl* | *naḥălâ 'el-hayyām haggādôl* |

All allocations are described identically except for three. The first (Danite, v. 1) and last (Gadite, v. 28) have been altered to connect with the summaries of the northern and southern borders; the initial wording of the eighth (Benjaminite, v. 23), *wĕyeter haššĕbāṭîm*, "As for the rest of the tribes," are a continuation required after the secondary insertion of verses 8–22 [721–22].

Following Block [722–24], the (corrected) list as a whole is characterized as follows:

1. The tribal list follows the premonarchic order. The twelve-tribe system (cf. Josh 13–19) is maintained by excluding Levi and replacing it with Joseph's two sons, Ephraim and Manasseh (cf. 47:13b). This map (Fig. 19) expresses concretely the prophet's hope for the unification of all the tribes of Israel as foretold in 37:16–23. In adhering to this ancient tribal structure, Ezekiel thereby repudiates the centralized administration of the monarchy (1 Kgs 4:7–19). Verse 1 picks up the reference to the northern boundaries of the land from 47:15, 17.

2. In accordance with 47:15–20, the territories of the transjordanian tribes—Reuben, Gad, and one-half of Manasseh—are completely rejected. These tribes receive their land allotment in Cisjordan, as if they had agreed with their fellow tribes that the land of Transjordan was *ṭĕmē'â*, "impure" (Josh 22:19). Moreover, actual northern tribes—Issachar, Zebulon, and Gad—are transferred to the south, and Judah is relocated to the north of Benjamin. Dan's position in the extreme north is in accordance with historic reality (Judg 18).

---

94. Duguid, *Ezekiel and the Leaders of Israel*, 143.

## The Land (Ezekiel 47–48)

3. Ezekiel's tribal borders all run in an east-west direction and thereby run against the grain of natural topography. The physical landscape is actually defined by north-south lines (the coastal plain, the central spinal region, the Jordan rift valley). Despite the plan's artificiality, it facilitates intertribal exchanges and access for all to the sacred *těrûmâ* [722]. In addition, as noted by Greenberg, "each [tribe would] share a bit of coastal plain, a bit of highlands, and a bit of the central valley... the scheme of Ezekiel 48 adopts the only way the topography of Palestine allows to parcel the land into roughly similar shares."[95]

4. Ezekiel's divisions confirm a pattern of tribal equivalence in accordance with *'îš kěnegdô*, "each like his brother" (47:14). Transferring the focus northward (5 : 7 tribes) corrects the distortion of the monarchic structure (2 : 10; 1 Kgs 11:30–31), thereby allotting both coveted and repudiated areas more equitably. However, stratification still abounds. "An ideal map, in which all tribes have identified sociopolitical status, and all enjoy equal access to the temple, would be designed like a wheel, with spokes for boundaries and the apex of each territory abutting the sacred area. In Ezekiel's plan distances alone create inequities" [723]. Moreover, as mentioned above, the eastern bulge north of the Sea of Galilee (see Fig. 19) is as much as 100 miles wide—the constraint of following the map of Num 34.

5. The tribal distribution distinguishes between Jacob's wives (Leah and Rachel) and their handmaidens (Bilhah and Zilpah)[96] by their relative distance from the *těrûmâ* [723–24]:

| | |
|---|---|
| Dan | (Bilhah [Rachel]) |
| Asher | (Zilpah [Leah]) |
| Naphtali | (Bilhah [Rachel]) |
| Manasseh | (Rachel) |
| Ephraim | (Rachel) |
| Reuben | (Leah) |
| Judah | (Leah) |
| ... *hattěrûmâ* ... | |
| Benjamin | (Rachel) |
| Simeon | (Leah) |
| Issachar | (Leah) |
| Zebulon | (Leah) |
| Gad | (Zilpah [Leah]) |

The tribes descending from Jacob's wives reap proximity to the sanctuary; the eight Leah and Rachel tribes apportioned equally, four on each side of the *těrûmâ*. The tribes descending from the handmaidens are located on the fringes, farthest from the

---

95. Greenberg, "Idealism and Practicality," 65.
96. See Cooke, *Ezekiel*, 531–32; Fohrer, *Ezechiel*, 262.

tĕrûmâ. This explains why the northern tribes, Issachar and Zebulon (Leah tribes), were moved to the south.[97]

6. Placing Judah's territory with the northern tribes neutralizes the disruptive regional loyalties and denies it (and any other tribe) the religio-political center [724]. Likewise, placing the capital Washington, DC between Maryland and Virginia rendered it independent of its neighbors (and of any other state).[98] The removal of Benjamin to the south, according to Block, may be due to the etymology of its name *binyāmîn* = *ben yāmîn* "son of the south" [724]

7. The current plan may be construed as a polemic against the increasing royal feudalism. In fact, only YHWH is king and the land is his. He alone apportions the tribal territories [724], and he alone (as shown in Ezek 44) constructs his sanctuary, into which no human may enter (except on Sabbath with a bread offering). Non-hierarchy reigns. The king is replaced by a *nāśî'* with only honorary powers. The high priest's office in the sanctuary is totally eliminated. The tribal portions are purportedly equivalent, and the city is equally accessible to all of Israel (see vv. 15–20, below).

## The Tĕrûmâ "District" (48:8–22)

### The Sacred Allotment (48:8–14)

TRANSLATION

8 The district that you will set up for YHWH will border on the territory of Judah, running from eastern limits to western limits. It will be 25,000 cubits wide and its length the same as that of the [tribal] allotments, running from east to west. The sanctuary will be within it.[99] 9 The district that you will set up for YHWH shall be 25,000 cubits long and 20,000 cubits[100] wide. 10 The sacred district will be designated for the following [order]: the priests will receive [an area] 25,000 cubits on the north side, 10,000 cubits wide on the west side, 10,000 cubits wide on the east side, and 25,000 cubits long on the south side. YHWH's sanctuary will be within it. 11 [This area will be set apart] for the consecrated priests, the descendants[101] of Zadok, who did guard duty for me, and who, unlike the Levites, did not go astray when the descendants

---

97. The superabundant fertility of the Jordan rift and erstwhile Dead Sea would give their adjoining tribes an agricultural advantage over their land-bloated but less fertile northern tribes.

98. According to Josh 18:28, Jerusalem was originally allotted to Benjamin, but the city was captured by David, a Judahite, and made his capital (2 Sam 5:4–9).

99. The masc. suffix of *bĕtôkô* relates to *ḥeleq*, rather than to its actual antecedent, fem. *tĕrûmâ*. Cf. Kethib *btwkh* in verse 21 [726, n. 113].

100. As in 45:1, the context requires that *'eśrîm 'ālep* should be read instead of *'ăśeret 'ălāpîm* (so LXX[967]) [726, n. 114].

101. Redividing MT *lkhnym hmqdš mbny* as *lkhnym hmqdšm bny*, with support from LXX, Tg., Pesh. Cf. 44:15 and 2 Chr 26:18. Hurvitz (*Linguistic Study*, 36, n. 36) suggests that MT *mqdš* can be retained if it refers to the "allotted portion," rather than "the priest." "The Pual passive of *qdš* occurs elsewhere in Isa 13:3, a noncultic context" [726, n. 118].

of Israel went astray. **12** It will be their own special district,[102] distinguished from the land district[103] as especially holy,[104] bordering on the territory of the Levites.

**13** The Levites[105] will receive an area bordering on the territory of the priests, 25,000 cubits long and 10,000 cubits wide. The entire length[106] will be 25,000 cubits and the width 20,000 cubits.[107] **14** None of this land will be sold,[108] neither traded nor transferred,[109] because it is sacred to YHWH.

## COMMENT

In the sacred district (25,000 x 25,000), the sanctuary and the city are as far from each other as possible, as shown in the chart, below. In verse 8a, instead of the standard tribal name plus ʼeḥād, the text reads tihyeh hattĕrûmâ, "the district will be." The key word in the entire subunit is tĕrûmâ, which occurs twelve times. The meaning of tĕrûmâ shifts from a strip of land stretching across the entire breadth of Israel (corresponding to the tribal allotments) to the sacred square at the center,[110] an example of the fluidity with which Ezekiel often uses his words. Following the opening statement (v. 8), the text divides into three panels dealing successively with the sacred district (tĕrûmat haqqôdeš, vv. 9–14), the common city property (ʼăḥuzzat hāʻîr, vv. 15–20), and the allotment of the prince (vv. 21–22).

---

102. tĕrûmiyyâ is a hapax form; cf. BDB, 929a [727, n. 120].

103. mittĕrûmat hāʼāreṣ, lit., "from the reserve of the land," with the prefixed min interpreted partitively [727, n. 121].

104. qōdeš qŏdāšîm. This is not the precise legal and cultic term, "most holy," but an expression of comparison, i.e., "holier," without stating a specific degree.

105. LXX and Vulg rightly read wĕlallĕwyim instead of MT wĕhalĕwyim, in keeping with the verse 11 parallel [727, n. 122].

106. kl h'rk Tg. and LXX instead of MT kl 'rk [727, n. 123].

107. As in verse 9, 'śr[y]m has been miswritten as 'śrt [727, n. 124].

108. yimkĕrû, lit., "they will not sell"/alternatively, "will not be sold." LXX ου πραθησεται may presuppose an original passive yimmākēr or impersonal yimkĕrû. Tg., Vulg, and Pesh. support MT [727, n. 125].

109. Reading yʻbyr with Qere instead of Kethib yʻbwr [727, n. 123].

110. The band of 5,000 cubits, although it is designated as ḥōl, "common, public," is needed in order to complete the larger 25,000 cubity square (Fig. 20). How can a square, Ezekiel's geographical symbol of holiness, comprise an area that includes a ḥōl component? The answer, I suggest, is that city property (ḥōl) is part of the larger tĕrûmâ (v. 20), i.e., Israel's "gift" to YHWH and, hence, it bears the quality of holiness (cf. Haran, Ezekiel, on 45:8).

PART TWO: EZEKIEL 40–48—THE VISIONARY SANCTUARY AND THE LAND

FIGURE 20: The Sacred District (Reserve)

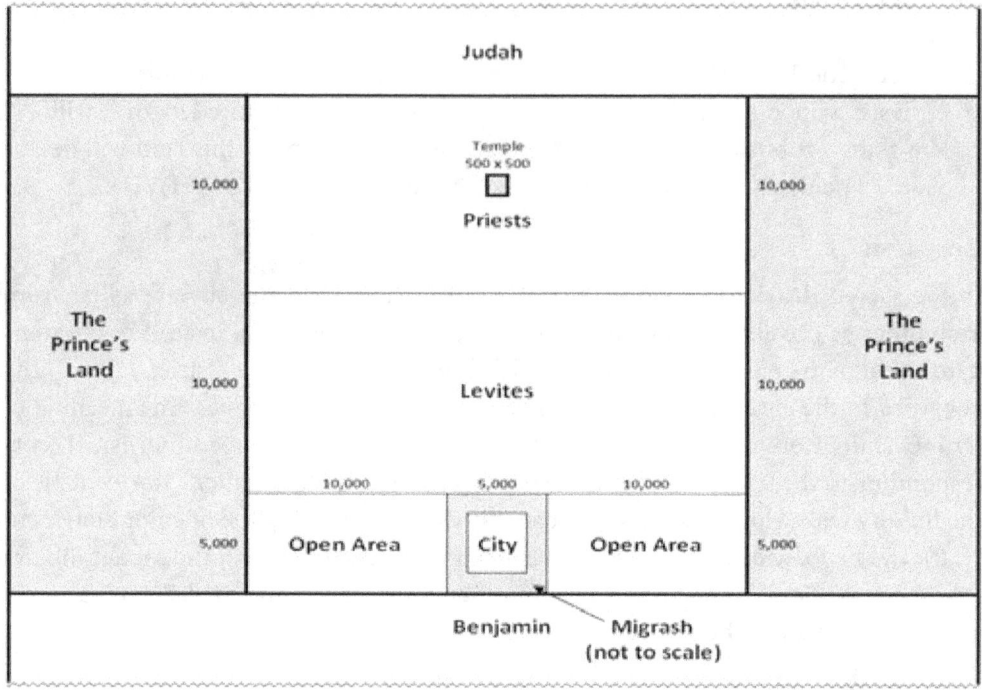

**48:8.** Parallel to the twelve-tribe territorial inheritances (*naḥălôt*) is a thirteenth strip of land, the *tĕrûmâ*, a technical sacrificial expression for a "gift" set aside [raised up] (*hērîm*) for YHWH, 25,000 wide (north to south) and the same length (*ōrek*) as the tribal areas (east to west).[111] Verse 8 calls the Israelites into action: They are to set aside [raise up] (*hērîm*) the territorial district as if it were an offering to the deity.[112] The inheritable sections (*naḥălôt*) are now called *ḥălāqîm* "portions" (cf. 45:7), aligning this text with Joshua's dividing up the territorial spoils.[113] The *tĕrûmâ* splits the *ḥălāqîm* into two unequal groups—seven in the north and five in the south [727–28]. This division enables the *tĕrûmâ* to overlap the site of Jerusalem, so that the new sanctuary can claim to be the "reconstructed" temple. Eliezer of Beaugency suggests that the purpose of stating (prematurely) that the sanctuary is "within" the *tĕrûmâ* is to stress that the temple is no longer in Jerusalem (i.e., "the city").

111. Milgrom, *Leviticus 1–16*, 473–81; Greenberg ("Design and Themes," 202) suggests that this land is called a *tĕrûmâ*, "gift," because each tribe had to surrender a little of its land so the strip might be available for national administrative purposes.

112. The use of the verb *hērîm* plus its cognate accusative *tĕrûmâ* in cultic contexts: 45:13 (grain offerings); Exod 35:27 (silver and bronze offerings for the tabernacle); Num 15:19–20 (dough offering); 18:19 (*qŏdāšîm*, "lesser holy offerings"); 18:24, 26, 28, 29 (the tithe).

113. The verb *ḥālaq*, "to divide, to share," is often used of dividing spoils (cf. Josh 22:8–9 [Qal]; Exod 15:9 [Piel]).

**48:9–12.** Verses 9–10a echo 45:1, with the phrase *tĕrûmat haqqōdeš*, "the sacred district," answering to *qōdeš min hā'āreṣ*, "the sacred area of the land." As demonstrated by Block, the dependence of verses 10b–12 on 45:3–4 for the description of the *tĕrûmâ* is manifest in the table below (Table 5).

TABLE 8: A Synopsis of Ezekiel 45:3–4 and 48:10b–12[114]

| Ezekiel 45:3-4 | Ezekiel 48:10b-12 |
|---|---|
| ûmin-hammiddâ hazzō't tāmôd | lakkōhănîm |
| 'ōrek ḥămiššâ we'eśrîm 'elep | ṣāpônâ ḥămiššâ we'eśrîm 'elep |
| wĕrōḥab 'ăśeret 'ălāpîm | wĕyāmmâ rōḥab 'ăśeret 'ălāpîm |
|  | wĕqādîmâ rōḥab 'ăśeret 'ălāpîm |
|  | wĕnegbâ 'ōrek ḥămiššâ we'eśrîm 'ālep |
| ûbô-yihyeh hammiqdāš | wĕhāyâ miqdāš-yhwh bĕtôkô |
| qōdeš qodāšîm |  |
| qōdeš min-hā'āreṣ |  |
| hû' lakkōhănîm | lakkōhănîm hamĕquddāš mibbĕnê ṣādôq |
| mĕšārĕtê hammiqdāš yihyeh | 'ăšer šāmĕrû mišmartî |
| haqqĕrēbîm lĕšārēt 'et-yhwh |  |
|  | 'ăšer lō'-tā'û |
|  | bit'ôt bĕnê yiśrā'ēl |
|  | ka'ăšer tā'û halĕwîyim |
| wĕhāyâ lāhem māqôm lĕbottîm | wĕhāyĕtā lāhem tĕrûmîyâ mittĕrûmat |
|  | hā'āreṣ |
| ûmiqdāš lammiqdāš | qōdeš qodāšîm |
|  | 'el-gĕbûl halĕwîyim |
| And from this measured-off area | For the priests |
| you shall measure off [an area] | there shall be [an area] |
| 25,000 cubits long | 25,000 cubits on the northern side, |
| and 10,000 cubits wide, | 10,000 cubits wide on the western side, |
|  | 10,000 cubits wide on the eastern side, |
|  | and 25,000 cubits long on the southern side. |
| and in it the sanctuary shall be, | The sanctuary of Yahweh shall be within it. |
| the most holy place. |  |
| It is sacred, set off from the land. |  |
| It shall be for the priests | [It shall be] for the consecrated priests, |
| who serve the sanctuary, | consecrated from the descendants of Zadok, |
| who approach to serve Yahweh. | who perform guard duty for me, |
|  | and who did not go astray, |
|  | when the Israelites went astray, |
|  | like the Levites went astray. |
| It shall be a place for their houses, | It shall be their own reserve, |
|  | distinguished from the land reserve, |
| and the holy area for the sanctuary. | the most holy place, |
|  | adjacent to the territory of the Levites. |

"The common elements are obvious: (1) identical dimensions, 25,000 by 10,000 cubits; (2) the sanctuary (*miqdāš*) within the priestly territory; (3) assignment to the priests who serve YHWH; (4) emphasis on the sanctity of the place [728]: *miqdāš* occurs four times in 45:3–4 and once in 48:10b–12; both characterize the priestly allotment as *qōdeš qŏdāšîm*, "the most holy [place]" [728, n. 131].

---

114. Adapted from Block, *Ezekiel 25–48*, 729.

But the differences are more striking: (1) The absence of the command to measure the area in 48:10b–12; (2) The four sides are measured in 48:10b–12; (3) The sanctuary is identified as YHWH's sanctuary (*miqdāš YHWH*) in 48:10b–12; (4) The priests' role is expanded in verses 10b–12. Whereas previously they were identified as the ones "who serve the sanctuary" (*měšārĕtê hammiqdāš*) and "who qualify to serve YHWH" (*haqqěrēbîm lěšārēt YHWH*), now they are: (a) "consecrated ones" (*hammĕquddāšîm*); (b) the sons of Zadok (cf. 40:46; 45:12); (c) the ones who perform guard duty for YHWH (*ăšer šāmĕrû mišmartî*; cf. 44:8, 15, 16); (d) "the ones who did not go astray" (*lō'-tā'û*; cf. 44:10, 15). The difference is only in language, not in meaning. (5) The priestly *tĕrûmâ* is distinct from the larger *tĕrûmâ* stretching across the breadth of the land (*tĕrûmat hā'āreṣ*, 48:12). (6) Failure to mention the residential function of the priests' allotment; (7) Explicit location of the priestly and Levitical reserves next to each other. Again, the differences are in language only, but there is no probable change in ideas [728]. That the priests' land is granted to the Zadokites (v. 11) shows that there are no other priests in Ezekiel's sanctuary and that both groups of priests mentioned in 40:45–46 are Zadokites.

**48:13a.** The reduced interest in the Levites' district calls attention to their demotion. There is no comment on their activities, nor do we learn how they will use this land [730].

**48:13b–14.** Verse 14 stresses the untransferable character of both the priestly and Levitical portions; absolutely no real estate transaction is permitted (i.e., gifting, Eliezer of Beaugency) deeding the property into anyone else's hands (cf. 45:8, also Lev 27:10, 33). As absolute owner of the land, YHWH has exclusive control of his property, though this text has nothing to say about the 500-cubits-square holy place referred to in 45:2.

The Public Allotment (48:15–20)

TRANSLATION

> **15** The remaining area—5,000 cubits-wide by 25,000 cubits—will be a common civic area.[115] The city will be central[116] containing a settled area and pasture. **16** Its size [the city's] on the north, 4,500 cubits; the south, 4,500 cubits;[117] the east side,[118] 4,500 cubits; the west 4,5000 cubits. **17** The pasture-land[119] will stretch 250 cubits to the north, 250 cubits to the south, 250 cubits to the east, and 250 cubits to the west. **18** The remainder that runs parallel to

---

115. *ḥōl hû'*, lit., "it shall be common, unconsecrated." In 2 Sam 20:15; 1 Kgs 21:23 and Lam 2:8, LXX προτείχισμα has misread *ḥōl* as *ḥēl* (*ḥyl*), "rampart" [730, n. 134].

116. Radak's ms, like the MT, has both Kethib and Qere, in which case the references of *bětôkâ* is the *tĕrûmîyâ* (v. 12) and of *bětôkô* (Qere) is the *nôtār*.

117. The dittography represented by the second *ḥmš* was recognized by the masoretes, who deliberately omitted any vowel points [730, n. 135].

118. MT *ûmippĕ'at* should be *ûpĕ'at* [730, n. 136].

119. For this rendering, see Milgrom, *Leviticus 23–27*, 2203–4; *Numbers*, 289.

the sacred district will measure 10,000 cubits on the east and 10,000 cubits on the west side.[120] Its harvest[121] will feed the city workers.[122] **19** Laborers[123] coming from all the tribes of Israel will work the land.[124] **20** The entire district will be a 25,000 cubit square.[125] You will set apart the sacred district together with[126] the city property.

## COMMENT

In 45:6 Ezekiel had introduced "the city possession/property" (*ăḥuzzat hā'îr*) as a 5,000-cubit wide strip of land contiguous with the sacred district (*tĕrûmat haqqōdeš*) belonging to all Israel (*lĕkol-bêt yiśrā'ēl*). Now he once again develops this theme, another example of Ezekiel's penchant for resumptive exposition [731].

**48:15–17.** Once the priestly and Levitical portions have been separated out, the 5,000-cubit wide rectangle remains of the 25,000-cubit square in the center of the greater *tĕrûmâ* (see Fig. 20) where the city is located (*bĕtôkāh*). The length of each side (*pē'â*) is mentioned separately, although the city is a square, contrary to the simpler description of the holy place (*haqqōdeš*), i.e., the sanctuary, in 45:2 as a 500 x 500 cubit square (*mĕrubba'at*). The city's four boundaries—north, south, east, and west—are all 4,500 cubits. The area totals a 5,000-cubit square including the *migrāš*, "pasture land," a 500-cubit square surrounding the city (see Fig. 20). The designation *ḥōl* for the city is neutral; not to be confused with its negative implications as in 22:26 [731].

Block claims that the city was laid out so as to provide accommodations *lĕmôšāb*, "for dwelling," for pilgrims from outlying tribal territories who came to worship at the sanctuary [732]. Hardly. The pilgrims from the north (the majority) would have to bypass the sanctuary and travel ("on foot," *'ălîyat regel*) another 15,000–20,000 cubits (about 5 miles) to reach the city and then reverse themselves another 5 miles to worship at the altar. Considering its centrality, the city had to have a more fundamental purpose.

As noted, the *naśî'* had an honorary status only in the sanctuary, chiefly to observe the immolation of his own sacrifices from a unique vantage point at the edge of the inner eastern gateway (46:1–2). But outside the sanctuary the *naśî'* was probably the king, ruling his kingdom in all of its other various components. This required a complex bureaucracy. Indeed, in the excavations at the site of Babylon, excluding all

---

120. MT adds *wĕhāyâ lĕ'ummat tĕrûmat haqqōdeš*, "and it will be alongside the sacred reserve." This is a case of vertical dittography from the identical phrase in the previous line. It must have occurred early since it is supported by the versions [730, n. 137]. Cf. Fig. 20.

121. *tĕbû'ātô* here referring to *hannôtār* "the remainder" (masc.) shall provide food for the city workers.

122. I.e., the civil servants, see the COMMENT.

123. MT *hā'ōbēd* is taken as a collective. LXX renders it as a pl. [731, n. 138].

124. The masculine suffix on *ya'abĕdûhû* also refers to *nôtār*. On attaching the suffix directly to the verb in later Hebrew, see Rooker, *Biblical Hebrew in Transition*, 86–87 [731, n. 139].

125. *rĕbî'ît* usually denotes "fourth." An emendation to *rĕbû'â* or *mĕrubba'at* is suggested by Block [731, n. 140]. MT's *'athnak* should stop here.

126. *'el* = *'im*, Radak.

the religious (the sanctuary) and royal (the palace) buildings, there still remain many large structures, which could only be administrative in purpose.[127] These many buildings are matched by the abundance of many titled office holders from ministers to governors down to the lowliest overseers.[128] Ezekiel was assuredly aware of all this, but since his objective was centered upon his visionary sanctuary and its functions he had no reason to mention the administrative details of the resurrected kingdom. Instead, Ezekiel collapsed these officials and their functions into a single edifice called "the city." Indeed, the fact that the *naśi'* was in charge of weights and measures (45:9–12) implies that he was the overall authority in economic matters. But where else would the financial and legal matters of the nation be contained? It had to be the city, the administrative capital of the nation.

Ezekiel took pains to emphasize that the city belonged neither to the *naśi'*—his holdings were vast, but far from the city—nor to the priesthood—the sanctuary was also deliberately distant from the city (Fig. 20). The city belonged to the *people*. Presumably, the city was the commercial and trade center of the nation to which all the tribes had recourse for their major economic needs. Also, one might reasonably assume that since the people comprised twelve tribes, each having its own gate, it was, therefore, likely that each tribe was responsible to supply the city workers for one month each year.

Block suggests that the two open area strips (each 10,000 by 5,000 cubits) east and west of the city provided compensatory land for workers, who were forced to abandon their own land to serve the city [732]. More likely, this land served the purpose of providing food for the city workers. Rashi, however, renders *'abdê hā'îr* as "city slaves," a reference to the Gibeonite descendants (Josh 9:27; Ezra 2:43; Neh 7:60), presumably dispersed among all the tribes. Radak, rejects this interpretation.

**48:20.** As illustrated in Fig. 14, the three rising levels of sanctity—summarizing verses 8–19—in reverse order include: priests (most holy), Levites (holy), and city (common); cf. Block [732–33].

## The Allotment of the Prince (48:21–22)

### Translation

> 21 What remains on both sides of the sacred district and the City holding belong to the prince. The territory extending eastward from the 25,000 cubits of the sacred district,[129] and westward from the 25,000 cubits, parallel to the tribal portions,[130] will be his. The center[131] is the place for the sacred district

---

127. Cf. Margueron, "Babylon," 1:564.

128. For details, see von Soden, *Ancient Orient*, 70–71; Alberts, *Israel in Exile*, 98–111; Middlemas, *Templeless Age*.

129. Thus MT, in agreement with Tg., but *těrûmâ* is missing in LXX and Pesh. On the basis of the next line, many emend to *qādîmâ* (cf. Zimmerli, *Ezekiel 2*, 525) [734, n. 147].

130. *ḥălāqîm* should be *haḥălāqîm*, Eliezer of Beaugency.

131. The suffix on Kethib *btkh* refers to the *těrûmâ*, not to the *nôtār*, as suggested by the Qere.

and the sanctuary, **22** [separated] from the holding of the Levites and the holding[132] of the city located in the midst of the prince's area. The prince[133] will also own [the area lying] between the territory of Judah and the territory of Benjamin.

COMMENT

Verses 45:7-8 provide the basis for the description of the prince's property and affirms its location on either side of the central square (see Fig. 18). According to the translation, verse 22 states that the prince's lands are separate (*min*) from the property of the Levites and the city [734], and also separate in equal measure from the territory of the priests (Fig. 20). Why was this fact omitted?

I believe that Rashi has the answer. He interprets *wĕhāyĕtâ tĕrûmat haqqōdeš* (v. 21bα) as a limited reference to the priestly territory. Supporting his suggestion is that this same phrase was mentioned earlier in the verse (v. 21a) where it had its customary identification of both the priestly and Levite territories. Therefore, it would hardly make sense for the fact to be repeated in the same verse. Also this phrase is followed by *ûmiqdaš habbayit bĕtôkōh*, a reference to the locus of the sanctuary, which has earlier been identified in the priestly territory (45:4). In sum, the territory of the prince borders the priestly land (v. 21b) and continues on either side of the Levites and city property.

Tg. renders the *mem* as "part of the property [of the Levites and the city] shall be in the middle of that which belongs to the prince," i.e., the *mem partitif*. Note also that the Levite property is designated as *ăḥuzzâ*, just like the city, and it is therefore different from the priestly property, which is rendered *tĕrûmîyyâ* and *qōdeš qŏdāšîm*, "special/most holy" (v. 12).

## The New City (48:30-35)

TRANSLATION

**30** And these are the exits[134] from the city:
For the tribes of Israel, on the north side,[135] [measuring][136] 4,500 cubits:
**31** The gates of the city are to be named after the tribes of Israel; three gates to the north;

---

Eliezer of Beaugency understands *bĕtôkōh* (Qere), lit., "in its midst," as *within* (i.e., between) the prince's territory.

132. Though attested in the versions, the preposition *min* prefixed to *ăḥuzzat* in both instances (the Levites and the city) is often deleted as a scribal error, but see Allen, *Ezekiel 20-48*, 276 [734, n. 150].

133. Many follow Pesh. in dropping *lannāśî' yihyeh* as a dittograph (Allen, *Ezekiel 20-48*, 276), but the versional omission may be the result of haplography [734, n. 151].

134. *tôṣĕōt*; cf. *môṣā'îm* (42:11; 43:11; 44:5); see the COMMENT. Alternately, render "outer limit" (with Block, 736), cf. Num 34:4; 1 Chr 5:26.

135. The preposition min on *mippĕ'at* is used locatively [734, n. 2].

136. *middâ*, lit., "measurement," occurs in connection with the north and south sides only [734, n. 3]; see the COMMENT.

Gate 1:[137] Reuben; Gate 2: Judah; Gate 3: Levi.[138]

32 On[139] the 4,500 cubits facing east there will be three gates: Gate 1: Joseph; Gate 2: Benjamin; Gate 3: Dan.

33 On the south side, [measuring] 4,500 cubits, there will be three gates: Gate 1: Simeon; Gate 2: Issachar; Gate 3: Zebulun.

34 On the 4,500 cubit west there shall be three gates: Gate 1: Gad; Gate 2: Asher; Gate 3: Naphtali

35 The distance around the city will be 18,000 cubits. And from that day[140] on the city will be called, "YHWH Is There."[141]

## Comment

The rendering "periphery, limits" for *tôṣā'ôt* (v. 31) is well attested (Num 34:4, etc.; 1 Chr 5:16) [736]. However, the context here is that of the city gates. Thus the focus of the term is the exit (verb *yāṣā'*, "to exit") from the city. Also, if the city limits were intended, the expected term would have been *ḥômâ* "the [city] wall" (26:4, 9, 10, 12; 38:20). As Block surmises, Ezekiel's twelve gates may have been influenced by the city of Babylon and its temple tower of Marduk, Etemenanki, whose sacred precinct was also laid out as a square and accessible through twelve gates, with which he may have been familiar [736].[142] Ezekiel's naming of the gates after the tribes of Israel compares with the naming of the nine imposing gates of Babylon: on the north side, Lugalgira (= Nergal) Gate, Ishtar Gate, Sin Gate; the east side: Marduk Gate, Zababa (= Ninurta) Gate; the south side: Enlil Gate, Urash Gate, Shamash Gate; the west side: Adad Gate[143] [738, n. 24]. Of course, Ezekiel would have had an imperishable memory of Jerusalem and its (at least) seven gates: Potsherd Gate (Jer 19:2, known as the Dung Gate, Neh 2:13; 3:13–14; 12:31); Corner Gate (Jer 31:37); Horse Gate (Jer 31:39); Benjamin Gate (Jer 20:2; 37:13; 38:7); People's Gate (Jer 17:19); Middle Gate (Jer 39:3, perhaps the same as Ephraim Gate 2 Kgs 14:13 = 2 Chr 25:23); Gate between the Walls (Jer 52:7) [736, n. 19].[144]

137. The numeral "one" after the name of the tribe is an ancient way of checking off individual items in a series. Cf. 48:1–7, 23–29; Josh 12:9–24. See also the Note on 48:1.

138. The function of the Levites in the city is explored in the Comment. Note that these three northern gates point to their respective northern tribal territories.

139. On *'el* in the sense of *'al*, see 40:16, etc.

140. On the use of *yôm*, "day," in the sense of "time," see Althann, "'Yom,' 'Time' and Some Texts in Isaiah," 3–8 [735, n. 10].

141. LXX either misread YWHW *šāmmâ* as YHWH *šĕmâ*, "YHWH is his name," or it is based on a different Vorlage. For example, Pesh., *mry' šmmh*, "the Lord is his name," and Tg.'s expansive *wšmh dqrt' ytprš mywm' dyšry škyntyh ywy tymn*, "And the name of the city, designated from the day that the Lord makes his Shekinah rest upon it, shall be: YHWH Is There." Cf. Levey, *Aramaic Bible*, 129, n. 6. Y. Qoler suggests the final *he* on *šāmmâ* functions as an abbreviation for the tetragrammaton. "Biblical Symbols, Abbreviations, and Acronyms," 317–24 [735, n. 11].

142. For the temple plan, see Wiseman, *Nebuchadrezzar and Babylon*, 69; Unger, *Babylon*, plate 24, Fig. 36.

143. For maps see Wiseman, *Nebuchadrezzar and Babylon*, 47–47; Unger, *Babylon*, plate 57.

144. See Pritchard, *ANEP*[2], 120–21.

## The Land (Ezekiel 47–48)

However, Jerusalem's gates were dwarfed by the size and magnificence of the Babylonian gates. Mere sight of the Ishtar gate in the present-day Pergamum Museum in Berlin suffices to underscore the difference. But the names of the gates in these two cities epitomize the difference, qualitatively and theologically. Babylon is the city of the gods (Akkadian *Bab-Ilu*, lit., "the gate of god"); Ezekiel's is the city of the tribes, i.e., of the people.

To be sure, naming the gates after the tribes to whose territories the gates lead is not an Ezekielian innovation (cf. Benjamin gate, Jer 20:2; Ephraim gate, 2 Kgs 14:13), but here their significance is not geographic but theological. First, the city is part of the *těrûmâ*, "the gift" (45:6), which Israel has contributed to God, and thus is bound to follow the laws of God. This is what is meant by the name of the city, *YHWH šāmmâ*, "YHWH Is There" (48:34, see COMMENT). Second, the city that the gates circumscribe does not belong to any single tribe (in contrast to Jerusalem, which virtually was a Judahite possession). Third, it is not the royal capital, since the nonexistent king, called *nāśî'*, was removed to the outskirts of the sacred area, the *těrûmâ*. Fourth, it is not the site of the sanctuary, the erstwhile domain of the high priest and his echelon, since the sanctuary, even though it was located in the heart of the *těrûmâ*, "the sacred district," was removed far from the city, and even there the high priest had neither place nor power. As suggested above, each tribe was responsible for one month's maintenance of the city; an equal distribution of labor.

It is no accident that two areas are circumscribed by a *migrāš*: the sanctuary (45:2) and the city. The former is a square (500 x 500 cubits); the latter is also a square (4,500 x 4,500 cubits), but whereas the former is *qōděš*, "sacred," the latter is *ḥōl*, "common" (thus public). The sanctuary is where the deity is worshiped; the city is where the transtribal (national) affairs are administered, including intertribal finances and trade.

The modification in sequence, from north-south-east-west (v. 16) to clockwise north-east-south-west follows the survey of the boundaries of the land (47:15–20; see Fig. 19). Perhaps, this represents an attempt to "portray the city as a microcosm of the land" [736].[145] Kasher suggests that the twelve tribal gates are structured like the twelve breast stones on the high priest's shield (Exod 28:17–21).[146] This configuration is conjectural. It is more likely that the image is the four groups of three tribes that circumscribed the tabernacle when the camp was at rest in the wilderness (Num 2). Perhaps this tribal arrangement of Ezekiel's city influenced Qumran's Temple Scroll [738]. The west side is least significant, being allocated to three of the concubines' children. The south side is represented by three of Leah's sons. The east side is shared by Rachel's two children, while Dan, a concubine's son, is promoted to join them. The north side is reserved for the three other Leah's sons: Reuben, Judah, and Levi (see Fig. 21). It is clear that the tribal list is based on genealogical grounds: Joseph has replaced Ephraim and Manasseh, and Levi has slipped in to fill the gap [737].

---

145. Allen, *Ezekiel 20–48*, 284.
146. Kasher, *Ezekiel*, 933.

## PART TWO: EZEKIEL 40–48—THE VISIONARY SANCTUARY AND THE LAND

FIGURE 21: The Gates of "The City"

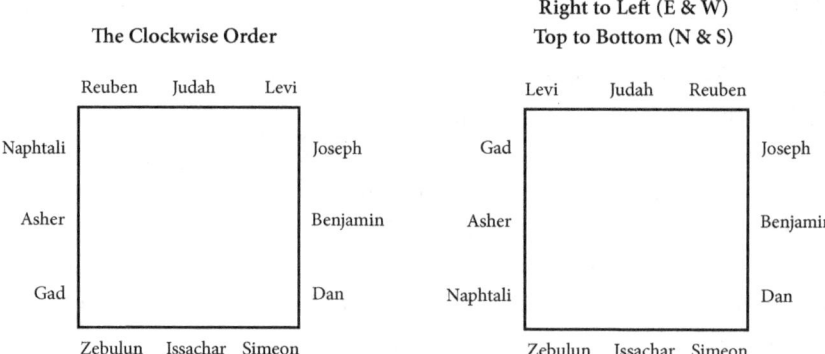

Revision of the location of the four groups of gates.
Two options: (from Block, 737; emended).

But what did Ezekiel have in mind by assigning the Levites a distinctive gate? Because it has been presumed (above) that the city was the economic (i.e., intertribal) center of the tribes, it had to include the tribe of Levi. After all, the Levites' forty-eight cities, hitherto dispersed among all the tribes, have centripetally coalesced into the single area allotted to the tribe Levi [740]. Already in Lev 25:32–34, the Levites were acknowledged as an urban population. It is, therefore, not unreasonable to presume that the Levites were prompted to expand their intratribal commerce, i.e., within the Levite tribal area into intertribal commerce, i.e., nationally, which could be accomplished in only one place—the capital city.

It is significant that the Levite territory is coupled with the city; both are called *ăḥuzzâ*. That is, the Levites are settled, like the priests, in the *tĕrûmâ*, but whereas the priests' holdings are called *tĕrûmiyyâ*, "special district" (48:12), the Levites holdings have the same status as the city, being termed *ăḥuzzâ* (45:5; 48:22). Also, no gates are named after Aaron, i.e., the "priests." It is insufficient to argue that the priests are subsumed under the patronym Levi, for in Ezekiel's system the priests and Levites do not mix. However, priests (differently from Levites) are subject to the pentateuchal restriction, *bĕ'arṣām lō' tinḥāl wĕḥēleq lō'-yihyeh lĕkā bĕtôkām 'ănî ḥelqĕkā wĕnaḥălātĕkā*, "you shall have no inheritance in their [the Israelites'] land, nor shall you have any [landed] portion among them; I am your inheritance and your portion" (Num 18:20; cf. Deut 18:2). In practical terms, the priests are fully supported by the sacrifices brought to the sanctuary and are given adequate living quarters and pasture land for their flocks in the area surrounding the sanctuary (see Fig. 20). Thus, the priests continue their pentateuchal independence in Ezekiel's cartography and have nothing to do with the city.

As the sanctuary is the (approximate) center of the sacred area, so the city is the center of the civic area. As the sanctuary is circumscribed by a *migrāš*, so is the city. As the sanctuary is the residence of YHWH (43:7), so is the city (48:35). Thus, the common (*ḥōl*) city is located and structured to counterbalance the sacred (*qōdeš*) reserve [739].

*The Land (Ezekiel 47–48)*

The arrangement of the city's twelve gates has counterparts in the numbers and names of gates in other theoretical structures, namely the wilderness (the book of Numbers) and Qumran's Temple Scroll, but there is no similarity in the arrangement of the gates, as illustrated below:

TABLE 9: The Tribal Encampment and Gates

|  | Wilderness (Numbers 2) | Ezekiel (Ezekiel 48) | Temple Scroll (30:9) |
|---|---|---|---|
| North | Asher, Dan, Naphtali | Reuben, Judah, Levi | Dan, Naphtali, Asher |
| East | Issachar, Judah, Zebulun | Joseph, Benjamin, Dan | Simeon, Levi, Judah |
| South | Simeon, Reuben, Gad | Simeon, Issachar, Zebulun | Reuben, Joseph, Benjamin |
| West | Manasseh, Ephraim, Benjamin | Gad, Asher, Naphtali | Issachar, Zebulun, Gad |

Why did Ezekiel not follow his pentateuchal model? And why did the Temple Scroll not follow its Ezekielian forerunner? The answer can only be that each document had its own agenda, which was expressed in the placement of its tribal names *sui generis*. Thus, the wilderness tribes were an army under "General" Moses, split into four battalions, headed respectively by Dan, Judah, Reuben, and Ephraim; Levi was assigned to sacral duties [Num 3–4] and removed from the tribal war camp, while Joseph was replaced by his sons. Reuben, Judah, and Levi are north of Ezekiel's city, as are their gates. Similarly, Simeon, Issachar, and Zebulun are south of the city, as are their gates. The logistic need to enable each tribe to have direct access to the city suffices to explain the orientation of the names of the tribal gates. Thus, it is not that the northern side was "most important" [Block, 738], but that it had an unobstructed and direct connection to the city via its own gate.

**48:35.** **"from that day on"** (*miyyôm*), i.e., from the time of the return of the *šĕkînâ* to the city (43:1–6; Radak). *miyyôm YHWH šāmmâ*, "from the day [the city was founded] YHWH Is There" in the temple, not in the city (Eliezer of Beaugency). However, the subject is the city, *not* the temple. Though the city may be planted on the site of Jerusalem, it does not bear its name. Jerusalem has only negative associations to Ezekiel [739]. As explained by his successor prophet, Isaiah of the exile, instead *wĕqārā' lāk šēm ḥādāš 'ăšer pî YHWH yiqqābennû*, "and you shall be called by a new name that the mouth of YHWH will bestow" (Isa 62:2).

The city is most likely Jerusalem, although Ezekiel masks this identity. The key to this identification is that the city lies in the midst of the tribal territories, seven tribes to the north and five tribes to the south. Why was the city not placed in between six and six tribes? The most likely answer is that the city was located on the site of Jerusalem, which geographically falls between seven and five tribes, as specified by the text. If it were placed between six and six tribes it would be too far north to be identified with Jerusalem.

## PART TWO: EZEKIEL 40-48—THE VISIONARY SANCTUARY AND THE LAND

The city is totally independent of the tribes. That is why David chose this erstwhile Jebusite city, Jerusalem, as his capital. It was *'îr dāwid*, "the city of David," and of his descendants. Ezekiel changes all that. The city belongs to *all* the tribes. They come to live and work in it (probably one month per year). For this reason the city, though it is *ḥōl*, "common," is part of the *tĕrûmâ*, "the district" (but not *tĕrûmat haqqōdeš*: "the sacred district," 45:6-7). It is the "gift" (*tĕrûmâ*) of the land by the tribes, that is, each tribe has donated a small part of its territory, to comprise the 25,000 x 25,000 cubit square known as the *tĕrûmâ*, "the district." This is the smaller district. The larger district includes the property of the *nāśî'*, which extends from the Jordan River to the Mediterranean (see Fig. 21 and Eliezer of Beaugency on v. 22).

However, the 25,000 x 5,000 southern strip of the *tĕrûmâ*, assigned to the national city is expressly designated as *ḥōl*, "common" (48:15). Herein, ostensibly, lies a theological conundrum. As we have seen throughout the description of Ezekiel's sanctuary and its laws (Ezek 40-46), an incessant demand was made to separate the *qōdeš*, "sacred," from the *ḥōl*, "common." How then can the prophet aver that in the explicitly secular city, *YHWH šāmmâ*, "YHWH [the quintessence and source of holiness] Is There"? Moreover, YHWH has literally locked himself inside his temple and promised never again to leave it (43:7-9), but here we find him in the city, far removed from the sanctuary? The answer is that God is unbounded (hardly anthropomorphic) in space. As expressed by the term *miškānî 'ălêhem*, "my presence over them" (37:27), probably based on *miškānî ... wĕhithallaḥtî bĕtôkĕkem*, "my presence ... [and I] shall walk about in your midst" (Lev 26:12), which indicates that YHWH can be and can operate in two areas simultaneously. It should also be noted that the divine presence must (somehow) be in the city to complete the perfect square (25,000 x 25,000), the unequivocal sign that this area is sacred.

### *Summary*

Thus, we see that in Ezekiel's thought, not only has Israel changed (from sinners to saints, to prophets), but God has also changed (from an anthropomorphic *kābôd* enthroned between the cherubim, to a ubiquitous presence, *miškān* [modern *šĕkînâ*]). An indication that Ezekiel changed his mind about God's anthropormorphism is discernable by focusing on his Presence in the sanctuary. There is no indication that the *kābôd* condescended into the adytum as is reported in the earlier tabernacle (Exod 25:22) and Solomon's temple (1 Kgs 8:6-9). Rather, the *kābôd* filled the entire sanctuary (Ezek 43:5; 44:4).[147] Furthermore, Ezekiel's sanctuary, without a candelabrum or incense altar, is no longer illuminated or activated, implying that YHWH is not to be treated anthropomorphically, as subject to human needs. The sanctuary building is not the focus of prayer. Rather, prayer rises with the smoke of the sacrifice and reaches the *kābôd-miškān*, wherever it may be.

---

147. Though temporarily the *kābôd* in the tabernacle (Exod 40:35) and in Solomon's temple (1 Kgs 8:11b) filled the tabernacle.

## The Land (Ezekiel 47–48)

One final objection to Ezekiel's utopian vision of Israel's transcendant "sainthood" and prophetic status remains. It is generally conceded by critics that outside of feeling shame, Israel need not express repentance for its sinful past. However, is it possible that Ezekiel maintains that humans are denied free will and are reduced to automatons, manipulated only by the divine will? As pointed out by Tova Ganzel (in an unpublished paper), the ubiquitous scholarly view that Ezekiel imposed no penitential demands upon Israel[148] is palpably wrong. Ezekiel 11:18 states explicitly that prior to YHWH's grant of a new heart and spirit, *ûbā'û-šammâ wĕhēsîrû 'et-kol-šiqqûṣêhā wĕ'et-kol-tôăbōtêhā mimmennâ*, "And when they return there [to the land of Israel], they will do away with all its detestable things and all its abominations." Thus, the elimination of idolatry in all its forms—the essence of repentance—is the prerequisite for the divine gift of moral perfection. Moreover, Ezekiel promises again the boon of a new heart and spirit (18:31; cf. 36:26), prefacing it with the direct second person address: *šûbû wĕhāšîbû mikkal pišĕ'êkem*, "Repent and turn from all your transgressions" (18:30b), using the specific term for prophetic repentance, *šûb/hāšîb*, as a requirement for the gift of new heart and spirit. Thus the ability to reject (or affirm) idolatry is indicative of choice! As opined by Fox, "When one has God's spirit in him he does God's will because he *wants* to do God's will."[149] Nonetheless, we are dealing with semantics: Wanting to do God's will is his *only* choice! God will see to it that mankind obeys.

Block avers that, "Ezekiel's cartographic vision is extremely narrow . . . The universalistic tendencies of the so-called Zion-tradition (cf. Isa 2:1–4; Mic 4:1–4) are deliberately reined in" [741]. Ezekiel is here misconstrued. This prophet of the exile was also the prophet of the destruction. In the exile he tries to reassemble the worthy survivors of his people and provide them with his vision of a new sanctuary and new society. Their erstwhile leaders are rendered powerless (e.g., the king, contrast 2 Kgs 11:15; the high priest, contrast 2 Kgs 11:2–18). The king, moreover, is demoted to the level of *nāśî'*. The Levites may no longer officiate at the altar (44:13). The lay leaders—the *zĕqēnîm*, "the elders," and the *śārîm*, "officers"—are condemned for their sin of idolatry (Ezek 8, 14, 20) and are accordingly punished, slain, or excluded from the land (11:13; 20:38). Even the prophets in the main were unfaithful to their charge and led the people astray (13:9; 14:9); they too will be slain or excluded from the land. Without spiritual leaders, Ezekiel is constrained to rebuild the nation *alone*. How then is he able even to see, much less to think beyond the borders and people of Israel?

Shorn of human leaders, Israel has been transformed into an exclusively theocentric people: YHWH alone is their leader. Having metamorphosed first into saints (incapable of sinning) and then into prophets (39:29; see COMMENT), there is no longer any need for intermediaries. Each Israelite is capable of accessing YHWH and receiving YHWH's response directly. As another prophet of the exile predicted, *wĕkol-bānayik limmûdê YHWH wĕrab šĕlôm bānāyik*, "All your children will be taught by YHWH and great will be the well-being of your children" (Isa 54:13). Implied in

---

148. See most recently Schwartz, "Bearing of Sin in Priestly Literature," 43–68.
149. Fox, "The Rhetoric of Ezekiel's Vision," 15.

Ezekiel's scheme, however, is that moral excellence (sinlessness) is a necessary and sufficient step to achieving prophecy.[150]

There is no doubt that Ezekiel is deeply pessimistic about the future of the human race. From the start God reluctantly endowed humanity with free will (Gen 3:22). The first experiment failed when the descendants of Adam and Eve chose violence (cf. Gen 4:23-24; 6:1-7). God tried again with righteous Noah, this time through legal means (Gen 9:1-6), and once again his progeny blundered (Gen 11:1-9). Finally God experimented with another just man, Abraham, "that he may instruct his children and their posterity to keep the ways of YHWH by doing what is just and right" (Gen 18:19). Taxing God's forbearance they invariably proved unregenerate (Ezek 20). But Israel will not change; "the inclination of the human heart is evil from youth" (Gen 8:21). Henceforth, Israel (and presumably all humanity) must become as incapable of sinning as God's angels.

As expressed by Greenberg, God will no longer gamble with Israel as in the old times, when Israel rebelled against him.[151] In the future no more experiments! God will put his Spirit into them; he will alter their hearts (their minds) and make it impossible for them to be anything but obedient to his rule and his commandments. Programmed to follow God's laws exclusively (36:26-27), human beings will no longer be able to choose evil. Nor will they become mute automatons. Endowed with the gift of prophecy (39:28) they will be free to consult with God on all issues that may confront the new theocentric society.

Why then were Ezekiel's rulings totally ignored by the rabbis? It can hardly be attributed to disagreements with the laws of the Torah. The example of R. Hananiah ben Hezekiah (*b. Shabb.* 13b; cf. *b. Men.* 45a, *b. Hag.* 13a), who is reputed to have successfully harmonized all the differences, indicates that the rabbis' problem with Ezekiel was not about law. The intractable impediment, in my opinion, is theological. The cost of sinlessness—namely the loss of free will—was counter to God's design of the universe, where the human being is the only creature with unprogrammed will. What was the point of it all if the human being could not be challenged? Thus, Ezekiel's visionary sanctuary and its rulings were retained in the tradition, but only as a fanciful, delusory utopia. One should, however, not overlook Radak's daring, unorthodox view that Ezekiel's visionary sanctuary was to be governed, not by the laws of the Torah, but by the rules revealed to Ezekiel (cf. Radak on 43:25; 45:18-20, 22, 25; 46:13). There can be no doubt that Radak regarded Ezekiel as the New Moses (cf. Excursus 8).

To recapitulate, Ezekiel's view of the restoration of Israel's exiles consists mainly of a detailed description of the architecture of his visionary sanctuary and the laws governing its use. Ezekiel's obsessive concern is lest this sanctuary might be defiled, provoking God's departure, followed by its destruction and Israel's exile to Babylon—

---

150. It is a striking coincidence that the thirteenth-century philosopher Maimonides independently intuited that moral (and intellectual) excellence is a prerequisite for attaining prophecy, the highest level of development attainable by the human race. See Pines and Strauss, *The Guide to the Perplexed*, II 12-38, 277-329; Kravitz and Orlinsky, *Shemonah Perakim*, 84-96.

151. Greenberg, "Three Conceptions of the Torah," 20.

precisely what took place in Ezekiel's time (597 and 586). To accomplish this goal, Ezekiel projects a sanctuary with maximal separation between the sacred and common areas; namely, three vertical platforms assigned respectively to God (YHWH), the (Zadokite) priests, and the (common) people.

Moreover, Ezekiel proposes that the redeemed people will neither be prone nor capable of deliberately sinning morally or ritually and thereby contaminating the sanctuary. All leaders accused of defiling the Jerusalem temple will lose their positions or have their status reduced. YHWH alone will be Israel's leader. Every Israelite will be endowed with prophetic powers (39:29) to communicate with God personally and directly. Israel's enemies will be annihilated so that the resettled people of Israel can create a theocentric community of prosperity and peace.

# Select Bibliography

Abba, R. "Priests and Levites in Ezekiel." *Vetus Testamentum* 28 (1978) 1–9.

Ackroyd, P. R. *Exile and Restoration*. Philadelphia: Westminster, 1968.

Aharoni, R. "The Gog Prophecy and the Book of Ezekiel." *Hebrew Annual Review* 1 (1977) 1–27.

———. "The Structure of the Prophecy on Gog from the Land of Magog (Ezekiel 38–39)." *Beth-Miqra* 64 (1974) 45–53 (Hebrew).

Aharoni, Y. *The Land of the Bible: A Historical Geography*. Trans. and edited by A. F. Rainey. Philadelphia: Westminster, 1979.

Albeck, C. *Six Orders of the Mishnah: Seeds*. Jerusalem: Bialik Institute, 1957.

Alberts, R. *Israel in Exile*. Atlanta: Society of Biblical Literature, 2003.

Albrecht, K. "Das Geschlecht der hebräischen Hauptwörter." *Zeitschrift für die Alttestamentliche Wissenschaft* 16 (1896) 41–121.

Albright, W. F. "Contributions to Biblical Archaeology and Philology." *Journal of Biblical Literature* 43 (1924) 363–393.

———. *From the Stone Age to Christianity: Monotheism and the Historical Process*. Garden City, NY: Doubleday, 1957.

———. *The Archaeology of Palestine*. Harmondsworth: Penguin, 1949.

Allen, L. C. *Ezekiel 20–48*. Word Biblical Commentary. Dallas: Word, 1990.

Althann, R. "'Yom,' 'Time' and Some Texts in Isaiah." *Journal of Northwest Semitic Languages* 11 (1983) 3-8.

Andersen, F. I., and A. D. Forbes. *Spelling in the Hebrew Bible: Dahood Memorial Lecture*. Rome: Biblical Institute Press, 1986.

Anderson, B. W. "The Place of Shechem in the Bible." *Biblical Archaeologist* 20 (1957) 10–19.

Anderson, G. A. *Sin: A History*. New Haven: Yale University Press, 2009.

Andrae, W. *Das Widerstandene Assur*. Leipzig: Heinrichs, 1938.

Astour, M. S. "Ezekiel's Prophecy of Gog and the Cuthean Legend of Naram-Sin." *Journal of Biblical Literature* 95 (1976) 567–79.

Balentine, S. E. *The Hidden God: The Hiding of the Face of God in the Old Testament*. New York: Oxford University Press, 1983.

Barkay, G. *Ketef Hinnom: A Treasure Facing Jerusalem's Walls*. Jerusalem: Israel Museum, 1986.

Barnett, R. D. *Ancient Ivories in the Middle East*, Qedem 14. Jerusalem: Hebrew University–Institute of Archaeology, 1992.

Barthélemy, D., et al. *Prophetical Books II: Ezekiel, Daniel, Twelve Minor Prophets*. Preliminary and Interim Report on the Hebrew Old Testament Text Project 5. New York: United Bible Societies, 1980.

## Select Bibliography

Beck, P. "The Drawings from Ḥorvat Teiman (Kuntillet 'Ajrud)." *Tel Aviv* 9 (1982) 3–68.

Beitzel, Barry J. *The Moody Atlas of Bible Lands*. Chicago: Moody Press, 1985.

Berry, G. R. "Priests and Levites." *Journal of Biblical Literature* 42 (1923) 227–38.

Biggs, C. R. "The Role of *nāśî'* in the Programme for Restoration in Ezekiel 40–48," *Colloquium* 16/1 (1983) 46–57.

Block, D. I. "Beyond the Grave: Ezekiel's Vision of Death and Afterlife." *Bulletin for Biblical Research* 2 (1992) 113–41.

———. *The Book of Ezekiel: Chapters 1–24*. New International Commentary on the Old Testament. Grand Rapids: Eerdmans, 1997.

———. *The Book of Ezekiel: Chapters 25–48*. New International Commentary on the Old Testament. Grand Rapids: Eerdmans, 1998.

———. "Divine Abandonment: Ezekiel's Adaptation of an Ancient Near Eastern Motif." In *The Book of Ezekiel. Theological and Anthropological Perspectives*, edited by M. S. Odell and J. T. Strong, 15–42. Atlanta: Society of Biblical Literature Symposium Series, 2000.

———. "Gog and the Pouring Out of the Spirit." *Vetus Testamentum* 37 (1987) 257–70.

———. "Gog in Prophetic Tradition: A New Look at Ezekiel XXXVIII 17." *Vetus Testamentum* 42 (1992) 154–72.

———. "Transformation of Royal Ideology in Ezekiel." In *Transforming Visions: Transformations of Text, Tradition, and Theology in Ezekiel*. Edited by W. A. Tooman and M. A. Lyons, 234–43. Eugene, OR: Pickwick Publications, 2010.

———. "The View from the Top: The Holy Spirit in the Prophets." In *Presence, Power and Promise: The Role of the Spirit of God in the Old Testament*. Edited by D. G. Firth and P. D. Wagner. Downers Grove, IL: InterVarsity, 2011.

Boadt, L. *Ezekiel's Oracles Against Egypt: A Literary and Philological Study of Ezekiel 29 – 32*. Biblica et orientalia 37. Rome: Pontifical Biblical Institute, 1980.

Botta, A. F. "*rḥq* in the Bible, a Re-Evaluation." *Biblica* 87 (2006) 418–20.

Bracke, J. M. "'*sûb sebût*': A Reappraisal." *Zeitschrift für die alttestamentliche Wissenschaft* 97 (1985) 233–44.

Brown, J. P. *Israel and Hellas*. New York: de Gruyter, 1995.

Brown, M. L. "Is It Not? Or Indeed!: *HL* in Northwest Semitic." *Maarav* 4/2 (1987) 201–19.

Burkert, W. *Ancient Mystery Cults*. Cambridge, MA: Harvard University Press, 1987.

———. *Greek Religion*. Cambridge, MA: Harvard University Press, 1985.

———. "Lescha-Liškah." In *Religiongeschichtliche Beziehung zwischen Kleinasien, Nordsyrien, und dem Alten Testament: Internationales Symposion Hamburg 17.-21, März 1990*, edited by B. Lanowski and G. Wilhelm, 19–38. Orbis Biblicus et Orientalis, 129. Göttingen: 1993.

———. *The Orientalizing Revolution*. Cambridge, MA: Harvard University Press, 1992.

Burrows, M. "Orthography, Morphology, and Syntax of the St. Mark's Isaiah Manuscript," in *Journal of Biblical Literature* 68 (1949) 195-211.

Busink, Th. A. *Der Tempel von Jerusalem: von Salomo bis Herodes: eine archäologisch-historische Studie unter Berücksichtigung des westsemitischen Tempelbaus*. 2 vols. Leiden: E. J. Brill, 1970–80.

Cansdale, G. S. *Animals of Biblical Lands*. Exeter: Paternoster, 1970.

Clements, R. E. *God and Temple*. Philadelphia: Fortress, 1965.

Cogan, M. *Joel*. Tel Aviv: Am Oved, 1994.

Cogan M. and H. Tadmor. "Gyges and Ashurbanipal." *Orientalia* 46 (1977) 65–85.

Cohen, M. *The Cultic Calendar of the Ancient Near East*. Bethesda, MD: CDL Press, 1992.

———. *Ezekiel, Haketer*. Ramat Gan: Bar Ilan University, 2000 (Hebrew).

Cook, S. L. "Innerbiblical Interpretation in Ezekiel 44 and the History of Israel's Priesthood." *Journal of Biblical Literature* 114 (1995) 193–208.

Cooke, G. A. *A Critical and Exegetical Commentary on the Book of Ezekiel*. International Critical Commentaries. Edinburgh: T. & T. Clark, 1985.

Cowley, A. *Aramaic Papyri of the Fifth Century B.C.* Oxford: Clarendon, 1923.

Crenshaw, J. L. *Joel*. Anchor Bible 24. New York: Doubleday, 1995.

Cross, F. M. "A Papyrus Recording a Divine Legal Decision and the Root *rhq* in Biblical and Near Eastern Legal Usage." In *Texts, Temples and Traditions: A Tribute to Menahem Haran*, edited by M. Fox, et al., 311–20. Winona Lake: Eisenbrauns, 1996.

Dalman, G. *Arbeit und Sitte in Palästina*. Gütersloh: C. Bertelsmann, 1928.

Darr, K. P. "The Wall Around Paradise." *Vetus Testamentum* 37 (1987) 271–79.

Davidson, A. B. *Introductory Hebrew Grammar: Hebrew Syntax*. Edingurgh: T. & T. Clark, 1901.

Davies, P. R. *Damascus Covenant*. Journal for the Study of the Old Testament Supplement 25. Sheffield: JSOT Press, 1982.

Day, J. "Whatever Happened to the Ark?" In *Temple and Worship in Biblical Israel*, edited by John Day, 250–70. Journal for the Study of the Old Testament Supplement Series London: T. & T. Clark International, 2005.

Dijkstra, M. "The Altar of Ezekiel."*Vetus Testamentum* (1982) 24–36.

Douglas, G. C. M. "Ezekiel's Temple." *Expository Times* 9 (1898) 365–67, 420–22, 468–70, 515–18.

Driver, G. R. "Linguistic and Textual Problems: Ezekiel." *Biblica* 19 (1938) 60–69, 175–87.

———. "Ezekiel: Linguistic and Textual Problems." *Biblica* 35 (1954) 308–9.

Driver, S. R. *The Book of Exodus*. Cambridge: Cambridge University Press, 1929.

Duguid, I. M. *Ezekiel and the Leaders of Israel*. Leiden: Brill, 1994.

Duke, R. K. "Punishment or Restoration? Another Look at the Levites of Ezekiel 44.6–16." *Journal for the Study of the Old Testament* 40 (1988) 61–81.

Ehrlich, A. B. *Randglossen zur Hebräischen Bibel: textkritisches, sprachliches und sachliches*. Leipzig: Hinrichs, 1908–14.

Eichrodt, W. *Ezekiel: A Commentary*. The Old Testament Library. Philadelphia: Westminster, 1970.

Elliger, K. *Leviticus*. Tubingen: J. C. Mohr [Paul Siebeck], 1966.

Ellis, R. S. *Foundation Deposits in Ancient Mesopotamia*. New Haven: Yale University Press, 1968.

———. "Gründungsbeigaben." In *Reallexikon der Assyriologie*, edited by Erich Ebeling and Ernst F. Weidner 3/9:655–61. Berlin: de Gruyter, 1971.

Eph'al, I. "The Babylonian Exile: The Survival of a National Minority in a Culturally Developed Foreign Milieu." *Gründungsfeier* 16 (2005) 21–31.

Falkenstein, A., and W. von Soden. *Sumerische und akkadische Hymnen und Gebete*. Zurich: Artemis, 1953.

Fishbane, M. *Biblical Interpretation in Ancient Israel*. Oxford: Clarendon, 1985.

## Select Bibliography

———. *Haftarot: The Traditional Hebrew Text with the New JPS Translation*. Philadelphia: Jewish Publication Society, 2002.

———. "Sin and Judgment in the Prophecies of Ezekiel." *Interpretation* 38 (1984) 131–50.

Fohrer, G. and K. Galling. *Ezechiel*. Handbuch zum Alten Testament 13. Tübingen: Mohr, 1955.

Fox, M. V. "The Rhetoric of Ezekiel's Vision of the Valley of the Bones." *Hebrew Union College Annual* (1980) 1–15.

Franklin, N. "Lost Tombs of the Israelite Kings." *Biblical Archaeology Review* (2007) 26–35.

Freedman, D. N. *The Nine Commandments*. New York: Doubleday, 2000.

Friedman, R. E. "The Biblical Expression *mastîr pānîm*." *Hebrew Annual Review* 1 (1977) 139–47.

———. *The Hidden Face of God*. San Francisco: Harper, 1995.

Frymer-Kensky, T. "Pollution, Purification, and Purgation in Biblical Israel." In *The Word of the Lord Shall Go Forth: Essays in Honor of David Noel Freedman in Celebration of His Sixtieth Birthday*, edited by C. L. Meyers and M. O'Connor, 399-414. Winona Lake: Eisenbrauns, 1983.

Fuhs, H. F. *Ezechiel II, 25–48*. Neue Echter Bibel., Altes Testament 22. Würzburg: Echter, 1988.

———. "*rā'â*." In *Theological Dictionary of the Old Testament*, edited by G. J. Botterweck, H. Ringgren, and H.-J. Fabry, and translated by D. E. Green, 13:208–42. Grand Rapids: Eerdmans, 2004.

Galambush, J. *Jerusalem in the Book of Ezekiel: The City of Yahweh*. Society of Biblical Literature Dissertation Series 130. Atlanta: Scholars, 1992.

Galil, G. "The Boundaries of Aram-Damascus in the 9th–8th centuries BCE." In *Studies in Historical Geography and Biblical Historiography: Presented to Zecharia Kallai*, edited by M. Weinfeld and G. Galil, 35–41. Leiden: Brill, 2000.

Ganzel, T. *The Concept of Holiness in the Book of Ezekiel*. PhD diss., Bar Ilan University, 2004 (Hebrew).

Garfinkel, S. P. *Studies in Akkadian Influences in the Book of Ezekiel*. PhD diss., Columbia University, 1983.

Gese, H. *Der Verfassungsentwurf des Ezechiel (Kap. 40–48): Traditionsgeschichtlich Untersucht*. Beiträge zur historischen Theologie 25. Tübingen: J. C. B. Mohr [P. Siebeck], 1957.

Ginsberg, H. L. *The Israelian Heritage of Judaism*. New York: Jewish Theological Seminary of America Publications, 1982.

Gordon, C. H. *The Common Background of Greek and Hebrew Civilization*. New York: W. W. Horton, 1965.

———. *Ugaritic Textbook*. Analecta orientalia 38. Rome, 1965.

Goshen-Gottstein, M. H. and S. Talmon, eds. *The Book of Ezekiel*. Jerusalem: Magnes, 2004.

Greenberg, M. "The Design and Themes of Ezekiel's Program of Restoration." *Interpretation* 38 (1984) 181–209.

———. *Ezekiel 1–20*. Anchor Bible 22. Garden City: Doubleday, 1983.

———. *Ezekiel 21–37*. Anchor Bible 22b. Garden City: Doubleday, 1997.

———. "Idealism and Practicality in Numbers 35:4–5 and Ezekiel 48." *Journal of the American Oriental Society* 88 (1968) 59–65. Reprinted in *Studies in the Bible and Jewish Thought*, 313–26. Philadelphia: Jewish Publication Society, 1995.

———. "Three Conceptions of the Torah in Hebrew Scriptures." In *Studies in the Bible and Jewish Thought*, 11–41. Philadelphia: Jewish Publication Society, 1995; translated from *Die Hebräische Bibel und ihre zweifache Nachegeschichte: Festschrift für Rolf Rendtorff zum 65. Geburtstag*, edited by E. Blum. Neukirchen-Vluyn: Neukirchen, 1990.

## Select Bibliography

Haak, R. D. "The 'Shoulder' of the Temple." *Vetus Testamentum* 33 (1983) 271–78.

Hale, J. R., J. Z. de Boer, J. P. Chanton, and H. A. Spiller. "Questioning the Delphic Oracle." *Scientific American* (August 2003) 67–73.

Hals, R. M. *Ezekiel*. The Forms of the Old Testament Literature. Vol XIX. Grand Rapids: Eerdmans, 1989.

Haran, M. "Biblical Topics: Yahweh's Presence in Israel's Cult and the Cultic Institutions." *Tarbiz* 38 (1969) 105–19 (Hebrew).

———. "Ezekiel." In *World of the Bible*, 204–18. Tel Aviv: Revivim, 1984 (Hebrew).

———. "The Law-Code of Ezekiel 40–48 and its Relation to the Priestly School." *Hebrew Union College Annual* 50 (1979) 45–71.

———. *Temples and Temple Service in Israel*. Oxford: Clarendon, 1978.

Helms, P. R. *Greeks in the Neo-Assyrian Levant and "Assyria" in Early Greek Writers*. PhD diss., University of Pennsylvania, 1980.

Holladay, W. L. *The Root šûb in the Old Testament*. Leiden: Brill, 1958.

Hurowitz, V. A. "Inside Solomon's Temple." *Bible Review* 10 (1994) 24–37, 50.

———. "Literary Structures in Samsuiluna A." *Journal of Cuneiform Studies* 36 (1984) 191–205.

———. "LORD YHWH's Exalted House: Aspects of the Design and Symbolism of Solomon's Temple." In *Temple and Worship in Biblical Israel*, edited by John Day, 63–110. London: T. & T. Clark, 2005.

———. "The Temple of Solomon." In *The History of Jerusalem: The Biblical Period*, edited by S. Ahituv and A. Mazar, 131–54. Jerusalem: Yad Izahak Ben-Zvi, 2000 (Hebrew).

Hurvitz, A. *A Linguistic Study of the Relationship between the Priestly Source and the Book of Ezekiel: A New Approach to an Old Problem*. Paris: J. Gabalda, 1982.

Irwin, B. P. "Molek Imagery, and the Slaughter of Gog in Ezekiel 38 and 39." *Journal for the Study of the Old Testament* 65 (1995): 93–112.

Jacob, B. *The Second Book of the Bible: Exodus*. Hoboken, NJ: Ktav Publishing House, 1992.

Japhet, S. *The Ideology of the Book of Chronicles*. Jerusalem: Bialik Institute, 1977 (Hebrew).

Jastrow, M. *Dictionary of the Targumim, the Talmud Babli and Yerushalmi, and the Midrashic Literature*. Peabody: New York: Putnam's Sons, 1903.

Joüon, P. and T. Muraoka. *A Grammar of Biblical Hebrew*. Subsidia Biblica 27. Revised edition. Roma: Editrice Pontificio Istituto Biblico, 2006.

Joyce, P. M. *Divine Initiative and Human Response*. Journal for the Study of the Old Testament Supplement 51. Sheffield: JSOT Press, 1989.

———. *Ezekiel: A Commentary*. New York: T. & T. Clark, 2007.

———. "Ezekiel 40-42: The Earliest 'Heavenly Ascent' Narrative?" In *The Book of Ezekiel and its Influence*, edited by H. Jan de Jonge and H. Tromp, 17–41. Aldershot: Ashgate, 2007.

———. "Temple and Worship in Ezekiel 40–48." In *Temple and Worship in Biblical Israel*, edited by John Day, 145–63. London: T. & T. Clark, 2005.

Kallai, Z. *Historical Geography of the Bible: The Tribal Territories of Israel*. Jerusalem: Magnes, 1986 (Hebrew).

Karageorghis, V. "Chronique de fouilles et decouvertes archeologiques a Chypre en 1969." *Bulletin de Correspondance Hellenique* 94 (1970) 191–300.

Kasher, R. "Anthropomorphism, Holiness and Cult: A New Look at Ezekiel 40–48." *Zeitschrift für die alttestamentliche Wissenschaft* 110 (1998) 192–208.

## Select Bibliography

———. *Ezekiel*. 2 volumes. Mikra Leyisrael. Tel Aviv: Am Oved, 2004 (Hebrew).

Kaufmann, Y. *The Religion of Israel: From its Beginnings to the Babylonian Exile*. Translated and abridged by M. Greenberg. Chicago: University of Chicago Press, 1960.

Kedar-Kopfstein, B. "חַג *chagh*." 201-13. *Theological Dictionary of the Old Testament*. Edited by G. J. Botterweck and H. Ringgren, and translated by D. E. Green, 4:201–13. Grand Rapids: Eerdmans, 1980.

———. *Biblische Semantik: Eine Einführung*. Stuttgart: Kohlhammer, 1981.

Kenyon, K. *Digging Up Jerusalem*. New York: Praeger, 1974.

———. *Jerusalem: Excavating 3000 Years of History*. London: Thames and Hudson, 1967.

Kissane, E. J. *The Book of Isaiah*, Vol. 1. Dublin: Browne and Nolan, 1960.

Kitchen, K. A. "Two notes on the subsidiary rooms of Solomon's Temple." *Eretz Israel* 20 (1989) 107–112.

Kletter, R. *The Judean Pillar-Figurines and the Archaeology of Asherah*. Oxford: Tempus Reparatum, 1996.

Knohl, I. *The Sanctuary of Silence: The Priestly Torah and the Holiness School*. Minneapolis: Fortress, 1995.

Kohn, R. L. "'With a Mighty Hand and an Outstretched Arm': The Prophet and the Torah in Ezekiel 20." In *Ezekiel's Hierarchical World*, edited by S. L. Cook and C. L Patton, 159-68. Atlanta: Society of Biblical Literature, 2004.

Kravitz, L. and K. M. Orlinsky, ed. and trans. *Shemonah Perakim: A Treatise on the Soul*. New York: Union of American Hebrew Congregations Press, 1999.

Kutsko, J. F. "Ezekiel's Anthropology." In *The Book of Ezekiel: Theological and Anthropological Perspectives*, edited by M. S. Odell and J. T. Strong, 119–41. Society of Biblical Literature Symposium Series. Atlanta: Society of Biblical Literature, 2000.

Lambert, W. G. *Babylonian Wisdom Literature*. Oxford: Clarendon, 1967.

Lane, D. *The Cloud and the Silver Lining*. Welwyn: Evangelical Press, 1985.

Lang, B. *Kein Aufstand in Jerusalem: Die Politik des Propheten Ezechiel*. Erträge der Forschung 153. Stuttgart: Katholisches Bibelwerk, 1978.

Langdon, S. *Die Neubabylonische Königsinschriften*. Leipzig: J. Hinrichs, 1911.

Lapsley, J. E. *Can These Bones Live?* Beihefte zur Zeitschrift für die Alttestamentliche Wissenschaft 301. Berlin: de Gruyter, 2000.

———. "Shame and Self-Knowledge in Ezekiel's View of the Moral Self." In *The Book of Ezekiel: Theological and Anthropological Perspectives*, edited by M. S. Odell and J. T. Strong, 143–73. Society of Biblical Literature Symposium Series. Atlanta: Society of Biblical Literature, 2000.

Lemaire, A. "Writing and Writing Materials." In *Anchor Bible Dictionary*, edited by D. N. Freedman, 6:999–1008. Garden City, NY: Doubleday, 1992.

Levenson, J. D. *Sinai and Zion: An Entry into the Jewish Bible*. San Francisco: Harper & Row, 1987.

———. "The Temple and the World." *Journal of Religion* 64 (1984) 275–298.

———. *Theology of the Program of Restoration of Ezekiel 40-48*. Harvard Semitic Monographs 10. Cambridge, MA: Scholars Press, 1976.

Levey, S. H. *The Targum of Ezekiel*. The Aramaic Bible. Volume 13. Collegeville, MN: Liturgical Press, 1990.

Levine, B. A., and J.–M. de Tarragon. "Dead Kings and Rephaim: The Patrons of the Ugaritic Dynasty." *Journal of the American Oriental Society* 104 (1984) 649–59.

## Select Bibliography

Levine, B. A. *Leviticus*. Jewish Publication Society Torah Commentary. Philadelphia: Jewish Publications Society, 1989.

Lewy, J. "The Biblical Institution of *D'rôr* in the Light of Akkadian Documents." *Eretz Israel* 5 (1959) 21–32.

Lipshitz, E. "On 'The Servant of LORD YHWH' and 'The servant of the King'." *Shenaton* 13 (2002) 157–71 (Hebrew).

Lipiński, E. "*'am*." *Theological Dictionary of the Old Testament*. Edited by G. J. Botterweck, H. Ringgren, and H.-J. Fabry, and translated by D. E. Green, 11:170–75. Grand Rapids: Eerdmans, 2004.

Maaß, M. "The Sanctuary of Apollo." In *Brill's New Pauly*, Vol 4, edited by H. Cancik and H. Schneider, 216–23. Leiden: Brill, 2004.

Mackay, C. "Why Study Ezekiel 40–48?" *Evangelical Quarterly* 37 (1965) 155–167.

Maiberger, P. "*pāgar, paegaer*." *Theological Dictionary of the Old Testament*. Edited by G. J. Botterweck, H. Ringgren, and H.-J. Fabry, and translated by D. E. Green, 11:477–82. Grand Rapids: Eerdmans, 2004.

Maier, J. "Die Hofanlagen im Tempel-Entwurf des Ezechiel im Licht der 'Tempelrolle' von Qumran." *Prophecy: Essays Presented to Georg Fohrer on his 65th Birthday*, edited by J. A. Emerton, 55–67. Berlin: de Gruyter, 1980.

Maimonides, Moses. *The Code of Maimonides*. Book 8, *The Book of Temple Service*. Yale Judaica Series 12. New Haven, CN: Yale University Press, 1957.

———. *The Guide to the Perplexed*. Translated with an introduction by S. Pines. Chicago: University of Chicago Press, 1963.

———. *Shemonah Perakim: A Treatise on the Soul*. Translation and commentary by L. S. Kravitz and K. M. Orlinsky. New York: Union of American Hebrew Congregations Press, 1999.

Malamat, A. *Mari and the Early Israelite Experience*. Oxford: Oxford University Press, 1989.

———. "Prophecy in the Mari Documents." *Eretz Israel* 4 (1956) 74–94 (Hebrew).

Margolit, E. "The Structure of the Prophecy on Gog from the Land of Magog (Ezekiel 38–39)." In *Sefer Tur-Sinai* edited by M. Haran and B.-Z. Luria, 99–103. Jerusalem: Kiriath Sefer, 1960 (Hebrew).

Margueron, J.-C. "Babylon." In *Anchor Bible Dictionary*, edited by D. N. Freedman, 1:564. New York: Doubleday, 1992.

Maur, J. "The Architectural History of the Temple in Jerusalem in the Light of the Temple Scroll." In *Temple Scroll Studies*, edited by G. J. Brooke, 23–62. Sheffield: Journal for the Study of the Old Testament Press, 1989.

May, H. G. "Ezekiel." In *The Interpreter's Bible*, edited by G. A. Buttrick, 6:39–338. Nashville: Abingdon, 1956.

Mazar, A. *Archaeology of the Land of the Bible*. Garden City, NY: Doubleday, 1990.

Mazar, B. "Canaan on the Threshold of the Age of the Patriarchs." *Eretz Israel* 3 (1954) 18–32 (Hebrew).

McCarter, P. K. *II Samuel*. Anchor Bible 9. Garden City, NY: Doubleday, 1984.

McConville, J. G. "Priests and Levites in Ezekiel: a Crux in the Interpretation of Israel's History." *Tyndale Bulletin* 34 (1983) 3–31.

McKeating, H. "Ezekiel, The Prophet like Moses." *Journal for the Study of the Old Testament* 61 (1994) 97–109.

Middlemas, J. *The Templeless Age*. Louisville: Westminster, 2007.

Milgrom, J. *Cult and Conscience: The Asham and Priestly Doctrine of Repentance*. Studies in Judaism in Late Antiquity 19. Leiden: Brill, 1976.

## Select Bibliography

———. "The Desecration of YHWH's Name: Its Parameters and Significance." In *Birkat Shalom: Studies in the Bible, Ancient Near Eastern Literature, and Postbiblical Judaism, Presented to Sahlom M. Paul on the Occasion of His Seventieth Birthday*, edited by C. Cohen, V. A. Hurowitz, A. Hurvits, Y. Muffs, A. J. Schwartz, and J. H. Tigay, 69–82. Winona Lake, IN: Eisenbrauns, 2008.

———. "Hittite *ḫuelpi*," *Journal of the American Oriental Society* 96 (1976) 575–76.

———. "*kipper 'ad/bě'adh*," *Leshonenu* 35 (1980) 16–17 (Hebrew).

———. *Leviticus 1–16*. Anchor Bible 3. New York: Doubleday, 1991.

———. *Leviticus 17–22*. Anchor Bible 3a. New York: Doubleday, 2000.

———. *Leviticus 23–27*. Anchor Bible 3b. New York: Doubleday, 2001.

———. "The Nature and Extent of Idolatry in Eighth-Seventh Century Judah." *Hebrew Union College Annual* 69 (1998) 1–13.

———. *Numbers*. Jewish Publication Society Torah Commentary. Philadelphia: Jewish Publication Society, 1990.

———. "Priestly Terminology and the Political and Social Structure of Pre-Monarchic Israel." *Jewish Quarterly Review* (1978) 66–76.

———. *Studies in Levitical Terminology, I: The Encroacher and the Levite, The Term 'aboda*. Near Eastern Studies, Volume 14. Berkeley: University of California Press, 1970.

———. "The Unique Features of Ezekiel's Sanctuary." In *Mishneh Todah: Studies in Deuteronomy and Its Cultural Environment in Honor of Jeffrey H. Tigay*, edited by N. S. Fox, D. A. Glatt-Gilad, and M. J. Williams, 293–305. Winona Lake, IN: Eisenbrauns, 2009.

Monson, J. M. "The New 'Ain Dara Temple: Closest Solomonic Parallel." *Biblical Archaeology Review* 26/3 (May/June, 2000): 20–35, 67.

———. "Solomon's Temple and the Temple at 'Ain Dara." *Qadmoniot* 29 (1996) 33–38 (Hebrew).

Moor, J. C. de, and H. F. de Vries, "Hebrew *hādād* Thunder–Storm." *Ugarit-Forschungen* 20 (1988) 173–77.

Moran, W. L. "New Evidence from Mari on the History of Prophecy." *Biblica* 50 (1969) 5–56.

Muraoka, T. *Emphatic Words and Structures In Biblical Hebrew*. Jerusalem: Magnes, 1985.

Na'aman, N. "Amarna *ālāni pu-ru-zi* (EA 137) and Biblical *'ry hprzy–hprzwt'* ('rural settlements')." *Zeitschrift für Althebräistik* 4 (1991) 72–75.

———. "Death Formulae and the Burial Place of the Kings of the House of David." *Biblica* 85 (2004) 245–54.

Neiman, D. "*PGR*: A Canaanite Cult–Object in the Old Testament." *Journal of Biblical Literature* 67 (1948) 55–60.

Neusner, J. *The Talmud of the Land of Israel*. Volume 17: *Sukkah: A Preliminary Translation and Explanation*. Chicago: University of Chicago Press, 1988.

———. *The Tosefta: Translated from the Hebrew with a New Introduction*. Peabody, Mass.: Hendrickson, 2002.

Noth, M. *Leviticus: a Commentary*. Philadelphia: Westminster, 1977.

Oates, J. and D. Oates. *Nimrud: an Assyrian Imperial City Revealed*. London: British School of Archaeology in Iraq, 2001.

Obermann, J. *Votive Inscriptions from Ras Shamra*. New Haven: American Oriental Society, 1941.

Odell, M. S. *'Are You He of Whom I spoke by My Servants the Prophets?' Ezekiel 38–39 and the Problem of History in the Neobabylonian Context*. PhD diss., University of Pittsburgh, 1988.

———. "The City of Hamonah in Ezekiel 39:11-16: the Tumultuous City of Jerusalem." *Catholic Biblical Quarterly* 56 (1994) 479-489.

———. *Ezekiel*. Smyth & Helwys Bible Commentary. Macon, GA: Smyth & Helwys, 2005.

———. "What Was the Image of Jealousy?" In L. L. Grabbe and Ogden Bellis eds., *The Priests and the Prophets*, 134-48. Journal for the Study of the Old Testament Supplement Series 408. London: T. & T. Clark, 2004.

———. "You Are What You Eat: Ezekiel and the Scroll." *Journal of Biblical Literature* 117 (1998) 229-48.

Olyan, S. M. "Some Thoughts on Isa 14, 19" *Zeitschrift für die alttestamentliche Wissenschaft* 118 (2006) 423-26.

Oppenheim, A. L. "Idiomatic Akkadian." *Journal of the American Oriental Society* 61 (1941) 251-71.

Pattai, R. *Ha-Mayim [Water]*. Tel-Aviv: Ha-maʿareb, 1936.

Patton, C. L. *Ezekiel's Blueprint for the Temple of Jerusalem*. PhD diss., Yale, 1991.

———. "Priest, Prophet and Exile: Ezekiel's Contribution to the History of the Old Testament as a Literary Construct." In *Ezekiel's Hierarchical World*, edited by S. L. Cook and C. L. Patton, 73-90. Atlanta: Society of Biblical Literature, 2004.

Paul, S. *Studies in the Book of the Covenant in the Light of Cuneiform and Biblical Law*. Supplements to Vetus Testamentum 18. Leiden: Brill, 1970.

Petersen, D. L. "Creation and Hierarchy in Ezekiel: Methodological Perspectives and Theological Prospects." Ezekiel's Hierarchical World, edited by S. L. Cook and C. L. Patton, 169-78. Atlanta: Society of Biblical Literature, 2004.

Pines, S. and L. Strauss. *The Guide to the Perplexed*, II 12-38. Chicago: University of Chicago Press, 1974.

Pope, M. H. "Review of K. Spronk, *Beatific Afterlife in Ancient Israel and in the Ancient Near East*." *Ugarit-Forschungen* 19 (1987) 462.

Powel, M. A. "Weights and Measures." In *Anchor Bible Dictionary*. Edited by D. N. Freedman, 6: 897-908. Garden City, NY: Doubleday, 1992.

Pritchard, J. B. *The Ancient Near East in Pictures Relating to the Old Testament*. 2nd ed. Princeton: Princeton University Press, 1969.

———, ed. *Ancient Near Eastern Texts Related to the Old Testament*. 3rd ed. Princeton: Princeton University Press, 1969.

———. *The Harper Atlas of the Bible*. New York: Harper & Row, 1987.

Procksch, D. G. "Furst und Priester bei Hezekiel, Zeitschrift für die alttestamentliche Wissenschaft" 58 (1940) 99-133.

Propp, W. H. C. *Exodus 1-18: A New Translation with Introduction and Commentary*. Anchor Bible 2. New York: Doubleday, 1999.

———. "The Priestly Source Recovered Intact." *Vetus Testamentum* 46 (1997) 458-78.

Qoler, Y. "Biblical Symbols, Abbreviations, and Acronyms," *Beth Mikra* 35 (1989-90) 317-24 (Hebrew).

Rabin, C. *Zadokite Documents*. Oxford: Clarendon, 1954.

Rad, G. von. *Holy War in Ancient Israel*. Translated and edited by M. J. Dawn. Grand Rapids: Eerdmans, 1991.

Rattray, S. and J. Milgrom, "בָּרָק *qarab*." In *Theological Dictionary of the Old Testament*, edited by G. J. Botterweck, H. Ringgren, and H.-J. Fabry, and translated by D. E. Green, 13:135-52. Grand Rapids: Eerdmans, 2004.

## Select Bibliography

Reviv, H. *The Elders in Ancient Israel: A Study of a Biblical Institution.* Jerusalem: Magnes, The Hebrew University, 1989 (Hebrew).

Rocchi, D., "Delphi," Volume 4, 215-20 in *Brill's New Pauly.* Leiden: Brill, 2004.

Rollinger, R. "Ancient Greeks and the Impact of the Ancient Near East: Textual Evidence and Historical Perspective (ca. 750–650 BC)." In *Mythology and Mythologies: Methodological Approaches to Intercultural Influences,* edited by R. M. Whiting, 233-264. Helsinki: The Neo–Assyrian Text Corpus Project, 2001.

Rooker, M. F. *Biblical Hebrew in Transition: The Language of the Book of Ezekiel.* Sheffield: Journal for the Study of the Old Testament Press, 1990.

Rubenstein, A. "The Anomalous Perfect with *Waw*-Conjunctive in Biblical Hebrew." *Biblica* 44 (1963) 62-69.

Schwartz, B. J. "The Bearing of Sin in Priestly Literature." In *Pomegranates and Golden Bells: Studies in Biblical, Jewish, and Near Eastern Ritual, Law, and Literature in Honor of Jacob Milgrom,* edited by D. Wright, D. N. Freedman, A. Hurvitz. Winona Lake, IN: Eisenbrauns, 1995.

———. "Ezekiel's Dim View of Israel's Restoration." in *The Book of Ezekiel: Theological and Anthropological Perspectives,* edited by M. S. Odell and J. T. Strong, 43–68. Atlanta: Society of Biblical Literature Symposium Series, 2000).

———. "Term or Metaphor: Biblical *nasa awon*," *Tel Aviv* 63 (1994) 149-71.

Scott, W. R. *The Booths of Ancient Israel's Autumn Festival.* PhD diss, Johns Hopkins University, 1993.

Seidel, M. "Parallels Between Isaiah and Psalms." *Sinai* 38 (1955–56) 149-72, 229–40 (Hebrew).

———. "Parallels between Isaiah and Psalms." In *Hiqrei Miqra,* 1-97. Jerusalem: Rav Kook Institute, 1978.

Sharon, D. M., "A Biblical Parallel to a Sumerian Temple Hymn? Ezekiel 40–48 and Gudea." *Journal of the Ancient Near Eastern Society of Columbia University* 24 (1997) 99–109.

Sharon, I. "Appendix E: Analysis of Homogeneity for the Distribution of Figurines in Strata 13–10." *Qedem* 35 (1996) 100–108.

Shiloh, Y. *Excavations at the City of David, vols. 1–6.* Jerusalem: Institute of Archaeology, Hebrew University, 1978–85.

Simon, B. "Ezekiel's Geometric Vision of the Restored Temple." *Harvard Theological Review* 102 (2009) 411–38.

Simons, J. J. *The Geographical and Topographical Texts of the Old Testament: A Concise Commentary in XXXII Chapters.* Leiden: E. J. Brill, 1959.

Ska, J. L. "La Sortie d'Egypte (Ex 7–14) dans le recit sacerdotal (P) et la tradition prophetique." *Biblica* 60 (1979) 203–215.

Smith, J. Z. *To Take Place: Toward Theory in Ritual.* Chicago: University of Chicago Press, 1987.

Smith, M. "A Note on Burning Babies." *Journal of the American Oriental Society* 95 (1975) 477–79.

———. *Palestinian Parties and Politics that Shaped the Old Testament.* New York: Columbia University Press, 1971.

Soden, W. von. *The Ancient Orient: An Introduction to the Study of the Ancient Near East.* Grand Rapids: Eerdmans, 1994.

———. "Ist im Alten Testament schon von Schwimmen die Rede?" *Zeitschrift für Althebräistik,* 165-170.

Sperber, A., ed. *The Bible in Aramaic.* Vol. 3, *The Latter Prophets according to Targum Jonathan.* Leiden: Brill, 1962.

Sperling, S. D. "Biblical 'rḥm' I and 'rḥm' II." *Journal of the Ancient Near Eastern Society of Colombia University* 19 (1989) 149–159.

Stager, L. "Jerusalem and the Garden of Eden." In *Traditions in Transformation: F. M. Cross Festschrift*. Winona Lake, IN: Eisenbrauns, 1981.

Stavrakopoulou, F. "Exploring the Garden of Uzza: Death, Burial and Ideologies of Kingship." *Biblica* 87 (2006) 1–21.

———. "*Gog's Grave* and the Use and Abuse of Corpses in Ezekiel 39:11-20." *Journal of Biblical Literature* 129 (2010) 67–84.

Stevenson, K. R. *The Vision of Transformation: The Territorial Rhetoric of Ezekiel 40–48*. Society of Biblical Literature Dissertation Series 154. Atlanta, GA: Scholars Press, 1996.

Sweeny, M. A., "Ezekiel, Zadokite Priest and Visionary Prophet of the Exile" In *Form and Intertextuality in Prophetic and Apocalyptic Literature*, 125–43. Tubingen: Mohr Siebeck, 2000.

Tadmor, H. "Chronology." *Encyclopaedia Miqrait* 4 (1962) 245–310 (Hebrew).

Talmon, S. "Double Readings in the Massoretic Text." *Textus: Annual of the Hebrew University Bible Project* 1 (1960) 144–84.

———. "The Judaean *'am ha'ares'* in Historical Perspective." *World Congress of Jewish Studies* 4 (1967) 71–76.

Talmon, S. and M. Fishbane. "The Structuring of Biblical Books: Studies in the Book of Ezekiel." *Annual of the Swedish Theological Institute* 10 (1976) 129–53.

Tigay, J. *Deuteronomy*. Jewish Publication Society Torah Commentary. Philadelphia: Jewish Publication Society, 1996.

Tuell, S. S., "Contemporary Studies of Ezekiel: A New Tide Rising," In *Ezekiel's Heirarchical World*, 251–52. Edited by S. L. Cook and C. L. Carvalho. Atlanta: Society of Biblical Literature, 2004.

———. "Ezekiel 40–42 as Verbal Icon." *Catholic Biblical Quarterly* 58.4 (1996) 649–64.

———. *The Law of the Temple in Ezekiel 40–48*. Atlanta: Scholars Press, 1992.

Tur-Sinai, N. H. *Pšuto šel-Miqrā'* III. Jerusalem: Kiryath Sepher, 1967 (Hebrew).

Unger, W. *Babylon: Die heilige Stadt nach der Beschreibung der Babylonier*, 2nd ed. Berlin: de Gruyter, 1970.

Vaux, R. de. *Ancient Israel: Its Life and Institutions*. Translated by John McHugh. London: Longman, 1961.

———. "Le pays de Canaan." *Journal of the American Oriental Society* 88 (1968) 23–30.

Viditch, S. "Ezekiel 40–48 in Visionary Context." *Catholic Biblical Quarterly* 48 (1986) 208–24.

Wagenaar, G. A. "The Priestly Festival Calendar and the Babylonian New Year Festival." In *The Old Testament in Its World*. Edited by R. P. Gordon and J. C. de Moor, 218–50. Leiden: Brill, 2005.

Waltke, B. K., and M. O'Connor. *Introduction to Biblical Hebrew Syntax*. Winona Lake, IN: Eisenbrauns, 1990.

Waterman, L. *Royal Correspondence of the Assyrian Empire, Part 2: Translation and Transliteration*. Ann Arbor, MI: University of Michigan Press, 1930–1936.

Weidner, E. F. "Hof- und Harems-Erlasse assyrischer Könige aus dem 2. Jahrtausend v. Chr." *Archiv für Orientforschung* 17 (1954–56) 257–93.

———. "Joachim, König von Juda in Babylonische Keilinschrifttexte." *Mélanges Syriens* (Festschrift R. Dussaud), vol. 2. Paris: P. Geuthner, 1939.

Weinfeld, M. *Deuteronomy and the Deuteronomistic School*. Oxford: Clarendon, 1972.

———. *Social Justice in Ancient Israel and in the Ancient Near East*. Minneapolis: Fortress, 1995.

## Select Bibliography

Wellhausen, J. *Prolegomena to the History of Ancient Israel.* Translated by J. S. Black and A. Menzies. New York: Meridian, 1957.

West, M. L. *The East Face of Helicon.* Oxford: Clarendon, 1997.

Wevers, J. W. *Ezekiel.* New Century Bible Commentary. Grand Rapids: Eerdmans, 1969.

Whybray, R. N. *Thanksgiving for a Liberated Prophet: An Interpretation of Isaiah 53.* Journal for the Study of the Old Testament 4. Sheffield: Department of Biblical Studies, University of Sheffield, 1978.

Wiseman, D. J. *Nebuchadrezzar and Babylon.* Oxford: British Academy, 1985.

Wright, D. P. *The Disposal of Impurity: Elimination Rites in the Bible and in Hittite and Mesopotamian Literature.* Atlanta: Scholars Press, 1987.

———. "Holiness in Leviticus and Beyond: Differing Perspectives." *Interpretation* 35 (1999) 351–64.

Wright, D. P., and R. N. Jones. "The Gesture of Hand Placement in the Hebrew Bible and in Hittite Literature." *Journal of the American Oriental Society* 106 (1986), 433–46.

Yadin Y. "The First Temple." In *Sefer Yerushalayim.* Edited by M. Avi-Yonah, 176–90. Jerusalem: Bialik Institute, 1956 (Hebrew).

———. *The Temple Scroll, Vol. 1.* Jerusalem: Israel Publication Society, 1983.

Yadin, Y. and N. Avigad. *A Genesis Apocryphon: A Scroll from the Wilderness of Judaea.* Jerusalem: Magnes Press of the Hebrew University and Heikhal Ha-Sefer, 1956.

Zeitlin, S. "The Titles High Priest and the Nasi of the Sanhedrin." *Jewish Quarterly Review* 48 (1957) 1–5.

Zimmerli, W. *Ezekiel 2.* Translated by R. E. Clements. Philadelphia: Fortress, 1983.

# Biblical Reference Index

## OLD TESTAMENT

### Genesis

| | |
|---|---|
| 1:20–21 | 232 |
| 1:26 | 18 |
| 1:28 | 18 |
| 2:8 | 230 |
| 2:10 | 230 |
| 3:22 | 264 |
| 4:23–24 | 264 |
| 6:11 | 182, 193 |
| 6:13 | 182, 193 |
| 6:1–7 | 264 |
| 7:11 | 62 |
| 7:14 | 18 |
| 7:21 | 18 |
| 7:23 | 18 |
| 8:4 | 62 |
| 8:5 | 62 |
| 8:13 | 62 |
| 8:14 | 62 |
| 8:17 | 18 |
| 8:21 | 50, 264 |
| 9:1–6 | 264 |
| 10:2–3 | 10 |
| 10:2 | 3, 7 |
| 10:3 | 3 |
| 11:1–9 | 264 |
| 13:10 | 196, 229 |
| 16:14 | 235 |
| 16:20 | 235 |
| 17 | 140 |
| 17:20 | 173 |
| 18:19 | 264 |
| 19:1–24 | 233 |
| 19:19 | 106 |
| 19:24 | 19 |
| 25:16 | 173 |
| 26:3 | 237 |
| 27:2 | 18 |
| 46:2 | 64 |
| 48:5 | 237 |
| 49:1 | 11 |
| 49:13 | 223 |
| 50:24 | 237 |

### Exodus

| | |
|---|---|
| 2:13 | 202 |
| 6:8 | 237 |
| 10:9 | 207 |
| 12:1–14 | 202 |
| 12:1–13 | 207 |
| 12:1 | 31 |
| 12:2 | 62 |
| 12:3–6 | 203, 208, 209 |
| 12:3–5 | 63 |
| 12:3 | 63, 206 |
| 12:5 | 206 |
| 12:7 | 121 |
| 12:14 | 199, 207 |
| 12:15 | 203, 207, 208 |
| 12:17 | 207 |
| 12:19–20 | 203, 208 |
| 12:19 | 245 |
| 12:22–27 | 207 |
| 12:22 | 121 |
| 12:28 | 207 |
| 12:43 | 124 |
| 12:48–49 | 244 |
| 12:48 | 244, 245 |
| 13:5 | 237 |
| 13:6 | 199, 206, 207 |
| 13:7 | 190, 203, 208, 245 |
| 13:11 | 237 |
| 14:2–4 | 6 |
| 14:8 | 6 |
| 14:17–18 | 6 |
| 15:9 | 252 |
| 16:1 | 62 |

## Biblical Reference Index

### Exodus (cont.)

| | |
|---|---|
| 18:13–25 | 248 |
| 19–24 | 60 |
| 19:1 | 62 |
| 19:3 | 61 |
| 20:21 | 121 |
| 20:22—23:33 | 124 |
| 20:22–23 | 124 |
| 20:26 | 122, 215 |
| 21–23 | 218 |
| 21:12–15 | 60 |
| 21:17 | 181 |
| 21:18–27 | 60 |
| 21:21 | 181 |
| 22:30 | 184, 186 |
| 23:12 | 244 |
| 23:16 | 57 |
| 23:17 | 207 |
| 24:1–11 | 61 |
| 24:3 | 215 |
| 24:6–11 | 215 |
| 24:6 | 217 |
| 24:9–15 | 171 |
| 24:12–18 | 61 |
| 24:12 | 61 |
| 25–10 | 215 |
| 25–Leviticus 7 | 115 |
| 25–40 | 60 |
| 25:1—40:38 | 61 |
| 25:1–40 | 61 |
| 25:1–30 | 215 |
| 25:9 | 65 |
| 25:22 | 47, 262 |
| 25:23–30 | 48, 95 |
| 25:23–29 | 41 |
| 25:25 | 96 |
| 25:29–30 | 42 |
| 25:29 | 225 |
| 25:30 | 41 |
| 25:41 | 50 |
| 26:23 | 223 |
| 26:27 | 223 |
| 27:2 | 120 |
| 27:21 | 168 |
| 28:17–21 | 259 |
| 28:28 | 61 |
| 28:30 | 51 |
| 28:35 | 181 |
| 28:38 | 150 |
| 28:42 | 33 |
| 28:43 | 150, 180, 181 |
| 29 | 214 |
| 29:15–18 | 202 |
| 29:18 | 50 |
| 29:20 | 121, 149 |
| 29:21 | 205 |
| 29:22 | 130 |
| 29:26 | 130 |
| 29:27 | 130 |
| 29:28 | 179 |
| 29:31 | 130 |
| 29:31–37 | 215 |
| 29:35–37 | 128 |
| 29:35 | 202 |
| 29:36–37 | 124 |
| 29:36 | 127, 202, 217 |
| 29:37 | 202 |
| 29:42 | 214 |
| 30:2 | 120 |
| 30:7 | 168 |
| 30:8 | 168 |
| 30:10 | 168 |
| 30:15 | 200, 200 |
| 30:17 | 44 |
| 30:20–21 | 44 |
| 30:20 | 180, 181 |
| 30:22–33 | 125 |
| 30:28–29 | 125 |
| 31:3 | 34 |
| 31:4 | 12 |
| 31:13 | 165 |
| 32 | 215 |
| 32:5 | 207 |
| 33:1 | 237 |
| 34:15–16 | 107, 109 |
| 34:22 | 57 |
| 34:23 | 207 |
| 34:25 | 199 |
| 35–40 | 104 |
| 35:12–13 | 95 |
| 35:27 | 198, 252 |
| 35:32 | 12 |
| 35:33 | 12 |
| 35:35 | 12 |
| 36:28 | 223 |
| 36:32 | 223 |
| 37:10–16 | 42, 95 |
| 39:28 | 33 |
| 40 | 115 |
| 40:2 | 62 |

## Exodus (cont.)

| | |
|---|---|
| 40:4 | 42 |
| 40:10 | 124 |
| 40:11 | 3 |
| 40:17 | 62 |
| 40:22 | 42 |
| 40:32 | 180, 181 |
| 40:34–38 | 30, 61, 104, 215 |
| 40:34–35 | 104 |
| 40:34 | 104 |
| 40:35 | 106 |

Leviticus 1:1–Numbers 10:28

61

## Leviticus

| | |
|---|---|
| | 218 |
| 1 | 77 |
| 1:1–13 | 77 |
| 1:4 | 79, 200 |
| 1:5 | 50, 77, 154, 157, 159, 171 |
| 1:6 | 154, 157 |
| 1:9 | 77, 154, 157 |
| 1:10 | 171 |
| 1:11 | 50, 159 |
| 1:12 | 77 |
| 1:16 | 77 |
| 2 | 224, 225 |
| 2:1–3 | 185 |
| 2:9 | 190 |
| 2:12 | 106 |
| 2:13 | 130 |
| 3 | 77 |
| 3:2 | 50, 154, 171 |
| 3:5 | 50 |
| 3:8 | 50, 171 |
| 3:13 | 171 |
| 3:16 | 50 |
| 4 | 77, 129, 131, 169, 215 |
| 4:1–5 | 224 |
| 4:1—5:13 | 225 |
| 4:2 | 44, 78, 115, 203, 245 |
| 4:3–20 | 205 |
| 4:5 | 200 |
| 4:12 | 44, 115, 129 |
| 4:13–21 | 128 |
| 4:13 | 44, 78, 245 |
| 4:14 | 128 |
| 4:18 | 200 |
| 4:21 | 129 |
| 4:22–26 | 108 |
| 4:22 | 44, 78, 109, 115, 245 |
| 4:25–26 | 43 |
| 4:25 | 55, 200 |
| 4:27 | 44, 78, 115, 245 |
| 4:30 | 200 |
| 4:34 | 200 |
| 5 | 77, 169, 201 |
| 5:1 | 150 |
| 5:2–5 | 44 |
| 5:4 | 78 |
| 5:5 | 78 |
| 5:6 | 150 |
| 5:7–11 | 186 |
| 5:11 | 210 |
| 5:14–26 | 224 |
| 5:14–16 | 43 |
| 5:15 | 44, 115 |
| 5:17 | 44, 78, 150 |
| 5:18 | 44 |
| 5:20–26 | 44, 78 |
| 5:23 | 44 |
| 5:24 | 44 |
| 5:26 | 78 |
| 6:13 | 33 |
| 6:19 | 43, 185, 225 |
| 6:20 | 179 |
| 6:23 | 200 |
| 6:27 | 179 |
| 7:2 | 129 |
| 7:7 | 43 |
| 7:8 | 80, 154 |
| 7:10 | 234 |
| 7:11–15 | 160 |
| 7:15–21 | 56 |
| 7:16–18 | 159 |
| 7:18 | 150 |
| 7:19–21 | 171 |
| 7:24–25 | 186 |
| 7:30–36 | 160 |
| 8 | 124, 129, 217 |
| 8:10 | 194 |
| 8:11 | 121 |
| 8:14–17 | 127 |
| 8:15 | 66, 130 |
| 8:18–21 | 202 |
| 8:22 | 130 |
| 8:23–24 | 121 |
| 8:23 | 122, 149 |

## Biblical Reference Index

### Leviticus (cont.)

| Reference | Page(s) |
|---|---|
| 8:29 | 130 |
| 8:30 | 205 |
| 8:33 | 202 |
| 8:34 | 200 |
| 8:35 | 156 |
| 9:2–7 | 104 |
| 9:4 | 105 |
| 9:5 | 105, 138 |
| 9:24 | 104, 105, 131 |
| 10:9 | 179, 180 |
| 10:10–11 | 215 |
| 10:10 | 102, 182, 242 |
| 10:11 | 182 |
| 10:17 | 150, 200 |
| 11:10 | 51 |
| 11:24 | 107 |
| 12–15 | 131 |
| 12 | 78 |
| 12:6 | 204 |
| 12:8 | 204 |
| 13–14 | 116 |
| 13 | 129 |
| 14 | 116 |
| 14:1–32 | 203 |
| 14:14–17 | 121 |
| 14:19 | 204 |
| 14:21 | 210 |
| 14:25–28 | 121 |
| 14:31 | 204, 210 |
| 14:54–57 | 116 |
| 14:54–55 | 116 |
| 14:54 | 116 |
| 14:55 | 116 |
| 14:56 | 116 |
| 14:57 | 116 |
| 15 | 78, 129, 203 |
| 15:13 | 183 |
| 15:14–15 | 183 |
| 15:14 | 183 |
| 15:28 | 183 |
| 15:29 | 183 |
| 15:31 | 109 |
| 15:39 | 107 |
| 16 | 63, 169, 201, 205, 215 |
| 16:4 | 33 |
| 16:5 | 200 |
| 16:6 | 199, 206 |
| 16:11 | 199, 206 |
| 16:12–20 | 104 |
| 16:12–16 | 168, 205 |
| 16:13–17 | 200 |
| 16:14–16 | 83 |
| 16:14 | 200 |
| 16:15–19 | 205 |
| 16:16 | 203 |
| 16:17 | 199 |
| 16:18–19 | 124, 200 |
| 16:18 | 55 |
| 16:21 | 203 |
| 16:24 | 199 |
| 16:32 | 199 |
| 17–26 | 124 |
| 17:1–9 | 124 |
| 17:3–5 | 56, 129 |
| 17:7 | 107 |
| 17:8–9 | 141 |
| 17:11 | 58, 197 |
| 17:15–16 | 186, 245 |
| 17:16 | 150 |
| 18:4 | 166 |
| 18:5 | 166 |
| 18:21 | 107, 166 |
| 18:22 | 25 |
| 18:25 | 109, 173 |
| 18:26 | 166 |
| 18:27 | 109 |
| 18:28 | 173 |
| 18:30 | 156 |
| 19:2 | 204 |
| 19:3 | 165 |
| 19:5–8 | 159 |
| 19:8 | 107, 109, 150 |
| 19:10 | 179, 244 |
| 19:12 | 107, 109 |
| 19:17 | 150 |
| 19:18 | 109 |
| 19:21 | 109 |
| 19:23–25 | 141 |
| 19:26–28 | 204 |
| 19:29 | 107 |
| 19:30 | 165 |
| 19:31 | 204 |
| 19:36 | 195 |
| 19:37 | 166 |
| 20:1–6 | 204 |
| 20:2 | 25 |
| 20:3 | 107, 109 |
| 20:4 | 25 |

## Leviticus (cont.)

| | |
|---|---|
| 20:5 | 107 |
| 20:6 | 107 |
| 20:8 | 204 |
| 20:17 | 150 |
| 20:19 | 150 |
| 20:22 | 166 |
| 21 | 218 |
| 21:1–3 | 183 |
| 21:2 | 183 |
| 21:5 | 109 |
| 21:6 | 107 |
| 21:7 | 218 |
| 21:8 | 204 |
| 21:10–12 | 183 |
| 21:10 | 179, 218 |
| 21:11–12 | 183 |
| 21:13–15 | 182 |
| 21:13 | 182 |
| 21:14 | 58, 204, 218 |
| 21:15 | 204 |
| 21:17 | 181 |
| 21:18 | 181 |
| 21:21 | 181 |
| 21:22 | 147 |
| 21:23 | 181, 204 |
| 21:24 | 140 |
| 22:2 | 109 |
| 22:8–9 | 186 |
| 22:9 | 156, 204 |
| 22:17–25 | 244 |
| 22:18 | 141 |
| 22:25 | 141 |
| 22:31–32 | 21 |
| 22:32 | 109, 204 |
| 23 | 217 |
| 23:3 | 182 |
| 23:5 | 62, 202, 206 |
| 23:6 | 207 |
| 23:19 | 212 |
| 23:21 | 57 |
| 23:22 | 244 |
| 23:23–25 | 57 |
| 23:24 | 62 |
| 23:26–32 | 63 |
| 23:27 | 62 |
| 23:33–43 | 217 |
| 23:39 | 62 |
| 23:41 | 62 |
| 24:3 | 168 |
| 24:8–9 | 51 |
| 24:8 | 41, 168 |
| 24:10 | 154 |
| 24:22 | 244 |
| 25 | 221 |
| 25:6 | 244 |
| 25:8 | 60 |
| 25:9 | 62 |
| 25:10–13 | 237 |
| 25:10 | 220, 222 |
| 25:18 | 11, 166 |
| 25:19 | 11 |
| 25:25–26 | 153 |
| 25:25 | 243 |
| 25:26 | 210 |
| 25:29 | 22 |
| 25:32–34 | 260 |
| 25:33–34 | 192 |
| 25:39–42 | 236 |
| 25:39–40 | 221 |
| 25:40 | 234 |
| 25:44–46 | 236, 244 |
| 25:45 | 244 |
| 25:47 | 244 |
| 25:49 | 210 |
| 26 | 110 |
| 26:1 | 155 |
| 26:2 | 165 |
| 26:4 | 141 |
| 26:5 | 11 |
| 26:6 | 6, 28 |
| 26:12 | 109, 262 |
| 26:15 | 166 |
| 26:40–42 | 32 |
| 26:40–41 | 163 |
| 27:8 | 210 |
| 27:10 | 254 |
| 27:15–16 | 186 |
| 27:28–29 | 185 |
| 27:33 | 254 |

## Numbers

| | |
|---|---|
| 1–10 | 218 |
| 1:1 | 62 |
| 1:2 | 9 |
| 1:18 | 62 |
| 1:44 | 9 |
| 1:53 | 215 |

## Biblical Reference Index

### Numbers (cont.)

| | |
|---|---|
| 2 | 259, 261 |
| 2:3 | 108, 248 |
| 3–4 | 261 |
| 3:7 | 141, 157 |
| 3:32 | 146 |
| 4:5–8 | 42 |
| 4:7–8 | 42 |
| 4:7 | 42, 95 |
| 4:9–14 | 42 |
| 4:34 | 9 |
| 4:46 | 9 |
| 5:17 | 72 |
| 5:31 | 150 |
| 6:10–11 | 204 |
| 6:18–19 | 226 |
| 6:22–27 | 162 |
| 6:25–26 | 31 |
| 6:27 | 210 |
| 7:2 | 109 |
| 7:3 | 109 |
| 7:10 | 109 |
| 7:11 | 109, 248 |
| 7:18 | 109 |
| 7:24 | 248 |
| 7:30 | 248 |
| 7:84–88 | 116 |
| 7:84 | 116 |
| 7:88 | 116 |
| 7:89 | 47, 51, 215, 217 |
| 8:2–3 | 168 |
| 8:9 | 177 |
| 8:16 | 187 |
| 8:19 | 187 |
| 9:1 | 62 |
| 9:3 | 208 |
| 9:6–14 | 201 |
| 9:6–7 | 245 |
| 9:9–14 | 203, 206 |
| 9:11 | 62 |
| 9:13–14 | 245 |
| 9:14 | 244 |
| 9:19 | 156 |
| 9:23 | 156 |
| 10:10 | 216 |
| 10:11 | 62 |
| 10:29 | 244 |
| 11:24–25 | 171 |
| 11:26 | 3 |
| 11:29 | 35, 37 |
| 14:30 | 237 |
| 14:33 | 109 |
| 14:34 | 150 |
| 15 | 201 |
| 15:2–12 | 57 |
| 15:3 | 154, 213 |
| 15:4–5 | 56 |
| 15:5 | 154, 199 |
| 15:7 | 199 |
| 15:8 | 213 |
| 15:10 | 199 |
| 15:14–16 | 244 |
| 15:14 | 141 |
| 15:15 | 244 |
| 15:19–20 | 252 |
| 15:19 | 189 |
| 15:22–26 | 128 |
| 15:24 | 128 |
| 15:26 | 245 |
| 15:29–30 | 244 |
| 15:30–31 | 141 |
| 15:38 | 61 |
| 15:39 | 107, 109 |
| 16–18 | 137, 141 |
| 16–17 | 186 |
| 16:3 | 136, 137, 139 |
| 16:5 | 76 |
| 16:6 | 146 |
| 16:7 | 136, 137, 139 |
| 16:9 | 136, 137, 152, 154, 155, 156, 157, 159, 160 |
| 16:10 | 151 |
| 16:14 | 185 |
| 16:35 | 152 |
| 17:5 | 136, 137 |
| 17:25 | 136, 137 |
| 18 | 136, 153 |
| 18:1–7 | 147, 150, 155, 186 |
| 18:1–4 | 138 |
| 18:1 | 136, 137, 138, 146, 150, 155 |
| 18:2 | 136, 137, 138, 177 |
| 18:3–5 | 151 |
| 18:3–4 | 137 |
| 18:3 | 136, 137, 138, 141, 146, 147, 150, 151, 152, 153, 155, 162, 186 |
| 18:4 | 136, 137, 138, 140, 150, 152, 153, 162 |
| 18:5 | 81, 119, 141, 143, 147, 148, 150, 152 |

## Numbers (cont.)

| | |
|---|---|
| 18:6 | 155 |
| 18:7 | 136, 137, 150, 152, 156 |
| 18:8 | 136, 137, 156 |
| 18:9 | 136, 137 |
| 18:11–13 | 136, 137 |
| 18:14 | 136, 137 |
| 18:20 | 59, 136, 137, 144, 151, 260 |
| 18:21–24 | 146 |
| 18:21 | 185 |
| 18:22–23 | 136, 137, 138, 155, 156 |
| 18:22 | 137, 138, 155, 160 |
| 18:23–24 | 59 |
| 18:23 | 150, 151, 152, 155, 185 |
| 18:24 | 59, 151, 185 |
| 19:11–22 | 25 |
| 19:12 | 200 |
| 19:13 | 129, 200 |
| 19:16 | 25 |
| 19:17–19 | 204, 206, 218 |
| 19:19 | 58 |
| 19:20 | 129, 200 |
| 20:1 | 62 |
| 20:2 | 190 |
| 20:22–29 | 241 |
| 21:13 | 117 |
| 21:23 | 117 |
| 22:4 | 31 |
| 23:17 | 207 |
| 24:14 | 11, 173, 248 |
| 26:7 | 185 |
| 26:53 | 185 |
| 26:54 | 185 |
| 26:56 | 185 |
| 26:62 | 185 |
| 27–36 | 214 |
| 27:1–3 | 153 |
| 27:4 | 185 |
| 27:7 | 185 |
| 27:8 | 185 |
| 27:9 | 185 |
| 27:10 | 185 |
| 27:11 | 185 |
| 27:12 | 24 |
| 27:14 | 235, 242 |
| 27:21 | 51 |
| 28–29 | 198, 202 |
| 28:2 | 213 |
| 28:3–8 | 56, 214 |
| 28:4 | 213 |
| 28:8 | 213 |
| 28:9–15 | 219 |
| 28:9–10 | 211 |
| 28:9 | 56 |
| 28:11–15 | 56 |
| 28:11–13 | 212 |
| 28:13–14 | 219 |
| 28:14 | 199 |
| 28:16–25 | 202 |
| 28:16 | 62, 206, 206, 208 |
| 28:17–25 | 206 |
| 28:17–23 | 208 |
| 28:19–24 | 57 |
| 28:26 | 57 |
| 28:29 | 214 |
| 29:1 | 57, 62 |
| 29:7 | 54, 62 |
| 29:12 | 62 |
| 29:12–34 | 5 |
| 29:13–34 | 57 |
| 30:11–17 | 181 |
| 30:15 | 150 |
| 31:20 | 200 |
| 31:23 | 200 |
| 32 | 214 |
| 32:5 | 185 |
| 32:11 | 237 |
| 32:18 | 185 |
| 32:22 | 185 |
| 32:28 | 185 |
| 32:29 | 185 |
| 32:32 | 185 |
| 33:3 | 62 |
| 33:8 | 241 |
| 33:38 | 62 |
| 33:50–56 | 189 |
| 33:54 | 185, 234, 238 |
| 34–35 | 214 |
| 34:1—35:34 | 61 |
| 34 | 64, 236, 237, 249 |
| 34:1–15 | 229 |
| 34:2 | 185 |
| 34:4 | 258 |
| 34:7–9 | 239, 240 |
| 34:7 | 241 |
| 34:10–12 | 242 |
| 34:13 | 238 |
| 34:15 | 237 |
| 34:18–28 | 222 |

*Biblical Reference Index*

## Numbers (cont.)

| | |
|---|---|
| 34:18 | 222, 247 |
| 35:1–8 | 192, 214 |
| 35:2 | 185 |
| 35:8 | 185 |
| 35:15 | 244 |
| 35:16–25 | 199 |
| 35:16–18 | 203 |
| 35:22–23 | 203 |
| 35:28 | 185 |
| 35:34 | 109, 173 |
| 35:50–56 | 214 |
| 36 | 214 |
| 36:1 | 153 |
| 36:2 | 185 |
| 36:3 | 185 |
| 36:4 | 185 |
| 36:7 | 185 |
| 36:8 | 185 |
| 36:9 | 185 |
| 36:12 | 185 |

## Deuteronomy

| | |
|---|---|
| 1:8 | 237 |
| 3:5 | 13 |
| 4:1 | 166 |
| 4:5 | 166 |
| 4:6 | 115 |
| 4:8 | 166 |
| 4:14 | 166 |
| 4:30 | 11 |
| 4:31 | 32 |
| 5:1 | 166 |
| 6:10 | 237 |
| 7:13 | 145 |
| 10:8 | 161 |
| 10:16 | 141 |
| 11:32 | 166 |
| 12–26 | 218 |
| 12:1–26:15 | 124 |
| 12:1–27 | 124 |
| 12:1 | 166 |
| 12:7 | 28 |
| 12:18 | 28 |
| 14:21 | 184, 186 |
| 14:22–23 | 59 |
| 14:23 | 28 |
| 14:26 | 28 |
| 15:20 | 28 |
| 16:2 | 206 |
| 16:10 | 57 |
| 16:11 | 207 |
| 16:14 | 207 |
| 16:16 | 207 |
| 17:11 | 182 |
| 17:18 | 161, 164 |
| 17:8–11 | 144 |
| 17:9 | 161, 164, 182, 194 |
| 18:1–6 | 144 |
| 18:1–2 | 59 |
| 18:1 | 144, 145, 161, 162, 164 |
| 18:2 | 184, 260 |
| 18:5 | 161 |
| 18:6 | 244 |
| 18:10 | 166 |
| 18:14 | 214 |
| 18:15 | 60 |
| 19:5–6 | 199 |
| 20:1 | 27 |
| 21:5 | 161, 164 |
| 21:22–23 | 24 |
| 24:8 | 161, 162, 164, 182 |
| 24:14–15 | 244 |
| 25:13–16 | 195 |
| 26:12 | 162 |
| 26:13 | 162 |
| 27:6–7 | 213 |
| 27:7 | 28 |
| 27:9 | 161, 164 |
| 27:15 | 145 |
| 28:32 | 187 |
| 29:16 | 166 |
| 30:6 | 141 |
| 31:9 | 164 |
| 31:29 | 11 |
| 32:9 | 234 |
| 32:15 | 242 |
| 32:48–52 | 61 |
| 32:49 | 215, 217 |
| 32:51 | 235 |
| 32:52 | 215, 217 |
| 34 | 60 |
| 34:1–4 | 215 |
| 34:3 | 235 |
| 34:27 | 91 |

## Joshua

| | |
|---|---|
| 3:3 | 161 |
| 4:19 | 63 |

## Joshua (cont.)

| | |
|---|---|
| 6:3 | 73 |
| 6:20 | 4 |
| 8:33 | 161 |
| 9:18–21 | 222 |
| 9:27 | 140, 256 |
| 11:4 | 27 |
| 11:17 | 242 |
| 12:7 | 242 |
| 12:9–24 | 246, 258 |
| 13–19 | 248 |
| 13:2 | 232 |
| 13:5 | 234 |
| 13:14 | 184, 185, 234 |
| 15:21 | 152 |
| 17:1–18 | 238 |
| 17:4 | 222 |
| 18:6 | 189 |
| 18:8 | 189 |
| 18:10 | 189 |
| 18:11–28 | 238 |
| 18:24 | 13 |
| 18:28 | 250 |
| 19:1–9 | 238 |
| 20:32 | 202 |
| 21 | 189, 192 |
| 21:4 | 189 |
| 21:9–19 | 189 |
| 21:13–16 | 59 |
| 22 | 185, 242 |
| 22:4 | 185 |
| 22:8–9 | 252 |
| 22:9 | 185 |
| 22:10–11 | 232 |
| 22:18 | 185 |
| 22:19 | 185, 242, 248 |
| 22:26 | 154 |
| 22:28 | 154 |
| 22:29 | 154 |
| 22:32 | 222 |
| 23:1 | 11 |

## Judges

| | |
|---|---|
| 13:11 | 18 |
| 13:14 | 180 |
| 14:10 | 180 |
| 16:22 | 61 |
| 17:7 | 244 |
| 18 | 248 |
| 19:1 | 244 |
| 20:24–25 | 202 |
| 21:19 | 207 |

## 1 Samuel

| | |
|---|---|
| 1 | 181 |
| 1:3 | 181 |
| 1:13–15 | 180 |
| 1:17 | 181 |
| 1:29–30 | 111 |
| 2:13–14 | 226 |
| 2:19 | 181 |
| 2:27–36 | 144 |
| 6:18 | 13 |
| 6:28 | 13 |
| 8:14 | 194, 221 |
| 10:24 | 216 |
| 11:6 | 34 |
| 11:7 | 190 |
| 14:32–34 | 199 |
| 20:5 | 216 |
| 20:18 | 216 |
| 22:7 | 172, 173, 193, 221 |
| 26:21 | 199, 203 |
| 30:16 | 207 |
| 30:21–30 | 248 |

## 2 Samuel

| | |
|---|---|
| 2:20 | 18 |
| 4:23 | 211 |
| 5:4–9 | 250 |
| 5:14–26 | 225 |
| 7:5 | 18 |
| 8:17 | 144 |
| 9:2 | 18 |
| 10:12 | 155 |
| 14:14 | 12 |
| 15:3–4 | 194 |
| 15:16 | 144 |
| 15:35 | 144 |
| 15:39 | 144 |
| 19:22 | 144 |
| 20:15 | 254 |
| 20:17 | 18 |
| 20:25 | 144 |
| 23:20 | 120 |

## Biblical Reference Index

### 1 Kings

| | |
|---|---:|
| 1:7 | 144 |
| 1:8 | 144 |
| 2:26–27 | 144 |
| 3:16–17 | 194 |
| 4:2 | 144 |
| 4:7–19 | 248 |
| 5:10 | 18 |
| 6–8 | 65 |
| 6–7 | 84 |
| 6:4 | 69, 71 |
| 6:5 | 87 |
| 6:6 | 88, 89 |
| 6:8 | 230 |
| 6:10–11 | 104 |
| 6:20–36 | 94 |
| 6:29 | 69 |
| 6:34 | 96 |
| 7:6 | 97 |
| 7:19 | 230 |
| 7:21 | 231 |
| 7:23–26 | 44 |
| 7:38–39 | 44 |
| 8:5 | 154 |
| 8:6–9 | 262 |
| 8:10–12 | 31 |
| 8:10 | 106 |
| 8:11 | 262 |
| 8:54 | 104 |
| 8:63 | 54 |
| 8:64 | 168 |
| 8:65 | 129, 239, 241 |
| 9:20 | 148 |
| 11:5 | 166 |
| 11:7 | 166 |
| 11:11 | 140 |
| 11:30–31 | 249 |
| 11:34 | 173, 222 |
| 13:2 | 142 |
| 13:14 | 18 |
| 14:10 | 155 |
| 18:7 | 18 |
| 18:17 | 18 |
| 18:29 | 56, 213 |
| 18:36 | 56, 213 |
| 20:1 | 27 |
| 20:30 | 4 |
| 21 | 194 |
| 21:23 | 254 |
| 22:22 | 34 |

### 2 Kings

| | |
|---|---:|
| 4:23 | 216 |
| 4:38 | 76 |
| 5:2 | 64 |
| 5:4 | 64 |
| 5:12 | 241 |
| 5:17 | 154 |
| 10:24 | 146, 151 |
| 11:2–18 | 263 |
| 11:4–8 | 140 |
| 11:4 | 148 |
| 11:5–6 | 198 |
| 11:6 | 152 |
| 11:11 | 230 |
| 11:15 | 263 |
| 12:11 | 59 |
| 12:22 | 177 |
| 14:13 | 258, 259 |
| 14:20 | 177 |
| 14:25 | 239, 241 |
| 16:7 | 62 |
| 16:10 | 62 |
| 16:12–14 | 54 |
| 16:12–13 | 168 |
| 16:15 | 56, 213 |
| 17:24 | 242 |
| 17:29 | 226 |
| 18:8 | 190 |
| 21:7 | 169 |
| 21:13 | 231 |
| 21:18 | 110, 111 |
| 21:26 | 107, 110, 111 |
| 22:4 | 59 |
| 22:8 | 59 |
| 22:10 | 59 |
| 23:6–16 | 156 |
| 23:9 | 145 |
| 23:13 | 166 |
| 23:17 | 25 |
| 23:20 | 142 |
| 23:24 | 59, 166 |
| 25:1 | 62 |
| 25:18 | 168 |
| 25:25 | 62 |
| 25:28 | 177 |

### Isaiah

| | |
|---|---:|
| 1:4 | 21 |
| 1:13 | 211 |
| 1:26 | 108 |

## Isaiah (cont.)

| | |
|---|---|
| 2:1–4 | 263 |
| 2:2 | 11 |
| 2:12 | 19 |
| 2:15 | 17 |
| 4:12 | 112 |
| 5:11 | 12 |
| 5:19 | 21 |
| 5:24 | 21 |
| 6:1 | 108 |
| 8:8 | 85 |
| 9:3 | 22 |
| 9:4 | 23, 155 |
| 9:11 | 91 |
| 10 | 16 |
| 10:1 | 108 |
| 10:3 | 12 |
| 10:20 | 21 |
| 10:28 | 8 |
| 11:11 | 242 |
| 12:6 | 21 |
| 13:3 | 250 |
| 14:1 | 246 |
| 14:18 | 111 |
| 14:25 | 4 |
| 14:35 | 19 |
| 15:3 | 232 |
| 17:7 | 21 |
| 22:11 | 88, 228 |
| 25:12 | 228 |
| 28:7 | 179 |
| 28:20 | 33 |
| 29:11–12 | 115 |
| 29:1–2 | 118 |
| 29:11 | 120 |
| 29:19 | 21 |
| 30:11 | 21 |
| 30:12 | 21 |
| 30:14 | 228 |
| 30:15 | 12, 21 |
| 31:1 | 21 |
| 33:15 | 69 |
| 33:21 | 233 |
| 33:24 | 150 |
| 34:6–7 | 28 |
| 34:6 | 28 |
| 34:11 | 231 |
| 34:17 | 231 |
| 37:23 | 21 |
| 41:14 | 21 |
| 41:16 | 21 |
| 43:3 | 21 |
| 43:14 | 21 |
| 44:3 | 34 |
| 44:13 | 231 |
| 45:10 | 21 |
| 47:4 | 21 |
| 48:9 | 107 |
| 48:11 | 107 |
| 48:17 | 21 |
| 52:5 | 107 |
| 54:5 | 21 |
| 54:8 | 33 |
| 54:13 | 263 |
| 55:5 | 21 |
| 56:6–9 | 236 |
| 56:7 | 246 |
| 57:5 | 145 |
| 59:13 | 33 |
| 60:9 | 21 |
| 60:13 | 109 |
| 60:14 | 21 |
| 62:2 | 261 |
| 65:3–4 | 111 |
| 66:1 | 106, 108 |
| 66:17 | 111 |
| 66:23 | 211 |

## Jeremiah

| | |
|---|---|
| 1–6 | 4 |
| 1:13–14 | 11 |
| 2:23 | 25 |
| 3:16–17 | 108 |
| 3:17 | 108 |
| 4–6 | 18 |
| 4:1 | 166 |
| 4:6–17 | 11 |
| 6:1–30 | 11 |
| 6:7 | 193 |
| 6:22 | 18 |
| 7:16–19 | 168 |
| 7:18 | 145 |
| 7:20 | 17 |
| 7:22 | 154 |
| 7:30 | 166 |
| 10:22–25 | 4 |
| 11:9–13 | 168 |
| 11:19 | 12 |

## Jeremiah (cont.)

| | |
|---|---:|
| 13:20–27 | 4 |
| 13:27 | 166 |
| 14:6 | 11 |
| 15:16 | 222 |
| 16:18 | 166 |
| 17:8 | 233 |
| 17:19 | 258 |
| 17:28 | 154 |
| 18:11 | 12 |
| 18:18 | 12 |
| 18:30 | 11 |
| 19:2 | 258 |
| 19:13 | 145 |
| 20:2 | 258, 259 |
| 20:8 | 193 |
| 22:15 | 195, 222 |
| 22:20 | 11, 24 |
| 23:5 | 222 |
| 25:9 | 18 |
| 25:46–51 | 4 |
| 26:15 | 187 |
| 29:11 | 12 |
| 30:24 | 11 |
| 31:31–34 | 36 |
| 31:37 | 258 |
| 31:39 | 231, 258 |
| 32:31 | 17 |
| 32:34 | 166 |
| 32:39–40 | 35 |
| 32:39 | 145 |
| 33:5 | 17 |
| 33:18 | 161 |
| 34:8 | 220 |
| 34:15–16 | 107 |
| 34:15 | 220 |
| 35:4 | 73 |
| 36:9–26 | 109 |
| 36:10 | 73 |
| 37:13 | 258 |
| 38:7 | 258 |
| 38:21 | 228 |
| 39:3 | 258 |
| 39:5 | 242 |
| 42:18 | 17 |
| 44:17–18 | 145 |
| 44:25 | 145 |
| 46:9 | 10 |
| 46:10 | 28 |
| 46:14 | 11 |
| 48:34 | 232 |
| 48:47 | 11 |
| 49:20 | 12 |
| 49:30–31 | 13 |
| 49:30 | 11, 12 |
| 52:7 | 258 |
| 52:24 | 9 |

## Ezekiel

| | |
|---|---:|
| 1–39 | 108, 170 |
| 1–11 | 6 |
| 1 | 48, 94, 229 |
| 1:1 | 61, 64, 103 |
| 1:3 | 64 |
| 1:4—3:11 | 114 |
| 1:4 | 114 |
| 1:7 | 65 |
| 1:24 | 103, 105, 106 |
| 2:1—3:21 | 217 |
| 2:3 | 64 |
| 2:5 | 170 |
| 2:6 | 170 |
| 2:7 | 139 |
| 2:8 | 170 |
| 2:25 | 165 |
| 3:6 | 132 |
| 3:9 | 170 |
| 3:12 | 117 |
| 3:16–21 | 151 |
| 3:22 | 64 |
| 3:26 | 170 |
| 3:29 | 170 |
| 4 | 245 |
| 4:1–3 | 115 |
| 4:2 | 103 |
| 4:3 | 242 |
| 4:4 | 150 |
| 4:5 | 150 |
| 4:6 | 37, 150 |
| 4:10 | 150 |
| 4:11 | 117 |
| 4:12 | 155 |
| 4:14 | 117, 186 |
| 4:15 | 155 |
| 5:1 | 33 |
| 5:5 | 117 |
| 5:7–8 | 32 |
| 5:7 | 26 |

## Ezekiel (cont.)

| | |
|---|---|
| 5:8 | 10 |
| 5:10 | 31 |
| 5:11 | 18, 149, 155, 171 |
| 5:15 | 31 |
| 6:2 | 9 |
| 6:3 | 165 |
| 6:4 | 155 |
| 6:8 | 33 |
| 6:9 | 107 |
| 6:24 | 117 |
| 7 | 229 |
| 7:3 | 34 |
| 7:4 | 33 |
| 7:8 | 34 |
| 7:9 | 33, 34 |
| 7:12–14 | 26 |
| 7:19 | 161 |
| 7:20 | 155 |
| 7:27 | 25, 197 |
| 7:28 | 34 |
| 8–11 | 31, 169 |
| 8 | 65, 263 |
| 8:1 | 36, 61, 64 |
| 8:3 | 64, 103, 168, 242 |
| 8:4 | 105 |
| 8:5 | 10 |
| 8:6 | 149, 153, 155, 191 |
| 8:7–11 | 172 |
| 8:10 | 72 |
| 8:11 | 33 |
| 8:12 | 32, 145 |
| 8:16 | 91, 242 |
| 8:27 | 107 |
| 9:2 | 65, 103 |
| 9:5 | 33 |
| 9:6 | 149, 172 |
| 9:9 | 32 |
| 9:11 | 149 |
| 10 | 48, 94, 104 |
| 10:1 | 103 |
| 10:3 | 177, 230 |
| 10:12 | 85 |
| 11 | 48 |
| 11:1 | 103, 172 |
| 11:6 | 172 |
| 11:7 | 32 |
| 11:8–10 | 172 |
| 11:9 | 31 |
| 11:10–11 | 117, 190 |
| 11:13 | 172, 263 |
| 11:15–17 | 155 |
| 11:15 | 153 |
| 11:17–21 | 35 |
| 11:17 | 8 |
| 11:18 | 155, 263 |
| 11:23 | 105, 133 |
| 12–17 | 24 |
| 12:2 | 170 |
| 12:3 | 170 |
| 12:8 | 213 |
| 12:9 | 139, 170 |
| 12:14 | 8 |
| 12:16 | 33 |
| 12:18 | 18 |
| 12:19 | 25 |
| 12:25 | 170 |
| 13:1–23 | 36 |
| 13:7 | 170 |
| 13:8 | 10, 170 |
| 13:9 | 36, 170, 263 |
| 13:13 | 32 |
| 13:17–23 | 170 |
| 13:17 | 9 |
| 13:19 | 145, 170 |
| 13:20 | 32 |
| 14 | 263 |
| 14:2 | 31 |
| 14:3 | 161 |
| 14:4 | 161 |
| 14:7 | 161 |
| 14:8 | 170 |
| 14:9 | 170, 263 |
| 14:10 | 146 |
| 14:13 | 31 |
| 14:19 | 34 |
| 15:8 | 31 |
| 16 | 112 |
| 16:4 | 31 |
| 16:5 | 33 |
| 16:16 | 107 |
| 16:17 | 107 |
| 16:24 | 85 |
| 16:26 | 107 |
| 16:28 | 107 |
| 16:29 | 107 |
| 16:30 | 107 |
| 16:31 | 85 |
| 16:34 | 107 |

## Biblical Reference Index

### Ezekiel (cont.)

| Reference | Pages |
|---|---|
| 16:37 | 8 |
| 16:39 | 85 |
| 16:46 | 230 |
| 16:52–54 | 44 |
| 16:52 | 152, 162 |
| 16:53–58 | 33 |
| 16:53–55 | 229 |
| 16:53–54 | 29, 163 |
| 16:54 | 113, 152, 163 |
| 16:61–63 | 44 |
| 16:61 | 113 |
| 16:62 | 152 |
| 16:63 | 152 |
| 17:12 | 139 |
| 17:17 | 7 |
| 17:20 | 19, 31 |
| 17:21 | 8 |
| 18:8 | 31 |
| 18:19 | 252 |
| 18:22 | 156, 220 |
| 18:24 | 31, 252 |
| 18:26 | 252 |
| 18:28 | 252 |
| 18:29 | 252 |
| 18:30 | 161, 263 |
| 18:31 | 263 |
| 19:13 | 34 |
| 20 | 165, 166, 263, 264 |
| 20:1 | 60, 61, 166 |
| 20:2 | 166 |
| 20:3 | 191 |
| 20:5 | 102, 165, 166 |
| 20:6 | 165, 166 |
| 20:7 | 155, 165, 172 |
| 20:8 | 155, 166 |
| 20:9 | 107, 109, 165 |
| 20:11 | 166 |
| 20:12 | 57, 165, 242 |
| 20:13 | 57, 165, 166 |
| 20:14 | 107, 109 |
| 20:15 | 165, 166 |
| 20:16 | 57, 165, 166 |
| 20:17 | 166 |
| 20:18 | 172 |
| 20:19 | 165, 166 |
| 20:20 | 57, 165, 242 |
| 20:21 | 57, 165, 166 |
| 20:22 | 107, 109 |
| 20:23 | 165 |
| 20:24 | 57, 165 |
| 20:25 | 166 |
| 20:26 | 73, 165, 172 |
| 20:27 | 31, 165 |
| 20:28 | 165, 166, 237 |
| 20:29 | 166 |
| 20:30 | 107, 155, 162, 165 |
| 20:31 | 145, 166, 172 |
| 20:32 | 166 |
| 20:33 | 108, 109, 166 |
| 20:34 | 8 |
| 20:35 | 166 |
| 20:37 | 165 |
| 20:38 | 165, 172, 263 |
| 20:39 | 107, 109, 165, 171, 175 |
| 20:41–44 | 60 |
| 20:41 | 8, 165, 166 |
| 20:42 | 165, 238 |
| 20:43 | 112 |
| 20:44 | 165 |
| 21:2 | 149, 235 |
| 21:7 | 9 |
| 21:8 | 10 |
| 21:12 | 22, 117 |
| 21:13 | 34 |
| 21:21 | 34 |
| 21:23 | 117 |
| 21:33–36 | 36 |
| 21:33 | 34 |
| 21:35 | 23 |
| 21:36 | 18 |
| 22:2 | 142 |
| 22:4 | 98 |
| 22:6–12 | 174 |
| 22:7 | 220 |
| 22:8 | 57, 165 |
| 22:19–20 | 8 |
| 22:20 | 17 |
| 22:21 | 18 |
| 22:22–25 | 174 |
| 22:22 | 34, 102 |
| 22:24 | 182 |
| 22:26 | 51, 57, 81, 101, 143, 144, 147, 148, 164, 165, 169, 170, 171, 182, 242, 255 |
| 22:28 | 33 |
| 22:31 | 18, 34 |
| 23:1 | 73 |
| 23:5 | 107 |

## Ezekiel (cont.)

| | |
|---|---|
| 23:6 | 7 |
| 23:7 | 172 |
| 23:12 | 7 |
| 23:14 | 72 |
| 23:17 | 25 |
| 23:19 | 107 |
| 23:21 | 133 |
| 23:22 | 8 |
| 23:24 | 31 |
| 23:30 | 107 |
| 23:32 | 107 |
| 23:36 | 162 |
| 23:38–39 | 117 |
| 23:38 | 57, 149, 165, 168, 172, 191 |
| 23:39 | 54, 149, 191 |
| 23:40–42 | 26 |
| 23:43 | 34, 107 |
| 23:45 | 73 |
| 23:47 | 154 |
| 24:1 | 60, 61 |
| 24:2 | 64, 115 |
| 24:3 | 76 |
| 24:8 | 18 |
| 24:18 | 213 |
| 24:21 | 117, 149 |
| 24:23 | 150 |
| 24:35–36 | 19 |
| 25–32 | 11, 36, 37 |
| 25:2 | 9 |
| 25:3 | 149 |
| 25:11 | 31 |
| 25:12 | 205 |
| 25:14 | 17 |
| 25:16 | 25 |
| 25:18–23 | 215 |
| 25:18–19 | 168 |
| 26:1 | 61 |
| 26:4–5 | 56 |
| 26:4 | 258 |
| 26:5 | 25, 232 |
| 26:7 | 7 |
| 26:9 | 258 |
| 26:10 | 18, 258 |
| 26:12 | 258 |
| 26:14 | 232 |
| 26:15 | 18, 21 |
| 26:16 | 25 |
| 26:17 | 25 |
| 26:18 | 21, 25, 34 |
| 27 | 114 |
| 27:3 | 21, 25, 173 |
| 27:4 | 173 |
| 27:6–7 | 21 |
| 27:6 | 11, 173 |
| 27:9 | 173 |
| 27:10 | 10 |
| 27:12–13 | 13 |
| 27:12 | 173 |
| 27:13 | 10 |
| 27:14 | 11 |
| 27:15–16 | 13 |
| 27:15 | 21 |
| 27:17–18 | 13 |
| 27:17 | 64 |
| 27:21–22 | 13 |
| 27:27 | 173 |
| 27:28 | 18 |
| 27:31 | 173 |
| 27:35 | 21 |
| 28:12 | 112 |
| 28:18 | 149 |
| 28:21 | 9 |
| 28:22 | 31 |
| 28:24 | 31 |
| 28:25 | 8, 237 |
| 29:1 | 60, 61 |
| 29:3 | 10 |
| 29:5 | 8 |
| 29:13 | 8, 37 |
| 29:14 | 33 |
| 29:15 | 37 |
| 29:16 | 37 |
| 29:27 | 7 |
| 29:38 | 175 |
| 30:9 | 261 |
| 30:14 | 31 |
| 30:19 | 31 |
| 31:1 | 61 |
| 31:12–13 | 18 |
| 31:16 | 18 |
| 32:1 | 61 |
| 32:2 | 13 |
| 32:3 | 7 |
| 32:11 | 12 |
| 32:26 | 10 |
| 32:38 | 7 |
| 33–36 | 12 |
| 33:11 | 153 |

*Biblical Reference Index*

Ezekiel (cont.)

| | |
|---|---|
| 33:21 | 60 |
| 33:22 | 213 |
| 33:24 | 237 |
| 33:25 | 173 |
| 34–37 | 12 |
| 34:2 | 106 |
| 34:10 | 217 |
| 34:13 | 8, 33 |
| 34:17 | 172 |
| 34:20 | 242 |
| 34:23–24 | 108, 173, 222 |
| 34:23 | 172 |
| 34:24 | 108, 134 |
| 34:25–29 | 12 |
| 34:26–27 | 13 |
| 34:28 | 29 |
| 35:3 | 10 |
| 35:15 | 185 |
| 36:6 | 18 |
| 36:10 | 12 |
| 36:12 | 185 |
| 36:17–18 | 25, 31 |
| 36:18 | 34, 173 |
| 36:20 | 109, 171, 177 |
| 36:22–23 | 16 |
| 36:22 | 153 |
| 36:23 | 109, 171 |
| 36:24–36 | 60 |
| 36:24 | 8, 12, 33 |
| 36:25–27 | 35, 36, 217 |
| 36:26–27 | 43, 115, 205, 264 |
| 36:26 | 263 |
| 36:27 | 35, 176 |
| 36:28 | 238 |
| 36:31–32 | 113 |
| 36:31 | 110, 112 |
| 36:32 | 44 |
| 36:37 | 43 |
| 36–37 | 3, 6, 172 |
| 37:1–15 | 170 |
| 37:1–10 | 24 |
| 37:1 | 64 |
| 37:7 | 18 |
| 37:10 | 35 |
| 37:14 | 35, 170 |
| 37:16–23 | 248 |
| 37:19 | 237 |
| 37:21 | 8, 33 |
| 37:22 | 108 |
| 37:23 | 44, 155 |
| 37:24–25 | 108 |
| 37:24 | 108 |
| 37:25 | 108, 134, 237 |
| 37:26 | 61, 149, 215 |
| 37:27 | 262 |
| 37:28 | 191 |
| 37:36–37 | 44 |
| 38–39 | 3, 4, 5, 6, 12, 37, 43, 215 |
| 38 | 5, 30, 34 |
| 38:1–13 | 7 |
| 38:1–9 | 4, 7, 21 |
| 38:1–4 | 4, 5 |
| 38:1–2 | 7, 8 |
| 38:1 | 3 |
| 38:2–23 | 4 |
| 38:2–13 | 3 |
| 38:2–9 | 7, 14 |
| 38:2–6 | 21 |
| 38:2–5 | 7 |
| 38:2–3 | 4 |
| 38:2 | 21 |
| 38:3 | 7 |
| 38:4–6 | 11 |
| 38:4–5 | 21 |
| 38:4 | 18, 21 |
| 38:5–9 | 8 |
| 38:5 | 16, 21 |
| 38:6 | 21, 31 |
| 38:7–8 | 11 |
| 38:7 | 21 |
| 38:8–9 | 15, 16 |
| 38:8 | 6, 8, 21, 34, 36 |
| 38:9–16 | 4 |
| 38:9 | 4, 8 |
| 38:10–19 | 22 |
| 38:10–13 | 4, 12, 14, 18, 22, 31 |
| 38:10–12 | 12 |
| 38:10–11 | 13 |
| 38:10 | 21, 32 |
| 38:11 | 8, 12, 36 |
| 38:12–13 | 13 |
| 38:12 | 6, 13 |
| 38:13 | 8, 13, 21 |
| 38:14–23 | 3, 15 |
| 38:14–16 | 14, 15, 16, 4 |
| 38:14 | 12, 15, 32, 36 |
| 38:15–16 | 15, 16 |
| 38:15 | 7 |

294

# Biblical Reference Index

## Ezekiel (cont.)

| | |
|---|---|
| 38:16 | 3, 5, 8, 17, 31, 34 |
| 38:17–23 | 4, 14, 17 |
| 38:17 | 15, 17, 18, 22 |
| 38:18–19 | 18 |
| 38:18 | 4, 16 |
| 38:19–20 | 18 |
| 38:19 | 32 |
| 38:20 | 21, 258 |
| 38:21–22 | 19 |
| 38:21 | 4 |
| 38:22 | 21, 31 |
| 38:23 | 5, 6, 8, 3, 18, 19, 30 |
| 38:28 | 21, 149 |
| 38:29 | 21 |
| 39 | 21, 28, 30, 34, 5 |
| 39:1–29 | 4 |
| 39:1–21 | 36 |
| 39:1–16 | 3, 4, 20 |
| 39:1–13 | 24 |
| 39:1–8 | 20 |
| 39:1–2 | 4, 5 |
| 39:1 | 21 |
| 39:2 | 11, 21, 34 |
| 39:4 | 4, 6, 8 |
| 39:6 | 3, 5, 7, 9 |
| 39:7 | 3, 18, 107, 109 |
| 39:8 | 8, 32, 34 |
| 39:9–11 | 28 |
| 39:9–10 | 5, 22, 23 |
| 39:9 | 11, 22, 160 |
| 39:11 | 24, 28, 32 |
| 39:11–16 | 23, 28 |
| 39:11–13 | 23 |
| 39:12–16 | 43 |
| 39:12–13 | 25 |
| 39:12 | 5, 6, 11, 25, 26, 28 |
| 39:13–15 | 24 |
| 39:13 | 25 |
| 39:14–16 | 26 |
| 39:14–15 | 25 |
| 39:14 | 5 |
| 39:15 | 24 |
| 39:16 | 6, 25 |
| 39:17–29 | 29, 37 |
| 39:17–24 | 4 |
| 39:17–20 | 27, 28 |
| 39:17–19 | 28 |
| 39:17 | 8, 24, 27, 34 |
| 39:20–29 | 30 |
| 39:20–24 | 30 |
| 39:21–29 | 29 |
| 39:21 | 28, 30 |
| 39:21–24 | 30, 32 |
| 39:21–22 | 30 |
| 39:22–23 | 30 |
| 39:22 | 3, 5, 32 |
| 39:23–24 | 30, 31 |
| 39:23 | 5, 31 |
| 39:24 | 31, 32, 34 |
| 39:25–29 | 30, 32 |
| 39:25 | 5, 30, 34 |
| 39:26–27 | 30, 33 |
| 39:26 | 12 |
| 39:27 | 8, 18, 28 |
| 39:28–29 | 3 |
| 39:28 | 3, 5, 30, 33, 264 |
| 39:29 | 30, 31, 34, 35, 36, 37, 43, 170, 176, 263, 265 |
| 40–48 | 41, 64, 102, 107, 108, 124, 164, 170, 214, 226 |
| 40–46 | 3, 6, 41, 43, 215, 262 |
| 40–45 | 5, 108 |
| 40–43 | 59, 60 |
| 40–42 | 66, 81, 88, 116, 124, 149, 210 |
| 40–41 | 68 |
| 40:1—43:27 | 61 |
| 40:1—43:12 | 66 |
| 40:1—43:11 | 114, 115 |
| 40:1—42:12 | 117 |
| 40:1–5 | 113 |
| 40:1–4 | 60 |
| 40:1–3 | 60 |
| 40:1 | 64, 106, 133 |
| 40:2–4 | 215 |
| 40:2 | 51, 61, 112, 113, 215, 217 |
| 40:3–5 | 231 |
| 40:3–4 | 61 |
| 40:3 | 61, 229, 231 |
| 40:4–6 | 113 |
| 40:4 | 113, 115, 133, 140, 61, 84 |
| 40:5–27 | 66 |
| 40:5 | 53, 66, 75, 81, 113, 118, 132, 227, 231 |
| 40:6–23 | 133 |
| 40:6–18 | 74 |
| 40:6–16 | 68 |
| 40:6–14 | 68 |
| 40:6 | 68, 103, 112, 132 |

295

## Biblical Reference Index

### Ezekiel (cont.)

| | |
|---|---|
| 40:7–8 | 229 |
| 40:7 | 72 |
| 40:8–10 | 71 |
| 40:8 | 66 |
| 40:9–10 | 68 |
| 40:9 | 66 |
| 40:10 | 132 |
| 40:11–15 | 71 |
| 40:12 | 68 |
| 40:14–16 | 69 |
| 40:14 | 68 |
| 40:15—41:13 | 101 |
| 40:16 | 68, 72, 94 |
| 40:17–19 | 72 |
| 40:17 | 56, 94, 97, 100, 223 |
| 40:18 | 72 |
| 40:19 | 53, 74 |
| 40:20 | 68, 103 |
| 40:20–27 | 73 |
| 40:20–23 | 74 |
| 40:21 | 68 |
| 40:22 | 5, 68, 73, 75 |
| 40:23 | 53, 74 |
| 40:24–27 | 74 |
| 40:24 | 73, 132, 229 |
| 40:25 | 102 |
| 40:26 | 5, 68 |
| 40:27–28 | 229 |
| 40:27 | 74 |
| 40:28–37 | 74 |
| 40:28–30 | 74 |
| 40:29 | 73, 75 |
| 40:30–37 | 75 |
| 40:30 | 75 |
| 40:31 | 68, 73, 75 |
| 40:33 | 73, 75 |
| 40:34 | 75 |
| 40:36 | 73 |
| 40:37 | 41, 68 |
| 40:38–46 | 75, 76 |
| 40:38–43 | 76 |
| 40:38 | 77 |
| 40:39–41 | 171 |
| 40:39 | 43, 58, 77, 100, 154, 159, 201, 204 |
| 40:40–41 | 79 |
| 40:40 | 72, 76, 79 |
| 40:41 | 68, 72 |
| 40:42–43 | 79 |
| 40:42 | 76, 79, 146, 154 |
| 40:43 | 66, 76, 80 |
| 40:44–46 | 80, 119, 186 |
| 40:44–45 | 229 |
| 40:44 | 72 |
| 40:45–46 | 81, 100, 119. 142, 143, 147, 148, 150, 169, 254 |
| 40:45 | 66, 81, 146, 147, 152 |
| 40:46 | 66, 80, 81, 100, 143, 147, 148, 254 |
| 40:47—41:26 | 82 |
| 40:47—41:4 | 82 |
| 40:47 | 53, 68, 82, 118, 119 |
| 40:48–49 | 83 |
| 40:48 | 66, 68 |
| 40:49 | 41, 75 |
| 40:51 | 101 |
| 41:1–4 | 83 |
| 41:2 | 125 |
| 41:3 | 5 |
| 41:4 | 54, 84, 95, 100, 117, 124, 125 |
| 41:5–12 | 85, 86 |
| 41:5–9 | 85 |
| 41:5 | 66 |
| 41:6 | 66, 87, 88, 89 |
| 41:7 | 66, 89, 90, 98 |
| 41:8–9 | 90 |
| 41:8 | 66, 98 |
| 41:9–12 | 86 |
| 41:9 | 66, 90, 118 |
| 41:10 | 66, 90, 92 |
| 41:12–15 | 54 |
| 41:12 | 90, 92, 97 |
| 41:13–15 | 91 |
| 41:13 | 66, 82, 91, 92 |
| 41:14 | 66, 92 |
| 41:15–26 | 87, 93 |
| 41:15–22 | 93 |
| 41:15–20 | 94 |
| 41:15 | 91, 92 |
| 41:16 | 229 |
| 41:17–20 | 94 |
| 41:17 | 66 |
| 41:18 | 72, 94, 223 |
| 41:19 | 66, 94 |
| 41:20 | 72 |
| 41:21–22 | 95 |
| 41:21 | 84, 97, 229 |
| 41:22–26 | 94 |

## Ezekiel (cont.)

| | |
|---|---|
| 41:22 | 41, 79, 81, 95, 96, 100, 225 |
| 41:23–25 | 96 |
| 41:23–24 | 96 |
| 41:25–26 | 96 |
| 41:25 | 72 |
| 41:26 | 66, 97 |
| 42 | 149 |
| 42:1–14 | 97, 224 |
| 42:1–13 | 158 |
| 42:1–6 | 100 |
| 42:1–4 | 97 |
| 42:2 | 54, 97 |
| 42:3 | 72, 118 |
| 42:4–11 | 98 |
| 42:7–12 | 100 |
| 42:7–8 | 47, 99 |
| 42:8 | 54, 148 |
| 42:9 | 224 |
| 42:10–12 | 100 |
| 42:11 | 257 |
| 42:12–14 | 99 |
| 42:12–13 | 229 |
| 42:13–14 | 100, 101, 124, 147 |
| 42:13 | 43, 58, 84, 112, 125, 143, 147, 186, 224, 225 |
| 42:15–20 | 66, 101, 102, 104 |
| 42:15 | 66, 68, 102 |
| 42:16–19 | 102 |
| 42:16 | 101 |
| 42:17–19 | 101 |
| 42:18 | 229 |
| 42:19 | 101, 225 |
| 42:20 | 41, 53, 99, 102, 191 |
| 43–46 | 226 |
| 43 | 83, 146 |
| 43:1–12 | 103 |
| 43:1–9 | 61, 102, 105, 118, 215 |
| 43:1–7 | 26 |
| 43:1–6 | 104, 261 |
| 43:1–5 | 31, 103 |
| 43:1–2 | 104 |
| 43:1 | 55, 68, 133 |
| 43:2–3 | 48 |
| 43:2 | 103, 105, 125, 133 |
| 43:3 | 103, 105, 134, 139 |
| 43:4–6 | 58 |
| 43:4–5 | 75 |
| 43:4 | 55, 68, 105, 211 |
| 43:5 | 139, 262 |
| 43:6–9 | 55, 91, 106 |
| 43:6–7 | 106 |
| 43:6 | 53, 107, 217 |
| 43:7–9 | 54, 107, 108, 109, 111, 171, 262 |
| 43:7–8 | 109, 171 |
| 43:7 | 61, 107, 108, 109, 110, 134, 167, 171, 217, 260 |
| 43:8 | 107, 111, 167, 171, 215 |
| 43:9 | 34, 107, 110, 112, 134, 171, 229 |
| 43:10–12 | 105, 112, 113 |
| 43:10–11 | 44, 51, 113, 115 |
| 43:10 | 112, 113, 114, 115, 117 |
| 43:11–12 | 113 |
| 43:11 | 44, 65, 66, 113, 114, 115, 149, 257 |
| 43:12–27 | 105 |
| 43:12 | 41, 53, 54, 61, 84, 102, 113, 116, 125, 146, 149, 205 |
| 43:13—46:24 | 115, 215 |
| 43:13–27 | 83 |
| 43:13–17 | 83, 104, 107, 118, 121 |
| 43:13 | 118 |
| 43:14–15 | 95 |
| 43:14 | 118, 120 |
| 43:15–16 | 120 |
| 43:15 | 79, 96, 120 |
| 43:16 | 120 |
| 43:17 | 118, 120, 122 |
| 43:18–29 | 215 |
| 43:18–27 | 83, 122, 124, 200, 202, 217 |
| 43:18–26 | 206 |
| 43:18–20 | 202 |
| 43:18–19 | 122 |
| 43:18 | 129, 217 |
| 43:19–27 | 123, 127 |
| 43:19–26 | 215 |
| 43:19–25 | 201 |
| 43:19–21 | 129 |
| 43:19 | 112, 127, 130, 161, 164, 169 |
| 43:20 | 102, 121, 122, 127, 129, 130, 198, 200, 205 |
| 43:21–26 | 202 |
| 43:21 | 127, 128, 130, 149 |
| 43:22–24 | 130 |
| 43:22 | 127, 128, 200 |
| 43:23–24 | 127 |
| 43:23 | 101, 127, 130, 200, 215 |
| 43:24 | 127, 128 |

## Biblical Reference Index

### Ezekiel (cont.)

| Reference | Pages |
|---|---|
| 43:25–27 | 127, 130, 201 |
| 43:25–26 | 128, 202 |
| 43:25 | 5, 127, 205, 214, 264 |
| 43:26 | 5, 122, 128, 130, 149, 199, 200 |
| 43:27 | 105, 125, 127, 128, 201, 202 |
| 44–46 | 59, 115, 116, 132 |
| 44 | 135, 186 |
| 44:1–9 | 132 |
| 44:1–6 | 43 |
| 44:1–3 | 53, 54, 58, 132 |
| 44:1–2 | 110, 230 |
| 44:1 | 77, 103, 117, 124, 130, 148, 156, 186 |
| 44:2–3 | 209 |
| 44:2 | 105, 132, 135, 186 |
| 44:3 | 28, 56, 134, 135, 186 |
| 44:4–8 | 134 |
| 44:4–5 | 134, 135 |
| 44:4 | 53, 54, 133, 138, 139, 187, 187, 262 |
| 44:5–31 | 188 |
| 44:5 | 54, 113, 117, 138, 140, 149, 187, 257 |
| 44:6–10 | 136, 137 |
| 44:6–8 | 135 |
| 44:6–7 | 170 |
| 44:6 | 124, 129, 139, 168, 170, 172, 187, 193, 194, 217 |
| 44:7–19 | 218 |
| 44:7–10 | 162 |
| 44:7–9 | 164, 171 |
| 44:7–8 | 168 |
| 44:7 | 117, 135, 136, 137, 140, 149, 160, 164, 187, 191 |
| 44:8 | 117, 141, 149, 164, 171, 191, 254 |
| 44:9–27 | 188 |
| 44:9–16 | 138 |
| 44:9–14 | 141, 148, 153 |
| 44:9–10 | 136, 137, 153 |
| 44:9 | 44, 117, 124, 129, 135, 137, 149, 150, 164, 217 |
| 44:10–14 | 154, 164 |
| 44:10–12 | 138, 169, 186 |
| 44:10–11 | 137 |
| 44:10 | 135, 145, 146, 150, 152, 153, 155, 160, 162, 164, 174 |
| 44:11 | 117, 130, 136, 137, 146, 148, 149, 150, 151, 154, 155, 156, 157, 159, 163, 164, 169, 171, 174, 205, 224, 226 |
| 44:12 | 124, 136, 137, 145, 146, 148, 149, 150, 151, 152, 153, 161, 174 |
| 44:13 | 29, 81, 85, 136, 137, 143, 146, 150, 151, 152, 156, 161, 162, 163, 164, 169, 215, 263 |
| 44:14 | 81, 136, 137, 142, 146, 147, 148, 149, 150, 151, 162, 163, 174, 205 |
| 44:15–31 | 36, 163 |
| 44:15–16 | 163, 164 |
| 44:15 | 100, 117, 124, 138, 143, 145, 149, 150, 152, 161, 163, 164, 169, 176, 191, 250, 254 |
| 44:16–31 | 218 |
| 44:16 | 28, 117, 135, 143, 149, 150, 152, 163, 164, 254 |
| 44:17–31 | 58, 168, 175 |
| 44:17–27 | 177 |
| 44:17–24 | 177 |
| 44:17–19 | 156 |
| 44:17 | 136 |
| 44:18 | 33, 179 |
| 44:19 | 163, 179, 204 |
| 44:20 | 156, 179 |
| 44:21 | 136, 157, 179, 181 |
| 44:22 | 58, 136, 153, 157, 182, 204, 218 |
| 44:23–24 | 136, 144, 157, 182 |
| 44:23 | 51, 161, 164, 175, 182, 194 |
| 44:24 | 57, 163, 165, 182, 194 |
| 44:25–27 | 157, 183 |
| 44:25 | 136, 183 |
| 44:26–27 | 183, 204, 218 |
| 44:26 | 5, 183 |
| 44:27 | 124, 136, 183, 184, 204 |
| 44:28–31 | 144, 184, 188 |
| 44:28–30 | 184, 189 |
| 44:28–29 | 157 |
| 44:28 | 136, 137, 184, 185, 189 |
| 44:29–30 | 59 |
| 44:29 | 58, 136, 137, 163, 184, 185, 201, 204 |
| 44:30 | 136, 137, 157, 185, 196 |
| 44:31 | 157, 186 |
| 45 | 208, 209 |
| 45:1–8 | 152, 187, 189 |
| 45:1–6 | 214 |
| 45:1–5 | 59, 60, 112, 185, 187 |
| 45:1 | 185, 189, 193, 247, 250, 253 |
| 45:2 | 53, 57, 118, 191, 254, 255, 259 |

## Ezekiel (cont.)

| | |
|---|---|
| 45:3–4 | 59, 193, 253 |
| 45:3 | 85, 117, 187, 191, 222 |
| 45:4–5 | 212 |
| 45:4 | 85, 107, 117, 143, 144, 187, 191, 257 |
| 45:5–8 | 188 |
| 45:5 | 59, 141, 144, 146, 147, 148, 149, 185, 187, 188, 193, 205, 224, 237, 260 |
| 45:6–7 | 189, 262 |
| 45:6 | 108, 185, 187, 192, 255, 259 |
| 45:7—46:12 | 134 |
| 45:7–9 | 108, 173 |
| 45:7–8 | 57, 193, 221, 222, 257 |
| 45:7 | 107, 185, 188, 192, 252 |
| 45:8—46:18 | 188 |
| 45:8–9 | 174, 220 |
| 45:8 | 185, 192, 217, 221, 251, 254 |
| 45:9–25 | 193 |
| 45:9–12 | 188, 192, 193, 194, 256 |
| 45:9 | 124, 193, 194, 217 |
| 45:10–15 | 60 |
| 45:10–12 | 195 |
| 45:12 | 118, 195, 254 |
| 45:13—46:15 | 188 |
| 45:13–17 | 196 |
| 45:13–16 | 171 |
| 45:13–15 | 196 |
| 45:13 | 193, 252 |
| 45:14 | 197 |
| 45:15–27 | 36 |
| 45:15 | 124, 197 |
| 45:16–17 | 197 |
| 45:16 | 171, 212 |
| 45:17 | 58, 201, 211 |
| 45:18–29 | 214 |
| 45:18–27 | 215 |
| 45:18–25 | 173, 198, 201, 216, 226 |
| 45:18–20 | 55, 104, 149, 198, 199, 201, 208, 214, 264 |
| 45:18–19 | 202 |
| 45:18 | 55, 117, 124, 149, 200, 205, 208, 217 |
| 45:19 | 55, 149, 200, 205, 216 |
| 45:20–25 | 199 |
| 45:20 | 5, 55, 149, 200, 201, 202, 205, 208, 216 |
| 45:21–24 | 201 |
| 45:21 | 199, 206, 207 |
| 45:22–25 | 57 |
| 45:22 | 57, 192, 203, 206, 212, 216, 264 |
| 45:23–25 | 201, 208 |
| 45:23–24 | 217 |
| 45:23 | 5, 206, 207, 208 |
| 45:25 | 5, 201, 217, 264 |
| 46 | 211 |
| 46:1–15 | 209, 214 |
| 46:1–8 | 44 |
| 46:1–2 | 54, 255 |
| 46:1 | 103, 124, 129, 132, 202, 209, 211, 217, 230 |
| 46:2–12 | 210 |
| 46:2 | 54, 58, 211, 213, 223, 226 |
| 46:3 | 196, 212, 226 |
| 46:4–15 | 226 |
| 46:4–8 | 192 |
| 46:4–7 | 219 |
| 46:4–5 | 213 |
| 46:4 | 212 |
| 46:5 | 212 |
| 46:6–7 | 56, 212 |
| 46:6 | 212 |
| 46:7 | 172, 212, 213 |
| 46:8 | 134, 212 |
| 46:9–11 | 172 |
| 46:9–10 | 44, 226 |
| 46:9 | 75, 103, 212, 227 |
| 46:10–20 | 147 |
| 46:10 | 213, 223 |
| 46:11 | 213, 219 |
| 46:12 | 54, 58, 103, 185, 212, 213 |
| 46:13–15 | 56, 211, 213, 214 |
| 46:13–14 | 213, 214 |
| 46:13 | 213, 216, 264 |
| 46:14–15 | 42 |
| 46:15 | 24, 213, 214, 216 |
| 46:16–18 | 172, 188, 214, 220, 221 |
| 46:16 | 124, 129, 185, 217, 222 |
| 46:17 | 61, 173, 220, 221 |
| 46:18 | 185, 192, 193, 194, 222 |
| 46:19–24 | 102, 104, 223 |
| 46:19–23 | 223 |
| 46:19–20 | 43, 224 |
| 46:19 | 43, 72, 113, 224 |
| 46:20 | 43, 58, 125, 148, 201, 204, 224, 225 |
| 46:21–24 | 224, 230 |
| 46:21–22 | 96 |

## Biblical Reference Index

### Ezekiel (cont.)

| | |
|---|---|
| 46:21 | 225 |
| 46:22–24 | 54 |
| 46:22 | 223, 225 |
| 46:23 | 94, 223 |
| 46:24 | 147, 148, 149, 158, 160, 205, 224, 226 |
| 47–48 | 3, 6, 210, 227, 238 |
| 47:1—48:35 | 61 |
| 47 | 52, 217, 239 |
| 47:1–12 | 227, 229, 232 |
| 47:1–4 | 227 |
| 47:1–2 | 44 |
| 47:1 | 229, 230, 233 |
| 47:2 | 73, 229 |
| 47:3–5 | 231 |
| 47:3 | 229, 233 |
| 47:4 | 233 |
| 47:5–12 | 228 |
| 47:5 | 229, 233 |
| 47:6–7 | 229 |
| 47:6 | 73, 232 |
| 47:7–9 | 232 |
| 47:7 | 229 |
| 47:8 | 229, 234 |
| 47:9 | 228, 229, 232, 234 |
| 47:10 | 229, 232, 234 |
| 47:11–12 | 233 |
| 47:12 | 117 |
| 47:13—48:29 | 214 |
| 47:13–23 | 229, 235, 243 |
| 47:13–20 | 214, 234, 243 |
| 47:13–16 | 234 |
| 47:13–14 | 235, 236, 243, 247 |
| 47:13 | 124, 129, 189, 217, 235, 236, 237, 248 |
| 47:14 | 185, 235, 236, 237, 249 |
| 47:15–20 | 235, 236, 237, 248, 259 |
| 47:15–17 | 239, 240 |
| 47:15 | 228, 235, 248 |
| 47:16–20 | 235 |
| 47:16 | 234, 235, 242 |
| 47:17 | 235, 248 |
| 47:18 | 60, 64, 227, 235, 242 |
| 47:19 | 228, 235, 242, 247, 248 |
| 47:20 | 228, 235, 236, 243 |
| 47:21–23 | 235, 236, 243 |
| 47:21 | 236, 243, 247 |
| 47:22–23 | 36, 153, 243, 244, 245, 246 |
| 47:22 | 185, 235, 236, 244, 247 |
| 47:23 | 124, 235, 236 |
| 47:28 | 185 |
| 48 | 36, 60, 172, 189, 217, 222, 237, 261 |
| 48:1–29 | 152 |
| 48:1–7 | 246, 258 |
| 48:1–2 | 246 |
| 48:1 | 234, 239, 240, 247, 248, 258 |
| 48:3–7 | 247 |
| 48:8–22 | 248, 250 |
| 48:8–20 | 189 |
| 48:8–17 | 247 |
| 48:8–14 | 59, 250 |
| 48:8–11 | 250 |
| 48:8 | 188, 192, 193, 251, 252 |
| 48:9–20 | 112 |
| 48:9–14 | 60, 251 |
| 48:9–12 | 253 |
| 48:9–10 | 253 |
| 48:9 | 193 |
| 48:10–12 | 59, 193, 253, 254 |
| 48:10 | 117 |
| 48:11–14 | 185 |
| 48:11–13 | 141 |
| 48:11–12 | 107, 144 |
| 48:11 | 81, 100, 143, 148, 169, 176, 191, 254 |
| 48:12–14 | 251 |
| 48:12 | 85, 117, 254, 254, 257, 260 |
| 48:13 | 193, 254, 262 |
| 48:13–14 | 59, 151, 153, 214, 254 |
| 48:14 | 144 |
| 48:15–20 | 251, 254 |
| 48:15–18 | 254 |
| 48:15–17 | 255 |
| 48:15 | 191 |
| 48:16 | 259 |
| 48:18–20 | 255 |
| 48:18 | 117 |
| 48:20 | 118, 185, 193 |
| 48:21–22 | 54, 57, 108, 112, 193, 251, 256 |
| 48:21 | 107, 149, 185, 250, 257 |
| 48:22 | 185, 242, 257, 260 |
| 48:23–29 | 246, 258 |
| 48:23–28 | 247 |
| 48:23 | 248 |
| 48:28 | 228, 242, 248 |
| 48:29 | 124, 185, 189, 234, 247 |

## Ezekiel (cont.)

| | |
|---|---|
| 48:30–35 | 36, 13, 108, 112, 257 |
| 48:30–34 | 55 |
| 48:30–31 | 257 |
| 48:31 | 258 |
| 48:34 | 259 |
| 48:35 | 26, 43, 54, 55, 61, 65, 260, 261 |

## Hosea

| | |
|---|---|
| 4:8 | 150 |
| 4:11 | 179 |
| 6:8 | 242 |
| 7:5 | 179 |
| 12:8 | 195 |

## Joel

| | |
|---|---|
| 2:18 | 33 |
| 3:1–2 | 35, 36 |
| 3:1 | 34 |
| 4:4 | 232 |
| 4:18 | 231 |

## Amos

| | |
|---|---|
| 1:8 | 12 |
| 2:7 | 107 |
| 3:10 | 193 |
| 4:12 | 11 |
| 6:14 | 241 |
| 7:17 | 242 |
| 8:5–6 | 195 |
| 8:5 | 216 |

## Jonah

| | |
|---|---|
| 3:3 | 100 |
| 3:4 | 100 |

## Micah

| | |
|---|---|
| 4:1–4 | 263 |
| 4:1 | 11 |
| 4:3 | 23 |
| 4:11–13 | 12 |
| 6:10–11 | 195 |

## Habakkuk

| | |
|---|---|
| 1:3 | 193 |

## Zephaniah

| | |
|---|---|
| 1:17 | 155 |

## Haggai

| | |
|---|---|
| 1:13 | 57 |
| 2:21–22 | 12 |

## Zechariah

| | |
|---|---|
| 1:16 | 231 |
| 2:5 | 65, 234 |
| 2:6 | 188 |
| 2:8 | 12 |
| 3:3 | 100 |
| 5:5–11 | 195 |
| 10:10 | 33 |
| 12:10 | 34 |
| 13:1 | 231, 234 |
| 13:7 | 12 |
| 14:5 | 19 |
| 14:8 | 232, 233 |
| 14:13 | 19 |
| 14:21 | 140 |

## Malachi

| | |
|---|---|
| 1:11–14 | 107 |
| 1:13 | 78 |

## Psalms

| | |
|---|---|
| 1:3 | 233 |
| 6:7 | 228 |
| 18:9 | 18 |
| 19:15 | 203 |
| 24:1 | 245 |
| 33:7 | 33 |
| 42:5 | 207 |
| 46:10 | 23 |
| 47:9 | 108 |
| 58:5 | 69 |
| 79 | 25 |
| 81:4 | 216 |
| 81:15 | 12 |
| 88:19 | 112 |
| 93 | 106 |
| 99:3 | 109 |
| 99:5 | 108 |
| 104:4 | 34 |
| 104:8 | 34 |

## Biblical Reference Index

### Psalms (cont.)

| | |
|---|---|
| 119:97 | xxiv |
| 132:7 | 108, 109 |
| 147:23 | 33 |

### Job

| | |
|---|---|
| 6:24 | 203 |
| 6:26 | 199 |
| 8:11 | 228 |
| 13:14 | 32 |
| 19:4 | 199, 203 |
| 26:5 | 25 |
| 38:5 | 231 |
| 40:21 | 228 |

### Proverbs

| | |
|---|---|
| 2:18 | 25 |
| 5:23 | 199, 203 |
| 9:18 | 25 |
| 11:1 | 195 |
| 16:11 | 195 |
| 17:28 | 69 |
| 20:1 | 179 |
| 20:10 | 195 |
| 21:13 | 69 |
| 27:19 | xvi |

### Ruth

| | |
|---|---|
| 2:2 | 60 |

### Song of Songs

| | |
|---|---|
| 5:3 | 211 |

### Lamentations

| | |
|---|---|
| 2:1 | 108 |
| 2:8 | 254 |
| 4:8 | 231 |

### Esther

| | |
|---|---|
| 1:6 | 72, 73 |
| 4:16 | 33 |
| 8:3 | 12 |
| 9:12 | 12 |

### Daniel

| | |
|---|---|
| 2:28 | 11 |

| | |
|---|---|
| 8:11 | 193 |
| 10:14 | 11 |
| 11:24 | 12 |

### Ezra

| | |
|---|---|
| 2:4 | 256 |
| 2:43–54 | 148 |
| 2:47–58 | 140 |
| 2:55 | 148 |
| 6:19–21 | 206 |
| 6:21 | 246 |
| 6:22 | 199, 207 |
| 8:16 | 120 |

### Nehemiah

| | |
|---|---|
| 2:6 | 100 |
| 2:10 | 115 |
| 2:13 | 258 |
| 3:13–14 | 258 |
| 3:38 | 225 |
| 7:46–60 | 140 |
| 7:47–56 | 148 |
| 7:57 | 148 |
| 7:60 | 256 |
| 8:13 | 202 |
| 10:29–30 | 246 |
| 10:38–40 | 73 |
| 12:14 | 33 |
| 12:31 | 258 |
| 12:47 | 187 |
| 13:5 | 187 |
| 26:11 | 187 |
| 26:46 | 187 |

### 1 Chronicles

| | |
|---|---|
| 1:5 | 7, 9 |
| 4:38 | 173 |
| 5:6 | 173 |
| 5:16 | 258 |
| 7:1 | 104 |
| 7:40 | 173 |
| 11:22 | 120 |
| 13:2 | 239 |
| 13:5 | 239 |
| 15:11 | 144 |
| 16:39 | 144 |
| 17:25 | 13 |
| 18:16 | 144 |

## 1 Chronicles (cont.)

| | |
|---|---|
| 20 | 191 |
| 22:2 | 33 |
| 28:2 | 108, 109 |
| 28:12 | 73 |
| 29:22 | 28 |

## 2 Chronicles

| | |
|---|---|
| 2:4 | 216 |
| 2:13 | 12 |
| 4:1 | 122 |
| 4:2 | 231 |
| 4:3 | 66 |
| 4:9 | 120 |
| 4:10 | 230 |
| 5:6 | 154 |
| 5:14 | 106 |
| 6:13 | 120 |
| 7:1 | 104, 129 |
| 7:3 | 72, 73 |
| 7:8 | 239 |
| 7:9 | 129 |
| 7:19 | 108 |
| 8:5 | 13 |
| 8:12–13 | 199, 207 |
| 8:13 | 216 |
| 14:6 | 13 |
| 21:3 | 220 |
| 22:9 | 177 |
| 23:10 | 230 |
| 24:24 | 31 |
| 24:25 | 177 |
| 25:23 | 258 |
| 25:28 | 177 |
| 26:16 | 12 |
| 26:18 | 250 |
| 30:13 | 199, 207 |
| 30:14 | 225 |
| 30:15–20 | 202 |
| 30:15–17 | 206 |
| 30:21 | 199, 207 |
| 30:22 | 206 |
| 30:24 | 206 |
| 30:25 | 246 |
| 31:3 | 216 |
| 33:11 | 11 |
| 35:7–17 | 206 |
| 35:17 | 199, 207 |
| 36:11 | 73 |
| 36:21 | 25 |

# NEW TESTAMENT

## Mark

| | |
|---|---|
| 14:53 | 179 |
| 14:63 | 179 |

## Revelation

| | |
|---|---|
| 20:8 | 9 |

# Ancient and Jewish Sources Index

| | |
|---|---|
| 11QT 20:6–8 | 160 |
| 11QT 30:30:3–31:89 | 89 |
| 11QT 33 | 72 |
| 11QT 33:11 | 72 |
| Josephus, *Antiquities* 1.6.1 §123 | 9 |
| Josephus, *Antiquities* 2.3 §36 | 111 |
| Josephus, *Jewish Wars* 5.5.6 §§222–26 | 122 |
| Philo, *Quast. In Exod.* 1.2 | 63 |
| Sira 2:8 | 33 |
| Sira 3:5 | 33 |
| Sira 38:4 | 229 |
| Sira 48:17 | 25 |
| Sira 50:2 | 120 |
| Strabo, *Geography* | 1.61 |
| Zincirli Stele | 11 |
| | |
| 'Aboda Zara | xxiv |
| 'Abot R. Nat. 2.38 | 155 |
| 'Abot R. Nat. A 40 | 125 |
| b. 'Arakin 12a | 61 |
| b. Baba Bathra 61a | 87 |
| b. Baba Bathra 90a–b | 195 |
| b. Baba Kama 67a | 97 |
| b. Ḥagiga 13a | 264 |
| b. Hulin | 141 |
| b. Menaḥot 45a | 264 |
| b. Sanhedrin 17a | 3 |
| b. Sanhedrin 8b | v |
| b. Shabbat 13b | 264 |
| b. Shabbat 33b | 111 |
| b. Yebamot 90b | 183 |
| b. Yoma 5b–6a | 178 |
| b. Yoma 77b | 231 |
| m. Giṭṭin 5:5 | 97 |
| m. Midot 2:3 | 68 |
| m. Midot 2:4 | 231 |
| m. Midot 2:5 | 225 |
| m. Midot 3:8 | 97 |
| m. Midot 4:3 | 86 |
| m. Midot 4:3–4 | 87 |
| m. Pesahim 9:5 | 63 |
| m. Shabbat 3.2 | 22 |
| m. Shevi'it 6:1 | 241 |
| m. Tamid 5:3 | 72 |
| m. Toharot 7:7 | 72 |
| m. Yoma 2:15 | 125 |
| m. Yoma | 206 |
| m. Zebaḥim 5:7 | 160 |
| Mekilta Bo', par. 8 | 207 |
| Midrash Songs on 4:8 | 241 |
| Numbers Rabbah 15:19 | 3 |
| Numbers Rabbah 15:7 | 69, 71 |
| Sipra, Ḥobah par. 4:12 | 122 |
| Sipra, Shemini par. 1:4 | 180 |
| Sipre, Numbers 78 | 244 |
| t. Soṭa 13:1 | 125 |
| t. Sukkoth 3:3–10 | 234 |
| t. Sukkoth 4:27 | 72 |
| t. Sukkoth | 5 |
| t. Terumoth 2:12 | 241 |
| | |
| Beaugency, R. Eliezer | xvii, xx, 7, 13, 20, 24, 25, 28, 29, 71, 73, 81, 86, 88, 93, 106, 107, 112, 114, 119, 129, 130, 132–34, 142–44, 147, 156, 178, 179, 183, 184, 186, 187, 191, 195, 197, 198, 211, 212, 214, 227, 229, 234, 242, 246, 252, 254, 256, 257, 261, 262 |
| Gaon, Saadiah | 63 |
| Ibn Ezra | 63 |
| Ibn Janah | 107, 155 |
| Isaiah of Trani | 24, 64, 107 |
| Japhet | 63 |
| Kara, R. Joseph | xvii, xx, 15, 20, 24, 28, 63 |
| Maimonides | 179, 180, 264, 273 |
| Menahem ben Simeon | 7, 8, 12, 13, 15, 20, 24 |

## Ancient and Jewish Sources Index

Mitrani  17
Radak  7, 8, 13, 17, 20, 22, 24, 29, 65, 69, 71, 76, 85, 93, 97, 106, 107, 110, 127, 129, 130, 154, 155, 179, 183, 184, 188, 190–92, 194, 197, 212–14, 225, 228, 230–32, 246, 254–56, 161, 264
Ramban  xxiii, 180
Rashi  7–9, 13, 15, 17, 24, 28, 61, 68, 69, 71, 86, 88, 90, 93, 97, 106, 107, 141, 184, 186, 190–92, 197, 212, 213, 230, 232, 235, 246, 256, 257

# Author Index

Abba, R., 138, 267
Ackroyd, P. R., 25, 267
Aharoni, R., 4, 11, 267
Aharoni, Y., 241, 242, 267
Albeck, C., 241, 267
Alberts, R., 256, 267
Albrecht, K., 118, 267
Albright, W. F., 9, 110, 120, 180, 267
Allen, L. C., 15, 68, 101, 123, 132, 196, 228, 257, 259, 267
Althann, R., 258, 267
Andersen, F. I., 68, 267
Anderson, B. W., 13, 267
Anderson, G. A., 267
Andrae, W., 111, 267
Astour, M. S., 267
Avigad, N., 278

Balentine, S. E., 32, 267
Barkay, G., 162, 267
Barnett, R. D., 94 , 267
Barthelemy, D., 106, 267
Baudissin, 155
Beck, P., 94, 268
Beitzel, B., 111, 268
Berry, G. R., 80, 268
Biggs, C. R., 200, 268
Block,[1] D. I., *xv, xvii, xviii, xxiii*, 3, 5, 8–10, 12, 18–20, 22–26, 28–31, 35, 61, 69, 71–73, 75, 79, 82, 91, 94, 97, 100–102, 104, 107, 113, 114, 118, 120, 124, 126–29, 133–35, 139, 169, 170, 173, 187–89, 191, 194, 196, 198–201, 206, 210, 216, 220, 221, 228, 229, 238, 239, 248, 250, 253, 255, 256, 258, 263, 268
Boadt, L., 133, 268
Boer, J. Z. de, 44, 45, 47, 271

Botta, A. F., 155, 268
Bracke, J. M., 33, 268
Brown, J. P., 49, 72, 268
Brown, M. L., 15, 268
Burkert, Walter, 49, 50, 51, 268
Burrows, M, 69, 268
Busink, Th. A., 94, 225, 268

Cansdale, G. S., 21, 268
Chanton, J. P., 44, 45, 47, 271
Clements, R. E., 228, 268
Cogan, M., 9, 35, 268, 269
Cohen, M., 269
Cook, S. L., 152, 269
Cooke, G. A., 80, 118, 154, 194, 223, 227, 249, 269
Cowley, A., 208, 269
Crenshaw, J. L., 35, 269
Cross, F. M., 155, 269

Dalman, G., 63, 269
Darr, K. P., 269
Davidson, A. B., 29, 269
Davies, P. R., 163, 269
Day, J., 269
Dijkstra, M., 118, 269
Douglas, G. C. M., *xvii*, 58, 269
Driver, G. R., 23, 133, 228, 269
Driver, S. R., 63, 269
Duguid, I. M., 35, 59, 80, 108, 110, 135, 138, 140, 146, 152, 163, 164, 167, 170–72, 176, 186, 194, 195, 200, 217, 222, 223, 248, 269
Duke, R. K., 80, 81, 143, 148, 151, 153, 269
Duman, Joel, *xv, xxi, xxiii*, 86, 90

Ehrlich, A. B., 228, 269
Eichrodt, W., 194, 269
Elliger, K., 62, 269
Ellis, R. S., 50, 111, 269
Eph'al, I., 49, 269

---

[1] References to Block identified by square brackets in the text (e.g., [544]) are not indexed.

## Author Index

Falkenstein, A., 128, 269
Fierstein, David, 45, 47
Fishbane, M., 66, 102, 138, 146, 152, 186, 269, 270, 277
Fohrer, G., 103, 249, 270
Forbes, A. D., 68, 267
Fox, M. V., 263, 270
Franklin, N., 111, 270
Freedman, D. N., 270
Friedman, R. E., 32, 270
Frymer-Kensky, T., 25, 270
Fuhs, H. F., 227, 232, 270

Galambush, J., 226, 270
Galil, G., 239, 270
Galling, K., 103, 270
Ganzel, T., *xv–xvi*, 117, 164, 167, 170, 176, 197, 263, 270
Garfinkel, S. P., 130, 177, 270
Gese, H., 62, 68, 69, 85, 106, 107, 132, 134, 196, 270
Ginsberg, H. L., 62, 270
Gordon, C. H., 228, 270
Goshen-Gottstein, M. H., 74, 270
Greenberg, M., *xv, xix*, 4, 21, 30, 36, 57, 58, 60, 64, 112, 145, 155, 224, 238, 249, 252, 264, 270

Haak, R. D., 72, 76, 79, 271
Hale, J. R., 44, 45, 47, 271
Hals, R. M., 194, 271
Haran, M., 59, 66, 79, 87, 99, 117, 142, 151, 155, 180, 192, 193, 207, 251, 271
Helms, P. R., 49, 271
Holladay, W. L., 8, 271
Hurowitz, V. A., 71, 72, 117, 271
Hurvitz, A., 33, 66, 82, 91, 93, 94, 101, 118, 250, 271

Irwin, B. P., 271

Jacob, B., 63, 271
Japhet, S., 129, 246, 271
Jastrow, M., 91, 225, 271
Jones, R. N., 158, 278
Joüon, P., 64, 69, 93, 99, 106, 220, 227, 271
Joyce, P. M., 16, 102, 117, 212, 227, 237, 271

Kallai, Z., 240, 271

Karageorghis, V., 71, 271
Kasher, R., 17, 18, 21, 28, 51, 64, 75, 77, 96, 106, 109, 110, 113, 114, 117, 126, 127, 137–39, 142, 168, 175, 182, 184, 185, 188, 190–92, 197, 205, 212, 213, 223–25, 228, 229, 243, 259, 271, 272
Kaufmann, Y., 6, 145, 146, 272
Kedar-Kopfstein, B., 207, 272
Kenyon, K., 168, 272
Kissane, E. J., 28, 272
Kitchen, K. A., 90, 272
Kletter, R., 145, 168, 272
Knohl, I., 109, 126, 272
Kohn, R. L., 165, 272
Kravitz, L., 264, 272
Kutsko, J. F., 272

Lambert, W. G., 32, 272
Lane, D., 58, 272
Lang, B., 58, 272
Langdon, S., 120, 272
Lapsley, J. E., 113, 162, 182, 272
Lemaire, A., 115, 272
Levenson, J. D., 52, 59, 120, 125, 214, 222, 272
Levey, S. H., 3, 13, 69, 76, 123, 225, 258, 272
Levine, B. A., 24, 62, 272, 273
Lewy, J., 221, 273
Lipshitz, E., 221, 273
Lipiński, E., 182, 273

Maaß, M., 44, 46, 273
Mackay, C., 58, 273
Maiberger, P., 110, 273
Maier, J., 48, 100, 273
Malamat, A., 110, 273
Margolit, E., 273
Margueron, J.-C., 256, 273
Maur, J., 273
May, H. G., 200, 273
Mazar, A., 69, 71, 273
Mazar, B., 239, 273
McCarter, P. K., 144, 273
McConville, J. G., 217, 273
McKeating, H., 273
Middlemas, J., 256, 273
Milgrom, J., *xvii, xviii, xix, xx, xxiii*, 5, 6, 22, 25, 26, 27, 28, 33, 48, 56, 57, 58, 59, 77, 80, 107, 109, 110, 115, 121, 123,

Milgrom, J. (cont.)
   125, 126, 128, 129, 138, 141, 142,
   144, 147–50, 152–55, 157–59, 163,
   167, 169, 175, 178, 179, 181, 182,
   184, 190, 192, 197–99, 203, 204, 206,
   208, 212, 214, 222, 226, 229, 232,
   237, 239, 243, 244, 252, 254, 273–75
Miller, Marr, 121
Monson, John M., 88, 274
Moor, J. C. de, 12, 274
Moran, W. L., 110, 274
Muraoka, T., 64, 69, 93, 99, 106, 220, 227, 271, 274

Na'aman, N., 13, 110, 274
Neiman, D., 110, 274
Neusner, J., 234, 274
Noth, M., 110, 274

Oates, D., 111, 274
Oates, J., 111, 274
Obermann, J., 110, 274
O'Connor, M., 134, 223, 277
Odell, M. S., 9, 10, 22, 24–28, 274, 275
Olyan, S. M., 28, 275
Oppenheim, A. L., 31, 275
Orlinsky, K. M., 264, 272

Pattai, R., 230, 275
Patton, C. L., 55, 204, 275
Paul, S., 124, 275
Petersen, D. L., 245, 275
Pines, S., 264, 275
Pope, M. H., 24, 275
Powel, M. A., 195, 275
Pritchard, J. B., 11, 111, 258, 275
Procksch, D. G., 275
Propp, W. H. C., 63, 165, 275

Qoler, Y., 258, 275

Rabin, C., 163, 275
Rad, G. von, 12, 275
Rattray, S., 107, 275
Reviv, H., 172, 276
Rocchi, D., 276
Rollinger, R., 49, 276
Rooker, M. F., 98, 99, 101, 106, 135, 154,
   187, 188, 209, 210, 220, 229, 242,
   246, 255, 276

Rubenstein, A., 154, 276
Schwartz, B. J., 150, 154, 263, 276
Scott, W. R., 207, 276
Seidel, M., 16, 105, 130, 224, 225, 276
Sharon, D. M., 65, 145, 230, 276
Sharon, I., 276
Shiloh, Y., 168, 276
Simon, B., 54, 276
Simons, J. J., 241, 276
Ska, J. L., 217, 276
Smith, J. Z., 54, 90, 91, 102, 103, 276
Smith, M., 145, 246, 276
Soden, W. von, 128, 228, 256, 269, 276
Sperber, A., 107, 276
Sperling, S. D., 33, 277
Spiller, H. A., 44, 45, 47, 271
Stager, L., 277
Stavrakopoulou, F., 27, 110, 111, 277
Stevenson, K. R., 44, 53, 54, 55, 90, 101,
   104, 129, 163, 232, 277
Strauss, L., 264, 275
Sweeny, M. A., 277

Tadmor, H., 9, 62, 63, 269, 277
Talmon, S., 17, 66, 74, 102, 277
Tarragon, J.–M. de, 24, 272
Tigay, J., 115, 155, 277
Tuell, S. S., 143, 165, 189, 221, 277
Tur-Sinai, N. H., 193, 277

Unger, W., 258, 277

Vaux, R. de, 62, 110, 172, 239, 241, 277
Viditch, S., 277
Vries, H. F. de, 12, 274

Wagenaar, G. A., 277
Waltke, B. K., 134, 223, 277
Waterman, L., 31, 277
Weidner, E. F., 49, 277
Weinfeld, M., 166, 221, 277
Wellhausen, J., 143, 150, 151, 156, 174, 202, 278
West, M. L., 49, 50, 278
Wevers, J. W., 194, 278
Whybray, R. N., 152, 278
Wiseman, D. J., 258, 278
Wright, D. P., 122, 158, 278

Yadin, Y., 71, 72, 89, 225, 278

## Author Index

Zeitlin, S., 58, 278
Zimmerli, W., 9, 10, 11, 12, 13, 22, 24, 27, 29, 58, 62, 68, 69, 72, 85, 91, 93, 99, 106, 109, 112, 118, 123, 132–34, 143, 154, 171, 187, 194, 205, 210, 223, 224, 243, 256, 278

# Subject Index

"Building" (*binyān*), 42, 54–55, 66, 72, 86, 90–92, 94, 97–100, 102–3, 105
"Restricted space" (*gizrâ*), 42, 54, 72, 86, 90, 92, 100, 103
Aaron/Aaronide, 31, 127–28, 161–63, 168, 177, 181, 186, 189, 237, 241, 260
Aaronic Blessing, 31
Aaronide priests/Levites, 161, 189, 237
Abandonment, divine, 29, 32, 104, 117, 155, 167, 169, 172, 174, 245
Abiathar, 144
Abomination, 33, 107, 112, 135, 137, 139, 162, 170, 195, 263
Adytum (*dĕbîr*, Holy of Holies), 47, 48, 51, 52, 54, 82–84, 91, 93–97, 104, 105, 109, 117, 123–25, 131, 187, 205, 230, 231, 262
Ain Dara, 87, 88
Akkadian, 8–10, 31, 50, 61, 72, 83, 91, 93, 110, 120, 130, 155, 177, 179, 194, 195, 259
Alarm Blast Festival, 57
Altar, 28, 41–44, 46–50, 52–55, 57–59, 63, 67, 72, 77, 79, 80–83, 87, 92, 93, 95–97, 100, 103–7, 110, 115, 116, 119–31, 132, 138, 141–51, 156–62, 164, 168, 169, 172, 175, 176, 180, 181, 183, 186, 187, 191, 198–205, 207–12, 214–17, 226, 227, 230, 232–33, 255, 262, 263
Apollo/ Temple of, 44–53, 65
Aramaeans, 239, 242
Aramaic, 66, 69, 85, 91, 106, 110, 155, 208
Ark of the covenant, 108, 109
Arrogance, 16, 19
Assyria/Neo Assyrian, 9, 10, 16, 49, 62, 71, 111, 241, 242
Atonement, Day of/Yom Kippur, 55, 60, 63, 104, 168, 175, 200, 201, 205, 206

Babylonian New Year's Festival (*Akitu*), 63, 104, 200
Babylon/Babylonian, 6, 10–11, 13, 33, 36, 49, 50, 51, 57, 61, 103, 104, 155, 180, 194, 195, 199, 200, 206, 207, 239, 242, 246, 255, 258, 259, 264
Beth-Togarmah, 5, 8, 10, 11
Book of the Covenant, 124
Booths, Festival of (Sukkoth), 57, 209
Bread [of presence], 41, 48, 55, 168, 175
Brook/wadi of Egypt, 235, 243, 247, 248
Bull [purification], 55–57, 123, 126–29, 198, 199, 201–4, 206, 208–10

Carites, 148
Chambers, priestly, 42, 67, 76, 80–85, 100, 143, 160, 224
Chambers, side, 85, 86, 89, 92
Chebar canal, 103, 105, 106, 114
Cherub/cherubim, 48, 93, 94, 96, 97, 103, 262
Chiasm, 15, 16, 30, 138, 188, 224, 225
Cimmerian, 9
City of David, 54, 55, 110, 262
City, The City, 55, 256, 257–63
Contamination, corpse, 58, 1–7, 109, 136, 182, 183, 186, 201, 203, 204, 206, 209
Corpses, 3, 6, 11, 21, 24, 25, 27–37, 58, 107, 109, 110, 129, 136, 161, 171, 182, 183, 186, 201, 203, 204, 206, 209, 218
Covenant (YHWH's covenant with Israel), 12, 31–33, 61, 130, 135, 138, 140, 153, 168, 170, 171, 185, 215, 222, 245
Covenant Code, 60
Covenant, new, 35
Cush/Ethiopia, 5, 7, 10

D (source), 60, 104, 161, 163, 165, 166, 182, 207

## Subject Index

Daily offering (*tāmîd*), 24, 56, 199, 232, 211, 213, 214, 216, 220
David, 34, 144, 195, 216, 231, 239, 241, 250, 262
Davidic ruler/house, 43, 108, 109, 134, 144, 172, 173, 195, 222, 234
Day of Atonement, 55, 60, 63, 104, 168, 175, 200, 201, 205, 206
Day of Purgation, 55, 63, 200, 201, 203, 217,
Dead Sea, 25, 231–33, 242, 250
Decalogue, 60
Deir Allah, 87
Delphi, 13, 44–53, 65, 174, 177
Deuteronomic law code, 124
Deuteronomic reform, 144, 145, 175
Diaspora/exiles, 11, 13, 32, 57, 216

Eden, Garden of, 52, 229, 230, 232
Egypt, Egyptians, 6, 8, 11, 33, 37, 90, 165, 207, 235, 239, 240, 241, 243, 247, 248
Exiles, 36, 103, 115, 239, 264

Feast of Tabernacles, 201
Foe [from the north], 4, 18, 22, 26
Foreigner/foreigners, 19, 24, 44, 51, 137, 140, 141, 148, 150, 153, 160, 164, 168–71, 243, 245

Gatehouses[s], 41, 43, 44, 51–55, 58, 66, 68–72, 73–77, 102, 103, 105, 132–35, 138, 141, 146, 148, 149, 151, 153–60, 163, 169, 210, 227
Glory/*kābôd* [of YHWH], 17, 23, 25, 29–31, 61, 102–6, 108, 114, 117, 125, 133, 139, 215, 262
Gog, 3–37, 215
Gomer, 5, 8, 10
Great Hall (*hêkāl*), 48, 49, 82–84, 91, 93, 94, 96–98, 123
Great Sea/Mediterranean, 13, 21, 25, 228, 231, 232, 234, 235, 240, 241, 243, 247, 248, 262
Greek influence/contact, 13, 49–51, 72, 155
Gudea, 65, 128, 230
Guidance formula, 72, 80, 229
Guide (temple/celestial), 54, 60, 65, 66, 70, 71, 79, 80, 83, 95, 100, 102, 105–8, 116, 119, 123–25, 129, 132, 133, 138, 139, 223–25, 227, 229, 230–32

Gyges/Gugu, 9, 10

H (source), 6, 12, 22, 56–60, 62, 107, 109, 126, 140, 155, 156, 163, 165, 173, 179, 182–86, 197, 204, 207, 214, 218, 236, 237, 243
Halves, halving, 4, 5, 21, 30, 34, 209, 224
Hamon-Gog, 25, 26
Heart, new, 35, 36, 43, 263
Hearth, 79, 118–20, 122, 215, 223, 225
Hezekiah, 25, 202, 216
High place, 107, 110, 151
High Priest, 36, 51, 55, 58, 59, 108, 123, 127, 130, 144, 167, 168–71, 173, 175, 176, 178–80, 182, 183, 186, 198, 200, 201, 204–6, 216, 218, 244, 250, 259, 263
Hittite/Hittites, 50, 229, 239, 240, 242
Holiness Code, xvii, 124, 195
Holocaust, 12
Holy One, 20, 21
Hostile orientation formula, 9

Idol/idolatry, 25, 31, 44, 107, 109, 112, 135, 138, 142–45, 147, 148, 151–56, 161, 166, 168, 169, 171, 172, 174, 175, 263
Impurity, 25, 32, 51, 56, 58, 59, 78, 102, 111, 112, 116, 121, 129, 130, 157, 169, 176–78, 183, 203, 208, 218, 245, 248
Incense/incense altar, 42, 44, 48, 49, 96, 120, 168, 175, 262
Inner court, 41–44, 48, 53–55, 58, 73–75, 79–83, 92, 97, 99, 100, 103–6, 139, 141–43, 146–53, 157, 160, 164, 167, 177–79, 181, 198, 204–6, 209, 223, 224
Ishtar, 31, 258, 259

Jaazaniah, 172
Jeremiah/prophecies of, 11, 18, 35, 36, 62, 108, 109, 163, 195
Jeroboam II, 62, 239, 241
Jerusalem, 3, 8, 25, 26, 51, 54, 59, 62, 64, 103, 105, 108, 110, 111, 120, 140, 142, 144, 145, 151, 156, 160–62, 168, 169, 171, 172, 189, 192, 231, 232, 234, 250, 252, 258, 259, 261, 262, 265
Joshua, 11, 185, 242, 247, 252
Josiah, 62, 142, 195, 202, 222

## Subject Index

Jubilees/ jubilee year, 60, 61, 62, 173, 220, 221, 222, 237

King (*melek*, Israelite), 32, 36, 44, 51–56, 78, 91, 107–9, 111, 112, 167, 173, 176, 193–95, 221–23, 237, 244, 250, 255, 259, 263
King, YHWH as, 250
Kitchens, temple/priestly, 42, 67, 102, 104, 147, 148, 158, 160, 223
Kohath/Kohathites, 146, 155, 186
Korah/Korahite, 137, 139, 141, 151, 152, 186

Law code/codes, 60, 124, 215, 218
Levites/Levitical priests, 33, 52, 53, 54, 59, 60, 72, 77, 81, 85, 103, 105, 108, 112, 123, 134, 135, 137, 138, 140, 141–65, 167, 168, 171, 174, 176, 177, 186, 187, 189–93, 209, 214–16, 224, 226, 244, 250, 251, 254–58, 260, 263
Levitical cities, 59, 144, 189, 192, 214, 260

Magog, 3–5, 7, 9, 10, 20, 21
Marduk, 32, 63, 104, 258
Medad, 3
Menorah/candelabrum, 42, 48, 168, 175, 262
Meshech, 3–5, 7, 9, 10, 20
Messenger formula, 124, 129, 217
Messiah, 3
Midas/Mitas, 10
Midian/Midianites, 4, 22, 173
*miqdāš*, sanctuary, 85, 85, 109, 117, 130, 130, 133, 134, 136, 138, 148, 149, 155, 164, 167, 170, 171, 174, 191, 200, 205, 233, 253, 254, 257
Mosaic Torah, 209, 219, 220
Moses, 12, 35, 37, 51, 61, 65, 104, 186, 207, 242, 261

*Nāśî'* [chief, prince], general, definition, 7, 9, 10, 36
The *nāśî'*, the prince, 44, 51–54, 56–58, 60, 107–9, 112, 116, 132–35, 167, 171–74, 188, 191–99, 200, 202, 206, 209–14, 216, 220–23, 226, 248, 250, 255–57, 259, 262, 263
Navel of the earth, 13
Nebuchadrezzar, 13, 18, 36, 120

New moon festival/sacrifices, 44, 56–58, 172, 192, 196, 197, 210–13, 216, 219
New Year, 57, 62, 63, 104, 200
Non–Zadokite Priests, 80, 81, 142, 143, 144, 147, 148, 156, 162, 167, 169, 170, 174, 176

Offering, purification (*ḥaṭṭā't*), 43, 44, 56–58, 76–80, 83, 99, 100, 121, 123, 126, 128, 129, 136, 137, 154, 156, 159, 178, 184–86, 196–206, 209, 214–16, 218, 223–25, 245
Offering, reparation (*'āšām*), 43, 44, 58, 76–80, 99, 100, 129, 137, 154, 156, 159, 184, 185, 198, 223–25
Outer court, 41–44, 53–55, 58, 72–75, 79, 90, 92, 97–101, 105, 133, 134, 138, 141, 146, 148, 150, 151, 153, 154, 156, 157, 164, 177, 178, 223–25

P (source), 44, 50, 55–57, 59, 60, 62, 77, 104, 125, 126, 146, 147, 151–53, 156, 165, 166, 178, 179, 186, 197, 202–4, 207, 208, 211, 214, 216, 225, 237
Paras, 10
Pelatiah, 172
Persia/Persian, 5, 7, 10, 73
Pesaḥ, *pesaḥ* offering, 57, 62, 63, 124, 192, 198–209
Phoenician, 51, 60, 233, 239
Priestly Code, xvii, 198
Prophecy, gift of, 170, 172, 176, 214, 264
Prophet/prophets, 3, 8, 10, 12, 17, 18, 21, 32, 34–37, 43, 44, 51, 61, 64, 65, 70, 73, 75, 79, 80, 83, 84, 94, 95, 100, 102, 103, 106, 107, 109, 113–16, 124, 126, 133, 138, 151, 163, 165, 167, 170, 172, 174, 176, 179, 180, 186, 192, 193, 195, 200, 203, 213–18, 221, 223, 224, 229–32, 236, 248, 261–63, 265
Purgation/decontamination of the temple, 55, 149, 171, 175, 199–209, 215, 215, 217
Purgation/decontamination of the altar, 121, 122–31
Put (Libya), 5, 8, 10

Rameses, 90
Recognition formula, 30, 217

## Subject Index

Red cow, 58, 204, 218
Rephaim, 24, 25
Resident alien[s], 36, 153, 172, 236, 243–46

Sabbath, 41, 51, 56, 57, 81, 103, 157, 165, 175, 176, 182, 209–13, 216, 219, 246, 250
Sabbaths, 44, 58, 169, 172, 178, 192, 195, 197, 223–26, 230
Sabbatical year, 25
Sacred land, *tĕrûmâ*, 54, 59, 60, 108, 112, 171, 188–93, 197, 198, 237, 247, 249–57, 259, 260, 262
Sacristies (*liškat haqqōdeš*), 43, 47, 54, 81, 97–101, 136, 149, 164, 177, 223, 225
Second Moses [Ezekiel], 59, 60, 114, 122, 125, 127, 128, 214–18, 264
Seidel, Seidel's law, 16, 105, 130, 224, 225
Shame/shameful, 29, 30, 33, 44, 55, 105, 112–15, 146, 152, 161–63, 263
Sheba, 13
Sheol/Netherworld, 10, 24, 25
Signatory formula, 3, 124, 197, 247
Slaughtering tables, 67, 76–79, 138, 159
Sodom [and Gomorrah], 229, 232–34
Solomon, 65, 144, 148, 168, 173, 216, 222, 241
Spine, sacred, 90–92, 103, 105, 125, 133, 158, 205, 209, 224
Spirit, God's, Holy, 3, 29, 34–36, 43, 114, 139, 170, 263, 264
Spirit, new, 35, 36, 43, 263
Steps (*maʿălôt*), 5, 25, 26, 41, 42, 43, 51, 68, 70, 73, 75, 77, 82, 83, 84, 92, 100, 105, 118, 119, 122, 158, 171, 211, 213,
Stream/river, 25, 47, 217, 228–34
Sumerian, 50, 83, 194

Tabernacle, 5, 41, 43, 48, 54, 87, 93, 95, 104–6, 115, 123, 125, 126, 128, 129, 131, 151, 152, 156–60, 181, 198, 202, 217, 230, 252, 259, 262
Table [for bread], 48, 51, 79, 81, 87, 95, 108, 125, 164, 168, 175
Table/tables, 76, 27, 28, 41, 42, 43, 48, 51, 67, 80
Tarshish, 13, 21
*Temenos*, 41, 43–48, 50, 52–56, 66, 81, 83, 84, 90, 105, 113, 114, 117, 124, 127, 135, 136, 138, 146–50, 160, 181, 183, 190, 191, 199, 216
Temple guards (Levitic), 72, 77, 80, 81, 119, 130, 135, 137, 138, 140–43, 146–60, 162–64, 167–69, 171, 174, 177, 186, 187, 215, 226, 250, 254
Temple Scroll, 48, 72, 89, 160, 259, 261
Temple, Solomonic, 54, 65, 69, 75, 84, 87, 94–96, 104, 105, 122, 129, 148, 168, 230, 262
Throne/throne room, 42, 65, 92, 104, 106, 108, 109, 114, 262
Torah, 56, 61, 62, 107, 113, 124, 134, 144, 145, 147, 148, 200, 209, 215, 216, 219, 220, 264
Tubal, 3–5, 7, 9, 10, 20
Tyre/Tyrian, 10, 11, 14, 18, 232, 241

Ugaritic, 12, 24, 50, 83, 110, 194, 228
Unleavened bread/Festival of, 57, 62, 162, 199, 201, 202, 206–9, 217

Vestments, 43, 99, 101, 151, 156, 179, 218, 225

Wall, inner, 43–46, 76, 82, 83, 86, 99, 138
Wall, perimeter, 4, 41, 44, 51–54, 66, 67, 84, 100–102, 104, 117, 130, 158, 160
Weeks, Festival of, 57
Well-being offering (*šĕlāmîm*), 56, 58, 105, 129, 133, 156, 158, 159, 171, 184, 189, 197, 206, 211–13
Wellhausen, Julius, 143, 150, 151, 156, 174, 202
Whole burnt offering (*ʿôlâ*), 5, 24, 56–58, 77–80, 100, 122, 123, 126, 128, 130, 154, 156, 159, 174, 196, 197, 199, 201, 202, 210–14, 216
Wooden altar, 93, 96
Word-event formula, 5

Yom Kippur/Day of Atonement, 55, 60, 63, 104, 168, 175, 200, 201, 205, 206

Zadok, 80, 100, 148, 250
Zadokite Priests, 59, 80, 81, 103, 105, 123, 127, 129, 135, 142–45, 147, 156, 162–164, 167, 169, 170, 174, 176, 191, 194, 199, 250, 254, 265

www.ingramcontent.com/pod-product-compliance
Lightning Source LLC
Chambersburg PA
CBHW080523020526
44112CB00046B/2771